CONTOURS OF A PEOPLE

New Directions in Native American Studies

Colin G. Calloway and K. Tsianina Lomawaima, General Editors

Contours
of a People

Metis Family, Mobility, and History

Edited by Nicole St-Onge, Carolyn Podruchny,
and Brenda Macdougall

Foreword by Maria Campbell

University of Oklahoma Press : Norman

Also by Nicole St-Onge
Saint-Laurent, Manitoba: Evolving Métis Identities, 1850–1914
    (Regina, Saskatchewan, 2004)
Also by Carolyn Podruchny
Making the Voyageur World: Travelers and Traders in the North American Fur Trade
    (Lincoln, Neb., 2006)
Also by Brenda Macdougall
One of the Family: Metis Culture in Nineteenth-Century Northwestern Saskatchewan
    (Vancouver, 2010)

Library of Congress Cataloging-in-Publication Data

Contours of a people : Metis family, mobility, and history / edited by Nicole
St-Onge, Carolyn Podruchny, and Brenda Macdougall.
    p. cm. — (New directions in Native American studies v.6)
    Includes index.
    ISBN 978-0-8061-4487-0 (paper)   978-0-8061-4279-1 (cloth)
1. Metis—History   2. Metis—Migrations.   3. Metis—Social life and customs.
I. St-Onge, Nicole.   II. Podruchny, Carolyn.   III. Macdougall, Brenda, 1969–
    E99.M47C66 2012
    305.8—dc23

                                                    2012015259

Contours of a People: Metis Family, Mobility, and History is Volume 6 in the New
Directions in Native American Studies series.

Copyright © 2012 by the University of Oklahoma Press, Norman, Publishing
Division of the University. Manufactured in the U.S.A.

To Maria Campbell, Jennifer S. H. Brown, and Jacqueline Peterson

Contents

Illustrations

Figures

Maps

TABLES

FOREWORD

Charting the Way

MARIA CAMPBELL

A couple of winters ago, I was asked to speak about Metis governance for a conference. When the conference was over I decided at the urging of Jennifer S. H. Brown to publish my talk as part of a collection of other writing. However, after a lot of thinking and several attempts to put my thoughts on paper, I put it away. As my great-granddaughter would say, "I couldn't find my words." Then, last summer after our annual clean-up day at the cemetery, which is all that is left of our road allowance community in northern Saskatchewan, I started to write. So, Jennifer, this is for you, *marci*.[1] This is also for my brothers Ben and Ray.

For those of you who are not familiar with the phrase "road allowance community," let me explain. Road allowance is the term used in Western Canada to describe the crown land that was surveyed and set aside for roadways that would be built in the future as the region developed. It was the surveying of their homeland by the Canadian government that culminated in the Metis resistances of 1869–70 in Red River and 1885 in Batoche. These events led to the dispossession of the Metis and

This paper was first given as a keynote address at the Conference on Métis Governance hosted by the University of Winnipeg, 25 March 2009.

Halfbreeds from there and created a diaspora that is the source of the poverty, rootlessness, and loss of identity being experienced by Metis people today. After the resistances were put down, the leaders hanged, imprisoned, or exiled, and their homelands settled by new immigrants, our people were forced out by fear of violence and imprisonment. Many fled to the United States or to isolated areas of the Northwest and were forgotten by authorities. They settled on crown lands, or road allowances, and were, according to the government, squatters; their inherent right to their land not recognized. They became known as Road Allowance People, and they were left alone, out of sight, out of mind, until it was again time for settlement or resource development.

Road allowance communities were unique to the three Prairie provinces of Manitoba, Saskatchewan, and Alberta, and at one point, prior to the early 1950s, they numbered in the hundreds. These communities were marked by small poplar log cabins and shanties strung out along old cart and wagon trails, provincial roads, and other crown lands. As more immigration was encouraged into the provinces by the 1920s, new land was opened for homesteading. A new era in development, coupled with a movement initiated by provincial governments to remove our people from the road allowances, became a horrific and untold story of bullying, cheating, burning, and forceful removal. That story ended in the mid-1960s with the Metis people of Crescent Lake in central Saskatchewan; they were lured to Yorkton and Regina with a promise of work that never materialized and, when they left for the summer, their homes were burned. But that's another story. Let me tell you briefly about my community, as we were also Road Allowance People.

When my family fled the racism and persecution of 1885, they went to the parkland of northern Saskatchewan to join Nehiyaw wah ko mah kahn ahk (Cree relatives) who had not signed Treaty 6 in 1876.[2] Not signing the treaty meant they were non-status Indians without reserves. The Metis were not encouraged to take treaty but instead were directed towards "scrip," a process by which, in exchange for extinguishing their rights to the land, they were granted individual parcels of land that they would be able to farm. My family applied for scrip in the late nineteenth/ early twentieth century and received certificates for land but never actually redeemed them. Under this process, the certificates the Metis received could only be applied to land already surveyed and open to homesteading. The parkland where we joined our Nehiyaw wah ko mah kahn ahk was not opened for homesteading until the 1920s and '30s, which meant that our family could not apply their scrip to this region. So, instead, they put the certificates away and went to join our Nehiyaw wah ko mah kahn ahk who were living on their traditional winter hunting and trapping territory in northern Saskatchewan. Indigenous people in those days had summer and winter territories, and they freely moved back and forth so as not to overhunt their territory.

Our *chapan* (great-grandmother), who along with other people did not take part in the treaty, moved to this area with her family, believing that no one would ever bother them again, and no one did until Grey Owl, an Englishman posing as an Indian, came to the area and decided to save the beaver. He along with several influential friends convinced the federal government to set aside the area as a national park. This place was the homeland of several groups of First Nations, Metis, and Half-breed people, and when the Prince Albert National Park was created, again people were dispossessed. Our family along with others moved out of the designated area onto crown land along the park's west boundary, and they had no sooner built their cabins than the land was opened to homesteading. Although some Metis families took homesteads, others, like my family, did not. Those Metis who took homesteads were not farmers and were desperately poor. Without experience, money, or equipment to farm the land, the majority of them lost it because they couldn't pay the taxes or they sold the land to speculators, who came "with lots of money," in the hopes of salvaging what they could. My grandmother who had never redeemed her scrip lost it to a man who came to the house and said he was from the government and that he wanted to see her papers proving the land was hers. My grandfather had just passed away, and she was destitute with eight children to raise, including my father, the oldest, who was eleven years old at the time. He remembers the man and how scared his mother was when he asked to see the papers. Dad said his mother sent him up to the rafters of the house to get a tin box, one he remembered his parents had always taken good care of. The box held the papers. His mother could not speak English, nor could she read or write, so my father, with his very poor English, spoke for her. He said the man looked at the papers and said he had to take them to Regina but that he would come back with them later. He never did, and several months later another man came and told my grandmother that they had to get out as it was now his place. The man who had said he was from the government had redeemed her certificates for land, and, since the area was now open to homesteading, he was able to apply for the land my family was living on. In turn, this man must have sold the land to the family that eventually homesteaded it. Grandma didn't know what to do, so she moved her family to the road allowance, where she was joined by other family members who had also lost their land or had nowhere else to go. This was the community I was born into and where my family lived until after my mother's death in 1953.

The dispossession of my family's land, however, is not the story I want to share with you now. Rather, I want to share stories of the annual trips we made out on the land because it exemplifies the way we lived not only while I was growing up but also when my father and his siblings were growing up. Our community was headed by my great-grandmother, her youngest daughter (my grandmother), my grandmother's sons, the oldest son (my father), and his sisters and their families. The other people who lived with us but not on a permanent basis were my great-grandmother's widowed and bachelor sons and my grandmother's adopted children and their families. We probably numbered about ten families at any given time. Scattered throughout that area were other families, related to us by blood or marriage. Offhand I can remember six such communities, but there were many more scattered throughout our area and across the province. Those communities no longer exist but our memories of them do. Every summer my family and our extended family members come home, as do other Metis and Halfbreed families across the prairies, to clean the graves, visit, tell stories, and eat together. On these days, families go for walks to the old homesites where only root cellars and burned out foundations are left. They re-remember family stories and take children to the places where they once played, as I did two years ago on a summer day when I walked to our old home place with my brother and he asked me if I remembered old uncle Pah cha neese. Of course I remembered him—he was one of our favorite people when we were kids.

Uncle Pah cha neese was our grandmother's oldest brother. He was a very old man when we were kids—I think he was probably an old man when he was born. He was tiny and wizened with long white hair and twinkling eyes. He always had a crooked brier pipe clenched in his mouth and he loved to wear blue scarves around his neck and pointed-toe moccasins or high-heeled cowboy boots. As a young man, he had worked on a ranch training, not breaking, horses. And the old "tunder grey horse" he rode was, he said, a descendant of the herd he once worked with. He called his horse "Chi gal," or little girl, which is also what he called my grandmother, my mom, myself, my girl cousins, and probably all the girlfriends he ever had. He was a pretty neat old man full of stories and songs. When he wasn't telling us kids about buffalo hunts he was snoozing under the poplar trees by the well. He said this was the coolest place in the yard because the well tapped into an underground river. It really did feel like the coolest spot in the yard on a hot July day. None of us ever sits under those trees without remembering that old man and recalling one of his stories. As did my brother and I, sitting down by the old well under the poplar trees two years ago. My brother reminded me of the times we used to leave, in the early summer, to go out on the land to dig Seneca roots and pick berries.

In the spring after we had finished cleaning and burning the yards and surrounding land we would begin the preparations to go out on the land for the summer.[3] Preparation meant oiling and mending the harness, sharpening the digging tools, and mending the tents that would house our large extended family. Finally, after the gardens were planted, we would get up early in the morning, loading up the wagons, and taking the old trail to the national park to dig roots and pick berries. When we had filled every box and bag we had, we would go to nearby small towns to sell or trade the roots and berries for things we didn't have. Things like wool for knitting socks and mittens or cloth for new dresses. Yards of bright and beautiful ribbon, spools of thread, shiny glass beads for our *nokoms* (grandmothers), and delicate silk embroidery thread for our moms and aunties. We also bought practical things like cloth for clothes, rubbers to wear over our moccasins, pants and shirts for our brothers and dads. But, I remembered most of all, how in the morning we would be up before the sun, and would pack up and harness the horses so that we were ready to go just as the sun came up over the trees. Old uncle Pah cha neese would climb on his Chi gal and ride to the front of the wagons—sometimes eight to ten of them—all loaded with mamas, papas, kids, *kookooms* (grandmothers), grub boxes, and tents. There would be dogs barking everywhere and uncles and older boys on horseback racing and showing off until someone yelled at them; then Uncle Pah cha neese would call out *"Hah kah sip way tah now"* and we were off.

We would be joined by other families along the way and there would be lots of loud greetings and laughter; you would think we had not seen each other in months when perhaps it was only yesterday. We'd spend the early summer travelling all over our old hunting territory, most of which was in the national park. We would dig Seneca roots which were dried and bagged to be sold later to a buyer from Winnipeg or taken to the nearest town by our fathers and uncles. Speaking of uncles, I remember one uncle in particular, who was my favorite in spite of my mother's complete disapproval of him. He never travelled with us but always arrived later in a big empty wagon. He would set up his tent at the edge of our camp and when we would come back after digging roots all day in the hot sun, there he'd be, sitting in his tent with the sides rolled up, drinking tea and playing solitaire. I remember my mom and aunties being upset when they saw him and calling him *"misi kee tim kun!"* (big lazy). Later, when the men had eaten, they would wander over to his tent and before you knew it there would be a poker game going on and pretty soon Uncle's wagon would be full of roots and off to town he'd go. We kids loved him because he always came back with candy, apples, and rich people's food like sardines, baloney, white bread, onions, and mustard in a jar. On the evening he came back he would have a dinner party with sandwiches and tea with lots of sugar and canned milk. While we ate he would play guitar and sing. When I think of him I have to laugh—he was so charming. I don't remember the cheating gambler but I remember the music, and songs like "Blue Velvet Band," "I Never Will Marry," and "The Wabash Cannon Ball." I don't think anybody suffered any real hardship because he won our roots in a poker game. He made up for it with the entertainment he provided and I certainly never forgot him after I grew up.

When the root digging was all done, we would pack up our camp and take the last load into town, checking out the berry patches as we went. We'd arrive at the outskirts of town, set up our camp for the night, then walk in, excited to do our shopping, go to a picture show, and have a bag of popcorn and an orange drink. I don't think I have ever tasted anything as good as that drink since. Early the following morning we would all leave together, old uncle Pah cha neese leading the way, and as the families left us to take their own trails home we called goodbye while we hurried home to, as mom would say, "chase the mice out and let them know this was still our home." Mice were the bane of my mother's existence.

We would only stay home long enough to weed and cultivate our gardens and then be off again. This time we would pick berries from early morning till the sun was setting and every afternoon the nokoms and little girls would sit by the side of the road selling bark baskets full of berries. During this time our fathers and uncles also hunted and fished. Two of our aunties would cut the meat into thin sheets and hang them on big racks made of saplings. Under the rack they would keep a hot little fire going until the sheets of meat were dry and crisp. They would then put it into a big canvas bag and pound it until it was like dry breadcrumbs and into that dry pulverized meat they poured dry berries. This is called *pimi kahn* by us and pemmican by white people. The bags were sewn shut and packed away. The aunties also smoked and dried the fish the same way. The dried meat and smoked fish were important staples in the late winter when we were running out of other food. The pimi kahn could be fried with grease and eaten as a side dish or it could also be made into a nourishing soup by adding water, a little flour, and smoked fat. We also dried medicinal plants, hanging them in bunches in a dark place, and we dried our blueberries by pouring them out on big sheets of canvas spread out on the ground in the hot sun. Then, all too soon, it was time to break camp and start for home, our wagons loaded down with provisions. We would stop and trade with local farmers, our berries and fresh meat for their wool and the flour and cereal they had ground from their grain. We would arrive home about mid-September and preparations would begin for winter.

When I read early settler history, writers go on and on about how hard the settlers worked, but when you read about us hard work is not what stands out. I remember when I was in graduate studies reading an article by a historian (and his name slips my memory at the moment) who wrote about kings and queens in Europe and their courts, which numbered in the hundreds, moving from winter castles and palaces to summer places. He wrote that the peasants and poor people hated the royalty and courtiers because they expected and, in fact, demanded that the peasants feed them as well as all their horses. The cupboards and land would be stripped of all food for people and animals after they had passed. This researcher also wrote that only rich people could hunt on the land. No other person could even hunt a rabbit without fear of being jailed or even killed. These aristocrats also had huge tracks of land set aside for their personal hunting and pleasure, and these they called parks. The people who settled in my area were Europeans who looked down on us and said we wasted our time going out on the land to hunt. They said we were lazy and wild and called us poachers. It was illegal for our people to hunt or trap anywhere because we had no treaty with the crown, and, if we were caught by the game wardens, we would be charged and prosecuted (and still are to this day). When I read that article I started to understand a great deal about these people. They saw us as mimicking the rich who had persecuted them in their own homelands, and when they came here to escape that, they brought that thinking and mind-set with them. The immigrants who settled in our area were certainly not aristocrats; in fact, most of them were poorly educated and were probably peasants or poor farmers in their countries. As far as they were concerned we should stay home and work the land and be good farmers like them. When I researched my particular community, I came across a letter written in the late 1940s by our local elected official to the government in Regina. He wrote that we must be moved from the road allowance and sent to an experimental farm, as "all they do is spend the summers racing horses and having picnics." We very seldom raced our horses as they were used for hunting and packing meat and we had to take care of them. However, they were raced when the game wardens were chasing a hunter out of the national park—then they raced like the wind, past the white farmhouses with the wardens in hot pursuit. Shades of the cowboys and Indians in John Wayne movies, or of the gentry and the poachers in England, or the poem "The Highwayman." As far as having picnics, we didn't even know the word much less ever go on one. However, every Monday, all summer for as long as the weather was good, our moms loaded up all the kids and laundry onto wagons and drove a mile to the gravel pit alongside the road, where they spent all day washing clothes. They would build a big fire, heat water from the gravel pit in big tubs and pots, then scrub on tin scrub boards all the clothes, towels, tea towels, and bedding for families as large as twelve children, two parents, and grandparents. The clean clothes would be hung on lines strung out in the trees to dry. This was also the day all the kids had a bath and were often taught to swim by a couple of aunties. Our lunch and supper would be eaten out there, and there would be lots of laughing, kids chasing each other around, and splashing of water. To someone driving by on the road and observing this, I guess it looked like a great picnic by them crazy, lazy breeds when in fact our moms, bent over tubs all day, scrubbed on those tin scrub boards with homemade lye soap until their knuckles were bleeding. Picnics indeed. Talk about two solitudes!

As my brother and I talked that day, I was struck with the realization that the annual summer and autumn excursions to pick roots, berries, and nuts, and to preserve fish and meat, were a reenactment of the old buffalo hunts of our ancestors. Of course! Why didn't I see that before— Uncle Pah cha neese was the grand chief, Dad was the captain, my uncles the guides and scouts. Instead of buffalo, it was roots, berries, nuts, moose meat, and fish that we harvested. And with each group that joined us, there was an old respected uncle serving as grand chief, a captain, and scouts. We even traded, not with the Hudson's Bay Company, but with the farmers, for the goods we needed. Later when I talked with other Road Allowance People of my generation, both in the north and the south, these life patterns were very similar. They didn't necessarily go into a national park, but they too travelled around on the land, picking rocks and roots for farmers, digging Seneca root and picking berries. All of this was similar to the buffalo hunts I had begun to research. This research told me that early observers saw a complex and orderly people with strong, experienced leadership who mobilized large groups of people. The buffalo hunt formed the basis of our social organization, they said, which was developed on our land and formed our leadership, identity, and unity. One of Canada's first historians, Alexander Ross, wrote that by 1840 there were 1,210 carts leaving Red River for the annual hunt and that he was present when the hunters left Red River that summer:

> Carts were seen to emerge from every nook and corner of the settlement bound for the plains. . . . From Fort Garry the cavalcade and campfollowers went crowding on to the public road, and thence, stretching from point to point, till the third day in the evening, when they reached Pembina, the great rendezvous on such occasions. . . . Here the roll was called, and general muster taken, when they numbered on this occasion, 1,630 souls; and here the rules and regulations for the journey were finally settled. The officials for the trip were named and installed into office; and all without the aid of writing materials.
>
> The camp occupied as much ground as a modern city, and was formed in a circle; all the carts were placed side by side, the trains outward. These are trifles, yet they are important to our subject. Within this line of circumvallation, the tents were placed in double, treble rows, at one end; the animals at the other in front of the tents. This is in order in all dangerous places; but where no danger is apprehended, the animals are kept on the outside. Thus the carts formed a strong barrier, not

only for securing the people and their animals within, but as a place of
shelter against an attack of the enemy without.[4]

Ross identified the basic rules, noting that with few variations, the laws
of the hunt were:

- No buffalo were to be run (chased) on the Sabbath.
- No party was to fork off, lag behind, or go ahead without per-
  mission.
- No person or party was to run buffalo before the general order to
  do so.
- Every captain and his men took turns patrolling the camp and
  keeping guard.
- On the first trespass against these laws, the offender had his sad-
  dle and bridle cut up.
- On the second offence, the offender's coat was taken from him
  and cut up.
- On the third offence, the offender was flogged.
- Any person convicted of theft was brought to the middle of the
  camp, then his or her name was called out three times, adding the
  word "thief" each time.[5]

Once these arrangements were determined, the Metis traveled in large
brigades of over one thousand people well into the nineteenth century.
They traveled together for hundreds of miles, until they reached buffalo
grazing areas where they would set up their camps.

Historians have said that we were adaptable and our organizational
skills unmatched. For the big hunts, there was one senior position held
by the grand chief; under him were ten captains, and below each captain were ten soldiers and ten guides. One of the responsibilities of the
guide for the day was the care and raising of the camp flag. The flag
remained raised until it was time for the camp to resettle at the end
of the day. The guide became the "chief of the expedition" for the day
he was guiding. All of the men in these positions worked and shared
the leadership responsibilities. The captains and soldiers were all responsible to this guide during the time that the flag was raised. Victoria Belcourt Callihoo, a grand old lady and longtime resident of Lac
St. Anne whom I was fortunate to meet in 1966 when she celebrated her

hundredth birthday, also provided us with a firsthand account of a buffalo hunt's organizational structure: "There were no police, no law. We
always had a leader in our caravan and his orders were respected. He
always had a flag flying on the top of his cart. He led his people ahead
and we followed."

At the end of the day, the soldiers and guides would again take over
and determine the placement of each cart in the camp. The carts were
moved together, side by side, forming a large circle. Tents and animals
were then all placed within the confines of this wall of wooden carts then
the children and old people inside. A reminder that children and old
people are the future and the past of a nation and must always be kept
in the inner circle to protect them. Around them the women, who are
the nurturers and protectors of the nation. In thinking of all this I am
reminded of two things—one of them, as I said earlier, is how hard my
mom and aunties worked. I do not remember any of them ever sitting
around, and if they did sit, they were beading, embroidering, making
baskets, or hooking and braiding rugs, all to be sold to the trader who
came from Winnipeg every spring or to local white people. This money
supplemented the family's income, and believe me there were times we
would not have made it were it not for this fine work. Women's roles
when I was a child were clearly defined, at least by our definition, as
were the roles of old people and men. In her recollections, Victoria Belcourt Callihoo elaborated on the role of women. In 1874, when she was
thirteen, she went on her first buffalo hunt from Lac St. Anne in the
spring. She recorded that when the buffalo hunt was finished, the women
would bring the meat in, while the girls worked to keep the fires going,
creating smoke to keep the flies away as the meat was hung to dry. She
told how the meat was pounded into a pulp and mixed with sundried
Saskatoon berries and grease to make pemmican, then sewn up in buffalo robes to help preserve it. On these hunts, Victoria specifically served
as a helper to her mother, Nancy Rowand. Victoria said, "I always used to
accompany my mother on these trips. She was a medicine woman who
set bones and knew how to use medicinal herbs. The riders who chased
the buffalo were often thrown, sometimes by bulls charging the riders'
horses or by the horses getting their feet in badger holes."[6]

A bonesetter and medicine person was vital to the hunt, and these
were usually the women who, like my own nokoms, were the midwives
and medicine people in our community. Even children, we included,

knew the basics of medicine—we had to; there was no drugstore nearby. I have also heard from old people I have interviewed (and I have also found documentation) about women who, as heads of families, like my great-grandmother, were respected and looked up to in their communities sometimes for leadership and often as hunters. Women like Cecelia Boyer, wife of Norbert Welsh, who published the story of his life in a book called the *Last Buffalo Hunter*, who mentioned that his wife had her own brigade but does not tell us of her hunting and leadership skills. She was known and respected as a leader and hunter and would lead her own brigades, owning her own carts, oxen, and hunting horses. As many as twenty families at a time depended on her. Isabelle Falcon was another woman who was known far and wide for her hunting and shooting skills. It was said of Isabelle that there was nothing to fear if she was among the Metis warriors during their fights with the Sioux. She was known as a crack shot both on the hunt and in wartime.

And everywhere in our communities you will hear stories of women who have not only raised children alone but who were also skilled hunters, trappers, and fishermen; who built their own cabins, made snowshoes, and ran dog teams. An example in our family was my grandmother's oldest sister Qui chich; after her husband's death she became a successful farmer, respected medicine woman, and money lender. Everybody came to her to borrow money, and she even charged interest. There are also many stories of the people she doctored with plants. She died on the Ahtakakoop Reserve at the age of approximately 110. She was an amazing woman and was certainly my role model. I am not sure at what point in our history, or why, the role of women became so denigrated and violence against them a norm, because women in our communities are still what keep us surviving and together.

The role of old people was equally important. They looked after the children because parents were busy working to provide. They taught us with stories; by doing activities, and having us help them, they were our teachers, historians, and archives. If we wanted to know anything, all we had to do was go to one of them, and if they didn't know what we wanted, they would find someone who did. By the time we left them as young men and women, we were grounded in our culture; we knew our land and environment and we could pull our own weight. They were, except in rare cases, kind and loving, and rarely did they have to punish us because, for some reason, we wanted to please them.

I know that First Nations, and especially Metis, understandings of the world are given little, if any, attention in contemporary academic discourse. But that is changing simply because we have more and more scholars, intellectuals, and artists looking at our worlds from outside the colonial box. Can you imagine—what if we brought storytellers, elders, artists, and scholars together? What would we look at? The comparison I just gave about our annual trips to pick roots and berries and the annual buffalo hunts—events one hundred years apart and yet still so similar to one another—is a reflection of the continuity of our history, not the end. We have always governed ourselves and we still do. Regulation and preference of some activities by the governments of Canada and the provinces do not mean the others will cease to exist. The proof of this is the lifestyle that many Metis people lived up to the 1940s, which included traditional forms of governance. This is evident in the story of old uncle Pah cha neese. There are many stories like this out there. What remains is for you, for us, to find them. There's still a living memory of this way of life.

When I think about all this and about the protocols, responsibilities, and obligations I grew up with, and I talk with other people of my generation and older who have had similar experiences, I am astounded by how much of our way of life was intact until the early 1950s. Yes, times had changed, new things were introduced, but Road Allowance People still lived, in most cases, by those old rules. Perhaps being marginalized and made invisible was not such a bad thing because culturally we were rich (and still are), but this is slowly being lost as we lose our old people. No one has ever researched and documented us from our perspective. Everything has been done by historians and done from a historical perspective until very recently. It is crucial for us to research and document our own stories and to share and discuss them at a community level. To celebrate them is a part of our decolonizing. I believe this must come first. Coming together to tell these stories is a beginning or a start to finding our way home. Home meaning the place where the spirit dwells.

Notes

1. *Marci* is the Michif spelling of *merci*. Michif is the language that Metis people speak in Canada.

2. The Cree words that appear in this text are written phonetically rather than in standardized Cree. This is done so that the reader will more easily be able to pronounce the words while reading them.

3. Aboriginal people in North America used fire in many ways, including altering their landscapes by clearing the prairie through burning. Fire cleared (and cleaned) the land, making it easier to hunt and improving the quality of the land for plant life. In both instances, fire improved the growth and yields of plants.

4. Alexander Ross, "The Red River Buffalo Hunt from Red River Settlement," *Manitoba Pageant* 5, no. 2 (1960): 1–5, at 1. http://www.mhs.mb.ca/docs/pageant /05/buffalohunt.shtml.

5. Ibid., 3.

6. Victoria Callihoo, "Our Buffalo Hunts," *Alberta Historical Review* 8, no. 1 (1960): 24–25, at 24.

ACKNOWLEDGMENTS

This volume began as a series of conversations that were facilitated by a Social Sciences and Humanities Research Council (SSHRC) of Canada Aboriginal Research Grant, "Patterns of Genesis: Identity, Culture, Communication and Mobility in the Emergence of Northwest Metis Populations." We thank Heather Devine, a member of the grant team (along with Nicole St-Onge, Brenda Macdougall, and Carolyn Podruchny), for her input, reflections, and wisdom. Our conversations were greatly enhanced by two conferences at the Congress of the Canadian Federation for the Humanities and Social Sciences: "Fur Trade and Metis Days" at the University of Saskatchewan in Saskatoon on May 27–28, 2007, hosted by the Canadian Historical Association and the Canadian Indigenous and Native Studies Association; and "Fur Trade and Metis History: Patterns of Ethnogenesis" at Carleton University in Ottawa on May 25–26, 2009, hosted by the Canadian Historical Association. We thank these organizations as well as the presenters and attendees. In particular, we acknowledge Jennifer S. H. Brown, who acted as a keynote speaker for the 2009 conference.

We are indebted to SSHRC, which provided us funds to organize conferences, to travel to meet members of the collaborative grant and work together in person, to take time away from teaching to research and write about Metis history, and to provide a subvention for the publication of this volume. We are also grateful to individual supporters and our institutional partners in our SSHRC Aboriginal Research Grant. These include the Metis elders Maria Campbell and Rose Fleury, and Saskatchewan Metis Angela Caron; the Gabriel Dumont Institute (GDI) executive director Geordy McCaffrey and Darren Préfontaine of GDI Curriculum and Publishing; Mark Calette, manager, National Historic Sites, Saskatchewan South Field Unit; Batoche National Historic Site manager Raymond Fidler; Société de Saint-Boniface directeur general Gilles Lesage; and the University of Athabasca president Frits Pannekoek. The University of Ottawa, the University of Saskatchewan, and York University also contributed to this project by providing funds to hire graduate assistants. We owe a debt of gratitude to the talented and dedicated people at the University of Oklahoma Press, particularly Colin Calloway for encouraging us to submit the volume to the press, Alessandra Jacobi-Tamulevich for overseeing the publication process, Emily Jerman for guiding us through production, and Kimberly Kinne for her excellent copy-editing, and to Bill Nelson for making the maps. The contributors to this volume are responsible for its insight and quality, and we thank them enthusiastically for their cooperation and patience over the duration of this volume's creation.

We are indebted to Neil Soiseth for his careful copyediting in the early stages of putting the collection together. We also thank Galen Perras for inspiration and Mark Guertin for technical advice. Kathryn White provided expert assistance with bibliographic citations, and Sara Howdle assisted with the creation of maps. We thank Stacy Nation-Knapper for doing an excellent job in preparing the index.

This volume is dedicated to three elders of Metis history: Maria Campbell, Jennifer S. H. Brown, and Jacqueline Peterson.

A Note on Terminology

Because the typographical designation of Metis people has such significant political implications, we decided to allow all authors to choose their own method for how to refer to Metis people rather than imposing a single term on the volume. Likewise, we have allowed authors to determine the means by which they refer to First Nations people and have not imposed single nomenclatures.

Many authors in this volume use the term Half-breed. Historically it was accepted as the English translation of Metis, and today it is often used politically to denote those Metis not descended from French ancestry. Although some may consider it pejorative, we consider it to be a term of historical significance with contemporary applicability used by many Metis people today.

ABBREVIATIONS

AM	Archives du Manitoba
ASGM	Archives des Soeurs Grises de Montréal
ASHSB	Archives de la Société historique de Saint-Boniface
BANQ	Bibliothèque et Archives nationales du Québec
CCF	Central Classified Files
CPFM	Centre du Patrimoine Franco-Manitobain
FRC	Federal Records Center (U.S.)
HBC	Hudson's Bay Company
HBCA	Hudson's Bay Company Archives
HMN	Historic Métis Nation
HMNH	Historic Métis Nation Homeland
LAC	Library and Archives Canada
MHS	Montana Historical Society
NA	National Archives (U.S.)
NARA	National Archives and Records Administration (U.S.)
NWC	North West Company (individuals in NWC known as Nor'westers)
OMI	Oblats de Marie-Immaculée
PAA	Provincial Archives of Alberta
RAC	Russian American Company
RCAP	Royal Commission on Aboriginal People
RG	Record Group
SAB	Saskatchewan Archives Board
SC	Small Collection
SCC	Supreme Court of Canada
WHC	Western Historical Company
WHS	Wisconsin Historical Society
XYC	XY Company (also known as the New North West Company)

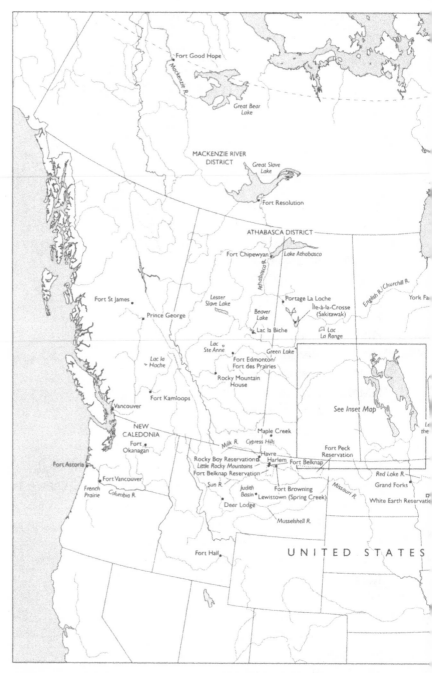

MAP 0.1. Canada and the northern United States. Map by Bill Nelson.

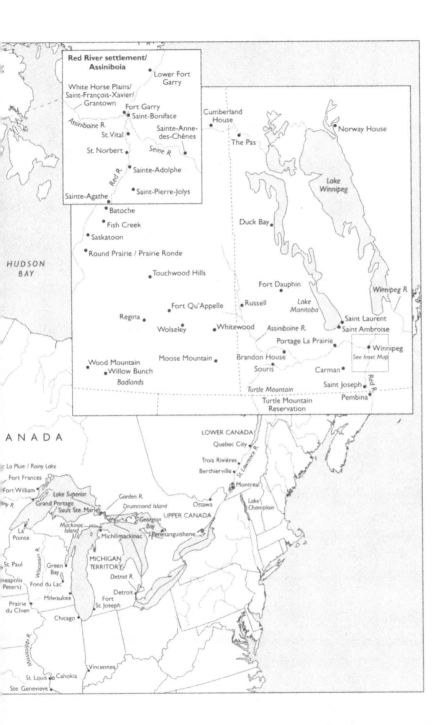

Red River settlement/ Assiniboia

Lower Fort Garry

White Horse Plains/ Saint-François-Xavier/ Grantown

Fort Garry
Saint-Boniface

Assiniboine R.

St.Vital

St. Norbert

Seine R

Red R.

Sainte-Adolphe

Sainte-Agathe

Saint-Pierre-Jolys

Sainte-Anne-des-Chênes

Cumberland House

Norway House

The Pas

Lake Winnipeg

Batoche

Fish Creek

Saskatoon

Round Prairie / Prairie Ronde

Duck Bay

Touchwood Hills

Fort Dauphin

Winnipeg R.

HUDSON BAY

Fort Qu'Appelle

Russell

Lake Manitoba

Saint Laurent
Saint Ambroise

Regina

Wolseley

Whitewood

Assiniboine R.

Portage La Prairie

Winnipeg
See Inset Map

Wood Mountain
Willow Bunch
Badlands

Moose Mountain

Brandon House

Souris

Carman

Saint Joseph

Red R.

Pembina

Turtle Mountain

Turtle Mountain Reservation

A N A D A

LOWER CANADA

Quebec City

Trois Rivières

Berthierville

St. Lawrence R.

Montreal

c La Pluie / Rainy Lake

Fort Frances

Fort William

Lake Superior

Grand Portage

Sault Ste. Marie

ny R.

Garden R.

Drummond Island

Ottawa

Lake Champlain

UPPER CANADA

La Pointe

Mackinac Island

Georgian Bay

Michilimackinac

Penetanguishene

Wisconsin R.

St. Paul

Green Bay

MICHIGAN TERRITORY

neapolis Peters)

Fond du Lac

Milwaukee

Detroit R.

MISSISSIPPI R.

Prairie du Chien

Detroit
Fort St. Joseph

Chicago

Vincennes

St. Louis Cahokia

Ste. Genevieve

CONTOURS OF A PEOPLE

INTRODUCTION

Cultural Mobility and the
Contours of Difference

BRENDA MACDOUGALL, CAROLYN PODRUCHNY,
and NICOLE ST-ONGE

In countless situations in history all over the world, trade between groups has led to sexual encounters and even intermarriage, including dual-heritage offspring. This circumstance became common in the North American fur trade, but this does not mean that Metis people can be found all over North America. Usually, dual-heritage offspring would join either their mothers' or fathers' communities and adopt their heritage and culture. But, in specific situations, when the dual-heritage children begin to intermarry and create families and communities with one another and to develop a distinctive culture based on novel practices—such as a new language, artistic production, or economic activity—and especially when a shared sense of collectivity is expressed, ethnogenesis, or the birth of a new people, occurs. This volume studies just such a situation in the northwestern part of North America in the eighteenth and nineteenth centuries. Groups of Metis people emerged on the Great Plains, in the boreal forests, and in the subarctic scrublands when successive generations of dual-heritage children intermarried and created communities. Not all of these communities acted together as a single collectivity or formed kinship ties or even were aware of one another, but a surprising number of them did. Regardless, in this place and time, the emergence of these groups constitutes the birth of a new people.

Having an Indian ancestor does not make one Metis; rather, Metis people emerged in and descended from communities of dual heritage with common interests and goals.

At several conferences from 2004 to 2006, a series of conversations about Metis and fur trade history began between Nicole St-Onge, Carolyn Podruchny, Brenda Macdougall, and Heather Devine. These discussions led to an innovative research collaboration to investigate the nature of Metis identification, shared group consciousness, cultural practices, communication, and mobility in northwestern North America.[1] We had each been conducting research in these areas independently, but we felt that we could more effectively advance Metis and fur trade historical inquiry by coordinating our efforts to understand what becoming and being Metis meant and means in historical and contemporary contexts. Although each of us dealt with different geographies and intellectual spaces, we were mutually intrigued by the nuances in the definitions, geographic contextualizations, economic behaviors, assertions of social and political collectivity, and rights expressed throughout Metis history. Equally intriguing was how the answers to these questions have evaded traditional studies of Metis communities over the past three decades.

After receiving a three-year Aboriginal Research Grant from the Social Sciences and Humanities Research Council of Canada to study the concepts of Metis identity and individual and collective consciousness in historic communities, we initiated our work by hosting two conferences to see whether we could bring together people to hold a focused conversation centered on Metis and fur trade history. Our approach was not new. Thirty years ago, the first conference on the "Métis in North America" was hosted by Jacqueline Peterson and Jennifer S. H. Brown at the Newberry Library's D'Arcy McNickle Center for the History of the American Indian[2] in Chicago, Illinois. The subsequent product of that conference was the seminal collection of essays edited by Peterson and Brown, *The New Peoples: Being and Becoming Métis in North America*.[3] Like many researchers engaged in Metis and fur trade scholarship, we were profoundly impacted by that collection. *The New Peoples* has since shaped intellectual discourse at the intersection of Metis and fur trade historiography. It provided the context for understanding various kinds of ethnogenesis across the continent, as the chapters explored diverse interpretive frameworks and theories to explain the psychological and physical diasporas experienced by the Metis throughout the eighteenth and nineteenth centuries and the diversity of Metis community histories and cultures spanning a geography that encompassed the Red River settlement in southern Manitoba, northern Montana, northern Ontario, and northern Alberta.

Perhaps one of *The New Peoples'* biggest contributions to academic discourse was the discussion begun in the introduction by Peterson and Brown of their understanding of and decision whether to use a lowercase or uppercase *m* when spelling "Metis."[4] Intentionally or not, Brown and Peterson introduced a debate that has been a preoccupation of scholars because the decision on how to spell the term is indicative of what type of people they were (and still are) designated by themselves and by outsiders—a race, a culture, or a nation.[5] The lowercase *m* was used inclusively for all mixed-ancestry people, and so the focus was on race, not nationhood. Peterson and Brown proposed that the lowercase *m* would also refer to those people with a sense of cultural distinctiveness but who perhaps did not engage in the same types of national development as was found in western Canada during the nineteenth century. Conversely, the usage of "Metis" was reserved only for those communities that formed a distinct indigenous nation with a shared history, culture, and homeland in western Canada.[6]

Inspired by *The New Peoples*, we hoped to contribute to the development of Metis history by providing a venue for scholars—many of whom previously had few opportunities—to engage in conversations with one another. Our goal was to promote a range of scholarly activity in these areas and to encourage scholars to ask new questions. Our first conference, "Fur Trade and Metis Days," was held at the University of Saskatchewan in 2007 as part of the annual Congress of the Canadian Federation for the Humanities and Social Sciences.[7] This one-day conference brought together a diverse group of graduate students, professors, professional researchers, government representatives, community scholars, and activists as both participants and observers interested in diverse topics, including Metis, voyageurs, trade economies, local histories, and indigenous rights. The enthusiasm with which this conference was met prompted us to host a second conference, "Fur Trade and Metis History: Patterns of Ethnogenesis," at the 2009 congress held at Carleton University.[8] The program was made up of some who had presented at the first conference, some audience members from the first, and newcomers. We witnessed the same level of enthusiasm, innovative research methodologies, intriguing research results, and desire to continue talking about Metis history.

When we originally conceived of the conferences and, subsequently, this collection, we were unsure whether any scholars would want to join our conversation. We were delighted to discover that many currently working in the field were excited to participate, and both the conference papers and the chapters collected for this book required little prompting. Fueled by the findings of other scholars in the field and interested in testing the boundaries of the existing discourse, the editors of this collection were keen to contribute to and expand the discussions about Metis studies.

What emerged was a realization that the intellectual dialogue about the Metis has moved beyond a conversation focused solely on their emergence as a new people. Researchers are now also asking questions centered around a Metis *state of being*, leading to broader discussions about Metis concepts of geography (not only how they used environments, but how they imagined themselves occupying space, giving meaning to place, and developing connections to multiple landscapes), their range of mobility as associated with various trade endeavors, and, finally, how family relationships sat at the center of their collective consciousness and way of being. Although scholars continue to explore and untangle the thorny issue of ethnogenesis, it is clear that they are also turning their attention to questions about who these people became—how they understood and moved about their world and, in turn, how they shaped their consciousness via large networks of families and communities. The emergent consensus among the scholars present in 2009 was that these three elements—geography, mobility, and family—defined Metis culture and society across North America, and that they were pivotal to a Metis worldview and way of life.

By now, the reader will have noticed our stance on spelling Metis. We have chosen to capitalize the *m* but remove the accent over the *e*. We feel that this spelling best reflects the lives and experiences of individuals and communities of people who descended from European fathers and Indian mothers during the fur trade. Our use of the word with an unaccented *e* (rather than *é*) is our effort to show that Metis people should not be considered simply as the descendents of French Canadian voyageurs; we recognize the patrilineal diversity of heritages beyond French Canadian to embrace Orcadian, Scottish, English, and so on. The capitalization of the term points to the existence of a group identification, if not nationhood, that was diverse and not tied solely to the political expressions of nationhood reflected in the resistance to Canadian annexation in the Red River settlement in present-day Manitoba and Batoche in present-day Saskatchewan. However, because of the complex political ramifications of terminology, we have allowed each of the authors in this collection to determine her or his own way to express the idea of Metis people.

Geographies, Migrations, and Families

One of the key intellectual exercises for scholars in Metis studies has been conceptualizing and articulating how the Metis differ from the maternal and paternal societies from which they emerged. The emphasis has, until now, been on the idea that the Metis blended their material culture to create things like embroidered or beaded frock coats that were made of tanned hide or the Red River cart that was styled after a common European wagon but made with no metal or steel parts so that it could be easily repaired out on the plains. These physical representations of Metis culture certainly point to their creativity in expressing distinctiveness, but such representations do not necessarily get at the essence of what it was to be a people who were neither European nor Indian. Clearly, geography, mobility, and family are all elements found within European and Indian cultures, but we contend that the Metis articulated and lived them differently.

The chapters in this collection illuminate aspects of the form and content of Metis culture[9] and, we hope, begin to formulate some answers to the overarching question of the contours of Metis lives. Although ethnogenesis is obviously the first step in the emergence of a new people, what else is required to transcend biracialism and biculturalism to become distinct, with corporate or even national interests? What are the contours of this new people? By and large, the collected chapters here accept that a new people—however they are defined—emerged in the workings of the fur trade between the seventeenth and nineteenth centuries. More important, the authors herein strive to analyze and explain how the Metis conceptualized themselves in relation to one another, to outsiders, to their homeland, and to their economy. We offer in this introduction a discussion about the themes that emerge in these essays and an attempt to broaden the conversation further by exploring the contours of Metis culture and nationhood.

Studied together, the three characteristics—an expansive geographic familiarity, tremendous physical and social mobility, and maintenance of strong family ties across time and space—appear to have evolved as a result of an entrepreneurial spirit in a variety of economic niches associated with the fur trade writ large. The Metis were involved most famously in the large scale, commercial buffalo hunt specific to Plains Metis culture, but they were also involved in other important activities, including trapping and freighting, working on vast transportation networks that operated along waterways and cart trails, taking part in subsistence and commercial hunting and fishing operations, free trading, and performing contract jobs within the fur trade industry, all practiced in a variety of geographies encompassing plains, parklands, woodlands, and the subarctic. All these economic endeavors, and the cultural practices that subsequently emerged from them, contributed to a sense of shared community and contributed to the nationalist sentiment felt by many Metis today.

Mobility emerges as a dominant theme in many of the chapters, but one should not presume that these communities were nomadic. The term "nomad" (and its derivatives) is laden with cultural baggage rooted in a discourse that posits that civilization is founded on agrarianism. Conversely, to be uncivilized is to have no fixed residence or, to be more specific, to "roam" the landscape gathering food. Nomadism often refers to a people or culture whose mobility is perceived as detrimental to their stability as a community. Nomad and settler are both concepts that are a part of an archaic classification system that posits humankind as evolving on a sociocultural scale. The achievement of any society was to move up the evolutionary scale toward civilization. There is, however, an alternative understanding of mobility that warrants some attention here. Hugh Brody's *The Other Side of Eden: Hunters, Farmers, and the Shaping of the World* explores the idea that the true nomads are, in fact, the settler farmers who were able to uproot themselves and transplant their way of life in new environments.[10] The "agrarian frontier" for millennia was ever expanding because the technology and economy associated with this way of life was such that the people were able to move about easily, looking for new, fertile regions where they could begin anew. Conversely, hunting, fishing, and gathering knowledge is far more site-specific. As such, the technological and cultural adaptation of those who harvest by hunting, fishing, and gathering are regionally or geographically specific traits and consequently not easily relocated unless their practitioners are prepared to fully transform themselves, including their entire knowledge system.

Brody's ideas about mobility are echoed by cultural theorist Stephen Greenblatt, who argues, "The reality, for most of the past as once again for the present, is more about nomads than natives."[11] In his introduction to *Cultural Mobility: A Manifesto*, Greenblatt asserts that cultures have never been whole, undamaged, or fixed, but rather mobility, fluidity, and change have been constant elements of human life in virtually all times and places. Like Brody, Greenblatt encourages us to reflect differently both on the idea that cultures belong to place and on the patterns of meaning that humans create for themselves.[12]

There is a tension between mobility and rootedness in Metis communities that can be better articulated if we reflect on the ideas of Brody and Greenblatt, and so, even as we use the term "mobility" here, it needs to be understood as a form of movement that establishes fixed communities. That fixedness, however, never quells their movement. The Metis are neither nomadic nor settled but, rather, are both. The Metis were spread throughout northwestern North America, the Great Lakes region, the Great Plains, along rivers used as major fur trade routes, in the subarctic scrublands, and in the boreal woodlands and parklands, where the physical and economic possibilities of those geographies informed the specific types of social and cultural communities that existed there. In each of these locations, fixed settlements were established, such as Red River, Île-à-la-Crosse, Lac La Biche, Batoche, and Michilimackinac. Inherent in these locations was a form of regional and interregional movement associated with trade. For example, the people of Red River—the largest fixed Metis community—continued to live according to a seasonal cycle predicated on movement, even as some of its residents themselves became rooted in place as merchants, clergy, or small-scale farmers. People came and went from this place to hunt buffalo on the plains, transport produce and goods to St. Paul, Minnesota, or work for a season or two on the northern boat brigades. As people and goods moved in and out of this inland port, they intersected with other fixed and mobile communities in other regions. The result of this fluid pattern of movement was a society that shared knowledge of various regions because its family members came and went with the seasonal cycles. The Metis lived and thrived at the intersection of mobility and fixedness.

There is certainly a relationship between Metis mobility and sense of geographic expanse, both of which were shaped by their economic interests in the fur trade and ideas of homeland, territory, and landscape. Their sense of space transcended ecological zones, but they also had a psychological understanding of their physical space as encompassing a far greater range of geography than what they might occupy in the short term. Thus, farmers on the banks of the Red River believed they could fish in Lake Manitoba or hunt buffalo in Montana because these places were part of their homeland. If they were buffalo hunters by occupation, their geographic worldview encompassed fixed sites across the plains, parklands, and forests that they regularly visited. Between the late eighteenth and nineteenth centuries, as the Metis spread out across western and northern Canada and the northwestern United States in various occupations associated with the peltry industry, they shaped for themselves a sense of homeland and connection to the territories where they lived and worked. Like other groups, they named the landscapes they occupied and shaped, and they created stories and songs linked to particular places, all of which rooted them to the new spaces they came to occupy. The physical landscape both shaped and was shaped by the mobility of a people who occupied or traversed these regions.

First Nations and European peoples, like many groups of people across the world, migrated and traveled across land, gaining knowledge of intersecting geographies to various degrees. As a people, the Metis emerged out of the migration (indeed, the mobility) of the French, Scottish, and English. All these nationalities or cultural groups from Europe migrated to North America and necessarily gave up something of who they were to become reborn in their newly adopted homes. These newcomers were not simply immigrating and reproducing their lives, rather they were engaging in a process of adaptation and acculturation to their new environs, becoming "native" to survive and prosper. The means by which they became native was rooted in their ability to produce homes in new landscapes by adapting place names, economies, and political structures that reflected both nostalgia for their old homes and excitement by the invention of new ways of living and being. Across the globe, European migration created new peoples—Afrikaners, Australians, Americans, Canadians, Acadians, Cajuns, Brazilians, and Chileans—in lands new to them. Yet, they remained connected to their European-ness by casting indigenous peoples as the foreigner, the exotic, and the nomad.

The maternal ancestors of the Metis were also mobile, traveling between summer and winter camps and following traditional routes for hunting, fishing, and gathering. When Europeans arrived on their lands, their mobility increased. European newcomers were intent on obtaining natural resources, engaging in trade, convincing indigenous people to convert religion, and, of course, colonizing the land. As a consequence, First Nations people responded to these new forces by adapting economically, culturally, politically, and socially to the expanding fur trade and settler economies, demands for political association and military alliances, and dispossessions. In some instances, they were reborn as new peoples, going so far as to adopt new tribal names, establish new lineages, and develop new lifestyles, even as others were able to hold onto their identities and adapt to a new space. For instance, the Crow, one of the most powerful Plains peoples of the nineteenth century, emerged as a new tribe. Once Hidatsa, a people from the woodlands ecology south of the Great Lakes, those who became the Crow migrated to the Plains in the seventeenth century. The Crow became Plains Indians after a prophetic vision received by their first chief, No Vitals, in which he was told to go west to high mountains and plant the seeds of a sacred tobacco plant. No Vitals and a group of fellow Hidatsa moved west until they found the place in his vision and planted those seeds. These Hidatsa became the Crow, a new tribe unaffiliated with any others. They developed an equestrian warrior culture that repelled everyone from their new homeland, which they believed was a sacred gift from the Creator for them alone, and they did so with a ferocity that overpowered other tribes.[13] At the other end of the spectrum, the Creek were removed from Georgia, Alabama, and Florida in the mid-nineteenth century and, despite the violence of their forced diaspora, managed to maintain themselves as Creek by adapting their religious institutions and beliefs to the Indian territories (now the state of Oklahoma). In short, the Creek became indigenous to Oklahoma.[14] A transformation halfway between the Crow and Creek experience was that of the Cree, some of whom turned from being subarctic, largely pedestrian, and boat-oriented woodlands peoples into a Plains equestrian society similar to that of the Crow. However, for the Cree who did move and adapt to new spaces, their decisions were based on range of economic factors, including optimizing their position in the trade economy, rather than religious prophecy.[15] The Plains Cree separated from the Swampy and Rock Cree, moved away from the shores of Hudson Bay and the woodlands and parklands of western Canada, and emerged, by the beginning of the nineteenth century, as a Plains people and a new type of Cree. This reinvention required adaptation to a new ecological zone, fully and completely, to not only survive but thrive. In each instance, these groups left behind territories and families and lost those connections and shared histories while simultaneously building new histories and family connections in their new homeland.

We must ask, however, what made the Metis different from other cultures around the world, which, according to Greenblatt, were necessarily shaped by mobility and cultural mixing. What, in particular, made the Metis different from their neighbors? It has long been argued that the Metis were a distinct North American people because they were mixed or biracial. Yet we know that other New World people have a history of biracialism because of their long history of contact and alliance building, dating to the wars of imperial conquest and fur trade economy. Historically, Indians intermarried with white traders and settlers, and, although some of their progeny became Metis, many more remained Indian. Many Acadians have ancestors who were Mi'kmaq yet identified historically as a distinct French North American society and did not claim to be Metis or even Indian. Certainly, the Metis, like many others, were shaped by the cultural mixing of such vastly divergent peoples from different parts of the globe, but, just as certainly, that alone did not make a people Metis. Instead, we suggest that the Metis were distinct because their mobility and sense of space were much more extensive, both in terms of influence and sheer ecological or geographic reach. The Metis world spanned the better part of a continent, and specific communities continuously transcended ecological zones. The Metis of the subarctic and Great Plains both made extensive use of parkland zones, just as the woodlands Metis around the Great Lakes easily made a transition to Red River. The connections between these diverse landscapes have shaped Metis notions of homeland and, indeed, their ideas of territoriality.

The link holding all of this together—mobility and geography—is found in the Metis conceptualization of family. Like many other societies throughout the world, the Metis created for themselves a system of extended family relationships within fixed communities and across these vast distances because of their tremendous mobility. Looking at subarctic Metis communities, Richard Slobodin argued that a widespread feature of Metis family and social life was an emphasis on family surnames as a means of inspiring and maintaining social and cultural unity. He attributed this particular cultural characteristic to the vastness of the region in which they lived, their relatively small population, and the range of economic activities in which they participated.[16] Within a generation or two, the Metis developed a complex genealogical structure and shared knowledge by emphasizing those surnames as a key aspect of their identity.

A wide range of family-based Metis studies have explored the centrality of family in Metis culture and history, but few studies have linked it to these notions of mobility and geographical expanse. Family studies have tended to focus on specific communities but rarely have looked at families within a regional configuration or across multiple and diverse regions.[17] They have focused on particular individuals or specific families but have not placed them within a matrix of community, cultural, or national behaviors common to all Metis people across a variety of geographies, even though few scholars would disagree that they were part of a highly mobile population. We could turn to the histories of other cultural groups that are characterized by the same types of mobility (either voluntary or because of racism-fueled diasporas) and sense of geography, but that comparative approach has not been very satisfying. For instance, Jewish history is replete with stories of various diasporas from a variety of regions, but they have nonetheless maintained a Jewish culture and identity across time and space. One of the means by which they have been able to perpetuate Jewish culture is through an emphasis on endogamy. The marital practice of Jew marrying Jew has been critical to the perpetuation of the faith and culture.[18] The Roma (Gypsies) have likewise had a history of movement and sociocultural exclusion from the communities and nations in which they reside, which has resulted in violent persecution and dislocation similar to that experienced by the Jews. Like Jews, they have maintained a tradition of inwardness and closing themselves off to others to protect and nurture their communities.[19]

The Metis, conversely, had no such tradition of inwardness and no explicit ideology or theology that emphasized endogamy. They were the products of population movements and maintained themselves in family or kinship networks that were both inward- and outward-looking. Although one could look at the Metis historically and see definite examples of endogamy taking precedence over exogamy, there was an inherent tension in those marital practices. The notion of building alliances through marriage was a mainstay of Metis social custom, which was then balanced against endogamous marital arrangements that supported the development of independent and distinct Metis communities. Overarching social norms within this vast and dispersed Metis world were the products of family values and a vast kinship matrix, both of which were informed by local economies dependent on the possibilities and constraints of mercantile capital. Family, relatedness, kinship—whatever the preferred term—is the basic building block in all human societies, and, of course, the idea of establishing family networks that inform political, economic, and social decision making is a principle found in other societies. Colin Calloway highlighted great similarities in Highland Scots and aboriginal families and clan structures, notably that, despite very real social and cultural differences, these peoples *recognized* each other.[20] Family is perhaps the best way to explain this human impulse to create connections, for the notion of family—and its offspring, clan, or tribe—is a way to show how relatedness was central to a variety of people. Family was the easiest means for people to establish other forms of alliances beyond the political, military, and economic.

Although the Metis differed from other groups, they were not monolithic. Although they shared the characteristics of kinship, mobility, and territoriality, there were distinctions between Metis communities based on where they lived, the types of work in which they engaged, and the religion they practiced. We take to heart Greenblatt's advice to patiently chart specific instances of culture mobility in great detail rather than construct grand new narratives.[21] We encourage scholars to study the variations and nuances proposed by the chapters in this collection to grasp the larger "Metis whole." The chapters here present case studies of a people who made physical mobility, economic entrepreneurship, and social and cultural exchange through family the cornerstones of their identity. The Metis were woven together by a mobility that bridged many human and physical geographies and by their kinship ties that bound the far-flung and dispersed human elements into a coherent functioning whole.

The Chapters

This collection of chapters covers many overlapping themes, both specific and broad. The chapters at the beginning and end of the volume embrace large conceptual issues, with earlier chapters examining ethnogenesis

and later chapters engaging with contemporary legal and historiographical questions, whereas the chapters in the middle are more focused on
particular conceptual, analytical, and geographic considerations. The
geographic organization of the chapters tends to run from east to west.
Those chapters that touch on like themes, such as women and language,
were placed side by side. The book opens with Jacqueline Peterson's exploration of the terms of identification, questioning whether the distinction she and Brown drew in 1985 between "Métis" and "metis" is still
useful today, and a reexamination of whether or not ethnogenesis of
Metis people occurred in the seventeenth- and eighteenth-century Great
Lakes region.

The subsequent three chapters look at the structures of Metis identification at its emergence. Focusing on the northern prairies, parkland, and
subarctic to the west of Hudson Bay and the Great Lakes, Nicole St-Onge
and Carolyn Podruchny use the metaphor of a spider's web to suggest
that the architecture of Metis culture was made up of extended kin networks in the fur trade and of mobility, both over great distances and in
socioeconomic terms. They argue that firm Metis identifications and self-
consciousness only crystallized in moments when external threats forced
group mobilization. Nevertheless, a sense of community, however mobile individuals and families may have been, permeated and linked together the inhabitants of the fur trade world. Gerhard J. Ens examines
one of these moments of crystallization, the 1816 Battle of Seven Oaks,
in which Red River Metis took up arms against the forces of Governor
Robert Semple, who prohibited the Metis from selling pemmican until all
the food needs of the Red River colonists had been met. Ens argues that
even though many claim this battle was the birth of the Metis Nation, the
conflict was not, at the time, an overt expression of nationalism but, rather,
a catalyst that awakened the Metis' sense of collectively held rights. In the
following chapter, Philip D. Wolfart echoes St-Onge and Podruchny in
highlighting mobility as a key characteristic of Metis ethnicity, asserting
that Metis cultural identity cannot be understood as emerging in a fixed
place, like a nation-state, but must be perceived in an aspatially organized
world. In this type of geographic organization of human populations,
connections among mobile individuals, families, and communities do not
conform to conventional mapping styles.

The next group of chapters examines different expressions of Metis
ethnicity, paying particular attention to language. Étienne Rivard's study

of the linkages between geography and oral histories among the nineteenth-century Metis on the prairies resonates with Wolfart's and with St-Onge and Podruchny's ideas about mobility. He shows us how narratives illuminate how some Metis understood their sense of place and collective consciousness and how place names reveal oral geographies or the relationship between orality and territoriality. Peter Bakker explores how the creation of new languages often accompanies the development of new ethnic identities, arguing that emerging languages are shaped by specific sociohistoric contexts and operate dialectically with one another. Bakker asserts that truly mixed languages, such as Michif, are very rare, that they do not necessarily accompany mixed cultures, and that it is difficult to say which comes first, the birth of a people or the new language.

Turning to a specific location with distinct politics, Victor Lytwyn describes the story of the Fort Frances Metis, the first Metis community to treat with the Canadian government (Treaty 3, signed in 1875) and be recognized as a distinct aboriginal nation. Although the Canadian government later denied their existence, these Metis considered themselves distinct from their Indian and European neighbors. Moving farther south and west, to Prairie du Chien, Wisconsin, Lucy Eldersveld Murphy draws our attention to Metis women. Her chapter traces how mixed-blood fur trade families lost autonomy, status, and land when the United States took over the region, and how women in these families used their networks, their roles as "public mothers," and family residence patterns to resist dispossession. Diane P. Payment continues the discussion about the central role played by Metis women in family networks, economic activities, and political movements. Payment focuses on the life of Marie Fisher Gaudet in the Northwest Territories, who assisted her husband's career with her economic skills, language proficiencies, and family networks and also taught her children Metis cultural practices in the face of growing community ambivalence about Metis heritage.

Michel Hogue takes us back south of the forty-ninth parallel to examine how shifting criteria for tribal membership and reservation access in the United States acted as a barometer for the changes in borderland communities. Metis migrated to northern Montana in the late 1860s and early 1870s, following the buffalo herds west, and intermarried with local Assiniboine and Gros Ventre peoples, creating multiethnic and fluid communities close to the Canada–United States border. These communities suffered a hardening of racialized identities and exclusion of Metis as a category. Northwest of the Great Plains, just beyond the Rockies, a group project by Mike Evans, Jean Barman, Gabrielle Legault, Erin Dolmage, and Geoff Appleby studies the origins of Metis ethnogenesis in New Caledonia among families connected to Red River. Like other contributors to this collection, these authors demonstrate how the historic Metis Nation is best understood as a mobile and expanding network, rather than fixed to a neatly delineated homeland. Further north, Daniel J. Blumlo shows us that descendents of Russian fur traders and Aleut, Alutiiq, and Tlingit women in what would become Alaska did not form distinct communities and identities apart from their parents' cultures. The Russian American Company strove to assimilate this Creole workforce by controlling social status, marriages, and upbringing and by undermining indigenous matrilineal traditions. Even though Creole people acted as go-betweens and cultural brokers in this fur trade, much like the Metis, Creoles came to identify themselves primarily as either Russians or members of an Indian group, depending on their location and life experience. These chapters show the extent to which local contexts mattered in the creation of Metis communities and identities.

The last two chapters in the collection take us to the present day by examining how scholarship about Metis peoples has evolved in court cases and historiography. Chris Andersen analyzes how Metis identification is expressed in Canadian legal proceedings, cautioning us that courts do not share the same nuanced and complex appreciation for ambiguities held by scholars, and that they manufacture fixed definitions of Metis identity. He identifies Metis historical use and occupancy as being lost in translation in the 2003 *Powley* ruling. Focusing on the problem of how to define Metis communities while recognizing the mobility of individuals and families, he explores how use and occupancy modalities of thought interrupt and restructure politically oriented understandings of territory. In the final chapter, Brenda Macdougall steps back to reflect generally on the question of ambivalence in Metis identification and historiography. She argues that rather than focus on Metis who celebrate a long-lost Indian grandmother to claim a Metis identity today, or on those Metis families who tried to hide their identities in the twentieth century to avoid racism and discrimination, we should instead examine the cultural ambivalence of scholars who have studied the Metis, who defy simple racial or cultural categorization, and their ontological systems.

Conclusion

Movement, geographic expanse, and family defined the elements and contours of Metis culture, community, and, eventually, nationhood. They became who they are—a people called Metis—not in spite of their mobility but because of it. Mobility allowed them to exploit a wide variety of economic and geographic niches in varied geographical regions along the sinews of the fur trade while permitting the maintenance and reproduction of far-flung ties of kinship. The Metis became a collectivity because they knew who they were and outsiders recognized them as such. Their mobility and spatial confidence allowed them to survive physically, spiritually, and intellectually. The chapters in this collection span a wide geographic area in northwestern North America, from Montana to Alaska, from British Columbia to the Great Lakes, and consider questions from the beginnings of the Metis in the Great Lakes region in the late seventeenth century to contemporary issues about defining Metis people and rights in Canadian law. They deal with questions as diverse as how the U.S. Library of Congress categorizes Metis scholarship, the nuances in Michif verbs, and the role of women in maintaining economic and social networks. The thread that holds all these chapters together is their focus on land, family, and mobility; this focus provides a way to better understand who the Metis were, who they became, and who they are today.

Notes

1. Our first conversation occurred in Winnipeg at the annual meeting of the Canadian Historical Association, and another conversation was initiated because of our mutual participation in the spring of 2006 at the Ninth North American Fur Trade Conference and the Twelfth Rupert's Land Colloquium held in St. Louis, Missouri.

2. This is now called the D'Arcy McNickle Center for American Indian and Indigenous Studies.

3. Peterson and Brown, "Introduction," 7–8.

4. Peterson and Brown (ibid.) cited the Métis National Council's statement to the United Nations Working Group on Indigenous Populations in 1984 as informing their decision. According to this statement, the lowercase *m* reflected the original French usage of the term as a racial designation for anyone of mixed ancestry who evolved into a distinct indigenous people throughout North America. The University of Manitoba Press insisted on lowercase *m* throughout the

volume for editorial consistency, despite the editors' reservations (personal communication from Jennifer S. H. Brown). The decision they made was largely driven by a desire for editorial and political consistency, but it incited a debate on terminology that has not yet been quelled. The issues of terminology and how best to apply the appropriate designations continue to perplex us today.

5. For more extensive discussions of terminology, see Peterson in this volume; Brown, "Noms et metaphors"; Brown, "Linguistic Solitudes in the Fur Trade"; Foster, "Origins of the Mixed Bloods in the Canadian West"; and Foster, "Métis."

6. Peterson and Brown, "Introduction," 5–7.

7. This conference was held at the Diefenbaker Canada Centre on the University of Saskatchewan campus and was cosponsored by the Canadian Historical Association and Canadian Indigenous/Native Studies Association.

8. This second conference was sponsored by the Canadian Historical Association (the Canadian Indigenous/Native Studies Association did not participate in the congress that year) and spanned two full days, with Jennifer S. H. Brown providing a keynote address.

9. None of the essays here engages directly with Metis material culture. For an excellent recent study of Metis clothing and decorative arts, see Racette, "Sewing Ourselves Together."

10. Brody, *Other Side of Eden,* 7.

11. Greenblatt, "Cultural Mobility," 6.

12. The authors in Greenblatt's volume explore the sixteenth-century Portuguese colony in India, German narratives of American slavery, tourism and migration in contemporary China, Islamic performativity traced over centuries, and Goethe's reading of world literature.

13. Lear, *Radical Hope,* explores the psychological impact of this initial transformation and what it then meant to this tribe when they were confined by the American government to reservations.

14. Ethbridge, *Creek Indians and their World.*

15. See Milloy, *Plains Cree;* and Mandelbaum, *Plains Cree.* Similarly, some Ojibwe moved west from the woodlands of the Great Lakes to become the Plains Ojibwe. See Peers, *Ojibwa of Western Canada.*

16. Slobodin, *Metis of the Mackenzie District,* 70–71, 163–64.

17. Devine, *People Who Own Themselves,* and Macdougall, *One of the Family,* are two exceptions.

18. These are recurring themes in most histories, both scholarly and popular, of people of Jewish descent. See, e.g., Johnson, *History of the Jews.*

19. Crowe, *History of the Gypsies.*

20. Calloway, *White People, Indians and Highlanders.* Although she does not discuss family per se, Nancy Shoemaker, *Strange Likeness,* explores the remarkable commonalities among Indians in eastern America and northwestern Europeans in the eighteenth century.

21. Greenblatt, "Cultural Mobility," 16.

Works Cited

Brody, Hugh. *The Other Side of Eden: Hunters, Farmers, and the Shaping of the World.* Vancouver, BC: Douglas and McIntyre, 2000.

Brown, Jennifer S. H. "Linguistic Solitudes in the Fur Trade: Some Changing Social Categories and Their Implications." In *Old Trails and New Directions: Proceedings of the Third North American Fur Trade Conference,* edited by Arthur J. Ray and Carol M. Judd, 147–59. Toronto, ON: University of Toronto Press, 1980.

———. "Noms et métaphores dans l'historiographie métisse: anciennes catégories et nouvelles perspectives." *Recherches Amerindiennes au Quebec* 37, nos. 2–3 (2007): 7–14.

Calloway, Colin. *White People, Indians and Highlanders: Tribal Peoples and Colonial Encounters in Scotland and America.* Oxford, UK: Oxford University Press, 2008.

Crowe, David M. *A History of the Gypsies in Eastern Europe and Russia.* New York, NY: St. Martin's Press, 1994.

Devine, Heather. *The People Who Own Themselves: Aboriginal Ethnogenesis in a Canadian Family, 1660–1900.* Calgary, AB: University of Calgary Press, 2004.

Ethbridge, Robbie. *The Creek Indians and Their World.* Chapel Hill: University of North Carolina, 2003.

Foster, John Elgin. "The Métis: The People and the Term." In *The Western Métis: Profiles of a People,* edited by Patrick C. Douaud, 21–30. Regina, SK: Canadian Plains Research Centre, University of Regina, 2007.

———. "The Origins of the Mixed Bloods in the Canadian West." In *Essays on Western History in Honor of Lewis Gwynne Thomas,* edited by Lewis H. Thomas, 71–80. Edmonton: University of Alberta Press, 1976.

Greenblatt, Stephen. "Cultural Mobility: An Introduction." In *Cultural Mobility: A Manifesto,* edited by Stephen Greenblatt, with Ines Zupanov, Reinhard Meyer-Kalkus, Heike Paul, and Pal Nyiri, 1–23. New York, NY: Cambridge University Press, 2010.

Johnson, Paul. *A History of the Jews.* New York, NY: Harper and Row, 1987.

Lear, Jonathan. *Radical Hope: Ethics in the Face of Cultural Devastation.* Boston, MA: Harvard University Press, 2006.

Macdougall, Brenda. *One of the Family: Metis Culture in Nineteenth-Century Northwestern Saskatchewan.* Vancouver, BC: University of British Columbia Press, 2010.

Mandelbaum, David G. *The Plains Cree: An Ethnographic, Historical and Comparative Study.* Regina, SK: Canadian Plains Research Centre, University of Regina, 1978.

Milloy, John S. *The Plains Cree: Trade, Diplomacy and War, 1780 to 1870.* Winnipeg: University of Manitoba Press, 1988.

Peers, Laura. *The Ojibwa of Western Canada, 1780 to 1870.* Winnipeg: University of Manitoba Press, 1994.

Peterson, Jacqueline, and Jennifer S. H. Brown. "Introduction." In *The New Peoples: Being and Becoming Métis in North America,* edited by Jacqueline Peterson and Jennifer S. H. Brown, 3–16. Winnipeg: University of Manitoba Press; Lincoln: University of Nebraska Press, 1985.

Racette, Sherry Farrell. "Sewing Ourselves Together: Clothing, Decorative Arts and the Expression of Metis and Half Breed Identity." PhD thesis, University of Manitoba, 2004.

Shoemaker, Nancy. *A Strange Likeness: Becoming Red and White in Eighteenth-Century North America*. New York, NY: Oxford University Press, 2004.

Slobodin, Richard. *Metis of the Mackenzie District*. Ottawa, ON: Canadian Research Centre for Anthropology, 1966.

1

RED RIVER REDUX

Métis Ethnogenesis and the Great Lakes Region

JACQUELINE PETERSON

The inclusion of the Métis in section 35 of the Canadian Constitution as one of Canada's aboriginal peoples (along with Indians and the Inuit) and the addition of "Métis" as an ethnic category of choice in the 1981 Canadian Census have served to enlarge Canada's Métis population and to expand the number of provincial Métis and non-status Indian[1] associations, particularly outside the Prairie provinces. In the past thirty years, the number of self-identified Métis throughout Canada has grown exponentially, as has membership in provincial Métis associations. Such organizations no longer advocate for non-status Indians because the addition of more than 100,000 C-31 Indians to the Indian Act since 1985 has effectively eliminated non-status Indian as a category.[2] Yet, between 1996 and 2006, the Canadian Census recorded an astonishing 91 percent increase in the "Métis identity population," from 204,000 in 1996 to about 390,000 in 2006. It is interesting that this growth of the self-identified Métis population in Canada has a parallel in the United States, where the number of self-identified American Indians has increased dramatically since the federal census allowed citizens to select their own ethnic/racial heritage. In 1970, the U.S. Census enumerated 827,108 Indians (including Inuit and Aleuts). Ten years later, in the 1980 census, 1,421,367 individuals listed themselves as Indian, a population increase of 75 percent. Of course, the larger American census numbers since 1980 do not reflect a growth in the actual number of tribally or federally recognized Indians.[3]

The expansion of the self-identified Native American population in the United States and of similar growth in the self-identified Métis population in Canada, narrowly affirmed by *R. v. Powley*, has been stunning. The elasticity and situational character of such modern identities raise questions about the boundaries of the groups to which they refer and about the genesis, fixedness, and persistence of those ethnic groups and tribes that precede them.[4] What are the historical connections, for example, between the original Métis Nation of western Canada and individuals of mixed ancestry in the eastern provinces who now use the term self-referentially? In the late 1970s, anthropologist Joe Sawchuk, writing for the Manitoba Métis Federation, described the modern Métis resurgence as a political reformulation of an ethnic identity. Métis sociologist Chris Andersen has recently countered that the Canadian policy definition of Métis, in its emphasis on race mixedness, has only further entrenched the symbolic power of race instead of legitimizing the ethnic identity of the Métis of the Canadian west and their descendants.[5] Following Andersen, it is necessary to ask whether the current political definition of the term Métis is consonant with its historical meaning, with the ethnic group that the Canadian Constitution intended to recognize when it named the Métis one of Canada's three aboriginal groups, or with the legal meaning of "peoples" as contained in section 35 (s. 35) of the constitution.

In this chapter I examine two aspects of the current debate over the identification of Métis people. The first concerns terminology and definition. What were the various terms used to describe the Métis people, including English-language equivalents, in the nineteenth century? How do these terms illuminate or confuse identification of Métis as a separate ethnic group and collective identity? And how are these terms to be separated from a colonialist vocabulary of "race," which reads social and moral characteristics into "blood mixture"?

The second aspect explores the relationship of several dozen multicultural fur trade settlements in the Great Lakes region, with roots stretching back to the seventeenth-century French regime, to the emergence of the Métis along the Red River. Given a long history of intermarriage, the development of visually distinct trading towns, and the growth of a sizeable population of mixed ancestry by the early nineteenth century, why did Métis ethnogenesis fail to occur in the Great Lakes region? What was the relationship, if any, between the multiethnic Great Lakes fur trade families and settlements and the emergence on the northeastern plains of a separate Métis ethnic group claiming rights to a tribal or national identity and to an aboriginal homeland by 1816?

Terminology and Definition

Over the past 150 years, the definition of Métis and the terms used to identify Métis people have often been a source of confusion and disagreement. Scholars generally have argued that Métis people emerged from the social milieu of the northwest fur trade during the final decades of Canadian and American colonization of the Great Lakes region and the northern plains. The usual storyline is as follows: between 1814 and 1816, a group of fur trade employees and former employees of mixed descent, known variously as *bois-brûlés* and "freemen," burst on the political scene along the Red River of the north, proclaiming themselves a new people with rights to the soil based on occupancy and aboriginal connection. These claims were made in opposition to those of Lord Selkirk and the Hudson's Bay Company. Although composed primarily of French speakers calling themselves *bois-brûlés*, the group subsumed both French and English speakers, nearly all of whom were former wintering employees of the North West Company or one of its competitors.

The subsequent socioeconomic and political history of the Red River Métis has focused on two subjects. First, scholars continue to explore the connections and differences between the English-speaking "Half-breed" and French Canadian Métis agricultural settlements at the Red River Colony on the one hand, and the predominantly French, Cree/Ojibwa, and Michif-speaking Plains Métis settlements of buffalo hunters and provisioners who split their residence between the colony and the plains on the other hand. Second, scholars continue to plumb the movement led by Louis Riel to establish self-rule and title to a Métis homeland between 1869 and 1885 and the migration of extended family groups out of Red River onto the western plains in search of buffalo in the same period. By the end of the nineteenth century, the resulting new Metis communities, many of them near former winter buffalo camps, stretched into the western and northern Prairie provinces and into North Dakota and Montana, where their descendants live today. This process is often termed the Métis diaspora.

The basic outlines of this integral aspect of western Canadian history, detailing the growth—from ethnogenesis to diaspora—of the members of a self-conscious nineteenth-century ethnic group whose members were of mixed European and Indian ancestry, enjoy fairly wide agreement among historians. There is less agreement about the causes for Métis ethnic group formation and about the dates, locations, and composition of groups subsequently drawn under the Métis mantle.[6]

In addition to Métis, the nineteenth-century vocabulary of mixedness used by both insiders and outsiders included a host of other terms to describe the residents of the Red River region. Some, such as *bois-brûlés*, *gens libres*, *li gens libres*, freemen, country born, "my countrymen," English Half-breeds, and Red River Half-breeds, were used by residents of the Red River Colony and speak to the several English and French language and Hudson's Bay Company and North West Company traditions of Métis and English Half-breed identity.[7]

Since the late 1970s, fur trade and Métis scholars searching for the genesis of the Métis Nation and of "Métis-like" groups outside the northeastern plains have also constructed a vocabulary of "mixedness" or "métis-ness" that includes analytic concepts such as the following: Great Lakes métis, proto-métis, Athabasca métis, Iroquois freemen, the Iroquois-métis, James Bay mixed-bloods, mixed-blood Saulteaux, mixed-bloods, voyageur-*hivernants*, outsider adult males, mixed-descent ethnic group, children of the fur trade, fur trade families, fur trade society, and peoples of mixed descent. This constructed vocabulary suggested that "the Métis" might encompass mixed individuals and groups ranging geographically from the Pacific Northwest, to the Athabasca, the shores of Hudson Bay, the northeastern plains and Red River, and to the Great Lakes, as well as individuals of French Canadian, English, Scots, Iroquois, Cree, Ojibwa, Assiniboine, Slavey, and Dene descent. An extremely lively debate on these issues in Canada and the United States has ensued, but it is important to note that historians and other scholars have not reached consensus on the use of "the Métis" outside of the original Métis Nation of what would become Manitoba and its diaspora region.[8]

An early effort to compare research among fur trade and Métis scholars occurred in 1981 at the Newberry Library in Chicago. Organized by

myself, Jennifer S. H. Brown, and Jeanne Oyawin Eder, the First Conference on the Métis in North America drew together more than twenty Canadian, American, Métis, and Native American scholars from the fields of
history, anthropology, geography, economics, art history, linguistics, literature, and Native American and Métis studies. The resulting publication,
The New Peoples: Being and Becoming Métis in North America, introduced
new work on the Red River Métis and related diaspora communities as
well as on other groups of mixed-descent individuals and families connected to the fur trade, most of whom had never called themselves either
métis or Métis.[9]

Were these other groups related to or part of the historical Métis
Nation of the west? In the introduction to the volume, Jennifer Brown
and I tried to draw a distinction between Métis with a capital *M* to designate the Red River Métis and its diaspora communities, and métis or
métisse with a small *m* (the French language terms for persons of mixed
descent) to designate mixed individuals or groups whose ethnic self-
consciousness and collective identity were unformed or unarticulated.
Although our intent was to recognize the potentiality of ethnic group formation, the use of the French terms *métis/métisse,* particularly when applied to English speakers, created confusion and eventual misuse by
those who failed to distinguish between Métis (historical ethnic/national
group of the west) and métis/metisse (denoting an individual of mixed
ancestry). Indeed, in my own earliest published work on the Great Lakes,
"Prelude to Red River," I erroneously conflated Métis and métis. Since
the mid-1980s, a majority of American scholars of the Great Lakes, including myself, Richard White, Susan Sleeper-Smith, Lucy Eldersveld
Murphy, and Tanis Thorne have variously used the lower case métis as
well as the English term "mixed-blood." Increasingly, however, the terminology of mixedness has shifted to less racialized constructions,
such as "mixed ancestry" or "mixed-descent families."[10]

Uses of the terms métis and Métis have taken on far greater importance
in the last several decades, as the discussion has moved to the courtroom.
Given that the term métis itself was rarely used in the nineteenth-century
Great Lakes by English speakers on either side of the Canadian–United
States border, the contemporary use in Ontario of the term Métis, as in
Ontario Métis Nation, is a misappropriation, as is the extension by schol-
ars of the French-language terms Métis or métis backward in time to re-
label those once known in the documentary record as "half-breeds" or

mixed-bloods, or by no distinct term at all. Yet, that is precisely what one sees in the expert witness reports prepared for *R. v. Powley* and in a spate of recent articles and theses by historians and lawyers attempting to prove the existence of historical "Métis" communities in Ontario. It is significant that in a recent analysis of the population of nineteenth-century Sault Ste. Marie, two prominent Ontario scholars have returned to the lower case métis to distinguish peoples of mixed ancestry at the Sault from the Red River Métis and the Métis Nation.[11]

Both current usages wrongly assume that the meanings of the term Métis (or métis) are timeless and immutable. Yet, prior to the last two decades of the eighteenth century, individuals of mixed ancestry, when they can be identified as such, were usually identified as Indian or Euro-Canadian or Euro-American, depending on their appearance and lifestyle. Even as the terms Half-breed, métis, and metif began to appear in fur traders' journals and travelers' accounts after 1800, only along the Red River after 1814–16 did the term Métis come to connote a separate ethnic group—the *bois-brûlés*—who viewed themselves as a new tribe or nation. Whereas Canadian and American Indian Affairs documents, written in English by English speakers after 1815, are replete with references to Half-breeds and mixed-bloods, the French language terms métis/métisse are rarely used outside of the northeastern plains.[12]

Instead, the awareness of a growing population of mixed-bloods both inside and outside tribal society in the American and Canadian Great Lakes inspired government officials to give preferential treatment to mixed-blood chiefs and to use traders related to Indian tribes as interpreters and informal treaty negotiators in securing Indian land cessions. In return for their services, the United States, between 1816 and 1830, offered gifts of land or individual reservations to such individuals. By the early 1830s, however, American officials came to view the growing body of mixed-blood claimants as Indians, who deserved some portion of the annual annuity paid to treaty bands based on the degree of their relatedness to a band member, or to receive a one-time payment, effectively extinguishing any future claim. American and Canadian Indian Department documents, treaties negotiated with Great Lakes tribes in the United States and Canada between 1816 and 1855, and lists of payments of land and money to Half-breeds and mixed-bloods all indicate that both governments struggled to identify those persons of mixed descent deserving to be treated as Indians, but by mid nineteenth century both saw only two categories: Indian or white.[13]

Thus, when contemporary scholars embrace terms such as the Ontario Métis Nation and consciously translate nineteenth-century English-language terms like Half-breeds or mixed-bloods from the documentary record into the politicized French-language term Métis (as in Métis Nation), they change the intended meanings of the original writers and of the terms themselves. Whatever the intent, the use of Métis in this context has implanted Métis communities, Métis identity, and Métis political consciousness into regions and times where they did not exist before.[14] After having anachronously inserted Métis consciousness into areas and eras where they did not previously exist, it has become easy for writers to slip into the erroneous assumption that the very use of the term "proves" the existence of distinct Métis communities outside Red River and its diaspora region in the nineteenth century. For example, Karl Hele has stated, "To continue to deny that the mixed race people of the Great Lakes lacked an identity by referring to them as 'métis,' is to deny them an existence as a people." Hele has thus "opted to capitalize 'Métis' in recognition of their distinct identity in their Great Lakes Homeland."[15] This logic is an example of circular reasoning and, like some other recent work, is a distortion of the historical record.

The modern usage and definition of Métis is equally problematic in its renewed emphasis on a vocabulary of "blood" or race mixture rather than ethnic or national identity. Although the terms métis and half-breed were not widely used before the early nineteenth century, the French-language term métissage (like its Spanish language equivalent mestizaje) referred in the early centuries of European colonial expansion to the mixing of civilized people and heathen or primitive peoples. This early usage emphasized culture as much as biology, allowing at least in principle highly acculturated Christianized Indians, Africans, or mulattos to become French or Spanish citizens. In fact, the terminology of racial amalgamation used from the sixteenth to the eighteenth centuries was pessimistic and derogatory. The English term "mulatto" shared the same root with "mule," and the epithet hurled at the offspring of Indian–African unions, "griffe," stemmed from "griffon," a mythical winged beast.[16]

The first documented usage of the terms métif and half-breed in the Great Lakes and northwest in the late eighteenth and early nineteenth centuries grew out of this paradigm and were an indication of the growing British and American obsession with classification systems that placed "races" on a continuum of humanity, stretching from savage to civilized. These systems confused and conflated biology with social and cultural behavior, and by the second half of the nineteenth century they were given legitimacy in the racist ideology of social Darwinism. This emerging ideology strongly influenced the development of U.S. and Canadian Indian policies and the attitudes of both governments toward the classification and treatment of "racial minorities," be they Indians, "half-breeds," Africans, or Asians in North America.[17]

Since the 1960s, scholars of ethnicity and nationhood have repudiated the idea of national and ethnic *"races* [italics added] grounded in the conflation of biology and culture."[18] We are all mixed, geneticists inform us. More to the point, Canada's First Nations and America's Indian tribes are as genetically mixed as the descendants of the Red River Métis. We know this intellectually, but the symbolic power of "race" is so pervasive in our post-colonial world that, in Métis sociologist Chris Andersen's words, it causes "fuzzy thinking." Race or "blood" quantum does not in itself create ethnic identities or cultures. There is no such thing, in reality, as a half-breed. Blood does not mix, and surely not in equal proportions. "Blood" is not ethnicity, nor is it culture. Yet, in the introduction to a recent anthology by well-known scholars on the Métis in the Canadian west, editor Patrick C. Douaud asserted, "A Métis now is a person with any degree of Indian blood who is not registered on a reserve." Where, then, one must insist on asking, is the original Métis ethnic group, the nineteenth-century people who proclaimed themselves a new tribe or nation, and where are their descendants?[19]

Rethinking Ethnogenesis and the Fur Trade in the Great Lakes Region

Perhaps we need to start anew. Most scholars of the latter half of the twentieth century have believed that the Métis coalesced as a separate ethnic group or nation only on the northeastern plains. However, since the 1980s, new work has sought to document examples of Métis ethnogenesis in other fur trade contact zones in Canada and the United States. The implicit assumption is that Métis ethnogenesis was not only closely related to, but was a direct outgrowth of, the fur trade.[20] As a form of intercultural colonial contact, the fur trade could well have engendered new multiracial groups and new identities in the borderlands between Indian and European societies, as happened in other contact spheres, such as the American Southeast or the Caribbean. However, there is surprisingly little evidence to suggest that there were multiple sites of Métis ethnogenesis in North America. Thus, as a new generation of scholars strains to locate the occasional reference to métis individuals and even less frequently to métis communities across 150 years of fur trade interaction and the entire St. Lawrence–Great Lakes and Hudson Bay drainage systems, it is important to recall the sheer force of Métis numbers and ethnic and political consciousness manifested at Red River after 1815. In contrast to what can be seen elsewhere, the reality of the Métis Nation on the northeastern plains is both incontrovertible and stunning. Perhaps we need to look again at the connection between the fur trade and the genesis of the Métis as a new and separate people.[21]

What we now know, after more than three decades of cumulative research and publication, is that the Great Lakes was the birthing ground of neither the Red River Métis nor a separate ethnic group of mixed ancestry and culture like the Red River Métis. My own early work documented the emergence and growth of a network of multicultural fur trade communities in the Great Lakes region in the eighteenth and early nineteenth centuries, whose members seemed to share some similarities with the peoples who coalesced at Red River as Métis. Given the paucity of documents written by women and fur trade employees at the lower ranks, it was impossible to discern how most Great Lakes people of mixed French Canadian and Indian descent viewed themselves. In the tumult and dislocations of the treaty and early reservation eras, however, as Great Lakes fur trade society gave way to a settler society, both men and women could and did reinvent themselves. At best, the Great Lakes métis were a "prelude" to Red River—metaphorically one of many roads to Red River but not themselves Métis.

From what can be gleaned from the Great Lakes documentary record, mixed-descent residents did not call themselves Métis or see themselves as a separate people aspiring to political power or autonomy. The multiethnic Great Lakes fur trade communities, sufficiently populous and connected by extensive regional kinship networks, might have been on the verge of a Métis ethnogenesis by 1815. However, this would have required a turn toward a new ethnic self-consciousness and a preference for marital endogamy. Instead, fur trade society, always centrifugal, was snuffed out in the

treaty era, its individual members transformed and reinvented as old settlers or as participants in other ethnogenesis or re-ethnification processes
involving native peoples, such as occurred within many of the Great Lakes
tribes during the late eighteenth and early nineteenth centuries.[22]

The hybrid culture complex of Great Lakes fur trade society was
shared, in part, by the Ottawa, Ojibwa, and Potawatomi and in fact may
have derived from the fur trade-oriented, Ojibwa-inspired pan-tribalism
that swept over the Great Lakes in the eighteenth century, reducing distinctions between bands, homogenizing cultures, and reducing the number of separate tribal groupings. The core denominator of fur trade
society's occupational identity was its connective and mediative stance
between the persons, labor, and products of Indian and Euro-American
societies. It was not as a separate or distinct people, but as a "network
people," or as a people in between, that members of Great Lakes fur trade
society served as guides, interpreters, negotiators, mail carriers, portage
and ferry tenders, barge and oar men, and officers and spies in the Indian
service, as well as tribal business agents and teachers and employees of
missions and Indian agencies. In each case, they functioned not as members of a separate ethnic group but as individual carriers, linking Indians
and Euro-Americans, and as buffers behind which the ethnic boundaries
of antagonistic Indian and Euro-Canadian and Anglo-American cultures
resisted transformation. These roles ensured the survival of individuals
but did not of themselves stimulate the emergence of a "new people"
within fur trade society.[23]

The three decades after 1780 were the high water mark of the Great
Lakes fur trade. In these years, as the great Canadian and American fur
trade companies expanded and clashed in violent competition, the growth
of a mixed-descent population accelerated. Not only did the competing
companies more than double the number of servants working in Indian
country, but established trading families, many of them of mixed descent,
enlarged their own commercial and kinship networks by forging new
partnerships with more distant Indian bands and establishing a host of
new hamlets and trading posts. By 1800, the first wave of Canadian traders and freemen, Ojibwa, and Ottawa hunters had permanently lodged
themselves in the western reaches of the Fond du Lac district and in the
Red River and Assiniboine River valleys and were building commercial
and social bridges with northeastern Plains tribes. It was from this nucleus that the plains-oriented Red River Métis were to multiply.

Mackinac, the corporate headquarters of the American Fur Company after the War of 1812, still had a very exotic look in 1820: "The present town of Michilimackinac . . . consists altogether of about one hundred and fifty houses, several of which are handsomely painted. Its permanent population does not differ far from four hundred and fifty, but is sometimes swelled by the influx of traders, voyageurs and Indians to one or two thousand." As late as 1830, according to the federal census for the territory of Michigan, the majority of Mackinac's 873 residents possessed French surnames, and many, along with a number of British Indian families, were of mixed ancestry.[24]

Descriptions of most of the other Great Lakes trading towns during the early nineteenth century were comparable. At Green Bay, where Henry Rowe Schoolcraft and Jedediah Morse visited in 1820, there were some 450–500 persons living outside the American fort, occupying "60 principal dwellings," besides temporary structures. The inhabitants were "except some half a dozen Americans . . . retired French voyageurs, and half breed French and Menomonee . . . [who] without let or hindrance [had] taken up the whole shore of the river above the fort, for six miles." Their wives were "part of the half, and the remainder of the full, aboriginal blood."[25]

In 1820, Morse likewise found at Prairie du Chien "an old French settlement, where are three or four hundred inhabitants, principally of mixed blood." Prairie du Chien grew only moderately over the next decade, to 449 civilians in 1830. As late as 1835, Henry Merrill characterized Prairie du Chien as a French Indian village with bark-covered houses, its residents gossiping, smoking their pipes, and sipping tea with native relatives and cronies.[26]

At Sault Ste. Marie, where after the War of 1812 a portion of the trading population moved to the British side of the river adjacent to the North West Company warehouses, the residents in 1826 were still primarily "voyageurs, and their Indian families, and their dogs," living in one-story bark-covered cabins. Although the town of 150 persons, according to Thomas McKenney's estimates, enjoyed the services of a cooper, tailor, baker, and blacksmith, as well as two groceries and three retail stores, it was still without a school, church, or legal representative.[27]

Yet in spite of such evidence of growth, occupational homogeneity, residential longevity, and a developing history, the multicultural and multiethnic Great Lakes trading communities had little hope of sustaining themselves. The fur trade may have been one of the more benign forms of the European invasion of North America, but it masked its exploitative fist most cleverly. It was, after all, a transitional extractive economy, and the society that organized around it was destined to be short-lived. The heyday of the trade in the Great Lakes was, in fact, its death knell. Between 1780 and 1815, English speakers took over the merchant houses at Montreal, systematized and engrossed the northwestern trade, and displaced French-speakers at the upper levels of the hierarchy. Ruthless competition and greed decimated the wildlife population and ravaged the Indian population. Caste lines around the voyageur class hardened, and those of mixed Indian ancestry found themselves pushed to the bottom of the occupational ladder. And, following the Peace of Ghent, the Yankees spread over the Midwest like a flood.

Signs of disequilibrium and change were not slow in coming. Traveling through Detroit in 1821, General Albert E. Ellis still described the population as "'mixed,' the French Canadian prevailing. . . . There were many Half-breeds, and it being the season of the year when the Indians usually come in from their wintering grounds, the wild Chippewa seemed to be in indisputed possession." But Ellis's vision was skewed by the summer crowds. Moreover, he noticed that while "a majority of the inhabitants of Detroit were of the plebian order, Canadian and mixed-blood prevailing, there was not wanting a good proportion of well-educated, intelligent, cultivated people, who would have graced any society."[28]

It is unlikely that Ellis was referring to the Canadian creole upper class. By 1821, many of the wealthy French Anglophiles and British merchant traders had already relocated to the British side of the Detroit River at Malden and Sandwich. Simultaneously, Detroit had attracted an impressive array of ambitious young American men, who soon came to wield political and economic power over the entire territory of Michigan (then including Wisconsin and part of Minnesota). Whereas in 1810 Detroit contained 2,114 non-Indian residents, most of whom were British sympathizers, by 1826 the city's 2,500 persons were overwhelmingly newcomers and American. In that year, Thomas McKenney proclaimed that the Canadian portion of the population was "declining fast."[29]

The dispersal of the Canadian and mixed-descent population within the American Great Lakes after 1815 was widespread, whether in the form of forced segregation into suburbs or rural margins or the selective migration to British Ontario or Indian reservations and reserves. According to a

British Indian Department official at Penetanguishene at the south end of Georgian Bay in 1829, some fifty families at the former British post at Drummond Island were in need of lands for resettlement in British territory. These "poor inhabitants," who "with few exceptions [were] connected with the Indians," had followed the British "from Michilimackinac at the time it was given up to the Americans." In 1829, they were in danger of losing "their dwellings with any little improvement they have made by the evacuation of Drummond Island."[30]

On the other hand, numerous old residents refused to quit their ancestral communities, even as the monopolization of the Great Lakes trade after 1815 by John Jacob Astor's American Fur Company contributed to another wave of fur trade terminations, this time of home-grown mixed-descent voyageurs who were British in sympathy and less docile than the French Canadian boatmen from the lower St. Lawrence. Faced with both unemployment and the loss of lands they had occupied without title in the trading settlements, many former trade employees went "free," turning to trapping, transporting, and logging as well as marginal employments peripheral to the Indian trade. Others relied on fishing in the cold waters about Michilimackinac, the shores of Lake Superior, and the rapids at Sault Ste. Marie. According to Philander Prescott, by the 1830s, fishing about Mackinac was "generally carried on by the French and Half-breeds with what they called gill-nets," and they caught "considerable quantities." For all this hard work, the overall pattern was one of economic impoverishment and decline in social status.[31]

The northern and western Great Lakes trading communities felt the impact of the American advance at a differential rate. In those towns lying within or adjacent to lands ceded to the American government by the Great Lakes tribes, the creole and mixed-descent population was soon outnumbered, as had been the case a generation earlier with the old French Canadian creole towns of the Illinois country. By the early 1830s, Milwaukee and Chicago were already viewed by some astute New York financiers as future metropolises, and less far-sighted promoters littered the streets of the East with dreams of "paper" towns like Baillytown, Indiana, the home of a prominent French Canadian trading family of mixed descent.[32]

A few of the more remote old villages escaped immediate notice and continued to prosper for a few decades longer. In the northwestern corner of Wisconsin and in Minnesota, trading posts maintained by one or two families of mixed descent remained intact until the 1850s, even though profits from the fur trade dwindled each year, gradually forcing into substantial debt those who clung to the occupation. However, the 1830s were a watershed. The scope of the predominantly Yankee migration from the East was so overwhelming that the French-speaking, multiethnic communities constructed during the fur trade era fell rapidly into oblivion. Most American county histories of the mid- to late-nineteenth century gave only passing mention, if any, to pre-American settlement and were loath to place the mantle of "first settler" upon French Canadian "half-breeds" and illiterate traders.[33]

American settlement may have been a catalyst for the dissolution of the old fur trade communities, but their economic and social underpinnings were already wobbling. John Jacob Astor's American Fur Company, while immensely profitable for a few individuals, was little more than a mopping up operation on the American side of the Great Lakes. Astor himself sold his interests in 1834. Moreover, the pro-British stance taken by most of the established Great Lake traders and their employees during the War of 1812 rendered them liable to American retaliation. For several disastrous years following the Peace of Ghent, traders and voyageurs who were not American citizens were excluded from the trade, prolonging the economic crisis of the war. In 1819, Louis Grignon of Green Bay cried in anguish, "British subjects are all Black Sheep." Four years later, the Grignons and John Lawe received permission to trade with the Menomini, but the situation for men at the lower ranks was dismal. "The Island of McKinac looks as gloomy as every Sunday," Lawe wrote to his uncle Jacob Franks, "no bustle nor noise no money stirring the 2/3 of the men hear find no employment & they have the best part of them hard times to leave the Island as they have no money to take them off you must walk the streets as Strait as a Shingle & there is only the Am Fur Co. that have large Extensive buildings."[34]

It was in this climate that the social and moral fabric of the old fur trade communities began to unravel. Disintegration was swift once it began. Robert Dickson had written to Lawe in 1813 to inquire after "the people" of Green Bay, drawing no distinctions except between that community and neighboring tribes, but by the 1830s, non-tribal participants at treaty payments were divided into "traders and Half-breeds," even though the two were sometimes related as closely as brothers or father and son. A chief, like the Menomini Caron, himself a descendent of an eighteenth-century Green Bay French Canadian trader and the relative of many Carons living in the former fur trade community of Green Bay, could observe in disgust in the early 1840s that his tribe had been "beset with a mongrel yelping race . . . who bite their red brethren." Caron's language suggests, at the least, that Indians as well as non-Indians were susceptible to the new derogatory vocabulary of social race."[35]

Fur trade society had always been loosely joined, its members' identity focused in the occupation itself and the intermediary range of services they performed that linked Indian and Euro-American societies. Intermarriage served to continually enlarge the circle of new Indian trading partners and to integrate influential white newcomers, but Great Lakes fur trade society marriage patterns were centrifugal, not centripetal or endogamous. Unlike the pattern of marriage between those of mixed descent, whether French or English speaking, that quickly developed along the Red River after 1810, Great Lakes fur trade society members of mixed descent did not prefer one another as marriage partners. Rather, mixed-descent sons were encouraged to marry native women so as to enlarge the family's economic relations with Indian bands; daughters were encouraged to marry incoming white traders or business partners. Thus, while the mixed-descent population in the Great Lakes had swelled into the thousands by the 1830s, endogamy—the most important criteria for building and sustaining a separate ethnic group and identity—was absent.[36] In other words, Great Lakes fur trade society was not a building block for future Métis communities.

Other identities—French Canadian, English, trader, Catholic, mixed French Menomini, voyageur—were subsumed under the fur trade's occupational mantle, but they had not disappeared by 1830. When the fur trade declined as a viable means of economically exploiting the vast landscape—a landscape that native peoples had once controlled but were steadily being separated from—group identity as related to the fur trade occupation collapsed. Fur traders, voyageurs, engagés, and laborers alike then had to adapt to changing conditions. In the backwash of the fur trade, they and their families patched together new livelihoods and new identities on a rapidly vanishing frontier or physically migrated north and west to northern Michigan, Wisconsin, Minnesota, and the Red River valley—places where the trade survived for a few decades longer.

A heightened race consciousness among British Canadians and Americans surely played a role in the demise of the multiracial Great Lakes fur trade universe. Racial (and religious) prejudice on the part of English speakers was partially responsible for the entrenchment of a French-speaking Canadian and mixed-ancestry caste at the bottom levels of the fur trade hierarchy after 1780 and for the dismissal of many of these men from the employee ranks after 1815. Whether these servants had previously been conscious of a "racial" identity is unclear. However, just as the 1821 merger of the North West Company and the Hudson's Bay Company—which cast more than a thousand employees, many of them of mixed ancestry, out of service—coincided with the coalescence of Métis ethnic and political consciousness at Red River, the plight of cast-off Great Lakes mixed-blood engages and voyageurs fashioned a new membership category: the "half-breed," defined by the dominant society as a confused amalgamation of racial (pseudo-biological) and sociocultural characteristics.

Unlike the Red River Métis after 1821, and those persons of mixed ancestry who purposely migrated to the eastern Plains to join them, the growing number of mixed-bloods in the Great Lakes region found the middling position untenable by the late 1830s. Persons of mixed ancestry who could not pass as white Americans were increasingly categorized as Indians, and vice versa, as if clothes made the man. It is worth noting, however, that in the more remote sections of the northwestern lakes region, the situation was fluid enough to persuade some who had grown up in the Great Lakes fur trade that they could continue to walk the fence. And many did. It was from the mixed-descent population that government sub-agents, interpreters, and blacksmiths were subsequently drawn. However, an 1831 petition for tribal annuities from three young men of Potawatomi and French Canadian ancestry attending Isaac McCoy's Carey Mission School in southwest Michigan reveals the ambiguities and pressures confronting those of mixed ancestry:

We went to the payment as usual at Chicago, but found the rules of the Agent much different from that of the previous one. A few of the half-blood, though they did not vote or pay taxes, did not receive their part of the annuity paid to the Indians. Even those that were quarter Indians received their portion because they were dressed like Indians. The Agent said to some of us if we did not vote nor pay taxes we should draw like the rest. But after we got there he observed we were not entitled to draw because we wore our dress like the whites. This all thought was not suitable reasons. We inquired of the principal Chief and he said of course you may draw for you are Indians as much as ourselves . . . For we heard that Genl Tipton gave to the half as the pure. And we should say nothing if they would stop all the half-blood or white-Indians for then we should have more than half of the Chiefs on our side for your Excellency knows well the immalgamation is powerful; nearly one half of the Putawatomies is part blood . . . Some of the half breed came in disguise and got their part . . . And this we deem an injustice for the Chiefs said they wanted us all to draw like themselves.[37]

The linguistic and commercial skills of educated mixed-bloods were useful to Indian tribes and First Nations as well as to the American and Canadian governments. By the early nineteenth century, a surprising number of chiefs of Great Lakes tribes and bands were of mixed descent, some of whom—like Shingwaukonse and Nebanigooching of the Garden River Ojibwa in Ontario, Richardville of the Miami, and Billy Caldwell and Claude Laframboise of the Chicago Potawatomi—traveled easily in American and British Canadian societies. Others, like Ottawa Augustin Hamlin (educated in Rome, Italy) and Potawatomi Madore Beaubien (educated at the Carey Mission School in Michigan and Hamilton College in New York), had to content themselves with the roles of business agents and guides in Washington, D.C., society. In the early decades of the nineteenth century, mixed-descent women born into Great Lakes trading communities also played important roles within the region's tribes as teachers, missionaries, and translators, disseminating French Canadian folk arts, Catholicism, and agricultural and business acumen to their Indian relatives.[38]

In the treaty era, Great Lakes mixed-bloods exerted seemingly contradictory influences. On the one hand, they introduced and modeled Euro-American technology, governance, and leadership styles; Christian religion; and values that ultimately altered Great Lakes Indian society in the latter half of the nineteenth century. On the other, it could be said that they shielded traditional Indian leaders, their families, and their way of life from Euro-American contamination, prolonging the period during which many native peoples were able to resist government and missionaries' demands for change. It was, after all, the mixed-descent members and relatives of the Great Lakes tribes who first turned to farming and filled the missions and schoolhouses of government- and church-sponsored philanthropists. Their apparent willingness to adopt "civilization" pacified well-intentioned Americans and British Canadians and also took the pressure off band society as tribal leaders explored how to adapt to innovation without losing their identity and cohesion as Indians or First Nations. The result was a late-contact form of ethnogenesis, a controlled set of changes that produced new Indian "nations" in the nineteenth century informed by pan-Indian claims to sovereignty and modeled to some degree after Euro-American nations.[39]

By the 1840s, the multiethnic, multicultural fur trade universe of the Great Lakes had all but vanished. The processes by which fur trade communities dispersed and their members metamorphosed were extremely complex. Members of the same family made contradictory choices. Half of the Vieau brothers of Milwaukee cast their lot with their Potawatomi kinsmen, and one of these, Louis Vieau, later signed himself as a Potawatomi chief. The others married an American and a women of mixed descent, slipping into anonymity in lower Wisconsin until called to give their oral reminiscences of the territory's "early days." Playing "first settlers," by then they identified themselves as "creoles," as native born.[40]

The numerous progeny of Joseph Bailly, reared near the mouth of the St. Joseph River in northwestern Indiana, similarly followed divergent paths. One daughter took the veil; another married a moderately successful American businessman at Chicago, and her offspring rewrote the family history by minimizing her Indian ancestry in favor of the family's "French" roots. Agatha Bailly, a daughter by an earlier marriage, dressed in semi-Indianized garb, spoke *français sauvage*, and married Nicolas Biddle, a Mackinac trader. Of Bailly's sons, Francis wed an Ottawa woman and reverted to his Ottawa mother's religion, becoming a medicine man. His step-brother, Alexis, on the other hand, followed a third route when he drove a head of cattle north from Prairie du Chien and sold it at a profit to the Métis and Selkirkers at Pembina and the Red River Colony. By this commercial transaction, Bailly opened a major overland traffic between the Red River Métis and the fur trade communities at St. Peters (Minneapolis) and Prairie du Chien.[41]

Was Alexis Bailly a Métis? That is, did he view himself as such, and did he live and marry among other members of a distinct ethnic group bounded by a set of face-to-face communities, a shared language, culture, history, and sense of homeland? In Bailly's case, the answer is likely no. He did not move to Red River, and there is no evidence that he ever used the terms Métis or *bois-brûlé* in reference to himself. Actually, there is no evidence that prior to, or even subsequent to 1815, mixed-descent residents of Great Lakes fur-trading communities had developed a separate ethnic group identity or political consciousness even though many of the cultural characteristics of Great Lakes fur trade communities were similar to those seen among the Red River Métis.

Does that mean that the traders and retired voyageurs and their families at Michilimackinac, Prairie du Chien, Sault Ste. Marie, and Green Bay and their tribal relations did not notice what was transpiring at Red River? The answer is clearly no. In addition to Bailly, members of a dozen prominent Great Lakes trading families, such as the Cadottes and Nolins from Sault Ste. Marie and La Pointe; the LaFramboises, Fishers, and Dousmans from Michilimackinac and Prairie du Chien; the LaRocques, Renvilles, and Rolettes from Prairie du Chien and St. Peters; and the Grignons from Green Bay established commercial and social relations with the nascent Red River Métis at Pembina and at the Forks as early as 1819. And in that same year, Robert Dickson, on behalf of Lord Selkirk, extended an invitation to John Lawe and the other major traders at Green Bay (including Jacques Porlier and the Grignon brothers) to move with their entire community—traders, voyageurs, and the neighboring Menomini—to the Red River Colony.[42]

This invitation, like those extended by the British Indian Department from Penetanguishene to Indian hunting bands in Michigan to move to Ontario, was a British strategy after the War of 1812 to maintain the strength and profitability of the British–Indian alliance. A similar invitation was extended by the Garden River chief Shingwaukonse to Ojibwa leaders as distant as Leech Lake. Although some Potawatomi moved to the Ontario peninsula, these efforts to persuade lower Great Lakes trading families and bands to move to either the Red River Colony or Ontario were mostly unsuccessful or, in the case of the several American Ojibwa chiefs who petitioned for permission to settle at Garden River on the Canadian side of the border, were denied. [43]

In the case of the Menomini and the Green Bay community, neither accepted Selkirk's offer. Amable Grignon, the youngest Grignon brother, joined the ranks of the Hudson's Bay Company long enough to take a Red River Métis wife before returning to Green Bay, but John Lawe and the others did not dislodge themselves from their homes. Although never able to compete with Yankee business acumen, and, like the Bailly family in Indiana, downwardly mobile after the war, they retained their status as traders and used their indebtedness to the American Fur Company as a lever to acquire contracts, jobs, and Indian claims payments through the territorial governor and the Office of Indian Affairs. In the end, they were unwilling to swap familiar surroundings, kin, and influential contacts for an uncertain future with the Hudson's Bay Company, harsh winters, and hostile Sioux on the Plains, knowing that they could rely on creditors such as Ramsay Crooks and Robert Stuart to keep them afloat. Like most of the traders and retired voyageurs of the Great Lakes trading towns a decade later, they petitioned for title to the lands that they had utilized and cultivated so that they might sell them for a profit, and they became American citizens. Thereafter, they would appear in the census and other official records as white Americans.[44]

Members of the fur trade elite, traders, and their offspring who received and retained title to their lands were the lucky ones. In later years, old settlers of French Indian ancestry would have the opportunity to present themselves as French Canadian creoles, to "hide in plain view," or to memorialize their dual heritage. Women seemed more likely to hide, whereas men bragged about their illustrious French or British and Indian forebears. One of J. G. Kohl's 1855 Lake Superior "half-breed" informants (possibly a Cadotte) provided a vivid example of the latter: "The Canadian half breeds often swagger with two genealogies—a European commencing with a 'lieutenant du roi,' and an Indian, from some celebrated chief. I met one Half-breed, a man tolerably well off, who had engraved both his French coat of arms and his Indian totem (an otter) on his seal-ring."[45]

But what of the fur trade proletariat at Mackinac, Sault Ste. Marie, Green Bay, Fond du Lac, and elsewhere on Lake Superior, the voyageurs and retired freemen who squatted with their mixed-descent families on narrow, marginal garden plots in the old settlements? After the American ascendancy, many were forced to relocate to trading posts farther west in unceded portions of Wisconsin or Minnesota or to fishing stations and logging camps, where their livelihood increasingly was gained through a patchwork of part-time work, fishing, logging, hunting, guiding, and transporting. These individuals, who were largely French Canadians, left few records.

From J. G. Kohl's footnotes, we learn that some French Canadian voyageurs were classified as *chicots*, even if they had no Indian ancestry, to distinguish them from the "Whites," meaning Anglo Saxons. The term chicot appears in Kohl's text as part of a lengthy French language soliloquy by a voyageur commenting on the multigenerational nature of the voyageur occupation: "Je suis Voyageur—je suis *Chicot*, monsieur. Je reste partout. Mon grand-pere etait vovageur. Il est mort en voyage." (I am a Voyaguer [a boatman and hauler in the fur trade], I am a *Chicot*, sir. I live everywhere. My grandfather was a voyaguer. He died in the service.) Kohl's assumption was that chicot stood for "half-breed," the term Kohl used to denote those of mixed ancestry. Subsequent scholars such as Marius Barbeau have connected chicot (referring to a stump of wood) and *bois-brûlés* (burnt wood), suggesting that one of chicot's meanings is Métis. Other meanings include deadhead, snare, and long in the tooth.[46]

But was the voyageur who called himself Chicot an incipient Métis? All subsequent historical usages of chicot as *bois-brûlés* or Métis can be traced to Kohl. There are no other known examples. Perhaps Kohl misunderstood. In Albert Lacombe's 1874 *Dictionnaire de la langue des Cris*, Timanaskatotak is rendered *chicot, souche*, the latter meaning stock or lineage. Of all the residents of the far-flung multicultural fur trade communities that evolved and briefly flourished in the Great Lakes region, the voyageurs were most capable, by their birthright and transportation and communication skills, to *"marche avec le vent"* (go with the wind). Ironically, however, in Kohl, the men of the lineage of voyageurs, the men who lived and died *en voyage*, did not dream of retiring to Red River or of carving out a Lake Superior homeland for themselves. They dreamed of Lower Canada (Quebec), their native country, their true home.[47]

> They regarded themselves as exiles—indeed, as doubly banished, first from France, and then again from Lower Canada. . . . Their mode of life exposes them to countless dangers and wants, and though they all say that they will soon return to Lower Canada, *their real home*, very few of them carry this into effect. And there are whole families of Voyageurs here on Lake Superior, who, from father to son, have sung of the "return to Canada," but who have all perished here.[48]

Though they dreamed of Lower Canada, most of these men and their offspring never returned to the French-speaking parishes of Quebec. Opportunities were severely limited for uneducated men with little means or connections. Even an educated North West Company clerk like Jean

Baptiste Perrault was forced to retire at Sault Ste. Marie after several unsuccessful attempts to settle himself and his large mixed-descent family in Quebec.[49]

A search of North West Company rosters between 1780 and 1820 indicates that surnames associated with the voyageur class of the old Great Lakes settlements also appear at the western and northern posts, including those of Upper and Lower Red River and the Assiniboine River, as well as in the Red River censuses, suggesting that some did move west. However, it is instructive to compare the names of settlers at trading towns and posts in the upper Great Lakes region prior to 1835 and employees in the Hudson's Bay Company, North West Company, and American Fur Company journals and rosters in the Lake Superior region with mixed-blood treaty payments, Half-breed scrip applications, and tribal annuity and band membership rolls in the Great Lakes after the 1830s. At Green Bay, for example, a large majority of the names of farmers, widows, traders, voyageurs, and their respective families that were listed as residents in 1818 reappeared on the Menomini mixed-blood payment rolls of 1836 and in an enumeration of Menomini mixed-bloods published in the Green Bay paper in 1849.[50]

Green Bay was not unique. Throughout the Great Lakes, the end of the fur trade and the writing of treaties that extinguished Indian title to vast hunting lands in exchange for reservations and periodic annuity payments and goods exposed the voyageur class and their mixed-descent families to impoverishment and rising Anglo-American race prejudice. Not surprisingly, many chose to identify as Indians or as kin to Indians, to take treaty payments or scrip, and eventually to join their tribal relatives living on or in close proximity to reservations. This process was well underway in the United States by the mid nineteenth century and in Ontario a decade or two later. However much the men and women of Great Lakes fur trade society might have looked like the Red River Métis, they did not become Métis in the nineteenth century. Contrary to the revolutionary transformation that occurred west of the Red River, no new economic niche or political opportunity roused the growth of a separate ethnic group consciousness and community in the Great Lakes. That history belongs to the northeastern plains.

Notes

I wish to thank Jennifer S. H. Brown, Chris Andersen, and Raymond DeMallie, Jr., for their helpful criticism of this chapter.

1. In Canada, a non-status Indian is an Aboriginal person who is not recognized by the Indian Act. In the West, non-status Indians were also non-treaty.

2. The Indian Act of Canada created a class of non-status Indians by granting citizenship to Aboriginal women who married non-Aboriginal men, and by reckoning status and treaty rights through the male line only. In 1985, the act was amended and the enfranchised women and their children were eligible to apply for re-instatement of their Indian status under Bill C-31. More than 100,000 Bill C-31 Indians were added to the Indian registry, among them several prominent leaders of Métis organizations.

3. Andersen, "From Nation to Population," *Nations and Nationalism*; Clifton, "Alternative Identities and Cultural Frontiers," 16; Thornton, *American Indian Holocaust and Survival*, 212–34; and Harmon, "Wanted: More Histories of Indian Identity."

4. Harmon, "Wanted: More Histories of Indian Identity"; Clifton, *Being and Becoming Indian*; Nagel, *American Indian Ethnic Renewal*; Harmon, *Indians in the Making*; and Blu, *Lumbee Problem*. For a discussion and examples of ethnogenesis in the Americas, see Hill, "Introduction"; and Albers, "Changing Patterns of Ethnicity in the Northeastern Plains," 1–19, 90–118. See also Sturtevant, "Creek into Seminole"; Merrell, *Indians' New World*; Galloway, *Choctaw Genesis*; and Gary Clayton Anderson, *Indian Southwest*.

5. Sawchuk, *Métis of Manitoba*; Andersen, "From Nation to Population"; and Giokas and Chartrand, "Who Are the Métis in Section 35?" See also Benedict Anderson, *Imagined Communities*.

6. Giraud's *Métis in the Canadian West* is the foundational source on the history of the Métis, the place where scholarly study of the Métis begins. However, Giraud was a product of his age and a Social Darwinist. *The Métis in the Canadian West*, like the work of A. S. Morton and George F. G. Stanley, is flawed by a racialism that assumed the instability and inferiority of "primitive races" and the superiority of European civilization. For a more positive view, see Sprague and Frye, *Genealogy of the First Métis Nation*; Ens, *Homeland to Hinterland*; and Payment, *Free People*. For an analysis of the relationship between and differences among the English Half-breeds and Métis in Rupert's Land, see Jennifer S. H. Brown, *Strangers in Blood*; Spry, "Métis and Mixed-Bloods of Rupert's Land"; Panekoek, *Snug Little Flock*; and Ens, *Homeland to Hinterland*.

7. For an analysis of the shifting meanings and terminology of mixedness, see Jennifer S. H. Brown, "Linguistic Solitudes in the Fur Trade." See also John Elgin Foster, "Origins of Mixed Bloods in Canadian West"; and John Elgin Foster, "Métis." Most recently, see the important work of Chris Andersen on the political significance of racial terminology in the Canadian courts and the conflation

of Métis with mixedness, especially, Andersen, *"Moya 'Tipinsook* [The People Who Aren't Their Own Bosses]."

8. Peterson, "Prelude to Red River," "Many Roads to Red River," and "Gathering at the River"; Devine, *People Who Own Themselves* and "Les Desjarlais"; Slobodin, *Métis of the Mackenzie District*; Nicks, "Iroquois and Fur Trade"; St-Onge, "Early Forefathers to the Athabasca Métis"; Thistle, "Twatt Family, 1780–1840"; Morantz, "Fur Trade and Cree of James Bay"; John Elgin Foster, "Wintering"; Sleeper-Smith, *Indian Women and French Men*; Murphy, *Gathering of Rivers*, xvii and passim; Thorne, *Many Hands of My Relations*, 3–12; and Jackson, *Children of the Fur Trade*, preface and passim.

9. See especially Dickason, "From 'One Nation' in the Northeast"; and Long, "Treaty No. 9," for other mixed-blood groups.

10. Peterson and Brown, "Introduction," 5–7; Peterson, "Prelude to Red River"; White, *Middle Ground*, 74, 190–91, and passim; Sleeper-Smith, *Indian Women and French Men*; Murphy, *Gathering of Rivers*; Thorne, *Many Hands of My Relations*; and Peterson, "Many Roads to Red River."

11. For the adoption of the term Métis for persons of mixed-blood and evidence of the pervasive reformulation of documentary references to mixed-bloods and "half-breeds" as Métis by current scholars writing about métis in Ontario, see Lytwyn, "Historical Report on Métis Community," 1, 2, 3, and throughout; Ray, "Economic History of Robinson Treaties Area," ii, 17, and passim; McNab, "Hearty Cooperation" and "Métis Participation"; Lischke and McNab, "Introduction," 2–3; Hele, "Manipulating Identity"; Travers, "Drummond Island Voyageurs"; Barter, "Searching for Silver Fox"; Hele, "Anishnabeg and Métis"; and Knight and Chute, "Shadow of Thumping Drum," 85–86.

12. Jennifer S. H. Brown, "Linguistic Solitudes."

13. Among the Ojibwa, both William Johnston, son of John Johnston of Sault Ste. Marie, and Oshanabunaqua, daughter of Waubojeeg, a prominent Ojibwa chief, were among the most important Half-breed interpreters in the American upper lakes during the treaty era. He was a literate and perceptive observer of both tribal and fur trade society. See his letters to his sister, Jane Schoolcraft, in Sharpless, ed., "Letters on the Fur Trade." For an enumeration of mixed-bloods as Indians in the American Great Lakes, see Henry Rowe Schoolcraft's 1832 statistical tables of the Indian population in Mason, *Schoolcraft's Expedition to Lake Itasca*, 158–60. See also Jameson, *Sketches in Canada and Rambles among the Red Men*, 188n. Mrs. Jameson noted that "in 1828, Major Anderson, our Indian agent, computed the number of Canadians and mixed breed married to Indian women, and residing on the north shore of Lake Huron, and in the neighborhood of Michilimackinac, at nine hundred. This he called his *lowest* estimate."

14. McNab, "Hearty Cooperation" and "Métis Participation"; Ray, "Economic History of Robinson Treaty Area"; Ltywyn, "Historical Report on the Métis Community"; Hele, "Manipulating Identity"; Travers, "Drummond Island Voyageurs"; Barter, "Searching for Silver Fox"; and Hele, "Anishnabeg and Métis."

15. Hele, "Manipulating Identity," 164–65. In his end notes, McNab revealed his intention to substitute "Métis" for "Half-breed" in his discussion of Ontario natives of mixed descent: "Métis are those individuals of mixed, largely Indian, British and French ancestry . . . The word commonly used to describe *métis* in Ontario prior to the twentieth century was 'Half-breed' and the word did not, at that time, have a pejorative meaning" (McNab, "Métis Participation," 77).

In contrast to the historians of Ontario cited above, American scholars of the past fifteen years have been more circumspect. Following Helen Hornbeck Tanner, a number of American historians and anthropologists studying the Great Lakes and northeastern Plains have either reiterated the terms used in the documentary record to avoid confusion or have used a more neutral terminology, such as the following: composite community, Ojibwa mixed bloods, French–Osage families of mixed descent, or mixed blood communities. See Tanner, "Glaize in 1792"; Sleeper-Smith, *Indian Women and French Men*; Thorne, *Many Hands of My Relations*, 3–12, 245–49; and Jennifer S. H. Brown and Schenck, "Métis, Mestizo, and Mixed Blood." In *Gathering of Rivers* (p. xvii and passim), Murphy alternatively used the lowercase métis to describe those of "mixed Indian and EuroAmerican ancestry," and Creole to designate those who participated in the region's blended culture.

16. Morner, *Race and Race Mixture*, 55–57. See, for instance, the late-sixteenth-century Portuguese Jesuit Alexandre Valignano, who opposed admission of Indians and *"mesticos"* to the priesthood because "all the dusky races are very stupid and vicious, and of the basest spirits" (Charles R. Boxer, *The Portuguese Seaborne Empire, 1415–1825*, as quoted in Anderson, *Imagined Communities*, 59).

17. See James McKenzie's characterization of the "Half-breed" as "a wretched species" and "a spurious breed" in Saum, *Fur Trader and Indian*, 206; Ross, *Red River Settlement*, for the use of "Half-breed" throughout; and West, *Substance of a Journal*, 136. See also Jordon, *White over Black*; and Blu, *Lumbee Problem*.

18. Barth, *Ethnic Groups and Boundaries*, Introduction, esp. 1–19; the more recent and revisionist collection of essays in Vermeulen and Govers, *Anthropology of Ethnicity*; Benedict Anderson, *Imagined Communities*, 5–7, 47–82; and Eric Hobsbawn, *Nations and Nationalism Since 1780*, 46–79. Also see James A. Clifton, "Alternative Identities and Cultural Frontiers," for a discussion of the confusion of race and ethnicity.

19. Andersen, "From Nation to Population," *Nations and Nationalism*; Douaud, "Genesis," 3. See, most recently, Andersen, *"Moya 'Tipinsook* [The People Who Aren't Their Own Bosses]."

20. Peterson and Brown's *New Peoples* is the best example of the new research in the 1980s linking Metis and fur trade studies. See more recently, Bakker, *Language of Our Own*, 51.

21. There is an impressive body of recently published work documenting ethnogenesis in the American Southeast, the Caribbean, and South America. See, e.g., the essays in Hill, *History, Power, and Identity*. For examples of recent scholarship seeking to identify Métis and métis in Ontario, see Reimer and

Chartrand, "Documenting Historic Métis in Ontario"; articles by Hele, Travers, and Barter in Lischke and McNab (eds.), *Long Journey of a Forgotten People*; articles by Hele, Knight, and Chute in Hele (ed.), *Lines Drawn Upon the Water*; Ray, "Economic History of Robinson Treaties Area"; and Lytwyn, "Historical Report on Métis Community." More fruitful has been new work on the Athabasca Region, including the work of St-Onge, "Early Forefathers to the Athabasca Métis"; and Thistle, "Twatt Family." For work on the expansion of Red River Métis into the Dakotas, Montana, Saskatchewan, and Alberta, see Peterson, "Gathering at the River"; Devine, *People Who Own Themselves*; Martha Harroun Foster, *We Know Who We Are*; and Payment, *Free People*.

22. Peterson, "Prelude to Red River," "Many Roads to Red River," and "Gathering at the River." See Sturtevant, "Creek into Seminole"; Blu, *Lumbee Problem*; and, more recently, Gary Clayton Anderson, *Indian Southwest*, for examples of ethnogenesis among the tribes.

23. Keating, *Narrative of an Expedition*, 1:104–105; Kohl, *Kitchi-Gami*, 66; and Clifton, "Personal and Ethnic Identity" and "Alternative Identities and Cultural Frontiers," 19–33. For the spread of a Pan-Indian Central Algonkian culture in the eighteenth century, partially in response to the fur trade, see Quimby, *Indian Life in the Upper Great Lakes*, 147–73.

24. Schoolcraft, *Narrative Journal of Travels*, 112; Hubbard, Recollections of First Year (1819), 11, Chicago Historical Society; Taft Harlan, Dubbs Millbrook, and Case Irwin, *1830 Federal Census*.

25. Schoolcraft, *Narrative Journal of Travels*, 369; Morse, *Report to Secretary of War*, 50, 58. For a description of Green Bay in the 1820s, see Ellis, "Fifty-four Years Recollections," 215–16. See also Fonda, "Early Reminiscences of Wisconsin," 235–36.

26. Taft Harlan, Dubbs Millbrook, and Case Irwin, "Crawford County," in *1830 Federal Census*; Merrill, "Pioneer Life in Wisconsin," 380; Morse, *Report to Secretary of War*, 316; and Keating, *Narrative of an Expedition*, 1:245.

27. McKenney, *Sketches of Tour to Lakes*, 191–92.

28. Ellis, "Fifty-four Years Recollections," 212–13.

29. Samuel R. Brown, *Western Gazetteer*, 171; McKenney, *Sketches of Tour to Lakes*, 126. See also *Aggregate Amount of Persons*, 88; and the lengthy description of French Canadian creole households in early nineteenth-century Detroit in Hamlin, "Old French Traditions."

30. Osborne, "Migration of Voyageurs." See also Travers, "Drummond Island Voyageurs," an interesting analysis of the original Drummond Island voyageur families and their descendants in the last half of the nineteenth century.

31. Parker, ed., *Recollections of Philander Prescott*, 13. See also Kohl, *Kitchi-Gami*, 314.

32. Pierce, *History of Chicago*, 1:57–58, 68–69; Haeger, *Men and Money*; Albert G. Ellis, Plat of Navarino, 1836, Special Collections, Newberry Library, Chicago; and Andreas, *History of Chicago*, 1:103. For examples of territory-wide land speculation, see the Lucius Lyon Papers, Clements Library, Ann Arbor, MI. For the decay and disappearance of the old French creole settlements on the American bottom,

see William Clark's Journal, 4–9 September 1797, Northwest Territory Collections, Indiana Historical Society, Indianapolis; and Reynolds, *Pioneer History of Illinois*.

33. St. Ignace, MI, one of the oldest French fur trade settlements, remained a haven for mixed-bloods well into the nineteenth century. See Reminiscences of David Corp, n.d., Emerson R. Smith Papers, Bentley Historical Library, University of Michigan, Ann Arbor. For declining profits in the fur trade after 1830 and the end of the trade following the removal of treaty tribes to reservations, see Porlier, "Narrative of Louis B. Porlier"; Peter Vieau, "Narrative of Peter J. Vieau," 466–67; and correspondence between Green Bay traders John Lawe and Augustin Grignon and the American Fur Company in the 1830s in the John Lawe Collection, Gurdon S. Hubbard Collection, Chicago Historical Society. For views of "first settlers," see Lockwood, "Early Times and Events in Wisconsin," 114. Western Historical Company's (WHC's) *History of Racine and Kenosha Counties* provides an instructive example: "Jambeau [Jacques Vieau] can, in no sense, be accredited with the honor of original settlement, for his purpose was solely that of trading with the natives, and his marriage with the squaw practically made him one of their number" (p. 286).

34. Louis Grignon to Robert Dickson, 6 February 1819, vol. 20, pp. 102–103; Lewis Cass to G. Boyd, Detroit, 17 July 1818, vol. 2, pp. 115–116; Declaration of Citizenship for John Lawe, 4 October 1821, vol. 20, p. 117; John Lawe to Jacob Franks, Michilimackinac, 3 September 1823, p. 216, all in WHC, *History of Racine and Kenosha Counties*, 20:102–103, 115–16, 117, 216, 308–10.

35. Morleigh [pseud.], *Merry Briton in Pioneer Wisconsin*, 84–85; William Johnston to Jane Schoolcraft, 28 August 1833, in Sharpless, "Letters on the Fur Trade," 163. For an increasingly rigid classification system of social race in the United States, see Bieder, *Science Encounters the Indian*.

36. See Gorham, "Families of Mixed Descent," 47, 50–51. The as-yet-unpublished work of Shawna Lea Gandey on fur trade families in the Oregon Country is also of interest here. See her "Fur Trade Daughters of the Oregon Country," 168–75, for a similar set of conclusions.

37. Joseph Bourassa, John Lalime, and Joseph LaFramboise to Lewis Cass, Secretary of War, Carey Station, 8 October 1831, in records of Chicago Agency, 1824–1834, Office of Indian Affairs (Central Office) Letters Received, RG 75, NA, Washington, DC. See Henry Rowe Schoolcraft's instructive "Statistical Tables of the Indian Population Comprised within the boundaries of the Consolidated Agency of the Sault Ste. Marie and Michilimackinac in the year 1832," in Mason, *Schoolcraft's Expedition*, 151–62, for numbers of "mixed bloods" in villages or permanent encampments stretching from Lake Huron to Pembina.

38. Kohl, *Kitchi-Gami*, 374–84; Keating, *Narrative of an Expedition*, 1:104–105. For an important and extremely well-researched analysis of one of the Great Lakes most illustrious half-blood chiefs, see Chute, *Legacy of Shingwaukonse*. See also Clifton, "Personal and Ethnic Identity" for Billy Caldwell; McClurken, "Augustin Hamlin, Jr."; and Peterson, "Goodbye Madore Beaubien." For a revealing analysis of the strategies and roles of mixed-descent women of early nineteenth-century

Great Lakes fur trade society, see Sleeper-Smith, *Indian Women and French Men*, especially 96–115 and 141–63.

39. For an illuminating correspondence regarding the education of Great Lakes mixed-blood children at the Carey Mission School, see Correspondence, 1823–1838, Isaac McCoy Papers, Kansas State Historical Society, Topeka. See also Kemper, "Journal of an Episcopalian Missionary's Tour," 406, for the lack of full-bloods at the Presbyterian Mission school at Mackinac established by Rev. W. M. Ferry in the 1820s, and State Historical Society of Wisconsin, "Documents Relating to Catholic Church," 165–66, 178–79, 183, and passim. For leadership roles, see Felix Keesing, "Leaders of the Menomini Tribe" (typescript), U.S. Manuscripts, State Historical Society of Wisconsin, Madison; Paquette, "Wisconsin Winnebagoes," 406; Warren, *History of the Ojibways*, 386; Parker (ed.), *Recollections of Philander Prescott*, 13–14; and Clifton, *Prairie Potawatomi*, 272–78. For a recent example of regional American Indian ethnogenesis, see Gary Clayton Anderson, *Indian Southwest*.

40. Andrew J. Vieau, Sr., "Narrative of Andrew J. Vieau, Sr."; Peter J. Vieau, "Narrative of Peter J. Vieau."

41. Moore, *Calumet Region*, 48–49; Bailly Family Papers, Chicago Historical Society, Chicago, IL, especially the biography of Alexis Bailly prepared in 1922. For a description and analysis of the mixed-descent members of the Bailly family, particularly the daughters and granddaughters, see Sleeper-Smith, *Indian Women and French Men*, 155–60, and "Être catholique et devenir indienne."

42. Chaput, "The 'Misses Nolin'"; Robert Dickson to John Lawe, 23 April 1819, in WHC, *History of Racine and Kenosha Counties*, 20:105–106. See also Gilman, Gilman, and Stultz, *Red River Trails*, 2–5, 11, 18–19, for the traders out of Prairie du Chien; and see Schenck, "Cadottes," 189–98, for the Cadottes of LaPointe. According to Schenck, "All of the sons of Michel Cadotte were active in the fur trade for as long as it lasted at LaPointe . . . and . . . all of whom had married Ojibwa women, stayed with their people" (p. 197).

43. Chute, "Ojibwa Leadership," 160–168; and Clifton, *Prairie Potawatomi*, 283–87.

44. John Lawe Collection, Chicago Historical Society. Most of the residents of the old trading towns petitioned the U.S. Congress for land titles once American territories were organized and civil government was installed at the county level. The 1829–33 petitions for land titles by the inhabitants of Brown County (Green Bay), Crawford County (Prairie du Chien), Michilimackinac County (Michili-mackinac), and Chippewa County (St. Mary's, or Sault Ste. Marie) affirm the long-term residency of numerous Canadian traders and voyageurs and their families of mixed descent. See Clarence Carter, *Territorial Papers of the United States*, 12:55–58, 67–71, 83–84, 109–12, 397–99, 605–606, 615–16; and Taft Harlan et al., *1830 Federal Census*. Maps of the plan of settlement of these pre-American settlement towns, all built on the French Canadian system of narrow and long river lots, may be seen in *American State Papers*, vol. 5. A good example, the "Plan of the Settlement at Green Bay," 1821, is facing 5:284.

45. Kohl, *Kitchi-Gami*, 216.

46. Ibid., 260–61; Barbeau, "Voyageur Songs."

47. Lacombe, *Dictionnaire de la langue des Cris*, available at http://peel.library
.ualberta.ca/bibliography/708/648.html. Thanks to Anne Lindsay for this reference. Kohl, *Kitchi-Gami*, 260–61.

48. Kohl, *Kichi-Gami*, 259–60; emphasis added. See also the "complainte" of
Jean Cayeux. According to Kohl, "One of the most celebrated of these elegies is
that in which the melancholy fate of Jean Cayeux, an old Voyageur, is lamented.
It describes a thoroughly Canadian tragedy, and is characteristic of the Voyageurs and the country." The complainte was very long, and Kohl met no one who
knew all of the verses or the entire story, but its conclusion is instructive. Driven
deep into the wilds by pursuing Iroquois and about to expire from lack of food,
Cayeux "dug himself a Christian grave. Over the grave he erected a cross, and
he cut and carved on the wood his complainte, the entire history of his tragic
fate . . . As he lay there before his cross, and dying, prayed, three French faces
appeared before him. 'Mais ils me donnaient une courte joie.' The delight was
too great for him. He spread out his arms to them. His eyes sparkled once more
with delight, and then they closed for- ever. He fell into the grave he had dug for
himself, and his three *countrymen* who read his complainte on the wood, buried
him with tears" (ibid., 261–65, emphasis added).

49. St-Onge, "Early Forefathers to the Athabasca Métis," 127–28.

50. See Wallace, *Documents Relating to the Northwest Company*, 219–21, for the 1805
company roster; Payette, *Northwest*, 250–62, for a more complete listing of North
West Company voyageurs and winterers for 1806; and HBC post journals from
Brandon House and Red River, including Peter Fidler's "census of Free Canadians
with their Indian Wives, also their Children of both Sexes, living with them, at
present residing in the Red River, February, 1814," HBCA, Winnipeg, Manitoba. For
mixed-descent residents of Great Lakes trading communities who claimed and
received treaty payments as mixed-bloods of various Indian nations, see "List of
Inhabitants at Green Bay, September 14, 1818 by J. B. S. Jacobs, Sr.," John Lawe Collection, Chicago Historical Society; "Statement showing the names of the relations & friends of mixed blood entitled to shares of the provisions made for them
in the 2nd article of the Treaty with the Menomenee of 3rd September 1836, with
the sum due & payable to each," in Indian Documents, Chicago Historical Society; "The List of Mixed Blood of the Menomonee Nation as Published in the *Green
Bay Advocate* June 28, 1849, copied by Sharon Belongeay," in Indian Documents,
Chicago Historical Society; and U.S. House, *Chippewa Half-Breeds of Lake Superior.*

Works Cited

Archival Sources

Ann Arbor, MI
  Corp, David. Reminiscences. Emerson R. Smith Papers. Bentley Historical
    Library, University of Michigan.
  Lyon, Lucius. Papers. William Clements Library.

Chicago, IL
  Bailly Family Papers.
  Chicago Historical Society.
  Elli, Albert G., Plat of Navarino, 1836. Newberry Library Special Collections.
  Hubbard, Gurdon S., Recollections of First Year (1819). Gurdon S. Hubbard
    Collection.
  Indian Documents.
  John Lawe Collection.
Indianapolis, IN
  Clark, William. Journal, 4–9 September 1797. Northwest Territory Collections.
    Indiana Historical Society.
Madison, WI
  Keesing, Felix. "Leaders of the Menomini Tribe" [typescript]. U.S. Manu-
    scripts. State Historical Society of Wisconsin.
Topeka, KA
  McCoy, Isaac. Papers. Kansas State Historical Society.
Washington, DC
  National Archives. Chicago Agency, 1824–1847. Copy no. 234, microfilm roll
    132. RG 75.
Winnipeg, MB
  Hudson's Bay Company Archives (HBCA).

Published Sources

Aggregate Amount of Persons Living Within the United States in the Year 1810. Wash-
  ington, DC, 1811.
Albers, Patricia C. "Changing Patterns of Ethnicity in the Northeastern Plains."
  In *History, Power and Identity: Ethnogenesis in the Americas, 1492–1992*, edited by
  Jonathan D. Hill, 90–118. Iowa City: University of Iowa Press, 1996.
*American State Papers, Documents of the United States Congress of the United States in
  Relation to the Public Lands*, Vol. 5. Washington, DC: Gales & Seaton, 1860.
Andersen, Chris. "From Nation to Population: The Racialization of 'Métis' in the
  Canadian Census." *Nations and Nationalism* 14, no. 2 (2008): 347–68.
———. "*Moya Tipimsook* [The People Who Aren't Their Own Bosses]: Racializa-
  tion and the Misrecognition of 'Metis' in Upper Great Lakes Ethnohistory."
  Ethnohistory 58, no. 1 (Winter 2011): 37–63.
Anderson, Benedict. *Imagined Communities: Reflections on the Origin and Spread of
  Nationalism*. London, England: Verso, 1991.
Anderson, Gary Clayton. *The Indian Southwest, 1580–1830: Ethnogenesis and Rein-
  vention*. Norman: University of Oklahoma Press, 1999.
Andreas, A. T. *History of Chicago from the Earliest Period to the Present*. 3 vols. Chi-
  cago, IL: A. T. Andreas, 1884–86.
Bakker, Peter. *A Language of Our Own: The Genesis of Michif, the Mixed Cree–French
  Language of the Canadian Métis*. New York, NY: Oxford University Press, 1997.

Barbeau, Marius. "Voyageur Songs." *The Beaver,* June 1842, 15–19.

Barter, Virginia (Parker). "Searching for the Silver Fox: A Fur Trade Family History." In Lischke and McNab, *Long Journey of a Forgotten People,* 247–303.

Barth, Frederik, ed. *Ethnic Groups and Boundaries: The Social Organization of Cultural Difference.* Boston, MA: Little Brown and Company, 1969.

Bieder, Robert E. *Science Encounters the Indian, 1820–1880: The Early Years of American Ethnology.* Norman: University of Oklahoma Press, 1986.

Blu, Karen I. *The Lumbee Problem: The Making of an American Indian People.* New York, NY: Cambridge University Press, 1980.

Brown, Jennifer S. H. "Linguistic Solitudes in the Fur Trade: Some Changing Social Categories and Their Implications." In Ray and Judd, *Old Trails and New Directions,* 147–59.

———. *Strangers in Blood: Fur Trade Families in Indian Country.* Reprint, Norman: University of Oklahoma Press, 1994. First published 1980.

Brown, Jennifer S. H., and Theresa Schenck. "Métis, Mestizo, and Mixed Blood." In *A Companion to American Indian History,* edited by Philip Deloria and Neal Salisbury, 321–38. Malden, MA: Wiley-Blackwell, 2004.

Brown, Samuel R. *The Western Gazetteer; or, Emigrant's Directory.* Reprint, New York, NY: Arno Press, 1971. First published 1817.

Carter, Clarence, ed. *The Territorial Papers of the United States.* Vol. 12, *The Territory of Michigan 1829–1837.* Washington, DC: The National Archives and Records Service, 1945.

Chaput, Donald. "The 'Misses Nolin.'" *The Beaver,* Winter 1975, 14–17.

Chute, Janet. *The Legacy of Shingwaukonse: A Century of Native Leadership.* Toronto, ON: University of Toronto Press, 1998.

———. "Ojibwa Leadership during the Fur Trade Era at Sault Ste. Marie." In *New Faces of the Fur Trade: Selected Papers of the Seventh North American Fur Trade Conference, Halifax, Nova Scotia, 1995,* edited by Jo-Anne Fiske, Susan Sleeper-Smith, and William Wicken, 153–72. East Lansing: Michigan State University Press, 1998.

Clifton, James A. "Alternative Identities and Cultural Frontiers." In Clifton, *Being and Becoming Indian,* 1–37.

———, ed. *Being and Becoming Indian: Biographical Studies of North American Frontiers.* Chicago, IL: The Dorsey Press, 1989.

———. "Personal and Ethnic Identity on the Great Lakes Frontier: The Case of Billy Caldwell, Anglo-Canadian." *Ethnohistory* 25, no. 1 (Winter 1978): 69–94.

———. *The Prairie Potawatomi: Continuity and Change in Potawatomi Indian Culture, 1665–1965.* Lawrence: University of Kansas Press, 1977.

Devine, Heather. "Les Desjarlais: The Development and Dispersal of a Proto-Métis Hunting Band, 1785–1870." In *From Rupert's Land to Canada,* edited by Theodore Binnema, Gerhard J. Ens, and R. C. McLeod, 129–60. Edmonton: University of Alberta Press, 2001.

———. *The People Who Own Themselves: Aboriginal Ethnogenesis in a Canadian Family, 1660–1900.* Calgary, AB: University of Calgary Press, 2004.

Dickason, Olive Patricia. "From 'One Nation' in the Northeast to 'New Nation' in the Northwest: A Look at the Emergence of the Métis." In Peterson and Brown, *New Peoples*, 19–36.

"Documents Relating to the Catholic Church in Green Bay, and the Mission at Little Chute, 1825–40." *Collections of the State Historical Society of Wisconsin*, vol. 14, 162–205. Madison: State Historical Society of Wisconsin, 1898.

Douaud, Patrick C. "Genesis." In Douaud, *Western Métis*, 1–19.

———, ed. *The Western Métis: Profile of a People*. Regina, SK: Canadian Plains Research Centre, University of Regina, 2007.

Ellis, Albert, Gen. "Fifty-four Years Recollections of Men and Events in Wisconsin." In *Collections of State Historical Society of Wisconsin*, vol. 7, edited by Lyman Copeland Draper, 207–68. Reprint, Madison: Wisconsin State History Society, 1908. First published 1876.

Ens, Gerhard. *Homeland to Hinterland: The Changing Worlds of the Red River Métis in the Nineteenth Century*. Toronto, ON: University of Toronto Press, 1996.

Fonda, John H. "Early Reminiscences of Wisconsin." In *Reports and Collections of the State Historical Society of Wisconsin for the Years 1867, 1868, and 1869*, vol. 5, 205–84. Madison, WI: Atwood & Rubless, State Printers, 1868.

Foster, John Elgin. "The Métis: The People and the Term." In Douaud, *Western Métis*, 21–30.

———. "The Origins of the Mixed Bloods in the Canadian West." In *Essays on Western History in Honor of Lewis Gwynne Thomas*, edited by Lewis H. Thomas, 71–82. Edmonton: University of Alberta Press, 1976.

———. "Wintering, the Outsider Adult Male and the Ethnogenesis of the Western Plains Métis." In Douaud, *Western Métis*, 91–103.

Foster, Martha Harroun. *We Know Who We Are: Métis Identity in a Montana Community*. Norman: University of Oklahoma Press, 2006.

Galloway, Patricia. *Choctaw Genesis: 1500–1700*. Lincoln: University of Nebraska Press, 1995.

Gandey, Shawna Lea. "Fur Trade Daughters of the Oregon Country: Students of the Sisters of Notre Dame de Namur." Master's thesis, Portland State University, Portland, OR, 2004.

Gilman, Rhoda R., Carolyn Gilman, and Deborah M. Stultz. *The Red River Trails: Oxcart Routes between St. Paul and the Selkirk Settlement, 1820–1870*. St. Paul: Minnesota Historical Society Press, 1979.

Giokas, J., and Paul Chartrand. "Who Are the Métis in Section 35? A Review of the Law and Policy Relating to Métis and 'Mixed Blood' People in Canada." In *Who Are Canada's Aboriginal People? Recognition, Definition, and Jurisdiction*, edited by Paul Chartrand, 83–125. Saskatoon, SK: Purich Publishers, 2001.

Giraud, Marcel. *The Métis in the Canadian West*. 2 vols. Translated by George Woodcock. Edmonton: University of Alberta Press, 1986. Originally published as *Le Métis Canadien* (Paris: Institut d'Ethnologie, Museum National d'Histoire Naturelle, 1945).

Gorham, Harriet. "Families of Mixed Descent in the Western Great Lakes Region." In *Native Peoples, Native Lands: Canadian Indians, Inuit, and Metis*, edited by Bruce A. Cox, 37–55. Ottawa, ON: Carleton University Press, 1987.

Haeger, John D. *Men and Money: The Urban Frontier at Green Bay, 1815–1840*. Pleasantville: Clarke Historical Library, Central Michigan University, 1970.

Hamlin, Carrie. "Old French Traditions." In *Michigan Pioneer and Historical Collections*, vol. 4, 70–78. East Lansing, MI: 1878.

Harmon, Alexandra. *Indians in the Making: Ethnic Relations and Indian Identities around Puget Sound*. Berkeley and Los Angeles: University of California Press, 1998.

———. "Wanted: More Histories of Indian Identity." In *A Companion to American Indian History*, edited by Philip J. Deloria and Neal Salisbury, 248–65. Malden, MA: Wiley-Blackwell, 2004.

Hele, Karl S. "The Anishnabeg and Métis in the Sault Ste. Marie Borderlands." In Hele, *Lines Drawn upon the Water*, 65–84.

———, ed. *Lines Drawn upon the Water: First Nations and the Great Lakes Borders and Borderlands*. Waterloo, ON: Wilfred Laurier University Press, 2008.

———. "Manipulating Identity: The Sault Borderlands Métis and Colonial Intervention." In Lischke and McNab, *Long Journey of a Forgotten People*, 163–96.

Hill, Jonathan D., ed. *History, Power, and Identity: Ethnogenesis in the Americas, 1492–1992*. Iowa City: University of Iowa Press, 1996.

———. "Introduction: Ethnogenesis in the Americas, 1492–1681." In Hill, *History, Power, and Identity*, 1–19.

The History of Racine and Kenosha Counties in Wisconsin. . . . Chicago, IL: Western Historical Company, 1879.

Hobsbawn, Eric. *Nations and Nationalism since 1780: Programme, Myth, Reality*. 2nd ed. Cambridge, England: Cambridge University Press, 1992.

Jackson, John C. *Children of the Fur Trade: Forgotten Métis of the Pacific Northwest*. Reprint, Corvallis: Oregon State University Press, 2007. Originally published 1995.

Jameson, Anna. *Sketches in Canada and Rambles among the Red Men*. New Edition. London, England: Longman, Brown, Green and Longmans, 1852.

Jordon, Winthrop. *White over Black: American Attitudes Toward the Negro, 1550–1812*. Baltimore, MD: Penguin Books, 1969.

Keating, William H. *Narrative of an Expedition to the Source of St. Peter's River, Lake Winnepeek, Lake of the Woods, etc. Performed in the year 1823*. . . . Minneapolis, MN: Ross & Haines, 1959.

Kemper, Jackson, Rev. "Journal of an Episcopalian Missionary's Tour to Green Bay, 1834." In *Collections of the State Historical Society of Wisconsin*, vol. 14, 394–449. Madison: Wisconsin State History Society, 1898.

Knight, Alan, and Janet E. Chute. "In the Shadow of the Thumping Drum: The Sault Métis—The People in Between." In Hele, *Lines Drawn upon the Water*, 85–114.

Kohl, Johann George. *Kitchi-Gami: Life among the Lake Superior Ojibway*. St. Paul: Minnesota Historical Society Press, 1985.

Lacombe, Albert. *Dictionnaire de la langue des Cris*. Montreal, QC: C.-O. Beauchemin & Valois, 1874.

Lischke, Ute, and David T. McNab. "Introduction: We Are Still Here." In Lischke and McNab, *Long Journey of a Forgotten People*, 1–9.

———, eds. *The Long Journey of a Forgotten People: Métis Identities and Family Histories*. Waterloo, ON: Wilfrid Laurier Press, 2007.

Lockwood, James H., Hon. "Early Times and Events in Wisconsin." In *Wisconsin Historical Collections*, vol. 2, 98–196. Madison: Wisconsin State History Society, 1856.

Long, John S. "Treaty No. 9 and Fur Trade Company Families: Northeastern Ontario's Halfbreeds, Indians, Petitioners and Métis." In Peterson and Brown, *New Peoples*, 137–62.

Lytwyn, Victor. "Historical Report on the Métis Community at Sault Ste. Marie." Exhibit 39. *Regina v. Powley*, 27 March 1998.

Mason, Philip P., ed. *Schoolcraft's Expedition to Lake Itasca: the Discovery of the Source of the Mississippi*. Reprint, East Lansing: Michigan State University Press, 1958. Originally published 1834.

McClurken, James M. "Augustin Hamlin, Jr.: Ottawa Identity and the Politics of Persistence." In Clifton, *Being and Becoming Indian*, 82–111.

McKenney, Thomas L. *Sketches of a Tour to the Lakes, of the Character and Customs of the Chippeway Indians, and of incidents Connected with the Treaty of Fond du Lac*. Baltimore, MD: Field Lucas, Jun'r, 1827.

McNab, David T. "Hearty Cooperation and Efficient Aid, the Métis and Treaty #3." *Canadian Journal of Native Studies* 3, no. 1 (1983): 131–49.

———. "Métis Participation in the Treaty-Making Process in Ontario: A Reconnaissance." *Native Studies Review* 1, no. 2 (1985): 57–79.

Merrell, James H. *The Indians' New World: Catawbas and Their Neighbors from European Contact through the Era of Removal*. Chapel Hill: University of North Carolina Press, 1989.

Merrill, Henry. "Pioneer Life in Wisconsin." *Collections of the State Historical Society of Wisconsin*, vol. 7, 366–404. Madison: Wisconsin State History Society, 1876.

Moore, Powell A. *The Calumet Region: Indiana's Last Frontier*. Indianapolis: Indiana Historical Bureau, 1959.

Morantz, Toby. "The Fur Trade and the Cree of James Bay." In Ray and Judd, *Old Trails and New Directions*, 39–58.

Morleigh [pseud.]. *A Merry Briton in Pioneer Wisconsin . . . Extracts from the Note Book of Morleigh. . . .* Reprint, Madison: State Historical Society of Wisconsin, 1950. Originally published 1842.

Morner, Magnus. *Race and Race Mixture in the History of Latin America*. Boston, MA: Little, Brown and Company, 1967.

Morse, Jedediah. *A Report to the Secretary of War of the United States on Indian Affairs, Comprising a Narrative of a Tour Performed in the Summer of 1820*. Reprint, St. Clair Shores, MI: Scholarly Press, 1972. Originally published 1822.

Murphy, Lucy Eldersveld. *A Gathering of Rivers: Indians, Metis, and Mining in the Western Great Lakes, 1737–1832*. Lincoln: University of Nebraska Press, 2000.

Nagel, Joanne. *American Indian Ethnic Renewal: Red Power and the Resurgence of Identity and Culture*. New York, NY: Oxford University Press, 1996.

Nicks, Trudy. "The Iroquois and the Fur Trade in Western Canada." In Ray and Judd, *Old Trails and New Directions*, 85–101.

Osborne, C. A. "The Migration of Voyageurs from Drummond Island to Penetanguishine in 1828." In *Papers and Records of the Ontario Historical Society*, vol. 3, 123–66. Toronto: Ontario Historical Society, 1901.

Panekoek, Frits. *A Snug Little Flock: The Social Origins of the Riel Resistance of 1869–70*. Winnipeg, MB: Watson & Dwyer, 1980.

Paquette, Moses. "The Wisconsin Winnebagoes." In *Wisconsin Historical Collections*, vol. 12, 399–433. Madison: Wisconsin State History Society, 1892.

Parker, Donald Dean, ed. *The Recollections of Philander Prescott, Frontiersman of the Old Northwest, 1819–1862*. Lincoln: University of Nebraska Press, 1966.

Payette, B. C., ed. *The Northwest*. Montreal: Payette Radio Ltd., 1964.

Payment, Diane P. *The Free People—Li Gens Libres: A History of the Métis Community of Batoche, Saskatchewan*. Calgary, AB: University of Calgary Press, 2009.

Peterson, Jacqueline. "Gathering at the River: The Metis Peopling of the Northern Plains." In *The Fur Trade in North Dakota*, edited by Virginia L. Heidenreich, 47–64. Bismarck: State Historical Society of North Dakota, 1990.

———. "Goodbye Madore Beaubien: The Americanization of Early Chicago Society." In *A Wild Kind of Boldness: The Chicago History Reader*, edited by Rosemary K. Adams, 24–36. Chicago, IL: Chicago Historical Society, 1998.

———. "Many Roads to Red River: Metis Genesis in the Great Lakes Region, 1680–1815." In Peterson and Brown, *New Peoples*, 37–71.

———. "Prelude to Red River: A Social Portrait of the Great Lakes Métis." *Ethnohistory* 25, no. 1 (Winter 1978): 41–67.

Peterson, Jacqueline, and Jennifer S. H. Brown. "Introduction." In Peterson and Brown, *New Peoples*, 3–16.

———, eds. *The New Peoples: Being and Becoming Métis in North America*. Winnipeg: University of Manitoba Press, 1985.

Pierce, Bessie Louise. *A History of Chicago, 1673–1848*. New York, NY: Alfred Knopf, 1937.

Porlier, Louis B. "Narrative of Louis B. Porlier." In *Collections of the State Historical Society of Wisconsin*, vol. 15, 439–47. Madison: Wisconsin State History Society, 1900.

Quimby, George Irving. *Indian Life in the Upper Great Lakes, 11,000 B.C. to A.D. 1800*. Chicago, IL, and London, England: University of Chicago Press, 1974.

Ray, Arthur J. "An Economic History of the Robinson Treaties Area before 1860." Report Prepared for *R. v. Powley*, 17 March 1998.

Ray, Arthur J., and Carol Judd, eds. *Old Trails and New Directions: Proceedings of the Third North American Fur Trade Conference*. Toronto, ON: University of Toronto Press, 1980.

Reimer, G., and J.-P. Chartrand. "Documenting Historic Métis in Ontario," *Ethnohistory* 51, no. 3 (2004): 567–607.

Reynolds, John. *Pioneer History of Illinois*. Belleville, IL: 1852.

Ross, Alexander. *The Red River Settlement: Its Rise, Progress and Present State*. Reprint, Rutland, VT: Charles E. Tuttle Company, 1972. Originally published 1856.

Saum, Lewis. *The Fur Trader and the Indian*. Seattle, WA, and London, England: University of Washington Press, 1965.

Sawchuk, Joe. *The Métis of Manitoba: Formulation of an Ethnic Identity*. Toronto, ON: Peter Martin Associates, 1978.

Schenck, Theresa M. "The Cadottes: Five Generations of Fur Traders on Lake Superior." In *The Fur Trade Revisited: Selected Papers of the Sixth North American Fur Trade Conference, Mackinac Island, 1991*, edited by Jennifer S. H. Brown, W. J. Eccles, and Donald P. Heldman, 189–98. East Lansing: Michigan State University Press, 1994.

Schoolcraft, Henry Rowe. *Narrative Journal of Travels from Detroit Northwest through the Chain of American Lakes to the Sources of the Mississippi River in the Year 1820*. Reprint, Readex Microprint, 1966. Originally published as *Travels through the Northwest Regions of the United States* in 1821.

Sharpless, J. Fox, ed. "Letters on the Fur Trade 1833 by William Johnston." In *Michigan Pioneer and Historical Society Collections, or Michigan Historical Collections*, vol. 37, 132–207. East Lansing: Michigan State Historical Society, 1877–1929.

Sleeper-Smith, Susan. "Être catholique et devenir indienne: Soeur Cecilia, une femme odawaisse." *Recherches Amérindiennes au Québec* 32, no. 1 (Spring 2002): 53–61.

———. *Indian Women and French Men: Rethinking Cultural Encounter in the Western Great Lakes*. Amherst: University of Massachusetts Press, 2001.

Slobodin, Richard. *Métis of the Mackenzie District*. Ottawa, ON: Canadian Research Center for Anthropology, St. Paul University, 1966.

Sprague, D. N., and R. P. Frye. *The Genealogy of the First Métis Nation: The Development and Dispersal of the Red River Settlement, 1820–1900*. Winnipeg, MB: Pemmican Publications, 1983.

Spry, Irene M. "The Métis and Mixed-Bloods of Rupert's Land Before 1870." In Peterson and Brown, *New Peoples*, 95–118.

St-Onge, Nicole. "Early Forefathers to the Athabasca Métis: Long-Term North West Company Employees." In Lischke and McNab, *Long Journey of a Forgotten People*, 109–61.

Sturtevant, William. "Creek into Seminole." In *North American Indians in Historical Perspective*, edited by Eleanor Leacock and Nancy Lurie, 92–128. New York, NY: Random House, 1971.

Taft Harlan, Elizabeth, Minnie Dubbs Millbrook, and Elizabeth Case Irwin, eds. *1830 Federal Census: Territory of Michigan*. Detroit, MI: Society for Genealogical Research, 1961.

Tanner, Helen Hornbeck. "The Glaize in 1792: A Composite Indian Community." *Ethnohistory* 25, no. 1 (Winter 1978): 15–39.

Thistle, Paul C. "The Twatt Family, 1780–1840: Amerindian, Ethnic Category, or Ethnic Group Identity?" In Douaud, *Western Métis*, 73–89.

Thorne, Tanis C. *The Many Hands of My Relations: French and Indians on the Lower Missouri*. Columbia, MO, and London, England: University of Missouri Press, 1996.

Thornton, Russell. *American Indian Holocaust and Survival: A Population History since 1492*. Norman: University of Oklahoma Press, 1987.

Travers, Karen J. "The Drummond Island Voyageurs and the Search for Great Lakes Métis Identity." In Lischke and McNab, *Long Journey of a Forgotten People*, 218–44.

U.S. House. *Chippewa Half-Breeds of Lake Superior; Letter from the Secretary of the Interior, in answer to A resolution of the House [of Representatives] of December 20, 1871, relative to the issuance of scrip to the Half-breeds or mixed-bloods belonging to the Chippewas of Lake Superior*. 42nd Cong., 2nd sess., March 15, 1872. H. Doc. 193, serial 1513

Vermeulen, Hans, and Cora Govers, eds. *The Anthropology of Ethnicity: Beyond "Ethnic Groups and Boundaries."* Amsterdam, The Netherlands: Het Spinhuis Publishers, 1994.

Vieau, Andrew J., Sr. "Narrative of Andrew J. Vieau, Sr." In *Collections of the State Historical Society of Wisconsin*, vol. 11, 218–37. Madison: Wisconsin State History Society, 1888.

Vieau, Peter J. "Narrative of Peter J. Vieau." In *Collections of the State Historical Society of Wisconsin*, vol. 15, 458–69. Madison: Wisconsin State History Society, 1900.

Wallace, W. Stewart, ed. *Documents Relating to the Northwest Company*. Toronto, ON: The Champlain Society, 1934.

Warren, William Whipple. *History of the Ojibways Based upon Traditions and Oral Statements*. Reprint, Minneapolis, MN: Ross and Haines, 1957. Originally published 1885.

West, John. *The Substance of a Journal During a Residence at the Red River Colony, British North America; and Frequent Excursions Among the North-West American Indians, in the Years 1820, 1821, 1822, 1823*. Reprint, Johnson Reprint Corporation, 1966. Originally published 1824.

White, Richard. *The Middle Ground: Indians, Empires, and Republics in the Great Lakes Region, 1650–1815*. Cambridge, England: Cambridge University Press, 1991.

2

Scuttling along a Spider's Web

Mobility and Kinship in Metis Ethnogenesis

NICOLE ST-ONGE *and* CAROLYN PODRUCHNY

Metis ethnogenesis is an ill-defined process of cultural creation for those who study it, just as it was for those who lived through it. Accessing the process is hard because those who experienced it often did not do so deliberately or consciously, and few recorded the process for historians to discover. Ancestors of the Metis, both European and indigenous, did not have categories of ethnic and cultural identity that match with those in use today. Indigenous ancestors in particular organized their worlds through relationships with people, landscapes, and the spirits they called on for assistance and guidance to survive and flourish.[1] When scholars write about men in the fur trade, it is often difficult to distinguish who was French Canadian, Metis, Cree, or Ojibwe. We can try to discover where someone grew up, who their parents were, what languages they spoke, those with whom they traded, and where they chose to live and work. But are these things the actual ingredients of a cultural identity? Do they suffice in defining a particular identity? Moreover, why do historians care about defining a Metis identity and understanding its formation? Why attempt to describe the process of Metis ethnogenesis if it was meaningless or murky for the people who supposedly initiated it, performed it, and lived it?

We do so for three reasons. First, Metis communities across the north-west of North America have for generations celebrated their distinct cul-ture, played Metis fiddle music, woven Metis sashes, spoken Michif, and waved the Metis flag, both literally and conceptually.[2] For these people and for their families, friends, neighbors, and fellow citizens, it is impor-tant to discern the beginnings of historical processes that, no matter how murky, later became defined, entrenched, and lived meanings of Metis-ness. The next two closely related reasons are that Metis people are po-litically recognized and their aboriginal rights affirmed in the Canadian Constitution Act of 1982 and the Supreme Court of Canada's 2003 decision to recognize the traditional harvesting rights of the Metis community of Sault Sainte Marie.[3] Neither the government nor the courts have yet worked out who is legally considered part of "the people." We believe that scholars of Metis history have an obligation to contribute to this pro-cess of defining Metis historical roots. Today's land and comprehensive claims processes, with their need to clearly define territories, do not accu-rately reflect eighteenth- and nineteenth-century mindsets of fur trade communities and their inhabitants. Echoing jurist Jean Teillet, we argue that court decisions such as *R. v. Powley*, which advance definitions of the Metis as a rights-bearing group as long as they can show that they are a "group of people living together in a stable and continuous community in the same geographic area," distort the lived reality and historical ex-perience of the Metis within the fur trade.[4] We caution researchers and jurists against focusing too closely on territorial delineations and worry that current notions of nation, rooted to state and with clear concepts of territoriality, may come to dominate definitions of a Metis Nation.[5] We must ask, What were historic Metis envisaging when they used the term *La Nation* or proclaimed "Nous sommes la nation" in the context of poten-tial or overt conflict and confrontation such as the Battle of Seven Oaks (1816) and the battle against the Sioux at Grand Coteau (1851)? Were the Plains Metis referring to an older concept of a large-scale community based on extended kin lineages, reciprocal ties, and access and use of common resources, rather than abstract identities with central authority and clear territorial boundaries? We suspect their use of the term "La Nation" reflected a crystallization of self-identification and commonality attributable to a need to mobilize in specific circumstances of time and space.[6] For example, the Battle of Seven Oaks (1816) was a collective de-fensive reaction to the activities of competing fur trade companies that coveted trade routes and favored wintering sites at the junction of the Red and Assiniboine Rivers for their own colonial settlement projects. In the Grand Coteau battle (1851), the Metis asserted their right to access the lucrative bison herds and to participate in the plains-provisioning trade against competing players on the plains, notably the Sioux.[7] Most inhabitants and descendents of fur trade communities did not need to mobilize in such fashion or take on an overt identification on a continuous basis, but we think they could have if they needed to.[8] The current concept of territory does not reflect the political reality for Metis communities in the northwest, who were future members of La Nation, at least not until 1870, when Canada's Manitoba Act introduced provincial boundaries and requirements to formally apply for river lot ownership and scrip claims.[9] Even in the 1869 and 1885 resistances, the Metis as a collective were primarily fighting for right of access—to bison herds, fishing grounds, and good wintering or gardening sites—and not necessarily individual plots of land to hold and own.[10]

In our attempt to describe Metis ethnogenesis, we consider those who worked in the fur trade in what became Canada's northwest. They came from the St. Lawrence valley, the British Isles, and the plains and boreal forests and have been identified as having French Canadian, Orcadian, Scottish, Cree, Ojibwe, Oji-Cree, Assiniboine, Blackfoot, Dene, Iroquoian, and Salish backgrounds. When European and Euro-Canadian men encountered indigenous societies, they traded with them and formed friendships and alliances with them, and sometimes children ensued from sexual unions. In some cases, the European and Euro-Canadian men and indigenous women formed long-lasting, stable unions, marrying *à la façon du pays* (in the custom of the country); their children married each other to form new and distinct communities and kin networks.[11] In this chapter, we attempt to put brackets around this murky process without pinning down individuals in one fixed and bounded category, instead tracing the movement of individual lives, loyalties, friendships, and kin ties. We argue that understandings of Metis-ness are distinct from other groups in the northwestern part of North America because the category of Metis was created from such a large variety of other ethnic groups and because, for the greater part of its history, it was not rooted to any particular place. The Metis carved economic niches within the fur trade as voyageurs and servants, as suppliers of pemmican, as freighters and trip men, as small traders and freemen, and as interpreters, guides, and go-betweens.[12] Metis probably thought of themselves as part of a far-flung network of commerce, and they probably had a distinct view of the world as a vast, mobile, and interconnected territory, as opposed to being long-term farmers with clear-cut quarter sections or river lots, held for generations within a bounded community. Most Metis social locations (including those that featured farming in addition to work as trip men and buffalo hunters) were rooted to a mode of life that happened to be mobile—the mercantile world of the fur trade and its contact points in the continental interior. The ever-expanding fur trade's water and land routes became the geographic architecture for Metis ethnogenesis because Metis communities emerged around the constantly opening and closing fur trade posts. In addition, during the eighteenth and nineteenth centuries Metis people generally moved westward to access new resources of fur, meat, fish, and fertile land to cultivate. In the midst of their migrations, both seasonal and permanent, they came to rely on kin and define themselves through kin networks.

Our metaphor for conceptualizing Metis ethnogenesis is a spider web, with finely spun connections of family, kin, and friendship obligations. Like spider webs, these connections were woven in surprising and complex patterns and multiple dimensions, could be hard to see, could be easily broken and re-spun, and yet were strong and durable. We take this metaphor from three distinct intellectual trajectories. First, Omushkego (or Swampy Cree) stories attribute the emergence of the first man and woman on the earth to the Giant Spider, or Ehap, who noticed the couple looking at a different dimension of life below them and admiring its beauty. Ehap offered to take them to that dimension by weaving a basket for them, and he lowered it down by spinning one of his strings. He warned the couple not to look down while they were being lowered or they would suffer a great tragedy. In all versions of the tale, the couple manages to resist looking down until they are close to their destination. When they look, some versions have them falling to the ground and hurting themselves, whereas other versions have them landing in a tree, where they are rescued by a bear, sometimes aided by a wolf.[13] Like these first humans, we acknowledge that our scholarship can suffer if we analyze too early, before collecting our evidence, and stereotype or mislabel processes, or if we try to precisely define a moment of origin. Like Ehap's humans, we will never easily land on earth or be able to see clearly the progression and recognizable instances of Metis ethnogenesis.

We also seek guidance from another old soul, Clifford Geertz, who, in his *The Interpretation of Cultures* (1973), so eloquently agreed with Max Weber that humanity is suspended in webs of signification that it has, itself, spun.[14] Rather than use the metaphor to designate strands of meaning in a web of culture or discourse, we view webs as material and emotional ties of kinship and loyalty.

We make similar use of postcolonial theorist Tony Ballantyne's work on Aryanism in the British Empire. Ballantyne used the metaphor of webs to transcend center–periphery models of empire and bounded models of nation-states. He outlined the advantages of a web metaphor to explain that empires were structures, complex fabrications fashioned from disparate parts and brought together in new relationships, and that the web metaphor "captures the integrative nature of this cultural traffic, the ways in which imperial institutions and structures connected disparate points in space into a complex mesh of networks." Like webs, empires are fragile and can be easily broken, yet they are also dynamic, "being constantly remade and reconfigured through concerted thought and effort." The web metaphor also emphasizes the horizontal linkages between colonies within empires, and it allows for the emergence of certain locales, individuals, or communities within the large web of empire as their own centers of intricate new webs.[15] In this chapter, we likewise emphasize the multiple processes of initiation of Metis ethnogenesis, rather than a main center in the Red River settlement and a periphery of the West; we also emphasize that that traffic along the web of Metis kin networks moved in all directions. Connections formed among many of the small communities and extended families along the fur trade routes, and new regional centers such as Fort St. Joseph, Île à la Crosse, Lac la Biche, Batoche, Wood Mountain, and St.-Laurent, were constantly emerging. The dynamics of the fur trade, the plains-provisioning economy, and the freighting business all informed the webs of kinship and loyalty being constantly forged, broken, and re-made.

Scuttling Around the Web

Many studies of Metis have focused on fixed communities, such as the Red River settlement; St.-Laurent, Manitoba; Batoche, Saskatchewan; and Prairie du Chien, Wisconsin.[16] But some scholars have started to recognize the centrality of extensive migrations to Metis culture and history.

The Metis demonstrated their mobility repeatedly, in multiple ways, beginning with voyageurs moving westward from the St. Lawrence valley to work in the trade and continuing both with the migration of individuals and families from the Great Lakes region to the Red River valley in the late eighteenth century and with the slow westward movement across the plains from the Red River settlement that accelerated after the 1870s, when it was clear that Metis were losing out on the rights to land and compensation that they had won in the Red River Resistance of 1869–70.[17] For example, Heather Devine's 2004 award-winning book, *The People Who Own Themselves*, traces the Desjarlais family across generations from France to New France, south to St. Louis at the confluence of the Mississippi and Missouri Rivers, downriver to Louisiana, north to the Red River settlement, and west to the prairies of Alberta. Michel Hogue's recent doctoral dissertation, "Between Race And Nation: The Plains Métis and the Canada–United States Border," which explores the question of why Metis communities flourished in Canada but not the United States, highlights the incredible mobility of Metis people back and forth across the international boundary from the moment of its inception.[18]

In a recent article in *Manitoba History*, Nicole St-Onge speculates about the role of geography in situational identities, noting that "Red River Métis families involved in the gillnet fisheries may have shared a greater sense of affinity with their parkland Saulteaux [Ojibwe or Anishinaabe] fellow fishermen than with the nearby trading and freighting Métis elite of Saint-Boniface [Winnipeg]." She contends, "There is a growing consensus among scholars that the key spatial expression of Métis life in the nineteenth and early twentieth centuries was mobility. The Métis economy included the harvesting of meat, fish and other country produce, but it was also based on trade and transport activities. This kind of economy resulted in spatial organization along networks of travel between specific locations for a variety of purposes."[19] Hence, we see Metis communities participating in annual or biannual buffalo hunts, organizing large-scale seasonal fisheries, and traveling together in small hunting bands, and sometimes returning to a home base, such as Mackinac, the Red River settlement, Île à la Crosse, or St-Albert. But rather than being tied to particular communities that sprung up among the fur trade routes, they were instead tied to communities of kin and attracted to the economic and social opportunities that these geographic points offered. Kin webs and economic ties coincided in those areas. When economic opportunities abated,

such as when the fur trade declined at Mackinac or the bison herds receded farther from the Red River settlement, the webs of kin found other
locales with new economic opportunities. These webs of kin were not
rooted to a tangible place, except in a very large sense—the Great Plains
region, nearby parkland, and the boreal forests to the north. But we also
see new home bases being established all the time, as Metis people
moved west to find new land to cultivate, to follow the fur trade posts to
continue selling country produce, and to follow the buffalo herds as they
shrank and moved farther away from the march of pioneers in the young
republic to the south.

The people from mixed origins who coalesced into these far-flung,
mobile fur trade communities descended from kin-based (and often clan-
based) societies that were also experiencing an accelerating history of mobility. From the eighteenth century on, more and more Scots were forced to
emigrate by changing economic and social circumstances. Many of these
migrants from the Scottish Highlands entered the fur trade and brought
their clan alliances with them.[20] Colin Calloway observed that both

> Highland and Indian society revolved around clan and kinship . . .
> The Gaelic term *clann* meant children or family and implied a kinship
> group that claimed descent from a common ancestor. Blood ties be-
> tween a clan chief and his people might be mythical rather than actual,
> but the assumption of kinship represented an emotional bond. Kinship
> bound people together in Native American societies, but there too it
> often had more to [do] with social relations than with biological con-
> nections, governing conduct between individuals and distribution of
> resources.[21]

In both groups, clan leaders were expected to act for the good of their
people. The similarities between Highlands and many Indian groups extended beyond clans: "They lived in tribal societies with a strong warrior
tradition, they inhabited rugged homelands, and they were accustomed
to deprivation and inured to hardship." Both Highlanders and Indians
also lived as tribal people on the edge of an empire that spanned the Atlantic, and their identities were forged by often-bitter experiences with British
colonialism and English cultural imperialism.[22]

Of course the parallels between Highlanders and Indians can only
go so far. Whereas the Highland Scots constituted a single ethnic group
with a common culture and language who inhabited a relatively small

homeland, Indian societies were numerous, possessed tremendous cultural and linguistic diversity, and inhabited a vast continent. Highland clans were feudally organized, clan chiefs had considerable control over members of their clan, and clans organized land distribution and defense, whereas Native American leaders rarely wielded the power, paraphernalia, or economic leverage of Highland clan chiefs.[23] And yet these similarities were strong enough that they shaped Highlander and Indian encounters and encouraged cultural mixing and intermarriages.[24]

The author Douglas J. Hamilton made the intriguing argument that Scots in the eighteenth and early nineteenth century successfully adjusted to an ever-expanding Atlantic World by adapting what could be considered their seemingly archaic and increasingly obsolete clan system. As Hamilton explained,

> To make the transition from a Scotland in a state of flux to a Caribbean beset by enormous challenges, Scots drew on the support and patronage of their networks. These groupings were, at their most fundamental level, based on precisely the kind of social relations within kinships that had characterised Scottish society for generations. More significantly, these apparently archaic forms of social relations, under attack at home, were adapted to provide the springboard for Scottish influence in what was regarded as a truly modern imperial enterprise. . . . As a result of the activity of the networks, the Scottish–Caribbean interaction emerges as a dynamic and symbiotic relationship, as an underpinning of the Atlantic World as a transnational world of exchanges.[25]

These networks must have fused with Indian clan and kin systems when the two groups met in the fur trade and must have contributed to the base of the extensive networks among Metis families.

In an earlier but parallel study, Christian Morissoneau observed that French Canadians from the St. Lawrence valley held family ties, even across vast continental distances, to be the most important characteristic of their consciousness. He explained that theirs "is a homeland writ small, a movable homeland, and it provides a basis for solidarity . . . and negates geography. Thus the people preserve their identity through their very instability."[26] French Canadians, like their Scottish counterparts, went into the interior in search of work and money and, sometimes, the quest for a better life. Between the 1700s and the early 1830s, over 34,000 fur trade contracts were signed before Montreal notaries by men eager to work in the "upper country" writ large.[27] Some might remain only one season, others a handful of years, and still others spent the balance of their lives in the North American interior.[28] Over the decades, a mercantile network was constructed and maintained across a broad crescent of interconnected waterways from Montreal to Michilimackinac, to the Red River settlement, to the Fort Des Prairies along the Saskatchewan River, farther north to the subarctic, to St. Louis, and finally to New Orleans. United by language, religion, and diffuse but very real webs of actual and fictive reciprocal kin obligations, this French River World endured and prospered into the nineteenth century.[29] Metis kin networks grew out of these Scottish and French Canadian familial and clan traditions, and the networks also incorporated indigenous kin and clan networks to adapt and create a unique web well suited to life in the Great Lakes, the Great Plains, and the northwestern boreal forests.[30]

Although kinship has not received the attention it deserves in the writing of North American indigenous history, Raymond J. DeMallie asserted that kinship is of central importance to understanding indigenous peoples, explaining, "Kin terminologies, descent and inheritance systems, marriage and residence patterns all combine in the family to shape the texture and dynamics of daily life, and serve as the foundations for Native American societies." He proposed that kinship is not simply a model for understanding social relations among families and tribal members but extends "to include the relationship of human beings to all other forms of existence in a vast web of cosmic interrelationship."[31] Robert Alexander Innes took up DeMallie's challenge to place kinship front and center by infusing kinship into our understanding of the indigenous people living in what became the northwest of Canada. In his work on the Cowessess First Nation in southeastern Saskatchewan, Innes found that kinship practices explain how this community came to be composed of Plains Cree, Saulteaux (western Ojibwe), Assiniboine, and Metis.[32]

Traders, both European and indigenous, were born into a fluid and mobile fur trade world where the smallest hunting camps and outposts were connected to global systems of trade and alliances over vast geographic expanses through extended webs of kin as well as economic, social, and cultural activities that bound people together. Bethel Saler and Carolyn Podruchny recently used the metaphor of a Russian nesting doll to envision the interconnectedness of the many spatial scopes of the fur trade, ranging from the macro views of global and hemispheric trade

networks to discrete company geographies and regional and local trading realms.[33] In the nineteenth century, this fur trade world was both
widening and shifting westward in geographic and demographic terms.
Montreal and Michilimackinac were slowly declining centers, whereas
Fort Chipewyan and York Factory (especially after 1821) were ascend-
ing.[34] Given these kin or tribal structures' roots in a mercantile economy
based on cross-cultural linkages and exchanges across vast swaths of the
North American continent, it would be an error to see them as anachro-
nistic. They were adaptive to the social, cultural, and geographic challenges faced in the North American interior. In the same vein, the mode
of life necessitated by successful Metis economic pursuits of freighting,
plains provisioning, and trading in the North American interior encouraged the preservation and adaptation of kin-based networks inherited
from both the maternal and paternal sides. In her examination of Indian
men and French women in the western Great Lakes, Susan Sleeper-Smith
found that the French Catholic kin ties, often expressed through god-
parenting, combined with the kin structures of indigenous people to
produce a widespread kin network and collective identity that subsumed
individuality, incorporated mixed-ancestry offspring, and facilitated the
expansion of the fur trade.[35] Likewise, Tanis Thorne's study of Metis
along the Missouri River, Diane Payment's account of the Batoche Metis
along the South Saskatchewan River, and Brenda Macdougall's description of the Metis at Lac Île à la Crosse in northwestern Saskatchewan, to
name a few examples, demonstrated a shared worldview that linked family, identification, self-understanding, and commonality into webs of connectedness.[36] The need for these ties may have been reinforced by the increased mobility and greater horizons of the eighteenth and nineteenth
centuries in the North American interior. The Metis were born into a world
where a degree of reciprocity and group cohesion was necessary. Beyond
the logistics of bridging the sheer distances involved and the logistics of the
economic endeavors pursued, there were competitions among fur trade
companies, clashes with competing Indian bands, epidemics, famines, and
struggles for access to bison herds, fishing grounds, and wintering sites.
Metis cohesion within the fur trade was necessitated by the internal dictates of trading and plains provisioning and by the ever-present possibility
of external competing interests and potential threats.

So, how should we view the contours of this emerging people? In the
eighteenth and nineteenth century, Metis people were defined by their

links to the fur trade; by networks of connectedness formed while working in the fur trade; by commonalities and relatedness formed in families; by inherited appreciation of family, kin, and clan structures; and
by their mobility. Certainly some appearances of stability, in the form
of fixed places, appeared in the northwest. Mackinac, Fort William, Red
River, La Loche, Lac la Biche, and French Prairie were examples of geographical rootedness to a site, and many of these endure to this day. But
these examples of geographical rootedness can give a false impression
of physical stability. People within these communities moved within
and between these and myriad other places, from large farming settlements to mobile hunting camps to temporary winter camps. Both their
economy and culture encouraged this mobility, which became one of
their prime societal markers. Such societal markers certainly could
exist within neighboring ethnic and occupational groups, such as Cree
middlemen and Iroquoian voyageurs, but what made the Metis distinct
were the particular combinations of occupational ranges and patterns
of mobility.

One could characterize the Metis as a variety of groups that drew on
mixed heritage in different ways in a wide range of circumstances. But
among this range of communities and families emerged a sense of commonality and eventually a sense of collectivity to survive, produce, and
reproduce in an environment of immense human, physical, and socioeconomic flux. They came from (to use Calloway's words) tribal peoples
both on the European and the Indian side. They recreated vast networks
of real or fictive kinships that they could call on for help and support
while maintaining the high degree of mobility required by the fur trade
economy. Places like the Red River settlement provided stability to support the movements and chain migration within the Red River families
and kin networks. Even those who were born and died at Red River were
mobile. This mobility becomes obvious when life histories and family
genealogies are reconstructed. Children were often born away from the
Red River settlement in wintering sites, at other trading posts, or on the
buffalo hunt. While working in the fur trade, Metis servants were left
alone or in groups to winter, hunt, fish, or work in families or clans like the
Delorme, Desjarlais, or Parenteau. These kin groups maintain to this day
an enduring presence in communities such as the Red River settlement,
but a great number of their members moved along the fur trade links to
Batoche, La Loche, English River, and Fort Chipewyan. To understand the

eighteenth- and nineteenth-century Metis, locale is less important than webs of kinship.

Ehap's Humans and Their Kin

In addition to seasonal migrations to follow resources and progressive westward migrations in search of new opportunities, a third type of migration pattern further complicates the tracing of Metis ethnogenesis: the movement of individuals in and out of different social and economic situations and in and out of different identifications, categories, and lifestyles. In this section, we briefly explore the lives of four people, three of whom were descended from Indians and Europeans and one who was descended from Europeans but was highly influenced by Indian kin. All four of these people lived in the northwest and moved in and out of various contexts and identities: Marie Madeleine Réaume L'archevêque Chevalier (ca. 1710–1780), Joseph Constant (1773–1853), Charles Racette (ca. 1804–1881), and Johnny Grant (1833–1907). We assess their reliance on kin networks and how mobility shaped their lives.

Our first example is an eighteenth-century Great Lakes woman who used kin connections to construct elaborate, powerful, and far-flung fur trade networks but remained rooted to a single place. Marie Madeleine Réaume L'archevêque Chevalier was the daughter of an Ilini woman, Simphorose Ouaouagoukoue, and a French Canadian father, Jean Baptisete Réaume, who worked as an interpreter for the French Crown at Fort St. Joseph on the south-eastern shore of Lake Michigan and Green Bay on the west side of the lake. Susan Sleeper-Smith provided a detailed sketch of Chevalier's life based on "baptismal and marriage registers, reimbursement records kept by fort commandants, letters and petitions written by her husband, and references made about her and her children in the letters of French and British officials."[37] At twenty-four, Chevalier married Augustin L'archevêque, an Illinois Country fur trader. Over the next fifteen years, she gave birth to at least four daughters, all of whom survived to maturity, and a son who probably did not reach adulthood. Her first husband died when Chevalier was in her thirties, and at forty-one she married Michilimackinac trader Louis Thérèse Chevalier.[38] Chevalier spent most of her life at Fort St. Joseph, a life fully shaped by the fur trade: she was the daughter of a fur trader and married two fur traders, and her five daughters also married fur traders. Mobility characterized her life not through migration or livelihood but, rather, through kin networks.

Marie Madeleine Réaume L'archevêque Chevalier's adult identity was defined by the ever-expanding Catholic kin network of the fur trade, which extended north of Michilimackinac, west to Green Bay, east to Montreal, and south to Cahokia and St. Louis.[39] She expanded and solidified kin networks by choosing godparents for her children. She chose Iliniwik women or her own daughters to serve as godmothers to her children. Each godfather, however, was French: the fort commandant, his sons, and an interpreter. Only for her last child did she select a godfather of mixed ancestry.[40] She dramatically increased her kin connections when she married Louis Thérèse Chevalier. One of her daughters married one of Louis's brothers, whereas another daughter married Louis's Montreal business partner. Other members of Louis's family married Winnebago women, and the merger of these two families integrated and extended their kin connections in many directions.[41]

By the mid-eighteenth century, as the French population at Fort St Joseph dramatically declined, the Pottawatomi, her kin, and her trading partners increasingly came to define Chevalier's world. About twelve hundred Potawatomi lived near or at the post, and several hundred Miami lived in an adjacent village.[42] By 1760, all but one of her children had moved to larger fur trade communities, but they all frequently returned to Fort St. Joseph to have their own children baptized or to serve as godparents. Chevalier expanded and adjusted her kin networks as her circumstances and environment changed. Sleeper-Smith explained, "Marriage served as a planned extension of kin networks, Catholicism further extended those linkages through fictive kinship, and mobility extended that kin network throughout the western Great Lakes."[43] Although Chevalier stayed in a single place, she manipulated her kin connections to move among different communities to trade.

In later times and places, she might readily have identified as Metis. But a crucial question is, What made her Metis? Can we know whether she thought of herself and her family as Metis, or as distinct from the Indian and French people living around her? It is clear that she operated successfully in multiple worlds, which included Illinois, Pottawatomi, Miami, and French.

Our second example, Joseph Constant, also shaped his life around opportunities in the fur trade, relied on his large family, and moved in and out of various contexts to follow economic opportunities. He was more geographically mobile than Chevalier, relocating from the Great Lakes to the Canadian northwest and eventually settling near The Pas in what is now northwestern Manitoba. Joseph Constant left many traces in the documentary record, and we have a fairly clear picture of the broad contours of his life.[44] Born to a French Canadian voyageur father and an Ojibwe mother in the western Great Lakes region, Constant followed in his father's footsteps by becoming a voyageur in the Montreal-based fur trade. Constant worked mainly for the North West Company (NWC) as a voyageur, but he quickly rose to prominence as a foreman in the trade through his skill in guiding and interpreting, as he spoke French, English, Cree, and Ojibwe, and possibly other aboriginal languages. The NWC hired Constant to spy on the Hudson's Bay Company (HBC), but Constant became a double agent, spying on the NWC for the HBC. Constant used his position as a spy to develop a widespread independent and covert trading operation, a clear violation of his terms of employment with both companies. When Constant either quit or was fired from fur trade service, he opened his own provisioning post with his Ojibwe wife and children near Cumberland House, north of Lake Winnipeg. Constant and his sons continued to perform short labor contracts and trade with the HBC after its merger with the NWC in 1821, and the family also sold provisions to explorers and missionaries who traveled through the area. He developed a trade network with neighboring Ojibwe and Cree communities, thanks to his wife's relatives and through the ties he had developed while working as a voyageur for the large trade companies. In addition to trading salt, sugar, tea, tobacco, pots, and other goods, the Constant family also hunted, fished, and cultivated grains and vegetables to sell at its post.

Like much of the northern plains and woodlands, the region north and west of Lake Winnipeg was a multiethnic environment. By the 1820s, Cree hunting groups and a minority of Ojibwe, Metis, and freemen inhabited the area around The Pas. Some Ojibwe families moved to the Saskatchewan River as part of larger westward and northward migrations in the late eighteenth and early nineteenth centuries.[45] Cree and Ojibwe communities engaged in similar lifestyles, living in small hunting parties for most of the year and travelling according to seasonal cycles to make use of resources on their land. They began to intermarry in the nineteenth century.[46] Significant numbers of retired French Canadian,

Metis, and, to a lesser extent, Orkney fur trade servants settled in the area and frequently acculturated into Indian communities.[47] Many lower Saskatchewan Cree accepted the increasing numbers of freemen in the area, developing good relations with them.[48] In the early years of the nineteenth century, Ojibwe, Cree, Metis, and freeman groups began to form mixed bands. Although these groups were beginning to compete with each other for resources, the complex web of kinship ties allowed them to combine their strengths.[49] Although The Pas coalesced as a multiethnic community, its members had similar lifestyles. The extended family remained the most important social and economic unit, and community members hunted, traded, gardened, and participated in the Midewiwin and Wabano, the Algonquian spiritual organizations most common among the Ojibwe.[50]

Constant's children became prominent members of the multicultural communities in the area. Two sons became leaders in the Midewiwin, and his descendents were Cree signatories of Treaty 5 with Canada. We cannot know how Constant thought about his own ethnic identification, but we do know that his fur trade employers, the Roman Catholic missionaries who converted him and his wife, and the Anglican missionaries who converted several of his children referred to Constant by a wide variety of labels, including Canadien (which meant a French-speaker from the St. Lawrence valley), Metis, Ojibwe, and Cree. However, he was most often called a freeman, which was a man who quit the fur trade service to live independently in fur trade country, residing neither at posts nor in aboriginal communities. Constant most likely had flexible self-identifications, self-understandings, and loyalties and adapted to changing economic and social circumstances to secure the optimal security and prosperity for his immediate family.

The quintessential French Canadian freeman (and one of the most famous) was Charles Racette, who called himself the Lord of Lake Winnipeg.[51] Although he was not descended from Indian and European parents, Racette's life closely resembled those of Metis. He and his children lived in the Lake Winnipeg and Lake Manitoba area, moving in and out of economic and social situations in search of prosperity. Racette was born in 1765 or 1773 in the parish of St. Augustin, just west of Quebec City along the St. Lawrence River. He entered the fur trade by at least 1790, joining a Michilimackinac-based group of Nipigon traders. We can be certain Racette's parents had managed to provide him with an education because he entered the service as a youthful clerk rather than a paddler. His start as a clerk probably explained his disdain for "common labourers," but he shared their language and probably suffered discrimination from Scottish and English bourgeois, especially when Racette worked on short-term labor contracts as a guide and interpreter. In the late 1790s, the HBC hired Racette to establish a post on the upper Red River. This venture failed because the Orcadian English-speaking servants, who could not understand the French-speaking Racette, refused to work under his authority. Some years later, Racette tried again to work within the confines of a large company, this time for the NWC, whose work force was primarily francophone. He procured several hundred pounds to establish a post near Grand Portage, but this venture failed as well. Disillusioned with working for companies, he began to trade on his own in the 1790s. By 1807 he was living as a freeman with his family on the west side of Lake Manitoba, near Fort Dauphin, while continuing to work informally for the NWC.

Racette began a family in the northwest in the last years of the eighteenth century, when he would have been either twenty-five or thirty-two. He married a woman of Ojibwe descent—referred to in the records as Josephte Sauteux, who would have been about twenty—and had at least five children with her between 1787 and 1824. Josephte, or "Mother" Racette, is regularly mentioned in sources as an active part of the family enterprise. She traded regularly with fur trade companies and probably trapped with her husband.[52] After this time, Racette began to refer to himself as the "lord of Lake Winnipeg."[53] Like Constant, Racette moved in and out of a variety of circumstances to find the best economic opportunities for his family, and he eventually settled on living as a freeman.

Some scholars, particularly John Foster and Heather Devine, consider the category of freeman as a part of Metis ethnogenesis, specifically the proto-generation of Metis. In his classic article "Wintering, the Outsider Adult Male and Ethnogenesis of the Western Plains Metis," Foster argued that the ethnogenesis of the Metis required a two-step process. The first was the wintering of an outside (European) male with an Indian band, which led to the outsider's marriage to a prominent Indian woman and the formation of close bond with adult Indian males, while still maintaining close bonds with the male outsider (European) fur traders. The second step involved the outsider male leaving the fur trade service, or "going free"—living apart from both the fur trade post and the wife's Indian band—and establishing bands of freemen and their families. The freeman relied on kin ties with Indian people and economic ties to fur trade companies to exploit economic niches in the fur trade. The social milieu of these freeman bands, which drew on but were distinct from European trading posts and Indian bands, created the circumstances for new cultural forms to emerge, and these were reinforced when the children of freemen married one another.[54]

Heather Devine built on Foster's work by closely tracing the lives of Dejarlais family members who joined the fur trade as servants and later left to become freemen in the Lesser Slave Lake region of Athabasca (now northern Alberta) in the first three decades of the nineteenth century. Like Foster and Jennifer S. H. Brown, Devine emphasized that children of mixed parentage followed trajectories shaped, in large part, by the social and cultural environment in which they were socially enmeshed, and that collective experiences lay at the root of Metis enthogenesis.[55] She showed that even within one family, children could take dramatically different paths that shaped their economic fortunes and cultural identities. Three Desjarlais men born in the St. Lawrence valley in the mid-eighteenth century, brothers "Old Joseph" (b. 1754) and "Old Antoine" (b. ca. 1760) as well as their relative François, entered the fur trade service with various Montreal partnerships as young men. But by the early 1800s all three lived as freemen. Old Joseph and Old Antoine fathered mixed families with their Ojibwe wives, forming a loosely connected band and prospering as fur traders, with Old Joseph based at the east end of Lesser Slave Lake and Old Antoine becoming master of the post at Lac La Biche.[56] Two of Old Joseph's known five sons, Baptiste (b. 1790) and Antoine (b. 1792), illuminate the range of options open to this first generation of mixed children. Antoine became the main interpreter at the HBC post at Lesser Slave Lake, and he cultivated ties with his relatives in the St. Lawrence valley via his uncle Old Antoine. Baptiste, on the other hand, was first employed at the HBC post as a hunter then later supplanted his brother as post interpreter. He then supplanted his step-brother Tullibii as the local trading chief and cultivated ties with his Ojibwe kin, seeking spiritual power and switching to his Ojibwe name, Nishecabo.[57]

Brenda Macdougall built on the work of Foster, Brown, and Devine by closely tracing the emergence of a Metis ethnicity in one place: the region around Lac Île à la Crosse in northwestern Saskatchewan. She followed forty-three Metis family groupings over five generations, from 1800 to 1912, starting from the French and Scottish fathers and Cree and Dene mothers, which she termed the "proto-generation." She found that Metis children took their fathers' last name but resided in the homelands of their mothers' families. This first generation of Metis children began to intermarry with each other and root themselves to the Lac Île à la Crosse region. Other individuals and families entering the region attached themselves to this core group, and this pattern of territorial intermarriage continued for at least two more generations.[58] The identity of the Metis in this region was based on family, relatedness, kin obligation, and interconnections within and among communities, all encompassed in the Cree term of relatedness, *wahkootowin*, adopted by these Metis to assert their prime social marker.[59] The Metis families in the region asserted their economic freedom, and especially their independence from the HBC, first by becoming freeman (with limited and occasional contracts with the HBC) and then by becoming free traders (independent operators trading solely for personal profit). They treated the HBC as a member of the family, relying on it for a variety of needs (investing savings, dispensing rations, and providing housing). But when the HBC failed to act as a good relative, putting profits ahead of the interests of Metis family members, the Metis turned away from the HBC to other family members to meet their economic needs.[60] For Macdougall, the key to Metis ethnogenesis lies in the idea of relatedness or wahkootowin. The work of Foster, Devine, and Macdougall provide parallel contexts in which to view the development of kin networks and communities that coalesced around Joseph Constant and Charles Racette; these men can be understood as the proto-generation of Metis, and we hope that more scholars will devote the same detailed attention to their families and regions as have Devine for the Desjarlais and Macdougall for Île à la Crosse.[61]

Johnny Grant, our fourth example of an individual Metis negotiating an identity in a variety of places throughout his life, was born in 1833 at Fort Edmonton. His grandfather William Grant was a Scottish-born Montreal and Trois-Rivières merchant. The community of Trois-Rivières was located in the St. Lawrence valley, a region with very deep roots to employment in the fur trade economy. William Grant "of Three Rivers," as the grandfather became known, was part of a large and active fur-trading family focused on the Michilimackinac Great Lakes trade. William's wife, Marguerite Fafard Laframboise, was the daughter of a prosperous Trois-Rivières merchant named Jean Baptiste Fafard Laframboise. William's son, and Johnny Grant's father, Richard Grant, was a HBC trader raised in Trois-Rivières. Johnny Grant was therefore born on his father's side to the dual French and British fur-trading elite of Lower Canada. These ties were reinforced after the death of Johnny's mother, when Richard Grant took him back to Trois-Rivières to be raised by his paternal grandmother until the age of seventeen.[62] Johnny's mother was a Metis woman, Marie Anne Breland, the daughter of Pierre Breland and Louise Umfreville. Here again the ties into the Metis world ran deep, especially in the vicinity of the Red River settlement and Fort Edmonton. Pierre Breland was a hunter and free trader along the Saskatchewan River who eventually moved with his family to the Red River settlement.[63] By 1832, Maria Anne's siblings resided in Grantown (St. Francois-Xavier), continuing the tradition of freighting, trading, farming, and bison hunting. They were considered one of the well-to-do and well-connected families of Red River.[64] Marie Anne was also partially raised by her stepfather, John Rowand, who was chief factor of Fort Edmonton from 1823 to 1854.[65] Several of John Rowand's sons and his daughter married into prominent Metis families and became active in the northwest fur trade. Johnny Grant considered all these relations and their descendants to be part of his kin network.

If the vertical webs of kin ran deep, Johnny Grant also ensured that horizontal lines of kinship and mutual obligations were quickly in place. In the 1850s, a few years after his return to the northwestern Great Plains, Johnny Grant struck out on his own and became a free trader in the vicinity of Fort Hall, Idaho, where his father was stationed. There, he married his first wife, a Shoshone woman, who helped cement his trading ties to her band. As Gerhard Ens noted, this was the beginning of a recurring theme for Johnny Grant. He had relationships with at least four different native women who bore him at least a dozen children in the Montana/ Idaho region. These kinship connections ensured good relations with the various Indian groups and enhanced his trading relations.[66] After making and losing several fortunes, he sold his ranch in Deer Lodge, Montana, and relocated to the Red River settlement. Prior to leaving, he sent a letter to John Rowand, Jr., his mother's half-brother, and asked whether he could bring his family to the Red River settlement to live near them. Rowand was dead by that time, and so the reply came from the Hon. John McKay, who was married to Margaret Rowand, Grant's mother's half-sister. It was McKay who told him to come up with his family.[67]

There is no evidence that Grant was in Red River prior to his initial scouting mission in the late 1860s, when he spent three months visiting with different kin and acquaintances, renewing friendships, and making new ones. He also organized the move of his large family and entourage, returning to Montana to fetch them.[68] When Grant finally set out for Red River, he led sixty-two wagons, twelve carts, and five hundred horses, two hundred of which were his. There were 106 men plus numerous women and children. Some of these people were heading "to the States," but many followed Grant to Red River settlement.[69] He used his tried-and-true strategy for securing a place in a community by immediately marrying Clotilde Bruneau, the Metis daughter of a judge in the Red River Colony.[70]

Grant lived in the Red River settlement from 1867 to 1892, standing apart from those Metis who opposed Canadian annexation and participated in the 1869 resistance. Grant instead supported Canadian officials and amassed another fortune in land speculation following the exodus of many Metis families further west after Manitoba's entry into Canadian Confederation. By 1882, Grant owned 13,000 acres of land, a substantial two-story house, and a large herd of cattle at Rivière aux Ilets des Bois (today the site of Carman, Manitoba).[71] Although Grant worked hard to become a member of the new commercial elite in Manitoba, he was not successful. He eventually lost his land, his home, and his cattle through unpaid debts and changing herding laws. Grant moved west to Alberta to start over as a homesteader and fur trader but with little success. He died in 1907 with little to his name.[72] Even if Grant was primarily a rancher throughout most of his life, his extended family illustrates the centrality of fur trade networks in creating patterns of economic opportunities and mobility, and these patterns were very easily adapted to an open-range ranching lifestyle.

Gerhard Ens described Johnny Grant as representative of many Metis traders and merchants in the last half of the nineteenth century: men who were able to amass wealth and property working as intermediaries between Native economies and incoming European-based capitalism. Success depended on their ability to move easily between Indian worlds and European settlement, using interpersonal and intercultural skills in the trade of furs and cattle. However, as Indians became dispossessed and their economies plummeted after the rapid demise of the buffalo, many Metis entrepreneurs could not adapt to the new capitalist environments, which required standardized management, accounting, planning, and knowledge of contracts and corporations. Furthermore, they lacked financial connections and access to capital in central Canada.[73]

Throughout his life, Grant fluctuated among a variety of identifications, including Euro-Canadian, Metis, and Indian, depending on which was most economically and socially advantageous.[74]

Some of the examples discussed above show that the development of Metis identifications and communities could be grounded in a region with core foci. Marie Madeleine Réaume L'archevêque Chevalier rooted her life and extensive kin network at Fort St. Joseph, though the family ties ranged throughout the Great Lakes basin. Joseph Constant, born in the Great Lakes region, eventually made a life and created a community on the north shore area of Lake Winnipeg. The family of Charles Racette gained prominence in the Interlake region of present-day Manitoba. Brenda Macdougall eloquently showed how the Metis community at Île à la Crosse was specific to that place. Macdougall explains,

> What makes the northwest truly compelling is that it is home to one of the oldest, most culturally homogeneous Metis communities in western Canada, a community of people who grounded themselves in the lands of their Cree and Dene grandmothers by adhering to a way of being embodied in the protocols of *wahkootowin*. The Metis family structure that emerged in the northwest and at Sakitawak [Lac Île à la Crosse] was rooted in the history and culture of Cree and Dene progenitors, and therefore in a worldview that privileged relatedness to land, people (living, ancestral, and those to come), the spirit world, and creatures inhabiting the space. . . . . Identity, in this conceptualization, is inseparable from land, home, community, or family.[75]

The locus for this community was clearly Île à la Crosse, though community members, especially men, moved throughout present-day northwestern Saskatchewan and northern Alberta, pursuing various economic opportunities. But even these regions may not have been particularly fixed, for they expanded, shifted, and contracted over time, depending on economic resources and possibilities. The nuclear unit may or may not have been especially mobile, but the larger web of kinship was diffuse and shifting, responding to new opportunities or socioeconomic pressures.

Mobility came in many guises. Although it could mean individuals and families moving around a great deal over varying distances, it also meant mobility in alliances and family connections as well as socioeconomic mobility and the constant search for new sources of livelihood. More often than not, the Metis themselves viewed it as a combination of all three. Yet, in whatever guise, this mobility was both anchored in and defined by expansive kinship networks rooted in the fur trade's innumerable trails and waterways. The multiple webs, both tangible and obscure, were made manifest by those who came to be called Metis. Although the people themselves may only have used collective terms such as Metis or La Nation in the nineteenth century when forced to deal with external and often hostile entities, they understood their unique position within multifaceted geographic, economic, social, and ideological networks. They lived a Metis life even if they did not have the need, time, or inclination to articulate it out loud or brand it with a label.

Gathering the Strands

The stories in the previous section lead one to wonder what was particularly Metis about the extended webs of kin and relatedness and the multiple guises of mobility. The same patterns could be found among other ethnicities, such as the Cree, Ojibwe, Assiniboine, and Dene on the northern plains and woodlands of what would become Canada's west. The Metis themselves lived in mixed bands. As early as 1988, J. R. Miller suggested that "the artificial barrier between Métis and Indians should be obliterated."[76] In his study of the history of the Cowessess First Nation, Innes noted that both the close relations from intermarriage and the similar cultural features among the Metis and Plains Cree, Assiniboine, and western Ojibwe (or Saulteaux) provide ample reasons to question both racial and cultural definitions of Metis.[77] Definitions of Metis that rely on the ingredients of hunting buffalo, practicing Roman Catholicism, speaking French, and wearing woven sashes imply that Metis cultural traits are static, exclusive, and singular, thus precluding cultural change and the creation of diverse ranges of Metis cultural expression (such as speaking Metif, Bungee, or English; practicing Anglicanism or Presbyterianism; and wearing tailored suits). Innes suggested that Metis ethnicities become more apparent when viewed from a band rather than tribal level.[78] We argue that a generalized vision of Metis-ness can be derived from the myriad of specific examples of Metis community and individual histories that have been published in the last twenty-five years. Metis are distinct from neighboring communities because of the sheer size of the area over which they traveled, lived, and worked; their emergence out of the fur trade; their close economic relationship to mercantile capital; their reliance on fur trade networks in the eighteenth and nineteenth centuries; and cultural practices passed down over generations. All these factors combine to give shape and coherence to their kin-structured communities.

Evidence suggests that Metis ethnogenesis in the eighteenth and nineteenth centuries in the northwest of North America was a singularly adaptive manifestation with a particular twist—the Metis used webs of kinship to succeed in an ever-expanding mercantile economy. The Metis represent not only an enduring form of organizing one's larger social, economic, and political world through webs of real and imagined kin, but one that could be fashioned and refashioned to meet eighteenth- and nineteenth-century realities. In these centuries, imperial trans-Atlantic economies consolidated and expanded, requiring ever-lengthening lines of secure communications and exchanges. Concurrently, emerging nation-states carved out territories, hardened their borders, and introduced national "state" categories of identification. Yet, all the while, groups variously termed classes,[79] tribes, peoples, and nations endured and adapted by transcending these national and state identifications. French Canadians, Scots, Metis, and the interior Indian tribes all survived, at least for a time, by proactively adapting older forms of social organizations, which allowed for stability through long-term and far-flung webs of reciprocity. These forms of social organization could endure even in situations of frequent mobility. As with other multicultural bands, the Metis web allowed for the incorporation of outsiders—including new Indian bands or incoming fur trade employees—via marriage and fictive kin practices such as god-parenting and adoption. The fur trade world certainly lent itself to such "stable mobility" with the regular back-and-forth movements of goods and people along its river routes and cart trails. The very emergence of fur trade mercantilism allowed old forms of tribalism or clanship to adapt and serve as a means of prospering and eventually creating a new people. The Metis were unique among other multicultural tribes because they embraced the opportunities that the expanding capitalist system provided. The rise of capitalism did not obliterate old forms of social organization but, rather, allowed the Metis to survive and refine themselves. In turn, the fur trade business needed the Metis as experienced suppliers, entrepreneurs, laborers, and middlemen in order to function effectively.

The concept of the fur trade world as constituted of webs and nodes, with people deriving from it their self-understandings and social locations through kinship ties, is a compelling one. Places like Red River or

Mackinac are important nodes in part because of their undeniable physical attraction in terms of geographic location and economic nexus, but also because of the webs of kinship that ran thick through them. Johnny Grant, after finally deciding to leave Montana, took his kin and entourage to the Red River settlement, a place he had never been, because he knew that the settlement offered both economic opportunity and a network of kin. Although he had never met his Red River settlement relatives, he knew that they would help him settle and take up his usual economic pursuits of ranching and trading. Webs as mental spaces and physical realities could be resilient and robust. On the ground, the "Northwest" was continuously being redefined. Western geographic centers, such as Red River, Fort Edmonton, Fort Chipewyan, Rocky Mountain House, and Fort Astoria, eclipsed eastern geographic centers, like Mackinac, Grand Portage, and Fort William. Equivalent social centers, like the forged ties of kin, alliance, and friendship between and within Metis communities, were also being continuously renegotiated as new Indian tribes were incorporated into the fur trade, populations moved farther west to follow bison herds, and old routes were abandoned and new ones opened, with attendant new trading posts. Continuous influxes of people were brought into the fur trade kin network not only from European arrivals and the interior Indian tribes, but also from eastern Indians who moved west to take advantage of trading opportunities. Many Iroquois from the Seven Fires communities[80] joined the fur trade as voyageurs, and at various points in time they comprised a tenth of the fur trade labor force operating out of Montreal. Some of these Iroquoian voyageurs settled in the northwest, and their communities have lasted to the present day.[81] This web of relatedness that spun Metis ties to one another, like the fur trade, was remarkably resilient.

Identifications based on expansive and extensive webs of kinship enabled Metis people to endure, survive, adapt, and prosper in changing, fluid, and sometimes hostile environments. This form of social adaptation and societal arrangement was a viable mechanism to maintain necessary social and economic cohesion over vast distances, in a milieu of merchant capitalism, and mingling with multiple cultures, societies, and economies. It was an effective basis for a group identification that could transcend local and regional ties and allow for economic pursuits predicated on mobility to flourish and, in turn, reinforce the far-flung kin-based structures. Being Metis and being part of a Metis world—whether one formally labeled oneself as such or not—was an intrinsically adaptive social construct given the conditions prevalent in the nineteenth-century fur trade world. Obviously the contours of this identification ebbed and flowed given specific conditions in specific moments and places. In some cases, internal and especially external pressures hardened Metis identification into a national militant category that used a clear us–them discourse. As Gerhard Ens suggests elsewhere in this volume, it occurred in Red River at specific times for specific reasons, but, for the *longue duree*, Metis identification was an embedded and adaptive category that incorporated or co-opted individuals rather than pushed them out.

Notes

We thank the following people who read either parts of or the whole chapter and provided guidance and information: Chris Andersen, Jennifer S. H. Brown, Richard Connors, Erin Dolmage, Timothy Foran, Douglas Hunter, Kathryn Magee Labelle, and Brenda Macdougall.

1. For a discussion on the instability of the term "identity," see Brubaker and Cooper, "Beyond 'Identity.'" Also see Albers, "Changing Patterns of Ethnicity." Blanche Cowley-Head, a member of the Opaskwayak Cree Nation, told Carolyn Podruchny that descendents of the Constant family did not focus on ethnicity or tribal affiliation. She explained that people did not ask whether they were Ojibwe, Cree, Oji-Cree, French, or Metis; rather, people emphasized both that they lived and flourished around the fur trade post of Cumberland House—and later the community of The Pas in northern Manitoba—and that families and community grew and members supported one another (Blanche Cowley-Head, personal communication to Carolyn Podruchny, 23 October 2008).

2. For examples, see the Gabriel Dumont Institute at http://www.gdins.org, and especially their Virtual Museum of Métis History and Culture at http://www.metismuseum.ca (accessed 13 October 2009).

3. On the *Powley* decision of 2003, see "*Powley* Case: Fulfilling Canada's Promise, Métis Nation of Ontario," at http://www.metisnation.org/harvesting/Powley_Case/legal01.html (13 October 2009), and Reimer and Chartrand, "Documenting Historic Metis in Ontario."

4. Teillet, "Metis of the Northwest," 1–8.

5. In this chapter we recognize that Metis people lived in the Pacific Northwest and the northern subarctic, but we draw most of our examples from the northwestern boreal forest, prairies, and Great Lakes region.

6. For a discussion of the emergence of diverse forms of nationalism in prestate contexts, see Adelman and Aron, "From Borderlands to Borders"; and Armstrong, *Nations before Nationalism*. For a discussion of the term "identification" used in lieu of "identity," see Brubaker and Cooper, "Beyond 'Identity,'" 14–21.

7. On the Battle of Seven Oaks, known to many Metis as la Victoire de la Gre-nouillière, or the Victory of Frog Plain, see Dick, "Seven Oaks Incident." On the Red River Metis and the lure of the buffalo hunt, see Ens, *Homeland to Hinterland*, 35, 38–43, 72, 75–76. On Sioux and Metis conflict, and occasional peace negotiations, see McCrady, *Living with Strangers*, 11–13, 19–27, 76–85.

8. And sometimes the overt identification was imposed from the outside, such as when mixed-blood employees in the post-1821 Hudson's Bay Company (HBC) could not advance their company careers beyond the lowest ranks. See Judd, "Native Labour and Social Stratification."

9. Sprague, *Canada and the Métis.*

10. We note, however, that many Metis practicing agriculture along rivers in the Red River settlement became concerned about their property to some degree. We suspect they used fences to keep livestock out of the crops, not to keep property in. On the chaotic system of land tenure in the Red River settlement in the 1830s, see Ens, *Homeland to Hinterland*, 30–35.

11. For the classic works on the relations between male fur traders and indigenous women, see Brown, *Strangers in Blood* and Van Kirk, *"Many Tender Ties."* Recently, some scholars have effectively traced the emergence of Metis families in specific locations, such as Macdougall for Île à la Crosse, Saskatchewan, in *One of the Family.*

12. For examples of the range of Metis economic activities, see Ens, "Dispossession or Adaptation?"; St-Onge, "Variations in Red River"; Devine, *People Who Own Themselves*; and Foster, "Plains Metis."

13. Bird, *Telling Our Stories*, 81–82; Bird, *Spirit Lives in the Mind* 15–17; and Scott, "Where the First People Came From" and "Arrival of People Here on Earth at the Very Beginning."

14. Geertz, *Interpretation of Cultures*, 5. Also see Vibert, *Traders' Tales*, 4, 6–7.

15. Ballantyne, *Orientalism and Race*, 14–15.

16. Ens, *Homeland to Hinterland*; Payment, *Free People*; St-Onge, *Saint-Laurent, Manitoba*; and Murphy, *Gathering of Rivers.*

17. On voyageurs and their extensive travels, see Podruchny, *Making the Voyageur World*. On the westward migrations of the Metis, see Ens, *From Homeland to Hinterland*, 14–15, 73, 77, 80, 92, 111–12, 114, 117–22, 139, 154, 170–72.

18. Devine, *People Who Own Themselves*; and Hogue, "Between Race And Nation."

19. St-Onge, "Uncertain Margins," 2–3, 4.

20. On the Highland traders and their clans, see Calloway, *White People, Indians, and Highlanders*, 23–28, 118–46.

21. Ibid., 7.

22. Ibid., 8–10; quote from p. 9.

23. Ibid., 8–10.

24. On Highland Scots becoming dominant in both the HBC and the Montreal-based companies, as well as in the upper echelons of the HBC after its merger with the North West Company (NWC), see ibid., 120–21. As for Highlander fur

traders marrying Indian women and having mixed-blood children, see ibid., 156–74.

25. Hamilton, *Scotland, Caribbean and Atlantic World,* 221.

26. Morissonneau, "The 'Ungovernable' People," 28.

27. Nicole St-Onge, "Tracing the Voyageurs: Understanding the Background to the Métis Nation and Métis Homeland—Voyageur Contract Database Project," University of Ottawa and the Saint-Boniface Historical Society, 2002–2009. The Voyageur Contract Database Project has collected approximately 34,000 voyageur fur trade contracts signed mostly in Montreal between 1700 and 1830. The original copies of the contracts are on microfilm at the Bibliothèque et Archives nationales du Québec (BANQ) and the St-Boniface Historical Society in Manitoba. The contracts have been digitized in a comprehensive database at http://shsb.mb .ca/en/Voyageurs_database. It is currently the largest organized collection of fur trade contracts. Also see Podruchny, *Making the Voyageur World.*

28. St-Onge "Early Forefathers to the Athabasca Metis."

29. Englebert, "Beyond Borders."

30. Sleeper-Smith, "Women, Kin and Catholicism."

31. DeMallie, "Kinship," 306.

32. Innes, "Elder Brother" and "Importance of Family Ties."

33. Saler and Podruchny, "Glass Curtains and Storied Landscapes." Also see Slattery, "Our Mongrel Selves."

34. Fur traders and Great Lakes Metis communities were not the only ones shifting westward. See Bowes, *Exiles and Pioneers.*

35. Sleeper-Smith, *Indian Women and French Men,* 42–44.

36. Thorne, *Many Hands of My Relations*; Macdougall, *One of the Family*; and Payment, *Batoche* and *Free People.*

37. Sleeper-Smith, "Furs and Female Kin Networks," 54.

38. Ibid., 56; and Sleeper-Smith, *Indian Women and French Men,* 46–47.

39. Sleeper-Smith, "Furs and Female Kin Networks," 54; and Sleeper-Smith, *Indian Women and French Men,* 45–49.

40. Sleeper-Smith, "Furs and Female Kin Networks," 56; and Sleeper-Smith, *Indian Women and French Men,* 46.

41. Sleeper-Smith, "Furs and Female Kin Networks," 58; and Sleeper-Smith, *Indian Women and French Men,* 48.

42. Sleeper-Smith, "Furs and Female Kin Networks," 55.

43. Sleeper-Smith, *Indian Women and French Men,* 50.

44. For an overview of Constant's life, see Podruchny, "Un homme-libre se construit une identité."

45. Peers, *Ojibwa of Western Canada,* 14–18. Also see Berens, *Memories, Myths and Dreams of an Ojibwa Leader*; and Innes, "Multicultural Bands on the Northern Plains."

46. Honigmann, Rogers, and Taylor all have asserted that language was the most important trait that distinguished the Swampy Cree from the northern Ojibwe and have claimed that their cultures were similar. Steinbring commented

on common patterns of intermarriage between Cree and Ojibwe in the nineteenth century. See Honigmann, "West Main Cree," 217; Rogers and Taylor, "Northern Ojibwa," 231; Steinbring, "Saulteaux of Lake Winnipeg," 245; and Smith, "Western Woods Cree." Paul Thistle found that a group of American Indians referred to as Bungees began to immigrate to the Cumberland House area in the 1780s and 90s, although he has argued that they were Swampy Cree rather than Ojibwe (Thistle, *Indian–European Trade Relations*, 69). Laura Peers also maintained that the closure of fur trade posts after the 1821 merger increased the number of Ojibwe trading at Cumberland House (Peers, *Ojibwa of Western Canada*, 102). For a good discussion of assessing identity at the band level in this region rather than the tribal level, see Innes, "Multicultural Bands on the Northern Plains."

47. For example, see Franklin, *Narrative of a Journey*, 48, 85.

48. Thistle, *Indian–European Trade Relations*, 73.

49. Peers, *Ojibwa of Western Canada*, 69; Innes, "Multicultural Bands on the Northern Plains"; and Albers, "Changing Patterns of Ethnicity."

50. James Hunter to the Secretaries, Rivière du Pas, 9 September 1845, Church Missionary Society (CMS), C.1/M.4, reel A-78, pp. 7, 37. In the summer of 1840, Reverend Henry Budd reported on a Midewiwin celebration at the Grand Rapids (John Smithurst's Journal, 25 December 1839 to 31 July 1840, 16 July 1840, CMS C.1/M.2, reel A-78, p. 517). Reverend James Hunter described another on 29 May 1848 (Rev. James Hunter's Journal, Cumberland, 9 April 1848–31 July 1848, CMS C.1/M-4, reel A-79, pp. 477–79).

51. For an overview of Racette's life, see Podruchny, *Making the Voyageur World*, 294–95.

52. George Nelson's Journal, 3 November 1807–31 August 1808, 14 May 1808, and 22 May 1808, pp. 31, 34, Baldwin Room, S13, Metropolitan Reference Library, Toronto; George Nelson's Journal, 1 September 1808–31 March 1810, entitled "Journal for 1808 &c &c &c," 14 September 1809, in ibid.; George Nelson's Journal, 1 April 1810–1 May 1811, 9 July 1810, in ibid.; George Nelson's Journal and reminiscences, 1 December 1825–13 September 1836, entitled "St. Judes, Dec 1st 1825," p. 82, in ibid.; and Cox, *Adventures on the Columbia River*, 15 July 1817, p. 276.

53. George Nelson's Journal and reminiscences, 1 December 1825–13 September 1836, entitled "St. Judes, Dec 1st 1825," p. 82, Baldwin Room, S13, Metropolitan Reference Library, Toronto, ON.

54. Foster, "Wintering, the Outsider Adult Male."

55. Devine, "Les Desjarlais," 130. Also see Foster, "Some Questions and Perspectives," 82–87; and Brown, "Diverging Identities," 204.

56. Devine, "Les Desjarlais," 133–40; and Devine, *People Who Own Themselves*, 76–91.

57. Devine, "Les Desjarlais," 135–40.

58. Macdougall, *One of the Family*, 17–20.

59. Ibid., 6–8.

60. Ibid., 215–16, 213–39.

61. We hope for more examples like Campbell, *Halfbreed*; Belcourt, *Walking in the Woods*; and Wishart, *What Lies Behind the Picture?*

62. Ens, "Introduction," p. x.

63. Grant, *Son of the Fur Trade*, 1; and Ens, "Metis Ethnicity," 164–65.

64. For example, one of her brothers, Pascal Breland, married Maria Grant, daughter of the settlement's founder and "warden of the plains," Cuthbert Grant (Grant, *Son of the Fur Trade*, 1).

65. Rowand's second country marriage was to Lisette or Louise Umfreville, likely Marie Anne's mother, who had separated from Pierre Breland prior to 1812 (ibid., p. xlvii).

66. Ens, "Introduction," 165.

67. Grant, *Son of the Fur Trade*, 135–36.

68. Ibid., 152–64.

69. Ibid., 170; Ens, "Introduction," p. xiv; and Ens, "Metis Ethnicity," 167–68.

70. Grant, *Son of the Fur Trade*, 180–84; and Ens, "Metis Ethnicity," 168–69.

71. Ens, "Introduction," pp. xiv–xxxiii; and Ens, "Metis Ethnicity," 168–71.

72. Ens, "Introduction," pp. xxiii–xxxix; and Ens, "Metis Ethnicity," 172.

73. Ens, "Metis Ethnicity," 172–73.

74. Ens, "Introduction," p. vii; and Ens, "Metis Ethnicity," 161–64, 174.

75. Macdougall, *One of the Family*, quote on 3, but also see 23–50, 241–42.

76. Miller, "From Riel to the Metis," 17.

77. See also Patricia K. Sawchuk, "Historic Interchangeability of Status," and Joe Sawchuk, "Métis, Non-Status Indians."

78. Innes, "Multicultural Bands on the Northern Plains."

79. Leon, *The Jewish Question*. Leon sees the Jews as constituting a "people-class."

80. Descendents of the Wendat (Huron), Abenaki, Algonquin, Nippissing, and Five Nations Iroquois settled in seven communities along the St. Lawrence valley: Wendake, Odanak, Wôlinak, Pointe-du-Lac, Khanawake, Kanesatake, and Akwesasne. These became known as the Seven Fires. See Sawaya, *La Fédération des sept feux*.

81. On Iroquois voyageurs, see Grabowski and St-Onge, "Montreal Iroquois Engagés"; Karamanski, "Iroquois and the Fur Trade"; and Nicks, "Iroquois and Fur Trade."

Works Cited

Archival Sources

Birmingham, UK
   Church Missionary Society Archives. University of Birmingham, Special Collections.
      Smithurst, John. Journal, C.1/M.2, reel A-78.

Hunter, James, to the Secretaries, Rivière du Pas, 9 September 1845, reel
A-78; and James Hunter's Journal, Cumberland, 9 April 1848–31 July
1848, reel A-79.
Toronto, ON
Metropolitan Reference Library, Baldwin Room, S13.
Nelson, George. Collection.

Published Sources

Adelman, Jeremy, and Stephen Aron. "From Borderlands to Borders: Nation-
States, and the Peoples in Between in North American History." *American
Historical Review* 104, no. 3 (June 1999): 814–41.
Albers, Patricia C. "Changing Patterns of Ethnicity in the Northeastern
Plains, 1780–1870." In *History, Power, and Identity: Ethnogenesis in the Americas,
1492–1992,* edited by Jonathan D. Hill, 90–118. Iowa City: University of Iowa
Press, 1996.
Armstrong, John. *Nations before Nationalism.* Chapel Hill: University of North
Carolina Press, 1982.
Ballantyne, Tony. *Orientalism and Race: Aryanism in the British Empire.* New York,
NY: Palgrave MacMillan, 2007.
Belcourt, Herb. *Walking in the Woods: A Métis Journey.* Brindle & Glass, 2006.
Berens, William. *Memories, Myths and Dreams of an Ojibwa Leader.* Edited by Jenni-
fer S. H. Brown and Susan Elaine Gray. Montreal, QC: McGill-Queen's Univer-
sity Press, 2009.
Binnema, Theodore, Gerhard J. Ens, and R. C. MacLeod, eds. *From Rupert's Land
to Canada: Essays in Honour of John E. Foster.* Edmonton: University of Alberta
Press, 2001.
Bird, Louis. *The Spirit Lives in the Mind: Omushkego Stories, Lives, and Dreams.*
Edited by Susan Elaine Gray. Montreal, QC: McGill-Queen's University
Press, 2007.
———. *Telling Our Stories: Omushkego Legends and Histories from Hudson Bay.* Edited
by Jennifer S. H. Brown, Paul W. Depasquale, and Mark F. Ruml. Peterborough,
ON: Broadview, 2005.
Bowes, John P. *Exiles and Pioneers: Eastern Indians in the Trans-Mississippi West.*
Cambridge, UK: Cambridge University Press, 2008.
Brown, Jennifer S. H. "Diverging Identities: The Presbyterian Métis of St. Gabriel
Street, Montreal." In Peterson and Brown, *New Peoples,* 195–206.
———. *Strangers in Blood: Fur Trade Company Families in Indian Country.* Vancou-
ver: University of British Columbia Press, 1980.
Brubaker, Rogers, and Frederick Cooper. "Beyond 'Identity.'" *Theory and Society* 29
(February 2000): 1–47.
Calloway, Colin. *White People, Indians, and Highlanders: Tribal Peoples and Colonial
Encounters in Scotland and America.* Oxford, UK: Oxford University Press, 2008.
Campbell, Maria. *Halfbreed.* Toronto, ON: McClelland and Stewart, 1973.

Cox, Ross. *Adventures on the Columbia River.* New York, NY: J. & J. Harper, 1832.

DeMallie, Raymond J. "Kinship: The Foundation for Native American Society." In *Studying Native America: Problems and Prospects,* edited by Russell Thornton, 306–56. Madison: University of Wisconsin Press, 1998.

Devine, Heather. "Les Desjarlais: The Development and Dispersion of a Proto-Métis Hunting Band, 1785–1870." In Binnema et al., *From Rupert's Land to Canada,* 129–58.

———. *The People Who Own Themselves: Aboriginal Ethnogenesis in a Canadian Family 1660–1900.* Calgary, AB: University of Calgary Press, 2004.

Dick, Lyle. "The Seven Oaks Incident and the Construction of a Historical Tradition, 1816 to 1970." *Journal of the Canadian Historical Association* 2 (1991): 91–113.

Ellis, C. Douglas, ed. *Cree Legends and Narratives from the West Coast of James Bay / âtalôhkâna nêsta tipâcimô wina.* Winnipeg: Algonquian Text Society, University of Manitoba Press, 1995.

Englebert, Robert. "Beyond Borders: Mental Mapping and the French River World." PhD diss., University of Ottawa, ON, 2010.

Ens, Gerhard J. "Dispossession or Adaptation? Migration and Persistence of the Red River Metis." *Historical Communications/Communications Historiques,* 1988, 120–44.

———. *Homeland to Hinterland: The Changing World of the Red River Métis in the Nineteenth Century.* Toronto, ON: University of Toronto Press, 1996.

———. "Introduction." In John Francis Grant, *A Son of the Fur Trade: The Memoirs of Johnny Grant,* edited by Gerhard J. Ens, vii–xxxix. Edmonton: University of Alberta Press, 2008.

———. "Métis Ethnicity, Personal Identity and the Development of Capitalism in the Western Interior." In Binnema et al., *From Rupert's Land to Canada,* 161–77.

Foster, John E. "The Plains Metis." In *Native Peoples: The Canadian Experience,* edited by R. Bruce Morrison and C. Roderick Wilson, 375–404. Toronto, ON: McClelland and Stewart, 1986.

———. "Some Questions and Perspectives on the Problem of Métis Roots." In Peterson and Brown, *New Peoples,* 73–91.

———. "Wintering, the Outsider Adult Male and Ethnogenesis of the Western Plains Métis." *Prairie Forum* 19, no. 1 (Spring 1994): 1–13. Reprinted in Binnema et al., *From Rupert's Land to Canada,* 179–92.

Franklin, Captain John. *Narrative of a Journey to the Shores of the Polar Sea in the Years 1819, 20, 21 and 22.* Edmonton, AB: Hurtig, 1969.

Geertz, Clifford. *The Interpretation of Cultures.* New York, NY: Basic Books, 1973.

Grabowski, Jan, and Nicole St-Onge. "Montreal Iroquois Engagés in the Western Fur Trade, 1800–1821." In Binnema et al., *From Rupert's Land to Canada,* 23–58.

Grant, John Francis. *A Son of the Fur Trade: The Memoirs of Johnny Grant.* Edited by Gerhard J. Ens. Edmonton: University of Alberta Press, 2008.

Hamilton, Douglas J. *Scotland, the Caribbean and the Atlantic World 1750–1820.* Manchester, UK: Manchester University Press, 2005.

Helm, June, ed. *Handbook of North American Indians.* Vol. 6, *Subarctic.* Washington, DC: Smithsonian Institute, 1981.

Hogue, Michel. "Between Race and Nation: The Plains Métis and the Canada–United States Border." Ph.D. diss., University of Wisconsin, 2009.

Honigmann, John J. "West Main Cree." In Helm, *Handbook of North American Indians,* 6:217–30.

Innes, Robert Alexander. "Elder Brother, the Law of the People and Contemporary Kinship Practices of Cowessess First Nation Members: Reconceptualizing Kinship in American Indian Studies Research." *American Indian Culture and Research Journal* 34, no. 2 (2010): 27–46.

———. "The Importance of Family Ties to Members of the Cowessess First Nation." Ph.D. dissertation, University of Arizona, 2007.

———. "Multicultural Bands on the Northern Plains and the Notion of 'Tribal' Histories." In *Finding a Way to the Heart: Feminist Writings on Aboriginal and Women's History in Canada,* edited by R. J. Brownlie and V. Korinek, 122–45. Winnipeg: University of Manitoba Press, 2012.

Judd, Carol M. "Native Labour and Social Stratification in the Hudson's Bay Company's Northern Department, 1770–1870." *The Canadian Review of Sociology and Anthropology* 17, no. 4 (1980): 305–14.

Karamanski, Theodore J. "The Iroquois and the Fur Trade of the Far West." *The Beaver,* Spring 1982, 5–13.

Léon, Abraham. *The Jewish Question: A Marxist Interpretation.* Mexico City, Mexico: Pioneras, 1950.

Macdougall, Brenda. *One of the Family: Metis Culture in Nineteenth-Century Northwestern Saskatchewan.* Vancouver: University of British Columbia Press, 2010.

McCrady, David. *Living with Strangers: The Nineteenth-Century Sioux and the Canadian–American Borderlands.* Lincoln: University of Nebraska Press, 2006.

Métis Nation of Ontario. "*Powely* Case: Fulfilling Canada's Promise." 2006. http://www.metisnation.org/harvesting/Powley_Case/legal01.html/ (accessed October 13, 2009).

Miller, J. R. "From Riel to the Metis" *Canadian Historical Review* 69, no. 1 (March 1988): 1–20.

Morissonneau, Christian. "The 'Ungovernable' People: French-Canadian Mobility and Identity." In *French America: Mobility, Identity, and Minority Experience across the Continent,* edited by D. R. Louder and E. Waddell, 15–32. Baton Rouge, LA, and London, UK: Louisiana State University Press, 1993.

Murphy, Lucy Eldersveld. *A Gathering of Rivers: Indians, Métis, and Mining in the Western Great Lakes, 1737–1832.* Lincoln: University of Nebraska Press, 2000.

Nicks, Trudy. "The Iroquois and Fur Trade in Western Canada." In *Old Trails and New Directions: Papers of the Third North American Fur Trade Conference,* edited by Carol M. Judd and Arthur J. Ray, 85–101. Toronto, ON: University of Toronto Press, 1980.

Payment, Diane P. *Batoche (1870–1910).* Saint-Boniface, MB: Éditions du Blé, 1983.

————. *The Free People—Les Gens Libres: A History of the Community of Batoche, Saskatchewan.* Calgary, AB: University of Calgary Press, 2009.

Peers, Laura. *The Ojibwa of Western Canada, 1780 to 1870.* Winnipeg: University of Manitoba Press, 1994.

Peterson, Jacqueline, and Jennifer S. H. Brown, eds. *New Peoples: Being and Becoming Métis in North America.* Winnipeg: University of Manitoba Press, 1985.

Podruchny, Carolyn. "Un homme-libre se construit une identité: Voyage de Joseph Constant au Pas, de 1773 à 1853." *Cahiers franco-canadiennes de l'Ouest, Numéro spécial sur La question métissage: entre la polyvalence et l'ambivalence identitaires* 14, nos. 1 and 2 (2002): 33–59.

————. *Making the Voyageur World.* Lincoln: University of Nebraska Press; Toronto, ON: University of Toronto Press, 2006.

Reimer, Gwen, and Jean-Philippe Chartrand. "Documenting Historic Metis in Ontario." *Ethnohistory* 51, no. 3 (Summer 2004): 567–607.

Rogers, Edward S., and J. Garth Taylor. "Northern Ojibwa." In Helm, *Handbook of North American Indians,* 6:231–43.

Saler, Bethel, and Carolyn Podruchny. "Glass Curtains and Storied Landscapes: Fur Trade Historiography in Canada and the United States." In *Bridging National Borders in North America,* edited by Andrew Graybill and Benjamin Johnson, 275–302. Durham, NC: Duke University Press, 2010.

Sawaya, Jean-Pierre. *La Fédération des sept feux de la vallée du Saint-Laurent, XVIIe–XIXe siècle.* Montreal, QC: Septentrion, 1990.

Sawchuk, Joe. "The Métis, Non-Status Indians and the New Aboriginality: Government Influence on Native Political Alliances and Identity." In *Readings in Aboriginal Studies,* vol. 2, edited by Joe Sawchuk, 70–86. Brandon, MB: Bearpaw Publishing, 1992.

Sawchuck, Patricia K. "The Historic Interchangeability of Status of Métis and Indians: An Alberta Example." In *The Recognition of Aboriginal Rights,* edited by Samuel W. Corrigan and Joe Sawchuk, 57–70. Brandon, MB: Bearpaw Publishing, 1996.

Scott, Simeon. "The Arrival of People Here on Earth at the Very Beginning." In Ellis, *Cree Legends and Narratives,* 8–13.

————. "Where the First People Came From." In Ellis, *Cree Legends and Narratives,* 3–7.

Slattery, Brian. "Our Mongrel Selves: Pluralism, Identity and the Nation." In *Community of Right / Rights of the Community,* edited by Ysolde Gendreau, 3–41. Montreal, QC: Editions Themis, 2003.

Sleeper-Smith, Susan. "Furs and Female Kin Networks: The World of Marie Medeleine Réaume L'archevêque Chevalier." In *New Faces of the Fur Trade,* edited by Jo-Anne Fiske, Susan Sleeper-Smith, and William Wicken, 53–72. East Lansing: Michigan State University Press, 1998.

————. *Indian Women and French Men: Rethinking Cultural Encounter in the Western Great Lakes.* Amherst: University of Massachusetts Press, 2001.

————. "Women, Kin and Catholicism: New Perspectives on the Fur Trade." *Ethnohistory* 47, no. 2 (Spring 2000): 423–52.

Smith, James G. E. "Western Woods Cree." In Helm, *Handbook of North American Indians*, 6:256–70.

Sprague, D. N. *Canada and the Métis, 1869–1885.* Waterloo, ON: Wilfrid Laurier Press, 1988.

St-Onge, Nicole. "Early Forefathers to the Athabasca Metis: Long-term North West Company Employees." In *The Long Journey of a Forgotten People: Metis Identities and Family Histories,* edited by David McNab and Ute Lischke, 109–61. Waterloo, ON: Wilfrid Laurier University Press, 2007.

————. *Saint-Laurent, Manitoba: Evolving Métis Identities, 1850–1914.* Regina, SK: Canadian Plains Research Center, University of Regina, 2004.

————. "Uncertain Margins: Métis and Saulteaux Identities in St-Paul des Saulteaux, Red River 1821–1870." *Manitoba History* 53 (October 2006): 2–10.

————. "Variations in Red River: The Traders and Freemen Métis of Saint-Laurent, Manitoba." *Canadian Ethnic Studies* 2 (1992): 2–21.

Steinbring, Jack H. "Saulteaux of Lake Winnipeg." In Helm, *Handbook of North American Indians*, 6:244–55.

Teillet, Jean. "The Metis of the Northwest: Towards a Definition of a Rights-Bearing Community for a Mobile People." Master's thesis, University of Toronto, ON, 2008.

Thistle, Paul. *Indian–European Trade Relations in the Lower Saskatchewan River Region to 1840.* Winnipeg: University of Manitoba Press, 1986.

Thorne, Tanis C. *The Many Hands of My Relations: French and Indians on the Lower Missouri.* Columbia: University of Missouri Press, 1996.

Van Kirk, Sylvia. *"Many Tender Ties": Women in Fur-Trade Society, 1670–1870.* Winnipeg, MB: Watson and Dwyer, 1980.

Vibert, Elizabeth. *Traders' Tales: Narrative of Cultural Encounters in the Columbia Plateau, 1807–1846.* Norman: University of Oklahoma Press, 1997.

Wishart, Vernon R. *What Lies behind the Picture? A Personal Journey into Cree Ancestry.* Edited by Linda Goyette. Red Deer: Central Alberta Historical Society, 2006.

3

THE BATTLE OF SEVEN OAKS AND THE ARTICULATION OF A METIS NATIONAL TRADITION, 1811–1849

GERHARD J. ENS

In 1991, Canadian historian Lyle Dick published an article in which he deconstructed the historical discourse in English Canadian historical writing regarding the Battle of Seven Oaks in 1816.[1] This battle, which took place near present-day Winnipeg, pitted the North West Company (NWC) and their Metis kinsmen against the Hudson's Bay Company (HBC) and the Selkirk Colonists. According to Dick, Anglo-Canadian historians, from George Bryce to W. L. Morton, have focused on Metis "savagism" in the battle and have used their accounts to justify the dispossession of Metis land by incoming settlers, discredit the legitimacy of the Riel Resistance to Canadian Confederation, and, by extension, question the validity of all Metis rights.[2] As interesting as Dick's analysis is in its particulars, his larger arguments obscure other narrative traditions. He examines the accounts of the battle in a narrow fashion: Who fired the first shot? Did the Metis mutilate the bodies of HBC governor Robert Semple's men? Who should bear most of the blame for the two dozen or so deaths? This type of analysis misses the much larger discourse that the Battle of Seven Oaks has become a crucial part of—the emergence of the Metis Nation. Since the early twentieth century, the various historical accounts of the Battle of Seven Oaks have not served to justify Metis dispossession or discredit Metis rights, as Dick argues, but rather have worked in exactly the opposite direction. Narration of the Battle of Seven Oaks as both the time and place of the political emergence of the Metis has, since the 1930s, served to naturalize and essentialize the Metis Nation as an unproblematic idea of national progress, providing the Metis with a story of national origins and a myth of a founding father.[3] This story, once established as unproblematic and natural, becomes the story of martyrdom at the hands of the Canadian state after the annexation of Rupert's Land.

In this chapter I reexamine the events of 1811–1816 in order to denaturalize this simple "Birth of Nation" narrative and to illustrate the competing narratives that emerged from it. These narratives, articulated by competing fur-trading companies, paid scant attention to the views and actual claims of the Metis themselves. Only in the succeeding thirty years did the Metis begin to articulate a series of claims as national rights that made the Battle of Seven Oaks the usable history it has become today.

The immediate context of the Battle of Seven Oaks was the decision in 1811 by Lord Selkirk and the London Committee of the HBC to establish a settler colony in the heart of Rupert's Land at the forks of the Red and Assiniboine Rivers and the increasingly violent competition for fur trade supremacy in the northwest, particularly in the Athabasca region, between the HBC and the NWC. Even before the Selkirk Colony was established in 1812, the Nor'Westers (employees of NWC) believed that it would disrupt their supply and communications routes between the Athabasca and Fort William. The colony's projected site would also sit astride the Nor'Westers' crucial provisioning route to the northwest, and they rightly suspected that the colony was a part of HBC plans to compete more effectively in the Athabasca. Up until 1811, the NWC had used intimidation, violence, and advantages in manpower and provisioning to monopolize the Athabasca fur trade, the last fur El Dorado of the northwest. If the Selkirk Colony provided the HBC with better provisioning and manpower, and if the colony infringed at all on the NWC's provisioning system, the Nor'Westers believed that their advantage in the Athabasca would be lost and with it their chance of victory in the so-called Fur Trade Wars.[4] For all these reasons, the NWC tried to prevent Lord Selkirk from acquiring land from the HBC. It disrupted Selkirk's recruiting of Scottish settlers, and, after the colony was established, it attempted to destroy the settlement by turning Indians, freemen, and Metis against the fledgling settlement.

On June 12, 1811, the HBC conveyed 116,000 square miles of territory (known as Assiniboia), centering on the forks of the Red and Assiniboine Rivers, to Lord Selkirk for colonization purposes. The first settlers from Scotland arrived in the fall of 1812, too late to plant crops and unprepared to feed themselves through the winter. Consequently, they were forced to relocate to Pembina for the winter, where they were provisioned by freemen and Metis buffalo hunters and aided by NWC traders. In the spring of 1813, the settlers returned to the forks, where they began building their houses on lots surveyed by Peter Fidler, in close proximity to the HBC's Fort Douglas. The next winter saw some colonists wintering at Fort Douglas, but the majority again retreated—along with their governor, Miles Macdonell—to Pembina, where they could be supported by the provisions provided by the buffalo-hunting freemen and Metis. By this time, however, the NWC partners in Montreal had informed their wintering counterparts that the Selkirk Colony posed a grave risk to their fortunes, and from this point on the Nor'Westers used their considerable powers of persuasion to separate Metis and freemen interests from the struggling colony.

Struggling to feed even his small contingent of settlers in the winter of 1813–14 and expecting a significant increase in colonists in the summer of 1814, Governor Macdonell issued his infamous Pemmican Proclamation in early January 1814. Although Macdonell's Pemmican Proclamation would have been ill-advised even during normal times, in January 1814 it was probably an act of desperation. James Bird, writing from Edmonton House in response to Macdonell's desperate request for pemmican (a nutritious, high-energy, concentrated, portable food made of dried meat and sometimes dried fruit) for the spring of 1814, replied that he had none to send.[5] Indeed, between 1810 and 1815 the northwestern plains were undergoing some of the worst provisioning years in more than two decades.[6] Although the supply of provisions improved very slightly at Carlton in the late spring of 1814, Macdonell had few prospects for collecting sufficient pemmican in the winter of 1813–14 to feed an expected increase of settlers.

The Pemmican Proclamation stated that no persons trading in furs or provisions could remove provisions from Assiniboia for the next twelve months except what was required for traders to carry them to their destinations. Even to take necessary provisions out of the territory required permission from the governor. Those provisions needed to feed the

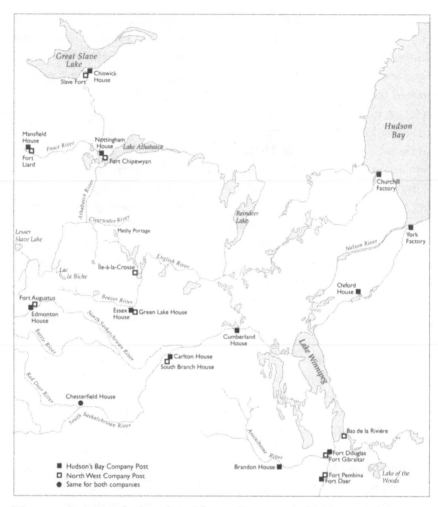

MAP 3.1.   Location of selected rival fur trading posts in Northwest, ca. 1815.
Map by Gerhard Ens.

settlers would be paid for at the customary rate, but failure to abide by
the proclamation would lead to seizure of the goods and prosecution.[7]
Meeting with little cooperation from the NWC, Governor Macdonell sent
Sherriff John Spencer to seize provisions from the Nor'Westers at White
Horse Plains on May 25, 1814.[8] Facing this threat to their supply system, a
NWC bourgeois stopped at the Selkirk Colony in June 1814, on his way to
Fort William, and negotiated a release of enough pemmican to supply
the NWC's northern brigades. The NWC was also given permission to

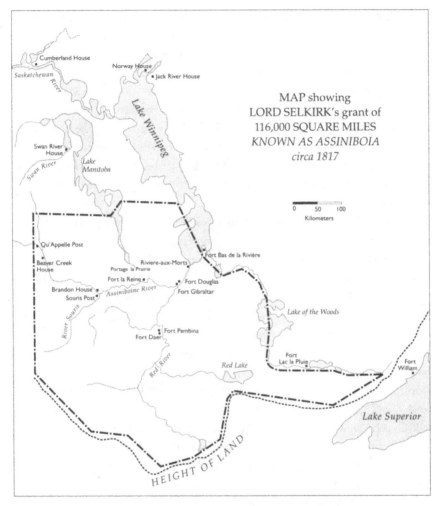

MAP showing
LORD SELKIRK's grant of
116,000 SQUARE MILES
KNOWN AS ASSINIBOIA
circa 1817

MAP 3.2.   Lord Selkirk's grant, 1811. Map by Gerhard Ens, adapted from George Bryce, *The Five Forts of Winnipeg* (Winnipeg, MB: Royal Society of Canada, 1885), plate III.

export more fat and pemmican in return for a commitment to help feed the colonists over the coming winter.[9] With this agreement, trouble seemed to have been averted. Evidence from the annual NWC meetings at Fort William, however, indicates that the NWC had little intention of holding to this agreement, and by the summer of 1814 the Nor'Westers were committed to both defending their property at all costs and destroying the colony.[10]

With more settlers in the colony, and expecting a hard winter, Governor Macdonell issued another precipitous proclamation in July 1814, this one prohibiting the hunting of buffalo on horseback for the remainder of the year, for fear that this type of hunting would drive the buffalo too far onto the plains and out of range of settlement hunters. If Macdonell's Pemmican Proclamation was understandable in the context of a provisioning crisis and NWC hostilities, his proclamation forbidding the hunting of buffalo on horseback was unwise. Given that there were few buffalo within range of the colony or HBC trading posts that winter, this proclamation had little effect other than to raise the ire of the freemen and Metis, who did not heed it anyway.

These two proclamations, coming one after the other, did much to turn many freemen, Metis, and Indians against the governor, if not the whole settlement. Commenting on the Pemmican Proclamation, Grandes Oreilles, a chief of the Ojibwa, is reported to have said,[11] How dare the "Landworkers" (his term for the colonists) deprive the NWC of the provisions that they (the Indians) had traded? This was not just an issue for the trading companies, but for the trading Indians as well. They were accustomed to encamping around the forts of their traders in spring (a typical time of scarcity), when the companies would feed their children with pounded meat and grease. Grandes Oreilles wished to see the settlers and NWC at peace, but if the so-called landworkers did not allow the NWC to trade as usual, he noted, "they shall be destroyed."[12] The prohibition on running the buffalo was also an interference with the practices of the freemen and Metis, and when the NWC traders saw the ill will that this proclamation had stirred up, they fed this resentment and refused to supply the colony with any meat.[13]

The winter of 1814–15 was a difficult one as the Metis buffalo hunters at Pembina were now increasingly hostile to the colony. Most settlers who wintered at the forks (Miles Macdonell and another group returned to Pembina for the third winter) became discouraged and were convinced by the NWC bourgeois at Fort Gibraltar, Duncan Cameron, to accept his offer of passage to Canada. And so, in June 1815, 133 settlers departed Red River in NWC canoes. For the remaining colonists, things only got worse. Later in June of that summer, a group of NWC servants and Metis headed by Cuthbert Grant laid siege to the settlement, burning their crops, killing their cattle, and eventually forcing Governor Macdonell to surrender. The remaining settlers and HBC personnel headed by Peter Fidler were forced to sign a capitulation to abandon the settlement.[14]

Colin Robertson, en route from Montreal to spearhead a northern trading expedition for the HBC, met these settlers at Norway House and convinced them to return under his protection. They reached the forks in the fall of 1815, reestablished their homes, and harvested what crops had not been destroyed. At that point the NWC post Fort Gibraltar was captured and later dismantled by the incoming governor of the colony, Robert Semple. Then, in November 1815, 120 new colonists arrived at the reestablished colony.

The NWC, infuriated that the colony had not disappeared and their own Fort Gibraltar had been destroyed, resolved to crush the colony for good, to which purpose they began to gather freemen and Metis associated with the NWC from across the northwestern plains at Fort Qu'Appelle in the late winter of 1816.[15] In May 1816, HBC boats loaded with furs and pemmican departed Qu'Appelle for Red River. Within a few miles they were captured by NWC servants and Metis, and the HBC and colony men manning the boats were imprisoned in the NWC post at Qu'Appelle. From there the Metis, again led by Cuthbert Grant, moved on to Brandon House, capturing the HBC post in early June, from whence they embarked for the forks, both on horseback and in boats, arriving at Portage La Prairie by mid-June. By this time Governor Semple and the Selkirk colonists had been warned by friendly freemen and Saulteaux that Alexander Macdonell of the NWC and a group of Metis were coming down the Assiniboine to destroy the settlement.

Semple kept a close watch from Fort Douglas, and in the early evening of June 19, 1816, the sentry spotted approximately sixty men on horseback with two carts crossing the prairie about one to two miles from the fort and headed to the settlers' houses north of the fort. From eyewitness testimony collected by W. B. Coltman in 1817 and various trials in Upper Canada in 1818, it is clear that the violence that occurred on June 19 was unplanned. The Metis, led by Cuthbert Grant, intended to circumvent Fort Douglas to avoid an immediate confrontation. Rather, it was Semple's action of marching out to confront the Metis party that led to the battle on June 19. Just as clearly, however, this was no peaceful pemmican run to resupply NWC boats coming from Fort William and heading north. Grant's intention was to avoid Fort Douglas, occupy the settler houses and cut off any retreat, and then lay siege to Fort Douglas until it surrendered. In

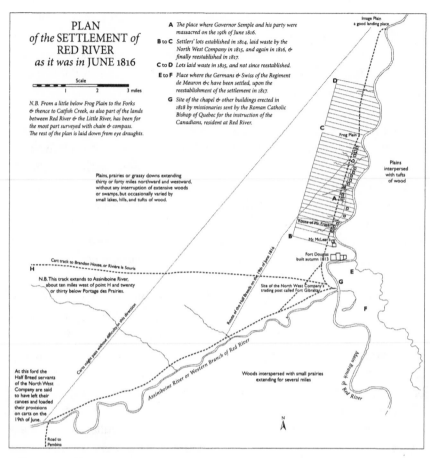

PLAN
of the SETTLEMENT *of*
RED RIVER
as it was in JUNE 1816

Scale

| 1   2   3 miles

N.B. From a little below Frog Plain to the Forks
& thence to Catfish Creek, as also part of the lands
between Red River & the Little River, has been for
the most part surveyed with chain & compass.
The rest of the plan is laid down from eye draughts.

A The place where Governor Semple and his party were
massacred on the 19th of June 1816.

B to C Settlers' lots established in 1814, laid waste by the
North West Company in 1815, and again in 1816, &
finally reestablished in 1817.

C to D Lots laid waste in 1815, and not since reestablished.

E to F Place where the Germans & Swiss of the Regiment
de Meuron &c have been settled, upon the
reestablishment of the settlement in 1817.

G Site of the chapel & other buildings erected in
1818 by missionaries sent by the Roman Catholic
Bishop of Quebec for the instruction of the
Canadians, resident at Red River.

Plains, prairies or grassy downs extending
thirty or forty miles northward and westward,
without any interruption of extensive woods
or swamps, but occasionally varied by
small lakes, hills, and tufts of wood.

Image Plain
a good landing place

Frog Plain

Plains
interspersed
with tufts
of wood

Route of Mr. Fraser

Mr. McLean's

Fort Douglas
built autumn 1813

Cart track to Brandon House, or Rivière la Souris

H

N.B. This track extends to Assiniboine River,
about ten miles west of point H and twenty
or thirty below Portage des Prairies.

Site of the North West Company's
trading post called Fort Gibraltar.

E

G

F

Carts might pass without difficulty in this direction

At this ford the
Half Breed servants
of the North West
Company are said
to have left their
canoes and loaded
their provisions
on carts on the
19th of June.

Route of the Half Breeds on the 19th of June 1816

Carts might pass without difficulty in this direction

Assiniboine River or Western Branch of Red River

Woods interspersed with small prairies
extending for several miles

Main Branch of Red River

N

Road to
Pembina

Map 3.3.   Metis movements, June 19, 1816. Map by Gerhard Ens, adapted from
Aaron Arrowsmith's map in *Report of Trials in the Courts of Canada, Relative to the
Destruction of the Earl of Selkirk's Settlement on the Red River With Observations*
(London: J. Murray, 1820).

other words, the strategy was to duplicate that of 1815—avoid a full-blown
battle but still manage to disperse and destroy the colony.

The Metis and NWC did not destroy the Selkirk Colony in 1815 or 1816
because it threatened their provisioning system, or because the Pemmican
Proclamation and the strictures against the mounted buffalo hunt jeopar-
dized the Metis buffalo hunting economy. By the summer of 1815 there
were neither restrictions on Metis buffalo hunts nor on the movement of
pemmican out of Assiniboia. The provisioning crisis was over. In the Red
River District, there were large quantities of dried meat and pemmican

in all posts by early summer of 1815,[16] and by the fall of that year buffalo were plentiful even near the Red River Settlement.[17] Indeed, there was an excess of pemmican everywhere, and the buffalo were numerous from Pembina to Brandon House and Edmonton.[18] Although one might make the case for residual Metis resentment toward the attempt to control their buffalo hunting in the Red River District in 1814, the NWC actions in gathering Metis from across the West to attack the colony (they came from as far away as Fort Augustus on the North Saskatchewan River) in 1816 belies this point.

James Bird's plausible answer to the question of why the NWC encouraged Metis aggression against the colony in 1816 is related to the abundance of provisions throughout the northwest by the summer of 1815. Traveling from Edmonton House to York Factory in the spring of 1816, he became aware of the NWC and Metis actions against HBC posts in the Qu'Appelle region and at Brandon House as well as the planned actions against the Red River Settlement. On reaching Cumberland House, he noted that in the present state of affairs Cumberland House should prepare to defend itself from NWC aggression. Otherwise, he feared that the NWC would seize the post, destroy its pemmican, and crush any attempt the HBC might make to expand their Athabasca campaign that year.[19] A few days later, he was even more explicit, and he noted that the uncommonly large amounts of dry provisions available at all provisioning posts defeated NWC hopes of being able to shut the HBC out from Athabasca. It was this dynamic that Bird believed was behind the NWC seizures at Qu'Appelle and Brandon House in May 1816 and the root of the NWC campaign against the Red River Settlement.[20] Although the provisioning crisis was over by the summer of 1815, the battle for Athabasca fur lands was still red hot. The reasons for the Battle of Seven Oaks are not to be found in the national aspirations of the Metis but, rather, in the attempts of the NWC to keep the HBC out of the Athabasca District. In other words, if the HBC were able to easily provision their brigades and posts in the Athabasca District, NWC dominance in the region would be threatened. The seizure of the HBC posts at Qu'Appelle and Brandon (both provisioning posts) and the destruction of the Selkirk Colony (a strategic settlement in the reorganization plans of the HBC) were all part of a NWC campaign to defend their interests in the Athabasca District.

The meaning of, and the blame for, the Battle of Seven Oaks was disputed almost as soon as peace had been restored. The extreme violence that had marked the competition between the two fur-trading companies, and especially the twenty-two deaths in the Battle of Seven Oaks, was regarded by Canadian and colonial officials in England as an affront to British control over the region, and so a commission of inquiry headed by William Coltman was convened to determine the causes of the conflict and apportion blame.[21] In this investigation, the officials of the NWC tried to deflect from their company any blame for the violence. According to William McGillivray, Lord Selkirk's and the HBC's colonizing efforts at Red River had from the start been aimed at destroying the NWC. The NWC, he testified, had acted only in self-defense and had scrupulously followed the law. It was Selkirk and the HBC who were the aggressors.[22] To explain the death of Semple and twenty other colonists at Seven Oaks, and to deflect blame from the NWC and its employees, McGillivray noted that the actions of the Metis were separate from those of the NWC. He portrayed the Metis as an independent band of Indians, who, in protecting their ancestral lands and rights, had attacked the colony on its own volition. The NWC had no control over this new nation.[23] William McGillivray's letter to William Coltman in 1818 is the most forceful statement of the view that the Metis were an independent nation:

> The assemblage of half-breeds requires a little further comment; we need not dwell here upon the organization of that class of men. You are yourself, Sir personally aware, that although many of them, from the ties of consanguinity and interest, are more or less connected with the North-West company's people, and either as clerks or servants, or as free hunters, are dependent on them; yet they one and all look upon themselves as members of an independent tribe of natives, entitled to a property in the soil, to a flag of their own, and to protection from the British Government.
>
> It is absurd to consider them legally in any other light than as Indians; the British law admits no filiation of illegitimate children but that of the mother; and as these persons cannot in law claim any advantage by paternal right, it follows, that they ought not to be subjected to any disadvantages which might be supposed to arise from the fortuitous circumstances of their parentage.
>
> Being therefore Indians, they, as is frequently the case among the tribes of this vast continent, as *young men* (the technical term for warrior) have a right to form a new tribe on any unoccupied, or (according to

Indian law) any conquered territory. That the half-breeds under the denomination of *bois brulés* and *metifs* have formed a separate and distinct tribe of Indians for a considerable time back, has been proved to you by various depositions.[24]

It was in the interest of the NWC to have the Metis be considered a "new nation" of Indians because if the Metis were regarded as an independent tribe of Indians who had attacked the Red River Settlement for their own reasons, the NWC could not be blamed for the bloodshed in 1816.

Lord Selkirk and the HBC officials took the opposite view both of the events and the role and affiliation of the Metis. According to Selkirk, the NWC had from the first resolved to obliterate the colony on the Red River. Having failed to induce the Indians to destroy Selkirk's budding settlement, the NWC's partners then turned to the Plains Metis. Closely tied to the various bourgeois of the NWC by consanguinity and employment, the Metis were encouraged to oppose the HBC's efforts to found a colony in Assiniboia and resist any attempts to impose government over them. From correspondence intercepted by Selkirk's agents at Red River, it was clear to Selkirk and his supporters that the NWC partners were encouraging the Metis to raze the Red River Settlement.[25] Far from being a new nation, according to Selkirk, these Metis were little more than "lawless banditti, technically termed, in that country, *Metifs, Bois Brulés*, or *Half-breeds*." Selkirk further asserted that, as the illegitimate progeny of Canadian traders in the service of the NWC, the Metis had "always been much under the control of that Company, by whom they are frequently employed as hunters, chiefly for provisions, an occupation in which they are very expert; hunting and shooting the buffalo on horseback."[26] Selkirk argued that, in order to destroy the colony, the NWC collected and organized the Metis from all parts of the northwest to descend on the colony. Although encouraged to consider themselves a separate tribe of men, a "Nation of Independent Indians," these Bois Brulés were, with few exceptions, Selkirk argued, in the employ of the NWC and their dupes.[27]

The "half-breeds" in the HBC system were also beginning to emerge as a separate collectivity, though with a decidedly anti-Metis bias. James Bird, the chief factor of Edmonton House in this period, and the HBC officer who took over control of the company's operations in the northwest when Semple was killed in 1816, noted that,

All the Half Breeds (sons of servants of the Company) that are here have expressed a wish to embody themselves under affairs of their own choosing and to come forward to arrest the alarming influences which the Canadian Half Breeds may now acquire by their atchievements in Red River; they are perhaps rather inferior in point of numbers to their Enemies yet if collected from all parts of the Country and regularly organized they cannot fail to be a powerful check. . . . I have thanked our young men for their offer & given them every encouragement in my power to take every measure that may enable them to come forward hereafter with Effect.[28]

Here, then, are the two major discourses that came to dominate the discussion of the Metis for the rest of the nineteenth century, and both arose in the aftermath of the killings and violence of Seven Oaks. The one authored by Selkirk and the HBC saw the Metis largely in racial terms— the hybrid offspring of fur traders and Native women who were not only in the employ of the NWC, but controlled by them. To be sure, the HBC regarded Metis as a new social grouping, but it did not accord them any distinct political independence. Choosing to blame all the troubles and violence on the machinations of the NWC, they saw the Metis merely as mixed-blood children of NWC servants who had been manipulated by NWC officers to do their dirty work. The other discourse, authored primarily by NWC officers wishing to deflect blame from themselves for the killing of Semple and his men, portrayed the Metis primarily in political terms as a "New Nation," with a sovereign claim to the soil, a political consciousness, and a flag. From the 1930s on, Canadian historians have increasingly accepted the latter discourse as more accurate because it fits more conveniently with subsequent events, especially the Riel uprisings of 1869 and 1885. An examination of developments after 1812, however, makes these assertions problematic. Although the Battle of Seven Oaks spurred the emergence of cultural, historical, and symbolic aspects of group consciousness that, when tied to a claim to the soil, became the hallmarks of Metis nationalism, this process was anything but straightforward.

The first of these symbolic markers to emerge in the period of 1812 to 1816 was the flag that the Metis carried into battle, described by Peter Fidler as a blue cloth about four feet square with a large horizontal figure 8 in the middle.[29] This flag has become the universal symbol of the Metis Nation today, but any attempt to read this meaning back to 1816, or even the mid-nineteenth century, meets with some serious roadblocks. We now know that the flag was designed and given to the Metis by the NWC to instill patriotic fervor.[30] As well, between 1816 and the twentieth century, this flag was nowhere to be seen. Indeed, during the Resistance of 1869–70 Riel chose a very different flag to symbolize his New Nation, one that featured the fleur-de-lis and a shamrock. This obvious association with Quebec and Irish Catholicism, however, became a stumbling block to a more inclusive Metis nationalism in the latter part of the twentieth century, and so the Metis reverted to the horizontal 8 as their national flag.

In order for the NWC to make their case that the Metis/Bois Brules were an independent nation or tribe of Indians with claims to the soil,[31] in 1816 the NWC had encouraged the Metis to paint themselves as Indians and put feathers in their hair. According to the testimony of Antoine Houle, this had never been the practice of the Metis or freemen before this point.[32] Although Cuthbert Grant, Bostonais Pangman, William Shaw, and Bonhomme Montour signed the capitulation of the Selkirk Colony as "The four chiefs of the Half-breeds,"[33] all four were employees of the NWC and sons of NWC partners. That this posing as a "separate and distinct tribe of Indians" was largely a fiction was obvious in 1816 when Grant assumed control of Fort Douglas after Seven Oaks and signed a nine-page inventory of goods seized as "Received on Account of the North West Company, by one Cuthbert Grant Clerk to the North West Company." As J. M. Bumsted notes, by signing as a clerk of the NWC rather than as chief of the "New Nation," Grant was suggesting "that he himself did not believe he was acting principally as an autonomous leader of his people."[34]

That Indians did not regard the Metis as an independent band/tribe/nation with claims to soil or territory is also clear from the treaty negotiations of 1817. From at least 1812, Miles Macdonell was under instructions to investigate the possibility of making a treaty or purchasing land from the Indian groups of Assiniboia so as to legitimate the colony at the forks.[35] To this end, Macdonell treated liberally with the Cree, Assiniboine, and Saulteaux (Ojibwa) of the region, and in 1813 he wrote to Selkirk that whatever the fears the NWC had stirred up against the colony, the Saulteaux, who occupied the region around the settlement, were all favorably disposed to it and were open to making a sale or signing a treaty. According to Macdonell, the Saulteaux referred to him as the "Master of the Soil" and their father who had come for their good. From that point on, the various Saulteaux chiefs of the region, including Peguis, supported, even defended the colony.[36] When Lord Selkirk's men recaptured Fort Douglas in January 1817, they were accompanied by Peguis and his warriors, who thereafter helped defend the colony from counterattack and also helped provision it.[37]

When Selkirk arrived at Red River in the summer of 1817, he quickly made arrangements to sign a formal treaty with the Indians of the region. The various Indian chiefs who had an interest in the territory were sounded out on this matter by William Coltman, and on July 18 an agreement was signed by Le Sonnant (Cree chief), Le Robe Noir (Ojibwa/Saulteaux chief), Le Homme Noir (Assiniboine chief), Peguis (Ojibwa/Saulteaux chief), and Premier (Ojibwa/Saulteaux chief) by affixing their totems to the agreement. The terms of this treaty included a payment of one hundred pounds of tobacco to be paid annually to the Saulteaux and Cree bands. In exchange, Selkirk was granted land "extending in breadth to the distance of 2 English statute miles" along the banks of the Red River from Lake Winnipeg to Grand Forks, and a similar strip of land along the Assiniboine River from its junction with the Red River to Musk Rat Creek near Portage La Prairie. In addition, three circles, each with a six-mile radius, were granted around Fort Douglas, Fort Daer, and Grand Forks.[38]

Throughout this process, no one—not Coltman, not Selkirk, not the Metis interpreters—believed it necessary to consult the Metis, and, indeed, during the speeches made at the various meetings, Chief Peguis is quoted by George Bryce as having said that the Bois-Brûlés were not acknowledged as an independent tribe.[39] Indeed, for a group so small and so young (barely one generation), it is not surprising that they were accorded no claims to territory. According to Peter Fidler's survey of the freeman and Metis population in the Red River/Qu'Appelle Region in 1814, this group amounted to only fifty-five families (sixty-five families if the Swan River District was included). Compare this to Fidler's count of 480 tents and 1,300 warriors of the Saulteaux, Cree, and Assiniboine bands in the region.[40] But if Metis claims went unacknowledged in 1817, even by the Metis themselves, the upheavals of 1814–1816, including the Battle of Seven Oaks, nevertheless set in motion a dynamic that rippled through the rest of the nineteenth and twentieth centuries.

Although the Metis military actions in dispersing the Selkirk Colony in 1815 and 1816 were largely a product of the NWC's organization and goading of their Metis kinsmen, they nevertheless acted as a powerful spur for both English and French Metis to reimagine who they were.

Over the next three decades, many Metis came to regard themselves both as British subjects, with the rights that entailed, and as natives with aboriginal claims to the soil. Though the term "nation" was seldom if ever used in the thirty years after 1816, the Metis actively defended and began to articulate a series of claims as national rights.

The first Metis expression of this newfound confidence was probably Pierre Falcon's[41] "Chanson de la Grenouillère," a song written to commemorate or celebrate the Metis victory at Seven Oaks.[42] Composed shortly after the battle—probably as the Metis camped at Frog Plain that night—the song directly appealed to Metis pride and sensitivity. Although hardly a national anthem, it portrays the Metis as a brave and honorable group prevailing over a group of outsiders with an overconfident and overreaching leader (Semple). The song defines the Metis by name—Bois-Brûlés—makes a claim to territory that needs defending from incursion by Orkneymen and English, and celebrates the military feats of the group.[43] As Kathy Durnin noted, whether Falcon intended to write a Metis anthem or merely commemorate the feat of a particular group of men, his song was destined to become both.[44]

"Chanson de la Grenouillère"

Voulez-vous écouter chanter
    une chanson de vérité!
Le dix-neuf de juin les
    "Bois-Brûlés" sont arrives
Comme des braves guerriers.
En arrivant à la Grenouillère
Nous avons fait trois prisonniers
Des Orcanais! Ils sont ici pour
    piller notre pays.

Etant sur le peint de débarquer
Deux de nos gens se sont écriés
Voilà l'anglais qui vient nous
    attaquer!
Tous aussitôt nous nous sommes
    devirés
Pour aller les rencontrer.

J'avons cerné la bande de
    Grenadiers,

Translation[45]

Will you come and listen to a song of
    truth!
On June 19th the Bois-Brûlés arrived

Like brave warriors
At Frog Plain.
We took three prisoners, Orkneymen
who had come to pillage our country.

Standing on the ridge
Two of our comrades cried out.
There are the English who come to
    attack us!
At once we turned around to meet
    them.

We surrounded the group of
    grenadiers.

Ils sont immobiles! Ils sont démontés!	They stood still! They were baffled!
J'avons agi comme des gens d'honneur	Acting as men of honor
Nous envoyâmes un ambassadeur.	We sent an ambassador to them.
Gouverneur! voulez-vous arrêter un p'tit moment!?	Governor! Stop for a moment!
Nous voulons vous parler.	We wish to talk to you.
Le gouverneur, qui est enragé,	But the governor was enraged and
Il dit à ses soldats—Tirez!	told his soldiers to fire!
Le premier coup l'Anglais le tire,	The English nearly killed our ambassador.
L'ambassadeur a Presque manqué d'être tué	
Le gouverneur se croyant l'Empereur	The Governor, thinking himself to be superior to us,
Il agit avec rigueur.	acted harshly.
Le gouverneur se croyant l'Empereur	The Governor, thinking himself superior to us,
A son malheur agit avec trop de rigueur.	to his misfortune acted too harshly.
Ayant vu passer les Bois-brûlés	Having seen the Bois-brûlés
Il a parti pour nous épouvanter.	He tried to frighten us.
Etant parti pour nous épouvanter,	He was wrong to attempt to frighten us.
Il s'est trompé; il s'est bien tué,	He was killed
Quantité de ses grenadiers.	along with many of his grenadiers.
J'avons tué presque toute son armée.	We have killed most of his army.
De la bande quatre ou cinq se sont sauvés.	Only four or five of his group were saved.
Si vous aviez vu les Ang'ais	If you had seen the English
Et tous les Bois-brûlés après!	And all the Bois-brûlés afterwards!
De butte en butte les Anglais culbutaient.	Exposed, the English fell.
Les Bois-brûlés jetaient des cris de joie!	The Bois-brûlés uttered shouts of joy.
Qui en a composé la chanson?	Who composed this song?
C'est Pierre Falcon! Le bon garçon!	It is Pierre Falcon! A good lad!

Elle a été fait et compose	It was composed
Sur la Victoire que nous avons gagné!	About the victory we have won!
Elle a été faite et compose	It was composed
Chantons la gloire de tous ces Bois-brûlés!	and sung to the glory of all those Bois-brûlés!

The song struck a nerve with the Metis, capturing a quality that they recognized in themselves. Easily remembered and repeated, the song took on a life of its own. Reverend J. A. Gilfillan, traveling through the Red River Valley in 1864 in the brigade of Antoine Gingras, complained that Gingras sang the song so often that it got on his nerves.[46] Isaac Cowie, a HBC trader in the Qu'Appelle District, noted that in 1869, during the Riel Resistance, the song that generated the most fire and fervor among the Metis was "La Chanson de la Grenouillère."[47] Even when the voyageur brigades and buffalo hunts were on their last legs, Henri de Lamothe, traveling through western Canada in the mid 1870s, noted that the song was still popular.[48]

Others remarked on the newfound Metis confidence and belligerence as well. The officers of the HBC noted that the Metis were harder to control and deal with after 1816. James Bird, the chief factor of the Saskatchewan District and acting inland governor after Semple was killed at Seven Oaks, noted in September 1816 that the Metis were unlikely to confine their depredations to Red River. Given their success at Red River and realizing their new strength, they might well conceive themselves sovereigns of the country and try to dictate laws to the trading companies.[49]

These fears did not come to pass. With the merger of the HBC and NWC in 1821, even Cuthbert Grant was brought into the new HBC as "Warden of the Plains" and convinced to settle in the Red River Settlement at White Horse Plains, where he helped George Simpson manage and control the Plains Metis.[50] But even as Grant abdicated his role as leader of an independent group of Metis for a paying position with the HBC, Metis claims to land and rights continued to evolve.

The catalyst for this new campaign for Metis rights arose not in response to the Battle of Seven Oaks, but the merger of the two companies that had brought peace to Rupert's Land. Indeed, the early leadership in this new campaign came from the very English Metis who in 1816 had earlier offered to battle the French Metis in defense of the HBC. As more

English Metis gravitated toward the Red River Settlement in the 1820s (after the merger reduced employment opportunities), they joined the French Metis in agitating for freer trade. When the HBC sought to prevent their participation in the fur trade, they adopted a new aboriginal rights position. In 1827, the writer of the Winnipeg Post journal noted that he had received information

> that the English halfbreeds have taken much umbrage at the late search for furs, which they consider an infringement upon their liberty and independence as natives. They affirm that by birth they are sovereign lords and Masters of the Soil, and consequently not subordinate to the laws and regulations of the place, like the White; whereas on the other hand, when occasion requires; they claim as settlers the same privilege as the European part of the community.[51]

For the HBC officials, like the colonial office later, this demand for both aboriginal and settler rights seemed inconsistent. As the journal writer went on to note, when the Metis incorporated themselves as citizens of the colony, surely they became subject to its laws and forfeited any birthright privileges, if such rights had ever been recognized to belong to them.[52]

A few years later, HBC governor George Simpson reported an upsurge in Metis activity in the Swan River District. He complained that he was at a loss as to how to respond, as these people were "native": "Were they whites we should insist on their settling in no other part of the country than Red River, but as natives of the country they conceive they have a right to settle where they please and to deal with the natives as they think proper, and this feeling and opinion I am sorry to say is beginning to obtain among the Red River half-breeds particularly those of European parentage . . ."[53] In these battles with the company, the English Metis were aided by their fathers, now retired from the HBC at Red River, who urged their sons to petition Britain for the right of free trade and, if denied, gain it by force.[54] Indeed, the concept of Metis as "natives of the country" was, according to Simpson, first broached by James Bird, an erstwhile chief factor of the HBC and father of at least three mixed-blood sons.[55] Simpson later also warned the governors of the HBC in 1831 that the Metis/"half-breeds" were planning to establish a village in the Swan River District. If this were allowed, Simpson argued, the village would attract other Metis, and in no distant future the Metis population in Swan River would become a threat to the trading interests of the HBC. This group, he warned, would not be able support themselves with agriculture, there being no markets, and would enter into the illegal trade of furs with the Indians, and thereby "revive the question of rights and privileges as natives of the soil." This assertion, he added, would be backed by strength and numbers.[56] Simpson argued that the HBC should lose no time in breaking up the infant settlement and removing it to the Red River Settlement.[57]

This nascent feeling of Metis rights became articulate in the free-trade controversy of the 1840s and the petition campaign to secure the rights to trade freely. The Metis, while seeing themselves as distinct from the Indians, argued that their native-born status and native ancestry gave them special rights above other British subjects. That is, they had the rights of both British subjects and aboriginals. In an exchange with the governor of the Red River Settlement, Alexander Christie, the Metis clearly articulated a position that "HalfBreeds, or natives of European origin" had both rights as natives of the country and as British subjects.[58] Christie's response reflected European perplexity over these claims. He noted,

Now as British subjects, the halfbreeds have clearly the same rights in Scotland or in England as any person born in Great Britain: and your own sense of natural justice will at once see, how unreasonable it would be to wish to place Englishmen and Scotchmen on a less favourable footing in Rupert's Land than yourselves.—Your supposition further seems to draw a distinction between halfbreeds and persons born in the Country of European parentage: and to men of our intelligence I need not say that this distinction is still less reasonable than the other.[59]

Receiving no satisfaction from the HBC, the Metis carried the debate to England. In 1846–47, A. K. Isbister and four other memorialists[60] presented a petition to the secretary of state for the colonies from "the Natives of Rupert's Land," who they described as "the Indians, and Half-Breeds residing in and near the Colony of Red River," praying for relief from the strictures of the HBC monopoly and its tyrannical rule.[61] The petitioners, who described themselves as "les humbles et loyaux sujets de sa Majesté Victoire," objected to the harsh administration of the HBC that kept them in a state of dependency, inhibited trade, and ignored the claims of the Indians and Metis as the original owners of the soil. As natives they wanted the right to trade freely, and as British subjects they wanted representative government and the right to import goods. If they were deprived of these rights, they warned, discontent and violence would follow.[62] J. H. Pelly, responding for the HBC, noted that the fact that the Metis were born in the country entitled them to call themselves native, but it neither conveyed to them any privileges belonging or supposed to belong to the aboriginal inhabitants, nor did it divest them of the character of British subjects. As such, Metis (unlike Indians) were precluded by the HBC's charter from trafficking in furs.[63] From the HBC's perspective, the petition and memorial to the colonial office had been inspired by the illegal traders of the Red River Colony who employed the Metis of the settlement, and who were trying to attack the monopoly of the HBC through the instrumentality of Metis rights.[64] In responding to Pelly, Isbister acknowledged that there was a distinction between Metis and Indians, but that this distinction did not divest the Metis of their aboriginal rights.[65]

After some investigation, Earl Grey ruled that the petition and memorial were without foundation and no further action would be taken on the matter.[66] Emboldened by this ruling, the HBC continued to harass the Metis to prevent them from trading in furs. The company regularly searched for and seized furs from Metis, culminating in the 1849 trial of Pierre-Guillaume Sayer and two other Metis for contravening the HBC monopoly in trading furs from Indians and smuggling them to American merchants. It was only after this trial, which found the three guilty, that the HBC realized they had no way of enforcing the court decision given that hundreds of armed Metis had surrounded the courtroom and would accept no punishment for the three. It was only after that point that the company stopped their policy of seizing illegally traded furs and initiating legal actions against Metis traders in the Red River Settlement.

Thus, by the 1850s the Metis in the Red River District had developed a view of themselves as holding both the rights of British subjects and aboriginal claims to the soil. They seldom if ever used the term "Metis Nation" in this period to articulate their rights, but it was a position that might easily be construed as "national." This was not a position or a sentiment, however, that was present in 1816 when Cuthbert Grant and the Metis destroyed the Red River Settlement. This sense of nationalism was spurred by the events of 1815–16, but it only emerged in any conscious way in the thirty years afterward.

Notes

1. Dick, "Seven Oaks Incident."

2. Ibid.

3. Among historians, the idea that the Battle of Seven Oaks was the central event in the birth of the Metis Nation found its first advocate in A. S. Morton. See his "New Nation," which was published in 1939. This argument was elaborated by Marcel Giraud in his *Métis Canadien*, where he devoted more than 130 pages to the events surrounding the Battle of Seven Oaks. Giraud argued that the battle revealed the Metis, led by Cuthbert Grant, asserting their collective rights to the Red River region and demanding the standing of an indigenous nation. Although more circumspect, W. L. Morton also took up this theme in his *Manitoba: A History* (see p. 63). The capstone of this argument was provided by Gerald Friesen, who noted in *Canadian Prairies* that the significance of the Battle of Seven Oaks lay in its impact of molding the Metis into a New Nation. The battle, he argued, was their ordeal by fire and gave them a sense of nationhood (see pp. 79–80).

4. A. S. Morton, *History of the Canadian West*, 518–32; and Bumsted, *Fur Trade Wars*, 93–110.

5. Edmonton House Journal, 8 February 1814, B.60/a/12, folio (fo.) 9-9d, Hudson's Bay Company Archives (HBCA).

6. This statement is based on an analysis of the fur trade journals of Edmonton House, Carlton House, and Brandon House from 1800 to 1821 (in HBCA).

7. A copy of this proclamation can be found in *Report of Disputes between Earl of Selkirk and North-West Company*.

8. The seized provisions consisted of 96 bags of pemmican, 94 kegs of fat, and 865 pounds of dried meat. These provisions were seized at gun and bayonet point.

9. The NWC bourgeois negotiating this agreement was John Macdonald of Garth.

10. See Bumsted, *Fur Trade Wars*, 105.

11. The early Manitoba historian and Selkirk sympathizer, George Bryce, has argued that that speech was a forgery and was actually penned by a NWC trader. See Bryce, *Remarkable History of Hudson's Bay Company*, 247.

12. Speech of Grandes Oreilles, a great chief of the Chipewas, made 19 June 1814 and addressed to partners of the NWC at Red River. Reprinted in Wilcocke (Ellice and McGillivray), *Narrative of Occurances in Indian Countries*, p. 36 of appendix 13.

13. Bumsted, *Lord Selkirk*, 250. In early August 1814, Alexander Macdonell noted that for some Nor'Westers, the destruction of the colony was the only solution to their problems (Alexander Macdonell to John McDonald, 4 August 1814, pp. 1207–1211, Selkirk Papers, MG 19 E1, Library and Archives of Canada [LAC]).

14. The capitulation was signed by Peter Fidler and James White, his lieutenant. The events of the spring and summer of 1815 at Red River can be followed in the Winnipeg Post Journal of 1814–15 written by Peter Fidler. See HBCA, B.235/a/3.

15. These dynamics and the following course of events have been recon-structed from evidence found in the HBC journals of Edmonton House, Carlton House, and Brandon House for the years 1814–16. For the events of the spring of 1816, I have relied on eyewitness testimony of individuals produced by William Coltman in his investigation of the Battle of Seven Oaks and the testimony of eyewitnesses during the trials in Upper Canada. For the Coltman report and evi-dence, see his "Papers Relating to Red River Settlement." For the testimony of witnesses during the trial, see *Report of Disputes between Earl of Selkirk and North-West Company*. Both of these latter two sources also contain numerous support-ing documents related to the events of 1815–16.

16. Brandon House Journal, 30 July 1815, HBCA, B.22/1/19, fo. 2.

17. Ibid., 13 October 1815, HBCA, B.22/a/19, fo. 7d.

18. Ibid., 26 January 1816, HBCA, B.22/a/19, fo. 15d; Carlton House Journals, 1815–17. HBCA, B.27/a/5-6; Edmonton House Journals 1814–1817, HBCA, B.60/a/ 12-17; and Edmonton District Report 1815, HBCA, B.60/e/1. Even as Peter Fidler noted a drought in the Red River District from 1816–19, he also noted that the buffalo were still numerous and indeed were teeming at the southern end of Lake Manitoba (see "General Report of Red River District by Peter Fidler, 1819 May," HBCA, B.22/e/1 and "General Report of the Manitoba District for 1820 by Peter Fidler," HBCA, B.51/e/1).

19. Edmonton House Journal, 30 May 1816, HBCA, B.60/a/15, fo. 40d.

20. Ibid., 11 June 1816, HBCA, B.60/a/15, fo. 43–43d.

21. The records of this commission headed by W. B. Coltman can be found in Coltman, "Papers Relating to Red River Settlement."

22. This interpretation emerges very clearly in Wilcocke (Ellice and Mc-Gillivray), *Narrative of Occurances in Indian Countries*.

23. Since 1816, McGillivray had been at great pains to defend both himself and the NWC from charges that they had been responsible for encouraging the Metis to attack the Red River Settlement. By asserting that the Metis were an indepen-dent tribe of Indians, McGillivray hoped to absolve himself and the NWC of any blame for the killings. W. B. Coltman, the officer who headed the inquiry, noted that the Metis had been tutored by NWC officers to call themselves a nation of Indians (W.B. Coltman to Sir John Coape, 14 May 1818, in Coltman, "Papers Re-lating to Red River Settlement," 308, 314).

24. "Statement of William McGillivray to W. B. Coltman, March 14, 1818," in Coltman "Papers Relating to Red River Settlement," 318 (emphasis in original).

25. Rich, "Introduction," pp. lxviii–lxix.

26. *Statement Respecting Earl of Selkirk's Settlement*, 17–18.

27. Ibid., 71–74; and Douglas, *Memorial of Thomas Earl of Selkirk*, 113–14.

28. Edmonton Post Journal 1815–16, 2 August 1816, HBCA, B.60/a/15, fo. 49d-50. Original spellings in direct quotes have been retained throughout.

29. Brandon House Journal, 1 June 1816, HBCA, B.22/a/19.

30. Ibid.; and D. McPherson to Selkirk, 4 September 1816, p. 2673, Selkirk Pa-pers, MG 19 E1, LAC.

31. "Statement of Wm. McGillivray to W. B. Coltman, March 14, 1818," in Coltman, "Papers Relating to Red River Settlement," 318.

32. W. B. Coltman, "A General Statement and Report Relative to the Disturbance in the Indian Territories of British North America, by the Undersigned Special Commissioner for Inquiring into the Offences Committed in the Said Indian Territories, and the Circumstances Attending to the Same," 30 June 1818, in Coltman, "Papers Relating to Red River Settlement," 372.

33. A record of the capitulation is recorded in Peter Fidler's Journal of 1815 and is also found in the Selkirk Papers, LAC, MG 19, E1, pp. 18514–16.

34. Bumsted, Fur Trade Wars, 150.

35. Miles Macdonell to Lord Selkirk, 17 July 1813, MG19, E1, p. 790, Selkirk Papers, LAC.

36. Ibid., pp. 790–91. See also Sutherland, Peguis, 32–70.

37. Miles Macdonell to Selkirk, 16 March 1817, MG 19, E1, pp. 3238–48, Selkirk Papers, LAC; Sutherland, Peguis, 32–70; and Campey, Silver Chief, 108.

38. The text of the treaty as well as the map accompanying it can be found in HBCA, E.8/1, Red River Settlement, Deeds and Agreements, 1811–1836. The two statute miles distance was decided to approximate what could be seen by looking under the belly of a horse out on the prairie.

39. For various aspects of the treaty signing, see Selkirk Papers, LAC, MG 19, E1, pp. 17295–313; and Bryce, Manitoba, 259.

40. This census of freeman and Indian bands can be found in Peter Fidler's Winnipeg Post Journal 1814–15, HBCA, B.235/a/3, fos. 32 & 39d.

41. Pierre Falcon was born on 4 June 1793 at Elbow Fort in the Swan River District, the son of a NWC clerk, also named Pierre, and a Cree woman. At the age of five years he was taken back to Quebec by his father. He was baptized in 1798 and received a rudimentary education. He returned to the west at the age of fifteen and entered the employ of the NWC. In 1812, he married Marie Grant, the daughter of Cuthbert Grant, and eventually settled down in Grant's village of White Horse Plain (later the parish of St. François Xavier) in the Red River Settlement. He lived there until his death in 1876. See Complin, "Pierre Falcon's 'Chanson.'"

42. There are many variants of this song, and the one reprinted here comes from J. J. Hargrave's Red River, published in 1871. According to Hargrave, he wrote the song down from the dictation of Falcon, who was still alive at the time. Hargrave believed that the song had never appeared in print before (see Hargrave, Red River, 488–89). A version of the song also appears in the Selkirk Papers (LAC, MG 19, E1, reel C-9, pp. 9207–9208), though the provenance of this version is unclear. For a fuller discussion of the various versions of the song and Falcon the author, see Macleod, Songs of Old Manitoba and "Bard of the Prairies"; Complin, "Pierre Falcon's 'Chanson'"; Dictionary of Canadian Biography Online, s.v. "Falcon, Pierre"; and Peel, Pierre Falcon.

43. For a longer analysis of the content of the song, see Durnin, "Mixed Messages," 57–66.

44. Ibid, 66.

45. My translation.

46. Gilfillan, "Trip through Red River Valley," 147.

47. Cowie, *Company of Adventurers*, 391.

48. De Lamothe, *Cinq Mois chez*, 308–309.

49. Edmonton House Journal, 2 September 1816, HBCA, B.60/a/15, fo. 54.

50. George Simpson to Colvile, 8 September 1821, pp. 1116–1116A, and Simpson to Colvile, 31 May 1824, pp. 1140–41, both in Selkirk Papers, LAC, MG 19, E1, reel A27.

51. Winnipeg Post Journal, 7 April 1827, fo. 22d, HBCA, B. 235/a/8.

52. Ibid.

53. George Simpson's report on districts, dated 20 June 1829, fos. 13d-14, HBCA, D4/96.

54. Winnipeg Post Journal, 7 April 1827, fo. 22d, HBCA, B. 235/a/8.

55. George Simpson's report on districts, dated 20 June 1829, fo. 14, HBCA, D4/96.

56. Letter of George Simpson, 10 August 1831, Correspondence Inward from George Simpson, fo. 465d-466, HBCA, A12/1.

57. Ibid.

58. James Sinclair et al. to Alex Christie, Governor of Red River Settlement, 29 August 1845, HBCA, D5/15, fo. 139a. This letter was signed by twenty-three Metis.

59. Alex. Christie, Governor of Assiniboia, to Messrs. James Sinclair, Bapti Larocque, Thomas Logan and others, 5 September 1845, HBCA, D5/15, fos. 139a–139b.

60. Alexander Kennedy Isbister was born at Cumberland House, the son of an Orkney clerk of the HBC and a mixed-blood daughter of Alexander Kennedy. He was educated in the Red River Settlement and briefly worked for the HBC but eventually moved to Great Britain, where he attended King's College (Aberdeen), the University of Edinburgh, and the University of London. He was a headmaster at various schools in Great Britain, edited a magazine, and fought hard on behalf of his Metis countrymen, whom he regarded as being under the tyranny of the HBC. See Bumsted, *Dictionary of Manitoba Biography*, 119–20. The memorial was also signed by Thomas Vincent, John M'Leod, D. V. Stewart, and James Isbister.

61. The petition, memorial, and considerable correspondence related to the question are found in "Hudson's Bay Company (Red River Settlement) Return to an Address of the Honourable the House of Commons, dated 9 February 1849; for Copies of any Memorials presented to the Colonial Office by Inhabitants of the Red River Settlement, complaining of the Government of the Hudson's Bay Company. . . . ," in *British Parliamentary Papers Relating to Red River Settlement* (hereafter cited as "HBC Address of the Honourable House of Commons").

62. This petition, which was written in French, was accompanied by a thousand signatures attested to by William Dease, J. Baptiste Payette, J. Louis Rielle, Charles Montigny, and Cuthbert M'Gillis. See pages 317–24 in "HBC Address of the Honourable House of Commons."

63. J. H. Pelly, "Report on the Memorial," 317–24, in ibid.

64. J. H. Pelly to Earl Grey, 24 April 1847, 316–17, in ibid.

65. A. K. Isbister's response to Pelly, 354–62, in ibid.

66. B. Hawes to A. K. Isbister, 23 June 1849, 409, in ibid.

Bibliography

Archival Sources

Winnipeg, MB

  Hudson's Bay Company Archives (HBCA)

    A12/1, London Correspondence Inward from George Simpson, Letter of August 10, 1831, folio (fo.) 465d-466.

    B.22/e/1. "General Report of Red River District by Peter Fidler, 1819 May."

    B.22/1/19. Brandon House Journal, July 30, 1815.

    B.27/a/5–6. Carlton House Journals, 1815–17.

    B.51/e/1. "General Report of the Manitoba District for 1820 by Peter Fidler."

    B.60/a/12–17. Edmonton House Journals 1814–17.

    B.60/e/1. Edmonton District Report 1815.

    B.235/a/3–8. Winnipeg Post Journal of 1814–27.

    D4/96, George Simpson's Report on Districts, dated June 20, 1829.

    D5/15, George Simpson's Correspondence Inward, 1845.

    E.8/1. Red River Settlement, Deeds and Agreements, 1811–36.

Ottawa, ON

  Library and Archives Canada (LAC)

    MG 19, E1. Selkirk Papers.

Published Sources

Arrowsmith, Aaron. *Report of Trials in the Courts of Canada, Relative to the Destruction of the Earl of Selkirk's Settlement on the Red River with Observations.* London, UK: J. Murray, 1820.

Ball, Timothy. "Climatic Change, Droughts and the Social Impact: Central Canada, 1811–20, A Classic Example." In Harrington, *Year without Summer,* 185–95.

———. "The Year without Summer: Its Impact on the Fur Trade and History of Western Canada." In Harrington, *Year without Summer,* 196–202.

British Parliamentary Papers—Reports, Correspondence and Other Papers Relating to the Red River Settlement, the Hudson's Bay Company and other Affairs in Canada, 1849—Colonies. Canada 18. Shannon, Ireland: Irish University Press, 1969.

Bryce, George. *The Five Forts of Winnipeg.* Winnipeg, MB: Royal Society of Canada, 1885.

———. *Manitoba: Its Infancy, Growth, and Present Condition.* London, UK: Sampson Low, Marston, Searle, & Rivington, 1882.

———. *The Remarkable History of the Hudson's Bay Company Including That of the French Traders of North-Western Canada and of the North-West, XY, and Astor Fur Companies*. London, UK: 1900.

Bumsted, J. M. *Dictionary of Manitoba Biography*. Winnipeg: University of Manitoba Press, 1999.

———. *Fur Trade Wars: The Founding of Western Canada*. Winnipeg, MB: Great Plains Publications, 1999.

———. *Lord Selkirk: A Life*. Winnipeg: University of Manitoba Press, 2008.

Campey, Lucille. *The Silver Chief: Lord Selkirk and the Scottish Pioneers of Belfast, Baldoon and Red River*. Toronto, ON: Natural Heritage Books, 2003.

Coltman, William. "Papers Relating to the Red River Settlement: viz Return to an Address from the Honourable House of Commons to His Royal Highness The Prince Regent, dated 24th June 1819 . . ." In *British Parliamentary Papers. Colonies. Canada 5*. Shannon, Ireland: Irish University Press, 1971.

Complin, Margaret. "Pierre Falcon's 'Chanson de la Grenouillère.'" In *Transactions of the Royal Society of Canada*, section 2. Ottawa, ON: Royal Society of Canada, 1939.

Cowie, Isaac. *The Company of Adventurers: A Narrative of Seven Years in the Service of the Hudson's Bay Company During 1857–1874 on the Great Buffalo Plains with Historical and Biographical Notes and Comments*. Toronto, ON: William Briggs, 1913.

De Lamothe, H. *Cinq Mois chez Les Français D'Amérique Voyage au Canada et à La Rivière Rouge Du Nord*. Paris, France: Librairie Hachette, 1879.

Dick, Lyle. "The Seven Oaks Incident and the Construction of a Historical Tradition, 1816–1970." *Journal of the Canadian Historical Association*, New Series, 2 (1991): 91–113.

Dictionary of Canadian Biography Online. s.v. "Falcon, Pierre" (by Bruce Peel), edited by John English and Réal Bélanger. http://www.biographi.ca/009004-119.01-e.php?&id_nbr=4977&interval=25&&PHPSESSID=uphrufdcueja8rmojdhp6i9nto (accessed December 2011).

Douglas, Thomas, Earl of Selkirk. *The Memorial of Thomas Earl of Selkirk*. Montreal, QC: Nahum Mower, 1819. Reprinted in *The Collected Writings of Lord Selkirk, 1810–1820*, vol. 2 in the *Writings and Papers of Thomas Douglas, Fifth Earl of Selkirk*, edited by J. M. Bumsted. Winnipeg: Manitoba Record Society, 1987. Page references are to the 1987 edition.

Durnin, Kathy. "Mixed Messages: The Métis in Canadian Literature, 1816–2007." PhD diss., University of Alberta, 2008.

Ellice, Edward. *The Communications of Mercator upon the Contest between the Earl of Selkirk, and the Hudson's Bay Company, on One Side, and the North West Company on the Other*. Montreal, QC: W. Gray, 1817.

Friesen, Gerald. *The Canadian Prairies: A History*. Toronto, ON: University of Toronto Press, 1987.

Gilfillan, J. A. "A Trip through the Red River Valley in 1864." *Collections of the State Historical Society of North Dakota* 2 (1908): 146–49.

Giraud, Marcel. *Le Métis Canadien: son role dans l'histoire des provinces de l'Ouest.* Paris, France: Institut d'Ethnoligie, 1945.

Hargrave, J. J. *Red River.* London, UK/Montreal, QC: John Lovell, 1871.

Harrington, C. R., ed. *The Year without Summer: World Climate in 1816.* Ottawa, ON: Canadian Museum of Nature, 1992.

Macleod, Margaret Arnett. "Bard of the Prairies." *The Beaver,* Spring 1956, 20–25.

———. *Songs of Old Manitoba.* Toronto, ON: Ryerson Press, 1960.

Morton, A. S. *A History of the Canadian West to 1870–71.* Toronto, ON: Thomas Nelson and Sons, 1939.

———. "The New Nation: The Métis." In *Transactions of the Royal Society of Canada,* section 2. Ottawa, ON: Royal Society of Canada, 1939.

Morton, W. L. *Manitoba: A History,* 2nd ed. Toronto, ON: University of Toronto Press, 1967.

Peel, Bruce. *Pierre Falcon.* Winnipeg: Manitoba Culture, Heritage and Recreation, Historic Resources Branch, 1984.

Report of the Proceedings Connected with the Disputes between the Earl of Selkirk and the North-West Company at the Assizes, Held at York in Upper Canada, October, 1818. Montreal, QC: James Lane and Nahum Mower, 1819.

Rich, E. E. "Introduction." In *Colin Robertson's Correspondence Book, September 1817 to September 1822,* edited by E. E. Rich. Toronto, ON: Champlain Society, 1939.

Statement Respecting the Earl of Selkirk's Settlement upon the Red River in North America; Its Destructions in 1815 and 1816; and the Massacre of Governor Semple and his Party. London, UK: John Murray, 1817.

Sutherland, Donna G. *Peguis: A Noble Friend.* Selkirk, MB: Chief Peguis Heritage Park, 2003.

Wilcocke, Samuel Hull (sometimes attributed to Edward Ellice and Simon McGillivray). *A Narrative of Occurances in the Indian Countries of North America, Since the Connexion of the Right Hon. The Earl of Selkirk with the Hudson's Bay Company, and His Attempt to Establish a Colony on the Red River with a Detailed Account of His Lordship's Military Expedition to, and Subsequent Proceedings at Fort William, in Upper Canada.* London, UK: B. McMillan, 1817.

4

AGAINST SPATIALIZED ETHNICITY

PHILIP D. WOLFART

The categories that have defined the discussion of Métis ethnogenesis—French, English, Indian, Métis, Bois-Brûlé, Mixed-Blood, Halfbreed—are those given in the written records of the fur trade companies and similar documents. Even in those contexts where they have been accepted without question, however, they should not be taken as natural but recognized as the artificial constructs of their age—the period immediately preceding the emergence of the Métis Nation and, much at the same time, the rise of the modern nation-states of Europe.

In looking for alternative constructs, it seems reasonable to examine the patterns of identity formation that are found in Europe at the end of the eighteenth century. Although the concepts of *jus sanguinis* and *jus soli*, for example, have attracted little attention among historians writing in English, they are critical to the study of the new states that emerged from the upheavals of the French Revolution, the collapse of the Holy Roman Empire, and the Napoleonic reshaping of continental Europe.

Best documented in the context of constitutional law, *jus sanguinis* refers to the person-based jurisdiction and consequent mobility that is grounded in feudal concepts of fealty and oaths, while *jus soli* reflects a more sedentary model and ultimately the increasing territorialization of early modern Europe.[1] They reappear in somewhat different form in such later concepts as the *pays* (roughly translatable, perhaps, as "country") of the *Annales* school (see note 26, below) and the *heimat* (just as roughly, perhaps, to be rendered as "hometown") of their less well-known German contemporaries. These new approaches arose in protest against the simplistic ethno-nationalist doctrines of the period between 1870 and 1918, and both stress the importance for history and the allied disciplines of going beyond constitutional sources to include *la vie quotidienne*: material culture and costume, music and processions, oral history, and ritual demarcations of space. A number of recent works, in fact, while not necessarily acknowledging the influence of the Annalistes, have once again begun to examine the evidence of ethnography and economics, concentrating on customary practice and ritual, on music and oral literature.[2]

Writing as a historical geographer, I concentrate on the effects, on both sides of the Atlantic, of a gradual development that culminated at the end of the eighteenth century—the shift in the dominant view of the geographical organization of the world from an *aspatial* to a *spatialized* one. In the new, spatialized model of the world, social, political, and economic relations are defined and demarcated on the ground. Where one goes to market, to church, to court; where contracts are concluded; where the marriage partner is chosen; and where countless other activities take place, is determined by the geographical boundaries that, in effect, enclose the space in which one's life is lived. In many places, in fact, the cycle of annual rituals calls for a procession around the boundaries of that space. Above all, such geographically bounded relationships, which are characteristic of a post-Napoleonic "modern" world, are "mappable." In an aspatial model of the world, by contrast, all these events and relationships defining one's "pays" are determined by parentage; by membership in a group, clan, or tribe; or by perennially competing political forces—in short, by a system of social obligations and fealty. Such systems typically represent a pre-"modern" world and are commonly found not only in nomadic and semisedentary communities, but also in the feudal and proto-industrial societies of Europe. Relations of this order are not readily susceptible to being mapped under the cartographic conventions of post-Napoleonic topographic map projects.[3]

In recognizing that the Métis lived and functioned in an aspatially organized world, I argue that an adequate account of their existence has seemed elusive to historians informed by a spatialized view of the world.[4] In relying, more specifically, on the methods of the Annalistes,

I concentrate on the analysis of the patterns embodied in the cultural activities of the Métis and the microhistorical and geographical contexts of their ethnogenesis.

The Nation-State Model

The ethnic categories of the written records suffer from various short-comings in addition to their fixation on linear history and descent. From the outset, for example, they force us into an excessively narrow, some-times even blinkered, reading of the documents. They are particularly restrictive with respect to time and place. Though we may not even real-ize it, moreover, they have for far too long tended to keep us dependent on written records exclusively. Finally, the surviving texts are almost never produced by the people in question. In sum, they are representative of the nation-state model that developed in the course of the nineteenth century. Characterized by the doctrine of a linear ascent from "savagery" to "civilization" and the nation-state as the epitome of "modern" achieve-ment, this view (often called "whiggish" or "liberal") has been widely held throughout the past two centuries. Many writers on ethnicity and nationalism regard tribal identities as natural.[5] In their view the nation with its tribally based collective consciousness perfectly coincides with the state, its politically and geographically precise expression. As a con-sequence, the nation-state cannot readily cope with social groups that have neither a universally recognized identity nor an unambiguously defined, nonoverlapping geographical space. It is one of the crucial failures of this model that it makes no allowance for those groups—the Métis along with the Palestinians, Kurds, Pashtos, and many others—for whom na-tion and state fail to coincide.

An alternative view insists that group identities are creatures of the early modern era, more specifically of the French Revolution.[6] Instead of the uniform and, ultimately, genetically defined units presumed by the nationalist camp, this latter view permits the coexistence of variously defined groups. It also challenges the liberal notion that a progression to nationhood is teleologically determined; instead, it stresses the crucial role of active processes in which the members of a group are collectively engaged.

The term *Métis* classically illustrates the kind of concept that makes sense only if it is interpreted dynamically.[7] Static categories, though they may at first appear useful in some well-defined context, almost invariably turn out to be oversimplifications. If identity is not, as the liberal model of the nation-state would have it, based on a predetermined set of parameters (e.g., position in a descent group), then it has to be constantly created and recreated through action and affirmation. More specifically, membership in a community is not automatically or essentially an issue of, say, residence but, much more importantly, of self-identification and community agreement. This is the crucial point of which Arthur J. Ray was able to convince the judges in *R. v. Powley* (1998, 2003) and *R. v. Goodon* (2008).[8] In this view, then, ethnogenesis is the recognition of a distinct group, established as distinct—and often with reference to a particular geographical space—both by self-ascription and by the acknowledgment extended by others.

My own position is that the categories defining these identities should not be taken as natural but recognized as the artificial constructs of their age. In that case, the genesis of a group such as the Métis rests not in the biological encounter between North American women and European men—*métissage* surely has been taking place in North America (and everywhere else) since first contact—but in the emergence of the *concept* of a distinct group, typically manifesting itself in a special term defining it, an ethnonym.

An Aspatial Model

It is ironic that, at the very moment early in the nineteenth century when the Métis had become a demographic force in their geographical space, their status underwent a radical change because the larger paradigm shifted. With the sophistication and scale of scientific cartography increasing at an exponential rate,[9] the aspatial (non-nation-state) model rapidly gave way to a strictly spatialized, territorially defined model, and a group like the Métis, who did not lead a settled life on bounded plots of land, became less and less visible. It should go without saying that the Métis have, of course, always had an *ecumene* (the world as known to the members of a given society), but their space has never been unambiguously filled, layered, and demarcated in the landscape as wholly theirs, politically, administratively, and culturally—in short, as a cultural landscape.[10]

Until the late eighteenth century, the European world (on both sides of the Atlantic) had been made up of loosely confederated principalities, an arrangement in which the Métis could readily have had a role and a history. But this multidimensional—and messy—structure was, practically at the stroke of a pen, replaced by a world of spatially demarcated nation-states that were not designed to accommodate any group that was not spatially organized.

In referring to the period at the turn from the eighteenth to the nineteenth century as the "Napoleonic divide," I want to draw attention to the end-point of a gradual transition from an aspatial world to a spatialized one. This point marks a critical juncture in the history of the Métis, ultimately reflecting the fundamental ideological shift in the concept of space that was implemented most dramatically in the cartographic projects and administrative reforms of Napoleon. It was precisely in this period of tumultuous transitions that the Métis came into their own but without being acknowledged by the governing conceptual and administrative frameworks since they fell outside the available categories. It was to take at least another century and the cataclysmic experience of World War I before the nation-state-constructing historiographies were at last challenged by the Annalistes and their successors, and only after this fundamental shift do we begin to see a history—and, therefore, the ethnogenesis—of the Métis people.

The cognitive categories, including the fundamentally aspatial concepts of lordship and jurisdiction, which defined pre-Napoleonic Europe were, of course, also applied in North America. In the notoriously fragmented center of Europe, for example, the rough divisions of geographical space were typically based on the drainage basins of the major rivers. For centuries, the Holy Roman Empire—a collection of infamously overlapping, intertwined, and aspatial entities at every political, economic, and social level—was organized into large-scale but loosely structured districts called *Kreise* or Circles: the Danubian Circle, the Rhenish Circle, and so on. It is not surprising—but also not at all obvious except perhaps for Rupert's Land as a whole (the proverbial "waters flowing into Hudson Bay")—that the districts of the North American fur trade were also defined by river basins: Red River, Saskatchewan, Athabasca, Columbia, and so on. And it is a key property of these fur trade districts, as it was for the Circles of the Holy Roman Empire, that their centers were clearly defined while the edges were largely left unspecified.

The new world of (proto-) nation-states brought about by the Napoleonic project was not limited to a mere redrawing of maps but also led to a brand-new emphasis on sharply defined edges. At the same time, the administrative reforms of the Napoleonic divide resulted in a process of the space that lay between the edges and the center being claimed and filled—and, for good measure, in many cases being newly labeled (e.g., when the Prince-Bishopric of Augsburg was absorbed into the new Kingdom of Bavaria).

In short, although the conflicts that had culminated in the French and American Revolutions may have been triggered by the bread price or the tea tax, one of the most important causes, I argue, was the rapid change in the way space, as a fundamental resource, was viewed—the hotly contested questions of how space had been and might be divided up or consolidated, how it should be used as the basis for rents and taxes, who should be entitled to survey, administer, and govern it.

In that multilayered, multidimensional, and multisite contest between old and new models, the more advanced nation-states like France and England (later and more painfully followed by Germany and Italy) succeeded at the expense of smaller, less visible, less territorially focused groups that to this day, like the Métis in North America, struggle for recognition within the nation-state framework: the Basques, Bretons, Catalans, Welsh, and all the others.

When I went to the Bavarian State Archives at Augsburg to study regional identity maintenance in the late eighteenth century in what is now southwestern Bavaria,[11] I almost immediately began to notice language and discussion that was strangely reminiscent of documents I had read much earlier in the Hudson's Bay Company Archives in Winnipeg. Above all, it was the land issues and the increasing role of surveyors that struck a familiar chord—the iconic image of Louis Riel, unforgettable in his defiant stance, standing on the surveyor's chain.[12]

The surveyor as the advance guard of railway construction is, of course, a topos of Western Canadian history—but there is, in fact, a much earlier scene in which the surveyor as the prime agent of modernity plays a leading role. One of the most intriguing cases I found in the archives at Augsburg is that of Ignaz Ambros Amman, who was vilified in his role as schoolmaster and ultimately chased out of town for his activities as surveyor and cartographer to the Prince-Bishop of Augsburg.[13]

Is it really a coincidence that the surveyor and cartographer David Thompson failed to convince the Hudson's Bay Company—large, old, and stodgy—of the value his work could provide, while the North West Company—younger, more dynamic, read: more modern—immediately[14] recognized the advantage of claiming and organizing their world in a clearly demarcated manner?

In the Canadian Northwest as in the Prince-Bishopric of Augsburg, we see an older, traditional world of seasonal movements and geographic fluidity—which I call aspatial—clashing with the modern, surveyed and parceled-out world—which I call spatialized or simply spatial. The old, aspatial model that prevailed at the time when North America was first colonized needed no adjustment to accommodate a previously unknown group such as the Métis (even if it remained more or less obscure and was not, perhaps, explicitly acknowledged at all times by the authorities in London). The new, spatialist model, by contrast, in effect denies the existence of the Métis as a distinct group.

In the context of the Red River Métis and Western Canada, we can document at least two early instances of this new spatialization: the Canada Jurisdiction Act of 1803 and the decree that has become known as the 'Pemmican Proclamation' of 1814. Both are contemporary with the European developments sketched above, and both predate the ultimate expression of spatialization in Western Canada: the Dominion Land Survey of the 1870s. But both also were already completely antithetical to the Métis way of life.

The Canada Jurisdiction Act, passed by the British Parliament in 1803, gave the courts of Upper and Lower Canada (as opposed to the British courts) criminal jurisdiction over "the North-West." [15] In so doing, it shifted the center of the geopolitical space of what was soon to become Red River from London to Montreal. At the same time, the act was remarkably vague (perhaps even deliberately so, as Hamar Foster seems to suggest) on the spatial extent of its applicability.[16]

The Pemmican Proclamation of 1814, by contrast, imposed edges on the Métis world. Irrespective of its larger political purpose,[17] the immediate goal of Miles Macdonnell's embargo on the export of food supplies produced in Assiniboia was, presumably, the survival of the colony at Red River. In the text of his proclamation, he went to extraordinary lengths to spell out the boundaries, describing the "tract of land or territory" the HBC had sold to the Earl of Selkirk as "bounded by a line running as follows" and then providing a detailed topographical description deploying (modern) degrees of longitude and latitude and (deceptively exact) cardinal directions along with (traditional, pre-modern) references to water courses and the height of land—and it was this "line" across which, and the territory from which, the provisions at issue were not to be "convey[ed] out" or "carrie[d] out" or "convey[ed] away."[18]

These constitutional edicts forced a spatial organization onto a world that was, at most, loosely spatial (edges and centers were defined, but nothing in between) and, more likely, completely aspatial. In short, by subtle and gradual changes in thinking, punctuated by changes in the law, the Métis were simply dismissed from the scene.

Legal/Historical Alternatives

The paradigmatic shift from aspatial to spatialized—which, ironically, left the Métis of Rupert's Land marginalized victims—seems to have been largely ignored in North American scholarship. The exception is Jacqueline Peterson, who proclaimed in 1985 that "Nationhood, wrung from revolution, was, in fact, the new paradigm for the age, on both sides of the Atlantic. The heroic nationalism of Napoleon Bonaparte touched even the northwestern prairies."[19] While no reasonable observer could disagree with Peterson's pointed remark that "nations do not, except metaphorically, spring from the soil," it should be kept in mind that she speaks of much loftier matters than the spatial issues examined here.[20] In his standard work on the survey of the Canada–United States border, for instance, Francis M. Carroll makes scant mention of Napoleon and none at all of the intellectual debt owed to his cartographic projects or to such practitioners as the Arrowsmith dynasty.[21]

The post-Napoleonic, spatialized model does not cope well with the Métis because their ecumene does not have well-defined external borders—in short, because there is no place called *Métistan*. By the obligatory categories of the territorially obsessed nation-state model, the Métis as a people were simply written out of the equation. In offering another way to analyze group identities, the pre-Napoleonic, aspatial model provides for a more sensible interpretation of the facts on the ground. At the very least, the aspatial model, which is person-based rather than territorially defined, allows us to see the Métis where they have not been seen before. I consider two versions of this person-based model: the first largely pre-dates the Napoleonic divide, the second is a creation of the period immediately following World War I.

The constitutional history of the past five centuries sharply distinguishes two principles for assigning citizenship: *jus sanguinis* and *jus soli*. While initially applied to questions of lordly jurisdiction, these terms gradually acquired much wider scope. *Jus soli* refers to jurisdiction based on territory; it unambiguously indicates that the subject is tied to the land and that citizenship is determined solely by residence. *Jus sanguinis*, on the other hand, has both a literal and a more general sense. Literally interpreted, it denotes biological descent or, more broadly, genealogical position.[22] In its general sense, it refers to jurisdiction based on the person rather than the land, as a consequence of which fact citizenship is portable. As a legal writer of the sixteenth century put it, *jus sanguinis* means that each individual "carries his citizenship on his back."[23]

These principles have not received much coverage outside Europe, and in practical terms they often lead to the same result. But in some cases, and that includes the Métis of the early nineteenth century, the *jus sanguinis* means that there is no territorial ascription; instead, one can be Métis wherever one lives.

The most powerful implication of choosing an aspatial, person-based definition of identity is that it is compatible with the claim that Métis identity does not depend on a simplistic rule of residence within a set of linear borders. In a spatialized nation-state model, the Métis are practically invisible. In an aspatial, person-based model, a Métis hunter of the twenty-first century can claim to "be from the bush (Turtle Mountain)" despite having his formal residence in Brandon;[24] both these points are key parts of Arthur J. Ray's evidence in the *Goodon* case.

The early modern concept of portable, person-based identity finds its twentieth-century counterpart in the work of the Annalistes. At the beginning of the twentieth century, the experience of the trenches—particularly when pitting French against German in the Alsatian borderlands, where most people could legitimately lay claim to both—taught a generation of young historians that the categories of the nation-state were wholly inappropriate not only for understanding the bloody conflict in which they found themselves, but also for the history that had created it.

Some of these historians went on to publish the *Annales d'histoire économique et sociale* (on the French side) and the *Vierteljahresschrift für Sozial- und Wirtschaftsgeschichte* (on the German side). Although there were close ties between the two editorial boards,[25] in the long run only the Annales group—led by Marc Bloch and Lucien Febvre and, later, by Fernand Braudel—succeeded in shifting the larger paradigm of history, geography, and the other *sciences humaines* toward a more thorough integration of the disciplines and, especially, a renewed emphasis on the interplay of social and spatial organization.[26] During their earliest phase, both sides struggled to define a different kind of identity, based not on territory or lines drawn on a map but rather on an attachment to place: a place "with its own identity," as Braudel paraphrases "pays," enacted through customary practice, song, costumes, architecture—in short, by recognizing a cultural landscape.[27]

The technical terms "pays" and "heimat" that emerged from this early work of the Annalistes and their unlabeled colleagues across the Rhine[28] are by no means identical, but they both include a reference to space in their (original) meaning.[29] It is much more important, however, that they both also accommodate an aspatial sense of identity. Moreover, this experience of one place can in fact be transferred to another, for instance, when colonists from Québec carried their iconic church steeples to the prairies. Finally, it may even be shared with others, so that one community's collective experience may, at least vicariously and temporarily, become someone else's (for instance when a modern Manitoban of, say, Polish and Punjabi parentage puts on his/her *ceinture fléchée* on the way to the *Festival du Voyageur*).

The "pays"/"heimat" approach first proposed in the aftermath of World War I seems especially promising in the analysis of aspatial groups.[30] Of course it has its own pitfalls, too. First and foremost, it should be obvious that the very same configurations of customary practice that the Annalistes et al. have been studying are also the domain of various more or less harmless merchants of nostalgia and kitsch. More disturbing, they have also been appropriated and used by all manner of political forces—and grotesquely misused by nationalist and fascist movements. But even where the circumstances are less extreme, the risk remains at all times—and for participants and observers alike—that they could imbue their sense of community, of belonging, and of history with a linear past and a reified myth of primeval origins. In short, the concepts of *jus sanguinis* and "pays"/"heimat" are powerful tools, but they are tools that have sharp edges, and if you use them uncritically, you may well cut yourself!

New Questions

The attempt to establish the parameters of the "pays"/"heimat" configuration as it manifests itself in the case of the Métis will require a wide range of microstudies to draw on. An obvious point of departure would be the dynamic interplay between individual (spatial) settlements and the overall (aspatial) community. Above all, the Métis way of life, then and now, exhibits a high degree of residential mobility, with particular locations treated as relatively transitory points within a larger, much more comprehensive, regional frame of reference. In critically reviewing this issue, we need to focus on the cultural landscape established through land use patterns and, ultimately, architecture.[31] In the domain of everyday life, too, more research is called for in such fundamental areas as kinship terms, marriage patterns, naming conventions, occupational choices, business alliances, and so on. Other cultural practices that bear directly on these issues range from dress and housing styles to food preferences and the role of hunting in food procurement. While the performance arts of song and dance; the iconic art of fiddling; and the visual arts of beadwork and finger-weaving are at last being recognized by the larger, non-Métis society, there is much less public awareness of the continuing use of the Michif language and the notable increase in the number of children's books on Métis subjects being published in Michif. Most of these books are the work of Rita Flamand and Norman Fleury; Fleury is also chiefly responsible for the introduction of a dramatically new approach, the graphic novel in Michif, to extend the reach of oral literature to the younger generation.[32]

Finally, there is the growing prominence of seasonal events that combine costume, song, and ritual with public display and, where appropriate, public participation. Besides family reunions and the festive celebration of High Mass, the most visible of these events are formal processions to sacred places, for example to Batoche and to Riel's grave in St-Boniface. At Red River, one of the defining points in the annual cycle is the Festival du Voyageur.

In a completely different language, self-identification even at the most informal level[33] is reported by the singer and song-writer Don Freed, who dedicated his collection of ballads, *The Valley of Green and Blue*, as follows: "Recently, I have been telling stories and singing songs to school children. When I asked the groups gathered before me how many of them are Métis I am pleased to see hands rise. There was once a dark and difficult time when this would not happen. It is to those generations who could not raise their hands that this recording is dedicated."[34]

While a comprehensive treatment of the Métis "pays" is not yet within reach, the influence of the Annalistes is nonetheless perceptible in a number of regional studies. Among recent historical works, Nicole St-Onge's study of St-Laurent stands out in stressing the relationship between settlement and subsistence patterns, between economic activity and the space in which it takes place. Situating the people of St-Laurent in the context of the fur trade, St-Onge in particular draws attention to the salt trade, which came to complement the fur trade as a unique aspect of St-Laurent.[35]

The approach of the early Annalistes is similarly reflected in the detailed work-up of all records of daily life that marks out Frits Pannekoek's demonstration that, in Red River, there were substantial economic disparities between English Halfbreeds and French Métis and that they also reacted very differently to the mounting economic and political pressures they both began to face by the middle of the nineteenth century. For the English-speaking Halfbreeds, Pannekoek writes, the negotiations of the 1850s were "constitutional conflict gone awry." For the French-speaking Métis, they were a "defensive reaction arising out of their fear of the threat posed by a Protestant Canadian religious and economic supremacy." In addition, the English Halfbreeds supported union with Canada; William Kennedy, for example, who had spent time in the East, was promoting the annexation movement as early as 1856.[36]

Pannekoek's study is one of the first also to draw attention to the "polarization" based on a "growing disparity between rich and poor" to be found within "Métis Society" itself (and which was not echoed to the same degree on the anglophone side). Among the francophones of the settlement, "Wealth was particularly concentrated in the parishes of St. Vital, St. Boniface, and St. Norbert . . . [which] produced more than half of Métis Red River's grain and potatoes and possessed most of the livestock." This distributional pattern looks very much like an emerging class distinction between the merchant-farmers of these central parishes, who also controlled the freight contracts to St. Paul on the Mississippi, and the "less buoyant" economy of the plains hunters and laborers of the outlying parishes, where "as late as 1867, for example, one-half of the Métis grew no grain."[37]

Against this background of social, economic, and geographical variability, the recently published memoirs of Johnny Grant (d. 1900) provide a fascinating case study. The editor simply speaks of "the Métis experience," while Grant does not seem to use any such term for himself. Scattered references to Métis hunters; to French, Scotch, and English Halfbreeds; to his maternal grandmother as a "quarter-breed of Scotch descent"; or his report, while claiming fluency in the Snake language (spoken in what is now Utah), that "I was not the only white man living with them" do not tell us what his *ethnie* might have been or if indeed that was a relevant category for him.[38]

In fact, in Grant's memoirs we have a rare text of someone who does not express a sense of grievance. Grant was not a follower of Riel and had clashed with him politically in the formative days of the provisional government.[39] As a successful entrepreneur he had much to gain by joining forces with the Canadians and seems to have made his political decisions very much in the light of economic circumstances. In modern discourse he might best be described as a self-made man and on the right of the political spectrum, a strong supporter of individual rights, self-evident liberties, and small government. Two key questions, however, remain to be explored critically: what it may have meant to Grant to be Métis, and what evidence his conduct might provide of either a spatial or an aspatial context.

The most dramatic venue for the reaffirmation of Métis identity, and thus also the one that has attracted the most attention from the larger society, are the courts. At least since 1982, when Canada gave itself a written constitution, the legal–constitutional route has held renewed promise, and a series of successful cases turning on aboriginal hunting rights have served to highlight many of the key issues of Métis identity and, more particularly, its persistence into the present. The most important of the recent cases is, arguably, *R. v. Powley*, dealt with in a comprehensive decision in the Ontario Court of Justice (Provincial Division) in 1998 and upheld in two appeal courts and, ultimately, in the Supreme Court of Canada. As Jean Teillet, lead counsel for the defense both in *Powley* and, subsequently, in *Goodon*, puts it: "*Powley* is now the governing law in Canada."[40]

In the present context, the most striking aspect of *Powley* are the three criteria proclaimed by the trial judge, Vaillancourt: besides the perennially thorny "genealogical connection" to "the historically identified Metis society" (or the "ancestral connection to a historic Métis community," to be established "by birth, adoption, or other means," as the confirming decision of the Supreme Court of Canada puts it), Vaillancourt's criteria are exactly the issues discussed here: "self-identification" and "community acceptance" (or "acceptance . . . into contemporary Metis society").[41] As an expert witness in *Powley*, and also in the more recent case of *Goodon*, Arthur J. Ray succeeded in introducing the teachings of historical geography—and, especially, the doctrine that membership in a group requires constant reaffirmation through action—to the courts. He is cited, particularly, for pointing out that "Metis people tend to be invisible or unidentifiable in official records," and this observation is echoed in Justice Vaillancourt's own words and again by the Supreme Court of Canada, which also quotes Ray's statement that, by 1846, "the people of mixed ancestry living there [at Sault Ste. Marie] had developed a distinctive sense of identity and Indian and Whites recognized them as being a separate people."[42]

In *Goodon*, the judge relied on Ray not only for the matters decided in *Powley*, but further quoted him on a specifically geographical issue: that "the Metis regional community was not defined by the boundaries of a single settlement" and that "[m]ovement was a central feature of Metis culture."[43] In this case, Justice Combs went so far as to acknowledge that the Métis hunting grounds in question are not limited to the Turtle Mountains but cover all of southwestern Manitoba (including the city of Winnipeg). Though he flinched from the further step—which would have been altogether extraordinary—of accepting the entire "Northwest" as Métis domain, the *Goodon* decision is provocative enough as it stands (as is obvious from the unusually broad press coverage it received).[44] As these two instances show, court cases have become an especially effective means of addressing the wider community on the traditional rights and practices of the Métis.

A domain where the reaffirmation of Métis identity remains at its most obscure and the expected effect turns out to be neither recurrent nor reliable is the system of subject headings used in the cataloging schemes of libraries. Subject headings may seem trivial (or, at least, innocuous), but the transfer of such headings to the realm of electronic databases looks set to make them as influential as the courts. The National Library of Canada gives an impression of murky waters, but the catalogue headings of the U.S. Library of Congress are absolutely clear-cut: where the term "Metis" appears at all, and without any cross-reference to "Halfbreed," the library restricts it to a group of people west of Lake of the Woods and north of the forty-ninth parallel—as if the Métis were limited to Canada. In its Subject Authority Files, moreover, which instruct librarians in the use of these terms, the Library of Congress is fully explicit: "Here are entered works on Canadians of Mixed European and Indian descent." (There is also a broader term, "Indians of North America—Mixed descent.") We might be tempted to be dismissive, but since the Library of Congress Catalogue is widely accepted as the ultimate authority in these matters, its cataloging rules are extremely powerful and, in effect, beyond contestation. As it turns out, they are also followed by every major database intended for the U.S. market. Thus these cataloging rules are both powerful and insidious, for they determine what we can look for and what we can find, and they may take even longer to change than the minds of the Canadian judiciary.

Conclusion

In contemporary descriptions, the emerging Métis are obliquely reflected at best, and very little light has been directed onto their existence as an enduring sociopolitical entity until well into the twentieth century. Only as the aspatial aspects of their existence began to be recognized and explored (and the nation-state model finally began to be challenged, notably by the Annalistes and their followers) did Métis society as such gradually start to emerge from obscurity.

Whatever happened on the ground (and notwithstanding the signal events at Seven Oaks or at La Barrière), in recent years Métis ethnogenesis has figured prominently in the work of historians, ethnologists, and legal scholars. Besides the evidence for a significant increase in self-identification, cultural activities, and general interest—whether in the anecdotal accounts of Métis fiddlers visiting Prairie schools or in the systematic study of census returns—the Métis resurgence of the present also manifests itself in the appearance of children's books and audio- and video-recordings in the Michif language. Scholarly efforts aside, the increasing assertiveness of various Métis communities and of the community at large, complemented by a flourishing cultural life, are clear signs that Métis ethnogenesis has at long last been—and is still being—achieved.

Notes

I am grateful to Patricia Kennedy at the Library and Archives Canada and Gerhard Immler at the Bavarian State Archives in Augsburg for their expert guidance through their collections, and I am also grateful to John Eaton, law librarian at the University of Manitoba, for his help with legal sources.

A set of research days provided by the University of Manitoba Libraries allowed me to prepare the original draft of this chapter. I owe special thanks to Brenda Macdougall and Carolyn Podruchny for their careful reading of the manuscript and, of course, also to the other readers and conference participants who offered critical comments; all errors or misinterpretations are undoubtedly mine.

1. As technical terms in constitutional law, *jus sanguinis* and *jus soli* figure prominently, along with various even more technical synonyms, in the constitutional thought of both insular and continental Europe and, especially, in the transition from Roman law to German law (cf. the fuller discussion below and, e.g., Wiedemann, *Der "Allgäuische Gebrauch"* and the references therein). In their use as technical terms, they rarely appear in other than their Latin form because a literal translation (e.g., as "the law of the blood" and "the law of the soil") would mainly serve to obscure the fact that these translations, referring to principles of descent and territoriality only in their narrowest readings, are part of a much wider and more complex system of juridico-constitutional concepts and practices.

2. In the field of Métis studies, see, e.g., St-Onge, *Saint-Laurent, Manitoba*; Saler and Podruchny, "Glass Curtains and Storied Landscapes"; Burley and Horsfall, "Vernacular Houses and Farmsteads"; and Dueck, "Public and Intimate Sociability."

3. The terms "spatialized" and "aspatial" are in common use in human geography. Although the aspatial model permits the recognition of a center and even of outer limits, it is defined primarily by social relationships that manifest themselves in regularly repeated activities and in accepted membership in a group. The practice—usually futile and often disastrous in its consequences—of squeezing such relationships into the straitjacket of modern topographic maps is a sad legacy of colonialism.

In historical geography, these concepts—along with the more general notion of boundaries—proved central to the methodological debate about the distinction between regional and national identities in which French and German scholars engaged before and after World War I; in addition to the discussion below, cf. Wolfart, "The 'Region' in German Historiography."

They also figure prominently in the by-now classical theoretical literature dealing with the construction and commodification of space, as illustrated in the gradual and piecemeal transition from aspatial to spatialized models of state organization in Europe; e.g., Gottmann, *Significance of Territory*; Lefebvre, *La production de l'espace*; Cosgrove, *Social Formation and Symbolic Landscape*; Sack, *Human Territoriality*; and Scott, *Freiburg and the Breisgau*.

4. Of course none of these theoretical arguments is to be construed as suggesting that the Métis themselves, either individually or as a group, were oblivious to the notion of territorial limits and their practical impact, with Riel's stand against the surveyors at La Barrière being the most salient illustration. Their social relationships and interactions, however, seem to have largely ignored such limits and even blatantly disregarded them. It is this defiance of a cognitive categorization founded in territoriality that appears to have made it difficult for nineteenth-century historians, working in an utterly spatialized world, to recognize the analytical categories in question as socially constructed.

5. Cf. Gellner, *Nations and Nationalism*; and Smith, *National Identity*; in the late twentieth century or Michelet and Treitschke in the nineteenth.

6. Cf. Hobsbawm, *Nations and Nationalism since 1780*; and Anderson, *Imagined Communities*.

7. This is not, of course, an attempt to revisit the distinction drawn by Peterson and Brown between the ethnonym *Métis* (with a capital *M*) and the more generic *métis* (with a lowercase *m*; Peterson and Brown, "Introduction," 4–6).

8. *R. v. Powley* (1998), Ontario Court of Justice (Provincial Division), Sault Ste. Marie: [1999] 1 C.N.L.R. 153; *R. v. Powley* (2003), Supreme Court of Canada: 2003 SCC 43; and *R. v. Goodon* (2008), Manitoba Provincial Court, Brandon: 2008 MBPC 59.

9. Cf. Wolfart, "Mapping the Early Modern State."

10. The existence of the river lots and the attachment that individuals and families may have felt toward them does not affect the generality of this model. The geographically inspired work of Burley, Horsfall, and Brandon, *Structural Considerations of Métis Ethnicity*, is the rare case of an explicit study of the impact of the Métis on the cultural landscape.

11. Cf. Wolfart, "Bishop's Peasants and the Lands below the Grünten"; and Wolfart, "Mapping the Early Modern State."

12. Why is there no monument at the place where this event took place? We should be grateful, I suppose, that at least the site of Riel's barricade has not yet been converted into a subdivision or mall but serves as a city park—la Barrière.

13. Wolfart, "Mapping the Early Modern State."

14. While most of Thompson's work for the Hudson's Bay Company (HBC) focused on surveys of routes, and is thus consistent with the pre-Napoleonic model, his very first assignment for the NWC was to survey the international boundary line west of Lake of the Woods. According to Nicks (Nicks, "David Thompson," 8:878–83), "Thompson's later claim that he left because he was ordered to cease his work as a surveyor cannot be substantiated."

15. The full title of the act reads *An Act for Extending the Jurisdiction of the Court of Justice in the Provinces of Upper and Lower Canada to the Trial and Punishment of Persons Guilty of Crimes and Offences within Certain Parts of North America Adjoining to the Said Provinces.*

16. Hamar Foster, "Long Distance Justice," especially p. 6.

17. For the wider context and a careful discussion of the nature of the Earl of Selkirk's tenure of these lands (purchased in fee simple, as confirmed by their subsequent sale, in 1836, to the HBC and, in 1870, to the Dominion of Canada), see Pritchett, *Red River Valley, 1811–1849*, chapter 12, where the issue of spatial relationships is dismissed in half a line: "outlining the boundaries of the grant" (p. 132).

18. Oliver, *Canadian North-West*, 1:184–85.

19. Peterson, "Many Roads to Red River," 38. Peterson adds a note of acknowledgement: "I am grateful to Dr. Lionel Demontigny, assistant surgeon general of the United States Public Health Service and a participant and speaker at the 1981 Newberry Library Conference on the Métis in North America for the suggestion that Napoleon Bonaparte and his Continental System were important early-nineteenth-century influences upon métis self- and group definition" (n. 4).

20. Ibid., 38.

21. Carroll, *A Good and Wise Measure*. Aaron Arrowsmith (1750–1823), who published his "historic" map of British North America in 1795, was given access to all HBC maps coming into London. His son Samuel and nephew John carried on his firm, "making this eminent cartographic family unofficial cartographers of the Hudson's Bay Company until the late nineteenth century" (Ruggles, *Country So Interesting*, 5, 58, and passim).

22. Even the notion of genealogical position is much less biological (and much less beholden to any kind of "blood-and-soil" doctrine) than an excessively literal word-by-word translation might suggest.

23. Crämer, *Das Allgäu*. Cf. Wolfart, "Bishop's Peasants and the Lands below the Grünten," 113–17, especially 115; Wiedemann, *Der "Allgäuische Gebrauch"*; and Baumann, *Geschichte des Allgäus*, vol. 2.

24. *R. v. Goodon* (2008), para. 64.

25. Veit-Brause, "Place of Local Regional History," especially p. 453.

26. Key titles from the early period include Bloch, *Les caractères originaux de l'histoire rurale française* (*French Rural History: An Essay on its Basic Characteristics*); Febvre and Bataillon, *La terre et l'évolution humaine* (*Geographical Introduction to History*); Demangeon and Febvre, *Le Rhin: Problèmes d'histoire et d'économie*; and Braudel, *L'identité de la France* (*Identity of France*). For general references, see Baker, "Reflections on Relations of Historical Geography"; Fink, *Marc Bloch*; and Burke, *French Historical Revolution*.

27. Braudel, *Identity of France*, 37; Wolfart, "'Region' in German Historiography."

28. The key work from that period is Aubin, Frings, and Müller, *Kulturströmungen und Kulturprovinzen in the Rheinlanden*. Cf. also Veit-Brause, "Place of Local Regional History"; and, for Aubin's career post-1929, Trüper, *Die Vierteljahresschrift für Sozial- und Wirtschaftsgeschichte*; and Mühle, *Für Volk und deutschen Osten*.

29. Ironically, an overly literal reading of "pays" as land or "heimat" as home would be just as inappropriate and misleading as reducing the person-based reading of "jus sanguinis" to mere blood.

30. In recent years the concept of pays as used by the later generation of Annalistes (e.g., Braudel) has been resurrected, albeit in a somewhat different form, in Pierre Bourdieu's concept of *habitus* (Bourdieu, *Outline of a Theory of Practice*).

31. Cf. Burley, Horsfall, and Brandon, *Structural Considerations of Métis Ethnicity*.

32. Murray, *Li Minoush*; Patton and Burton, *Li Daanseur di vyaeloon / Fiddle Dancer*; and Fleury et al., *Lii Zistwayr di la naasyoon di Michif / Stories of our People*.

33. For the formal context of census returns, see Andersen, "From Nation to Population."

34. Freed, *Valley of Green and Blue*.

35. St-Onge, *Saint-Laurent, Manitoba*, 9–13.

36. Pannekoek, "Some Comments on Social Origins," 39–40. Pannekoek's claim that Red River society was increasingly becoming polarized along class lines has been challenged by Spry, "Métis and Mixed-Bloods." Irrespective of his conclusions, Pannekoek's analysis, methodologically reminiscent of the approach of the Annalistes, is exemplary in drawing out social and geographical variability in Métis Red River.

37. Pannekoek, "Some Comments on Social Origins," 43–44.

38. Ens, "Introduction," p. vii; and Grant, *Son of the Fur Trade*, 1, 39, 157.

39. Ens, "Introduction," p. xix.

40. Reported as [1999] 1 C.N.L.R. 153 and 2003 SCC 43. Jean Teillet, "Resume of Jean Teillet."

41. *R. v. Powley* (1998), para. 47, cf. also paras. 65, 66; *R. v. Powley* (2003), para. 32, cf. also paras. 30, 49.

42. *R. v. Powley* (1998), paras. 45, 80–81; *R. v. Powley* (2003), paras. 24, 22.

43. *R. v. Goodon* (2008), paras. 34, 46.

44. *R. v. Goodon* (2008), paras. 48, 19–20.

Bibliography

Andersen, Chris. "From Nation to Population: The Racialisation of 'Metis' in the Canadian Census." *Nations and Nationalism* 14, no. 2 (2008): 347–68.

Anderson, Benedict. *Imagined Communities: Reflections on the Origin and Spread of Nationalism*. London, UK: Verso, 2006.

Aubin, Hermann, Theodor Frings, and Josef Müller. *Kulturströmungen und Kulturprovinzen in den Rheinlanden: Geschichte, Sprache, Volkskunde*. Veröffentlichungen des Instituts für Geschichtliche Landeskunde an der Universität Bonn. Bonn, Germany: Röhrscheid, 1926.

Baker, Alan R. H. "Reflections on the Relations of Historical Geography and the Annales School of History." In *Explorations in Historical Geography: Interpretative Essays*, edited by Alan R. H. Baker and Derek Gregory, 1–27. Cambridge, UK: Cambridge University Press, 1984.

Baumann, Franz Ludwig. *Geschichte des Allgäus*. 3 vols. Kempten, Germany: J. Kösel, 1883.

Bloch, Marc. *Les caractères originaux de l'histoire rurale française*. Oslo, Norway: H. Aschehoug, 1931. Translated as *French Rural History: An Essay on its Basic Characteristics* by Janet Sondheimer (London, UK: Routledge & Kegan Paul, 1966).

Bourdieu, Pierre. *Esquisse d'une théorie de la pratique, précédé de trois études d'ethnologie kabyle*. Geneva, Switzerland: Droz, 1972. Translated with revisions as *Outline of a Theory of Practice* by Richard Nice (Cambridge, UK: Cambridge University Press, 1977). Page references are to the 1977 English translation.

Braudel, Fernand. *L'identité de la France [I]: Espace et histoire*. Paris, France: Arthaud-Flammarion, 1986. Translated as *The Identity of France*, vol. 1, *History and Environment* by Siân Reynolds (London, UK: Collins, 1988). Page references are to the 1988 English translation.

Brown, Jennifer S. H. "People of Myth, People of History: A Look at Recent Writing on the Metis." *Acadiensis* 17 (1987): 150–62.

Burke, Peter. *The French Historical Revolution: The Annales School, 1929–1989*. Oxford, UK: Clarendon Press, 1990.

Burley, David V., and Gayel A. Horsfall. "Vernacular Houses and Farmsteads of the Canadian Metis." *Journal of Cultural Geography* 10, no. 1 (1989): 19–33.

Burley, David V., Gayel A. Horsfall, and John D. Brandon. *Structural Considerations of Métis Ethnicity: An Archaeological, Architectural, and Historical Study*. Vermillion: University of South Dakota Press, 1992.

Carroll, Francis M. *A Good and Wise Measure: The Search for the Canadian–American Boundary, 1783–1842*. Toronto, ON: University of Toronto Press, 2001.

Cosgrove, Denis E. *Social Formation and Symbolic Landscape*. London, UK: Croom Helm, 1984.

Crämer, Ulrich. *Das Allgäu: Werden und Wesen eines Landschaftsbegriffs*. Remagen, Germany: Verlag der Bundesanstalt für Landeskunde, 1954.

Demangeon, Albert, and Lucien Febvre. *Le Rhin: Problèmes d'histoire et d'économie*. Paris, France: Armand Colin, 1935. Dueck, Byron. "Public and Intimate Sociability in First Nations and Métis Fiddling." *Ethnomusicology* 51, no. 1 (2007): 30–63.

Ens, Gerhard J. "Introduction." In *A Son of the Fur Trade: The Memoirs of Johnny Grant*, edited by Gerhard J. Ens, pp. vii–xxxix. Edmonton: University of Alberta Press, 2008.

Febvre, Lucien, and Lionel Bataillon. *La terre et l'évolution humaine: Introduction géographique à l'histoire* (Evolution de l'humanité: Synthèse collective, 4). Paris, France: Renaissance du livre, 1924. Translated as *A Geographical Introduction to History* (London, UK: Kegan Paul, Trench, Trubner; New York, NY: A.A. Knopf, 1925).

Fink, Carole. *Marc Bloch: A Life in History*. Cambridge, UK: Cambridge University Press, 1989.

Fleury, Norman, Gilbert Pelletier, Jeanne Pelletier, Joe Welsh, Norma Welsh, Janice DePeel, and Carrie Saganace. *Lii Zistwayr di la naasyoon di Michif / Stories of our People: A Métis Graphic Novel Anthology*. Saskatoon, SK: Gabriel Dumont Institute, 2008.

Foster, Hamar. "Long Distance Justice: The Criminal Jurisdiction of Canadian Courts West of the Canadas, 1763–1859." *American Journal of Legal History* 34, no. 1 (1990): 1–48.

Foster, John E. "Some Questions and Perspectives on the Problems of Métis Roots." In Peterson and Brown, *New Peoples*, 72–91.

Freed, Don. *The Valley of Green and Blue*. Produced by Danny Greenspoon. Original sound recording published by Gabriel Dumont Institute, Saskatoon, SK, 2004. CD 1006.

Gellner, Ernest. *Nations and Nationalism*. Oxford, UK: Basil Blackwell, 1983.

Gottmann, Jean. *The Significance of Territory*. Charlottesville: University Press of Virginia, 1973.

Grant, Johnny. *A Son of the Fur Trade: The Memoirs of Johnny Grant*. Edited by Gerhard J. Ens. Edmonton: University of Alberta Press, 2008.

Hobsbawm, Eric J. *Nations and Nationalism since 1780: Programme, Myth, Reality*. Cambridge, UK: Cambridge University Press, 1992.

Lefebvre, Henri. *La production de l'espace*. Paris, France: Editions Anthropos, 1974. Translated by Donald Nicholson-Smith as *The Production of Space* (Oxford, UK: Blackwell, 1991).

Mühle, Eduard. *Für Volk und deutschen Osten: Der Historiker Hermann Aubin und die deutsche Ostforschung* (Schriften des Bundesarchivs, 75). Düsseldorf, Germany: Droste Verlag, 2005.

Murray, Bonnie. *Li Minoush*. Translated by Rita Flamand. Illustrated by Sheldon Dawson. (Michif Children's Series.) Winnipeg, MB: Pemmican Publications, 2001.

Nicks, John. "David Thompson." In *Dictionary of Canadian Biography*, vol. 8, 878–83. Toronto, ON: University of Toronto Press, 1985.

Oliver, E. H., ed. *The Canadian North-West: Its Early Development and Legislative Records, Minutes of the Councils of the Red River Colony and the Northern Department of Rupert's Land*. 2 vols. (Publications of the Canadian Archives, 6.) Ottawa, ON: Government Printing Bureau, 1914.

Pannekoek, Frits. "Some Comments on the Social Origins of the Riel Protest of 1869." *Transactions of the Historical and Scientific Society of Manitoba*, Series 3, no. 34 (1977): 39–48.

———. *A Snug Little Flock: The Social Origins of the Riel Resistance of 1869–1870*. Winnipeg, MB: Watson and Dwyer, 1991.

Patton, Anne, and Wilfred Burton. *Li Daanseur di vyaeloon / Fiddle Dancer*. Translated by Norman Fleury. Illustrated by Sherry Farrell Racette. Saskatoon, SK: Gabriel Dumont Institute, 2007.

Peterson, Jacqueline. "Many Roads to Red River: Métis Genesis in the Great Lakes Region, 1680–1815." In Peterson and Brown, *New Peoples* 31–71.

Peterson, Jacqueline, and Jennifer S. H. Brown. "Introduction." In Peterson and Brown, *New Peoples* 3–16.

———, eds. *The New Peoples: Being and Becoming Métis in North America*. Winnipeg: University of Manitoba Press, 1985.

Podruchny, Carolyn. "Baptizing Novices: Ritual Moments among French Canadian Voyageurs in the Montreal Fur Trade, 1780–1821." *Canadian Historical Review* 83, no. 2 (2001): 165–95.

Pritchett, John Perry. *The Red River Valley, 1811–1849: A Regional Study.* New Haven, CT: Yale University Press; Toronto, ON: Ryerson Press, 1942.

Ruggles, Richard I. *A Country So Interesting: The Hudson's Bay Company and Two Centuries of Mapping, 1670–1870.* Montreal, QC; Kingston, ON: McGill-Queen's University Press, 1991.

Sack, Robert David. *Human Territoriality: Its Theory and History.* Cambridge, UK: Cambridge University Press, 1986.

Saler, Bethel, and Carolyn Podruchny. "Glass Curtains and Storied Landscapes: The Fur Trade, National Boundaries, and Historians." In *Bridging National Borders in North America: Transnational and Comparative Histories,* edited by Benjamin H. Johnson and Andrew R. Graybill, 275–302. Durham, NC: Duke University Press, 2010.

Scott, Tom. *Freiburg and the Breisgau: Town–Country Relations in the Age of Reformation and Peasants' War.* Oxford, UK: Clarendon Press, 1986.

Smith, Anthony D. *National Identity.* London, UK: Penguin, 1991.

Spry, Irene M. "The Métis and Mixed-Bloods of Rupert's Land before 1870." In Peterson and Brown, *New Peoples,* 95–118.

St-Onge, Nicole. *Saint-Laurent, Manitoba: Evolving Métis Identities, 1850–1914.* Regina, SK: Canadian Plains Research Center, University of Regina, 2005.

Teillet, Jean. "Resume of Jean Teillet." [Updated 2005.] Accessed January 16, 2010, at www.pstlaw.ca/resources/Jean_Teillet-Resume.doc.

Trüper, Henning. *Die Vierteljahresschrift für Sozial- und Wirtschaftsgeschichte und ihr Herausgeber Hermann Aubin im Nationalsozialismus.* (Vierteljahresschrift für Sozial- und Wirtschaftsgeschichte, Beihefte, 181.) Stuttgart, Germany: Steiner, 2005.

Veit-Brause, Irmline. "The Place of Local Regional History in German and French Historiography: Some General Reflections." *Australian Journal of French Studies* 16, no. 5 (1979): 447–78.

Wiedemann, Rudolf. *Der "Allgäuische Gebrauch" einer Gerichtsbarkeit nach Personalitätsprinzip.* (Schriftenreihe zur bayerischen Landesgeschichte, 11.) Munich, Germany: Verlag der Kommission für bayerische Landesgeschichte, 1932.

Wolfart, Philip D. "The Bishop's Peasants and the Lands below the Grünten: The Origins of Territoriality in the Late Eighteenth Century." PhD thesis, Queen's University, Kingston, ON, 1997.

———. "Mapping the Early Modern State: The Work of Ignaz Ambros Amman, 1782–1812." *Journal of Historical Geography* 34, no. 1 (2008): 1–23.

———. "The 'Region' in German Historiography." In *Histoire Mythique et Paysage Symbolique / Mythic History and Symbolic Landscape: Actes du projet d'échange Laval-Queen's, Octobre 1995 / Octobre 1996, rencontres de Québec et de Kingston,* edited by Serge Courville and Brian S. Osborne, 88–95. Cheminements, Sainte-Foy, QC: CIEQ [Centre interuniversitaire d'études québécoises], 1997.

Court Cases

R. v. Goodon (2008), Manitoba Provincial Court, Brandon: 2008 MBPC 59.
R. v. Powley (1998), Ontario Court of Justice (Provincial Division), Sault Ste. Marie: [1999] 1 C.N.L.R. 153.
R. v. Powley (2003), Supreme Court of Canada: 2003 SCC 43.

Legislation

An Act for Extending the Jurisdiction of the Court of Justice in the Provinces of Upper and Lower Canada to the Trial and Punishment of Persons Guilty of Crimes and Offences within Certain Parts of North America Adjoining to the Said Provinces. 43 George III, cap. cxxxviii.

5

"Le Fond de l'Ouest"

Territoriality, Oral Geographies, and the Métis in the Nineteenth-Century Northwest

ÉTIENNE RIVARD

The emergence and development of the Métis Nation in the nineteenth-century Canadian northwest has drawn much attention over the years and deeply shaped Canadian imagination. The Métis "rebellions" of 1870 and 1885, the creation of the province of Manitoba in 1870, and the emblematic character of Louis Riel figure even more predominantly in Canada's imagination for they profoundly marked the colonial history of the country. Since the late 1960s, this rather "classic," or "colonial," stance on history has been challenged by two major changes that have brought to the forefront Métis perspectives and voice. The first one lies with increasing Métis involvement in academic research, including individual scholarship as well as editing (les *Éditions Bois-Brûlés* or the Pemmican Press), and in institutions such as the Gabriel Dumont Institute. The second change has to do with the expanded use of oral material—narratives, songs, or in-depth interviews are just a few examples[1]—which has demonstrated that oral traditions are fundamental to Métis social–cultural reality. This shift to a more Métis-centered viewpoint certainly enhances our knowledge of Prairie Métis history, particularly with regard to its organization, its materiality (tools, means of transportation, food, clothing, housing), and its cultural distinctiveness.

In this chapter, my goal is to provide a geographical reading of oral material by asking what it reveals about nineteenth-century Prairie Métis territoriality and oral geographies. The first section scrutinizes four individual narratives and some collective narratives in order to portray Métis territoriality (or Métis sense of identity and place). Although these narratives represent only a fraction of the available oral material,[2] they nonetheless draw a fairly rich and diverse portrait of Prairie Métis identity and territorial reality. The second part of the chapter focuses on Métis place names and how they expose oral geographies, or, put another way, the close relationship between orality and territoriality. Ultimately, inbetweenness, spatial mobility, and oral culture itself may well be considered to be forming *la toile de fond*,[3] the backdrop, against which Métis relation to land and identity stands.

Métis Territoriality: The Intermingling of Identities and Places

Broadly defined, territoriality refers to a people's relationship to a specific and delineated geographical area, or, as the geographer Robert D. Sack would have it, "how people use the land, how they organize themselves in space, and how they give meaning to place."[4] This definition emphasizes the material, political, and symbolic dimensions of territoriality. The concept of *territorialité* is more often described as the relationships between a people's sense of identity and their sense of place. Thus defined, territoriality is not simply an existing sociospatial structure, but also an ongoing reality. Territoriality is both the process by which a people appropriate space and create territory through their identity markers and the process by which they redefine, at least partially, their identity and sense of belonging in relation to that territory. "Otherness"—interaction with "others" or institutional structures, for example—constitutes the backbone of such a territorial and identity process.[5]

In this section, I rely largely on the memoirs of four individuals: Louis Goulet, Peter Erasmus, Norbert Welsh, and Antoine Vermette. Even though most were born at Red River at about the same period, all four lived distinct lives and, as their respective narratives suggest, had specific views of Métis identity and territorial reality. Whereas Louis Goulet, Antoine Vermette, and Norbert Welsh clearly self-identified as Métis, Peter Erasmus's sense of identity is only indirectly suggested. Their sense of identity heavily depended on their distinct ethno-linguistic and religious backgrounds. Goulet and Vermette were Catholic French; Erasmus, whose Danish father worked for the Hudson's Bay Company (HBC), was Protestant and spoke English. Welsh kept strong links with his English origin, though he mostly adopted the religion of his French Métis mother and in-laws. Erasmus (1833–1931) had considered becoming an Anglican priest and had been teacher for some time before he was hired by the Canadian government as an interpreter in the treaty process. Goulet principally pursued his family's trading and freighting activities, but he also became a scout for the U.S. Army. Welsh divided his time between his trading activities, the buffalo hunts—he and his family followed the last of the buffalo to the Cypress Hills—and farming. In other words, although these Métis individuals all performed roughly the same activities in the Northwest and went through the same events (colonization, depletion of the buffalo herds, the uprisings of 1870 and 1885), they also made sense of these activities and events in their own ways.

On the other hand, and paradoxically, these individual narratives also reveal a relatively narrow collective view. If they offer a fairly good glance at the diversity of roles played by Métis males on the plains—as traders, freighters, buffalo hunters, or interpreters—they seem to overlook many other parts of Métis life. All these men shared a similar set of socio-economic activities that only partially account for being Métis in *le Nord-Ouest*. None was a full-time farmer, fur trade employee, or fisherman, but they were all mostly involved in the free trade and buffalo hunt. Except for Goulet's description of the voyageurs' old brigading songs[6] and Erasmus's mention of the "most hazardous experiences of the north country,"[7] there are but a few observations from Métis about their involvement in the fur trade.[8] Although it is true that a great proportion of the Métis in the nineteenth century hunted buffalo and lived at *Rivière-Rouge* (Red River, in present-day Manitoba), the parkland–woodland environment, fur trade routes, and proximity of the posts were also important components of Métis sense of place.[9] In a similar manner, and despite the fact that at times they account for the role played by women on the Plains, these narratives are likely to convey some gender bias.[10]

Identity Mobility and a Discourse of In-Betweenness

A few elements stand out in these narratives. One is a sense of "in-betweenness," which has the Métis as neither Indian nor European, but

partly both. Prairie Métis consciousness of their so-called in-between condition likely emerged because they were occupying a very specific socioeconomic niche within the Northwest economy, one where their role as
intermediaries was an asset.[11]

At first sight, Métis individuals' accounts draw on very specific cultural lines, making clear-cut distinctions between Métis and the "other,"
either Indian or Euro-American. In Goulet's memoirs, Indians are frequently depicted as those *mauvais chiens* (dirty dogs) or enemies who can
never be trusted.[12] Following is what he claimed in his comparison of
Métis and Indian horses:

> In our day we used to call the Metis' horses cayuses and the Indians'
> broncos. . . . There were more fine animals, proportionately, among the
> cayuses than the broncos. The big difference between the two, besides
> their physique, was that the cayuse was like a dog; you always knew
> pretty well what you had on your hands, whereas the bronco was like
> an Indian; you couldn't trust him until you'd known him for a while.[13]

Welsh also suggested at times the "primitive" nature of Indians, portray-
ing them as superstitious or ignorant.[14] His memoirs offer other illustrations of the differences between Métis and Indians; for example, he explained that Métis traders occasionally performed Indian dances and
songs mainly as a matter of good business and sociability, implying that
it had nothing to do with their common cultural practices.[15]

The Métis' urge to distinguish themselves from their Indian forebears
is also conveyed by their collective narratives. Métis consciousness arises,
in no small part, from their collective battle for land and for control over
the buffalo, also a necessary resource for many Indian tribes.[16] The Métis'
need to protect themselves from potential Indian attacks, particularly
from the Sioux, is depicted in the Métis story of the "Sixty Seven Bois-
Brûlés."[17] According to this story, which likely refers to the 1851 battle of
Grand Coteau, the Bois-Brûlés are those courageous ancestors who once
faced 2,000 Sioux warriors, defending themselves and their right to use
the land. The story also emphasizes the age of this event—"only the
prairie wind is left to know," when the Bois-Brûlés were already a distinct people and they left "home" with "nine hundred carts" travelling
"the ox-cart trail." The spirit of this story is that the Métis should be
proud of their glorious past, of what they are, and of the land from

which they originate. There could hardly be a better way to feed collective feelings.

These narratives also clearly distinguish the Métis from *les Anglais* and *les Américains* (or the "Yankees," as Welsh would have it). As the so-called newcomers became more influential and modified the geography of the Northwest, they were often depicted as those who troubled the quietude of the old days—or, as Goulet would have it, as "the devil . . . in the woodpile."[18] Euro-Canadians were generally depicted as being hardly suited to survive on the prairie, ill-adapted to this vast wilderness. Hiding from the sight of some Canadian troops during the 1885 uprising, Goulet said, "We'd have been goners if they hadn't been White men!"[19] meaning that if these men had been Indians or Métis, Goulet and his friends would have been detected. Norbert Welsh's few comments about the pointlessness of possessing a watch to tell the time on the prairie was another way that the Métis distanced themselves from Euro-Canadians and Euro-Americans.[20] Another illustration of such a separation is found in Welsh's critique of Yankee hunters, who, he claimed, "shot more buffalo for their hides than all the Indian and half-breed hunters put together."[21]

Collective narratives can also emphasize the distinction between Métis and Euro-Canadians. On the evening of June 19, 1816, Pierre Falcon composed "La Chanson de la Grenouillère," a song that described an event of the same day that came to be known as the "Battle of Seven Oaks," the other name for the "Frog Plain" in Rivière-Rouge. This song is much more than an objective description of a fight that took place in a specific site at a given time. It is a call for Métis mobilization against the "outsider" and a claim for Métis collective sovereignty over the land. Falcon's song drew definite ethnic boundaries between Métis and "outsiders." The Bois-Brûlés were not to be confused with les Anglais or *les prisonniers des Arkanys* (Orkneymen who worked for the HBC). That they were also employees of the fur trade and that the companies were also important actors in the making of Rivière-Rouge was ignored. The song became a de facto national anthem during the uprising of 1870, reinforcing its use as a vehicle of Métis distinctiveness.

"Chanson de la Grenouillère"[22]

1: *Voulez-vous écouter chanter / Une chanson de vérité? / Le dix-neuf de juin la bande des Bois-Brûlés / Sont arrivés comme de braves guerriers.*

2: *En arrivant à la Grenouillère / Nous avons pris trois prisonniers / Trois prisonniers des Arkanys / Qui sont ici pour piller notre pays.*

3: *Étant sur le point de débarquer / Deux de nos gens se sont mis à crier / Deux de nos gens se sont mis à crier / Voilà l'Anglais qui vient nous attaquer!*

4: *Tout aussitôt nous avons deviré, / Nous avons été les rencontrer / J'avons cerné la bande de grenadiers / [Ils] sont immobiles, ils sont démontés.*

5: *J'avons agi comme des gens d'honneur / J'avons envoyé un ambassadeur / "Le Gouverneur, voulez-vous arrêter / Un petit moment, nous voulons vous parler?"*

6: *Le Gouverneur qui était enragé / Il dit à ses soldats: "Tirez!" / Le premier coup, c'est l'Anglais qu'a tiré / L'ambassadeur a manqué tuer.*

7: *Le Gouverneur qui se croit empereur / Il veut agir avec rigueur / Le Gouverneur qui se croit empereur / À son malheur, agit trop de rigueur.*

8: *Ayant vu passer tous ces Bois-Brûlés / Il a parti pour les épouvanter / Étant parti pour les épouvanter / Il s'est trompé, il s'est fait tuer.*

9: *Il s'est trompé, il s'est fait tuer / Une quantité de ses grenadiers / J'avons tué presque tout son armée / Rien que quatre ou cinq ça l'ont pu se sauver.*

10: *Si vous aviez vu tous ces Anglais / Tous ces Bois-Brûlés après / De butte en butte, les Anglais culbutaient / Les Bois-Brûlés lâchaient des cris de joie!*

However, a closer look at these narratives indicates some permeability in the Métis process of separating themselves from the Other. The narratives were not exclusively constructed on differences from Others but, rather, also on mediation and dialogue. They amalgamated diverse voices[23] and moved between two cultures, making Métis identity exceedingly mobile. Métis individuals seemed to borrow, alternately, the way of thinking of both Indians and Euro-Canadians and build their own sense of identity through a double looping movement between divergence and convergence. Sometimes they spoke the voice of their Euro-Canadian ancestors, such as Goulet and Erasmus labeling Indians as "savages." Sometimes they thought the way of their Indian forebears, showing sympathy for them and being critical of Euro-Canadian behaviors and ideologies.[24] This is what happened when Louis Goulet described one of his fellows, William Gladu , as a *"métis sauvage,"*[25] for although Goulet did not completely reject the colonial ideology of primitive people, he challenged it somewhat by showing Métis potential for occasional savageness. Peter Erasmus experienced similar in-between situations as he had to make sense of the opposition between his enjoyable life with Woodland and

Prairie Indians and a more settled life achieved by the advance of colonization. He also had to face the discordance between Indian and Euro-Canadian beliefs. In addition to the "conflict between Indian mysticism and Protestant rationalism"[26] experienced by Erasmus was the antagonism between scientific (i.e., European) and Indian medicines. In spite of his initial doubts with regard to Indian medicines,[27] Erasmus was later "convinced that [his old friend and Methodist minister, Rev. Woolsey] could have been saved his present misery if he had not been prejudiced against Indian medicines."[28] Norbert Welsh's memoirs offer another example of this in-between condition. Although he emphasized the strangeness of Indian camps, he also described in great detail how he set a tent for and by himself in the Indian way.[29]

It would be misleading to think that the Métis experience of in-betweenness was completely unconscious. Indeed, it made Métis successful intermediaries between Indians and Euro-Canadians, a role that most of the narrators performed and were often pleased to play.[30] This role is likely what Welsh had in mind when he displayed his linguistic skills: "I spoke to [the Indian] in Cree, asking where he had come from, and what he wanted. He shook his head and answered in Assiniboine that he did not understand Cree. We then talked in Assiniboine."[31] Welsh's account is filled with similar comments that bring to light his knowledge of English, French, and many Indian languages.[32] This intermediary role led the Métis to consider themselves indispensable. "Many of the early famous travellers," Erasmus said, "would have been hopelessly lost, starved, or frozen to death without the guidance and advice of the Indians and half-breeds."[33] Reading Goulet's narrative, it seems that in-betweenness became, over the years, the focus of Métis political awareness and distinctiveness. Quoting Charles Nolin, who spoke at the meeting in 1884 that decided that a party would be sent to Montana to bring Louis Riel to the Northwest, Goulet mentioned that "the problem with us Metis right now is that we're like a cart with only one wheel. If we want to get moving, we'll have to go find the other one we need, in Montana, beside the Missouri."[34] Nolin referred to the cart as a metaphor for Métis sociopolitical reality, one made of both Indian (filled by Gabriel Dumont, the "child of the plains") and Euro-Canadian (the literate Louis Riel, the missing wheel) origins. For Nolin, there was only one way for the Métis to resist the advance of colonization and the Dominion of Canada—to mobilize a cart that contained the two essential components of their identity. Nolin's comment demonstrated that Métis in-betweenness was not just ambivalence and mobility, but also collective consciousness and a sense of distinctiveness. Indeed, Goulet, Erasmus, and Welsh were not ambiguous when they referred, indirectly or not, to their in-betweenness.

Spatial Mobility and the Extended Territoriality of the Métis

Along with in-betweenness, spatial mobility was another central component of Métis territorial experience in the nineteenth-century Northwest. Despite their importance in Métis life, settlements were not continuously inhabited, for many Métis would leave them, often for years. Settlements were points of both departure and arrival. There were elements of a broader network of places dispersed over the prairie, which included winter camps or hunting areas. Métis mobility was the backbone of this network. It was what connected all these places together.

In the course of the nineteenth century, the Métis created a socioeconomically diverse array of settlements across the Northwest. They were generally located in the parkland—Lac Sainte-Anne, Lac La Biche, Île-à-la-Crosse (where fishing, trapping, and hunting activities were dominant), but also Saint-Albert, Petite-Ville, and Batoche—and at the proximity of numerous wooded hills scattered over the grassland (the montagnes de Bois, de Cyprès, de l'Orignal). Rivière-Rouge was, however, the dominant Métis settlement.

Métis individual accounts contain many references to the material (or economical) importance of Rivière-Rouge, notably about its agricultural activity. Louis Goulet explained that *la rivière aux Marais* (west of today's Dufrost) was where the Métis used to *"faire du foin"* (make hay). He also told how the *tourtes* (a type of pigeon), known as pests among farmers, made the settlement difficult for agriculture.[35] Norbert Welsh also mentioned the importance of la Rivière-Rouge when he recalled, "Long ago, near Fort Garry there were a lot of farmers along the Red River. They were rich farmers, although they had small farms."[36] Besides these comments about agriculture, there were other indications of the material reality of Rivière-Rouge, as illustrated by Goulet's mention of the durability of the Métis log houses—the Charette house built in the *rivière Sale* settlement (which later became known as the Saint-Norbert parish) in 1800 was still standing when Goulet told his story.[37]

The material life of other settlements was described in similar ways. For example, Welsh, along with Father Hugonard, was the first to farm in Fort Qu'appelle in 1878.[38] Later still, in 1884, he started ranching in *Prairie Ronde* (about sixty miles south of Batoche) and provided a good idea of Métis land tenure: "It was now the beginning of September [1884]. I had brought my plow and harness, so I broke three acres of land that could be used for potato and vegetable garden in the spring. *The plowing marked my claim. Nobody else would take it. That was the law of the country.*"[39]

Métis accounts also provide a sense of the importance of settlements in Métis community life. Describing the moral importance of Father Ritchot, Goulet emphasized the central role of the Catholic Church.[40] Indeed, churches and religious figures regulated most of the central activities of community life in settlements—marriages, baptisms, funerals, and masses. The churches also affected patterns of settlement when they divided territory into parishes of specific religious adherence.[41] Furthermore, Goulet stated that newcomers from Ontario in the 1850s affected the Red River communities, recalling his father's sense of loss for the "feeling of unity and friendship that had always been felt among those people of different races and religions."[42] In the same vein, Erasmus recorded the words of his family's neighbor and friend of Red River, the Scot Murdoch Spence, who lamented the quietude of the old days of the community before they were compromised by a young French Métis "agitator" named Louis Riel.[43]

Because of the prairie's importance in their economic life and development, the Métis spent a considerable part of their lives there. It is no surprise that the Welshes delivered their own baby on the plains in the mid-1860s while trading at *Prairie Ronde*.[44] According to Goulet, the "unsettled" prairie also greatly affected Métis elders' sense of territory and identity:

> Those days of my childhood and adolescence were so beautiful, I wouldn't hesitate to say they were the most exciting years in all Metis history (with the stress on Metchiff). We had the virgin prairie, with all the buffalo we could use, and no competition from the Indians since they were pacified. The old-timers who'd lived through the old days and the wars on the prairies were still with us.[45]

Goulet's words described the plains as "virgin," as if there had only been Métis living on and from it. Indian competition for the land was depicted as something that belonged to the past. Similarly, the numerous fur trade posts scattered across the parkland and grassland seemed to have had little significance for Métis elders, for they were not even mentioned.

If many consider the prairie to be limited to grassland, a distinct landscape mostly of low-prairie vegetation (grasses, wild flowers, or mosses), and exclude the parkland, known as the ecological transition between grassland and woodland, the Métis narratives do not often make these distinctions. From the Métis narratives under scrutiny here, "prairie" was defined as wherever the buffalo were. Some species of bison, such as the wood bison, occupied both parkland and woodland zones.[46] Even the plains bison, the most economically significant type of bison, which generally ranged within the grassland, was often chased up to Edmonton, in the parkland, by Métis hunters.[47]

The buffalo was basic to Métis geography, as illustrated by Louis Goulet's description of the different species of bison hunted by the Métis, or by the numerous hunt expeditions Vermette, Welsh, and Erasmus participated in during their lives.[48] Although the hunt itself reached its peak in the 1840s, the importance of the buffalo-robe trade to St. Paul grew during that period in terms of both the number of carts involved and the value.[49] Although seasonal, the buffalo hunt nevertheless occupied the Métis for much of the year. Antoine Vermette reported that there were no fewer than three buffalo seasons: summer, fall, and winter.[50] Goulet provided further detail of how the buffalo hunt organized Métis life and geography:

> We usually left for the prairie early in spring, as soon as the grass was long enough for grazing—nippable, as we used to say. We would come back around the month of July, stay at the house one, two or three weeks and leave again, not to return this time until late in autumn. Sometimes we even spent the winter on the prairies. That's what we used to call wintering-over, in a tent, a cabin or a makeshift house built on the plain. Normally we went to Wood Mountain, but when the buffalo drew back into the area of the Cypress Hills, we followed them. Finally, later on, when they took refuge in the rough country of Montana, Wyoming, Nebraska and Colorado, it was along the Missouri River we went to find the few remaining herds.[51]

The buffalo hunt affected not only broad geographical movements, but also more specific spatial patterns, such as organization of the camps. If Métis individuals often slept outside simply, with only a blanket,[52] the settling of a buffalo-hunting brigade camp was generally a far more complex matter:

> Some caravan leaders had a habit of forming a circle at every stop so that the people would get used to the manoeuvre and learn with practice how to do it quickly. *Former la ronde* meant to place the carts parallel, side by side, wheel to wheel, in a line, with the shafts lifted in the air so that the carts tipped backwards and rested on their rear bottom edge, forming a circular enclosure. . . . Thanks to this system, the camp could be instantly transformed into a fortress preparing its defenses.[53]

Goulet's description of the camps as a circular distribution of carts for defensive purposes reveals the importance of both human geography on the plains and conflicts with Indians for available resources.

The prairie was also the site of more permanent structures: the winter camps. These winter camps were generally situated near a river and a source of wood, and their construction demonstrated the Métis relation to land:

> The great majority of winter shacks were made of poplar, which was the most common wood in the forests of the upper Missouri. It was by far the most abundant tree and the easiest to work, but once it was squared and dried in the shade it could be as durable as oak. So I wouldn't be surprised if some of those houses I saw built are still standing, especially the ones made of cedar or cypress.[54]

Norbert Welsh, a native of the Red River Settlement who traded all over the plains for most of his life, claimed, "in all I must have had about twenty wintering houses on the Saskatchewan plains."[55]

The Métis experience of the prairie was also political. Although the Rivière-Rouge was the center of institutional organization in the Northwest for both Euro-Canadians and Métis, the prairie was not without political importance for the latter. As Welsh pointed out, "We fur traders had a law of our own in the North-West. Before we left the country we appointed a Chief officer and four sub-officers to police the trip."[56] In contrast to colonial organizations in the settlements—the Council of Assiniboia in Rivière-Rouge, the Legislative Assembly of Manitoba, or the diverse religious orders—the hunting organization, often called *le conseil des chasseurs*, was a temporary and itinerant sociopolitical structure. The

Métis hunting council was meant to achieve specific tasks and be dissolved and reconstituted as needed. The power it exercised, its authoritative and coercive functions, disappeared once the hunt was over. However, the election of a new hunt council was fairly consistent and ongoing. Elections were called at specific meeting points, such as Pembina or near Beaver Lake, Alberta.[57] The laws that regulated the hunting expedition and the hunt itself were another element. According to Vermette, "There was a law that you couldn't shot cows after July 15, and if a man was found guilty of this he was fined by the chief of the party. They would also fine a man if he could not skin all he had killed."[58] Communal sharing of the meat and labor was another feature of buffalo-hunting expeditions.[59] Moreover, the structure and function of le conseil des chasseurs eventually became the basis of the political organization of the new permanent settlements in the Batoche area in the 1870s and 1880s, even before such a political structure was used at Rivière-Rouge.[60]

A Shifting Hierarchy of Places

Métis spatial mobility underlined a persistent and paradoxical feeling—the excitement of departing for the "free life" of the plains, yet the heartbreak of leaving the settlements. Both Louis Goulet and Peter Erasmus expressed this feeling, as well as the pleasure of coming back to Rivière-Rouge after months of enjoying the prairie life.[61] Such a mix of feelings conveys the complexity and depth of Métis relation to land. Contrary to colonial perspective, settlements were not the continuous core of Métis experience of place, and the prairie was not simply a peripheral region subordinate to settlements, a mere potential hinterland to be cultivated. The individual narratives under scrutiny reveal a fluctuating hierarchy of places, a spatial priority oscillating between settlement and prairie. Although some parts of the Métis narratives suggest a centrality of settlements, others suggest the lure of the "margins." A similar conclusion can be drawn from collective oral narratives, such as the song "la Chanson de la Grenouillère" and the story "Sixty Seven Bois-Brûlés" mentioned above. Whereas the former depicts Rivière-Rouge as the home of the Métis, the latter portrays the prairie as the focal point of their experience of space.

When Goulet referred to Rivière-Rouge (more specifically, the parish of Saint-Norbert) as *"la maison"* and *"le pays natal,"*[62] or when he discussed how, in 1870, Louis Riel and the Métis prevented the Dominion from taking it over,[63] he certainly centered the settlement in his narrative. Erasmus also wrote about Rivière-Rouge as "home."[64] And yet, most of Goulet's and Erasmus's memoirs focus on the prairie as vital to the Métis way of life, setting Métis settlements at the margins of their narratives. As a result of the buffalo hunts of his childhood,[65] as well as his work as freighter and as a scout for the U.S. Army during his adult life, Goulet spent little time in Rivière-Rouge. More important, their descriptions of prairie life are deeply and sincerely positive, if not nostalgic, reflecting their specific attachment to that space. Erasmus was convinced that his attraction to the prairie life compromised his chance to marry Florence, a Métis woman from Lac Sainte-Anne: "Suddenly I realized that the real reason for doubt or hesitation in declaring my intentions was not actually the difference in religious adherence but in my own dislike for a settled existence and my love for travel."[66]

The shared centrality of both settlements and the prairie was sometimes expressed through a rapid switch between the two, even on the same page of a narrative:

> Many a young love ending in happy marriage saw its first spark during one of those memorable journeys [toward wintering places]. It was the ideal time for a girl or a widow to pick a husband from the cream of the crop! . . . The communal, pastoral life we enjoyed all the way across the plains from Red River to Wood Mountain or the Cypress Hills or to the steep-cut banks of the Missouri River, went on even after the caravan had reached its destination [Red River]. Once there, we'd rest a few days and spend that time picking up again with old friends and relatives. Back then, family ties among the Metis could stretch to infinity, so to speak. If two grandfathers traded dogs one day, that was enough for their grandchildren to call themselves relatives. Children of cousins two or three times removed turned into uncles and aunts.[67]

This comment suggests that there was more than one specific center to Métis socialization. From Goulet's perspective, Métis communal life was determined as much by the months of pastoral life spent in the prairie— where, he said, marriages occurred—as by life in Rivière-Rouge—where the extended family assumed its significance.

Oral Geographies: Ground for a Primary Writing

Orality—the condition of oral cultures or the state of reliance on oral traditions—provides much more than the evidence from which Métis territoriality can be examined. In fact, orality and territoriality are deeply interconnected. Memory is the cement that binds them. It thickens the experience of space by giving meaning to places, justifying collective and individual appropriation of space, and enhancing a sense of belonging to them. In spite of their great mobility, Métis behavior in space was socially structured. It often followed the prescriptions of elders, bearers of memory and knowledge about land and resources. Finding bison, berries, or firewood were all activities facilitated by landmarks and geographical knowledge and were expressions of Métis historical land use.

Orality, memory, and territoriality (or, more broadly, spatiality) form the triad upon which are built oral geographies. The concept of oral geography has two main meanings. First, it can be defined as oral history—the historical and critical analysis of oral material—mediated through space or, more specifically, territory or landscape. Second, it represents the connection between spatial structures—the material, political, and symbolic orderings of space—and social structures (e.g., cultural practices, norms, or institutions) inherent to oral cultures.

Among the studies addressing, explicitly or not, oral geographies,[68] those that focus on place names are numerous.[69] Such emphasis on toponyms is not surprising. For oral cultures, place naming represents more than simply a symbolic appropriation of space or the cultural dimension of territorialization. It constitutes a significant process of social–spatial production. As Julie Cruikshank notes of Athapaskan toponyms, they "are more than names; they are metaphors bringing together varieties of information in one small word."[70] Place names are mnemonic devices that follow and lead a narrator through a story.[71] The mnemonic role of indigenous place names is reflected in the terse grammatical style in which these toponyms are composed. Toponyms are generally not precise geographical descriptions but, rather, are pictorial and summarized versions that act as guides for remembering and communicating.[72] Globally, place names convey individual and collective memories, stories, the mythic baggage of a people, and geographical knowledge. Whereas naming is the result of a close time-related experience of the land, the passing of these names from one generation to another is a means of communicating a people's history and geography.[73]

Naming Is Knowing: Resources, Land Use, and Territorial Occupancy

Métis toponyms are no different, hence our interest for the Prairie Métis toponymic nomenclature.[74] The Métis-named landscape—which largely borrows from both Indian and Euro-Canadian names—is the text in which is recorded their historical land use. The descriptive and pictorial nature of Métis toponymy, in which place names are the mental presentations of the physical and human geography they name, provides a wealth of geographical information.

Toponyms constitute a text that describes the physical geography of the prairie. First, they relate its broad topographical features. The prairie itself was described with names such as *la Prairie Ronde* (Saskatchewan) and *la Prairie de la Tête de Bœuf* (Calf Mountain area, Manitoba). The numerous hills where the Métis had a number of camp sites were descriptively named—*la Montagne de l'Orignal* (Moose Mountain), *la Montagne de Cyprès* (Cypress Hills), *la Montagne de Bois* (Wood Mountain), *la Montagne Sale* (Dirt Hills), and *la Butte du Cheval Caille, la Butte au Carcajou,* or *la Butte du Foin de Senteur* (Sweetgrass Hills). So are the *coulées* and rivers that incise the prairie, such as *la Grande Coulée de la Grosse Butte,* which derived "its name from a large conical hill about two hundred feet high."[75] Certain place names offered a precise description of land. *La rivière aux Gratias* (Morris River, Manitoba) recalled the presence of *gratias,* an old-French word for burdocks, also referred to by the name "Scratching River" on some nineteenth-century maps of the Red River area. Some other place names described available resources. *La Talle de Hart-Rouge* (Willow Bunch, Saskatchewan) is one example, as Métis used to fill their pipes with the bark of the red willow that grows in the region.[76] The name *la rivière aux Îles-de-Bois* (Boyne River, Manitoba) is another illustration: along this river, only a few miles west of Rivière-Rouge, was a forest of oak where the Métis used to gather most of the wood they needed to build or repair their carts. The place named *Tas d'Os* (Regina, Saskatchewan) was where Métis gathered to make pemmican, and the name was derived from the accumulation of buffalo bones. In the 1880s, some Métis, especially those from la Montagne de Bois and La Talle de Saule, moved there to gather these bones (and those spread all over the prairie), which were then sent to the United States to be powdered and processed into fertilizer.[77]

Place names were also textual expressions of Métis experiences on the northern margins (the boreal forest and the parkland), lands often shared with the *Canadiens*, at the very heart of the fur trade geography. In Manitoba, there was *les eaux-qui-remuent* (series of portages near the mouth of Winnipeg River), *la rivière de la Tête Ouverte* (Brokenhead River), *la rivière Bouleau*, *la rivière Blanche*, and the upper section of *la rivière au Rat*. Northern Saskatchewan and Alberta featured places such as *Lac La Biche*, *Lac La Ronge*, *Île à la Crosse*, *Portage La Loche* (Methy Portage), *Décharge du Rapide Croche* (Crooked Rapids), *Portage du Diable* (Great Devil Rapids), *Pointe au Sable* (Sand Point), and *Rapide du Genou* (Knee Rapids). All these names, often descriptive, also highlighted a way of life distinct from the one on the plains. Rivers, lakes, rapids, and portages—all basic geographical components of the fur trade geography—were predominant features in Métis/Canadien toponymic nomenclature.[78]

Métis place names also referred to human geography, with toponyms such as *Batoche*, the place where Xavier Letendre dit Batoche had his ferry and store; *la traverse à Gabriel* (Gabriel's Crossing), named after Métis leader Gabriel Dumont, who used to operate another ferry service; or *la Fourche des Gros-Ventres* (south branch of the Saskatchewan River), which referred to the upstream presence of "Big Belly" Indians.[79] In a similar manner, *la Coulée-Chapelle* or *la Coulée des Prêtres* (Saint-Victor), in the vicinity of *la Montagne de Bois*, referred to the chapel built in the early 1870s to welcome the Oblate father Jean Lestanc, the first Roman Catholic priest to establish himself in the region.

"Writing" Métis History Books: Names, Memory, and Spatial Mobility

These examples highlight the relationship between place names, information about land, and Métis collective memory. Toponyms form, at the very least, a memory of land. To return to individual narratives, there is hardly a recollection or description that is not linked to specific place names. Describing a buffalo expedition, Louis Goulet explained,

> The old people wanted to go [to *La Coquille Pilée*, near present-day Whitewood in Saskatchewan] because it used to be a popular spot for wintering-over sixty or seventy years before. One year, a group of one

hundred to one hundred and fifty Metis families from Red River were set up there for the winter, with a big camp of Cree Indians nearby. During the winter, the Cree camp was hit with a bad epidemic of smallpox. Dogs carried the germs of the terrible disease into the Metis' winter camp, which was totally wiped out in a matter of days. There wasn't even anybody to bury the dead who became carrion for wolves the rest of the winter and for crows in the spring.[80]

The hunting caravan did not head toward la Coquille Pilée for a material reason. Rather, the rationale for the detour, Goulet explained, was to re-member those who had died there years ago.

The example of la Coquille Pilée also stressed the thread that held to-gether orality, memory, and relation to land, for it reveals one important element of Métis territoriality—spatial mobility. The elders' will to reach this place showed that Prairie Métis were not a "wandering" people, as many nineteenth-century observers had it. Métis mobility was a spatial practice that was socially structured and based on a precise and well-established network of deliberately named places. The Métis-named landscape (or more broadly, the aboriginal-named landscape), and the geographical and historical knowledge it contained, had the capacity for guiding spatial mobility. The opposite was also true. Deflected from its original course, a party of Métis could be exposed to unknown or long-unvisited lands. Such encounters could generate new historical and territorial experiences and feed Métis collective memory and their toponymic baggage. *Les Mauvais Bois* on the Assiniboine (near *les Grands Rapides de l'Assiniboine*, or today's Brandon, Manitoba) is an illustration of how names could inscribe a specific event and unique experience of space into collective memory. Geologist and explorer Henry Youle Hind met this place and referred to it in his narrative of the Red River expedition:

Leaving Prairie Portage on the morning of the 19th [June 1858], we took the trail leading to the Bad Woods, a name given to a wooded district about thirty miles long, by the buffalo hunters in 1852, who, in conse-quence of the floods of that year, could not pass to their crossing place at the Grand Rapids of the Assiniboine by the Plain or Prairie Road. There were four hundred carts in the band, and the hunters were com-pelled to cut a road through the forest of small aspens which forms the Bad Woods, to enable them to reach the high prairies. This labour occupied them several days, and will be long remembered in the settlements in consequence of the misery entailed by the delay on the children and women.[81]

An In-Between Geography of the Nord-Ouest: Naming Distinctiveness

Métis place names were symbolic expressions of in-betweenness and identity mobility. If many derived from direct Métis experience, others originated from both Métis cultural backgrounds, Indian and Euro-Canadian. This variability in naming exposes the duality of Métis collective memories, stories, and mythic baggage. It explains why toponyms of Native origin, such as the *rivière Queue d'Oiseau, rivière Calumet, lac la Vieille*, or *Côteau des Festins* lie alongside place names of Euro-Canadian extraction: (a) toponyms like *Portage-la-Prairie*, derived from the Pierre Gaultier de Varennes, sieur de La Vérendrye's exploration expeditions of the 1730s and 1740s; (b) toponyms shared with the voyageurs, such as *la fourche des Gros-Ventres* or *la rivière du Pas* (north branch of the Saskatchewan River); and (c) hagionyms (names with religious meaning) brought to the Northwest by missionaries, such as Saint-Boniface, Saint-Norbert, Saint-Anne, Saint-Vital, and Saint-Albert. The Métis did more than translate Native place names into French (or *Mitchif*), they often integrated the original stories associated with these names. *La Prairie du Cheval Blanc* (White Horse Plain, today Saint-François-Xavier, on the Assiniboine River in Manitoba) is one example. The general belief is that the name comes from Indians and is related to a story of a mysterious and unapproachable horse. Although he agrees that the name comes from an Indian story, Elliot Coues suggests that the story is also rooted in Métis oral tradition.[82] If la Prairie du Cheval Blanc is a name whose meaning borrows from Indians, it also finds its form in Euro-Canadian language, thus adding another dimension to the in-betweenness of Métis naming.

In addition to this general picture, there are more specific indications of the in-between reality of Métis naming. One is the coexistence of multiple names for the same place. Again, la Prairie du Cheval Blanc is a good example. This Native place name was used for a while in parallel with the hagionym Saint-François-Xavier (1850s) as well as another "official" toponym, Grantown, named after Cuthbert Grant. *Fond du Lac/Saint-Laurent* (1861) and *Prairie à Fournier/Baie-Saint-Paul* (1834) in Manitoba, *Batoche/Saint-Laurent de Grandin* in Saskatchewan, and *Lac des Esprits* (1830)/*Lac-Sainte-Anne* (1850) in Alberta are other eloquent examples. It is not surprising that the appearance of church names in existing Native/ Métis-named land coincided with the spread of missions in the North-west and was mostly initiated by the priests (symbolizing, to some extent, the importance of the church and priests). Louis Goulet, Peter Erasmus, and Norbert Welsh, notably, used both Indian–Métis names and hagionyms, often interchangeably.

However, in many cases, the earlier Métis name was eventually re-placed by the church name, indicating an important shift in the power of naming. Such a substitution process developed at a rapid pace after the creation of the province of Manitoba in 1870. Many Métis dispersed to far corners of le Nord-Ouest and were often replaced by newly arrived French Canadian settlers. *La Pointe-à-Grouette*, which became Sainte-Agathe in 1876; *la Pointe-Coupée*, renamed Saint-Adolphe at about the same period; or *Rivière-aux-Rats* (Saint-Pierre and, later, Saint-Pierre-Jolys) are good il-lustrations. In a sense, these church names erased, at least symbolically, the Métis presence. In other cases, amalgamation was the norm, the Mé-tis name only partially covert. Such amalgamation is how *la Coulée des Loups* was "christianized" to become *Sainte-Anne-de-la-Peau-du-Loup* (be-fore it was changed to *Sainte-Anne-du-Loup*, and finally Wolseley in Sas-katchewan), a name that assimilated the "savage" into the patroness of the voyageur. A similar argument can be made for *Pointe-des-Chênes* in Manitoba, which became *Sainte-Anne-des-Chênes*. Despite representing the shifting power of naming in the late nineteenth-century Northwest, these amalgamations or hybrid names nevertheless suggest the pre-eminence of the Métis geo-cultural layer in the region and the difficulty in simply erasing it from land and memories.

Conclusion

Métis oral culture expressed the diversity of meanings contained in Louis Goulet's phrase "le fond de l'Ouest."[83] This phrase suggests how extended, diverse, and rich Métis territoriality was. The individual nar-ratives analyzed in the first section depict a far-reaching Métis experi-ence of space, both socially and spatially. This space was composed of a vast array of places scattered over the whole Northwest, with different places coming to the vanguard of importance at different times, depend-ing on life contingencies, seasonal activities, and spatial mobility. Like this shifting Métis hierarchy of places, Métis sense of in-betweenness, which frames the extent of the mobility of their identity and their intermediary role in the Northwest, also conveys the diversity of Métis territoriality.

As revealed by the investigation of Métis place names, spatial mobility and in-betweenness represented the "bottom line" (or *le fond de l'histoire*) of the Métis sense of territory and identity—what is buried under the surface. Given the descriptive nature of place names and their importance to oral tradition, they prove to be an excellent source of geographical information, historical land use, and collective memory. Along with the landscape they describe, toponyms are, in many respects, the Métis history book. And as such, they constitute a window into the interaction between territoriality and orality, or oral geographies.

Notes

1. Cass-Beggs, *Seven Metis Songs of Saskatchewan*; Jannetta, " 'Travels through forbidden geography' "; and Payment, *"Les gens libres—Otipemisiwak."*

2. Some of the individual narratives were, in fact, written by their literate Métis authors. Nonetheless, they often suggest the importance of the Métis oral culture, revealing at times collective narratives and songs. For example, see Charette, *L'espace de Louis Goulet*, 65; Dempsey, "Foreword," p. x; and Weekes, *Last Buffalo Hunter*, 25. For a more extensive use of Métis oral material, see Rivard, "Prairie and Québec Métis Territoriality," 86–124.

3. Hence the use of Louis Goulet's phrase—"Le fond de l'Ouest"—as the chapter title (see Charette, *L'espace de Louis Goulet*, 78). My use of this phrase likely carries more meanings than Louis Goulet intended. For the Métis, *le Fond de l'Ouest* was merely a geographical reference; it would translate as "the far west."

4. Sack, *Human Territoriality*, 2.

5. Raffestin, *Pour une géographie du pouvoir*, 145.

6. Charette, *L'espace de Louis Goulet*, 65.

7. Erasmus, *Buffalo Days and Nights*, 63.

8. As an explanation, I would suggest that the "free life of the prairie" in the early twentieth century, when all these accounts were recorded, was much more gratifying to Métis storytellers (as opposed to the contemporary sociospatial marginalization that they faced) and much more "romantic" and "exotic" to interviewers.

9. Tough, *"As Their Natural Resources Fail."*

10. One might as well mention a possible "translation" bias. These "oral" accounts had to be recorded on paper, most often by non-Métis, which meant losing the true way of speaking of the Métis in the process. The great efforts made by the publisher of Goulet's memoirs to keep alive the spirit of the Métis elder's

speech should not hide the fact that it was written in standard French, not in its original French-Métis language. Moreover, most of these recollections were performed years after the events described (late nineteenth century). Louis Goulet was in his seventies when Charette interviewed him, and Norbert Welsh was eighty-seven in 1931 when he told his life to Mary Weekes. The men's age when interviewed might explain their stories' rather nostalgic tone regarding the "free life of the prairie," particularly given that this way of life was long gone.

11. Foster, "Some Questions and Perspectives."

12. Charette, *L'espace de Louis Goulet*, 16, 17, and 146. The translated excerpts provided here are, for the most part, from the English version of the narrative. See Charette, *Vanishing Spaces*.

13. "De notre temps, l'on appelait les chevaux des Métis cayousses et ceux des Indiens, broncos . . . La proportion des bonnes bêtes était plus forte chez les cayousses que chez les broncos. La grande différence entre les deux, en dehors de leur physique était que le cayousse ressemblait au chien: vous saviez à peu près toujours ce que vous aviez dans vos mains, tandis que le bronco, c'était comme un sauvage, vous ne pouviez pas vous y fier avant de l'avoir connu" (Charette, *L'espace de Louis Goulet*, 97).

14. Weekes, *Last Buffalo Hunter*, 17, 44.

15. Ibid., 47.

16. Ray, *Indians in the Fur Trade*, 206, 227, 231.

17. One may find this story in Sealey's *Stories of the Métis*, 90–93. The author attributes this story to "the era of Louis Riel." I am not aware of any French version. According to Norbert Welsh's account, the remembrance of this event had been important for the Métis (Weekes, *Last Buffalo Hunter*, 161).

18. "Le diable . . . dans la cabane" (Charette, *L'espace de Louis Goulet*, 77).

19. "Si ce n'eût pas été des blancs, ça y était!" (ibid., 174).

20. Weekes, *Last Buffalo Hunter*, 20, 40.

21. Ibid., 43.

22. Quoted from Complin, "Pierre Falcon's 'Chanson de la Grenouillere,' " 49–50. Please see pp. 107–109 in chapter 3 for an English translation of the song lyrics.

23. Jannetta, " 'Travels through forbidden geography,' " 65.

24. Erasmus, *Buffalo Days and Nights*, 201.

25. The *métis sauvage* expression was found in the transcripts of Charette's original manuscript notes in the Provincial Archives of Manitoba (MG9A6, folio 112). The editor has preferred the term *métis indien*. If this last term efficiently shakes the distinction between Métis and Indians, it does not carry the colonial ideology that the original expression implies. That said, the French term sauvage was used in the nineteenth century as a general expression, just like "Indian" in English at the same period or "aboriginal" today. It was not meant to be as pejorative as "savage."

26. Spry, "Introduction," p. xxviii.

27. Erasmus, *Buffalo Days and Nights*, 154.

28. Ibid., 171.

29. Weekes, *Last Buffalo Hunter*, 10–11.

30. Charette, *L'espace de Louis Goulet*, 146, 150; Erasmus, *Buffalo Days and Nights*, 239–64; and Weekes, *Last Buffalo Hunter*, 84, 107.

31. Weekes, *Last Buffalo Hunter*, 15.

32. Ibid., 84.

33. Erasmus, *Buffalo Days and Nights*, 75.

34. "La question métisse . . . est comme une charrette. Pour la faire marcher il faut deux roues et, dans le moment, il nous en manque une. Si nous la voulons, il nous faut aller la chercher dans le Montana, le long du Missouri" (Charette, *L'espace de Louis Goulet*, 137).

35. Ibid., 24, 51.

36. Weekes, *Last Buffalo Hunter*, 119.

37. Charette, *L'espace de Louis Goulet*, 59.

38. Weekes, *Last Buffalo Hunter*, 119.

39. Ibid., 144 (emphasis added).

40. Charette, *L'espace de Louis Goulet*, 90–93.

41. The Roman Catholic Church was the most important religious institution. It was established in the region in 1818 by Father Jean-Norbert Provencher in response to Lord Selkirk's and the Métis' expressed demands.

42. "[L']esprit d'union et de camaraderie qui avait toujours existé chez les gens d'origines raciales et de religions différentes" (Charette, *L'espace de Louis Goulet*, 77).

43. Erasmus, *Buffalo Days and Nights*, 140, 191.

44. Weekes, *Last Buffalo Hunter*, 35.

45. "ces années de mon enfance et de mon adolescence ont été si belles! je n'hésite pas à dire qu'elles ont été les plus enivrantes de toute notre histoire à nous Métis, avec l'accent, Métifs. Nous avions la prairie vierge où il y avait encore assez de buffalos pour nous suffire, et les Indiens pacifiés n'étaient plus là pour la disputer. Nous avions avec nous tous les anciens qui avaient vécu le temps de la prairie et de ses guerres" (Charette, *L'espace de Louis Goulet*, 60).

46. Ibid., 36.

47. Ibid., 78.

48. Ibid., 36–37.

49. Ens, *Homeland to Hinterland*, 80.

50. *Manitoba Free Press*, "Antoine Vermette," 26 August 1910.

51. "Nous avions coutume de partir de bon printemps pour la prairie, dès que l'herbe était assez longue pour être broutée, pour la pincer, comme on disait. Nous revenions vers le mois de juillet. Nous restions à la maison pendant une, deux ou trois semaines pour repartir et ne revenir cette fois que tard à l'automne, quand nous ne passions pas l'hiver dans la prairie. C'est ce que nous appelions passer l'hiver en hivernement, sous la tente, dans une loge ou dans une maison d'occasion construite sur la plaine. Nous allions ordinairement à la montagne de Bois; quand le buffalo recula du côté des environs de la montagne Cyprès, nous l'y suivîmes. Enfin, plus tard, lorsque le buffalo se réfugia dans les terrains

difficiles d'accès du Montana, du Wyoming, du Nebraska et du Colorado, ce fut le long du Missouri que nous allions à la rencontre des troupeaux qui restaient encore" (Charette, *L'espace de Louis Goulet*, 32).

52. Ibid., 177; *Manitoba Free Press*, "Antoine Vermette," 15; and Weekes, *Last Buffalo Hunter*.

53. "Certains chefs de caravane avaient l'habitude de former le rond à chaque arrêt afin d'habituer les gens à cette manœuvre et d'en acquérir la rapidité à force d'exercice. On appelait former le rond, placer les charrettes parallèlement à côté l'une de l'autre, roue à roue, puis lever les timons en l'air de façon à asseoir la charrette sur sa fonçure d'arrière et présenter ainsi une clôture circulaire. . . . Grâce à ce système le camp pouvait se mettre immédiatement en état de siège et préparer sa défense" (Charette, *L'espace de Louis Goulet*, 40).

54. "La grande majorité des maisons d'hivernement étaient construites de liard, qui était l'essence la plus commune des forêts du haut Missouri. C'était de beaucoup l'arbre le plus abondant et le plus facile à travailler, mais une fois qu'il avait été équarri, puis mis à sécher à l'ombre il valait le chêne comme durée. Alors, je ne serais pas étonné qu'il y eût encore de ces maisons que j'avais vu construire. Surtout parmi celles qui étaient d'épinette rouge ou de cyprès. (Charette, *L'espace de Louis Goulet*, 59).

55. Weekes, *Last Buffalo Hunter*, 96.

56. Ibid., 24.

57. Erasmus, *Buffalo Days and Nights*, 200.

58. *Manitoba Free Press*, "Antoine Vermette," 15.

59. Erasmus, *Buffalo Days and Nights*, 183, 229; and Weekes, *Last Buffalo Hunter*, 20.

60. Payment, *Batoche (1870–1910)*, 95.

61. Charette, *L'espace de Louis Goulet*, 77; and Erasmus, *Buffalo Days and Nights*, 141.

62. Charette, *L'espace de Louis Goulet*, 32, 45, 95, 113.

63. Ibid., 89.

64. Erasmus, *Buffalo Days and Nights*, 14.

65. Goulet's family once spent over two years away from Rivière-Rouge.

66. Erasmus, *Buffalo Days and Nights*, 61.

67. "C'était au cours des ces voyages mémorables [toward wintering places] que s'allumaient les amours qui aboutissaient à d'heureux mariages. C'était la belle occasion pour les filles et les veuves de se trouver un mari choisi sur la crème de toute la race! . . . La vie pastorale en commun au cours de la traversée des plaines depuis la Rivière-Rouge aux montagnes de Bois, de Cyprès, ou aux bords escarpés du Missouri se continuait même après que la caravane eût atteint sa destination [Rivière-Rouge]. Un repos de quelques jours succédait à notre arrivée et nous en profitions pour retrouver des connaissances ou de la parenté. C'était le temps où les liens de parenté chez les Métis s'étiraient pour ainsi dire à l'infini. Il suffisait à des grands-pères d'avoir une fois échangé des chiens pour que leurs petits-enfants se considèrent comme des parents. Ceux issus des cousins de deuxième et troisième degré redevenaient des oncles et des tantes" (Charette, *L'espace de Louis Goulet*, 61).

68. See, e.g., Hewitt, " 'When the Great Planes Came' "; and Lytwyn, *Muskekowuck Athinuwick.*

69. See, e.g., Aporta, "Trail as Home"; Collignon, *Les Inuit*; Fair, "Inupiat Naming and Community History"; and Pearce, "Native Mapping."

70. Cruikshank, "Getting the Words Right," 63.

71. Fair, "Inupiat Naming and Community History," 473.

72. Pearce, "Native Mapping," 159–60.

73. Cruikshank, "Getting the Words Right," 63; Linklater, "Footprints of Wasahkacahk"; Ray, *I Have Lived Here since the World Began*, 1; and Rivard, "Territorialité métisse," 26–27.

74. In addition to the individual memoirs analyzed in the first section, and otherwise specified, the principal sources for this toponymy analysis are as follows: Coues, *New Light on the Early History of the Greater Northwest*; Geographic Board of Canada, *Place-Names of Manitoba*; Hind, *Narrative of the Canadian Red River*; Léonard, "Une toponymie voilée"; Létourneau, *Henri Létourneau raconte*; Morice, *L'Église catholique*; Rondeau, *La Montagne de Bois*; and Taché, *Esquisse sur le nord-ouest de l'Amérique.*

75. Hind, *Narrative of the Canadian Red River*, 1:18.

76. Rondeau, *La Montagne de Bois*, 104.

77. Ibid., 112.

78. Léonard, "Une toponymie voilée"; and Rivard, "Territorialité métisse."

79. Charette, *L'espace de Louis Goulet*, 84.

80. "Les vieux tenaient à passer par [la Coquille Pilée], parce qu'il y a soixante ou soixante-quinze ans c'était un lieu populaire d'hivernement. Une année, un groupe de cent à cent cinquante familles métisses de la Rivière-Rouge s'y étaient installées pour hiverner. A côté, se trouvait un gros camp d'Indiens cris qui fut attaqué durant l'hiver par une forte épidémie de grosse picote. Des chiens transportèrent des germes de la terrible maladie dans le camp d'hivernement métis, ce qui le décima totalement dans l'espace de quelques jours. Pas un seul Métis ne s'en réchappa. Il n'y resta même personne pour donner la sépulture aux victimes, qui devinrent la pâture des loups pour le reste de l'hiver, et des corneilles au printemps" (Charette, *L'espace de Louis Goulet*, 79).

81. Hind, *Narrative of the Canadian Red River*, 1:283–84.

82. Coues, *New Light on the Early History of the Greater Northwest*, 1:288.

83. Charette, *L'espace de Louis Goulet*, 78.

Works Cited

Aporta, Claudio. "The Trail as Home: Inuit and Their Pan-Arctic Network of Routes." *Human Ecology* 37, no. 2 (2009): 131–46.

Cass-Beggs, Barbara. *Seven Metis Songs of Saskatchewan, with an Introduction on the Historical Background of the Metis.* Don Mills, ON: BMI Canada, 2009.

Charette, Guillaume. *L'espace de Louis Goulet.* Winnipeg, MB: Bois-Brûlés, 1976.

———. *Vanishing Spaces (Memoirs of a Prairie Métis)*. Translated by Ray Ellen-wood. Winnipeg, MB: Bois-Brûlés, 1980.

Collignon, Béatrice. *Les Inuit, ce qu'ils savent du territoire*. Paris, France: L'Harmattan, 1996.

Complin, Margaret. "Pierre Falcon's 'Chanson de la Grenouillere.'" *Proceedings and Transactions, Royal Society of Canada* vol. 33, no. 2 (1939): 49–58.

Coues, Elliott, ed. *New Light on the Early History of the Greater Northwest: The Manu-script Journals of Alexander Henry, Fur Trader of the Northwest Company and of David Thompson, Official Geographer of the Same Company 1799–1814. . . .* 3 vols. New York, NY: F. P. Harper, 1897.

Cruikshank, Julie. "Getting the Words Right: Perspectives on Naming and Places in Athapaskan Oral History." *Arctic Anthropology* 27, no. 1 (1990): 52–65.

Dempsey, Hugh. "Foreword." In *Buffalo Days and Nights (as told by Henry Thomp-son)*. Calgary, AB: Fifth House, 1999.

Ens, Gerhard J. *Homeland to Hinterland: The Changing Worlds of the Red River Metis in the Nineteenth Century*. Toronto, ON: University of Toronto, 1996.

Erasmus, Peter. *Buffalo Days and Nights (as told by Henry Thompson)*. Calgary, AB: Fifth House, 1999.

Fair, Susan W. "Inupiat Naming and Community History: The *Tapqaq* and *Sani-niq* Coasts near Shishmaref, Alaska." *Professional Geographer* 49, no. 4 (1997): 466–80.

Foster, John E. "Some Questions and Perspectives on the Problem of Métis Roots." In *The New Peoples: Being and Becoming Métis in North America*, edited by Jacqueline Peterson and Jennifer S. H. Brown, 73–91. Winnipeg: University of Manitoba, 1985.

Geographic Board of Canada. *Place-Names of Manitoba*. Ottawa, ON: Department of the Interior, 1933.

Hewitt, Kenneth. "'When the Great Planes Came and Made Ashes of our City . . .' Towards an Oral Geography of the Disasters of War." *Antipode* 26, no. 1 (1994): 1–34.

Hind, Henry Youle. *Narrative of the Canadian Red River Exploring Expedition of 1857 and of the Assinniboine and Saskatchewan Exploring Expedition of 1858*. 2 vols. London, UK: Longman, Green, Longman and Roberts, 1860.

Jannetta, Armando E. "'Travels through forbidden geography': Métis Trappers and Traders Louis Goulet and Ted Trindell." *Ariel: A Review of International English Literature* 25, no. 2 (1994): 59–74.

Léonard, Carol. "Une toponymie voilée: Problématique des noms de lieux partic-ulière à une minorité canadienne, la Fransaskoisie." PhD dissertation, Départe-ment de géographie, Université Laval, QC, 2005.

Létourneau, Henri. *Henri Létourneau raconte*. Winnipeg, MB: Bois-Brûlés, 1980.

Linklater, Eva Mary Mina. "The Footprints of Wasahkacahk: The Churchill River Diversion Project and Destruction of the Nelson House Cree Historical Land-scape." Master's thesis, Department of Archaeology, Simon Fraser University, BC, 1994.

Lytwyn, Victor P. *Muskekowuck Athinuwick: Original People of the Great Swampy Land*. Winnipeg: University of Manitoba Press, 2002.

Manitoba Free Press. "Antoine Vermette, Red River Pioneer, Tells of Manitoba's Buffalo." August 26, 1910.

Morice, A. G., o.m.i. *L'Église catholique dans l'Ouest canadien: Du lac Supérieur au Pacifique (1659–1905)*. 3 vols. Winnipeg, MB, 1912.

Payment, Diane P. *Batoche (1870–1910)*. Saint-Boniface, MB: Éditions du Blé, 1983.

———. *"Les gens libres—Otipemisiwak": Batoche, Saskatchewan 1870–1930*. Ottawa, ON: Parks Canada, 1990.

Pearce, Margaret Wickens. "Native Mapping in Southern New England Indian Deeds." In *Cartographic Encounters: Perspectives on Native American Mapmaking and Map Use*, edited by Malcolm G. Lewis, 157–86. Chicago, IL: University of Chicago Press, 1998.

Raffestin, Claude. *Pour une géographie du pouvoir*. Paris, France: LITEC, 1980.

Ray, Arthur J. *I Have Lived Here since the World Began: An Illustrated History of Canada's Native People*. Toronto, ON: Lester Publishing Limited & Key Porter Books, 1996.

———. *Indians in the Fur Trade: Their Role as Trappers, Hunters, and Middlemen in the Lands Southwest of Hudson Bay, 1660–1870*. Toronto, ON: University of Toronto, 1998.

Rivard, Étienne. "Prairie and Québec Métis Territoriality: *Interstices territoriales* and the Cartography of In-Between Identity." PhD diss., Department of Geography, University of British Columbia, 2004.

———. "Territorialité métisse dans le Nord-Ouest canadien au XIXe siècle: exploration cartographique et toponymique." *Cahiers franco-canadiens de l'Ouest* 14, nos. 1–2 (2002): 7–32.

Rondeau, Clovis, Rév. *La Montagne de Bois (Willow Bunch Sask): Histoire de la Saskatchewan méridionale*. Quebec, QC: L'Action Sociale, 1923.

Sack, Robert David. *Human Territoriality: Its Theory and History*. Cambridge, UK: Cambridge University Press, 1986.

Sealey, Bruce D. *Stories of the Metis*. Winnipeg: Manitoba Metis Federation, 1975.

Spry, Irene M. "Introduction." In *Buffalo Days and Nights (as told by Henry Thompson)*, pp. ix–xxxii. Calgary, AB: Fifth House, 1999.

St-Onge, Nicole. *Saint-Laurent, Manitoba: Evolving Me¥tis Identities, 1850–1914*. Regina, SK: Canadian Plains Research Center, University of Regina, 2004.

Taché, Alexandre A. *Esquisse sur le nord-ouest de l'Amérique*. Montréal, QC: Typographie du Noveau Monde, 1869.

Tough, Frank. *"As Their Natural Resources Fail": Native Peoples and the Economic History of Northern Manitoba, 1870–1930*. Vancouver: University of British Columbia Press, 1996.

Weekes, Mary. *The Last Buffalo Hunter (as told to her by Norbert Welsh)*. Saskatoon, SK: Fifth House, 1994.

6

ETHNOGENESIS, LANGUAGE, AND IDENTITY

The Genesis of Michif and Other Mixed Languages

PETER BAKKER

The Red River Métis in Canada and the United States are a population with a mixed ancestry, and some speak a mixed language. In this chapter, I discuss the connection between ethnogenesis and the emergence of new languages, the different social situations that lead to the genesis of mixed languages, and the extent to which the structure of a new language correlates with certain social situations. My main argument is that a new ethnic identity is connected with the emergence of a new language, and the type of language that emerges is connected to a specific sociohistorical context.

Michif and the Métis

The name Michif is used for a few different languages. One is a distinct variety of French spoken today mostly by the Métis in Saint Ambroise and Saint Laurent, Manitoba, as well as pockets in Manitoba, Saskatchewan, northern Alberta, and elsewhere. It is also called Michif French or Métis French. It must have come into being as a result of French speakers from the St. Lawrence River area and Acadia coming into contact with aboriginal languages of northern regions. Except for pronunciation, a few deviant verb forms, some minor syntactic differences, and a handful of loanwords from Ojibwe and Cree, it is a variety of French.[1] It is a distinct and instantly recognizable variety, different from both eastern and western Canadian French.[2]

The second language called Michif is a mixed language that combines Michif French and southern Plains Cree, a Native American language of the vast Algonquian family. This Michif is spoken by some Métis in Manitoba, Saskatchewan, North Dakota, Montana, and elsewhere.

The third language called Michif is spoken in northwestern Saskatchewan, notably Île-à-la-Crosse and the communities between Green Lake and Buffalo Narrows. In some of the literature it has been called Northern Michif. This language is a variety of northern Plains Cree with a considerable number of loans from mission French (acquired in church, school, and the missions) and Métis French.[3] Today, most speakers in that region, especially the younger ones, tend to replace almost all the French words with English. This language has been called Michif primarily only in the last few decades. Before that, it was called *Cris* in French, *Cree* in English, and *Niihiyawiiwin* in the local Cree language. The last word is the usual Cree term for the Cree language. In southern Plains Cree it is *Neehiyaweewin*, which is the language of the *Neehiyaw(ak)*, or Cree. Use of this word does not mean that the people identify as Cree; rather, they identify as Métis. The second language called Michif is also called *Cree* by its speakers (*ãn kri/en Cris*).[4] Thus, several different languages are called Michif, and different languages are called Cree among the Métis.

In this chapter, I focus on the second of these languages, the mixed language with roughly equal numbers of Cree and French elements, without claiming that the other Métis languages or varieties do not deserve the same degree of attention. When I write "Michif" in this paper, I mean the mixed Cree–French language. In order to illustrate the nature of the language, I start with a fragment of a story, as narrated by Norman Fleury from Manitoba. In the text, spelled in a phonemic way, French words are given in *italics* and Cree words in Roman **boldface** type. Under each line, I provide a translation of each part of each word so that the readers can get a sense of the structure of words and sentences. Beneath that, I give a rough overall translation in quotation marks.[5]

(1) A Michif fairy tale (fragment)
(1a) *Zha parii*   **chi-aachimo-yaan**   *mon istweer pur* **awa** *la pchit*
                                                fiy, la Sandrieuz

I-am ready   to-tell-I   *my story about* this *the little*
                                             girl the Cinderella

"I am ready to tell my story about this little girl, Cinderella"

(1b) **Kiitaaw,**   **kii-ishinihkaashow**
This-was-said-about-her   She-was-called

"This was said about her, that was her name"

(1c) **E-kii-kitimaahikaasho-t**
that-she-was-pitiful

"She was pitiful"

(1d) *la pchit fiy* **awa**   *sitenn*   *pchit orfalinn*
The little girl this   *she-was-a*   *little orphan-girl*

"This little girl, she was a little orphan"

(1e) **and** *pi* **o-paapaa-wa   kiiwiikimeeyiiw**   **onhin** *la fam*-**a**
eetikween
And *and* her-father-OBV   he-had-been-married-to   this *the*
her it-is-said   *woman*OBV

"And her father, it is said, had married this woman."

This is a fragment of the Cinderella story, which is part of the Métis oral tradition. It is told throughout the Métis homeland, and storytellers usually trace it back to their grandparents. That Cinderella is called La Cendrieuse, instead of the ubiquitous Cendrillon as heard in France, Quebec, and the French creoles of the Caribbean, points to a different tradition, not one learned in school or from films.[6] To my knowledge, Cendrieuse was or is also used only in rural Acadia and Newfoundland.[7]

The most striking feature of this very special language in which the story is told is that the verbs are all Cree (the equivalents of "to tell, to say, to be called, to be pitiful, to marry"), but the nouns are all French (*histoire* "story," *fille* "girl," *Cendrieuse* "Cinderella," *orpheline* "orphan girl," and *femme* "woman"). There are two exceptions: the verb "to be" in *sitenn* (*c'est une,* "it is a") is French; the forms of the copula are indeed normally from French. Second, the noun *paapaa* "father" is one of a handful of Cree nouns used in Michif. English adjectives translate as French adjectives (*petite* "little," *prêt* "ready") or as Cree verbs ("to be pitiful"). Furthermore, demonstratives (this, that) are all Cree, and possessive pronouns (my, his, her) are French with French nouns (*mon histoire* "my story") and Cree with Cree nouns ("her father"). French nouns preserve the definite and indefinite articles from French (*le, la* "the"; *un, une* "a") with French gender marking, and Cree demonstratives are inflected for Cree animate/inanimate gender and also for a functional distinction that distinguishes subjects or agents from objects or patients/undergoers of an action. All words are either completely Cree or completely French, with one exception in this fragment: the last French noun gets a Cree noun ending -*a*, again one that distinguishes subjects from objects. This fragment is not at all exceptional—the noun–verb dichotomy is pervasive through all of the language.[8]

Michif is not spoken by all Métis. It has probably always been a minority language among Métis. Some were predominantly or exclusively French speakers, whereas others were speakers of Saulteaux, Swampy Cree, or Plains Cree. Until the first half of the twentieth century, most Métis spoke several of these languages.

It could be said that Michif shows "cohabitation" of two structural systems in one language. The table below shows how the different categories or parts of speech are either predominantly Cree or French, and that there is a roughly equal distribution between the languages. These numbers are based on samples of the speech from approximately twenty-five speakers from all over the Metis homeland (Manitoba, Saskatchewan, North Dakota).

Who are the people who speak the Michif discussed in this chapter? They are all descendants of the Red River Métis, the early nineteenth-century inhabitants of the area of present-day Winnipeg. Only some Red

TABLE 6.1.   Approximate Proportion of Language Source for Each Grammatical Category

Category	Language(s)
Nouns	83–94% French, rest Cree, Ojibwe, English
Verbs and copulas	88–99% Cree, few French verbs, some mixed Cree–French
Question words	Almost all Cree
Personal pronouns	Almost all Cree
Adverbial particles	70% Cree, 30% French
Postpositions	Almost all Cree
Coordinate conjunctions	55% Cree, 40% French, 5% English
Prepositions	70–100% French, rest Cree
Numerals	Almost all French
Demonstratives	Almost all Cree
Negation	Roughly 70% French, 30% Cree

Adapted from Peter Bakker, *"Language of Our Own."*

River Métis were Michif speakers, presumably the buffalo hunters and their descendants, whereas the farmers were predominantly French speakers.[9] The evidence is threefold: first, the location of Michif-speaking communities coincides with the wintering camps of the bison-hunting Métis; these were Saint Joseph/Walhalla, ND, Pembina, Wood Mountain, SK, Touchwood Hills, Cypress Hills, SK, and the Souris, MB, area near Turtle Mountain, ND, all in Manitoba, Saskatchewan, and North Dakota.[10] The second piece of evidence includes remarks on language use by contemporary observers. In farming communities, visitors mentioned the use of French; with hunters, visitors mentioned the use of an indigenous language.[11] Finally, family histories and genealogy often end up with ancestors involved in bison hunt.[12] The Métis Nation and the language both developed in the early 1800s, based on the available evidence. (I do not discuss other mixed groups here, such as the Scottish "halfbreeds.")

The Métis are persons of mixed European (French) and Native American (mostly Ojibwe and Cree) ancestry and descendants of marriages between French and British fur traders and Native American women. The word Michif (from the Métis pronunciation of the older French word *Mitif*) means the same as Métis or Mestizo—a person of mixed Native American–European ancestry. Michif and Michif French speakers use the word "Michif" for both the language and their ethnicity. Thus, there is a clear connection between identifying as Métis and speaking a Michif language.

Language and Identity

How did the Michif language come into being? The answer is tightly connected to the question of identity. Language and identity are associated in two ways. Language is part of one's collective identity (i.e., as an individual, one shares part of one's identity with those who speak the same variety, dialect, or language as oneself). Language is also part of one's individual identity (i.e., one's individual linguistic traits are part of one's personal identity). These two sides of identity are connected with two social–psychological tendencies in humans that partly contradict each other. Individuals want to belong to some group or collectivity, yet they want to be different from others, sometimes also from individuals in the same group. People express both their belonging and their individuality through language, clothing, hair styles, or tattoos. A distinct identity may lead to different appearances and distinct ways of speaking.

When one uses a language, one communicates in two different ways. On the one hand, there is the content of the message. This message can be expressed directly ("I want to go to bed") or indirectly ("It is getting late," implying and meaning, "I want to go to bed"). On the other hand, there is the way that the message is delivered. Speakers can reveal a lot by their particular way of speaking. They do this, for instance, by choosing a particular language or dialect (e.g., choosing English when among francophone Quebeckers, or Cockney English in rural Britain), by having a foreign accent (an accent might reveal one as an immigrant or a person from a dialect-speaking region), by word choice (e.g., interlacing the message with swears or not), or by using polite or less polite forms (*Du* or *Sie* in German, or *tu* or *vous* in French). Many of these choices reveal an attitude that a speaker may have toward the conversation partner. Listeners are usually quite sensitive to such clues, however subtle they may be. Even minute differences may reveal speakers' ethnic identity, gender, class, and/or perceived relationship to the listener.[13] Some of these clues are largely subconscious, whereas others are obvious to all.

Thus, language use can be adjusted to a certain extent in order to express a desired change of identity. One can try to change one's language and try to speak like others in order to belong to a different or additional group. Sociolinguists—scholars who study the connection between language and society—use the term "convergence" if speakers choose to speak the same way as the group to which they want to belong, and "divergence" if they choose to speak differently from the group, whether to express individuality or to show adherence to a different group.

Convergence and divergence are two sides of the same coin. When trying to be more similar to members of group A, one may also become more different from members of group B. The desire to be different is closely related to the desire to belong. These aspects of one's individual and group identity can be expressed in a range of different ways beyond language and language use: clothing, choice of food, body decoration, or music choice.

In the desire to belong to some other group, and the ensuing development and adoption of certain language features, one can distinguish three groups: innovators, trendsetters, and trend followers. Innovators are those who start using a certain new word, a new sound, or a new construction and introduce it into the community. Perhaps they have "invented" the innovation themselves or have heard it from someone else outside the community. These innovations may or may not be adopted by others. Whether or not the innovation is adopted probably depends on the status of the innovator in the society, community, or network. If the innovation is adopted, trendsetters take it over, and people are often aware of these changes, at least in the initial stages. Later, the rest of society may take over such changes—as trend followers—when the changes are no longer considered odd.[14] Such patterns are quite typical of all kinds of changes, not only in language, but also in fashion or art.

A language-related issue in this connection is the use of deviant writing in electronic text messages, a medium used primarily by young people. The standard spelling of words in electronic messages is changed and sent either via mobile phones or during computer chats or in e-mail messages. Some of these are abbreviations ("4get"), some require an equal effort from the writer (Danish *knus* "hug" written as *knuz*), and some are actually more time consuming, such as when writing words with alternating uppercase and lowercase letters. Such changes can affect not just a simple modification, but a wholesale change of a language, as has happened with the Michif language.

Linguistic Engineering: Hanging One's Language on Purpose

Most research on language change relates to more-or-less subconscious changes in language. Research on different types of conscious innovations in language is more marginal. In recent years, researchers have been trying to come to grips with what has been called linguistic engineering,[15] which, in extreme cases, can lead to "genetically modified" language or languages. Both monolinguals and bilinguals can do this, but bilinguals have more codes at their disposal, thus allowing a wider range of choices.

Monolinguals can change their language by modifying existing words in their language in some systematic way. One can, for instance, add a fixed syllable after each vowel. This happens in languages of the Pig Latin type: *Yougou agoudd agou sygoullagoublegou*, in which (in this case) a syllable /gu/, written "gou," is added after each vowel sound. Even though the pattern is simple and transparent, such modified languages are impossible to decode for the untrained ear.

Monolinguals can also reverse words or syllables. In French suburbs, for instance, a language called Verlan is spoken. The word *Verlan* is based on the French word *l'envers* (the reverse), which is based on the spoken, not written, language. Somewhat simplified, words with two syllables reverse their order (*céfran* from *français*, "French"). In a one-syllable word, the consonants shift position, a vowel is added to the end, and the first vowel is always "eu" (*reupé* from *père*, "father"). Such languages are always in-group languages, usually based on the spoken language of the surrounding community but occasionally based on the written language.

Monolinguals typically manipulate the syllables, letters, or phonemes (sounds) of their mother tongue. Multilinguals, however, have additional means at their disposal. Speakers of several languages can use words from one of those languages (always the ones not known locally) and insert them into the patterns of the other language. Only the bilingual group members can understand utterances containing elements from several languages. For example, the language structure of the Romanichals in Britain, also known as Gypsy-Travellers, is quite clearly English—the sound system, the endings, and the sentence structure are identical to English—but all of the content words are not:

> *Puri mOnušini* and a *puri* old *rai*. They had *yek chavi*, a *rakli*, and *yeka divés* there was a *muš jal* in' on the *drom dikin'* for *buti*.

The grammatical system (word order, endings, sound system) is English, but the vocabulary is completely Romani (Romani elements italicized), the language of the Roma, or Gypsies. It may be possible to understand an utterance such as this one only if one knows the equivalent Romani words (*phuri* "old," *manušni* "woman," *raj* "gentleman," *yekh* "one," *haj* "girl, daughter," *rakli* "non-Gypsy girl," *dives* "day," *murš* "man," *džal* "he goes," *drom* "road," *dikh-* "to see, look," and *buti* "work"). But even for those who speak English and know Romani (e.g., recent Romani immigrants from outside Britain), it might initially be unintelligible.[16]

In another example, the language of the Island Carib men, who originally inhabited some of the Caribbean islands, combines the vocabulary of a Carib language with the grammatical structure of an Arawak language, especially in conversations involving women. Carib and Arawak are two very different, nonrelated languages. In the men's language, the morphemes in italics are from Arawak and other elements (in Roman boldface type) are from Carib.

nemboui-*a-tina*	*t*-**ibonam**	(male style)
chile-*a-tina*	*t*-**one**	(female style)
come-*PAST-I*	*her*-towards	

"I have come to her"

This language is the result of a rather catastrophic event. According to the oral history of this group, Carib-speaking warriors from the mainland of South America invaded some of the islands where Arawak-speaking people were living. The local Arawak men were killed by the Carib invaders, and the Arawak women were taken as wives by the Caribs, creating a new ethnic group in the next generations. The mixture of their groups became part of their collective identity, and their language likewise blended Arawak and Carib elements.[17] The endings are Arawak, and the content words Carib.

Such radical changes as in the case of Michif, Angloromani, or Island Carib are not natural changes, at least not when they take place at such grand scale. They cannot be unconscious changes, from one generation to the other. The changes must be the result of conscious manipulation.

What could be the motive for these intentional changes to languages, both among monolinguals and bilinguals? It must be a perception, or a desire, to be different. The theoretical contributions of social scientists like Frederik Barth and Benedict Anderson come to mind.[18] Anderson discussed how people create the community, or an image of the community, of which they are part, even though they know only a minor part of the population of that community. In addition, the pillars of that community are just as often real as they are fictitious. In his book *Ethnic Groups and Boundaries*, Barth discussed the (real or perceived) differences between ethnic groups and the symbolic boundaries that group members uphold—or create—in order to distinguish their own group from others.

Both ideas appear to fit what happened in the cases of the Romanichals and the Island Caribs. The Romanichals are a distinct community in British society, whose members often live separated from others in caravan sites, and they usually choose their partners among their own group rather than the society at large. Their language, or their variety of

English, sets them symbolically apart from the rest of society, just as their dwelling sets them physically apart. Their language creates a boundary between themselves and other English speakers. The language is generally used only at special occasions, not as a means of daily interaction, typically when solidarity within the group, or distancing from others, is at stake.[19] The first generation of Island Caribs did not want to be assimilated into their fathers' group, the Carib speakers who had massacred their relatives. They expressed their distinctness by not adopting the Carib language of their fathers and by preserving as much of the indigenous Arawak language of their mothers as possible, meanwhile using some Carib words with their fathers. Thus, they resisted assimilation and created new boundaries and a new community, and they intentionally created a new, mixed language that symbolized their special position in local society.

Michif is also a mixed language, but it does not show the same dichotomy as the examples of the mixed languages discussed above. Michif displays a mixture of nouns from one language and verbs from another. However, the social situation in which Michif came into being is quite similar to those by which some other mixed languages came into being. The Garifuna, the Métis, and others all descend from new, ethnic groups that came about by men from one group having wives from some other group. Their descendants identify as a mixed group and speak a mixed language. In most cases, this is a mixture of one lexicon with another grammatical system, but in the case of Michif it is the nouns of one language and the verbs of another. This combination has been explained by taking the complexity of the Cree verb into consideration.[20] In theory, Cree verbs can consist of more than twenty consecutive morphemes, and even the stems consist of smaller elements.[21] Furthermore, it is very difficult to find exact boundaries between roots and derivational and inflectional elements in Cree. If one considers the Cree verbs to consist solely of bound, grammatical morphemes, then the outcome of the mixture of Cree grammar with French verbs would rather consist of Cree verbs and French nouns. In the next section, I try to locate the genesis of Michif in space and time, and I discuss in more detail the motivation for the genesis or creation.

Michif Genesis: When, Where, and Why?

The biological mixture of two individuals speaking different languages never leads to a systematic language mixture among their descendants.

Children of mixed marriages speak the language, or languages, of their parents; they do not create a new language or a mixture of the two, except, of course, for occasional loanwords. A collectivity of people is apparently needed for a new language to be created out of the two spoken in a community. Furthermore, Olive Dickason showed that the descendants of Europeans and Native Americans along the Canadian east coast did not develop a distinct sense of identity. The children were raised as Indians in their mother's families, or as French in their father's family. Even today in aboriginal communities, physical appearance is much less important than appropriate behavior, which could mean that skin color, for example, at that time in aboriginal families did not play a role. A casual comparison of cases of intermarrying communities suggests that a certain quantity of mixed couples is required for the development of a new, mixed identity.[22] However, more research is required to establish the exact conditions. The crucial difference between the East and the West in Canada seems to have been that only the people of mixed French–Native American ancestry in the West started to identify as a separate group rather than as members of their mothers' or fathers' ethnic groups. As adults, they called themselves "La Nouvelle Nation" in the early 1800s, and there is reason to assume that the genesis of the mixed Michif language took place in the same period.[23]

The western Canadian Métis were connected to the land, some as farmers, others as hunters. They were considered distinct from both French and Indians. This distinctiveness was manifested in their clothing, identity, cultural utterances, and hybrid mythology. They had a distinct society not only in their own eyes, but also in the eyes of the Europeans and the First Nations.

Many Métis individuals were multilinguals, speaking the languages of their mothers and the language of their fathers, a multilingualism that continued into the twentieth century, with the mixed language added to the preexisting aboriginal and European languages. The bilinguals had every opportunity to combine their languages into a new system, which they apparently did in or around the first decades of the nineteenth century. The creation of Michif was an "act of identity" in which a language was created for the expression of a new identity.[24]

When considering other cases of linguistic creativity elsewhere in the modern world, it is apparent that teenagers are mostly responsible for the creation of new language varieties, such as the multilingual ethnolects[25] of the urban centers of western Europe (e.g., Murks and Straattaal in the Netherlands; Kanakisch in Germany; the unnamed immigrant varieties of Denmark; and the above-mentioned Verlan of Paris). These multi-ethnolects are used by second-generation immigrants and symbolize their distinctness in society but, at the same time, their connections to both the new land and the parents' country of origin.

The creation of Michif was also an act of resistance. The newly emerged Métis identity and the new language symbolized a break with their parents and parent cultures. Not all Métis became speakers of the mixed language. Métis farmers were culturally closer to the French culture, and they predominantly transmitted the French language to their children, whereas the buffalo hunters were much closer to the First Nations in their lifestyle. The linguistic act of identity was the creation of a new language, which expressed both a connection with the ancestral cultures and, at the same time, a form of resistance against them.

The Gradual Emergence of New Languages and the Sudden Genesis of Mixed Languages

In the preceding sections, we have seen that neither the Métis people nor the Michif language existed before a certain date. It is impossible to provide an exact date for the genesis of the population or the language (nothing before 1780–90?). It is also clear that Metis people emerged as a separate ethnic group fairly suddenly, within a very short time frame of a few decades. Furthermore, indirect evidence suggests that the language also emerged rapidly. This swiftness contrasts with the more common development of new ethnicities, such as the Dutch, Italians, or French or, in North America, Ojibwe or Montagnais. In the European context, we can distinguish between an identity connected to a certain state (e.g., the Netherlands, Italy, and France) from an ethnic identity connected to a different heritage within a state (e.g., Frisians in the Netherlands, Sardinians in Italy, and Bretons and Basques in France). For the Dutch, it is very difficult to pinpoint when they became a distinct ethnic group. State borders have changed frequently in the past five centuries or so, and a range of foreign powers (Spanish, Austrian, French, German) have dominated portions of the area of what is today the Netherlands. Italy existed for much of its history as independently governed regions, united only in relatively recent times, and ethnic and regional minorities still aspire to more autonomy. France is a centralized state where the French language has dominated the past 200 years at the expense of at least a half-dozen ethnic minorities with their own language or patois. It is impossible to say when France became French—that is, a country once dominated by a Celtic language (Gaulish) in a country named after a Germanic group (the Franks) and now speaking a Romance language. Both at the state level and that of ethnicity of minorities, these collective identities developed relatively slowly.

In most cases, languages also evolve or change slowly, even if it is almost always impossible to point out a distinct point of transition. Grandchildren speak slightly different from their grandparents, and the inhabitants of one village speak slightly different than those in the next village, but the language is still considered the same. However, at some point the varieties will be considered distinct enough for its speakers to claim that it is a different language (e.g., German and Dutch; French and Spanish). Linguists are unable to give fixed criteria as to when vulgar Latin became French or Italian or when the Dutch language split off from a broader Germanic language. The fluidity of borders between different languages is true not only through time, but also through space. Dialect continua of Germanic and Romance languages typically straddle state borders, and neighboring languages often share dialectal features across linguistic borders.

These dialect continua are natural and universal as are developments through time, where a language may split into dialects, and these dialects into separate languages no longer understandable to others. Regional and ethnic dialects emerge. Newfoundland English, Toronto English, and Cree English may all be partly unintelligible to speakers of the standard language. The same can be seen in First Nations languages, where we also find continua and dialect splits.[26] In other words, the default pattern for the genesis of a new ethnic group is slow, occurring over many centuries, without clear boundaries in time, and with often arbitrary boundaries in space. Languages also develop slowly into new, distinct varieties.

Ethnicity and language are often connected, and the emergence of a new ethnic or state identity is often connected with the development of a new language. When Norway became independent from Denmark in the 1800s, after centuries of domination by the Danish language, attempts were made to develop a Norwegian language based on rural varieties, as different as possible from Danish. More recently, the independence of Bosnia led to an emphasis on and implementation of minor differences between the language spoken in Bosnia compared with varieties of the same language spoken in Serbia and Croatia. In just a few years, a new language, Bosnian, came into being. In the case of Bosnian and Norwegian languages, the newly labeled languages are not radically distinct from their predecessors. It is not only via new state formations that new languages get labeled. New languages can also develop when a new ethnicity emerges from the combination of two earlier separate groupings. However, in the case of these newly emerged ethnic groups, circumstances may also lead to the genesis of new languages, but here the result may be much more radical.

Sudden Genesis of New Languages: Four Types

This chapter focuses on new peoples who came about in ways similar to the Métis. That is, men from one ethnic/language group immigrated to an area where they married women of another ethnic/language group, and their descendants—perhaps even their children, just the second generation—came to consider themselves a new ethnic group, characterized by the double ancestry of their paternal and maternal lineage. Here, these new ethnicities created a new language as an act of identity. Their distinctness as a people was reflected in their language. The new language was created as a conscious action and emerged in a very short time. It must have been conscious, because such languages are associated with very specific social events (métissage, or intercultural mixing, and the emergence of a new intermediate group; or bilingual nomads who settle). It also must have been rapid in that the Michif language must have existed in the 1840s if not earlier—just a few generations (possibly only one) after the first mixed marriages. From other cases, we know that a mixed language can develop within one generation.[27]

Let me emphasize that such ethnogenesis and language genesis are not the only examples of identity acts connected with the creation of a new language. One can distinguish at least four main types of new languages connected with an act of identity: in-group languages (e.g., Verlan), pidgins (e.g., West Africa), creoles (e.g., Tok Pisin), and intertwined/mixed languages (e.g., Angloromani). Pidgins and creoles emerge in quite different circumstances: when two people meet who have no language in common, a pidgin may develop to facilitate understanding. Pidgins are makeshift languages that allow only direct communication and a limited range of subjects. A creole can be said to be a pidgin that becomes a native language, or a main language, and hence a "real" and complete language. As pidgins and creoles are only marginally relevant for the genesis of mixed languages, these are not discussed further here. I focus on mixed languages.

In-group Languages

Members of social groups who wish to distinguish themselves from mainstream society, or even from their slightly larger microsocial group, such as classmates, may develop their own distinct speech variety more or less consciously. In major and minor language groups, there are subsets of individuals who add syllables to the words of their language, reverse existing words, add words from foreign languages, or just pronounce a few words differently in order to create a means of communication intelligible only to the intimates of the subgroup. If the members of the group are monolinguals, one typically finds phonological changes, such as the addition of a syllable after each vowel or the reversal of words.

Mixed Languages

In the preceding sections, we have seen two examples of languages of mixed people, Island Caribs and Michifs. Two more examples of newly developed mixed groups from different parts of the world may illustrate the connection between a new hybrid ethnicity and the creation of a new mixed language.

In South Africa, marital units of speakers of Dutch/Afrikaans and speakers of the local Khoenkhoen language created a community of people who call themselves Basters (also Oorlams or Griekwas). Their ethnic name is derived from Dutch "bastaard," related to English "bastard," stressing their special status as children of the country, the result of the contact between Europeans and the local population. They also developed a mixed language combining Khoenkhoen (in italics below) with Dutch (in Roman boldface type below):

Heeltemaal-*se*	**natuur**-*a-xu*	**bedorven**-*he* (Basters: Khoenkhoen and Dutch)
completely–ADV	nature–CAS–PREP	rotten–PASS

Van nature helemaal bedorven (Dutch)
"totally rotten in nature"

The Peranakans are a group who descend from Chinese fathers and Indonesian mothers from Java. The Chinese fathers came as traders some centuries ago and used the pidgin Bazaar Malay as their language of communication. The language of this newly emerged ethnic group combines the lexicon of their fathers' (contact) language and the grammatical system of their mothers' language. The elements in italics are from Malay, the words in Roman boldface type are from Javanese:

Mama-e	*itu*	*sudah*	**rondo**	**dadine**	*ngerja* -**qno**	**japet**
Mother-her	*that*	*already*	widow	so	*make*–T	cake

"her mother who is a widow made these cakes"

The examples in this section (Angloromani, Island Carib, Basters, Peranakans) show a dichotomy between languages that has been observed in almost all of the few dozen mixed languages. Some are spoken by biologically and culturally mixed groups such as the Basters, Island Carib, and Peranakans, whereas others are spoken by settled nomads, as exemplified by Angloromani. All four languages display a dichotomy between grammatical elements (bound morphemes, phonology, syntax) from one language and lexicon (vocabulary) from another. Of course, there is a gliding scale between grammatical and lexical elements, such as in certain free grammatical elements like pronouns or certain adverbs. In those areas, we find variation in whether the words come from one language or the other, or from both. This variation is found with both individual speakers or between speakers of the same language, and, at a more abstract level, also between the different mixed languages. Some speakers of Michif use more French adpositions (prepositions before and after the nouns) or adverbs, whereas others use more of them from Cree.

Most of these groups tend to use an autonym (ethnic name people give themselves, e.g., the Dutch call themselves "Nederlander") that refers to their double ancestry. There are about ten such mixed groups from all over the world that use, or until recently used, a mixed language and take pride in their mixed ancestry. Undoubtedly there are other groups elsewhere who may not have attracted the attention of scientists or travelers.

Mixed-Descent Groups and Mixed Languages: What Is the Relation?

The groups thus far identified as mixed-descent groups are Métis (Cree, French), Basters (Dutch/Afrikaans, Khoenkhoen), Petjo/Indo-Europeans (Malay, Dutch), Javindo (Javanese, Dutch), Chindos (Javanese, Malay), Island Carib (Arawak, Carib), Philippine mixed group (Tagalog, Spanish), and perhaps the Okrikas (Igbo, Ijo).

We can formulate a number of generalizations about these groups. Their members are not monolinguals; rather, they speak other languages in the mixed group beside the mixed language. Usually the local language is known, sometimes also other languages. This finding is not surprising as the groups are not large or dominant enough to impose their in-group language on others, and they need to have a command of other languages in order to communicate with outsiders. The mixedness is reflected in many aspects of their cultures, such as distinctive clothing, food, music, and language; thus, they display a hybrid culture with its own unique developments. Many of these groups played an important role in the history of the region or states where they came into being—as traders, middlemen and explorers—but they often ended up on the margins of the greater society, and other groups started to dominate economically and politically. The nature of the mixed language makes clear that the first generation of speakers must have had a full command of the two source languages. There is hardly any loss of lexical or grammatical features in comparison to the source languages and in sharp contrast to what we find in creoles. Their mixed languages are of two structural types. Most combine the grammar (grammatical morphemes, function words, sound system) of one language with lexical words of another language. The language of the mothers—the local population—provides the grammatical system, and the language of the fathers, the lexical words. The mixed languages are typically based on vernacular forms of the languages, and in contrast to creoles, the new language displays no or only minimal reduction in the grammatical categories existing in the language from which the grammatical system is drawn. On the other hand, there are a few languages in which nouns from one language are combined with verbs from another. There are only two known to do this, Michif and Okrika of Nigeria.

For all of them, mixedness is a major part of their identity, and only a few mixed languages are spoken by groups where mixedness is not considered characteristic of their identity. Thus, there are mixed languages and there are self-identifying mixed peoples. The question posed here is, How big or significant is the overlap? Do all mixed peoples speak mixed languages, and are all the groups who speak a mixed language also biologically and culturally mixed?

Let us first look at the group of Gypsies and Travellers with mixed languages. Consider the Angloromani language example. Such groups have been identified in, among others, Britain (English), Spain (Spanish, Catalan, Basque), Scandinavia (Norwegian, Swedish, Low German), Turkey (Turkish), France (French), and perhaps also Germany (German), Hungary (Hungarian), and the Czech Republic (Czech). Other groups include the Irish Travellers (a non-Romani vocabulary with Gaelic or English), Armenian Gypsies (Lom vocabulary, Armenian grammar), Abdals (Persian vocabulary and Turkic grammar), and Iranian iron mongers (Gypsy vocabulary, Persian grammar).

Most of these groups keep a clear social distance from the surrounding societies, with whose members they rarely intermarry despite extensive contact. All of them have taken over major sociocultural traits of the surrounding populations, but there are attempts to stick to traditional economic activities (music, transport, services). Biological or cultural mixedness is never characteristic of their identity. In other words, the existence of mixed languages is not limited to groups who consider themselves mixed.

In preceding sections, three mixed groups and their mixed languages were discussed: the Peranakan, whose name means "locally born, creole, half"; the Basters, whose name refers to their dual ancestry; and the Island Carib, where the mixture is not reflected in their ethnic label and which is not the name they gave to themselves. In the seventeenth century they called themselves, according to a contemporary observer, *Callinago*, or *Calliponan* in the women's language.[28] The meanings of these terms are unknown to me.

Mixed Ethnic Groups with No Mixed Language

There are also many groups who are characterized as blended, and who consider themselves such, without there being a mixed language. In Mexico, for example, the main groups are Indians and Mestizos. The indigenous groups, if they have not shifted to Spanish, continue to speak their many indigenous languages, albeit it with different levels of Spanish influence.[29] The main mixed population in Mexico is generally called Mestizo, contrasting with the indigenous groups; however, with very few exceptions, they are speakers of Spanish, not speakers of a mixed language.

In other cases, DNA research has revealed that some ethnic groups are actually of mixed descent, even though this is not part of their identity. Research on Chukchi groups in Siberia has shown that their male ancestry is predominantly local, whereas their female ancestry is mostly Eskimo. Their language is not a mixed language but Chukchi, even though research has pointed out considerable influence on Chukchi from Eskimo, especially in the grammatical domain. This influence was apparently transmitted through the Eskimo mothers. There are countless other examples spread over the globe where a real or perceived dual ancestry is not connected to the existence of a mixed language.

Old Ethnic Groups with Mixed Languages

There are a few mixed languages spoken by "old" ethnic groups who do not belong to the category of settled nomads. Perhaps the best known of them is Media Lengua, or Little Quechua, spoken in a few communities in Ecuador.[30] People of clearly Native American affinity mix Spanish vocabulary with a Quechua grammatical system. Unmistakably identifying as Quechuas, the first generation of speakers may have acquired sufficient Spanish while working as manual workers during a period of industrialization. They are speakers of a mixed language, but they are ethnically Quechua.

In Australia, a number of aboriginal groups have witnessed younger generations developing new ways of continuing their ancestral languages, often by mixing it with exceptional amounts of English Creole. This mixing has been documented for Tiwi, Dyirbal, Gurinji, and Warlpiri. The nature of the mixtures is unique in all cases, but there are some common traits.[31] Some of the aboriginal morphology is lost, case marking is reduced and applied in ways different from the ancestral language, Kriol auxiliaries are used, and in some cases there is a split in categories (e.g., verbs and nouns). Their languages are mixed, but their identity is aboriginal. In short, there are non-mixed indigenous groups who speak mixed languages. There is no one-to-one correspondence between mixed languages and biologically mixed ancestry. On the other hand, the structures of these language do not show the combination of grammar and lexicon that we encounter in the other cases. Possibly these aboriginal mixed languages came into being in a more subconscious way.

Conclusion

The Michif language was created by French–Cree bilinguals as an act of identity when the new ethnic group emerged, thus expressing a form of resistance toward the cultures of both parents. Michif culture and language combine elements from both ancestral cultures yet also show certain innovations.

Forms of linguistic creativity resulting in the manipulation of existing languages into something (at least partially) new are commonly found in all places and times. However, the creation of mixed languages is relatively uncommon in the history of the world. Only a few dozen cases of mixed languages have been documented, which is a modest number, taking into account that around 7,000 languages are known to exist, or to have existed. Not all mixed languages are spoken by self-identifying mixed populations, and not all mixed populations speak mixed languages, regardless of how important the hybridity is to their identity.

We can now make a number of concluding observations. First, it is clear that creole languages came about in situations of multilingualism, with only limited immersion into the language of power but concurrent sudden loss of ancestral identity. The lack of a common language forced the population to create a makeshift language. These makeshift languages are comparatively less complex in that many distinctions and categories less crucial for communication do not get transferred into the new language, whereas some categories get reinstituted as soon as the speakers of the language need them. The forced process of ethnogenesis led to the unavoidable creation of a new language in a multilingual situation.

With regard to mixed languages, we have seen that there is significant overlap between self-defined mixed ethnic groups and the existence of mixed languages. Even though there is a clear correlation here, it is not certain whether ethnicity developed first or if there was a simultaneous process of genesis. In contrast to the creole situation, the genesis of the language is a voluntary process, instigated by a need to express a separate identity. The act of identity here is the expression of difference from ancestral groups. Nevertheless, there are also non-mixed groups with mixed languages. However, in the case of Media Lengua, some special historical events have been held responsible for the genesis. In the voluntary and conscious creation of new languages, complexities of the source languages are preserved, but in a forced situation the creators drop unnecessary complications because they are superfluous to communication. There are no mixed languages that developed in the absence of special social events that led to their genesis. This special event may be ethnogenesis, the formation of a social group, or resistance to ancestral groups.

Thus, there is a connection between ethnogenesis and the emergence of a new language, but this connection is not a mechanical and necessary one. The structural type of the emerging language is connected to the specific sociohistorical context, and mixed, new populations like Métis often have a grammatical system that is copied from an ancestral language rather than created anew, as in the case of creoles.

Notes

1. Dickason, "From 'One Nation' in the Northeast."
2. See, e.g., Papen, "Le parler français des Métis," "Sur quelques aspects structuraux du français," and "Le Mitchif."
3. An excellent dictionary of this variety is Ahenekew, *Michif/Cree Dictionary*. For an analysis of the French elements, see also Peter Bakker and Papen, "French Influence on the Native Languages."
4. For clarification, see Peter Bakker, "What is Michif?" See also Papen, "Langue(s) et identité(s) des Métis."
5. The language examples given in this chapter have the following structure: The first line gives the sentence in the original language. The second line gives a translation, where each meaningful part of the utterance is translated—a so-called "gloss." Here, content elements are in plain type, and grammatical elements in CAPITALS. The third line, between quotation marks, provides a translation into English. For details, see http://www.eva.mpg.de/lingua/resources /glossing-rules.php.
Abbreviations for grammatical terms used in the glosses are as follows: ADV = adverb; CAS = case marker, OBV = obviative, PASS = passive marker,

PAST = past tense, PREP = preposition, T = tense, 1 = first person (i.e., "I"), 2 = second person (i.e., "you"), and 3 = third person, (i.e. "he/she").

6. Belmont and Lemirre, *Sous la cendre.*

7. Haden, "La petite Cendrillouse"; and Thomas, *Two Traditions,* 182.

8. For more details on the language, see Peter Bakker, *"Language of Our Own"* and "What is Michif?"; Peter Bakker and Papen, "Michif"; Papen, "Le métif" and "Le Mitchif,"; and Barkwell, *La Lawng.*

9. Peter Bakker, *"Language of Our Own."*

10. Ibid., 171–73; and Giraud, *Le Métis Canadien,* 817–20.

11. Peter Bakker, *"Language of Our Own,"* 161–69.

12. Ibid., 169–71, 176.

13. Hay and Drager, "Sociophonetics."

14. Milroy, "Social Networks."

15. Golovko, "Language Contact and Group Identity."

16. Matras, *Romani in Britain.*

17. de Pury, "Le garifune, une langue mixte."

18. Anderson, *Imagined Communities;* and Barth, *Ethnic Groups and Boundaries.*

19. Matras et al., "Angloromani."

20. Peter Bakker, *"Language of Our Own."* See also Matras, "Mixed Languages"; and McConvell, "Unraveling Languages."

21. Peter Bakker, "Algonquian Verb Structure."

22. Dickason, "From 'One Nation' in the Northeast."

23. See Peter Bakker, *"Language of Our Own,"* for argumentation.

24. LePage and Tabouret-Keller, *Acts of Identity.*

25. An ethnolect is a variety of a language characteristic of an ethnic group (e.g., Cree English). In mixed communities—for example, among urban immigrants—it can be a multi-ethnolect, spoken by several ethnic groups. See Quist and Svendsen, *Multilingual.*

26. For Algonquian languages, see Rhodes and Todd, "Subarctic Algonquian Languages."

27. Muysken, "Media Lengua." Media Lengua was at the time spoken in a community where the older generation was monolingual in Quechua, the youngest generation was monolingual in Spanish, and the intermediate generation spoke Media Lengua as well as either Quechua or Spanish. Muysken relates the genesis of the language to the return of the Quechua speakers to their communities after having worked on the building of the local railroad. The fact that the new language was unintelligible for the parents is indicative enough for the fact that it must have been a conscious act: by speaking Media Lengua, these young people exclude the older people from their social world.

28. de Pury, "Le garifune, une langue mixte"; and de Pury and Lewis, *Language of the Callinago People.*

29. See, e.g., Dik Bakker et al., "Spanish Meets Guaraní, Otomí and Quichua"; Hill and Hill, *Speaking Mexicano;* Stolz and Stolz, "Funktionswortentlehnung in

Mesoamerika" and "Universelle Hispanismen?"; and Rendón, "Typological and Social Constraints on Language Contact."

30. Muysken, "Media Lengua"; and Rendon, "Typological and Social Constraints on Language Contact."

31. See McConvell, "Unraveling Languages."

Works Cited

Ahenekew, Vince. *Michif/Cree Dictionary. Nëhiyawêwin Masinahikan*. Saskatoon, SK: Saskatchewan Indian Cultural Centre, 1997. Reprint, Saskatoon, SK: Gabriel Dumont Institute, 2009.

Anderson, Benedict. *Imagined Communities: Reflections on the Origins and Spread of Nationalism*. New York, NY: New Left Books/Verso, 1983.

Bakker, Dik, Jorge Gómez Rendón, and Ewald Hekking. "Spanish Meets Guaraní, Otomí and Quichua: A Multilingual Confrontation." In *Aspects of Language Contact: New Theoretical, Methodological and Empirical Findings with Special Focus on Romancisation Processes*, edited by Thomas Stolz, Dik Bakker and Rosa Salas Palomo, 165–238. Berlin, Germany: Mouton de Gruyter, 2008.

Bakker, Peter. "Algonquian Verb Structure: Plains Cree." In *What's in a Verb?* (LOT Occasional Series 5), edited by Grazyna Rowicka and Eithne Carlin, 3–27. Utrecht, The Netherlands: LOT, 2006.

———. *"A Language of Our Own": The Genesis of Michif, the Mixed Cree–French Language of the Canadian Métis*. New York, NY: Oxford University Press, 1997.

———. "What is Michif?" In *La Lawng: Michif Peekishkwewin: The Heritage Language of the Canadian Metis: Manitoba Metis Federation Michif Language Program*. Vol. 1, *Language Practice*, edited by Lawrence Barkwell, 5–7. Winnipeg, MB: Pemmican Publications/Manitoba Metis Federation Michif Language Program, 2004.

Bakker, Peter, and Robert A. Papen. "French Influence on the Native Languages of Canada and Adjacent USA." In *Aspects of Language Contact: New Theoretical, Methodological and Empirical Findings with Special Focus on Romancisation Processes*, edited by Thomas Stolz, Dik Bakker, and Rosa Salas Palomo, 239–86. Berlin, Germany: Mouton de Gruyter, 2008.

———. "Michif: A Mixed Language Based on Cree and French." In *Contact Languages: A Wider Perspective*, edited by Sarah Grey Thomason, 295–363. Amsterdam, the Netherlands: John Benjamins, 1997.

Barkwell, Lawrence, ed. *La Lawng: Michif Peekishkwewin. The Heritage Language of the Canadian Metis*. 2 vols. Winnipeg, MB: Pemmican Publications/Manitoba Metis Federation Michif Language Program, 2004.

Barth, Frederik, ed. *Ethnic Groups and Boundaries: The social organization of culture difference*. Boston, MA: Little, Brown, 1969.

Belmont, Nicole, and Élisabeth Lemirre, eds. *Sous la cendre: figures de Cendrillon*. Paris, France: José Corti, 2007.

de Pury, Sybille. "Le garifune, une langue mixte." In *Langues de diaspora: Langues en contact*, edited by Anaïd Donabédian, special issue, *Faits de Langues* 18 (2001): 75–84.

de Pury, Sybille, and Marcella Lewis. *The Language of the Callinago People: Father Breton's Dictionnaire caraïbe–français (1665) compared with Garifuna*. Paris, France: Editions Sup-Infor, 2001.

Dickason, Olive P. "From 'One Nation' in the Northeast, to 'New Nation' in the Northwest: A Look at the Emergence of the Métis." In *The New Peoples: Being and Becoming Métis in North America*, edited by Jacqueline and Jennifer S. H. Brown, 19–36. Winnipeg: University of Manitoba Press, 1985.

Giraud, Marcel. *Le Metis Canadien. Son role dans l 'histoire des provinces de l 'Ouest*. Paris, France: Institut d'Ethnologie, Musée Nationale d'Histoire Naturelle, 1945.

Golovko, Evgenij V. "Language Contact and Group Identity: The Role of "Folk" Linguistic Engineering." In *The Mixed Language Debate*, edited by Y. Matras & P. Bakker, 177–207. Berlin, Germany: Mouton de Gruyter, 2003.

Haden, Ernest F. "La petite Cendrillouse, version acadienne de Cendrillon: étude linguistique." *Archives de folklore* 3 (1948): 21–34.

Hay, Jennifer, and Katie Drager. "Sociophonetics." *Annual Review of Anthropology* 36 (2007): 89–103.

Hill, Jane, and Kenneth Hill. *Speaking Mexicano: The Dynamics of Syncretic Language in Central Mexico*. Tucson: University of Arizona Press, 1986.

LePage, Robert, and Andrée Tabouret-Keller. *Acts of Identity: Creole-Based Approaches to Language and Identity*. Cambridge, UK: Cambridge University Press, 1985.

Matras, Yaron. "Mixed Languages: Re-examining the Structural Prototype." In *The Mixed Language Debate: Theoretical and Empirical Advances*, edited by Yaron Matras and Peter Bakker, 151–76. Berlin, Germany: Mouton de Gruyter, 2003.

———. *Romani in Britain*. Edinburgh, Scotland: Edinburgh University Press, 2010.

Matras, Yaron, Hazel Gardner, Charlotte Jones, and Veronica Schulmann. "Angloromani: A Different Kind of Language?" *Anthropological Linguistics* 49, no. 2 (2008): 142–84.

McConvell, Patrick. "Unraveling Languages: Multilingualism and Language Contact in Kalkaringi." In *Children's Language and Multilingualism: Indigenous Language Use at Home and School*, edited by Jane Simpson and Gillian Wigglesworth, 247–64. New York, NY: Continuum, 2008.

Milroy, Leslie. "Social Networks." In *The Handbook of Language Variation and Change*, edited by J. K. Chambers, P. Trudgill, and N. Schilling-Estes, 549–72. Oxford, UK: Blackwell, 2002.

Muysken, Pieter. "Media Lengua." In *Contact Languages: A Wider Perspective*, edited by Sarah Thomason, 365–426. Amsterdam, the Netherlands: John Benjamins, 1997.

Papen, Robert A. "Langue(s) et identité(s) des Métis de l'Ouest canadien." In *Patrimoine et identités en Amérique française*, edited by Par André Charbonneau et Laurier Turgeon. 211–49. Québec, QC: Presses de l'Université Laval, 2010.

————. "Le métif: Le nec plus ultra des grammaires en contact." *Revue Québécoise de Linguistique Théorique et Appliquée* 6, no. 2 (1987): 57–70.

————. "Le Mitchif: Langue Franco-Crie des Plaines." In *Le Français en Amérique du Nord: État Présent*, edited by Albert Valdman, Julie Auger, and Deborah Piston-Hatlen, 327–48. Saint-Nicolas, QC: Les Presses de l'Université Laval, 2005.

————. "Le parler français des Métis de l'Ouest canadien." In *Français d'Amérique: Variation, Créolisation, Normalisation*, edited by Patrice Brasseur, 147–61. Avignon, France: CECAV, Université d'Avignon, 1998.

————. "Sur quelques aspects structuraux du français des Métis de l'Ouest canadien." In *Variation et Francophonie*, edited by Aidan Coveney, Marie-Anne Hintze, and Carol Saunders, 105–29. Paris, France: L'Harmattan, 2004.

Quist, Pia, and Bente Ailin Svendsen, eds. *Multilingual Urban Scandinavia: New Linguistic Practices*. Bristol, UK: Multilingual Matters, 2010.

Rendón, Jorge Gómez. "Typological and Social Constraints on Language Contact: Amerindian Languages in Contact with Spanish" LOT diss., University of Amsterdam, 2008.

Rhodes, Richard, and Evelyn M. Todd. "Subarctic Algonquian Languages." In *Subarctic. Handbook of North American Indians 6*, edited by June Helm, 52–66. Washington, DC: Smithsonian Institution, 1981.

Stolz, Christel, and Thomas Stolz. "Funktionswortentlehnung in Mesoamerika: Spanish–amerinindischer Sprachkontakt." *Sprachtypologie und Universalienforschung* 49, no. 1 (1996): 86–123.

————. "Universelle Hispanismen? Von Manila über Lima bis Mexiko und zurück: Muster bei der Entlehnung spanischer Funktionswörter in die indigenen Sprachen Amerikas und Austronesiens." *Orbis* 39 (1997): 1–77.

Thomas, Gerald. *The Two Traditions: The Art of Storytelling amongst French Newfoundlanders*. St. John's, NF: Breakwater, 1993.

7

IN THE SHADOWS OF THE
HONORABLE COMPANY

Nicolas Chatelain and the Métis of Fort Frances

VICTOR P. LYTWYN

In the fall of 1875, a group of Métis at Fort Frances met with John S. Dennis, surveyor general of Canada, and agreed to join Treaty 3—the 1873 accord between the "Saulteaux Tribe of the Ojibbeway Indians" and Queen Victoria that involved a large tract of land in present-day northwestern Ontario and part of eastern Manitoba. Called "half-breeds" at the time, the Métis were part of what is now called the Métis Nation, comprising a distinct, self-identifying community with shared cultural and economic values. They were linked by internal marriages as well as external ties to other Métis communities in the Red River region of present-day Manitoba and other parts of the fur trade northwest, including Fort William and Sault Ste. Marie. They developed their own collective identity, elected their own leaders, and entered into political dialogues with the Canadian state. Known as the "Halfbreed Adhesion," the Fort Frances Métis Treaty promised reserves, annuities, and other treaty benefits to the Métis. It was the first treaty agreement in Canada to recognize the Métis as a distinct community with rights to land and other resources on par with the Anishinabeg First Nations who signed Treaty 3. Led by Nicolas Chatelain, an influential and charismatic veteran of the War of 1812, the Fort Frances Métis joined the treaty with expectations that they would be treated the same as the Anishinabeg of Treaty 3.

Chatelain was identified as the chief of the Fort Frances Métis in the treaty agreement that affirmed their interest or title to land in the Treaty 3 territory. However, within a few years of the treaty adhesion, the government of Canada reversed its position and refused to uphold its treaty promises. In this chapter I trace the origins of the Fort Frances Métis and their struggle for recognition as a distinct nation.

Fur Trade Origins

In 1805, the North West Company (NWC) and XY Company merged, setting the stage for a major reorganization of the Montreal-based fur trade operations. In the aftermath, the NWC closed trading posts and made deep cuts to its labor force. In 1810, the London-based Hudson's Bay Company (HBC) followed suit with a major reorganization of its fur-trading business in North America. This reorganization, too, led to post closures, pay cuts, and job losses.[1] In 1821, the HBC merged with the NWC, ending decades of fiercely competitive fur trade rivalry and once again signaling cost-cutting measures. After opting to keep the HBC name, one of the first orders of business was to again cut the new company's labor force. Within three months, 250 men were discharged,[2] and five years later more than 1,300 men were out of a job.[3] Some returned to their homes in Europe or Canada, and about 15 percent found new homes in the new Red River settlement in present-day Manitoba.[4] Many, however, continued to live in and around the trading posts where they had once been employed. Some engaged as part-time or seasonal labor for the HBC, whereas others, known as freemen, lived independently from the company. Many married local aboriginal women and raised families in the vicinity of the fur trade posts.[5] Known as Métis in the Red River area, and "half-breeds" in other parts of Rupert's Land, they established communities around many HBC trading posts. These communities emerged separately around the fur trade posts but were linked by the fur trade transport routes that moved people and goods in an ebb and flow from the St. Lawrence valley to Red River and the greater northwest. Red River was the hub, but Métis communities developed along the many spokes of the canoe routes that spiraled in and out of the fur trade regions of the Great Lakes and Northwest.[6] This pattern of Métis ethnogenesis was similar to that described by Jacqueline Peterson about fur trade communities south and west of the Great Lakes.[7]

After downsizing its labor force, the HBC increasingly filled new positions with Métis recruits. By the 1830s, more than 25 percent of its labor
force was native-born, rising to about 60 percent by 1860.[8] The HBC's
labor policy in the nineteenth century was shaped in part by difficulties
in obtaining suitable recruits in Europe and Lower Canada. However,
the company came to value the services of native-born recruits who
possessed valued skills, such as canoe-building, guiding, and interpreting. These skills were obtained from parents who were well versed
in obtaining a livelihood from the land.

Métis settlements were more prominent around the larger trading es-
tablishments of the HBC. These district headquarters maintained relatively large labor forces and continued to demand provisions and other
"country products" that could be supplied locally by freemen and their
families. In the Red River country, Métis communities supplied the HBC
with much-needed provisions. As Nicole St-Onge explained, "This surplus population specialized in the production of commodities indirectly
tied to the fur economy. A fluid Métis underclass of bison hunters, fishermen and salt makers emerged."[9] At Fort William, the former grand _en-
trepôt_ (warehouse) of the NWC on Lake Superior, a group of Métis continued to live in the vicinity of the post long after it faded from being the
busy rendezvous it was before 1821. Also known as freemen, they were
employed seasonally as fishermen, hunters, and canoe-builders as well as
in other occupations that required local knowledge and wilderness skills.
The distinction between freemen, "half-breeds," and Indians was often
blurred in the Fort William records. For example, a man named Louis
Ross was employed by the HBC in 1824–25 and referred to as a "half-
breed." In 1835, Louis Ross was called an Indian and hunted with other
Anishinabeg in the Fort William area; in the spring of 1836 he was associated with a group of freemen led by Michel Collin.[10]

The fur trade post on the Rainy River that came to be known as Fort
Frances[11] was another place where a Métis community developed in the
early nineteenth century. Fort Frances was located on the north bank of
the Rainy River, just below the Chaudière (Kettle) Falls (see fig. 7.1). The
falls were circumvented by a portage that cut across a neck of land
formed by a bend in the Rainy River. Fort Frances was the district headquarters of the HBC Lac la Pluie (Rainy Lake) district, which included
outposts from Sturgeon Lake in the east to Fort Alexander in the west
(see map 7.1). Before 1821, the Lac la Pluie post was an important depot

FIGURE 7.1.   Camp below the Chaudière Falls at Fort Frances in 1857. By Henry Y. Hind, *Narrative of the Canadian Red River Exploring Expedition of 1857 and of the Assiniboine and Saskatchewan Exploring Expedition of 1858* (London: Longman, Green, Longman and Roberts, 1860), 1:81.

along the NWC's main transport line into the Northwest. It was here that canoe brigades from Montreal and the Athabasca country met and exchanged furs and trade goods, which allowed crews from each brigade to return home before the onset of cold weather and the annual freeze-up. The Lac la Pluie post also served as a canoe-building center and collection place for provisions such as wild rice, Indian corn, and sturgeon. Nicholas Garry, visiting the Lac la Pluie post just after the union of the two companies in 1821, noted the strategic importance of the post, but predicted its demise under the new regime. He wrote, "The Post of Lac La Pluie or Rainy Lake before the Union of the two Companies was one of great Importance. Here the People from Montreal came to meet those who arrived from the Athabascan Country and exchange Lading with them receiving the Furs and giving the Goods to trade in Return. It will now become a mere trading Post as the Athapascans will be supplied from York Fort."[12] Garry was partially correct in his prognostication. The HBC did reorient its transportation network to focus on York Factory and abandoned the Montreal trade route that had previously run through Rainy River. However, the HBC was soon faced with competition in the Rainy River region from independent traders and the American Fur Company,

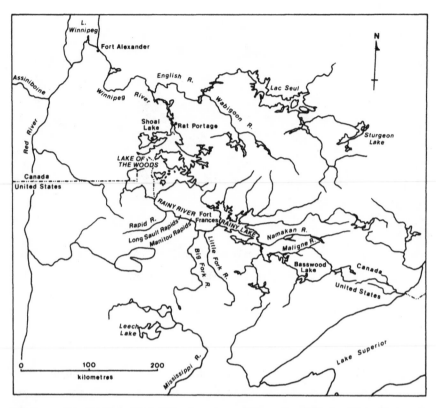

MAP 7.1. Lac La Pluie District and surrounding region. Map by Victor Lytwyn. Previously published in Tim E. Holzkamm, Victor P. Lytwyn, and Leo G. Waisberg, "Rainy River Sturgeon: An Ojibway Resource in the Fur Trade Economy," *The Canadian Geographer* 32, no. 3 (1988), 196.

and this competition necessitated maintaining a larger establishment in that area.[13] Although the HBC pushed the American Fur Company out of the Rainy River region in 1833 by a cash compensation deal, independent traders from Sault Ste. Marie, Red River, and St. Louis continued to operate in the Rainy River region. The fur trade continued to be a valuable enterprise in the region long into the nineteenth century, and the Métis community at Fort Frances was a vital part of the fur trade economy.

After the 1821 coalition, a group of freemen and their families established an independent settlement on the Rainy River at the confluence with the Little Fork River. Vincent Roy, who had previously worked for the NWC and HBC, established a farm there and attracted others who had been let go by the company.[14] According to HBC records, he had previously been allowed to clear some land beside the old NWC fort (located near Fort Frances). In 1823, the HBC manager bought Roy's claim to the land, explaining, "Old Roy was here today agreed to feed his cow and grind nine bushels of wheat for the spot of land that he cleared alongside the NW fort—it is true that he cannot sell it to any one but this is the cheapest mode of purchasing his claims—he was allowed to clear this spot by the late NWC and dwells in it this summer when he removed to the little forks."[15] Roy's son, Vincent Junior, was described as "a half Breed [who] speaks very little French[,] unacquainted with trade but acquainted with every part of the country and feared by the Natives."[16] Roy's establishment at the Little Fork River operated until 1837, when he and others left for Red River and other places. William Sinclair, HBC post manager at Fort Frances, recorded the end of the "little settlement" in his journal entry of June 1, 1837:

> The little settlement of the *little Forks* below this, is almost wholly abandoned by its inhabitants—one Simon Sayer only remaining to take care of the remaining property, moveable and immoveable, during the proprietor's absence [Vincent Roy Jr.] now on his voyage to Sault St. Mary's, where he is gone to settle his affairs and *square* his accounts with his American Employers if he can, with whom no doubt and it is hoped he has made a *slick bargain*. Old Vincent Roy is also off for Red River, where he intends to settle and end his well spent life amongst some of his quondam friends, may he be a good substantial farmer and a more fortunate one than hitherto—we wish him all success poor old man, at all events he will be more safe from Indian insults and aggressions.[17]

While Roy and others moved out of the region, other freemen and their families stayed in the Fort Frances area and developed a sense of community in the shadows of the HBC post. The post journals, reports, and correspondence referred to them as "half-breeds," and some were employed by the HBC as interpreters, guides, and clerks.[18] Nicolas Chatelain, the son of French Canadian fur trader Jacques Chatelain and an Anishinabeg woman named Josephte, rose to become a leader of the local Métis community.[19] Born around 1792 at Fort William, Chatelain fought in the War of 1812 and was well respected by Métis and Anishinabeg alike.[20] In 1825, HBC trader Simon McGillivray described Nicolas Chatelain as "a Half Breed Interpreter [who] is an acquisition to the Post—speaks the Saulteaux language well and is feared by the natives, and is perfectly acquainted with the Geographical part of the country, particularly to the north side of Lac la Pluie, in short he is a man that ought not be lost sight of."[21] In 1826, John D. Cameron offered this description of Nicolas Chatelain:

> Nicholas Chatelin (*sic*), Interpreter. This man is the first of his class in the Indian Country because he is a very sober man, a rare virtue among Interpreters. Young, hardy & ambitious for the interest of his employers. Brave & haughty with the Indians, particularly when alone amongst them. He will suffer more insults from them at the Fort than at their Lodges. A good Fisherman and ready at every work he is put to. Has twenty five pounds a year according to contract but with Governor Simpson's approbation is to be allowed five pounds gratuity each year. Has a wife & two children. Winters with myself.[22]

Other prominent Métis names in the Fort Frances area included Jourdain, Mainville, and Morriseau. Although some were employed by the HBC, others retained their freeman status. An 1873 account book recorded twenty-five freemen with debts owing at Fort Frances, about half of whom can be positively identified as Métis.[23] An 1871 paylist identified nine men as "Halfbreeds of Fort Frances" (see table 7.1).

Aside from John Linklater, the "half-breeds" of Fort Frances on the 1871 paylist were Catholics who had links to the Ste. Anne Catholic Church in Ste.-Anne-des-Chenes, Manitoba. Located on the Seine River about 40 kilometers west of the forks of the Red and Assiniboine Rivers, Ste.-Anne-des-Chenes was on a well-travelled route that connected with Lake of the Woods and Rainy River.[24] The registers of baptisms, marriages, and deaths there contain numerous references to people from Fort Frances. The Fort Frances Métis intermarried within their own community and with those of Red River and other places, such as Fort William. Tables 7.2 and 7.3 show baptisms of people from Fort Frances in 1873 and 1874, as recorded by R. M. Racicot, the priest of St. Norbert Catholic Parish.

It is interesting to note that a number of so-called "English half-breeds" were recorded in the Ste.-Anne-des-Chenes registry books. These included members of the Linklater, Flett, and Calder families, originally Orkney names of men employed by the HBC. By 1871, many of these families had mixed with Métis of French Canadian origin. For example, Isabelle

TABLE 7.1. "Half-breeds" of Fort Frances

Name	Men	Women	Boys	Girls	Total	Per head	Total amount
Jean Bpt. Jourdain	1	1	0	1	3	$3	$9
John Jourdain	1	1	1	3	6	$3	$18
Joseph Jourdain	1	1	0	3	5	$3	$15
Simon Jourdain	1	1	4	1	7	$3	$21
Louis Jourdain	1	0	0	0	1	$3	$3
Francois Mainville	1	1	2	3	7	$3	$21
Michel Morrisseau	1	1	4	3	9	$3	$27
John Linklater[a]	1	1	7	1	10	$3	$30
Xavier Ritchot	1	0	0	0	1	$3	$3
Total	9	7	18	15	49		$147

Source: The paylist titled "Half-breeds of Fort Frances" was compiled 17 October 1871 by Robert Pither (vol. 1,675, p. 71, RG 10, LAC). The paylist may have been connected to work done on the transportation route later known as the Dawson Road.
[a]John Linklater was listed in the 1891 census as a Presbyterian, and he was likely identified as an "English Half-breed." His 1875 scrip application indicated that he was born in 1805 to a "Scots" father and an "Indian" woman. Like the so-called "French Half-breeds," he had been employed by the HBC and was likely the son of an Orkney fur trader and Anishinabe woman. An 1874 map entitled "Plan of Claims between Rainy Lake and Ft. Francis" showed the claim of John Linklater, with an explanation that sixty acres had been purchased by Duncan Sinclair (Department of the Interior, Dominion Lands Branch, Headquarters Correspondence, D-II-1, vol. 232, file 2,808, RG 15, LAC). On 28 May 1877, J. S. Dennis reported that Duncan Sinclair was sent to survey the timber limits granted to S. H. Fowler on Rainy Lake, and that he purchased a squatter's right from a man named Linklater, who had built a shanty and garden near Fort Frances (ibid.).

Linklater was married to Joseph Guimond, and Charles Flett was married to Mary Guimond. This situation is similar to the findings of historian Irene Spry, who pointed out that some of the children of Red River Orkneymen and aboriginal women were fluent in French, including James McKay, who played a key role in the negotiations leading up to Treaty 3. Spry noted that "many marriages spanned the alleged gulf between the mixed-blood and métis groups."[25] The historical data she examined indicated that the people of Orkney and French Canadian origins were also connected in business operations, such as trading and freighting, and in buffalo hunts. The Fort Frances data reveal that the evolution of the Métis community was complex and came to incorporate people from various ethnic backgrounds.

TABLE 7.2.   Fort Frances Baptisms in 1873 at St. Norbert Catholic Parish

Name	Name of father	Name of mother	Godfather	Godmother
Marie Anne Jourdain	Simon Jourdain	Archange Mainville	Nicolas Chatelain	Merguerite Chatelain
Julie Jourdain	John Jourdain	Marguerite Chatelain	Nicolas Chatelain	Rose Chalotqui
Patrice Cyr, Jr.	Patrice Cyr	Zoe Jourdain	J. B. Cyr	Julie Serre
Pierre Mainville	Francois Mainville	Mary Jourdain	Joseph Guimond	Charlotte Jourdain
Pierre Guimond	Joseph Guimond	Isabelle Linklater	None	Angeline Mainville
Basil Jourdain	Joseph Jourdain	Julie Saulteuse	Simon Jourdain	Marie Guimond
Jean Vincent	Vincent Vincent	Marguerite Saulteuse	Francois Mainville	Julie Saulteuse
Simon Jourdain, Jr.	Simon Jourdain	Archange Mainville	Patrice Cyr	Marie Anne Jourdain
Paul Jourdain	Louis Jourdain	Angelique Mainville	Guillaume Briere	Cecile Saulteuse

TABLE 73. Fort Frances Baptisms in 1874 at St. Norbert Catholic Parish

Name	Father	Mother	Godfather	Godmother
Louis Jourdain, Jr.	Louis Jourdain	Angelique Mainville	Nicolas Chatelin	Archange Mainville
Marie Anne Saulteuse (20 yrs)	None	None	Father Giroux	Marie Anne Jourdain
Vincent Nichikitas, Jr.	Vincent Nikichitas	Margaret Kakikepines	Nicolas Chatelain	Archange Mainville
Isabelle Matthews	Richard Matthews	Rose Chabot	James McKay	Mrs. McKay
Marie Anne Chatelain	David Chatelain	Marie Saulteuse	Father Giroux	None
Mary Jane Calder	William Calder	Nancy Luttit	Francois Mainville	Marguerite Chatelain
William Charles Flett	Charles Flett	Mary Guimond	Father Giroux	None

Other Métis communities developed around trading posts within the Fort Frances district. At Fort Alexander, for example, Captain John Palliser noted a "half-breed population" when he visited that post in the summer of 1857.[26] An anonymous officer in General Garnet Wolseley's military expedition of 1870 noted a Métis village near Fort Alexander and wrote, "The banks of the river are high at this place, and on account of the numerous clearings and nice thatched cottages of Half Breeds, it presents a very fine appearance."[27] When General Wolseley visited Fort Frances in the summer of 1870, he disparaged the Métis community: "The half-breed race to which the officers of the Hudson Bay Company at such posts generally belong now is extremely apathetic—there is no go-aheadness about it; and in these out-of-the-way localities the half-breeds quickly go back to the manners, customs, and mode of living of their Indian mothers. They live upon fish as their Indian ancestors did, and, like them, have no appreciation of the value of cleanliness or order."[28]

Treaty Negotiations

The Wolseley military expedition had been sent from Upper Canada through the Rainy Lake area, using the old canoe route from Fort William to Red River, in order to defend against an expected Métis uprising led by Louis Riel. The Red River Métis had resisted the Canadian government's attempt to survey their lands after the HBC surrendered its claim to the area. In 1859, Simon J. Dawson, then the surveyor of the Red River expedition, had first advocated the building of a government transportation route using steamboats and wagons.[29] Government support was lacking, however, and by 1869 only twenty-five miles of the "Dawson Road" had been built west of Fort William.[30] The Métis uprising in Red River spurred development of the transportation route, and many in Wolseley's military expedition were recruited to work on the road. The Red River uprising was arrested, but the Canadian government was alerted to the need to make treaties with aboriginal people west of Lake Superior in order to achieve lasting peace.

The Fort Frances Métis possessed interpretive skills that came to be valued in political meetings between government officials and the Anishinabeg. When Simon Dawson was sent by the Canadian government in 1868 to meet with the Lac la Pluie Anishinabeg to discuss the transportation route and other matters, he was assisted by Nicolas Chatelain, who was then in charge of Fort Frances. Dawson recommended that Chatelain would be a valuable person to assist in future treaty negotiations. He remarked, "There resides at Fort Frances a half-breed of the name of Chatelain, an aged man, who is highly esteemed by the tribe and who, it may be added, has on previous occasions, rendered valuable service in dealing with them."[31] Chatelain knew about the 1850 Robinson treaty negotiations at Sault Ste. Marie. About a month prior to the treaty, Chatelain met HBC governor George Simpson at Fort Frances and advised him that he had a claim to land on Lake Superior because his mother and grandfather were "Indians of the Old Grand Portage." Simpson wrote to treaty commissioner William B. Robinson and informed him that he had obtained a power of attorney to act for Chatelain and had in turn given it to John Swanston, who was in charge of the HBC post at Sault Ste. Marie. Simpson, who was a friend of Robinson's, told Robinson that Swanston had "promised to request your good offices in Securing his claims."[32] Jesuit missionary Nicolas Frêmiot reported that the Métis had been purposely excluded from a meeting that had been organized by HBC chief trader John Mackenzie. Frêmiot confided to his superiors, "The meeting began with a roll call from the list prepared the evening before by Mr. Mackenzie. The half-breeds were passed by in silence, for they have not the right to speak at such gatherings. Is this wise? Do some people fear that they, better informed than the Indians themselves, might be in a better position to defend their rights?"[33] Although treaty commissioner William B. Robinson had verbally promised the Sault Ste. Marie Métis that their lands would be protected, the government failed to live up to that promise after 1850.[34] Chatelain's specific request for inclusion in the treaty also fell on deaf ears.

Chatelain and others at Fort Frances were also probably aware of the treaty negotiations in the United States that had included Métis. For example, the 1830 treaty at Prairie du Chien included an article demanded by the Sioux Nation that set aside a tract of land for the "half breeds of their nation." The treaty stated, "The United States agree to suffer said half Breeds to occupy said tract of country; they holding by the same title, and in the same manner that other Indian Titles are held."[35] This Métis reserve, however, was never realized. According to James Hansen, "The 'half-breed tract' granted to the eastern Sioux in 1830 was not divided and made available for more than twenty-five years, despite continued importunities from the individuals involved. By the time it was available the

pressure for white settlement was so strong that, in exchange for relin-
quishing their claims to the tract, the mixed bloods were granted certificates to obtain federal land elsewhere."[36] Closer to home, the 1863 treaty at
Old Crossing of Red Lake River also included Métis considerations. That
treaty provided for 160 acres to be granted to "each male adult half-breed
or mixed-blood who is related by blood to the said Chippewas."[37] A detailed list of Métis claimants was recorded in a report of a U.S. commission
investigating "Half-Breed Scrip" relating to the 1854 treaty at La Pointe.
That report identified several individuals named Jourdain who were living at Red Lake at the time of the treaty.[38] It is not known whether they
were related to the Jourdains at Fort Frances, but the HBC records indicate
that people from the Red Lake area frequented the trading post.[39]

In 1870, Nicolas Chatelain was hired to assist Wemyss Simpson[40] during the first treaty negotiations at Fort Frances. Chatelain was employed
as interpreter, and he was expected to "prepare the minds of the Indians
for the negotiation of a treaty with them."[41] Simpson failed to achieve a
treaty, but he succeeded in obtaining for the government a temporary
right of way to transport troops under General Wolseley through the Lac
la Pluie area. It was later recalled that Nicolas Chatelain was instrumental in these negotiations and had "used his great influence over the Indians of the District, in their allowing the volunteers to pass through their
territory in 1870."[42] In 1871, the government appointed Simpson, along
with Simon J. Dawson and Robert Pither, to act as commissioners for another attempt at a treaty. Chatelain again served as interpreter, but the
negotiations failed to achieve their objective. The commissioners tried
and failed again in the summer of 1872. The recent discoveries of gold
and silver in their territory had made the Anishinabeg chiefs difficult to
deal with, and so making a treaty at that time was impossible. A newspaper reporter from Winnipeg who attended the treaty negotiations described the chiefs as "cranky, obstinate, and difficult to manage."[43] Dawson and Pither met with a smaller number of chiefs at Fort William in
October 1872 but were unable to change the chiefs' position.[44]

Meanwhile, negotiations between the HBC and the government of
Canada produced an agreement in 1869 that involved the surrender of
the company's charter rights in the territory draining into Hudson Bay
(known as Rupert's Land). On November 18, 1869, the HBC signed a deed
of surrender to the Crown. The deed of surrender included the granting
of titles to lands around HBC posts in the affected territory. An attached

schedule listed the posts and acreage to be given to the company. In the Lac la Pluie district, fourteen posts were listed and 1,300 acres specified. Fort Frances was included on that list, with 500 acres around the post set aside for the company.[45] The HBC deed of surrender was accepted and confirmed by an order in council dated June 23, 1870.[46] On June 1, 1872, Donald A. Smith, chief commissioner of the HBC, wrote to Secretary of State James Aikins and requested permission to instruct the surveyor general to survey blocks of land around eight HBC posts, including Fort Frances.[47] On June 13, 1872, Smith wrote again to Aikins and advised him that the HBC had been granted an additional 140 acres at Fort Frances, bringing the total to 640 acres.[48] In the winter of 1872–73, dominion land surveyor Charles F. Miles was sent to the Lac la Pluie district to establish the boundaries of the HBC "reserves." His survey plan, dated January 7, 1874, depicted an area of 640 acres marked off around Fort Frances, including the company's buildings and cemetery.[49]

The appearance of a government surveyor at Fort Frances after several failed treaty negotiations was a cause for alarm among the Anishinabeg and Métis. When another treaty party arrived in 1873—led by Alexander Morris, the Lieutenant-Governor of Manitoba and the Northwest Territories—the surveying of HBC claims was an impediment to negotiations. The Fort Frances chief told Morris that if he saw survey stakes around the HBC post, he would "put them aside." He explained, "I see signs that the H.B.Co. has surveyed. I do not hate them. I only wish they should take their reserves on one side. Where their shop stands now is my property, I think it is three years now since they have had it on." Morris was evasive in his answer, saying, "I do not know about that matter; it will be enquired into. I am taking notes of all these things and am putting them on paper."[50]

The HBC issue was one of many that was brought into the treaty negotiations. Chief Mawedopenais raised the issue of including the Métis in the treaty: "I should not feel happy if I was not to mess with some of my children that are around me—those children that we call the Half-breed—those that have been born of our women of Indian blood. We wish that they should be counted with us, and have their share of what you have promised. We wish you to accept our demands. It is the Half-breeds that are actually living amongst us—those that are married to our women." Morris evaded a direct answer, but assured them that he would communicate their desire to his superiors in Ottawa: "I am sent here to treat with the Indians. In Red River, where I came from, and where there is a great body of Half-breeds, they must be either white or Indian. If Indians, they get treaty money; if the Half-breeds call themselves white, they get land. All I can do is to refer the matter to the Government at Ottawa, and to recommend what you wish to be granted."[51]

On October 3, 1873, twenty-four Anishinabeg chiefs signed the treaty later known as Treaty 3. It was later recalled that Nicolas Chatelain used his great influence "in inducing the Indians to make a Treaty with the Government in 1873."[52] The text of Treaty 3, however, did not specify how the HBC or Métis issues were to be resolved. Despite Morris's assurances to enquire into complaints about the HBC land claim at Fort Frances, the government of Canada had already promised the company 640 acres of land around its post. The HBC did not immediately receive a land patent at Fort Frances, but those 640 acres were still effectively removed from availability to the Anishinabeg or Métis.[53] The issue involving the Métis was left entirely silent until Simon J. Dawson was sent to investigate the boundaries of Indian reserves in Treaty 3 territory. In January 1875, Dawson reported on the Indian reserves and noted that the Métis had decided to join the treaty. He explained, "The Half-breeds in the Rainy River District, numbering about 90 persons, have decided on joining the Indians. They will require a Reserve laid out for them next summer."[54] Surveyor General John S. Dennis was sent to Fort Frances in September 1875 to determine the reserve boundaries. When he arrived, he was met by a "half-breed" delegation seeking admission to Treaty 3. On September 12, 1875, Dennis, representing Queen Victoria, and Chatelain, acting on behalf of the "Half-breeds at Fort Frances," signed a "memorandum of agreement" concerning an adhesion to Treaty 3. The text of the agreement was written as follows:

> This memorandum of Agreement made and entered into this twelfth day of September one thousand eight hundred and seventy-five—Between Nicholas Chatelaine, Indian Interpreter at Fort Francis [sic] and the Rainy River and acting herein solely in the latter capacity for and as representing the said Halfbreeds, on the one part—And John Noughton [Stoughton] Dennis, Surveyor General of Dominion Lands as representing Her Majesty the Queen, through the Government of the Dominion on the other part.
>
> Witnesseth as follows:

Whereas the Halfbreeds above described by virtue of their Indian blood claim a certain interest or title in the lands or Territories in the vicinity of Rainy Lake and the Rainy River for the commutation or surrender of which claim they ask compensation from the Government.

And whereas having fully and deliberately discussed and considered the matter, the said Halfbreeds have elected to join in the treaty made between the Indians and Her Majesty at the North West angle of the Lake of the Woods, on the third day of October, 1873, and have expressed a desire thereto and to become subject to the terms and conditions thereof in all respects saving as hereafter set forth. It is now hereby agreed upon by and between the said parties hereto (this agreement however to be subject in all respects to approval and confirmation by the Government without which the same shall be considered of no effect) as follows, that is to say:—

The Halfbreeds through Nicholas Chatelaine their Chief above named, as representing them herein agree as follows, that is to say:—

That they hereby fully and voluntarily surrender to Her Majesty the Queen to be held by Her Majesty; and Her successors forever any and all claim right title or interest which they by virtue of their Indian blood have or possess in the lands or Territories above described and solemnly promise to observe all the terms and conditions of the said treaty (a copy whereof duly certified by the Honourable the Secretary of State of the Dominion has been this day Placed in the hands of the said Nicholas Chatelaine.

In consideration of which Her Majesty agrees as follows, that is to say:

That the said Halfbreeds keeping and observing on their part the terms and conditions of the said treaty shall receive compensation in the way of reserves of land, payments, annuities and presents in manner similar to that set forth in the several respects for the Indians in the said treaty. It being understood, however, that any sum expended annually by Her Majesty in the purchase of ammunition and twine for nets for the use of the said Half-breeds shall not be taken out of the fifteen hundred Dollars set apart by the Treaty for the purchase annually of those articles for the Indians, but shall be in addition thereto and shall be a pro-rata amount in the proportion of the number of Halfbreed parties hereto to

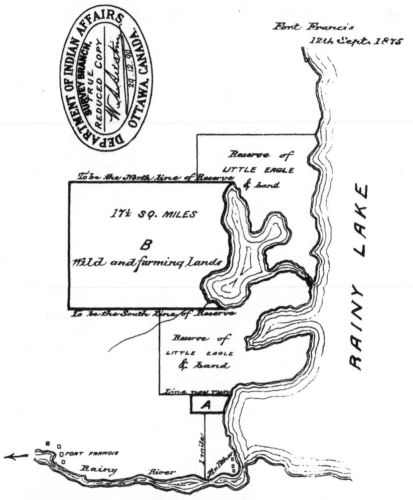

This is the rough diagram alluded to in the agreement to which the same is attached shewing the Reserves for the Half-breeds on the westerly shore of the Rainy Lake

Fort Francis
12th Sept. 1875

DEPARTMENT OF INDIAN AFFAIRS. SURVEY BRANCH. TRUE REDUCED COPY 29.12.00 OTTAWA, CANADA.

RAINY LAKE

Reserve of
LITTLE EAGLE
& band

To be the North line of Reserve

17½ SQ. MILES
B
Wild and farming lands

To be the South line of Reserve

Reserve of
LITTLE EAGLE
& band

Line now run

A

1 mile

FORT FRANCIS
Rainy   River   Mr. Dilke

A. To be 160 acres for Halfbreeds to build and live on as a village

B. To extend from south to north limit of large Bay as shewn and to extend westerly to embrace 17½ square miles.
(Sgd) J.S.D.
       N.C.

MAP 7.2. "Half-Breed Reserves" on Rainy Lake, 1875. © Government of Canada. Reproduced with the permission of the Minister of Public Works and Government Services Canada (2011). Source: RG 10, D-10-a, Vol. 1846, Microfilm Reel T-9939, No. IT 270, LAC/Indian Affairs.

the number of Indians embraced in the Treaty, and it being further understood that the said Halfbreeds shall be entitled to all the benefits of the said Treaty as from the date thereof as regards payments and annuities in the same manner as if they had been present and had become parties to the same at the time of the making thereof.

And whereas the said Halfbreeds desire the land set forth as tracts marked (A) and (B) on the rough diagram attached hereto and marked with the initials of the parties (aforementioned) to this agreement, as their reserve, (in all eighteen square miles) to which they would be entitled under the provisions of the treaty, the same is hereby agreed to on the part of the Government.

Should this Agreement be approved by the Government, the reserves as above to be surveyed in due course.[55]

A sketch map showing the proposed "Halfbreed" reserve is shown in map 7.2.

Unkept Treaty Promises

Two years after the treaty adhesion, the Métis still had not received treaty payments and Nicolas Chatelain was unable to receive an explanation from Robert Pither, the Indian agent at Fort Frances. Chatelain wrote to J. S. Dennis to remind him, "When I met you at Fort Francis [sic], you kindly consented to grant to the French Half Breed of that place, a certain tract of land along the Rainy Lake to be their Reserve. Those Half Breed [sic] were to receive annuities like the Indians, some cattle and tools for farming and I was to be the chief of the Fort Francis [sic] Half Breed."[56] Chatelain informed Dennis that he could not continue to be Métis chief because he was still being paid by the government,[57] but he had written on their behalf in order to get the government's attention to their situation. Dennis forwarded Chatelain's letter to the Indian Department, and Pither was instructed to report how many "Half-breeds" at Fort Frances had been admitted into treaty by being paid an annuity in past years. He was also told to meet with them and ascertain whether they would be willing to join Chief Little Eagle's (Mickeseese) band on Rainy Lake, whose reserve adjoined land set apart for the Métis.[58] The instructions further stated that the department could not encourage separate "Half Breed

Bands" and added that "Half breeds" who were paid as Indians prior to the passing of the Act of 1876 must continue to be so paid, as well as receive cattle and farming implements as Indians.[59]

Robert Pither investigated the matter and reported that the Métis who had received annuities numbered seven families containing forty-eight people. Pither also interviewed Chief Mawandopenais and recorded his answers to questions about the Fort Frances Métis and their inclusion in Treaty 3. Chief Mawandopenais said, "During the Treaty at the N.W. Angle one of my requests was that the Half Breeds of Fort Frances should be taken into the Treaty and paid as Indians, and the Governor promised to represent my request to the Department." He further explained, "When I requested the Half Breeds to be taken into the Treaty it was not as a separate Band but to join whichever band they chose." However, he also added what he had been told by Nicolas Chatelain: "In the summer of 1875 the Surveyor General came to settle the question of Reserves, and Mr. Chastellain [sic] and some of the Half Breeds had an interview with him, and he told them that the Department had consented to their proposition sent down by Mr. Dawson, and a separate Reserve was directed to be surveyed for them."[60]

On January 12, 1877, Pither wrote to Joseph A. N. Provencher, commissioner of Indian Affairs in Winnipeg, and forwarded a request from Nicolas Chatelaine and other "Half-Breeds" stating that they still had not been receiving the same payments as Indians. They wished to know whether the department intended to give them an allotment of land or allow them to take homesteads as whites.[61] On February 12, 1877, Provencher wrote to Pither and asked him to report on the number of "half-breeds" asking for a grant of land at or in the vicinity of Fort Frances. He also asked for the number of payments already received by the "half-breeds" of Fort Frances as Indians, and on the extent and exact locality of the reserve surveyed for them, on whose instructions, and at whose demand such a reserve was surveyed.[62] On February 20, 1877, Pither replied that the reserves were surveyed under the instructions of the surveyor general (J. S. Dennis) and that the demand had been made by Nicolas Chatelain on behalf of himself and the other "Half Breeds" of Fort Frances.[63] On February 28, 1877, Pither wrote again to Provencher and specified that the "half-breeds" who had not taken pay as Indians were "Nicholas Chastellain [sic], Louis Jourdain, John Linklater,"[64] his wife, and six children. Pither noted that there were other "half-breeds" there, but they belonged to Red River or Winnipeg and were entitled to land in that vicinity.[65]

After receiving no answer to the petition, Nicolas Chatelain traveled to Winnipeg to make a claim for "Half-breed Scrip." On August 27, 1878, he appeared before a Dominion Lands agent and made his mark on a scrip claim. The application noted that the information had been read back to Chatelain in French and was perfectly understood. Chatelain claimed that he had been living with his son-in-law, Jean Baptiste Ritchtot, in St. Vital, Manitoba, for about six months before and after 15 July 1870.[66] Chatelain further explained that he had waited so long to file his claim because he had received "promises from the officers of the government that I was to get my scrip at Fort Frances with many other people of that locality." He also explained that after the government failed to live up to its promise, he decided to file his claim in Winnipeg. Chatelain would have to wait ten years, only to find out that his Manitoba scrip application had been disallowed by the Deputy Minister of the Interior after consulting with Ebeneezer McColl of the Indian Department.[67]

While Chatelain waited for an answer, the government began to formulate a plan to extinguish the distinct identity of the Fort Frances Métis. On April 9, 1880, James F. Graham, the acting Indian superintendent in Winnipeg, wrote to Pither regarding a grandson of Nicholas Chatelain who wanted to take advantage of the amended Indian Act of 1876 by refunding the annuity money paid to him and receiving scrip instead. Nicholas Chatelain, who was admitted into treaty in 1875 but never received any annuity money, also sought to receive scrip.[68] Ebeneezer McColl, inspector of Indian agencies in Winnipeg, wrote to Pither and instructed him as to how to deal with half-breeds who were connected to Treaty 3. McColl stated that he had been directed by the Department of Indian Affairs to prohibit any Métis who had taken scrip from being paid treaty annuities. McColl explained that this measure would "prevent complications and impositions upon the government."[69] This new policy was designed to exclude any Métis who did not join Little Eagle's band, including Nicolas Chatelain. Pither's annual report for 1880 on the Couchiching Agency included a description of Little Eagle's Rainy Lake reserve. Pither noted, "The half-breeds who receive annuities are paid with this band."[70] McColl's 1882 annual report on the Manitoba Superintendency region described the "Rainy Lake Band under Chief Mickesee":

This band is principally composed of French half-breed settlers, who were living at Fort Francis [sic] at the time treaty was made with the

Indians. It embraces thirty-one families, of whom about one-half have gardens and houses on the reserve. They produce annually sufficient corn and potatoes for their own use. The interpreter, Chastellain, is desirous of severing his connection with this band, and withdrawing from the treaty, as he wishes to obtain a homestead where he is living on Rainy River. I would respectfully recommend that the application of this worthy, venerable half-breed be favorably entertained.[71]

Chatelain's request was not granted, and the Métis' struggle to secure treaty rights continued. On June 27, 1885, a letter and attached census was sent to the prime minister of Canada from the "Half Breeds of Fort Frances." They asserted that in the Treaty of 1873 they were promised twelve dollars per person for the first year and five dollars for the second year, which they had not received. They also stated that when Surveyor General Dennis passed through Fort Frances in 1875, he promised them seven head of cattle, farm implements, and other equipment in similar proportion to the Anishinabeg bands in Treaty 3. An attached list provided the names of the Métis who had not received annuities in 1873 and 1874. Eight families with a total of forty-five people were owed $782.00 for unpaid annuities (see list below).

Unpaid Annuities for the "Half-Breeds of Rainy Lake"
John Jourdain
> Marguerite Oscchipuee (wife)
> Rosette Jourdain (daughter)
> Marie Anne Jourdain (daughter)
> Marie Jourdain (daughter)
> John Jourdain (son)
> Julie Jourdain (daughter)

Francois Mainville
> Marguerite Jourdain (wife)
> Alexis Mainville (son)
> William Mainville (son)
> Francoise Mainville (daughter)
> Joseph Mainville (son)
> Elizabeth Mainville (daughter)
> Pierre Mainville (son)

Joseph Jourdain
  Isabelle Menassaokyikok (wife)
  Charlotte Jourdain (daughter)
  Suzanne Jourdain (daughter)
  Eliza Jourdain (daughter)
  Basile Jourdain (son)

Simon Jourdain
  Archange Mainville (wife)
  Pierre Jourdain (son)
  Isabelle Jourdain (daughter)
  Joseph Jourdain (son)
  Simon Jourdain (son)
  Marie Anne Jourdain (daughter)

John Jourdain
  Julie Serro (wife)
  Zoé Jourdain (daughter)

Louis Jourdain
  Angelique Mainville (wife)
  Paul Jourdain (son)

Nicholas Chatelain
  David Chatelain (son)
  Xavier Chatelain (son)

Joseph Guimond
  Elizabeth Linklater (wife)
  Charles Guimond (son)
  Marie Guimond (daughter)
  Catherine Guimond (daughter)
  Joseph Guimond (son)
  Marguerite Guimond (daughter)
  Leonille Guimond (daughter)

Duncan Campbell Scott, then a clerk in the Indian Department, launched an investigation into the unpaid annuities issue and found that none of the Métis had been paid in 1873 or 1874. Scott noted that some of the women may have been paid under their aboriginal names, but it was

impossible to trace them.[72] Lawrence Vankoughnet, deputy superintendent general of Indian Affairs, reported Scott's findings to Sir John A.
Macdonald, prime minister and superintendent general of Indian Affairs.
Vankoughnet reported that the Métis had not been paid annuities in 1873
and 1874, but because they had become members of the "Rainy Lake Band
of Indians of Chief Mickasisi," they were not entitled to the additional
cattle or farm implements they had claimed in their petition.[73]

On August 1, 1885, J. D. Raine of Port Arthur wrote to Simon J. Dawson,
now a member of the Canadian Parliament, and reported on a meeting
with the "Half-Breeds of Rainy Lake and Rainy River" at Fort Frances.
Raine noted that John Jourdain had replaced their appointed chief, Nicolas
Chatelain, because Chatelain was still employed as an interpreter for the
government. The Métis complained that although they had elected to be
treated as Indians, they had not been paid annuity and other treaty benefits.[73] Dawson forwarded Raine's letter to the Indian Department, and local
Indian agent Pither was again instructed to investigate the matter. Pither
reported that the Métis entered the treaty in 1875 and had been paid as
Indians. He added that when Chief Little Eagle received his cattle, he gave
two cows to the "Half Breeds"—one to Simon Jourdain and one to Francois
Mainville—and they had been receiving their share of agricultural implements.[75] On September 18, 1885, Pither wrote again to McColl and reported
that the Fort Frances "Half Breeds" had not been promised a treaty payment of $12.00 per capita in 1873 because they had not joined the treaty
until 1875. He added that in 1875 Louis Jourdain had been paid in Long
Sault Band No. 1 under his Indian name. Joseph Jourdain's wife had been
paid alone in 1874–1875, and none of the other wives had been paid until
1875, with their husbands. Pither concluded that he found no information
that the Métis had been promised treaty payments in 1873 and 1874.[76]

Duncan Campbell Scott was again assigned the task of sorting out the
Fort Frances Métis issue in Treaty 3. Scott reported that it had always been
the custom of the Department of Indian Affairs to pay arrears of annuity from the date of the treaty to those Indians who signed after the
treaty had been made. He noted that it remained to be decided whether
this would be allowed in the case of the "half-breeds of Rainy Lake and
Rainy River." If they signed the treaty, Scott believed they had a right to
arrears.[77] On October 13, 1885, Lawrence Vankoughnet wrote to Ebeneezer
McColl and advised him that there was no reason why the arrears from
the date of Treaty 3 should not be paid to the so-called half-breeds of Fort

Frances, as such had invariably been the custom when Indians came into treaty.[78] McColl then wrote to Pither on October 19, 1885, and provided the same explanation.[79]

On August 9, 1886, the "Half Breeds of Fort Frances" wrote to the deputy minister of Indian Affairs and complained again about not receiving what had been promised in the treaty.[80] This time, J. D. McLean, another clerk in the Indian Department, was assigned the task of investigating the issue. He reported that the "half-breeds" of Fort Frances had accepted the treaty in 1875 and had been paid arrears on the annuity for 1873 and 1874 on December 14, 1875. McLean also asserted that the Métis had joined Rainy Lake Band No. 1 under Chief Little Eagle or Mickeseese.[81] On October 1, 1886, McColl wrote to the superintendent general and reported that the records in his office showed that the Fort Frances Métis appeared to have received all that was due them, in accordance with treaty stipulations.[82] On October 11, 1886, Vankoughnet wrote to McColl and enclosed a copy of a letter from "Halfbreed Indians of Fort Frances" concerning promises alleged to have been made to them in 1875. He asked McColl to confirm that they had received all that they were due under the treaty.[83] On October 29, 1886, Vankoughnet wrote again to McColl and advised him to instruct Pither to inform the "half-breeds" of Fort Frances that they had received all the supplies to which they were entitled under the treaty.[84]

The Department of Indian Affairs annual account book for the year 1886 shows that the Fort Frances Métis were finally paid their arrears on treaty annuities for the years 1873 and 1874.[85] The list of payees was similar to the 1885 petition, with the addition of several family members. The names and amounts are shown in table 7.4.

After being paid their arrears in 1887, Nicolas Chatelain and his sons David and Xavier joined the Couchiching Indian Band.[86] On July 12, 1887, L. J. Arthur Leveque, inspector of Indian agencies at Rat Portage, wrote his annual report and included a description of the "Coutcheeching [sic] Band and Reserve." He reported, "These Indians nominally belong to the Ojibbewa tribe, but many are half-breeds with a large admixture of French blood. . . . This band is composed of one hundred and two Roman Catholics, five of the Church of England and twenty-six pagans. There is no church situated on the reserve, but the Roman Catholic priest stationed at Fort Frances holds service every alternate Sunday in the school-house, which is well attended."[87]

TABLE 7.4.   Payments in 1886 to Fort Frances Métis
for Arrears on Treaty Annuities

Name	Amount
J. B. Jourdain, family of 3	$51.00
John Jourdain, family of 7	$119.00
Simon Jourdain, family of 8	$136.00
Francis Mainville, family of 8	$136.00
Joseph Jourdain, family of 6	$97.00
Joseph Guinard [Guimond], family of 8	$136.00
Louis Jourdain, family of 3	$51.00
Nicholas Chatelaine, family of 3	$51.00
Catherine Mainville	$17.00
Total	$794.00

On August 9, 1887, Pither reported on the Coutcheeching Agency and
wrote, "I held a council meeting and re-elected councilors; gave out the
supplies, paid the band, delivered the two oxen sent for the Coutcheeching [sic] band, and settled the dispute between the half-breeds and the Indians, in reference to their reserves, to the satisfaction of both parties."[88]
However, a year later the issue resurfaced when Simon J. Dawson wrote to
Vankoughnet and reported that "the Indians of Rainy River and the Lake
of the Woods held a meeting at Hungry Hall, at which the claims of the
Half breeds living among them came under their consideration." Dawson noted that during the negotiations preceding the signing of Treaty 3,
"a promise was made to them, the Indians, that their kindred the Half-
breeds living among them should in respect to rights, privileges and
land grants, be treated as the Half breeds of Manitoba had been." Dawson added,

> The Half breeds in the section of country to which I refer are not nu-
> merous. At the time of the outbreak in 1869–70 they were steadfastly
> loyal and it seems hardly fair that they should be placed in a worse
> position than were the half-breeds of Manitoba who took up arms to
> enforce their rights and, I may add, with perfect success. The answer,
> heretofore always given to the effect that nothing can be done until the
> question of the disputed territories is settled is not, in my opinion a
> very fair answer. The claims of these poor people can be easily dealt
> with, if the government will only set about the matter in the determi-
> nation to have it arranged.[89]

Despite Dawson's eloquent plea, the reply from the Indian Department repeated the same old excuse for inaction. The department's position stated that when the promises were made to the Métis, the lands in Treaty 3 were supposed to have belonged to Canada, but Ontario had advanced a claim to that territory. "The question of ownership is, however, being tested by a suit which is at present before the Imperial Privy Council and when a final decision has been rendered this whole matter will receive special and early consideration."[90] In December 1888, the Privy Council decided in favor of Ontario in *Regina v. St. Catherine's Milling and Lumber Company.*[91] Suffice it to say that the Fort Frances Métis claim for fair inclusion in Treaty 3 never received "special" or "early consideration" after the St. Catherine's decision.[92]

Nicolas Chatelain died on March 6, 1892, and his passing signaled an end of an era in the fight by the Fort France Métis to be recognized as a distinct nation within Treaty 3. He had long since given up on the idea of leading the Fort Frances Métis on their small reserve on Rainy Lake. He had also failed in his attempt to obtain scrip in Manitoba. The HBC, on the other hand, had obtained a large grant of land at Fort Frances. It was the land where Chatelain and many other Métis had worked and lived and likely expected to remain after they joined Treaty 3 in 1875. The HBC sold the land and profited handsomely. The Métis, on the other hand, were forced to move to the shore lands of Rainy Lake and become members of Chief Little Eagle's band. Chatelain must have been disillusioned with the Canadian government for breaking the treaty promises made to him in 1875. However, he remained until his death a respected figure among the Fort Frances Métis and Anishinabeg. Ebeneezer McColl described him in 1889 as "a French Half-Breed, one of nature's noblemen of commanding presence, being six feet four inches in height, 98 years of age and totally blind. Even now, neither agent, nor any other person within the District has a greater influence over the Indians than this remarkable man."[93]

Conclusion

The Fort Frances Métis evolved as a fur trade community in the shadows of the HBC trading post. They were part of a larger Métis nation that evolved principally in the aftermath of the major reorganizations of the fur trade industry that began in 1805. The Fort Frances Métis self-identified as a distinct community apart from the Anishinabeg and were linked together by ties of marriage, both within the community and with other Métis communities in the Red River area and wider fur trade territory. They elected their own leaders and met together to discuss political issues. At the time of treaty negotiations with the Canadian government in the period 1873–1875, the Métis were recognized as a distinct group of aboriginal people with an interest in or right to the land. They joined the treaty expecting to obtain the same benefits as the Anishinabeg. Nicolas Chatelain, acting as their chief, was promised that the Fort Frances Métis would have their own reserve lands and treaty benefits. These promises rang hollow when Canadian government officials decided to extinguish their distinct Métis identity. Forced to choose to become either Indian or white, many opted to join the Anishinabeg on Rainy Lake under the leadership of Chief Little Eagle. Nicolas Chatelain reluctantly followed and ultimately accepted treaty payments, but in doing so he and the other Fort France Métis were no longer recognized by the government as a distinct nation. The Canadian government's position, however, did not prevent the Métis from continuing to self-identify as a distinct community in the Fort Frances area. Currently, talks are under way between representatives of the Fort Frances Métis and the federal and provincial governments in order to come to a political agreement on resource harvesting and other issues linked to the legal rights of the historic Métis community.

Notes

1. Lytwyn, *Fur Trade of the Little North'*, 112–39.
2. Judd, "'Mixt Bands of Many Nations,'" 130.
3. Goldring, *Papers on the Labour System*, 32–33.
4. Sprague and Frye, *Genealogy of the First Métis Nation*, 15.
5. Brown, *Strangers in Blood*, 170–76.
6. Some scholars have argued that the Métis Nation properly includes only those who originated in the Red River settlement. For example, Paul L. A. H. Chartrand and John Giokas stated, "This historic nation is 'Riel's people' of western Canada, whose history includes negotiations that led to the birth of Manitoba, and military encounters with both Indians and colonial and Canadian authorities, which crystallized their distinct identity as a unique people" (Chartrand and Giokas, "Defining 'The Métis People,'" 294). Chris Andersen applied similar logic in his writing about the use of terminology. He noted "the importance of 'the Métis' at Red River lay not in their mixed-ness (whatever anxiety or consternation it caused historical officials or produces in contemporary ethnohistorians) but rather in their ability to force the Canadian government to halt, however briefly, its an-

nexation desires to territories now known as western Canada, in their earlier treat-ing with the Sioux and other indigenous nations, or in their collective self-consciousness *as Métis*" (Andersen, *Moya 'Tipimsook*, p. 47, emphasis in original).

7. Peterson, "Many Roads to Red River."

8. Goldring, "Labour Records of the Hudson's Bay Company," 56.

9. St-Onge, "Race, Class and Marginality," 76.

10. Lytwyn, "Anishinabeg and the Fur Trade," 29.

11. The trading post was known as Lac la Pluie post. It was re-named Fort Frances in honor of Sir George Simpson's wife, Frances, after she visited in 1830.

12. Garry, "Diary of Nicholas Garry (1821)," 125.

13. Nute, "Posts in Minnesota Fur-Trading Area."

14. A similar settlement was established in 1817 on the north bank of the As-siniboine River by a group of free Orkneymen and their Cree wives and native-born families. Known as Birsay Village, after the home parish of the oldest set-tler, Magnus Spence, it was located west of the Red River because it was closer to good fisheries and buffalo hunting grounds. However, Birsay Village was beset with a grasshopper plague and a disease epidemic that led to its abandonment in less than two years. Historical geographer Barry Kaye noted that "most of the Birsay freemen were eventually absorbed into the main colony on the Red River" (Kaye, "Birsay Village on the Assiniboine," p. 21).

15. Lac la Pluie Post Journal, 18 December 1823, B.105/a/9, p. 38, Hudson's Bay Company Archives (hereafter HBCA), Winnipeg.

16. McLoughlin, Lac La Pluie District Report, 1822–1823, B.105/e/2, folio 7d, HBCA.

17. Sinclair, Fort Frances Journal, 1 June 1837, B.105/a/20, folio 1d, HBCA.

18. Reimer and Chartrand, "Documenting Historic Métis in Ontario," 572–73.

19. McNab, "Chatelain, Nicolas." Information on Chatelain's father and mother comes from his scrip application in Manitoba, 27 August 1878, vol. 567, p. 17108, RG 15, Library and Archives Canada (hereafter LAC).

20. E. McColl, Inspector of Indian Agencies, Winnipeg, to L. Vankoughnet, Deputy Minister of Indian Affairs, 18 November 1889, Personnel file on N. Chas-tellaine, vol. 3,830, file 62,423, RG 10, LAC.

21. McGillivray, Lac La Pluie District Report, 1824–1825, B.105/e/3, folio 4d-5, HBCA.

22. Cameron, Lac La Pluie District Report, 1825–1826, B.105/e/6, folio 14d, HBCA.

23. Reimer and Chartrand, "Documenting Historic Métis in Ontario," 575.

24. The Dawson Route would later follow the old trail that led from Lake of the Woods to Ste.-Anne-des-Chenes.

25. Spry, "Métis and Mixed-Bloods of Rupert's Land before 1870," 99.

26. Journal of John Palliser, PRO, CO 6/36, pp. 150–52, NA Kew.

27. Officer of the Force, "Red River Expedition of 1870," 349.

28. Wolseley, "Narrative of the Red River Expedition," 286.

29. Arthur, *Simon J. Dawson, C.E.*

30. Dawson, *Report on the Line.*

31. Memorandum by Simon J. Dawson, 17 December 1869, Adams G. Archibald Papers, no. 1, Provincial Archives of Manitoba.

32. George Simpson, Sault Ste. Marie, to William B. Robinson, 20 September 1850, Governors' Records, Correspondence Outward (General), 1848–51, D.4/42, pp. 31d–32d, HBCA.

33. "Report of Father Frêmiot to his Superior in New York, 18 October 1849," in Arthur, *Thunder Bay District, 1821–1892*, 14.

34. Lytwyn, "Echo of the Crane."

35. "Articles of a treaty made and concluded by William Clark Superintendent of Indian Affairs and Willoughby Morgan, Col. of the United States 1st Regt. Infantry, Commissioners on behalf of the United States on the one part, and the undersigned Deputations of the Confederated Tribes of the Sacs and Foxes; the Medawah-Kanton, Wahpacoota, Wahpeton and Sissetong Bands or Tribes of Sioux; the Omahas, Ioways, Ottoes and Missourias on the other part," 15 July 1830, Prairie Du Chien, in Kappler, *Indian Affairs: Laws and Treaties*, vol. 2, *Treaties*, 305–10.

36. Hansen, " 'Half-Breed' Rolls," 162.

37. "Articles of a treaty made and concluded at the Old Crossing of Red Lake River, in the State of Minnesota, on the second day of October, in the year eighteen hundred and sixty-three, between the United States of America, by their commissioners, Alexander Ramsey and Ashley C. Morrill, agent for the Chippewa Indians, and the Red Lake and Pembina bands of Chippewas; by their chiefs, headmen, and warriors," 2 October 1863, Old Crossing of Red Lake River, in Kappler, *Indian Affairs: Laws and Treaties*, vol. 2, *Treaties*, 853–55.

38. Jones, King, and King, *Report of Commission Investigating Half Breed Scrip*, 202.

39. Nicole St-Onge explained in a personal communication that the 1837 treaty with the Chippewa, signed on 29 July 1837 at St. Peters, included a "half-breed roll." The roll taker was based on Madeline Island, Lake Superior, and included heads of families identified as Peter, Bazil, Eustache, and Joseph Jourdain— young men in their twenties, all listed as "1/2 Chippewa" from Red Lake.

40. Wemyss Mackenzie Simpson was a cousin of HBC governor George Simpson and had been employed by the company from 1841 to 1864. He was a member of the Canadian Parliament for Algoma from 1867 to 1871 and served as a treaty commissioner in 1871 for Treaties 1 and 2 in Manitoba.

41. Memorandum by S. Stewart, Department of Indian Affairs, Ottawa, to L. Vankoughnet, Deputy Minister of Indian Affairs, 29 November 1889, Personnel file on N. Chastellaine, vol. 3,830, file 62,423, RG 10, LAC.

42. E. McColl, Inspector of Indian Agencies, Winnipeg, to L. Vankoughnet, Deputy Minister of Indian Affairs, 18 November 1889, Personnel file on N. Chastellaine, vol. 3,830, file 62,423, RG 10, LAC.

43. "Letter from Fort Frances," *The Manitoban*, 12 July 1872.

44. Wemyss Simpson to Joseph Howe, 17 July 1872, copy in Irving Papers, MS 1514 (75/16), file 1,027-3-3, Archives of Ontario.

45. "Deed of Surrender from the Hudson's Bay Company to Queen Victoria," in Ollivier, *British North America Acts and Selected Statutes, 1867–1962*.

46. "Order in Council accepting the Deed of Surrender from the Hudson's Bay Company to Queen Victoria," in Ollivier, *British North America Acts and Selected Statutes, 1867–1962.*

47. Smith to Aikens, 1 June 1872, Land records belonging to the Governor and Committee, Copies of correspondence . . . , A.72/6, p. 1, HBCA.

48. Smith to Aikens, 13 June 1872, Governor and Committee official inward correspondence . . . , A.12/14, pp. 136–136d, HBCA.

49. Miles, "Plan of the H.B.Co's. Reserve at Fort Francis in the Lac la Pluie District," RG 1/87/10/1A/i, HBCA.

50. "Indian Treaty: Closing Proceedings," *The Manitoban,* 18 October 1873.

51 "Letter from Alexander Morris to unknown [likely Howe]," in Morris, *Treaties of Canada with Indians of Manitoba,* 69.

52. E. McColl, Inspector of Indian Agencies, Winnipeg, to L. Vankoughnet, Deputy Minister of Indian Affairs, 18 November 1889, Personnel file on N. Chastellaine, vol. 3,830, file 62,423, RG 10, LAC.

53. The company's claim to land at Fort Frances became embroiled in the dispute between Canada and Ontario over jurisdiction of the Treaty 3 territory. The matter was finally resolved, and, in 1898, the federal government issued an order in council advising the Ontario government that the HBC was entitled to a patent for 640 acres of land at Fort Frances. In 1910, the HBC was actively engaged in subdividing and selling town lots in its patented tract (Land records belonging to the Governor and Committee, Secretary's loose papers on land matters, A.72/3, pp. 97–98d, HBCA).

54. Report by S. J. Dawson to E. A. Meredith, copy in Irving Papers, MS 1514 (75/16), file 1,027-3-3, Archives of Ontario.

55. Memorandum of Agreement between J. S. Dennis on behalf of Queen Victoria and Nicholas Chatelaine on behalf of Halfbreeds at Fort Frances, vol. 1,846, no. IT 270, RG 10, LAC.

56. Chatelain to Dennis, 10 August 1876, Fort Frances District Office, vol. 12,370, file 1,876, RG 10, LAC.

57. Chatelain continued to be paid $250 per year as an interpreter in the Couchiching Indian Agency until his death in 1892. He did not actually serve as an interpreter, and Ebeneezer McColl explained in 1889: "I always understood that the amount of $250.00 was given to this veteran of the war of 1812 as an acknowledgement of the great service he had rendered to his Country, not only during the invasion of Canada in that year by the Americans, but also for his great influence over the Indians of the District, in their allowing the volunteers to pass through their territory in 1870 and afterwards in inducing the Indians to make a Treaty with the Government in 1873" (E. McColl, Inspector of Indian Agencies, Winnipeg, to L. Vankoughnet, Deputy Minister of Indian Affairs, 18 November 1889, Personnel file on N. Chastellaine, vol. 3,830, file 62,423, RG 10, LAC).

58. Little Eagle, or Mickeseese, was chief of the band that would come to be known as the Couchiching band. Their reserve was located on Rainy Lake and adjoined the "Half-breed Reserve."

59. Provencher to Pither, 8 September 1876, Fort Frances District Office, vol. 12,370, file 1,876, RG 10, LAC.

60. Pither to Provencher, 3 January 1877, "Couchiching Agency—Treaty Payments to Halfbreeds and a Reserve for their use," Black Series, vol. 3,558, file 30, RG 10, LAC.

61. Pither to Provencher, 4 January 1877, in ibid.

62. Provencher to Pither, 12 February 1877, Fort Frances District Office, vol. 12,370, file 1,877, RG 10, LAC.

63. Pither to Provencher, 20 February 1877, "Couchiching Agency—Treaty Payments to Halfbreeds and a Reserve for their use," Black Series, vol. 3,558, file 30, RG 10, LAC.

64. John Linklater was not identified as one of the "Half-breeds" who joined Treaty 3.

65. Pither to Provencher, 28 February 1877, "Couchiching Agency—Treaty Payments to Halfbreeds and a Reserve for their use," Black Series, vol. 3,558, file 30, RG 10, LAC.

66. The *Manitoba Act of 1870* used 15 July 1870 because it was the date that Rupert's Land was transferred to Canada.

67. Chatelain, Scrip Application in Manitoba, 27 August 1878, vol. 567, p. 17108, RG 15, LAC.

68. Graham to Pither, 9 April 1880, Fort Frances District Office, vol. 12,370, file 1,880, RG 10, LAC.

69. McColl to Pither, undated [but evidently 1880], in ibid.

70. Canada, Parliament, "Report from Pither," 69.

71. Canada, Parliament, "Report from McColl," 180.

72. Unsigned memorandum [evidently by D.C. Scott] to the Deputy Minister, 10 July 1885, "Couchiching Agency—Half-Breeds of Rainy Lake . . . ," Black Series, vol. 3,715, file 21,809 (microfilm reel C-10,191), RG 10, LAC.

73. Memorandum by Vankoughnet to Macdonald, 17 July 1885, Fort Frances District Office, vol. 12,370, file 1,885, RG 10, LAC.

74. Raine to Dawson, 1 August 1885, copy in ibid.

75. Pither to McColl, 6 September 1885, "Couchiching Agency—Half Breeds of Rainy Lake . . . ," Black Series, vol. 3,715, file 21,809, RG 10, LAC.

76. Pither to McColl, 18 September 1885, in ibid.

77. Memorandum by D. C. Scott to Vankoughnet, 6 October 1885, in ibid.

78. Unsigned letter [likely by Vankoughnet] to McColl, 13 October 1885, in ibid.

79. McColl to Pither, 19 October 1885, Fort Frances District Office, vol. 12,370, file 1,885, RG 10, LAC.

80. Half Breeds of Fort Frances to the Deputy Minister, 9 August 1886, "Couchiching Agency—Half Breeds of Rainy Lake . . . ," Black Series, vol. 3,715, file 21,809, RG 10, LAC.

81. Memorandum by J. D. McLean to the Deputy Superintendent General, 16 September 1886, in ibid.

82. McColl to the Superintendent General, 1 October 1886, in ibid.

83. Unsigned letter [likely by Vankoughnet] to McColl, 11 October 1886, in ibid.

84. Unsigned letter [likely by Vankoughnet] to McColl, 29 October 1886, in ibid.

85. Canada, Parliament, "Table of Payments to Indians of Manitoba," 142–43.

86. Paylist for Couchiching Indian Band, 1887, vol. 9,362, RG 10, LAC.

87. Canada, Parliament, "L. J. Arthur Leveque's Report," 107–108.

88. Canada, Parliament, "Robert J. N. Pither to the Superintendent General," 53.

89. Dawson to Vankoughnet, 13 June 1886, "Claims of Half-Breeds in the Rainy Lake and Lake of the Woods Districts . . . ," Black Series, vol. 3,788, file 43,362, RG 10, LAC.

90. Unknown author, Indian Department, to Dawson [draft letter], 17 July 1888, in ibid.

91. See Cottam, "Indian Title as a 'Celestial Institution.'"

92. In 1901, the Indian commissioner for Manitoba and the Northwest Territories reported on how the Métis of Fort Frances had been treated after 1875. He noted that they had been forced to join Chief Little Eagle's band and had ever since been identified as the Couchiching band. He wrote, "Reserves 16A and 16D were laid out for the halfbreeds of Rainy River district, who had entered treaty. These individuals afterwards were told by the Department that they could not be recognized as a separate Halfbreed band, and as far as Mr. Wright [probably Indian Agent John Wright] can find out (and the Indians and Halfbreeds are also under that impression) Little Eagle's and Nicholas Chatelaine's band have ever since held reserves 16A, 16D and 18B in common under the name of Couchiching band" (Indian Commissioner to the Secretary of the Department of Indian Affairs, 25 November 1901, Case file on Couchiching Reserve in Indian and Northern Affairs Canada, Gatineau, QC).

93. E. McColl, Inspector of Indian Agencies, Winnipeg, to L. Vankoughnet, Deputy Minister of Indian Affairs, 18 November 1889, Personnel file on N. Chastellaine, vol. 3,830, file 62,423, RG 10, LAC.

Works Cited

Archival Sources

Gatineau, QC
    Case file on Couchiching Reserve. Indian and Northern Affairs Canada.
London, UK
    Journal of John Palliser. PRO, CO 6/36: 150–52. National Archives, Kew (previously Public Record Office, or PRO).
Ottawa, ON
    Library and Archives Canada (LAC).
        Chatelain, Nicolas. Scrip Application in Manitoba, 27 August 1878. RG 15, vol. 567, p. 17108.

"Claims of Half-Breeds in the Rainy Lake and Lake of the Woods Districts, to Rights and Privileges Similar to those Accorded to the Manitoba Half-Breeds." RG10, Black Series, vol. 3,788, file 43,362.

"Couchiching Agency—Half-Breeds of Rainy Lake Claiming Arrears of Annuities for the Years 1873–1874." RG 10, Black Series, vol. 3,715, file 21,809. Microfilm reel C-10,191.

"Couchiching Agency—Treaty Payments to Halfbreeds and a Reserve for Their Use." RG 10, Black Series, vol. 3,558, file 30.

Department of the Interior, Dominion Lands Branch, Headquarters Correspondence. RG 15, D-II-1, vol. 232, file 2,808.

Fort Frances District Office. RG 10, vol. 12,370.

"Memorandum of Agreement between J. S. Dennis on Behalf of Queen Victoria and Nicholas Chatelaine on Behalf of Halfbreeds at Fort Frances." RG 10, vol. 1,846, no. IT 270.

Paylist for Couchiching Indian Band, 1887. RG 10, vol. 9,362.

Paylist of "Halfbreeds of Fort Frances," 17 October 1871, compiled by Robert Pither. RG 10, vol. 1,675, p. 71.

Personnel file on N. Chastellaine, interpreter for the Coutcheching [sic] Agency. RG 10, vol. 3,830, file 62,423.

Toronto, ON
Irving Papers, MS 1514 (75/16), file 1,027-3-3. Archives of Ontario.
Winnipeg, MB
Hudson's Bay Company Archives (HBCA).
Cameron, John D. Lac La Pluie District Report, 1825–1826. B.105/e/6, folio 14d.

Governor and Committee official inward correspondence, Correspondence from commissioners, 1871–1912. A.12/14.

Lac la Pluie Post Journal, 18 December 1823. B.105/a/9.

Land records belonging to the Governor and Committee, Copies of correspondence concerning disposition of HBC lands under Deed of Surrender, 1871–1913. A.72/6.

Land records belonging to the Governor and Committee, Secretary's loose papers on land matters. A.72/3.

McGillivray, Simon. Lac La Pluie District Report, 1824–1825. B.105/e/3.

McLoughlin, John. Lac La Pluie District Report, 1822–1823. B.105/e/2, folio 7d.

Miles, Charles F. "Plan of the H.B.Co's. Reserve at Fort Francis in the Lac la Pluie District." RG 1/87/10/1A/i.

Governors' Records, Sir George Simpson, Correspondence Outward (General), 1848–51. D.4/42.

Sinclair, William. Fort Frances Journal, 1 June 1837. B.105/a/20, folio 1d.
Provincial Archives of Manitoba.
Adams G. Archibald Papers.

Published Sources

Andersen, Chris. *Moya 'Tipimsook* ("The People Who Aren't Their Own Bosses"): Racialization and the Misrecognition of "Métis" in Upper Great Lakes Ethnohistory." *Ethnohistory* 58, no. 1 (Winter 2011): 37–63.

Arthur, Elizabeth. *Simon J. Dawson, C.E.* Thunder Bay, ON: Thunder Bay Historical Museum Society, 1987.

———, ed. *Thunder Bay District, 1821–1892: A Collection of Documents*. Toronto, ON: University of Toronto Press, 1973.

Brown, Jennifer S. H. *Strangers in Blood: Fur Trade Families in Indian Country*. Reprint, Norman: University of Oklahoma Press, 1994. First published 1980.

Canada, Parliament. "L. J. Arthur Leveque's Report on the Rat Portage Agency." *Sessional Papers of Canada*, no. 14 (1889): 107–108.

———. "Report from McColl to the Superintendent General of Indian Affairs." *Sessional Papers of Canada* 5, part 2 (1883): 180.

———. "Report from Pither to the Superintendent General of Indian Affairs." *Sessional Papers of Canada*, no. 7 (1881): 69.

———. "Robert J. N. Pither to the Superintendent General of Indian Affairs." *Sessional Papers of Canada*, no. 14 (1889): 53.

———. "Table of Payments to Indians of Manitoba and the North-West, Annual Report of the Department of Indian Affairs for the Year Ended, 31st December 1886." *Sessional Papers of Canada*, no. 14, part 2 (1886): 142–43.

Chartrand, Paul L. A. H., and John Giokas. "Defining 'The Métis People': The Hard Case of Canadian Aboriginal Law." In *Who Are Canada's Aboriginal Peoples?: Recognition, Definition, and Jurisdiction*, edited by Paul L. A. H. Chartrand, 268–304. Saskatoon, SK: Purich, 2002.

Cottam, S. Barry. "Indian Title as a 'Celestial Institution': David Mills in the St. Catherine's Milling Case." In *Aboriginal Resource Use in Canada: Historical and Legal Aspects*, edited by Kerry Abel and Jean Friesen, 247–65. Winnipeg: University of Manitoba Press, 1991.

Dawson, Simon J. *Report on the Line of Route between Lake Superior and the Red River Settlement*. Ottawa, ON: I. B. Taylor, 1869.

Garry, Francis N. A., ed. "Diary of Nicholas Garry, Deputy Governor of the Hudson's Bay Company from 1822–1835: A Detailed Narrative of His Travels in the North West Territories of British North America in 1821." *Royal Society of Canada, Proceedings and Transactions*, 2nd ser., no. 6 (1900), sec. 2: 73–204.

Goldring, Philip. "Labour Records of the Hudson's Bay Company, 1821–1870." *Archivaria* 11 (Winter 1980–81): 53–86.

———. *Papers on the Labour System of the Hudson's Bay Company*. Manuscript Report Series, no. 362. Ottawa, ON: Parks Canada, 1979.

Hansen, James L. " 'Half-Breed' Rolls and Fur Trade Families in the Great Lakes Region—An Introduction and Bibliography." In *The Fur Trade Revisited: Selected Papers of the Sixth North American Fur Trade Conference, Mackinac Island,*

Michigan, 1991, edited by Jennifer S. H. Brown, W. J. Eccles, and Donald P. Heldman, 161–69. East Lansing: Michigan State University Press, 1994.

Holzkamm, Tim E., Victor P. Lytwyn, and Leo G. Waisberg. "Rainy River Sturgeon: An Ojibway Resource in the Fur Trade Economy." *The Canadian Geographer* 32, no. 3 (1988): 194–205.

Jones, Thomas C., Edward P. King, and Dana E. King. *Report of the United States Commission Investigating Half Breed Scrip under the 7th Clause of the 2nd Article of the Treaty with the Chippewa Indians of Lake Superior and the Mississippi, Concluded at La Pointe, in the State of Wisconsin, September 30, 1854.* Washington, DC: Government Printing Office, 1874.

Judd, Carol M. " 'Mixt Bands of Many Nations': 1821–1870." In *Old Trails and New Directions: Proceedings of the Third North American Fur Trade Conference*, edited by Carol M. Judd and Arthur J. Ray, 127–46. Toronto, ON: University of Toronto Press, 1980.

Kappler, Charles J., comp. and ed. *Indian Affairs: Laws and Treaties.* Vol. 2, *Treaties.* Washington, DC: Government Printing Office, 1904.

Kaye, Barry. "Birsay Village on the Assiniboine." *The Beaver* 213, no. 3 (Winter, 1981): 18–21.

Lytwyn, Victor P. "The Anishinabeg and the Fur Trade." In *Thunder Bay: From Rivalry to Unity*, edited by Thorold J. Tronrud and A. Ernest Epp, 16–37. Thunder Bay, ON: The Thunder Bay Historical Museum, 1995.

——. "Echo of the Crane: Tracing Anishnawbek and Métis Title to Bawating (Sault Ste. Marie)." In *New Histories for Old: Changing Perspectives on Canada's Native Pasts*, edited by Ted Binnema and Susan Neylan, 41–65. Vancouver: University of British Columbia Press, 2007.

——. *The Fur Trade of the Little North: Indians, Pedlars, and Englishmen East of Lake Winnipeg, 1760–1821.* Winnipeg, MB: Rupert's Land Research Centre, 1986.

McNab, David T. "Chatelain, Nicolas." In *Dictionary of Canadian Biography*, vol. 12, edited by Francess G. Halpenny and Jean Hamelin, 187–88. Toronto, ON: University of Toronto Press, 1990.

Morris, Alexander. *The Treaties of Canada with the Indians of Manitoba and the North-West Territories Including the Negotiations on Which They Were Based, and Other Information Relating Thereto.* Toronto, ON: Belfors, Clarke and Company, 1880.

Nute, Grace Lee. "Posts in the Minnesota Fur-Trading Area, 1660–1855." *Minnesota History* 11 (December 1930): 353–80.

Officer of the Force. "Red River Expedition of 1870." *The Manitoban*, 1870.

Ollivier, Maurice, ed. *British North America Acts and Selected Statutes, 1867–1962.* Ottawa, ON: Queen's Printer, 1962.

Peterson, Jacqueline. "Many Roads to Red River: Metis Genesis in the Great Lakes Region, 1680–1815." In Peterson and Brown, *New Peoples* 37–71.

Peterson, Jacqueline, and Jennifer S. H. Brown, eds. *The New Peoples: Being and Becoming Métis in North America.* Winnipeg: University of Manitoba Press, 1985.

Reimer, Gwen, and Jean-Philippe Chartrand. "Documenting Historic Métis in Ontario." *Ethnohistory* 51, no. 3 (Summer 2004): 567–607.

Sprague, D. N., and R. P. Frye. *The Genealogy of the First Métis Nation: The Development and Dispersal of the Red River Settlement, 1820–1900.* Winnipeg, MB: Pemmican Publications, 1983.

Spry, Irene M. "The Métis and Mixed-Bloods of Rupert's Land before 1870." In Peterson and Brown, *New Peoples*, 95–118.

St-Onge, Nicole. "Race, Class and Marginality in an Interlake Settlement: 1850–1950." In *The Political Economy of Manitoba*, edited by James Silver and Jeremy Hull, 73–87. Regina, SK: Canadian Plains Research Center, University of Regina, 1990.

Wolseley, Garnet. "Narrative of the Red River Expedition." In *Travel, Adventure and Sport from Blackwoods Magazine.* Vol. 1. New York, NY: White and Sons, ca. 1871.

8

Women, Networks, and Colonization in Nineteenth-Century Wisconsin

Lucy Eldersveld Murphy

uphrosine Peltier *dit* Antaya was born in 1796 at Prairie du Chien, where the Wisconsin River flows into the Mississippi. She was the seventh of ten children born to a Mesquakie Indian mother and a French Canadian father. About twenty years earlier (around 1777), Euphrosine's parents, Pokoussee and Pierre Peltier *dit* Antaya, had married and settled at the old rendezvous grounds at Prairie du Chien, where Pierre worked as a fur trader. No doubt, Pokoussee assisted Pierre in trading cloth, kettles, beads, knives, and guns for furs and other items produced by Native people.[1] Together with other mixed families, they made their community an important fur trade center with strong links to Mesquakie, Sauk, Dakota, Ho-Chunk, and other Midwestern tribes (see map 8.1).

Millions of Americans today, like Euphrosine Antaya, have ancestors from both Native American and European or African peoples. Some identify as Native, but others tend to check a box designating themselves as white or African American. In Canada, people of mixed Indian and white ancestry can be legally identified as Métis (and aboriginal) if they meet certain conditions, but in the United States the term Métis has a legal meaning only on the Turtle Mountain Reservation of North Dakota.[2]

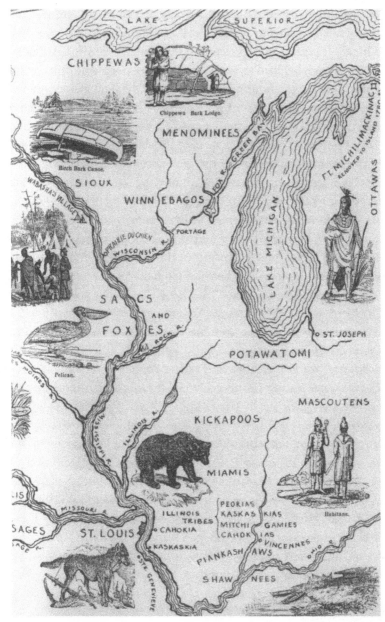

MAP 8.1.   Western Great Lakes fur trade territory. Detail of an illustration
from "Trade Territory of St. Louis in the Late XVIII Century," 1939, in James
B. Musick, *St. Louis as a Fortified Town* (St. Louis, MO: Press of R. F. Miller, 1941).

What happened to Euphrosine Antaya, her brothers and sisters, and her many neighbors from mixed families? Thousands of people like her lived in what is now the American Midwest when the United States colonized the region, beginning with the Revolutionary War. But we still do not know very much about how families like the Antayas weathered the changes of the nineteenth century. Few have studied the ways that these families responded to the challenges of changing politics, economies, and social patterns. We also know very little about the process of assimilation of Native people into mainstream society. Furthermore, although Indian land loss through treaties, allotment, and termination has attracted the attention of scholars, the process by which individual Native families lost land has not received much scholarly treatment.

This chapter, taken from a larger study about the mixed families of the western Great Lakes region, examines the ways that many women lost autonomy, status, and land when the United States took over territories from prior European colonizers.[3] It also explores the ways that women used their networks, their roles as "public mothers," and family residence patterns as resources to cope with these challenges. My focus is primarily on Prairie du Chien, but it occasionally wanders to other midwestern sites.

Marriages like Pokoussee's and Pierre Antaya's were a way to create ties between people of different cultural traditions. Unlike many ethnic groups, Indian peoples in the Midwest had approved of—and even encouraged—intermarriage. During the fur trade era of the eighteenth and early nineteenth centuries, Euro-American traders learned that their Native customers expected them to marry local daughters and create bonds of obligation to their in-laws and their communities. Native wives became interpreters who learned and taught both their own Native families and their husbands about each other's expectations and cultures. Their bicultural children grew up to continue the patterns of mediation.

In the nineteenth century, outsiders used various terms to describe these individuals and their families, including "half-breed," French, Canadian, *habitant*, or Creole. Except for the first, these terms included people of both mixed and unmixed ancestry.

For example, an 1840 newspaper article about Prairie du Chien stated that "the population consisted almost exclusively of Canadians of French descent, and half-breed Indians" and also referred to residents as "the old French settlers."[4] "The Americans generally consider the Canadians as ignorant," remarked an Italian traveling in the region in 1828. "Whether this be true, I know not; but I do know that I invariably found them very polite and obliging, even among the lower classes."[5] Yankee politician James Duane Doty used the term "old Inhabitants" in reference to Green Bay residents, probably as an Anglicization of the French *habitants*.[6] Treaties provide examples of the term "half-breed" in use: one typical instance was an 1830 document in which the "Sioux" provided land to "the half breeds of their Nation."[7] For the most part, the word "half-breed" was not inclusive enough to cover all the people of these old fur trade communities and was used to refer only to those with mixed ancestry.

The reality was more complex. A typical fur trade family might include a French Canadian husband (who might or might not have had some intermarried Native ancestors); a wife of mixed Sauk and Mesquakie ancestry; and kin, servants, and other employees, who might have Pawnee, Dakota, Menominee, Odawa, Scottish, or even African ethnic heritages. In addition, their neighbors might represent different ethnicities. This variety bothered some Anglo-Americans. For example, Caleb Atwater, an agent sent as part of an 1827 treaty delegation, described the people of Prairie du Chien in this way: "They are a mixed breed, and probably more mixed than any other human beings in the world; each one consisting of Negro, Indian, French, English, American, Scotch, Irish, and Spanish blood! And I should rather suspect some of them, to be a little touched with the Prairie wolf. They may fairly claim the vices and faults of each, and all the above named nations and animals, without even one redeeming virtue."[8] As social relations in the United States were being racialized during the nineteenth century, mixed communities like these did not fit into the neat categories that people in the eastern states were developing. The U.S. federal censuses in the mid-nineteenth century, for example, were not designed to record the complex families and ancestries of these people. There was a column in which census takers were supposed to record a person's "color," but the only options were "White, black, or mulatto," so in the Great Lakes region, they generally left the column blank unless someone was "black or mulatto," making others "White" by default.[9] Decades earlier, Anglo-American factor John W. Johnson had given up and used his imagination, writing in a letter from Prairie du Chien, "I have spent a winter of more pleasure than one could calculate on from the society around me, <u>we</u> (I use this word meaning the americans here) had to immagin them to be a white people, their manners were very much in favor under this impression."[10]

Anglo-Americans might not have been able to racialize the residents of the fur trade towns, but they did sense that they were very different culturally. One of the terms they used was "Creole." In the most neutral sense, this term was one that had come to convey the idea that the people and their culture were already in place before the arrival of the Yankees. They were what vacationers today might call "the locals" when away from home—residents who had arrived beforehand and established a society of their own.

Strictly speaking, French dictionaries defined Creoles as people of pure European ancestry born in colonies, but actual usage changed over time and varied from place to place and user to user. A study of Mississippi Valley French during the eighteenth and early-nineteenth centuries found that the noun *Créole* was formally defined as "a white person born in America of European ancestry" but sometimes applied to American-born blacks. Furthermore, when lowercased and used as an adjective, *créole* meant "anything produced by Creoles, anything native to the land of the Creoles."[11]

But in communities in which many people were of mixed ancestry but cultural elements such as French language and Christianity were prevalent and unifying characteristics, the term Creole became more inclusive as to ancestry but retained the sense that the people had been born in the region. In the upper Mississippi Valley, the word Creole was used infrequently but inclusively. In Illinois, a 1797 census divided the adult males into four categories: *"français, creole, canadien, américain."* Historian Carl Ekberg found that some people of mixed ancestry were certainly included in the category of *creole.*[12] Anglos were using the term Creole to describe the residents of the fur trade communities as early as the late eighteenth century. For example, the English commandant at Mackinac, Arent Schuyler DePeyster, wrote in a report to the governor of Canada, General Frederick Haldimand, in 1780 about the dangers of Sioux attacks upon the "Habitations of the Creoles."[13] This usage continued and increased in the nineteenth century. To illustrate, in 1819 the *Detroit Gazette* printed a description of Edward Tanner's travels through Wisconsin and mentioned the residents of Prairie du Chien: "In the settlement are about fifteen hundred inhabitants . . . who are principally Creoles."[14] In the preface to their 1987 book, *The Wisconsin Creoles* genealogists Les and Jeanne Rentmeester documented nineteen examples during the eighteenth, nineteenth, and early twentieth centuries of the use of the word Creole to refer to the francophone, often mixed-ancestry peoples of Wisconsin. For them, "The first 200 years of Wisconsin's recorded history . . . is dominated by French-Creoles, a mixture of French newcomers with the Indian natives."[15] The *Iowa Patriot* newspaper in 1839 reprinted a short article, previously published in the *New Orleans Picayune*, defining the word: "A Creole is but a native of the state or country where he or she may have been born."[16] In other words, the term had come to refer to the people who had been living in the region and established communities and cultures well before the high tide of anglophone in-migration began in the early to mid-nineteenth century.

What should we call people like Pierre, Pokoussee, and Euphrosine? They did not call themselves or each other Métis. It is hard to find more than a few sources in which the residents of the fur trade communities of the Midwest used terms to refer to themselves as a group distinct from others. An 1887 interview with septuagenarian Andrew J. Vieau, a former fur trader and son of the founder of Milwaukee, referred to the "French Creoles" of Green Bay.[17] It is unclear whether the francophone Vieau or the Anglo interviewer chose this word. Joseph Brisbois, a justice of the peace and francophone member of an old fur trade family, used the word "Inhabitants," which may be an Anglicization of the French word *habitants*.[18] A voyageur's grandson born in the late nineteenth century, Albert Coryer, was interviewed in 1951, and he referred to his childhood neighbors in Prairie du Chien's Frenchtown neighborhood as "the old French settlers."[19] Jeanne Rioux Rentmeester, herself a descendent of mixed ancestry, promoted the use of the word Creole.

Because Native people and fur trade families thought of themselves and each other more often in reference to culture than color, this terminology is appropriate. The word Creole best reflects the idea that people of many backgrounds created a culture with roots in several cultures, but also with original elements, and that this culture was in place before the United States took control of the region. I use the word métis only when I seek to make a point about someone's ancestry, for these people never used the term themselves.

Like Green Bay, St. Louis, Detroit, Mackinac Island, and dozens of other towns that grew out of the fur trade era in New France, early-nineteenth-century Prairie du Chien had developed a culture that combined elements of both Native and European traditions. One might hear French spoken but also Mesquakie, Dakota, Ho-Chunk, Ojibwe, and other languages. Wives and mothers continued maple-sugar making, often taking their chickens (a European introduction) with them to the sugar camps. Most people were at least nominally Catholic, so Easter celebrations combined crêpes with maple syrup and Easter eggs. Some men hitched plows to their oxen or horses to prepare the ground for European crops, but many wives cultivated family gardens, continuing Native ways of growing corn, beans, and squash together in hills without need for plows or live-stock to pull them. The cultural negotiations were made at both the fam-ily and community level. This was a type of "middle ground" based on personal, social, and economic relationships, rather than the political and diplomatic associations examined by historian Richard White.[20]

These old Midwestern fur trade towns had much in common with other communities across North America—places such as Santa Fe, Santa Barbara, St. Augustine, and New Orleans—where people's many cultures came into contact and where contests of social, economic, and political control were played out. Like these other borderlands, the Great Lakes region experienced multiple waves of colonization and immigration, hav-ing been part, first, of New France, then of British North America before the United States took control in the late eighteenth and early nineteenth centuries. These histories can be better understood in the context of the larger demographic changes taking place across the Americas.

After thousands of years as the western hemisphere's only peoples, Native Americans' absolute and proportionate population decreased after the arrival of Europeans and Africans, both because of imported diseases and because of the violence of conquest and colonization. In the late eighteenth century, Native people became a minority of the overall population of the Americas.[21] These demographic changes, of course, were played out with many variations at the local and regional levels, based on local and regional events. Where there were multiple waves of colonization, intermarriage, and several immigrant groups, the dynam-ics of population changes became complex and created conflicts over the control of resources and politics.

The controversies and the accommodations often occurred on the cultural, ethnic, and racial borders or frontiers, where mixed relation-ships blurred distinctions, prejudices were fluid, and human contacts teetered precariously between appropriation and generosity, assimilation and exile. The identity and affiliation of people "in-between" (as historian Jacqueline Peterson has called them), people like Euphrosine Antaya, were important to many on both sides of these "borders," especially during demographic shifts. Understanding these people on the cultural borders can help us understand the dynamics of these transitions and the evolution of societies, economies, and polities.

Great Lakes Fur Trade Communities

Before the late eighteenth century, most fur trade couples resided at least part of the year in Indian villages, but after the Seven Years War more and more mixed couples and their children moved to newly established villages, where they created a culturally syncretic society and economy based on the fur trade. These communities included Detroit, Mackinac Island, Vincennes, St. Louis, Green Bay, and Prairie du Chien. The ethnically diverse nature of these towns is evident in the following partial reconstruction of Prairie du Chien's adult population as of 1817, based on church and land claims records and other documents (see list below).

Prairie du Chien Ethnicity, 118 Females, 1817

Wives and mothers (whose names appeared in records):

11 Dakota
 5 Mesquakie
 2 Ojibwe
 1 Pawnee
 1 Sauk
 1 Menominee
 1 Ho-Chunk (Winnebago)
17 Métis
 2 Afro-French
 3 French
 3 Not ascertained
47 Total

Daughters:

57 Métis
 7 Afro-French
 6 French
 1 Not ascertained
71 Total

The total population was estimated at about 600.[22] These Native women maintained connections to their tribal communities (with the exception of the Pawnee), keeping open lines of communication between their hometowns and the cosmopolitan Prairie du Chien. In a way, these women were delegates in a regional United Nations, playing important social, economic, and political roles.

As residents in a community where cultures mixed to create a new, locally born culture, these women and their husbands, brothers, and sons were perceived by incoming Anglo-Americans as ethnically different. The term Creole designated them both as having lived there before the Anglo-Americans arrived and as participating in this local culture. It also was a way of designating them as "other," and it usually implied some French ethnic connection, such as language or kinship connections.

Becoming Minorities

By the 1820s, the United States had established a series of forts garrisoned by soldiers around the Midwest to control people and resources. The prospect of available land drew anglophone settlers from the eastern United States, especially after the opening of the Erie Canal. The old fur trade towns experienced significant population changes, resulting in political, social, and economic transitions. For example, Prairie du Chien's largely francophone Creole population declined slightly whereas Anglo immigration rose sharply during the two decades before 1836, when Wisconsin became a territory independent of Michigan. The demographic shift continued thereafter (see table 8.1). The Creoles were soon minorities in the old fur trade town, a transformation that caused a change in town and county political control away from the old fur trade elites and toward Yankee newcomers. Economic changes included shifts in land ownership and commercial patterns. Many Creoles found themselves marginalized socially, economically, and even geographically to two "French" neighborhoods.

Networks

Pokoussee and Pierre Antaya and their neighbors belonged to networks of kin, friends, and others connected by love, blood, adoption, obligation, clans, tribal affiliation, and god-parenting. As they raised their children,

TABLE 8.1.   Prairie du Chien Creole Proportion of the Population

Year and no. of Creoles	French surname
1817: Men identified by name in sources: $n = 60/72$	83.3%
1820: Household heads, U.S. Census: $n = 39/53$	73.5%
1830: Household heads, U.S. Census: $n = 45/62$	72.6%
1836: Household heads, Wisc. Census, County $n = 79/157$	50.3%
1840: Household heads, U.S. Census, County $n = 63/187$	33.7%
1850: All residents (Creoles[a]) $n = 425/1,406$	30.2%
1860: All residents (Creoles[a]) $n = 380/2,398$	15.8%

Sources: Hansen, "Prairie du Chien's Earliest Church Records, 1817"; Lockwood, "Early Times and Events in Wisconsin," 125–26; Hoffmann, *Antique Dubuque*, 51–59; U.S. Congress, *American State Papers*, Class VIII, *Public Lands*, 5:47–98, 270–72, 283–328; Russell, ed., *Michigan Censuses 1710–1830*, 146–47; Harlan et al., *1830 Federal Census*; [Butterfield], *History of Crawford and Richland Counties, Wisconsin* 1:294–95; "Population Schedules of the Seventh Census," 1850 manuscript, Crawford County, WI, microfilm M432, reel 995, NA, Washington, DC; "Population Schedules of the Eighth Census," 1860 manuscript, Crawford County, WI, microfilm M653, reel 1402, NA, Washington, DC; and U.S. Census Office, *Population of the United States in 1860*, 534.
[a]"Creoles" includes residents with French surnames who were born in Wisconsin, Michigan, Minnesota, Missouri, Illinois, or Canada before 1820, their children, and/or those who were known from genealogical and treaty records to be members of fur trade families. Data for the years before 1850 were for those with French surnames. All residents appeared in the records without ethnic or racial designations or as "white."

others moved to their communities and became similarly linked to these Creole families and towns. Like many social networks the world over, these webs connected Creoles to others across long distances and perhaps facilitated migration. As in other countries, Creole marriages were often arranged by parents (or other kin) and affected the social and political status and authority of both brides and grooms. In times of difficulty, kin and friends might help people to overcome health problems, political conflicts, and financial difficulties.

The networks of Creole women were, in some ways, similar to those of white frontier women. In studies of frontier Michigan and Ohio, historians have shown that white women, through visiting and correspondence, maintained relationships that served as a resource for all family members, but particularly for women made vulnerable by laws and economic realities that limited their autonomy.[23] The same was true for Creole women. However, a key difference was that many Creoles approved of women's activism in a wide range of arenas, including independent economic management, religious leadership, diplomacy, and, to some extent, political participation.[24] Thus, many of the networks in which Creole women and their children participated connected them to business partners, religious associates, and political allies, in addition to friends and relatives.

Another difference was that Native and Creole cultures valued exogamy (marrying someone outside one's group). Whereas Europeans and Euro-Americans ideally married within their groups (class, religion, race, and ethnicity), Native and Creole people in the Midwest encouraged and appreciated women who espoused well-connected outsiders. Midwestern Indians traditionally assimilated immigrants into their communities by arranging marriages for them or, less frequently, by adopting.

We can see these patterns in the social network of a woman who was a neighbor of the Antayas during her infancy. Elizabeth Thérèse Fisher Baird came from three generations of fur trade marriages. She was the daughter of a Scots-American father and a mother of French and Ottawa Indian ancestry; her father and brothers were fur traders, and so were her maternal grandmother and great aunt. Her great grandfather Jean Baptiste Marcotte had been a fur trader who enhanced his chances for business success and political authority by marrying Marie Nekesh, the daughter of an Ottawa chief, around 1775.[25]

The United States' conquest and colonization of the Midwest disrupted Elizabeth's family. Born in 1810 at Prairie du Chien, she moved with her mother to Mackinac Island to be with her grandmother and great-aunt when her father left for Canada to avoid U.S. rule during the War of 1812. In 1824, at the age of fourteen, Elizabeth married a young Scots-Irish lawyer named Henry Baird and moved with him to Green Bay in present-day Wisconsin.[26] With this marriage, her family allied themselves with a man who knew not only the new court language, English, but also the laws of the new courts. Fortunately for Elizabeth, the marriage was not only beneficial to her family but also affectionate, as her correspondence reveals. For example, she wrote to him in 1825 while visiting her relatives at Mackinac Island and awaiting the birth of her first child: "Do not forget to write by every opportunity if it is possible do take care of your self for you know I cant help being uneasy about you, and think of me. . . . I remain dear husband your ever affectionate wife Eliza T Baird."[27] For his part, Henry benefited greatly from his wife's linguistic skills because he spoke neither French nor any Indian languages, and few of his clients spoke English. Elizabeth, who spoke French, Ojibwe, and Ottawa, soon learned to speak English and served as interpreter for his law practice, in a classic métis mediator role.

Elizabeth Baird's memoir presents an example of other ways that Creole women added people to their social networks. On a summer day in 1820, Baird's grandmother, Thérèse Marcotte Schindler, approached the wigwam of a family that had recently arrived at Mackinac Island and set up camp near the shore. Madame Schindler, or Tó-e-ak-qui, a forty-six-year-old Ottawa-French métisse and member of an elite fur trade family, extended a customary welcome and found that the parents had four children with them, including an infant only a few days old.[28] Fluent in the Ojibwe language, she mediated a separation between the quarreling husband, John Tanner, and his Ojibwe wife (who appears in the memoir under the nickname "La Sateuse").[29] Schindler and her adult daughter, Mary Ann Lasallière Fisher, became patrons to La Sateuse, helping her to find a house nearby and to become economically self-sufficient, and they encouraged her conversion to Catholicism. According to Baird, her grandmother also adopted the newborn baby girl.[30]

In these ways, through marriage, adoption, patronage, or friendship, strangers gained kin networks, patrons, mentors, and interpreters but also supervisors, responsibilities, and commitments. Daughters of elite families became the brides of immigrants who were thought to be important to the community. Immigrants also gained status by affiliating with prominent Indian families. Native traditions of arranging young women's first marriages were tempered by the option of divorce and by greater choice for women in selecting subsequent marriage partners.[31] Creole networks put these wives in positions as intercultural mediators, enhancing both their authority and usefulness to their communities.

The Baird–LaFramboise Network

The geographic and ethnic range of these networks is illustrated by a collection of letters saved by Elizabeth Baird's family.[32] She, her mother, grandmother, and great-aunt were linked across hundreds of miles by ties of kinship, friendship, religious association, and business interests with an extremely diverse assortment of people.

For example, within a year after Elizabeth's marriage and move to Green Bay, her step-grandfather wrote to her from Mackinac Island: "Dear Betsey, . . . I am glad to see that you will be here shortly." The young bride was pregnant and planned to return to Mackinac where her kin could help her through the childbirth and teach her to care for her new baby. George Schindler, who was from Switzerland, reported that "your mother [h]as passed the winter with the unfortunate Mrs. Bailley."[33] Elizabeth's mother, Marianne Fisher, was probably at L'Arbre Croche, an Ottawa village on the mainland, with Angelique McGulpin Bailly, another French-Ottawa fur trade daughter who had experienced some misfortune. Elizabeth Baird's and Marianne Fisher's traveling to be with family and friends in times of childbirth, disease, or distress was typical of Anglo women and suggests that Creole women followed similar patterns.[34]

These networks also included workers who were not free, including Native American slaves. "Catish says that she will go and stay with you [when your baby comes],"[35] George Schindler wrote to Elizabeth. Catish was the nickname of Catherine La Croix, one of the family's Osage Indian slaves, who with her brother, niece, and nephew were considered members of the Ottawas, the tribe of their owners.[36] Catish's mother, Catherine Angelique, had probably been captured as a child around 1790 in what is now southern Missouri and sold or given to the Laframboise family.[37]

Elizabeth's great-aunt, Madeleine Laframboise (also known as Shaw-we-no-qua) at Mackinac, received a short letter written in French from Domitille Gauthier Brisbois of Prairie du Chien, inviting her to spend the winter of 1829–1830 with the Brisbois family.[38] Madame Brisbois descended from Ottawa and Illini Nations of Indians as well as from French Canadian fur traders. Historian Susan Sleeper-Smith has shown how the networks of Madame Brisbois's grandmother expanded from Cahokia in the Illinois Country to St. Joseph, Mackinac, and Green Bay.[39]

Another document among the family's correspondence illuminates Creole women's organizations in the region. Laframboise received a letter in French written in 1830 from Green Bay by Rosalie Laborde Dousman, who was Menominee and French.[40] It explained that the ladies of her religious society had been meeting on Mondays for prayers, and they sent their respects and prayers to the Mackinac ladies' society.[41] These Native-descended women who organized Christian women's groups seem similar to the Ojibwe groups that historian Rebecca Kugel described for the later nineteenth century. She found that in Minnesota, Ojibwe women's politically active traditional councils were transformed into women's church groups after the adoption of Episcopalian Christianity. These Ojibwe groups participated in community political discourse and continued seeking to influence local politics, to the dismay of male Anglo church leaders. The correspondence between Catholic women's organizations raises questions about whether they, too, had political agendas.[42]

Madame Laframboise was active in promoting Catholicism, serving as a lay minister to teach church doctrines to many women and girls in the area. In 1834, she received a letter in English to "My beloved Mamma" from Margaretta Maccotebinnessi at St. Clare's Seminary near Pittsburgh, dated March 18, 1834. After responding to news from home, Maccotebinnessi reported, "I did not receive the letter and Mocasins that you sent me," in care of Father Mazzuchelli. Laframboise regretted that she, herself, had not received an education, so she hired tutors for other young women and encouraged them to attend school. Maccotebinnessi, who was probably Laframboise's goddaughter, signed her letter, "From your most obedien[t] Child."[43] Through her patronage of girls such as Maccotebinnessi, Laframboise expanded her network, connecting them to hers.

Elizabeth Baird's step-niece, Emilie Rolette of Prairie du Chien, was the granddaughter of a Dakota woman. Rolette married U.S. Army Lieutenant Alexander Simon Hooe, who had been appointed a commissary and quartermaster and posted to Fort Winnebago, located at Portage in present-day Wisconsin.[44] In July 1831, Emilie wrote to Elizabeth of her trip to her new home ("We had a delightful journey . . . we had good weather, no musketoes") and of how pleased she was to find that "there is 9 married ladies and the two Miss[es] Low" living at the Fort. "I am delighted with this place . . . it is near[er] home and the country about is beautiful, [I take a] great many pleasant walks around the fort."[45] Emilie's father had been a prominent fur trader at Prairie du Chien. Her marriage to an army officer connected her family to the muscle of the new regime, and she cultivated friendships with the other officers' wives.

The fondness of friends and relatives comes through in many of the letters. "It is impossible for me to say how much I miss you. For the first few days of your absence I felt really desolate," wrote Eliza H. Platt, a recent migrant to the Green Bay area from Vermont, while Elizabeth Baird was away in 1837. "I went over to your house yesterday afternoon, and wandered through its silent and deserted apartments. The spirit of the place was gone. When will you come back and cheer us by your presence?"[46] Soon enough, Elizabeth was back home in Green Bay after visiting friends and relatives in Mackinac.

Taken together, this correspondence reveals that Elizabeth Baird's family and friends were part of a large network that connected people whose grandparents had lived in places as far apart as Switzerland and Missouri. They included Ottawa, Dakota, Osage, Menominee, and Illinois Indians as well as immigrants from France, Switzerland, Ireland, Scotland, and Canada. Between 1825 and 1837, they were located in Green Bay, Prairie du Chien, Portage, Mackinac Island, L'Arbre Croche, and Pittsburgh. Elizabeth and her relatives maintained ties to old friends in both Creole and indigenous communities while connecting with the newest immigrants, settlers, soldiers, and priests.

The New Regime

Increasing Anglo immigration and the introduction of U.S. social and political systems changed the dynamics of political power, ethnicity, and social hierarchy in the Great Lakes region. Women's status in Creole communities was negatively affected. The U.S. colonization of the Midwest accelerated a challenge to Native women's roles that had begun under the French regime. During their lifetimes, Elizabeth Baird, Pokoussee, and Euphrosine Antaya experienced a decline in legal status and property rights.

Wives like Pokoussee came from communities in which mature women had a substantial amount of autonomy in their personal lives and economic activity, both because they controlled key resources and forms of production and because the norms of Midwestern Native societies emphasized communalism and individual autonomy for women and men. Political traditions acknowledged Native women's right to have a voice in community decision making, and some tribes included women's, as well as men's, formal political organizations and roles.[47]

Native women managed their production of foods, such as corn, beans, squash, and maple sugar, and were considered to own the usufruct rights to the fields and sugar groves in which they worked.[48] And wives as mothers owned the family's property. A knowledgeable Indian agent reported, "It is a maxim among the Indians that every thing belong[s] to the woman or women except the Indian [man]'s hunting and war implements, even the game, the Indians bring home on his back."[49] Divorce was relatively easy, based upon the choice of spouse (although in a very few cases of diplomatic marriages, parents tried to prevent it).

But Europeans brought different ideas about marriage with them to the Americas. Roman Catholic priests taught that women should be subordinate to men, especially wives to their husbands. They opposed both divorce and pre- or extramarital sexual relations and expected that priests would perform weddings as religious ceremonies. Most other Europeans accepted patriarchy as a pattern for gender and family relations, but some adapted their views in America to conform to Native ways, especially when they intermarried. Native people tended to resist the patriarchal European ideas, although some were influenced by these norms. Women's status in Creole communities was also influenced by the French legal code, the *Coutume de Paris*, which was in force during the French and British regimes in the Great Lakes and Illinois regions roughly until the 1790s. This code was less permissive than Native practices, but it was more protective of wives' property than U.S. laws.[50]

The transition to U.S. control of the region in the early nineteenth century brought a legal and social system that reduced women's rights and stigmatized and marginalized Creoles. The newly dominant society not only brought different gender ideals, but also tried to enforce those values with laws and courts that constricted the rights of wives and rigidified the concept of marriage.[51] Euphrosine Antaya ran afoul of this system in 1824. She and her second husband, who had the wonderful name of Strange Powers, were targeted by the new court system with an indictment for fornication, even though they had been together for five years and had two children.[52] Local norms had recognized marriages contracted "according to the custom of the country" (according to Indian custom, without Christian ceremony or official licenses), but under the new regime these marriages were considered illicit, so couples in such partnerships came under the critical scrutiny of the new territorial courts.[53]

Fornication and adultery charges demonstrated the new territorial government's right to regulate people's intimate relations and also humiliated Creoles who followed Native domestic patterns. In 1824 and 1825, as Judge James Duane Doty inaugurated the Additional Circuit Court of Michigan Territory at Prairie du Chien and Green Bay, he instructed the grand juries to indict thirty-one men for fornication, including many of the Creole elites, because their marriages had been contracted according to the "custom of the country."[54] These boilerplate indictments usually contained strong language, alleging, in a typical example, that "Augustin Asselin . . . being an unmarried person of Lewd, Lascivious, depraved and abandoned mind and disposition, and wholly lost to all sense of decency, morality and religion . . . did unlawfully and wickedly . . . live and cohabit as man and wife with a woman by name the *little Pine alias La grosse Boulanger* of Lewd and dissolute habits, and . . . did comit whoredom and Fornication . . . divers disturbances and violations of the Peace of our said Territory and dreadfull filthy and Lewd offences in the same house." Furthermore, the indictment alleged that Asselin had done this "with intent to corrupt the morals of the Citizens of this territory, stir up and Excite in their minds filthy, Lewd and unchaste desires and inclinations to the great scandal and subversion of religion and good order to the great corruption of the morals and manners of the citizens . . . in contempt of the laws of this Territory."[55]

Such language may have been derived from standard court practices of the northeastern states, but those states' courts rarely prosecuted fornication by this time, and the New York Supreme Court had issued a ruling in 1809 legalizing common-law marriage, a decision that was widely accepted.[56] Thus, the new Additional Court was not extending to Wisconsin the legal practices of eastern states but, rather, was making a complex statement about Creole couples and intermarriage. Besides asserting the right of the new government to dictate the terms of their intimate relationships and challenging the very bases of their families, the courts insulted Creole mothers and fathers and attributed "evil" motives to them. The court's action against Euphrosine Antaya and Strange Powers caused her to file for divorce from her previous husband. After official court approval of the split, she formally married Strange Powers the following year.[57]

By requiring couples to conform to marriage laws, the U.S. courts ensured that Native-descended women like Little Pine and Euphrosine Antaya would be considered part of the "American" community, as would their children, potentially disengaging them legally from Native tribes. Officially licensed marriage acknowledged the domination of the U.S. government over Native and Creole societies as well as their intimacies, and the domination of husbands over their wives' property and behavior. The courts enforced this subordination of wives. For example, in 1825 Prudent Langlois went to a justice of the peace, James Lockwood, to complain that his wife, Margaret Manikikinik, had been sleeping with Louis Cardinal. Twice that summer she was summoned to answer to the court about her relationship with Cardinal, where witnesses testified about her personal life.[58] Divorces were not easy to obtain. They could be granted by the territorial legislature or a circuit court only for impotence, adultery, or bigamy, essentially requiring public scrutiny of intimate personal information.[59] Under this system, these women became wives who could not own property or make contracts on their own.[60] Thus, when Julia Gardipie was sure that François St. Jean had stolen "seven yards of blue nankin" cloth from her and took the matter to the local magistrate, she had to give a deposition stating that he had stolen the cloth from her husband.[61]

When land claims were recorded, beginning in 1820, most were entered only in the names of men. Because wives could not own property, husbands entered claims for land belonging to women. The claims map labeled each lot by its claimant, such as "Charles Menard who claims in right of his reputed wife Marianne Labuche Menard," and "Joseph Rolette for his wife Jane Fisher Rolette."[62] The land on which Strange and Euphrosine Antaya Powers's house was located had been in her family for a long time. The Mesquakies (Pokoussee's people) who lived nearby had in 1781 confirmed a land grant to Pierre Antaya and two other men. This grant became the village of Prairie du Chien.[63] Adjacent to the "Powers's" land in 1820—under the U.S. regime—were lots legally belonging to her sisters' husbands but probably family land from their mother Pokoussee. The records show that land as the property of Strange Powers, Michael Brisbois, Jr., Andre Basin, Pierre La Riviere, and Charles La Pointe. Their wives were Pokoussee's and Pierre's daughters Euphrosine, Catherine (who married Brisbois first, then Basin), Marguerite, and Josette Antaya, respectively. Their neighbors were other relatives.

Strange Powers died in 1838 without leaving a will. Euphrosine and a family friend, François Chenevert, were appointed to administer the estate, even though neither could read nor write. Under the laws of the territory, widows were entitled only to one-third of the couple's real estate and personal property and were not protected from creditors.[64] Minutes of court hearings about the estate's administration show evidence of the judge's concern for the creditors but none in protecting Euphrosine's dower rights.[65] For fifteen years the process continued, as Strange Powers's debts by far exceeded the value of his and Euphrosine's property, including four parcels of land, which were sold. The widow subdivided one lot, which she had owned long before marrying Strange Powers, into what became known as the "Mrs. Powers Plat," in an attempt to earn funds to settle the estate. (Her sons-in-law and a niece's husband bought some of the land but had trouble keeping up with tax payments.) Euphrosine bought back the land on which her house stood and mortgaged it, losing it to foreclosure in 1869.[66]

In this way, land belonging to these Native-descended women passed legally out of their hands into the possession of men whom the law had forced them to marry under threat of court action. Furthermore, their husbands' debt separated them from their land, in a system rigged to favor men's claims to land and to favor creditors over widows. Thus, they were "divorced from the land," to use the phrase of historian Jean O'Brien, who described the Native women of eighteenth-century Natick, Massachusetts.[67]

Turning Inward: Residential Patterns

Even as newcomers flooded into the Great Lakes region, Creole families continued to maintain relationships among family branches and between Creole communities and tribal friends and relations, maximizing available resources and nurturing Creole culture. In a way, we might invert an old metaphor and say that they were circling the wagons to defend against Anglo "pioneers." Their residential patterns reflected a clustering of extended kin, with women as the connecting links.

The Creoles' values were notably communal. In towns like Prairie du Chien, Detroit, Green Bay, and St. Genevieve, they built their homes along the rivers in close proximity to their neighbors, with their fields behind them or nearby. Historian Jacqueline Peterson argues that they "valued harmony and unanimity over competition; leisure over excess productivity; family and clan over economic interest and class; hospitality over exclusivity; generosity over saving; and today over tomorrow." She attributes these values to Native American cultural influences.[68]

Women were central to these families and relationships. We can see this in many of the residential patterns evident in the census of 1850. Historian Jennifer S. H. Brown has argued that Métis women in Rupert's Land were "centre and symbol in the emergence of Métis communities," and that their families were matrifocal in organization.[69] As census takers often walked door-to-door, a sense of neighborhoods emerges in the sequence of families on the population lists. If we add wives' maiden

TABLE 8.2.   U.S. Census, Prairie du Chien, Wisconsin, 1850

Dwelling	Name	Maiden name	Age	Sex	Occupation
229	Louis Barrett		26	M	Farming
	Caroline Barrett	Powers	19	F	
	2 children				
	Michael Barrett		15	M	Farming
230	Peter Barrette		49	M	Ferryman
	Theresa Barrett	LaPointe	40	F	
	8 children				
231	Charles Barrett		24	M	Farming
	Emily		20	F	
232	Frazini (Euphrosine) Powers[a]	Antaya	58	F	
233	Michael La Point		46	M	Farming
	4 children				
234	Mary La Point	Antaya	67	F	
	Michael La Point		22	M	Farming

Sources: "Population Schedules of the Seventh Census," 1850 manuscript, Crawford County, WI, microfilm M432, reel 995, 496–7, NA, Washington, DC; "Reminiscence of Theresa Barrette," in Martell, *Our People the Indians*, 52–53; and Hansen, "Crawford County, Wisconsin Marriages, 1816–1848," 50.
[a]This matrifocal cluster was anchored by Euphrosine Antaya Powers (in dwelling 232) and her cousin, Mary Antaya LaPointe (dwelling 234). Nearby lived Euphrosine's daughter Caroline Powers Barrette (dwelling 229) and grandchildren, Mary's son Michael and grandchildren, and niece Theresa LaPointe Barrette.

names to family lists, the records of census takers' rounds reveal a clustering of Prairie du Chien families related through the wives and mothers. In 1850, for example, the Antaya women still maintained a family cluster as they had in 1820. Euphrosine Antaya Powers was fifty-eight years old in 1850. Living next door on one side was her cousin Mary Antaya (widow of Francis La Pointe), with Mary's son Michel La Pointe, and five children (see table 8.2). Living on the other side of Euphrosine Antaya Powers were three houses of the Barrette family, including Barrette wives Caroline Powers (Euphrosine's daughter) and Theresa La Pointe (whose mother was Susan Antaya). These families had several Native connections: Euphrosine Antaya Powers and her siblings were half Mesquakie, and La Pointes and Barrettes appear on the official lists of "Sioux Mixed Bloods." For example, Emily Dousman Barrette, who lived next door to Euphrosine Antaya Powers, was one-quarter Dakota Sioux.[70] The residential pattern of Euphrosine Antaya Powers's family is typical of many Creole families in Prairie du Chien. It clearly demonstrates family clusters of kin connected through wives, mothers, and sisters.

This pattern of female kin and their families clustering together reflects the matrilocal residence patterns of many Midwestern tribes and Native women's habits of performing agricultural and other work in female kin groups. These residence patterns at Prairie du Chien suggest that the matrifocal pattern Brown noted in Rupert's Land was also practiced in Wisconsin. Family residential clustering of this type also suggests that this was a way of sharing resources and labor to cope not only with life's ordinary routines, but also with the challenges posed by the demographic shift and Anglo invasion. When I shared these observations with some of Euphrosine's and Strange's descendents, they noted that a large number of their family members still live within a few blocks of each other.[71]

Maintaining Ties and Reaching Outward

Although Creole people lost political power, status, and sheer numbers during the mid-nineteenth century, women could draw upon their networks and traditional roles as intercultural mediators to help one another and to enhance their usefulness to their communities. They served in roles that I refer to as "public mothers."[72] As Creoles and Native people lost power and numbers, the work of Creole women's mediation often revolved around charity work and hospitality. For many, this was part of their religious obligations. Native people believed (and many still believe) that "we are all related," including all people, all living things, and the earth. And they believed that it was their obligation to help all in need.[73] For example, in northern Illinois trader Stephen Mack learned this philosophy from his wife Hononegah, who was Ho-Chunk (also known as Winnebago). When she died, he wrote that "in her the hungry and naked have lost a benefactor, the sick a nurse, and I have lost a friend who . . . taught me to reverence God by doing good to his creatures." He continued, "Her funeral proved that I am not the only sufferer by her loss. My house is large but it was filled to overflowing by mourning friends who assembled to pay the last sad duties to her who had set them the example how to Live and how to Die."[74] Examples of other Native and Creole women's efforts are numerous in the historical record. As public mothers, they frequently provided healthcare in addition to these other forms of assistance.

Although there were proportionately fewer Native brides in frontier communities, many older Native women and their daughters and sons continued to live in areas of mixed population, where they provided hospitality and charity for Indians suffering the effects of land seizures, late or inadequate annuities, poorly administered Indian Bureau policies, disease, and other social, economic, and political disruptions.

One such instance was evident in testimony taken in Prairie du Chien during 1838–39, relating to distribution of treaty money earmarked for Ho-Chunk "half-breeds." The leading men of Prairie du Chien and Green Bay testified that a woman named "Man-ne-te-se is the full sister of . . . the most influential Chiefs of the Tribe." As the wife of Jean Lequyér,

> having plenty in the world, her house was called the home of the naked & hungry Indian. . . . When she was left a widow, she had a fine lot of goods, horses, waggons, fine stock of cattle, and was considered wealthy. . . . All her valuable property . . . was sacrificed in support or harboring of Winnebago Indians, who applied to her in all cases for relief, as being the hospitable sister of their principal chiefs.

In 1839, she lived with her daughter, Julia Grignon, in Prairie du Chien, and their house, it was said, "is known to the citizens of Prairie du Chien as the resting place of the Winnebagoes when in the Village. . . . Julia Grignon has given her last loaf of bread to hungry Indians, & on some occasions *sold her own clothes to relieve their distress.*"[75]

Prairie du Chien's county and local government records detailed the names of those who cared for the community's paupers, receiving reimbursement from local funds. Euphrosine Antaya Powers was among a small number of residents (mostly Creoles) who took care of paupers around 1844.[76] In addition, many Creole women reached out to newcomers, to people who were from very different backgrounds and ethnic groups. In Michigan, Wisconsin, and northern Illinois, mature Native and métis women commonly worked at creating ties between the Anglo newcomers, their francophone Creole neighbors, and Native American villagers during the early years of Anglo American immigration. Many women continued these mediation efforts during the later nineteenth century and into the twentieth century, passing the tradition from mother to child.

An example of this pattern may be found in a family genealogy compiled by Mary Martell during the 1940s, which recalled her ancestor, Mary La Pointe La Tranche, born in Prairie du Chien about 1838, who married and moved across the river to Iowa during the late 1850s. Madame La Tranche "would go around with an old Indian woman doctor and do the talking for her as this lady could not speak one word of English—only made the Indian sign signals. In doing this, Mary learned a great deal about taking care of the sick and in later years she went herself. She brought a good many of the now [1950] old-timers . . . into the world. Many a cold, stormy night she braved the storm to go to someone in distress. She kept up this practice until she was quite old."[77] Clearly, both the "old Indian woman doctor" and Madame La Tranche were reaching across the cultural borders from Native to Creole to Anglo in their community. There are many similar examples of this type of healthcare-related mediation in accounts by both Anglos and Creoles around the Midwest.

Interviews reveal some of the details of this continuing legacy. Take, for example, Pokoussee's granddaughter (Euphrosine Antaya's niece), Clara LaPointe Hertzog (born ca. 1835), who married an immigrant from Luxembourg (another exogamous marriage). Clara's daughter Adaline Hertzog Barrette was interviewed by a genealogist in 1949 and recalled, "I can remember . . . the Indians dancing in our back yard, my mother never minded them at all, she herself had Indian blood and she knew their languages and was able to carry on a conversation with them, they always treated mother very well, and looked to her for advice and instructions, she was often invited to their abode to eat."[78] Her descendants told me that Adaline Hertzog Barrette (born 1861) continued these relationships in the late nineteenth century and into the twentieth century. She and her husband socialized and traveled with Indian friends or relatives. Some families kept camping grounds on their farms for Indian friends and relatives, the Barrette family among them. I was told, "Grandmother [Barrette] used to take care of them. . . . And if they were sick, she used to nurse them to health, do what she could for them. If they were hungry, she'd feed them. And in turn, if she had a problem [with a threatening visitor] the Indians came and took him away."[79]

Many other families have similar stories; I have found examples of relationships very much like these—relationships that women facilitated between Native, Creole, and Anglo individuals and groups—in many communities in Illinois, Iowa, Wisconsin, and Michigan.[80] Even today, when their descendents talk about the values and practices of their neighborhoods, they stress that people looked out for each other and fed the poor.

Conclusion

Changes to the Midwest after the United States took control had important implications for Native and Creole women's status. Colonization reduced the property rights of wives, forced women into legal roles of subordination to their husbands, and separated women from their land. Courts (in which women could not serve as judges or jurors) also enforced new control of their personal lives. Immigrants streamed into their communities, bringing with them their prejudices against Indians, mixed marriages, and Canadians. Native, métis, and other Creole women responded by extending their networks outward, shifting patterns of intermarriage, clustering their kin residentially, and maintaining spaces for Native people to visit. Women were central to the networks that served as such important resources in coping with the transitions of the nineteenth century in the Great Lakes region.

Notes

I would like to thank The Ohio State University (OSU) for sabbatical leave and the Committee on Institutional Cooperation American Indian Studies Consortium and the Newberry Library, Chicago, D'Arcy McNickle Center for a 2006–2007 fellowship to work on this project. Additional funding was provided by Ohio State Newark, for which I am grateful. An earlier version of this chapter was presented on 24 October 2007, for the American Indian Studies Program lecture series at Ohio State University. Portions of this chapter were presented on 26 May 2007 at "Early American History, 1600–1877, in Global Perspective: An International Conference," in Tianjin, China. The conference was sponsored by the Fulbright Foundation, the Institute of American History and Culture, and the Research Center for the History of the Modern World, Nankai University, Tianjin, China. I would like to thank fellow conference participants for helpful comments. Thanks also to Rebecca Kugel, Alcira Dueñas, and Katey Borland for suggestions on earlier drafts of this chapter and to my former research assistant, Cecily Barker McDaniel, for her work with the census data.

A note on terms: The terms "American Indian," "Native American," "Native," and "Indian" are used interchangeably according to American Indian Studies usage to refer to the indigenous peoples of the Americas. The term "Métis" is commonly used in Canada, but only sporadically in the United States, to refer to people of mixed Indian and European ancestry. In order to distinguish ancestry from culture, I use the term "Creole" to refer to people of any race who participated in the syncretic society and culture discussed in this chapter. Not only the métis children, but also their Indian mothers and Euro-American fathers were Creoles. Most were francophones (French speakers) but also spoke Indian languages. Because the term "American" can be confusing and misleading, I generally refer to those who immigrated to the Midwest of North America from the United States as anglophones (English speakers) or Anglos, or, if they came from the U.S. northeast, as Yankees. These might include African Americans, but they were usually Euro-Americans. I also refer to the Great Lakes region (the area around the western Great Lakes) and the Midwest, the latter including the present states of Michigan, Wisconsin, Ohio, Indiana, Illinois, Iowa, and Minnesota. The Ho-Chunk people are sometimes called the Winnebagos; the Fox Indians now prefer Mesquakie; and Ojibwe Indians were previously known as the Chippewa (some still use that term, whereas others prefer Anishnaabe). Ottawa Indians are sometimes called Odawa.

1. Forsyth, "A List of the Sac and Fox half breeds who claim land according to the Treaty made at Washington City with the Chiefs Sac and Fox Tribes on 4th August 1824," Thomas Forsyth Papers, Lyman Draper Manuscripts, microfilm, 2T, p. 22, State Historical Society of Wisconsin Library, Madison (hereafter cited as WHS Library).

2. Brown and Schenck, "Métis, Mestizo, and Mixed-Blood," 332.

3. Lucy Eldersveld Murphy, "After the Fur Trade," work in progress.

4. "Prairie du Chien," *Madison Wisconsin Enquirer,* 26 February 1840.

5. Beltrami, *Pilgrimage in Europe and America,* 2:174.

6. James Duane Doty, Green Bay, to Joseph Brisbois, Prairie du Chien, 3 May 1831, letterbook (microfilm), pp. 148–149, Doty Papers, Bentley Library, Ann Arbor, MI.

7. "Treaty with the Sauk and Foxes, etc.," 15 July 1830, in Kappler, *Indian Affairs: Laws and Treaties,* vol. 2, *Treaties,* p. 307. Originally published by the GPO in 1904 and now available at http://digital.library.okstate.edu/kappler/ (accessed 29 October 2010). The word choice was clearly made by the interpreters and officials.

8. Atwater, *Remarks on Tour to Prairie du Chien,* 180.

9. For example, "Population Schedules of the Eighth Census," 1860 manuscript, microfilm M653, reel 1402, NA, Washington, DC; and U.S. Census Office, *Population of the United States in 1860,* 534.

10. John W. Johnson to George C. Sibley, 28 April 1817, Prairie du Chien, Sibley Papers, Missouri Historical Society collections, St. Louis.

11. McDermott, *Glossary of Mississippi Valley French,* 60–62. Folklorist Nicholas R. Spitzer traces the word *creole* to the Portuguese *crioulo* ("native to a region") and

finds that, "It is especially significant for folklorists (given our penchant for expressive culture) that the root verb in Latin, *crear*, means 'to create.' Indeed creole peoples are often the makers of memorable and significant new cultural expression." He points out that although "European control of the word *creole* initially defined 'native to a region' as a white person of European descent born and raised in a tropical colony . . . this meaning shifted in practice to include people of non-European origin, and especially those perceived as having multiracial, 'mixed' ancestry" (Spitzer, "Monde Créole," 59).

12. "Etat et dénombrement de la population . . . ," compiled by Pierre-Charles de Lassus de Luzières in 1797 and located in the Archivo General de Indies in Seville, legajo 2365; and Carl Ekberg, personal correspondence with Lucy Murphy, 27 October 2006. Thanks to Carl Ekberg for sharing this source.

13. DePeyster, letter to General Frederick Haldimand, 8 June 1780.

14. The article was apparently extracted from the report of a committee that interviewed Tanner about his travels. The committee is given as "Messrs. Woodward, Rowland, and Shattuck" (Woodward et al., "Wisconsin in 1818 by Edward Tanner," 8:289).

15. Rentmeester and Rentmeester, *Wisconsin Creoles*, v–iii (quote is from p. v).

16. "Creole," *(Iowa) Patriot*, 6 June 1839.

17. Thwaites, "Narrative of Andrew J. Vieau, Sr.," 234.

18. Joseph Brisbois, Prairie du Chien, to Morgan L. Martin, Member of the Legislative Council, Detroit, 10 December 1832, Green Bay and Prairie du Chien Papers, micro. p. 144, frame 340, WHS Library.

19. Albert E. Coryer, Interview, broadcast, and anecdotes, WHS Library.

20. Some works on this topic include Peterson, "People in Between"; Kidwell, "Indian Women as Cultural Mediators"; Van Kirk, *"Many Tender Ties"*; Brown, *Strangers in Blood*; Thorne, *Many Hands of My Relations*; Sleeper-Smith, *Indian Women and French Men*; Ekberg, *French Roots in the Illinois Country*; and Murphy, *Gathering of Rivers*. The reference is to Richard White, *Middle Ground*.

21. McEvedy and Jones, *Atlas of World Population History*, 280.

22. The names of 133 males appear in records. Of these, fifty-four were Métis, six were Anglo-American (including one Jew), five French Canadian, three Afro-French, one Mandan Indian, and sixty-five "not ascertained." Hansen, "Prairie du Chien's Earliest Church Records, 1817," 329–42; Lockwood, "Early Times and Events in Wisconsin," 2:125–126; Hoffmann, *Antique Dubuque, 1673–1833*, 51–59; and U.S. Congress, *American State Papers*, 5:47–98, 270–72, 283–328. Thanks to James L. Hansen for help gathering information about these people.

23. Motz, *True Sisterhood*; Miller, " 'Those with Whom I Feel Most Nearly Connected' "; and Sleeper-Smith, *Indian Women and French Men*.

24. For an extended discussion of this issue, see Murphy, "Public Mothers."

25. Peterson, "People in Between," 161, 163; Elizabeth T. Baird, Memoranda, box 4, folder 1, Henry S. Baird Papers, WHS Library.

26. Probably, Marie Nekesh's mother was Mejakwataw. Peterson, "People in Between," 161, 163; Elizabeth T. Baird, memoranda, Henry S. and Elizabeth

Baird Papers, WIS MSS V, box 4, folder 1, WHS Library; and Elizabeth T. Baird, "O-De-Jit-Wa-Win-Wing: Contes du Temps Passe," box 4, folder 9, Henry S. Baird Papers, WHS Library.

27. Elizabeth T. Baird to Henry Baird, 22 July 1825, WIS MSS V box 1, folder 1, Henry S. Baird Papers, WHS Library.

28. She was mentioned in the 1821 treaty with the Ottawa, Chippewa, and Pottawatomi Indians as "Theresa Chandler or Tó-e-ak-qui, a Potawatamie woman." Both she and her "daughter" Betsey Fisher (actually her granddaughter) were to receive land. However, the terms of the treaty were later changed, and they were allocated money instead (Kappler, *Indian Affairs*, vol. 2, *Treaties*, 199).

29. La Sateuse meant "the Ojibwe woman" (McDermott, *Glossary of Mississippi Valley French, 1673–1850*, s.v. "Saulters," 136). John Tanner was a white captive who wrote a narrative of his life titled *The Falcon, A Narrative of the Captivity & Adventures of John Tanner During Thirty Years Residence Among the Indians in the Interior of North America* that was published in 1830.

30. Elizabeth T. Baird, "O-De-Jit-Wa-Win-Wing; Contes du Temps Passe," box 4, folder 9, Henry and Elizabeth Baird Papers, WHS Library; McDowell, "Therese Schindler of Mackinac"; and Sleeper-Smith, "Women, Kin, and Catholicism," 432–38.

31. Van Kirk, *"Many Tender Ties"*; Brown, *Strangers in Blood*; Peterson, "People in Between"; Thorne, "For the Good of Her People" and *Many Hands of My Relations*; Bruce M. White, "Woman Who Married the Beaver"; Lurie, *Mountain Wolf Woman*; and Kidwell, "Indian Women as Cultural Mediators."

32. The letters are in the Henry and Elizabeth Baird Papers, WHS Library.

33. George Schindler to Elizabeth Baird, 7[?] May 1825, box 1, folder 1, Henry S. Baird Papers, WHS Library; Angelique Bailly was an Odawa woman married to fur trader Joseph Bailly. Mission of St. Ignace de Michilimakinak, "Mackinac Register," 19:141; and Sleeper-Smith, *Indian Women and French Men*, 155–59, 218n56, 219n69.

34. Smith-Rosenberg, "Female World of Love and Ritual"; and Miller, "Those with Whom I Feel Most Nearly Connected."

35. George Schindler to Elizabeth Baird, 7[?] May 1825, box 1, folder 1, Henry S. Baird Papers, WHS Library.

36. Elizabeth T. Baird, "O-De-Jit-Wa-Win-Wing; Contes du Temps Passe," box 4, folder 9, pp. 6–7, Henry S. Baird Collection, WHS Library. This memoir originally appeared as a serial in the *Green Bay (WI) State Gazette*, 4 December 1886–19 November 1887. Treaty with the Bands of the Ottawa and Chippewa, 28 March 1836, "Claim of Charles (or Isaac) Butterfield," special file 124 in Special Files of the Office of Indian Affairs, microfilm M574, roll 230, NA, Washington, DC; Ste. Anne's Church (Mackinac Island, MI), "Mackinac Register, 1695–1888" (electronic resource), 15 August 1823, 15 October 1825, and 21 July 1829, WHS Library. Thanks are extended to James L. Hansen of the WHS Library for locating this information about the La Croix family. This comment suggests that Catish did have some say in where she worked.

37. Waldman, *Atlas of the North American Indian*, 45. For these slaves, colonization by the U.S. meant emancipation, but only gradually. Judge Augustus Woodward of Detroit declared in 1807 that slaves born after 1793 should be freed at age twenty-five (Magnaghi, "Red Slavery in the Great Lakes Country").

38. Kappler, *Indian Affairs*, vol. 2, *Treaties*, 200. Domitille Brisbois to Madame Laframboise, 29 June 1829, box 1, folder 2, Baird Papers, WHS Library.

39. Mission of St. Ignace de Michilimakinak, "Mackinac Register," 18:490, 492; Peterson, "People In-Between," 161; and Sleeper-Smith, "Women, Kin, and Catholicism."

40. WIS MSS BU, Account Book of 1849 Payment, pp. 9, 22, Menominee Indian Papers, WHS Library.

41. Rosalie Dousman to Madame Laframboise, [?] October 1830, box 1, folder 2, Baird Papers, WHS Library.

42. Kugel, "Leadership within the Women's Community." Interestingly, Father Samuel Mazzuchelli, the priest who ministered to the region, did not mention these groups in his memoir, though he did acknowledge Métis women's important roles as catechists. This evidence suggests that the women's groups were self-initiated rather than organized by the priest or the church. Mazzuchelli, *Memoirs of Father Samuel Mazzuchelli*.

43. Margaretta Maccotebinnessi to Mrs. M. Laframboise, 18 March 1834, WIS MSS V, box 1, folder 3, Baird Papers, WHS Library.

44. Hansen, "Roll of Sioux Mixed Bloods, 1855–56," 603; and James L. Hansen, letter to author, 9 April 2007.

45. Emilie Hooe to Elizabeth Baird, 19 July 1831, box 1, folder 2, Henry S. Baird Papers, WHS Library.

46. Eliza H. Platt, Navarino, to Elizabeth Baird, Mackinac, 10 September 1837, box 1, folder 2, Henry S. Baird Papers, WHS Library.

47. Thorne, "For the Good of Her People"; and Kugel, "Leadership within the Women's Community."

48. Lurie, "Indian Women"; Pond, "1740–1175: Journal of Peter Pond," 335; and Forsyth, "Account of the Manners and Customs," 218. For an extended discussion of Native women's status, see Murphy, "Autonomy and Economic Roles."

49. Forsyth, "Account of the Manners and Customs," 218.

50. Greer, *People of New France*, 69–71; and Boyle, "Did She Generally Decide?"

51. A parallel situation was occurring in western Canada at a later date. See Sarah Carter, *Importance of Being Monogamous*.

52. *United States v. Strange Poze*, Indictment for Fornication, Circuit Court of the United States for the County of Crawford of the term of May 1824, courtesy of Dale Klemme; and Hansen, "Pelletier dit Antaya Families."

53. Greer, *People of New France*, 69–71; Lockwood, "Early Times and Events in Wisconsin," 121–22, 176; Peterson, "People In-Between," 1; and Childs, "Recollections of Wisconsin since 1820," 167.

54. Jung, "Judge James Duane Doty," 31; and Peterson, "People In-Between," 1, counted thirty-six at Green Bay. See also Saler, "Treaty Polity," 259.

55. *United States v. Augustin Asselin*, Indictment for fornication, 9 May 1825, Iowa Series 20, WHS Library, Platteville. Emphasis in original.

56. Nelson, *Americanization of the Common Law*, 110; and Hall, *Magic Mirror*, 154. The case was *Fenton v. Reed* (1809).

57. *United States v. Strange Poze* (1824); and Rentmeester and Rentmeester, *Wisconsin Creoles*, 322–23. I have been unable to discover the story behind this man's remarkable name.

58. *United States v. Louis Cardinal*, Iowa Series 20, folder 16, WHS Library, Platteville.

59. *Laws of the Territory of the United States North-West of the Ohio*, 182–83.

60. Kulikoff, *From British Peasants to Colonial American Farmers*, 231–32.

61. Crawford County Clerk Board Papers 1817–1848, box 1, folder 2, WHS Library.

62. "Plan of the Settlement at Prairie des Chiens from the Report of J. Lee Esqre Agent" (1820), reproduced in Scanlan, *Prairie du Chien*, 186–87.

63. Scanlan, *Prairie du Chien*, 70–71. At least one of the other two men had a Mesquakie wife.

64. *Some of the Acts of Territory of Michigan*, 61. Wives could veto the sale of land, however (p. 45). *Statutes of the Territory of Wisconsin*, 308–309.

65. Crawford County [Wisconsin] Courthouse, county court minutes, Prairie du Chien, WI, book A, 110; probate book A, 312–21, passim; book B, 14–396, passim; and probate file, 3–4.

66. Catherine was married first to Michael Brisbois, Jr., and then to Andre Basin. Hansen, "Pelletier dit Antaya Families"; *National Register of Historic Places Inventory*, 2; Klemme, "So, What Do We Know?" [pamphlet]. Thanks to Dale Klemme of Prairie du Chien for sharing this with me.

67. O'Brien, "Divorced from the Land."

68. Peterson, "Goodbye, Madore Beaubien," 101.

69. Brown, "Woman as Centre and Symbol."

70. Hansen, "A Roll of Sioux Mixed Bloods, 1855–56," 604.

71. Rosemary Stephens, Geri Curley, and Philip Barrette, interview with author, 12 September 2007, Prairie du Chien, WI.

72. Murphy, "Public Mothers."

73. For example, the motto of the Native American Indian Center of Central Ohio (NAICCO) in Columbus, Ohio, is *"Mitakuye Oyasin,"* a Lakota phrase or prayer meaning "all my relations," or the concept that "we are all related" and that we have obligations to "people, animals, and everything that God has created" (NAICCO website, www.naicco.org, accessed 10 September 2009; and Carol Welsh, executive director of NAICCO, conversation with author).

74. Bishop and Campbell, *History of the Forest Preserves*, 35.

75. Waggoner, *"Neither White Men Nor Indians,"* 31–32. Emphasis in original.

76. Wisconsin Territorial Papers, County Series, Crawford County, "Proceedings of the County Board of Supervisors," 155.

77. Martell, *Our People the Indians*, 7.

78. Ibid., 53.

79. Rosemary Stephens, Geri Curley, Phil Barrette, and Doris Barrette, interview with author, 1 August 2002, Prairie du Chien, WI. Myra Lang also said that grandparents kept a place on their farm for Indians to stop on their travels and "always treated them right, and fed them and so on." Myra Lang and Chuck Lang, interview with author, 2 August 2002, Prairie du Chien, WI.

80. Murphy, "Public Mothers."

Works Cited

Archival Sources

Ann Arbor, MI
  Bentley Library.
    James Duane Doty Papers. Microfilm.
Madison, WI
  State Historical Society of Wisconsin Library (WHS Library).
    Baird, Elizabeth T. Papers.
    Baird, Henry S. Papers.
    Coryer, Albert E. Interview, broadcast, and anecdotes.
    Crawford County Clerk Board Papers 1817–1848.
    Draper, Lyman. Manuscripts.
      Forsyth, Thomas. Papers.
    Green Bay and Prairie du Chien Papers.
    Menominee Indian Papers.
    Ste. Anne's Church, "Mackinac Register, 1695–1888" (electronic resource).
Prairie du Chien, WI
  Crawford County [Wisconsin] Courthouse, county court minutes.
Seville, Spain
  Archivo General de Indies.
    "Etat et dénombrement de la population du Poste de la Nouvelle Bourbon des Illinois." Compiled by Pierre-Charles de Lassus de Luzières in 1797. Legajo 2365.
St. Louis, MO
  Missouri Historical Society.
    Sibley Papers.
Washington, DC
  National Archives.
    "Population Schedules of the Eighth Census." 1860 manuscript. Crawford County, WI, microfilm M653, reel 1402.
    "Population Schedules of the Seventh Census." 1850 manuscript. Crawford County, WI, microfilm M432, reel 995.
    Special Files of the Office of Indian Affairs. M574, roll 230.

Published Sources

Atwater, Caleb. *Remarks Made on a Tour to Prairie du Chien in 1829*. Columbus, OH: Isaac Whiting, 1831.

Beltrami, Giacomo Constantino. *A Pilgrimage in Europe and America*. Vol. 2. London, UK: Hunt & Clarke, 1828.

Bishop, David, and Craig G. Campbell. *History of the Forest Preserves of Winnebago County, Illinois*. Rockford, IL: Winnebago County Forest Preserve Commission, 1979.

Boyle, Susan C. "Did She Generally Decide? Women in Ste. Genevieve, 1750–1805." *William and Mary Quarterly* (3rd series), 44, no. 4 (October 1987): 775–89.

Brown, Jennifer S. H. *Strangers in Blood: Fur Trade Company Families in Indian Country*. Vancouver: University of British Columbia Press, 1980.

———. "Woman as Centre and Symbol in the Emergence of Métis Communities." *The Canadian Journal of Native Studies* 3, no. 1 (1983): 39–46.

Brown, Jennifer S. H., and Theresa Schenck. "Métis, Mestizo, and Mixed-Blood." In *A Companion to American Indian History*, edited by Philip J. Deloria and Neal Salisbury, 321–38. Malden, MA: Blackwell Publishers, 2002.

[Butterfield, C. W.]. *History of Crawford and Richland Counties, Wisconsin*. 2 vols. Springfield, IL: Union Publishing Company, 1884.

Carter, Sarah. *The Importance of Being Monogamous: Marriage and Nation Building in Western Canada to 1915*. Edmonton: University of Alberta Press and University of Athabasca Press, 2008.

Childs, Ebenezer. "Recollections of Wisconsin since 1820." In *Wisconsin Historical Collections*, 4:153–96. Madison: Wisconsin State History Society, 1859.

"Creole." *(Iowa) Patriot*, 6 June 1839.

DePeyster, Arent Schuyler. Letter to General Frederick Haldimand dated 8 June 1780. *Wisconsin Historical Collections* 12 (1892): 50.

Ekberg, Carl J. *French Roots in the Illinois Country: The Mississippi Frontier in Colonial Times*. Urbana: University of Illinois Press, 1998.

Forsyth, Thomas. "An Account of the Manners and Customs of the Sauk and Fox Nations of Indians Tradition." In *The Indian Tribes of the Upper Mississippi Valley and Region of the Great Lakes*, edited by Emma Helen Blair, II, 183–245. Cleveland, OH: Arthur H. Clark, 1911.

Greer, Allan. *The People of New France*. Toronto, ON: University of Toronto Press, 1997.

Hall, Kermit L. *The Magic Mirror: Law in American History*. New York, NY: Oxford University Press, 1989.

Hansen, James L. "Crawford County, Wisconsin Marriages, 1816–1848." *Minnesota Genealogical Journal* 1 (May 1984): 39–58.

———. "The Pelletier dit Antaya Families of Prairie du Chien." Forthcoming.

———. "Prairie du Chien's Earliest Church Records, 1817." *Minnesota Genealogical Journal* 4 (1985): 329–42.

————, ed. "A Roll of Sioux Mixed Bloods, 1855–56." *Minnesota Genealogical Journal* 7 (November 1987): 601–20.

Harlan, Elizabeth Taft, Minnie Dubbs Millbrook, and Elizabeth Case Erwin, trans. and eds. *1830 Federal Census: Territory of Michigan*. Detroit, MI: Detroit Society for Genealogical Research, 1961.

Hoffman, M. M. *Antique Dubuque, 1673–1833*. Dubuque, IA: 1930.

Jung, Patrick J. "Judge James Duane Doty and Wisconsin's First Court: The Additional Court of Michigan Territory, 1823–1836." *Wisconsin Magazine of History* 86, no. 2 (Winter 2002–2003): 31–41.

Kappler, Charles J., comp. and ed. *Indian Affairs: Laws and Treaties*. Vol. 2, *Treaties*. Washington, DC: Government Printing Office, 1904.

Kidwell, Clara Sue. "Indian Women as Cultural Mediators." *Ethnohistory* 39, no. 2 (1992): 97–107.

Klemme, Dale. *So What Do We Know?* [Pamphlet]. Prairie du Chien, WI, privately printed.

Kugel, Rebecca. "Leadership within the Women's Community: Susie Bonga Wright of the Leech Lake Ojibwe." In *Midwestern Women: Work, Community, and Leadership at the Crossroads*, edited by Lucy Eldersveld Murphy and Wendy Hamand Venet, 17–37. Bloomington: University of Indiana Press, 1997.

Kulikoff, Allan. *From British Peasants to Colonial American Farmers*. Chapel Hill: University of North Carolina Press, 2000.

Laws of the Territory of the United States North-West of the Ohio. Cincinnati, OH: W. Maxwell, 1796.

Lockwood, James H. "Early Times and Events in Wisconsin." In *Wisconsin Historical Collections* 2:98–196. Madison: Wisconsin State History Society, 1856.

Lurie, Nancy Oestreich. "Indian Women: A Legacy of Freedom." In *Look to the Mountain Top*, edited by Charles Jones, 29–36. San Jose, CA: Gousha, 1972.

————, ed. *Mountain Wolf Woman, Sister of Crashing Thunder: The Autobiography of a Winnebago Indian*. Ann Arbor: University of Michigan Press, 1961.

Magnaghi, Russell M. "Red Slavery in the Great Lakes Country during the French and British Regimes." *The Old Northwest* 12, no. 2 (Summer 1986): 201–17.

Martell, Mary. *Our People the Indians: A Genealogy of the Indians and French Canadians, 1750–1950: In the Areas of Prairie du Chien, Wisconsin, Harpers Ferry, Iowa, and Pembina-Red River of the North in N. Dakota and Minnesota*. Privately published, ca. 1950.

Mazzuchelli, Samuel. *The Memoirs of Father Samuel Mazzuchelli, o.p.* Chicago, IL: Priory Press, 1967.

McDermott, John Francis. *A Glossary of Mississippi Valley French, 1673–1850*. St. Louis, MO: Washington University Studies, 1941.

McDowell, John E. "Therese Schindler of Mackinac: Upward Mobility in the Great Lakes Fur Trade." *Wisconsin Magazine of History* 61, no. 2 (1977–78): 125–43.

McEvedy, Colin, and Richard Jones. *Atlas of World Population History*. New York, NY: Facts on File, 1978.

Miller, Tamara G. " 'Those with Whom I Feel Most Nearly Connected': Kinship and Gender in Early Ohio." In *Midwestern Women: Work, Community, and Leadership at the Crossroads,* edited by Lucy Eldersveld Murphy and Wendy Hamand Venet, 121–40. Bloomington: University of Indiana Press, 1997.

Mission of St. Ignace de Michilimakinak. "The Mackinac Register." In *Wisconsin Historical Collections* 19:1–162. Madison: Wisconsin State History Society, 1910.

Motz, Marilyn Ferris. *True Sisterhood: Michigan Women and Their Kin, 1820–1920.* Albany, NY: State University of New York Press, 1983.

Murphy, Lucy Eldersveld. "Autonomy and the Economic Roles of Indian Women of the Fox-Wisconsin Region, 1763–1832." In *Negotiators of Change: Historical Perspectives on Native American Women,* edited by Nancy Shoemaker, 72–89. New York, NY: Routledge Press, 1994.

———. *A Gathering of Rivers: Indians, Métis, and Mining in the Western Great Lakes, 1737–1832.* Lincoln: University of Nebraska Press, 2000.

———. "Public Mothers: Native American and Métis Women as Creole Mediators in the Nineteenth-Century Midwest." *Journal of Women's History* 14, no. 4 (Winter 2003): 142–66.

Musick, James B. *St. Louis as a Fortified Town.* St. Louis, MO: Press of R. F. Miller, 1941.

National Register of Historic Places Inventory—Nomination Form. [Pamphlet for Strange Powers's House]. In the author's possession.

Nelson, William E. *Americanization of the Common Law: The Impact of Legal Change on Massachusetts Society, 1760–1830.* Cambridge, MA: Harvard University Press, 1975.

O'Brien, Jean. "Divorced from the Land." In *After King Philip's War: Presence and Persistence in Indian New England,* edited by Colin G. Calloway, 144–61. Hanover, NH: University Press of New England / Dartmouth College, 1997.

Peterson, Jacqueline. "Goodbye, Madore Beaubien: The Americanization of Early Chicago Society." *Chicago History* 9 (Summer 1980): 98–111.

———. "The People in Between: Indian–White Marriage and the Genesis of a Métis Society and Culture in the Great Lakes Region, 1680–1830." PhD diss., University of Illinois at Chicago Circle, 1981.

Pond, Peter. "1740–75: Journal of Peter Pond." In *Wisconsin Historical Collections* 18:314–54. Madison: Wisconsin State History Society, 1908.

"Prairie du Chien." *Madison Wisconsin Enquirer.* 26 February 1840. Reprinted from *Galena (IL) Gazette and Advertiser.*

Rentmeester, Les, and Jeanne Rentmeester. *Wisconsin Creoles.* Melbourne, FL: privately printed, 1987.

Russell, Donna Valley, ed. *Michigan Censuses 1710–1830.* Detroit, MI: Detroit Society for Genealogical Research, Inc., 1982.

Saler, Bethel. "The Treaty Polity: Gender, Race, and the Transformation of Wisconsin from Indian Country into an American State, 1776–1854." PhD diss., University of Wisconsin, 1999.

Scanlan, Peter Lawrence. *Prairie du Chien: French, British, American*. Menasha, WI: Collegiate Press, 1937.

Sleeper-Smith, Susan. *Indian Women and French Men: Rethinking Cultural Encounter in the Western Great Lakes*. Amherst: University of Massachusetts Press, 2001.

———. "Women, Kin, and Catholicism: New Perspectives on the Fur Trade." *Ethnohistory* 47, no. 2 (Spring 2000): 423–52.

Smith-Rosenberg, Carroll. "The Female World of Love and Ritual: Relations between Women in Nineteenth-Century America." *Signs: Journal of Women in Culture and Society* 1, no. 1 (1975): 1–29.

Some of the Acts of the Territory of Michigan with the Titles and a Digest of all the Acts of the Said Territory; Now in Force. Detroit, MI: Theophilus Mettez, 1816.

Spitzer, Nicholas R. "Monde Créole: The Cultural World of French Louisiana Creoles and the Creolization of World Cultures." *The Journal of American Folklore* 116, no. 459 (Winter, 2003): 57–72.

Statutes of the Territory of Wisconsin. Albany, NY: Packard, Van Benthuysen & Co., 1839.

Thorne, Tanis C. "For the Good of Her People: Continuity and Change for Native Women of the Midwest, 1650–1850." In *Midwestern Women: Work, Community, and Leadership at the Crossroads*, edited by Lucy Eldersveld Murphy and Wendy Hamand Venet, 95–120. Bloomington: University of Indiana Press, 1997.

———. *The Many Hands of My Relations: French and Indians on the Lower Missouri*. Columbia: University of Missouri Press, 1996.

Thwaites, Reuben Gold. "Narrative of Andrew J. Vieau, Sr." In *Wisconsin Historical Collections* 11:218–237. Madison, WI: Democrat Printing Co., State Printers, 1888.

Van Kirk, Sylvia. *"Many Tender Ties": Women in Fur-Trade Society*. Winnipeg, MB: Watson and Dwyer; Norman: University of Oklahoma Press, 1980.

Waggoner, Linda M., ed. *"Neither White Men nor Indians": Affidavits from the Winnebago Mixed-Blood Claim Commissions, Prairie du Chien, Wisconsin, 1838–1839*. Roseville, MN: Park Genealogical Books, 2002.

Waldman, Carl, ed. *Atlas of the North American Indian*. Rev. ed. New York, NY: Checkmark Books, 2000.

White, Bruce M. "The Woman Who Married the Beaver: Trade Patterns and Gender Roles in the Ojibwa Fur Trade." *Ethnohistory* 46, no. 1 (1999): 109–47.

White, Richard. *The Middle Ground: Indians, Empires, and Republics in the Great Lakes Region, 1650–1815*. New York, NY: Cambridge University Press, 1991.

Wisconsin Territorial Papers, County Series, Crawford County. "Proceedings of the County Board of Supervisors, Nov. 29, 1821–November 19, 1850." Madison: Wisconsin Historical Records Survey, 1941.

Woodward, Rowland, and Shattuck, Messrs. "Wisconsin in 1818 by Edward Tanner." *Wisconsin Historical Collections* 8 (1879): 289. Originally published in the *(Detroit) Gazette*, 8 and 15 January 1819.

U.S. Census Office. *Population of the United States in 1860.* Washington, DC: Government Printing Office, 1864.

U.S. Congress. *American State Papers: Documents, Legislative and Executive, of the Congress of the United States . . . ,* 38 vols., Class VIII, *Public Lands,* 8 vols., edited by Walter Lowrie et al. Washington, DC: Government Printing Office, 1832–1861.

Court Cases

United States v. Augustin Asselin, Indictment for Fornication, 9 May 1825, Iowa Series 20, Wisconsin Historical Society Library, Platteville.

United States v. Louis Cardinal, Iowa Series 20, folder 16, Wisconsin Historical Society Library, Platteville.

United States v. Strange Poze, Indictment for Fornication, Circuit Court of the United States for the County of Crawford of the term of May 1824, courtesy of Dale Klemme.

9

Une femme en vaut deux—"Strong Like Two People"

Marie Fisher Gaudet of Fort Good Hope, Northwest Territories

DIANE P. PAYMENT

Une femme en vaut deux (strong like two people) is an expression often heard in reference to Métis women in the North.[1] Women were the backbone of society, the ones who kept the family together and passed on values of caring, giving, and sharing. "Work, work, and more work" was their motto. In addition to changing moss bags (baby carriers in which moss acts like a diaper) and feeding and clothing large families, they had the skills to live independently or survive on the land because the men were often absent—"visiting," hunting, trading, and working on the boats. Many women worked "unofficially" at the trading posts and some even had dog teams to visit their trap lines, transport goods, and carry mail from one community to another. They were the traditional healers, midwives, and counselors, skills that they passed on to newcomers in Territorial healthcare services. Because of their knowledge and experience as translators and missionary assistants, northern Métis women played a particularly important role in the reassertion and resurgence of Métis political rights in the north in the late twentieth century.

Métis Women in the Context of Nineteenth-Century
Fur Trade and Imperialism

Silence surrounds most aboriginal women in North America.[2] We rarely hear their voices, and much of their lives are left to the researcher's imagination. In Western literature, we reconstruct them through our own cultural biases and often inadvertently misinterpret the reality of their everyday lives and values. The stereotypes of aboriginal women as beasts of burden or princesses may be largely dispelled, but we are still in the process of documenting them as players in their own societies. Marie Fisher Gaudet's life story is that of a northern Métis woman who walked two worlds, blended elements of the two, and found her own in the society of the time. She was a strong and powerful woman, but she demonstrated public respect and deference toward men according to nineteenth-century Métis custom. Her life probably had little in common with women who lived primarily off the land or worked in the bush, for she lived in the manager's residence of a Hudson's Bay Company (HBC) trading post. But it was not a life of domesticity in the western tradition, as Marie Gaudet processed raw materials, produced trade goods, and fostered kinship networks indispensable to the fur trade. The Gaudet family considered itself part of the landed elite,[3] and it seems that Marie Fisher conformed, at least outwardly, to the role of the commissioned officer's wife.

She also found a special mission in the propagation of the Roman Catholic faith, and on that issue she was resolute and outspoken. The Oblate missionaries of the region acknowledged her invaluable contribution. She developed a special relationship with the Grey Nuns (Sisters of Charity of Montréal) who established a convent boarding school on the Mackenzie River in Fort Providence in 1867. They were impressed by Mme Gaudet's devotion and piety, and these religious women found a strong ally and mentor in influential Métis women such as Mme Gaudet. Her daughters became associates of the Grey Nuns, assisting them in their work while pursuing their own formal education and perfecting skills in decorative arts, music, and painting. As a Dene woman, Marie Fisher had a strong respect for men as hunters and providers, and she maintained those traditions. She also dutifully "served" the HBC, but wives were "unpaid servants" who were rarely mentioned in official records. Traders, explorers, and outsiders who visited the post referred to Marie derisively as "M. Gaudet's little nun," and she was mostly ignored by the numerous male visitors to the post.

It is not surprising that it was the sisters and nonaboriginal female "explorers" or travelers who provided more specific descriptions of Marie Fisher and her contemporaries. Only one letter that Mme Gaudet wrote or dictated has survived. The most incisive personal insights can be gleaned from family photographs, the rich legacy of artwork of Marie Fisher Gaudet and three daughters—Bella, Christine, and Dora—who lived into adulthood, and the family history that was passed down to present-day generations, both in oral and written form. She belonged to a tightly knit and loyal family with a strong sense of its unique history. It is my hope that the reconstruction of her life will ensure that she and her generation of Métis women will be better known and recognized.

Origins and Family History

Marie, the daughter of HBC chief trader Alexander Fisher[4] and Élise Taupier, was born in the vicinity of Fort Liard/Fort Simpson (Northwest Territories) on June 24, 1843. Fisher was a Montréal fur trader whose Loyalist family had settled in the Lake Champlain district in the mid-eighteenth century, and Taupier was the daughter of a French Canadian voyageur[5] and an unidentified aboriginal woman of Beaver or Slavey (today, collectively known as Dene) ancestry. Marie's birth was the result of a brief relationship between Fisher and Taupier that illustrates the racism and double standard that dominated many relationships between fur traders and aboriginal women in the nineteenth-century Northwest. Alexander Fisher exhibited the rather condescending attitudes and licentious behavior of many of his peers. He was reportedly also a rather flighty and disreputable character. HBC governor George Simpson, whose comments were admittedly rarely complimentary and who particularly disliked former *Canadiens* Nor'Westers, described him as a "trifling thoughtless superficial lying creature."[6] Other correspondents support these claims, referring to him as an unscrupulous and vindictive man. Fisher had reportedly assaulted Charlotte, a Cree woman, around Norway House in 1829, and he was censured and fined for the abduction of a laborer's wife at Fort William in 1830. In letters to his nephew Henry

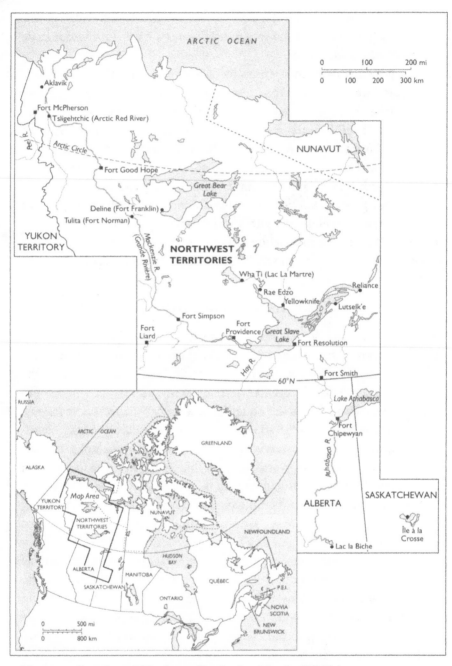

MAP 9.1. Canada and Northwest Territories. Map by Bill Nelson.

Fisher, a fur trade clerk in the Saskatchewan district, Alex Fisher revealed his views of aboriginal women and marriage *à la façon du pays* (according to the custom of the country):

> You must not on any account get yourself entangled with the squaws for if you do, you are a lost man, you will get a family and of a spurrious kind, that you will regret as long as you live. Now if you have any send them from you. Do not let such a weakness get the better of you. It would require a chapter to write you the evils that attend such a concubinage.[7]

Alexander Fisher did not heed his own advice and contracted a customary marriage with a Métis woman, Angélique Savard, in New Caledonia in the early 1830s. The relationship lasted over ten years, and they had at least eight children. She was recognized in fur trade society as Mme Fisher, and Fisher referred to her as "milady" and the mother of my "adopted" children.[8] However, she may have been insecure in the marriage, as the following events illustrate. In 1840, Fisher was transferred to the Athabasca District, and the following year he was demoted to the remote Mackenzie District, at Fort Good Hope. Perhaps not wishing to bring his family to such an isolated post, he left Angélique and the children to winter at Fort Chipewyan. Possibly fearing being "turned off" to another fur trader or abandoned by Fisher, who had already advised her of his plans to retire to Canada, the vulnerable Angélique Savard had a relationship with the local postmaster. When the pregnant Angélique and children arrived in Fort Good Hope in the summer of 1842, Fisher could not forgive his wife for committing "a woman's greatest sin," and he summarily left her at Fort Chipewyan on his return to Montréal in 1843, taking their children with him. Many HBC officers, such as James Hargrave, applauded Fisher's behavior, stating that he "was obliged to leave his wife if she deserves the name," and "if there is hell on this earth to a man it must be the bitter sting of a wife's infidelity."[9] There is no mention of Angélique's subsequent fate, but it is safe to say she was probably alone, heartbroken, and left at the mercy of relatives if they were in the vicinity.[10] Separating her from her children was a cold and vindictive act on Fisher's part but not an unusual one among fur traders of the time. Some abandoned or destitute aboriginal women found refuge with the Grey Nuns in St. Boniface in the 1840s, but Angélique Savard is not mentioned in their annals or correspondence.

After his separation from Angélique, and perhaps seeking revenge for her "fall," the sanctimonious Alex Fisher sought the companionship of another woman. Élise Taupier was one of the few Métis women hired by the HBC as a "bully" (disciplinarian) on the boats between Fort Liard and Fort Simpson. Oblate missionaries described her as a strong and resolute woman who carried a dagger on her belt and was respected and feared by all, especially her faltering husbands.[11] She had a relationship with the older (fifty-nine-year-old) Alexander Fisher in the summer of 1842 when he was in the Fort Simpson region, and in June 1843 she gave birth to their daughter, Marie, just before he left for Montréal. Fisher did not mention Mme Taupier in his subsequent correspondence, nor is it clear if this daughter was included in his will.[12] But he was a wealthy man, and it is probable that he provided for Élise and his child before he left the country, as Marie was given the surname Fisher. Élise Taupier married Métis interpreter François Houle,[13] and although Marie was raised by her mother and step-father and is occasionally identified by the surname Houle, she was acknowledged as Alexander Fisher's daughter.[14] According to missionary accounts, Élise Taupier Houle went to meet Father Thibault at Portage la Loche around 1845 and subsequently traveled to the Red River Settlement (St. Boniface), where she received religious instruction and was baptized.[15] Alexander Fisher had many relatives at Red River, including the extended family of his nephew, Henry Fisher, who also became a HBC chief trader,[16] whereas Houle was originally from Red River and was there on leave in 1848–50. The scarcity of records makes it almost impossible to confirm these activities, but it is probable that Élise Taupier Houle brought her infant daughter Marie with her to Red River to meet her relatives. In 1850, the Houle family returned to Fort Liard/Fort Simpson, where François resumed his work as an interpreter for the HBC. A zealous Catholic, Élise Taupier Houle became active as a missionary assistant. She taught the Oblates the Chipewyan and Slavey languages and customs, and she acted as their interpreter.

Youth and Marriage

Not much is known about Marie Fisher's youth. Her strong-willed and enterprising mother probably inculcated similar values to her daughter, who also became a zealous Catholic. As the daughter of an HBC commissioned officer, or bourgeois, and a renowned Métis mother, Marie Fisher was a member of the fur trade elite, a position that probably helped her secure a husband of the same rank. In 1858, at the tender age of fifteen, the attractive Métis girl married Charles-Philippe Gaudet,[17] the HBC postmaster at Fort Resolution, in a Catholic ceremony in Fort Simpson. Gaudet was a French Canadian trader who had come north from Montréal in the employ of the company in 1851. He was fifteen years her senior and had a newborn daughter, Eliza, from a relationship with Natitele, a Slavey or Gwich'in woman.[18] Fur traders needed aboriginal women as helpmates to survive and conduct business in the Canadian Northwest, but church or western-style marriages were usually the result of long-term unions or social pressure.

In the case of Marie, her youth and status as a westernized or acculturated woman of Scottish, French Canadian, and Métis origins made her a very desirable spouse. Marie Fisher brought indispensable economic skills and social networks to the union. She had relatives among the Slavey and Gwich'in, and she was fluent in Chipewyan, Slavey, "convent" French, and Michif French. She was an expert in dressing hides and had mastered the art of silk embroidery and beadwork, skills that were highly valued in the production of clothing and household articles.[19] Marie's schooling was probably limited to religious instruction until the 1860s. Father Gascon, who served at Fort Good Hope, reported that he gave her daily lessons in French reading and writing. The Gaudets lived at Fort Resolution in 1858–59 and at Peel River (Fort McPherson) from 1859 to 1863, where C. P. Gaudet occupied the position of postmaster. In 1863, he was appointed clerk at Fort Good Hope, where the couple lived for over fifty years. In 1878, Gaudet was promoted to chief trader, a position that he owed to his ability and dedication to the company, but also to his wife and her extended family's prestige and trade connections.

Fur Trader's Wife, Mother, and HBC "Servant"

Evidence shows that the first years of her marriage were difficult for Marie Fisher. Gaudet was an amiable and hard-working man, but family tradition and accounts also suggest that he was a strict husband and father who was "loyal in the extreme to the HBC."[20] It was traditional for the father, or *paterfamilias,* to rule in French Canadian society, but interracial marriages could accentuate social tensions. C. P. Gaudet was a French Canadian employed by a company in which very few French

Canadians reached the rank of officer. Much to Mme Gaudet's chagrin, it seems that her husband felt that if he were to rise in the ranks, he had to adopt the dominant language and religion of the HBC. In 1859, he followed the orders of anti-Catholic chief factor Bernard Ross and refused hospitality to the admittedly disagreeable Father Henri Grollier, who had married him a year earlier. M. Gaudet openly supported the Anglican priest, Rev. Kirkby, and subjected Marie Fisher to an Anglican ceremony or "second" marriage that undoubtedly caused some anguish to his devoutly Catholic wife (even though this may have been a formality to appease the anti-Catholic chief factor). Mme Gaudet gave birth to eleven children between 1860 and 1877, and even though her husband did not reconcile with the Catholic Church until the early 1870s, she ensured that her children born in the 1860s were baptized and instructed in the Catholic faith. It also seems that her parents, François Houle and Élise Taupier, were often close by for support.

Marie also endured the long absences of her husband, whose business required visits to other posts in the district. The enterprising and adventurous M. Gaudet loved to travel with his colleagues, and he participated in many hunting expeditions with the Gwich'in and Inuit to the north.[21] From 1859 to 1861, he accompanied Smithsonian naturalist Robert Kennicott during his expedition to the Mackenzie River District. Kennicott was a favorite companion, and M. Gaudet, fluent in Inuktitut, used his contacts among the Inuit to collect and identify ornithological specimens for the Smithsonian. Kennicott spent several months with the Gaudet family at Peel River and noted Mme Gaudet's serious manner compared with her jovial husband. Marie could not speak English and was naturally reserved with outsiders, especially men. However, it is highly probable that Mme Gaudet and her Houle relatives collected and preserved for the Smithsonian some Gwich'in and Slavey ethnological specimens, especially women's clothing, tools, and ornaments.[22] Local women also produced some clothing specimens and articles for the Smithsonian. In return, the women received clothing dyes, belt buckles, glass necklaces, beads, silk thread, handkerchiefs, hairnets, "crying doll babies," and other prized gifts.[23]

As was custom, Mme Gaudet was often alone at home with her young children, even on holidays such as New Year's Day when her husband would go off to drink and celebrate with his male friends. She could easily have hired help for domestic chores in the "Big House" at Fort Good

Hope, and probably did have someone to perform rigorous work such as wood chopping. Contrary to European fur trade wives of the era, aboriginal wives were expected to produce all the food and clothing for the household. Marie Fisher's parents had a fishing camp at some distance from the fort, and Marie liked to accompany them on hunting and trading expeditions. Like other local Métis and Slavey women, she filleted and dried fish—an important food staple—snared rabbits, trapped small fur-bearing animals, and cultivated a large root vegetable garden. Berry-picking was another important seasonal activity that ensured a supply of dried and preserved fruit to supplement a diet of meat, fish, and potatoes. Like many Métis women of her generation, she was strong and healthy and gave birth to many children, but she almost died during a scarlet fever epidemic that swept Fort Good Hope and other northern posts in 1865.

C. P. Gaudet went on furlough in 1867–68, and the family, which then included Marie (who was pregnant) and five young children (Elizabeth, Isabelle, Sara, Christine, and Frédéric), "went down" or traveled "outside" via the Red River Settlement to visit his elderly mother, Elizabeth Short Gaudet, in Ottawa and family near Montréal. The trip was a long and arduous one undertaken before the advent of steamboat and rail transportation in the Northwest. The Gaudets traveled to Red River via Norway House by York boat, and then to St. Paul (Minnesota) either by steamboat or stagecoach.[24] From St. Paul they traveled by rail to Ottawa, where family photographs were taken.[25]

The joy of family reunions, however, was soon shattered by the death of three of her six children during the trip: "*le bon Dieu les prit tous, mes trois jolis enfants.*"[26] A daughter, Sara, died in Ottawa at the age of five in the spring of 1868, and two other daughters, Elizabeth (aged eight) and baby Marie, died during the return trip in June 1868 and were buried at Cumberland House on the Saskatchewan River. It was a devastating blow to the couple and illustrates the prevalence of contagious diseases such as measles, diphtheria, and whooping cough at the time as well as the dangers associated with rigorous long-distance travel. Marie Fisher refused to travel south after that unhappy experience and did not accompany her husband in 1887 when he attended the officers council meeting in Winnipeg and visited their sons who attended college in neighboring St. Boniface.[27] Between 1869 and 1877, Mme Gaudet had five more children: Jean-Pierre (John Peter), Timothy, Dorothy, Léon, and Dora. Dorothy

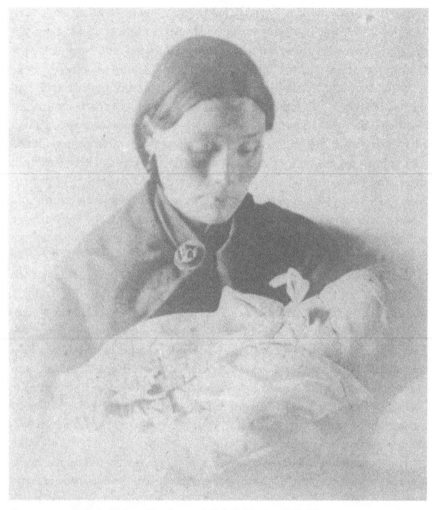

FIGURE 9.1.   Marie Fisher Gaudet and "bibi" Marie, 1868. Photo courtesy of Gaudet family.

died of whooping cough at Fort Good Hope in 1874, and in 1909 Mme Gaudet suffered the loss of two adult daughters. Christine, who was anemic, had traveled to St. Boniface with her brother Léon to seek medical treatment. She died in the hospital in October at the age of forty-five. The family did not learn about her death until mail arrived the following year. The youngest daughter, Dora, died suddenly the following month of *la grippe* (influenza) in Fort Good Hope at the age of thirty-two.[28] Only one daughter, Isabelle (known as Bella), survived to old age.[29] Four sons

FIGURE 9.2.   Charles-Philippe Gaudet and children, 1868. Photo courtesy of
Gaudet family.

lived to adulthood and followed their father's footsteps with careers in
the HBC as post managers and clerks.[30]

Mme Gaudet wanted a French Catholic education for her children,
whereas her husband favored an English one. In 1870, Marie and her

young children (including her step-daughter) traveled to the mission at Île-à-la-Crosse to ask for help. She wrote to Bishop Taché in St. Boniface, entreating him to take her son at the college and added that she wanted to send her daughters to be educated by the Grey Nuns in St. Boniface. She pleaded with the bishop to assist her so that the children could go to Red River: "I was glad to take them away from their poor father's influence . . . the sooner that my children go to Red River, the sooner the better as I fear that my husband will come and get them."[31] Her letter confirmed her anguish and resolution on this matter, and it seems that she was actually contemplating leaving her husband, becoming a nun, and sending her children to St. Boniface in the care of the bishop. She eventually succeeded in her mission, for her daughters attended the Grey Nuns boarding school at Île-à-la-Crosse in the 1870s and 1880s, where they were taught English, music, and painting by Sister Sara Riel (sister of Louis Riel). In the 1890s, they went to the school at Fort Providence, closer to home. The sons attended school in St. Boniface and Winnipeg. Marie Fisher Gaudet returned to live with her husband, who "mended his ways" and reconciled with the Roman Catholic Church when it became more politically acceptable for him to do so in the 1870s. Missionary accounts confirm that he was never a devout Catholic, although he was very generous and supportive. The daughters adopted the religious zeal of their mother, but the sons followed their father, as was usually the case in Catholic French Canadian and Métis families. All the family, however, was imbued with a strong sense of discipline and dedication to the church.

As a dutiful HBC officer's wife, Mme Gaudet was reportedly very loyal to the company, and this may have placed her in a somewhat awkward position with her relatives who were free or independent traders in competition with the HBC. A local free trader remarked, "She doesn't approve of me and makes a point of not seeing me as she passes here."[32] Daughters Bella and Christine worked with their brothers at various posts doing journals and processing accounts, as they were better bookkeepers. Ed Nagle, a free trader in opposition to the HBC in the Mackenzie District in the 1890s and early 1900s, reported that Fred and his spinster sister (Bella) were from the old HBC school and worked actively against him and other traders. He referred to Bella as a snob who ostracized him, though he grudgingly admired her business skills. Bella often acted as an intermediary to resolve disputes between the HBC and

FIGURE 9.3. *Standing at back,* Charles-Philippe Gaudet; *front row, left to right:* Christine, Isabelle (Bella), and Marie Fisher Gaudet. Photograph taken at Fort Good Hope, Northwest Territories, ca. 1892–94. Photo courtesy of Hudson's Bay Company Archives, Archives of Manitoba, 1987/13/204 (N8896).

independent traders. She also capably nursed Mrs. McKinley (the Anglican missionary's wife) back to health at Fort Resolution.[33] She would have gained her knowledge of medicinal plants and healing techniques from her mother, the Grey Nuns, or medical practitioners who occasionally visited northern posts.

Religious Leader: "la providence du fort Good Hope"

The Oblate missionaries acknowledged the crucial role of women in the spread of Catholicism in the Northwest. Father Giroux summed it up when he wrote to Bishop Grandin that "You must first gain the support of the women to be successful."[34] Métis women were and remain the transmitters of culture,[35] and Marie followed the example of her mother in her support of the Catholic Church and education of her children. The role of women in the Roman Catholic Church in the nineteenth century was restricted to that of an auxiliary or assistant, but because of their power and influence within the community, many Métis women assumed leadership roles similar to that of a present-day deaconess.[36] Father Séguin and Brother Kearney, who were at Fort Good Hope during most of Marie Fisher's lifetime, praised the generosity and piety of "the excellent Mme Gaudet, what a heart of gold," and her invaluable influence: "nothing is more powerful than the words of the big boss lady."[37] Mme Gaudet *prenait les devants* (took the lead) or preached to the women on her own initiative, and her word was law. M. Gaudet rounded up people in the community for Sunday Mass. Marie Fisher memorized the catechism in Slavey and Gwich'in so that she could teach it in the priest's absence. She also settled questions of conscience, and her judgments were accepted as final, a rare position for Catholic women in the nineteenth and twentieth centuries.[38] She provided on-going economic support to the mission in the form of mass offerings and altar linens that she sewed and embroidered (as well as laundered). Marie Fisher Gaudet and her daughters were sacristans, responsible for the decoration and maintenance of the altar and liturgical linens. The Gaudets donated a valuable statue of the Virgin Mary to the church and made regular gifts of food staples, such as flour, caribou tongues, and dried meat, as well as luxuries such as syrup and tea. In recognition of the family's services, Mme Gaudet's in particular, they received a special blessing and indulgence from Bishop Faraud.[39]

Marie Fisher's apostolate extended to the teaching and training of Dene women to oppose *inkonze*, or some of the teachings of traditional leaders, particularly those whom she associated with bad power.[40] Slavey women were known for their assertiveness, strength, and moral influence. Father Émile Petitot noted that they were headstrong women who resisted outsiders and Christianity, but once they were won over they became true apostles.[41] Mme Gaudet was familiar with and respected traditional Dene customs—belief in good and evil forces, visions and revelations, and the interrelationship between human and animal spirits. It was natural for her to integrate those traditions with Christian dogma, or indigenize Catholicism, and make it acceptable to her people. Dene spirituality was rooted in personal communication with the spirits, prophecy, and invocation, which were compatible with Catholic beliefs in prayer, guardian angels, miracles, and the existence of a supreme being. The influence and support of respected Dene and Métis women such as Marie Fisher, who understood their language and shared aspects of their culture, was indispensable to the missionaries. Mme Gaudet's influence on the Gwich'in at Fort McPherson, particularly the training of a Gwich'in auxiliary, Cécile Uzpichi'è, helped the Oblates secure a foothold among them despite the very strong Anglican presence. Cécile was a leader of her people, and Marie called her "the mother of the Gwich'in" in acknowledgement of her power and influence.[42] Marie also adopted or mentored young orphaned girls, of which at least three, Cécile Lecou, Marie Kahppaxconne (Sister Donatien), and Noelia Voedz-Jen, became Grey Nuns.[43]

What is not known, specifically, is what Dene—or, more specifically, Beaver Slavey—beliefs and customs Mme Gaudet maintained and passed on to her family, especially her daughters. Her grandson, Julien, later recalled that Aunt Bella and his uncles spoke "an Indian language" between themselves and exchanged stories that gave them much pleasure, but they did so secretly and did not want to be questioned about them. They upheld Dene practices, such as respect for animals and the land and the Métis tradition of honoring the saintly Louis Riel.[44] It can be argued that like many Métis of her time, Marie Fisher Gaudet respected and maintained core Dene Métis traditions and beliefs but, like her mother, embraced Christianity because it was a source of influence and comfort. Mme Gaudet's activities illustrate the indigenization of Catholicism in the nineteenth century, in which strong and powerful Métis women played a key role in the church (contrary to Euro-Canadian women and twentieth-century women). Conversely, it can also be argued that the patriarchal church fostered submissiveness among traditionally assertive and powerful aboriginal women.

The Gaudet daughters followed in their mother's footsteps. Bella's, Christine's, and Dora's lives were dominated by service and dedication to the mission at Fort Good Hope. The privileged Gaudet daughters were not required to perform tedious domestic chores like other boarders at the Fort Providence school but instead developed their artistic and musical skills. On their return home, they played a key role in the church liturgy, music, and decoration. The church of Notre Dame de Bonne-Espérance (Our Lady of Good Hope), built by the Oblate Fathers between 1865 and 1885, is remarkable for its architecture and interior artwork.[45] Missionary records credit noted ethnologist and author Father Émile Petitot and other Oblate fathers with most of the interior decoration of the church, but Bella Gaudet made an important contribution that was never officially recognized or that was attributed to others. According to family and local oral tradition, Bella, who worked with Father Petitot in

8757

FIGURE 9.4. Charles-Philippe Gaudet wearing deerskin clothing and beaded belt, 1868. Photo courtesy of Gaudet family.

the 1870s, decorated the altar and executed many of the paintings.[46] Brother Kearney was the only one to note that Bella, a gifted artist, painted the Jesus Christ frescoes and decorations on the communion table.[47] It was not unusual for female artists of the time to work on the sidelines or assist "masters." As a young devout Catholic woman, Bella would have been compelled to downplay her artistry and relinquish her role in favor of the brilliant but obstinate and egocentric Petitot. As she matured, Bella Gaudet grew more assertive and independent, but she always remained subservient to the church. She generously contributed her time and income to missionary causes. When the Gaudet family retired to Montréal in 1917, she donated valuable household articles to the mission and a bursary of $2,000 for the training of priests for the North. In contrast with the women, the Gaudet men were able to develop more egalitarian and informal relationships with the missionaries, which was possible between men. C. P. Gaudet and his sons Fred and Léon often socialized with the priests in the evenings, engaging in political discourse and listening to music on the phonograph while smoking and imbibing *un p'chi coup*.[48]

Identity and Culture: Ambivalence and Conflict

Marie Fisher Gaudet and her daughters spent most of their evenings in the dark northern winter sewing. They made moccasins, coats, and mitts, which they decorated with silk, beads, porcupine quills, and moose hair. The Fort Liard region, where Marie Fisher came from, was known for its moose hair tufting. The daughters perfected their embroidery techniques with the Grey Nuns at Fort Providence. Their artwork, of which sixty-three items have survived, is probably the best expression of their Métis identity and culture.[49] They used the Métis embroidered flower beadwork pattern and vivid colors. Shortly after her marriage, Mme Gaudet made a complete deerskin suit decorated with intricate beadwork, fringe, and fur trim and a fur hat for her husband. The Gaudet women made clothing articles, such as gloves, mittens, moccasins, garters, and purses, as well as harnesses, whips, and *tapis* (tuppies, or blankets) for their sled dogs. These items were usually made of textiles (such as wool, silk, and velvet) and decorated with beads, embroidery, and feathers. They also made household items, such as velvet shelf valances and runners, elaborate wall pockets, jewelry boxes, tobacco pouches, and furniture covers, all decorated with beadwork and embroidery. Marie Fisher had *ulus* (Inuit scrapers), which she acquired when her husband was stationed at Peel River, and, according to her family, she was an expert at preparing hides. Mother and daughters made snowshoes for the whole family. Furthermore, "the Gaudet sisters and their mother would place and visit the animal traps themselves."[50] They did not make these articles for sale but, rather, for personal use. They were brought from Fort Good Hope in 1917 in large wooden steamer trunks and kept by the family in St. Lambert in their little home museum until 1989. It was only after Bella's and Frédéric's deaths in 1955 that these items were displayed. They were precious souvenirs from their aboriginal or Métis past, articles that were hidden because they could have been the source of mockery and prejudice in the community. Nephew Julien Gaudet recalled that people sometimes referred to the Gaudet home and other former fur traders' residences nearby as the "Indian camp" and made derisive remarks about Bella's clothing and her trap lines in the countryside.[51]

Although Marie Fisher Gaudet was ethnically Métis and living among her Dene relatives in the Northwest, there is evidence that she identified primarily, or at least outwardly, with her French Canadian and British heritage. This identification may have been the result of pressure from her husband or the patrilineal society of the times as well as pressure to conform to HBC culture. Missionaries and outsiders who wrote about Mme Gaudet were either silent about her aboriginal heritage or referred to her as French Canadian. Fathers Duchaussois and Dugré referred to her as French Canadian in their publications in the 1920s, possibly out of deference to the family and the prejudice toward *les sauvages* (Native peoples), especially in southern Canada.[52] This was a time when Métis women married to French Canadian men were pressured to integrate into the dominant group and hide their heritage, claiming "We are not Métis, us."[53] An account by Father Séguin in the late 1880s illustrates Marie's sensitivity on this issue. Bishop Faraud had sent a number of gifts to Mme Gaudet and her daughters in return for their dedication and service to the church. A beautiful shawl and religious pictures were destined for Marie, but, fearing offense, the priest decided not to give her the shawl, claiming, "She would not have appreciated the shawl and perhaps it would even have offended her. I decided to keep it rather than risk displeasing her."[54] Elizabeth Taylor of St. Paul, Minnesota, who stopped at Fort Good Hope during her travels in the Mackenzie region in 1892, was greeted warmly in French by the Gaudet women, whom she described as "kindly, bashful and simple."[55] She noted that the mother was dressed in the dark Victorian colors of the period and wore a small black cape made perfectly plain (not the traditional Métis shawl or *couverte*), and the daughters were dressed in brightly colored 1860s European-style hooped skirts—not quite up to date with the current American fashions!

British traveler and author Agnes Deans Cameron, who visited Fort Good Hope on her northern journey in 1908, was impressed by the Gaudet women, particularly the queen-like matriarch Marie. She recalled "one of the sweetest homes in the world,"[56] and described Mme Gaudet as "a dear old lady with a black cap, the pinkest of pink cheeks, and the kind of smile that brings a choky feeling into your throat and makes you think of your mother."[57] Perhaps unknown to Miss Cameron, Marie served the visitors several Métis specialties, homemade wine (*piquette*) and bannock (*galettes*), and they engaged in a long conversation about the North. Oblivious of or politely avoiding Mme Gaudet's aboriginal heritage, Miss Cameron summed up Marie's life as mother-love and devotion to the company. In clothing and manner, the Gaudet women presented themselves to outsiders as prim and proper Euro-Canadian women. They spoke the French language of their cultured visitors and presented the ideal domestic household. They only privately expressed their Métis heritage in their art, spirituality, and day-to-day language, a mixture of French and Slavey.

Marriage was an issue that illustrated the family's ambivalence toward their Métis identity. Mme Gaudet expected her children to marry Catholics first and foremost. Two of her sons who remained in the North married Métis women.[58] Sarah Hardisty, Timothy's wife, was Anglican, which reportedly upset Marie, and she ensured that their children were raised as Catholics by pressuring her son to remove them from their mother's influence or send them to the boarding school in Fort Providence. Marie's three daughters who lived to adulthood did not marry. Was it because, as suggested by Sylvia Van Kirk and corroborated by their nephew, miscegenation was feared, racist attitudes intensified during that period, and the acculturated and socially respectable Mlles Gaudets could not find suitable mates?[59] They became associates of the Grey Nuns but did not enter the order, possibly because they were devoted to the family and wanted to help their mother. It was customary to have children around the home, and Marie and Charles-Philippe "adopted" a young grandson, Frédéric-Alexandre, which brought much comfort and joy to the family in their last years at Fort Good Hope.[60]

FIGURE 9.5.   Frédéric Gaudet and Frances Théroux, 1913. Photo courtesy of
Gaudet family.

The other two sons, Frédéric and Léon, were over forty when they
married. They "went out" yearly on company business and on furlough
to Montréal every five years. During a trip to Montréal in 1908, Frédéric
became engaged to his second cousin, Frances Théroux (or Terroux). According to family accounts and photographs, the idyllic couple, deeply
in love, married in January 1913. Frédéric, who was only two years away
from retirement, tried to persuade his wife to wait for him in Montréal
or Edmonton, but she was determined to accompany him to Fort Good
Hope. The headlines of the *Montreal Daily Star* of February 1, 1913, read,
"The bride and groom start on their journey to the frozen north where
there is no other [white] woman within a thousand miles and family in
Great Bleak Land faces young wife." The account carefully avoided the
groom's northern origins, mentioning only that he had returned East
after a long absence. It also confirmed a strong prejudice toward aboriginal people, women in particular, suggesting that they were invisible or
sub-human. "Mme Fred" arrived in Fort Good Hope with her husband

in July after a long journey by train, wagon, and steamboat. When Marie Fisher, who had lost two daughters to illness four years earlier, first saw her daughter-in-law Frances, she was apprehensive because Frances had respiratory problems and life in the Arctic was harsh. Marie had a premonition of Frances's death and said, "Death is upon us. Poor little woman, she will not be with us very long."[61] Frances died a few months later while giving birth to her first child.[62] It was a hard blow for the family and for Marie, who was already sick and frail.

Marie Fisher and Charles-Philippe Gaudet lived to celebrate their fiftieth wedding anniversary in 1908, a rare occurrence at the time. It was the last time that the whole family was together for photographs and celebrations at various posts, including Fort Providence, where the sisters made special cakes for a feast.[63] Marie's last years were marked by loss and illness. As usual, she found refuge and consolation in prayer. She usually attended church twice a day, and when she became too frail to go, the priest brought daily communion to her at home. On April 26, 1914, he reported that Mme Gaudet's wish to leave this world had been fulfilled and that she had died like a saint. All the aboriginal people came to pay their respects: "Mrs. Gaudet died last night at 7pm. She had a very edifying death. Death did not surprise her; she longed for it. She had taken communion in the morning. We sent a messenger to inform the Indians of the area and they all came to pray for her."[64] Marie Fisher Gaudet was almost seventy-two years old and weary beyond her years. A few years later, in 1917, the elderly Mr. Gaudet, accompanied by Frédéric, Bella, and grandson Freddy, left Fort Good Hope to retire in Montréal. C. P. Gaudet suffered a stroke during the journey and died en route in St. Boniface, far from "the solitudes [of the North] which he loved so dearly."[65]

Marie Fisher Gaudet's Legacy

We can document Mme Gaudet's activities and lifestyle quite extensively, if often indirectly, through missionary accounts and family memoirs, and especially through photographs and artwork. She is rarely mentioned directly in HBC records, for nineteenth-century women were silent partners in the public sphere. Marie Fisher's labor was central to the success of her husband and, by association, the HBC and the fur trade economy in the Northwest. Perhaps inevitably, she was eclipsed by her formidable husband and sons, who, in their own words, "gave one hundred and

FIGURE 9.6.   Charles-Philippe Gaudet and Marie Fisher, with family, on their
fiftieth wedding anniversary, 1908. *Front row*: Charles-Philippe Gaudet holding
grandson, Frédéric; Marie Fisher; and protégée, Cecilia. *Back row*: Isabelle
(Bella), Léon, Frédéric, and Dora. Photo courtesy of Missionary Oblates,
Grandin Collection, Provincial Archives of Alberta, Jane Gaudet Album,
OB14144.

ninety years of service to the Honourable Company by one family in two
generations,"[66] although Mme Gaudet and her daughters also "served"
unofficially. The male bias of history, which persisted until the 1970s and
beyond, meant that women such as Marie were forgotten or ignored in
the literature or not identified by name. For example, the father's obituary
did not mention his late wife or surviving daughter, Bella, who nursed
him and was with him when he died.

Marie Fisher's life was one of devotion to the church and family (probably in that order) and deference to men in the francophone Métis Catholic tradition of the time, though she was outspoken on religious and
social issues. Mme Gaudet passed on her strength and knowledge to her
daughters and granddaughters. Her daughter Bella, who lived into her
nineties, was respected for her traditional and Western medical knowledge. She made herbal medicines for various illnesses and treated burns,
cuts, and frostbite, and even amputated limbs.[67] Her granddaughter, who
was interviewed in the 1970s, noted a Slavey tradition of respect for
man as hunter and certain rituals that were observed by her mother's

and grandmother's generations. Women were required to wash men's clothing separately and could not touch their personal belongings.[68] Children were taught to respect and share the land and its resources. They were taught mainly by example and storytelling, though *la discipline* was also the Métis way. Like their grandmother, Jane Gaudet and Bella Gaudet Trindell were independent and enterprising women who were involved in the fur trade in the 1930s and 1940s, but unlike Marie they were paid employees and independent traders. Possibly Marie Fisher Gaudet's most tangible Métis legacy—one that she passed on to her daughters—was her artistry, examples of which have survived for posterity. Another contribution was a large number of Michif French words that were incorporated into the Slavey language, especially in the Sahtu region of the Northwest Territories (Fort Good Hope and Fort Norman), where the Gaudet family was most prominent.[69] Considering that it was Mme Gaudet and her daughters who were more attached to or spoke French (and a mixture of French and Slavey) in day-to-day activities at the post, they were the transmitters of what could be described as a Michif Slavey dialect or mixed language.

Marie Fisher Gaudet's life illustrates the complex intersection of the dynamics of nineteenth- and early twentieth-century Métis identity, culture, class, and gender. It is probably unfair to ascribe a specific identity to her. She was multicultural—Slavey, Métis, French Canadian, and Scottish—and she blended various elements of these cultures, as was evident in her values and lifestyle. Before her marriage, she used the various surnames of her parents: Fisher, Taupier, and Houle, depending on circumstances, and as Mme Gaudet she assumed the French Canadian identity of her husband, who experienced prejudice from the HBC and compensated by cultivating his Englishness. Mme Gaudet lived at a time when there was a certain stigma to being Métis, "half-breed," or a mixed people, among both Dene and Euro-Canadians (whites). Many Métis identified as Dene or according to their European origins—in particular French and Scottish—until the 1970s, when the Métis were officially recognized as a distinct aboriginal people in the Northwest Territories. Unlike in western Canada, many Métis in the North continue to identify as both Métis and Dene. Marie Fisher definitely considered herself a northerner, and family history confirms that she was unwilling to "retire" in the south amongst *les étranges* (strangers). The North was her home and native land, and she was comfortable "in the bush" among her Dene and

FIGURE 9.7.   Isabelle (Bella) Gaudet, Montréal, ca. 1925. Photo courtesy of Gaudet family.

FIGURE 9.8.   Julien Gaudet, Montréal,
ca. 1989. Photo courtesy of Gaudet
family.

Métis relatives as well as in the company residence at Fort Good Hope. The
Roman Catholic Church and its French and French Canadian missionaries
and sisters had a strong influence on Marie Fisher. What they identified as
her extreme piety, communion with the spirits, and special powers, however, were also expressions of her Native spirituality and culture.

Her descendants in the Northwest Territories and western Canada
identified as Métis. Her sons Timothy and John took Métis scrip in 1921,
stating that they were not Indians and wanted to remain "their own
boss." They spoke Slavey and other Dene languages and probably some
Michif French and Cree in northern Alberta, and the older generations
spoke French. They were and remain active in the Métis community.
Timothy's grandson, Richard Hardy, was president of the Métis Association of the Northwest Territories in the 1970s, a respected lawyer, and
advocate of Métis rights and culture.[70] Marie Fisher Gaudet's family in
Québec integrated into the francophone community, though they also
acknowledged their anglophone heritage and northern roots. Her
grandson Julien Gaudet[71] pursued the family history and discovered his
northern French Métis heritage. He remembered the precious stories and
family history passed on by his Aunt Bella and Uncle Fred, who were
like grandparents to him. He questioned his cousin Freddy, who denied
his aboriginal heritage, claiming that Marie Fisher was British, and destroyed "incriminating evidence." There had been only occasional

FIGURE 9.9.　Richard Hardy, Fort Good Hope Cemetery, 1998. Reproduced courtesy of Richard Hardy.

contact between the northern and southern families since Marie Fisher's death in 1914, and the last visit to the North by Bella and Frédéric was in 1925. Julien renewed contact with his cousins in Fort Norman (Tulita) in the 1980s and ensured that family artwork, photographs, correspondence, and oral history were preserved for posterity.

In conclusion, Marie Fisher Gaudet's life provides a glimpse of a Métis woman who walked "both worlds," aboriginal and Euro-Canadian, and forged an identity of her own. Perhaps her indomitable spirit lives on in her descendants, and her little grave in Fort Good Hope lies amidst the wild roses and blue columbines in the portal of the Arctic that was her beloved home for over half a century. Today, Marie's descendants in the Northwest Territories, western Canada, and Québec acknowledge and celebrate their Métis identity and culture. The families share a proud family history, and first names such as Marie (Mary), Christine, and Isabelle (Bella) have passed from generation to generation. The family in the Northwest Territories is more firmly entrenched in its culture, and the family in Québec remains less connected to its Métis heritage, where it was largely hidden and marginalized.

Notes

I would like to dedicate this article to Marie's descendants "all over the country," who inspired me to tell "herstory," in particular the Gaudet family of St. Lambert (Québec), the Gaudet and Hardy families of the Northwest Territories, and the Fisher family of Saskatchewan.

Some of the information for this chapter was obtained from conversations with Pierrette Marquis Gaudet (St. Lambert, QC) and Richard Hardy (Yellowknife, NT).

1. North Slave Métis Alliance, *North Slave Métis History*, 11, citing an interview with Marie Dautel, Fort Rae, 1999.

2. The silence or absence from Western literature should not be interpreted as powerlessness. Power and gender have dominated the discourse on Euro-Canadian and Euro-American women in the last century, but it may not be appropriate or relevant to many North American aboriginal women. Scholars must search for culturally appropriate concepts and recognize the diverse experiences of each woman or group of women. For a valuable discussion on these issues and an assessment of the current state of research, see Klein and Ackerman, *Women and Power in Native North America*, 3–16.

3. That the Gaudets considered themselves part of the landed elite is frequently mentioned in the fur trade and missionary literature, such as, for example, by free trader Ed Nagle, who knew the family (Zinovich, *Battling the Bay*, 149).

4. Alexander Fisher (1783–1847) was the brother Henry Monroe Fisher (ca. 1776–1827), who left descendants in the Great Lakes, Prairie du Chien (Wisconsin), and Canadian Prairies. Both brothers became involved in the western fur trade in the 1790s and sired Métis families. Alexander had entered the service of the North West Company (NWC) around 1815 and then the HBC in the English River and New Caledonia districts.

5. It is not known whether Taupier was her father or mother's surname. Taupier, Topier, and Taupié *dit* Vigeant appear in Drouin, *Répertoire des mariages des Canadiens Français 1760–1935*. The family was from the Montréal region. A François Taupié was hired by McTavish and Frobisher to go to Lac La Pluie in 1803, and many Métis from the Great Lakes eventually made their way to the Northwest. See Répertoires des engagements pour l'ouest, Centre du Patrimoine Franco-Manitobain (CPFM), Archives de la Société historique de Saint-Boniface (ASHSB), Winnipeg, MB.

6. "Simpson's Character Book, No. 10, Alex Fisher," in Williams, *Hudson's Bay Company Miscellany 1670–1870*, 191–92.

7. Fonds Fisher-d'Eschambeault, April 1820, CPFM, ASHSB. He reiterated the same themes in other letters to his nephew in the 1830s and 1840s.

8. Ibid., 15 March 1832.

9. Reported in Van Kirk, *"Many Tender Ties,"* 166–67, 275n73; and Glazebrook, *Hargrave Correspondence 1821–1843*, 453.

10. Unfortunately we do not have access to Angélique's own thoughts on the situation.

11. Dugré, "Les Missionnaires Oblats," 374; and Duchaussois, *Aux Glaces Polaires*, 348. She is also mentioned in McCarthy, *From the Great River*, 109.

12. Will of Alexander Fisher drawn 1 May 1846 and probated in 1853, A36/6, microfilm 426, Hudson's Bay Company Archives (HBCA), Archives du Manitoba (AM). He lists his "adopted" children: Charlotte, Nancy, Elizabeth, Mary, John, Duncan, James, and Donald, all living with him in Canada (Montréal) as his beneficiaries. Fisher had numerous properties in and around Montréal.

13. It is not known whether Élise was "turned off" by Fisher or subsequently married François Houle. Houle (ca. 1798–1885) was the son of Antoine of St. François-Xavier (Red River Settlement), who had participated in the battle of La Grenouillère (also known as Seven Oaks) in 1816. François Houle is listed in HBC biographical files as interpreter at Fort Simpson, 1821–48. One of his sons, Antoine (ca. 1827–68), interpreter at Fort Yukon, worked as an interpreter and guide for Smithsonian ornithologist R. Kennicott while Kennicott was in the Mackenzie district in 1859–62. Antoine was well liked by the Gwich'in.

14. She is identified as Marie Fisher in the parish register of Fort Good Hope and in her children's Métis scrip applications. See also McCarthy, *From the Great River*, 227n9. In a letter, she signed Marie Gaudet née Topier [*sic*], her mother's birth name.

15. Grollier, "Souvenirs," 417.

16. Henry (Henri) Fisher (ca. 1798–1871) was the son of Henry Monroe Fisher and Madeleine Gauthier, a Métisse from Makinac. Around 1810, Henry M.

Fisher relocated to Prairie du Chien, Wisconsin, where he became a prosperous landowner and trader. As a result of the British–American War of 1812, he went north to Red River (Pembina area) with his eldest sons, Alexander and Henry, and a nephew, Charles Brisebois. Henry *fils* (Henry, Jr.) remained in the Red River area, working first as a clerk for the NWC and then as an employee of the HBC and also as a free trader. He became one of the few French Canadians to achieve the rank of a commissioned officer in the HBC. He spent most of his career in the Saskatchewan District and retired to Saint-Boniface in 1855. He had numerous wives and children and left many Métis descendants in present-day Manitoba and Saskatchewan.

17. Charles-Philippe Gaudet was born in Montréal in 1828 and died in St. Boniface, Manitoba, in 1917. The Gaudet family was of Acadian origin. The first male ancestor arrived in Port Royal from France in 1632, and the descendants suffered the expulsion of the Acadians by the British in 1755. It is probable that he had Mikmaq or Maliseet heritage, as recent inquiries suggest. The family spoke English, and his oldest brother served as commissioner in the British army and died in England. This British connection may have been a factor in securing employment with the HBC (Gaudet, "Chief Trader Charles Philip Gaudet," 45). He is extensively documented in Overvold, *Our Métis Heritage.*

18. Eliza was born in 1857 or 1858 and lived with Marie and the Gaudet family in Fort Good Hope in the 1860s. She married a Slavey man, Julien Denegouli or Goulay and Passepartout, in 1872 and lived in Fort Smith, where she has descendants.

19. The family in Montréal kept a collection of beautiful artwork (clothing and household) made by Marie and her daughters that was deposited in the McCord Museum by descendant Julien Gaudet in 1989 and 1994 (Gaudet Fisher Collection, ME988.136.1–44 and 137.1–9, McCord Museum, Montréal, QC).

20. This is the memory that was passed on to his great grandson, Richard Hardy, in the Northwest Territories and family in Montréal. His loyalty to the company is corroborated in his son Léon's account (Gaudet, "Chief Trader Charles Philip Gaudet").

21. See numerous references to trips by the hardy and adventurous Gaudet to Fort McPherson on the Peel River, and to La Pierre House and Fort Yukon across the mountains on snowshoes during the winter months. In the summer, he would make at least two boat trips to district headquarters at Fort Simpson and other posts on Great Slave Lake.

22. Table 5.1 in Lindsay, *Modern Beginnings of Subarctic Ornithology,* 174. Gaudet, one of the top six HBC collectors, sent over 170 specimens to the Smithsonian between 1861 and 1871. Aboriginal women were instrumental in these transactions.

23. Ibid., 257.

24. Steamboat travel on the Red River had been available since 1859, but service was irregular until 1868. The Anson Northup and the International operated on the Red River, and the Minnesota Stage Company linked St. Paul and Winnipeg. The family may also have traveled by slower but more dependable Red River carts operated by Métis between Red River, Pembina, and St. Paul.

25. See account in newspaper article published in 1868, which I have been unable to trace, and family photographs courtesy of Pierrette (Marquis) Gaudet from material collected by her husband, Julien Gaudet (1925–99), son of Léon and grandson of Marie and Charles-Philippe. There is a photograph of Mr. Gaudet in his so-called buckskin outfit that Mme Gaudet made, one of Marie and her baby, and one of Mr. Gaudet with their five other children.

26. "The good Lord took them all, my three beautiful children," cited in Cameron, *New North*, 210.

27. Mission de Saint-Boniface, Registre des écoliers, 1844–94, Archives des Soeurs Grises de Montréal (ASGM).

28. Codex of Mission of Fort Good Hope, 97.109, book 10, 2 November 1909 and 26 February 1910, Fonds Oblats de Marie-Immaculée (OMI), Provincial Archives of Alberta (PAA), Edmonton, AB.

29. Isabelle was born on the trail on Peel River near Fort McPherson in 1861 and died in St. Lambert, Québec, in 1955, the same year as her brother, Frédéric, with whom she lived. Family genealogy of Julien Gaudet, Gaudet Family Collection (private collection).

30. Biographical files, HBCA, AM; Gaudet, "Chief Trader Charles Philip Gaudet," 45. The four sons were Frédéric (1866–1955), HBC clerk and postmaster in the Mackenzie District, 1885–1916; John Peter (1869–1941), clerk in the Peace River and Athabasca Districts, 1888–1904; Timothy (1872–1952), clerk and post manager in the Mackenzie District, mainly at Fort Norman, 1895–1930; and Léon (1875–1943), clerk and post manager with his father at Fort Good Hope, 1894–1915, and then in the south, retiring as post manager at Bersimis in the St. Lawrence District (Gaspé Peninsula, Québec) in 1931.

31. Author's translation. Original quote: *"j'ai été heureuse de les éloigner de leur pauvre père . . . le plus vite que mes enfants seront à la Rivière-Rouge, le mieux je crois ce sera, car je crains que mon époux vienne les chercher"* (Fonds Taché, T8002, 25 September 1870, CPFM, ASHSB). The same sentiments are reiterated in a letter from Sister Agnès to Mother-General, 10 January 1871, Île à la Crosse, ASGM. Sister Agnès was completely mesmerized by Marie's piety and reported that she was like an angel and spent most of her time in prayer.

32. Cited in Cameron, *New North*, 210.

33. Zinovich, *Battling the Bay*, 191.

34. Author's translation. Original quotation: *"gagner les femmes c'est gagner la partie"* (10 February 1890, Letters, 91.345, Fonds OMI, PAA).

35. See Brown, "Women as Centre and Symbol."

36. McCarthy, *From the Great River*, 107–117. A deacon is the highest lay person in the Roman Catholic Church, just below a priest.

37. Author's translation. Original quotations: *"l'excellente dame Gaudet, quel coeur d'or . . . rien de plus fort que la parole de la grosse bourgeoise"* (Breton, *Au Pays des Peaux de Lièvres*, 118–19, citing Father Séguin). The petite Mme Gaudet grew rounder with age, and the missionaries referred to her as *"la petite boule ambulante"* (a little ball always in motion).

38. Duchaussois, *Aux Glaces Polaires*, 414–15.

39. Father Séguin to Bishop Faraud, 31 July 1889, Letters, 91.345, Fonds OMI, PAA.

40. *Inkonze* is a Dene Chipewyan term that roughly translates into medicine power, spiritual helpers, or source of supernatural abilities. Medicine power could be used for good and evil. Inkonze was fundamental to Dene and Dene–Métis life. Men and women with inkonze could make medicine to cure the sick, predict where animals could be found, or conjure away evil spirits. See Coutu and Hoffman-Mercredi, *Inkonze*; and Smith, *Inkonze*.

41. Petitot, *En route pour la mer glaciale*, 375.

42. Duchaussois, *Aux Glaces Polaires*, 414–16.

43. Sutherland, *Northerners Say*, 70–71, 73–74, 82–83. They were auxiliary sisters. Sister Sutherland is Métis.

44. Interview with Alice Hardy née Gaudet (1976), p. 14, Prince of Wales Northern Heritage Centre, Métis Heritage Association Collection, Yellowknife, NWT; and Dorval, "Entrevue auprès d'un donateur du musée McCord [Julien Gaudet]," p. 34, Université de Montréal, Faculté des Études Supérieures, Programme de muséologie, 1990, McCord Museum, Montréal, QC.

45. Wright, *Église Notre-Dame de Bonne Espérance*. The church was declared a National Historic Site in 1977.

46. Bella's artistic contribution was mentioned to the author by the Hardy family. It was also suggested that Bella had a relationship with Father Petitot, which may be gossip or an acknowledgment of a certain intimacy between the two artists. In any case, Petitot preferred young male companions.

47. Journal of Brother P. Kearney, cited in Breton, *Au Pays des Peaux de Lièvres*, 93.

48. "A little drink and good times," Codex of Mission of Fort Good Hope, 97.109, 1879–1917, books, 3–11, various entries, Fonds OMI, PAA.

49. ME988.136.1–44 and 137.1–9, Gaudet Collection, McCord Museum. A number of artifacts were also deposited in the Prince of Wales Northern Heritage Centre in Yellowknife by Timothy Gaudet's family of Fort Norman (Tulita).

50. ME988.136.37A-B and 38A-B (translation), Gaudet Collection, McCord Museum.

51. Dorval, "Entrevue auprès d'un donateur du musée McCord [Julien Gaudet]," 49, 66, McCord Museum.

52. Dugré, "Les Missionnaires Oblats," 374; and Duchaussois, *Aux Glaces Polaires*, 415. The former refers to her as French Canadian and the latter as of French origin, albeit born in the Mackenzie District.

53. Author's translation. Original quotation: *"on n'est pas mitchifs nous-autres"* (Payment, " 'On n'est pas mitchifs nous-autres' ").

54. Author's translation. Original quotation: *"elle ne l'aurait pas prise à sa valeur, qui sait même si ça ne l'aurait pas choquée. J'ai préféré le garder que de m'exposer"* (31 July 1889, Letters, 91.345, Fonds OMI, PAA). The shawl, especially a decorated fringed style, was worn extensively by Aboriginal women in the nineteenth century and became a traditional Métis clothing item or marker. Perhaps the priest thought

that she might have been insulted if presented with a gift traditionally worn by Métis women or that he identified her as such.

55. Nute, "Down North in 1892," entry from June 1948, p. 43. Elizabeth was the daughter of John W. Taylor, American consul in Winnipeg, Manitoba, between 1870 and 1893.

56. Cameron, *New North*, 208.

57. Ibid.

58. Timothy married Sarah Hardisty of Fort Simpson, NWT, daughter of Métis Lenoir [Allen] Hardisty and Mary Ann Koketta, a Slavey woman. John (Jean-Pierre) married Marguerite St. Germain, a Métis from the Peace River region in northern Alberta.

59. Van Kirk, "Tracing the Fortunes," 176. Julien Gaudet also reported that there was family pressure to marry "white" women, and that the family considered Tim's wife, Sarah, to be "Indian," whereas John Peter's wife was "white" despite having Métis heritage.

60. Known as Freddy (1907–1981), he was the son of John and Marguerite St. Germain of Peace River, Alberta. He went to live with his grandparents in Fort Good Hope in 1908, and he went with Frédéric and Bella to St. Lambert, Québec, in 1917. His sister Christine also spent a few years in Québec in her youth.

61. Author's translation. Original quotation: *"voilà la mort qui arrive, pauvre petite elle ne sera pas longtemps avec nous"* (Dorval, "Entrevue auprès d'un donateur [Julien Gaudet]," 58, McCord Museum, and reiterated to the author by Richard Hardy in Yellowknife in 2000).

62. Codex of Mission of Fort Good Hope, 97.109, book 10, Fonds OMI, PAA. Frances had an attack of the croup and died on 28 November 1913. The child, Nancy, was baptized and died two days later. They were buried together on 1 December. Her husband cherished Frances's memory. Nephew Julien reported that he would cry at the mention of her name and kept souvenirs of her at his bedside all his life.

63. Fort Providence, Chroniques, 1867–1915, 29 June 1909, ASGM: "Mr. and Mrs. Gaudet arrived on the steamer 'Mackenzie' and we made cakes to mark their 50th anniversary [actually married in 1858]" (translation).

64. Author's translation. Original quotation: *"Mme Gaudet est morte ce soir à 7 heures. Elle a fait une mort bien édifiante. La mort ne l'a pas surprise, elle la désirait depuis longtemps. Elle avait communié hier matin. On a envoyé avertir les sauvages des environs et ils sont tous venus prier pour la défunte"* (Codex of Mission of Fort Good Hope, book 10, Fonds OMI, PAA).

65. He died in St. Boniface Hospital on September 22, 1917, and was buried beside his daughter Christine in St. Norbert parish cemetery, south of Winnipeg. See obituary in *Manitoba Free Press*, 24 September 1917. Among the witnesses who signed the parish register were his old HBC friend and colleague, Roderick MacFarlane, and this author's great-uncle, Joseph Lecomte, husband of Anna Payment. The Lecomtes are buried next to the Gaudets.

66. Gaudet, "Chief Trader Charles Philip Gaudet," 45. In the article, it is mentioned that he had four sons, "all in the service," but there is no mention of his wife Marie and the three daughters.

67. Dorval, "Entrevue auprès d'un donateur [Julien Gaudet]," 67, McCord Museum; and account by Pierrette Gaudet about the elderly Bella, who fell and treated her broken hip herself in the early 1950s.

68. Transcript of interview with Alice Hardy née Gaudet, daughter of Timothy Gaudet and Sarah Hardisty, Fort Norman, 1976, Métis Heritage Association Collection, Prince of Wales Northern Heritage Centre, Yellowknife, NWT.

69. List compiled by Father Henri Posset of Fort Simpson in late 1970s. Courtesy of Richard Hardy.

70. See, e.g., Hardy, "Métis Rights in the Mackenzie River District." The Gaudets played a key role in the first official publication on the Métis in the Northwest Territories. See Overvold (Burger), *Our Metis Heritage*, with preface by Richard Hardy and contributions by elders Alice Gaudet Hardy, Jane Gaudet, Ted Trindell, and other extended family members.

71. Julien was the younger son of Léon Gaudet and Georgianna Rioux, who were married in St. Lambert, Québec, in 1921 and had three children, Amédée, Julien, and Georgette. I am indebted to Julien's wife, Pierrette Marquis (1925–2010), for sharing family records and answering numerous inquiries.

Works Cited

Archival Sources

Edmonton, AB
Provincial Archives of Alberta (PAA). Fonds Oblats de Marie-Immaculée (OMI).
Codex of Mission of Fort Good Hope (Notre Dame de Bonne-Espérance) 1868–1917, Books 1–11. 97.109.
Letters. 91.345.
Montréal, QC
Archives des Soeurs Grises de Montréal (ASGM).
Fort Providence, Chroniques, 1867–1915. L25.
Île-à-la-Crosse, 1860–1917. Lettres à Mère-Générale Chroniques, 1860–1917. L18.
Mission de Saint-Boniface, Registre des écoliers, 1844–94.
Gaudet Family Collection (private collection).
McCord Museum.
Dorval, Nicole. "Entrevue auprès d'un donateur du musée McCord [Julien Gaudet]." Université de Montréal, Faculté des Études Supérieures, Programme de maîtrise en muséologie, 1990, 111p.
Gaudet Fisher Collection, 136.1–44; 137.1–9. ME988.

Winnipeg, MB
    Hudson's Bay Company Archives (HBCA).
        Biographical files.
        Will of Alexander Fisher. A.36/6, microfilm 426.
    Centre du Patrimoine Franco-Manitobain (CPFM), Archives de La Société
    historique de Saint-Boniface (ASHSB).
        Fonds Fisher-Deschambeault.
            Fonds Taché, T8002–04.
        Répertoires des engagements pour l'ouest.
Yellowknife, NWT
    Interview with Alice Hardy née Gaudet, 1976. Prince of Wales Northern Heri-
    tage Centre, Métis Heritage Association Collection.

Published Sources

Breton, P. E. *Au Pays des Peaux de Lièvres*. Edmonton, AB: Éditions de l'Ermitage,
    1962.
Brown, Jennifer S. H. "Women as Centre and Symbol in the Emergence of Métis
    Communities." *The Canadian Journal of Native Studies* 3, no. 1 (1981): 39–46.
Cameron, Agnes Deans. *The New North: Being Some Account of a Woman's Journey
    through Canada to the Arctic*. New York and London, UK: D. Appleton & Co.,
    1910.
Coutu, Phillip R., and Lorraine Hoffman-Mercredi. *Inkonze: The Stones of Traditional
    Knowledge*. Edmonton, AB: Thunderwoman Ethnographies, 1999.
Drouin, R. *Répertoire des mariages des Canadiens Français 1760–1935*. Vol. 61. Mon-
    tréal, QC: Éditions histoire et généalogie Pépin, 1998.
Duchaussois, R. P. *Aux Glaces Polaires*. Ville La Salle, QC: L'Oeuvre Apostolique,
    1921.
Dugré, Adélard. "Les Missionnaires Oblats de Marie Immaculée aux Glaces
    Polaires." *Missions des Oblats de Marie Immaculée* 216 (June 1922): 371–81.
Gaudet, J. Léon. "Chief Trader Charles Philip Gaudet." *The Beaver* 15, no. 2 (Septem-
    ber 1935): 45–46.
Glazebrook, G. P., de T., ed. *The Hargrave Correspondence 1821–1843*. New York, NY:
    Greenwood Press, 1968.
Grollier, Henri. "Souvenirs." *Missions des Oblats de Marie Immaculée* 24 (1886):
    409–22.
Hardy, Richard. "Métis Rights in the Mackenzie River District of the Northwest
    Territories. *Canadian Native Law Reporter* 1 (1980): 1–33.
Klein, Laura F., & Lillian A. Ackerman, eds. *Women and Power in Native North
    America*. Norman: University of Oklahoma Press, 1995.
Lindsay, Debra J., ed. *The Modern Beginnings of Subarctic Ornithology: Correspon-
    dence to the Smithsonian Institution 1856–69*. Winnipeg, MB: Manitoba Record
    Society, 1991.
Manitoba Free Press, September 24, 1917.

McCarthy, Martha. *From the Great River to the Ends of the Earth: Oblate Missions to the Dene, 1847–1921*. Edmonton: University of Alberta Press, 1995.

North Slave Métis Alliance. *North Slave Métis History*. Rae-Edzo, NWT, 2003.

Nute, Grace Lee. "Down North in 1892" [Diary of Elizabeth Taylor]. *The Beaver* 28, no. 1 (June 1948): 42–46.

Overvold (Burger), Joanne, ed. *Our Metis Heritage: A Portrayal*. Yellowknife, NWT: Métis Heritage Association of the Northwest Territories, 1976.

Payment, Diane P. " 'On n'est pas mitchifs nous-autres': relations entre les missionnaires catholiques et les Métisses au Nord-Ouest entre 1818 et 1920." *Western Oblate Studies/Études Oblates* 3 (1994): 139–58.

Petitot, Émile. *En route pour la mer glaciale*. Paris, France: Létourzey et Ane, 1887.

Smith, D. M. *Inkonze: Magico–Religious Beliefs of Contact–Traditional Chipewyan Trading at Fort Resolution, NWT, Canada*. Ottawa, ON: National Museum of Canada, Mercury Series, 1973.

Sutherland, Agnès. *Northerners Say: "Thanks Sisters."* Montréal, QC: L'Oeuvre de Mère Youville, 1996.

Van Kirk, Sylvia. *"Many Tender Ties": Women in Fur Trade Society, 1670–1870*. Winnipeg, MB: Watson and Dwyer Publishing, 1980.

———. "Tracing the Fortunes of Five Founding Families of Victoria, B.C." *B.C. Studies* 115/116 (Autumn–Winter 1997–98): 149–78.

Williams, G., ed. *Hudson's Bay Company Miscellany 1670–1870*. Winnipeg, MB: Hudson's Bay Record Society, 1975.

Wright, Janet. *Église Notre-Dame de Bonne Espérance, Fort Good Hope, Northwest Territories*. Ottawa, ON: Environment Canada-Parcs, 1986.

Zinovich, Jordan. *Battling the Bay: The Turn of the Century Adventures of Fur Trader Ed Nagle*. Edmonton, AB: Lone Pine Publishing, 1992.

10

THE MONTANA METIS AND THE SHIFTING BOUNDARIES OF BELONGING

MICHEL HOGUE

O n November 1, 1921, a handful of families who lived on Montana's Fort Belknap Indian Reservation learned from the commission charged with drawing up new tribal rolls that they were no longer eligible for enrollment on the reservation. The decision unsettled Antoine Gladue and Antoine Azure, two men whose families had deep and lasting connections to Montana Metis communities, but whom Indian agents had counted among the Fort Belknap Assiniboines since the late nineteenth century. "The greater part of my life has been spent among the Indians," Gladue wrote to the U.S. secretary of the interior, "and I am familiar with the mode of living and with their habits and peculiarties." Gladue went on to sketch his family's history and detail his links to the reservation in an effort to convince the secretary that the commission had made an error. To provide additional evidence of such ties, Gladue even included with the letter the pass that the Fort Belknap Indian superintendent John Marshall had issued him the previous summer allowing him to travel to the nearby Rocky Boy Reservation to celebrate the Fourth of July holiday.[1] In his appeal, Azure likewise pointed to his family's long history among the Assiniboines. He lamented that those charged with enrollment denied his children "the right here when my father had went through so much danger and trouble to get me and my children the right which they have a comming to them."[2]

The enrollment commission's mandate to determine who belonged on the Fort Belknap Reservation and was eligible for land allotments there forced the members of the Azure and Gladue families to document the ties that bound them to the other members of the reservation. These ties extended deep into the past. After all, the Azures were of part Assiniboine ancestry, and they and the Gladues had established a presence in Montana's Milk River Valley as early as the 1860s. They were part of a cluster of Metis families who, since their arrival in Montana, had married one another and had lived and worked together. But they had also been singled out by the U.S. Army as "American half-breeds" and, because of their kin ties to the Assiniboines at Fort Belknap, were allowed to remain on the reservation even as other "foreign" Metis or Indians had been forcibly expelled in the 1870s. Indian agents added their names to the Fort Belknap tribal censuses of the 1890s. Now, several decades later, the tribal enrollment commission expunged their names on the grounds that they were "half breeds, half French Canadian and Cree."[3]

That these families could be counted among the Fort Belknap Indians in the late nineteenth century, yet later be denied rights to the reservation because they were "Canadian half breeds," illustrated the complicated and shifting criteria for belonging as well as the stakes involved in the enrollment process for these families. Indeed, the enumeration of Fort Belknap members generated a need both to define who belonged on the reservation and to elaborate the characteristics that would entitle someone to reservation land and resources.[4] Asked to decide who belonged on the reservation, the resident tribes and federal representatives weighed these families' claims. The resulting dialogue illustrated how descent, blood quantum, residency, community or kin ties, and even lifestyle were potential markers of belonging on the reservation. The result, as historian Alexandra Harmon has argued, was the product of negotiations between officials intent on applying federal policies and law and indigenous people whose notions of belonging both yielded to and shaped those laws.[5]

At Fort Belknap, these variables were intimately linked to politics and life on the reservation and to the perception that the Azure and Gladue families lacked a demonstrated and continued attachment to Assiniboines and Gros Ventres. Metis families had long sustained their presence in the Milk River Valley through their kin and economic ties to Assiniboines, but the density of those ties had lessened as the environmental, economic, and social conditions that had enabled the creation of earlier borderland communities changed. The changes were evident in the labels used to describe these families in the agency records. Identified variously as "half breeds" or "mixed bloods," they were nonetheless listed among the Assiniboines in the administrative records. In their own appeals, these individual likewise sought to accent those ties that bound them to the reservation and its members. The enrollment commission's rejection of their claims in 1921 pointed to an unraveling of ties that had underpinned these earlier borderland communities. The descendants of the early Metis borderland settlers occupied a marginal space on the reservation, married members of other tribes less frequently, and were seemingly less involved in the reservation's cultural and social life. In the eyes of the enrollment commission—which had to weigh the Azures' and Gladues' claims against emerging government policies and local notions of belonging—this growing distance made their claims to membership less compelling.

The Plains Metis in the Borderlands

Antoine Gladue's grandfather was among a group of itinerant Metis traders who crossed the U.S.–Canadian border to do business on the northern Montana Indian reservation in the 1860s. In the fall of 1866 or 1867, Antoine Gladue (he and his grandson shared the same name) and his brother-in-law and fellow trader, James Francis Whitford, set up winter quarters among a group of about twenty-five Métis families who had settled in the Milk River Valley. The group was also one of the first organized bands of Metis buffalo hunters to set down more permanent roots in the Milk River Valley. Most descended from Pembina Metis families and were of mixed French Canadian, Chippewa, and Assiniboine ancestry. They relied on traders like Gladue to supply them with the ammunition they needed to hunt buffalo and then to purchase the products of their hunts.[6]

Gabriel Azure was one of the leaders of this group of Metis families. Born in 1824 at Pembina, he was the second son of Antoine Azure and Marguerite Assinibwan. With his parents, he had lived on both sides of the forty-ninth parallel. The Azures had moved north from Pembina to settle among the Metis community in the parish of St-François Xavier in the 1820s, but Gabriel and his new wife, Cecelia Laframboise, were among the various Azure family members who moved in the 1840s to reestablish homes just south of the border.[7] The buffalo trade appears to have drawn these families westward. Azure and the members of his extended family were among the Metis who arrived in northern Montana to hunt and, in the late 1860s and early 1870s, to set up more permanent settlements. Their migrations conformed to the broader pattern evident across the northern plains whereby extended families migrated together or followed in chain migrations. Kin relations remained central to the subsequent organization of the new, mobile settlements they established farther west.[8]

These Metis hunters and traders, however, became increasingly entangled with U.S. federal and Montana territorial officials who were determined to stake their claims to the region. Since 1851, the U.S. government had formally recognized as Indian Country the land east of the Continental Divide and north of the Musselshell and Missouri Rivers to the forty-ninth parallel. The Fort Laramie Treaty of that year, and the treaty concluded with the Blackfeet four years later, parceled out north-central Montana to its resident tribes: the Blackfeet, Gros Ventres, Assiniboines, and River Crows.[9] It was only in the late 1860s, when growing numbers of Euro-American settlers began to arrive in Montana, that federal officials took more decisive steps to organize Indian agencies and administer federal Indian policies. In 1868, the Indian Bureau established the Milk River Agency approximately ninety miles upstream from the Missouri River. There, Indian agents attempted to implement federal directives for the management of the Assiniboines, Gros Ventres, and River Crows.[10] U.S. officials believed that Metis traders, by trading in Indian Country, undermined the administration of Indian affairs

As a result, those Metis families who established themselves in northern Montana were subject to repeated raids by U.S. officials who sought to drive them off the Indian reservation. In the fall of 1867, Deputy Marshal John X. Beidler attempted to expel the Canadian-based Metis traders off the reservation. In a surprise raid, Beidler confiscated goods worth $15,000 from traders Gladue and Whitford, set fire to their cabins, and told them to return at once to Canada.[11] In following years, Metis traders like Gladue were repeatedly subjected to fines, imprisonment, and seizure of their goods based on the argument that they had "smuggled" goods across the border and were trading with Indians on an Indian reservation without a license.[12] Because Gladue was neither American nor affiliated with the local Indian agency, officials felt that he did not belong.

Other Metis families, however, had greater success remaining in Montana. Indeed, as many as one hundred Metis families wintered year after year along the banks of Frenchman's Creek, just south of the forty-ninth parallel. They were the primary customers in the early 1870s at a trading post known as Fort N. J. Turney, located at the confluence of Frenchman's Creek and the Milk River.[13] Although U.S. officials routinely cracked down on efforts by Metis or other Canadian-based traders to conduct trade in northern Montana, they allowed their Metis clients to remain.

The ability of these Metis communities to remain in the region also hinged on maintaining good relations with the region's indigenous peoples. Their migrations west in search of buffalo had occurred in tandem with the migrations of Assiniboines, Crees, and Ojibwas. Members of these groups traveled, hunted, and traded together and were often linked through marriage and kinship. Although the degree of mixing varied across space and time, in some instances, the close connections forged over generations prompted close alliances and even patterns of fusion or ethnic merger. Indeed, more and more Ojibwas, Crees, and Assiniboines were incorporated into the ranks of the emergent Metis community on the Dakota plains in the mid-nineteenth century, and related dynamics propelled closer relations between bands of Crees and Assiniboines and ultimately led to the formation of hybrid Cree–Assiniboine bands (known as the *Nehiopwat* in Cree).[14]

The shifting ethnic and political landscape also prompted realignments among the Gros Ventres and Assiniboines after their migration to the Milk River region in the 1850s and 1860s. The contraction of the buffalo and the westward expansion of their enemies, the Lakota, had pulled them west, which caused them to forge closer relations with one another. Both had been repeatedly weakened by disease and were outnumbered by the more populous and expansionist Lakota. Their ties, promoted through trade and cemented through marriages, offered a measure of protection on the volatile northern Plains. A similar desire to bolster their position led them to cultivate closer ties with other indigenous nations, like the River Crows, and with U.S. officials and traders after the establishment of the Milk River Indian Agency at Fort Browning in 1868.[15]

The Metis, then, were one of the groups jockeying for access to the region's resources. As these contests became more pitched in the 1870s, Metis experienced more determined attempts to force them from the reservation. With groups pressing in from the north and east, Gros Ventres and Upper Assiniboines agitated for assistance in guaranteeing access to the buffalo herds. During that decade, the U.S. Army, at the prompting of local indigenous populations and Indian Affairs officials, launched repeated army campaigns to drive out those whom they deemed "foreign." Although these operations targeted many Metis, Crees, and others, some were able to secure permission to remain. Because of their demonstrable ties to the local Assiniboine, Gros Ventres, or Yanktonai Indians, authorities allowed Gabriel Azure and members of his camp to remain on parts of the reservation.[16] His son Antoine later recalled that Gabriel had been "made a ward of the Government" at the conclusion of the first treaty between the Assiniboines and U.S. government representatives and had later worked for the Indian agency established at Fort Browning.[17] Fort Belknap Indian agent Wyman Lincoln, too, sanctioned their presence. Azure and his family were eventually incorporated onto the rolls of the Assiniboine band at the Fort Belknap Agency. Their inclusion reflected the U.S. government practice of only recognizing Metis as members of "full-blood" Indian groups so long as those groups consented to their inclusion.[18] The continued power of local indigenous peoples to decide who belonged on their reservations continued to influence Metis claims to belonging in subsequent decades.

Reshaping Fort Belknap

The accommodations forged in the context of these borderland settlements came under increasing scrutiny as the federal presence increased across the northwestern plains. U.S. federal land policies, and specifically the push for the allotment of Indian lands between the 1880s and 1920s, prompted an enumeration of indigenous peoples across the United States and the creation of tribal base rolls on reservations. Although bureaucrats had long kept records of agency Indians, the impetus behind the creation of enrollment commissions to compile official tribal rolls stemmed from the federal General Allotment Act (or Dawes Act), which authorized in 1887 the survey and allotment of land on Indian reservations to individual Indians.[19] The legislation's provisions allowed for the assignment of 160-acre allotments to heads of families (and lesser amounts to children or orphans). Policymakers and Christian reformers alike believed that such legislation would bring about two interrelated benefits. First, proponents thought that allotting lands in severalty would promote a broader goal of "civilizing" indigenous peoples by breaking their communal ways and inculcating habits of hard work, thrift, and the other virtues that supporters presumed would flow from private property ownership. Second, the legislation also promised to open any "surplus" lands—that is, lands left over once all eligible members received their allotments—for sale to non-Indians.[20] But before officials could allot reservation lands, they needed to know who belonged on the reservation.

Yet years elapsed between the passage of this legislation and the allotment of the Fort Belknap Indian Reservation. The delay arose from a number of factors. First, much of the urgency to open reservation lands in northern Montana to outside settlement subsided after 1887. In that year, the Northwest Commission visited Fort Belknap to negotiate the land cessions that broke up the large Indian reservation that spanned the northern reaches of the territory into three distinct, and much smaller, reservations: Fort Peck, Fort Belknap, and Blackfeet. The land cessions were the culmination of years of agitation among white settlers in Montana, but the unusually harsh winter of 1887 devastated area stock and effectively ended the large open-range outfits that drove the earlier ranching boom. Thereafter, aridity checked further homestead development in the eastern two-thirds of Montana until reclamation, new dry-farming techniques, and enlarged homestead provisions helped prompt a renewed land rush in the first two decades of the twentieth century.[21] As outside pressure to open more reservation lands subsided, so too did interest among Bureau of Indian Affairs officials in pursuing the matter. Although local Indian agents repeatedly asserted that allotting lands to individuals and families was essential to making Indians self-supporting, the Indian Bureau showed little interest in pursuing the matter.[22]

The delay also reflected opposition to allotment among Fort Belknap Indians, or at least among a majority of Assiniboines. The growing split between Assiniboines and Gros Ventres regarding the desirability of allotment came to the fore in 1894, when the U.S. Congress sent another commission to treat with the Assiniboines and Gros Ventres for the cession of the southernmost portion of their reservation. This time the impetus for the reduction came after outsiders discovered gold and silver deposits in the Little Rocky Mountains and began to stake mining claims.[23] Ultimately, a majority of the adult males on the reservation agreed to cede a strip of land of roughly four by seven miles and, in return, received $360,000, to be disbursed over a period of four years. The agreement also stipulated that the reservation would remain "as a communal grazing tract," and that Indian Affairs officials would not allot land in severalty until a majority of adult males specifically requested such a course. In the end, five-sixths of the Assiniboine population and a majority of the older men approved the agreement, but most Gros Ventre men and a number of the younger men did not.[24]

The differences that emerged in 1894 were rooted deep in reservation politics and continued in subsequent years to cloud discussions about enrollment and allotment at Fort Belknap. The Assiniboines, who at the time were more destitute than their Gros Ventres neighbors, favored outright cession. For them, the agreement was a way to curry favor with government officials and to secure an extension to the soon-to-expire annual payments and supplies that they had been receiving as a result of the 1887 cession of the reservation. Given the exceedingly bleak economic circumstances on the reservation in the 1890s, the promise of continued annuities would have offered at least some guarantee for their future well-being.[25] The Gros Ventres, by contrast, opposed the land cessions because they hoped to take advantage of the gold deposits on their reservation by mining the gold themselves. They also objected to provisions in the final agreement that blocked allotment. Unlike most Assiniboines, many Gros Ventres favored allotment because it seemingly promised a solution to the grinding poverty at Fort Belknap and a way to minimize government intrusions in their daily lives. With title to their lands, they hoped that they could also obtain revenues from leases or other arrangements. Allotment also raised hopes for greater self-determination. It offered a check against the ongoing pressure from the surrounding community for further land cessions and a guard against the chronic mismanagement and corruption among Fort Belknap Indian agents. Finally, allotment also served another longstanding Gros Ventre goal—to convince officials of their progressiveness and determination to become "civilized." The attempt to portray themselves as "civilized," and to contrast themselves with the Assiniboines, was part of a broader political strategy to gain prominence and primacy on the reservation.[26]

Although this goal had long animated relations between individual Gros Ventres and group relations among the Gros Ventres, neighboring tribes, and representatives of the United States, the equation shifted along with a growing realization that Assiniboines now outnumbered them at Fort Belknap. Close relations with Assiniboines had, historically, improved their political position by bolstering their numbers and helping them deflect pressure for further land cessions. Assiniboine growth, however, threatened Gros Ventres' ability to secure their political goals. Assiniboine ranks at Fort Belknap had swelled in the final decades of the nineteenth century, as growing numbers of Assiniboine families from the Fort Peck Reservation and reserves in Canada, as well as a smaller number of Cree–Chippewa families, arrived at Fort Belknap.[27] Thus, for many leading Gros Ventres, the 1895 cession underscored the importance both of securing allotment and of slowing the growth of the Assiniboine population. The Gros Ventres continued to believe that allotment provided their best hope for greater autonomy, and so they pressed local and federal officials to allot the reservation. Between 1911 and 1921, they traveled to Washington, D.C., on four separate occasions to make their case.[28] In so doing, they focused attention on the people, including the various Metis families, who had helped bolster Assiniboine ranks in the preceding decades.

The Fort Belknap Enrollment Commission

The enrollment commission officially began its work drawing up its lists in the summer of 1921. Its three members included the Indian superintendent, John T. Marshall, and two elected representatives of the Gros Ventres and Assiniboines, George Cochran and William Bigby, who were chosen at a special council held for that purpose. From its headquarters at the agency office near Harlem, Montana, the commissioners posted notices and sent word to neighboring reservations, non-reservation schools, and nearby towns calling all would-be applicants to the agency to make their claims for enrollment. For each applicant, the commissioners recorded the applicant's name, age, and birthplace; the birthplace of their parents and grandparents; the names of their spouses and living children; and the extent of their education. The commissioners posted the names of all persons enrolled each month for a twenty-day period at different points on the reservation. In those cases where tribal members contested someone's enrollment, the commission launched a further investigation. Their goal was to determine who, "by virtue of blood and affiliation" with the Assiniboines and Gros Ventres, ought be enrolled as members of the Fort Belknap Reservation.[29]

After only a single day of hearing claims, the commissioners encountered a series of cases that underscored just how difficult it would be to determine how and when blood or other ties would entitle certain individuals to enrollment. The commissioners wondered, for example, if they should enroll a man who was the son of a "full-blood" Gros Ventre woman and a white man who had left the reservation, proved up on a "citizen's homestead" off the reservation, but sold the land and returned to the reservation. Could someone who had applied for, received, and proved up on a homestead as a non-Indian now become an enrolled member of an Indian tribe? In another instance, three siblings based their claim on their relationship to their grandmother, a "full-blood" Gros Ventre woman. Their mother (who was of mixed Gros Ventre and white ancestry) had married a white man, and the entire family had never lived on the reservation. Was this blood connection enough to recommend enrollment? And if a man of mixed Piegan (Pikuni) and white ancestry who was raised on the Fort Belknap Reservation married a Gros Ventre woman, was he eligible for enrollment?[30]

Their questions underscored the difficulty of the task that the commissioners faced. Deciding who did or did not belong on the reservation involved pulling apart many of the tangled historical relationships that had promoted the mingling of Natives and newcomers and indigenous peoples of varied tribal backgrounds. In their place, the commissioners were meant to delineate clearer tribal and, eventually, racial boundaries. The claims that Antoine Azure and the members of his extended family presented to the commission showed that this task was rarely straightforward.

The stories the Azures told, combined with the Indian agency records, illustrated a long-standing presence in and around the reservation. For example, the Azure family traced its presence in the Milk River Valley back to Gabriel Azure and Cecelia Laframboise's arrival in the 1860s from Dakota Territory. As we have seen, Gabriel was of part Assiniboine ancestry. He had also worked directly for the U.S. government when it began to establish a more formal (and permanent) presence in the region. Indeed, the ties that Azure (who also went by the name Swift, Swift Runner, or Sky Man) had to the surrounding Indians were significant enough to merit his inclusion on a list of so-called "American half-breeds" who were allowed to remain on the reservation through the 1870s.

By decade's end, however, many of these Métis families had chosen to leave the reservation. The Azure family reportedly left the Milk River Valley in 1879, along with a group of about forty families bound for the Judith Basin. Many of these families formed the nucleus of the Metis settlement at Spring Creek (later, Lewistown).[31] Some, like the Azures and Gladues, did not remain there long. Instead, they moved west to the Jesuit mission of St. Peter's near Sun River, where a small Metis community had sprung up. By 1880, Gabriel and Cecelia Azure, and their son Antoine, had taken up forty-acre plots and had established small farms near one another. So had Modeste Gladue and about a half a dozen other Metis families.[32]

Why the various members of the Azure family sold their land at Sun River and returned to Fort Belknap several years later is not clear, but their return seems to have coincided with the dramatic cessions of Indian lands in 1887. In return for their land, the tribal members at Fort Belknap would share in $115,000, disbursed over a ten-year period. The money came with strings attached—it could only be used for the purchase of stock, clothing, subsistence, agricultural supplies, education, and the like—but the promise of a regular annuity may have been reason enough to draw some of them back.[33] Thereafter, the Azures and Gladues appeared frequently in the records of the Fort Belknap Indian Agency. Indian agents began noting some of the Azure family members on the annual Indian census beginning in 1893—they received rations at the agency, their children attended St. Paul's Catholic mission school on the reservation, and they apparently added their names to the various petitions that the Fort Belknap Assiniboines sent to their agent or to Washington, D.C.[34]

At the commissioners' prompting, Antoine Azure narrated many of these aspects of his family's history and their connections to the Fort Belknap tribes.[35] The other members of his family who appeared before the commission in support of their own enrollment applications, or as witnesses who corroborated their testimony, added to the picture Azure created. Asked about aspects of their own lives, they told the commission of the varied routes that had led them to and from Fort Belknap and the different ties that bound them to the reservation and its people.[36]

It became clear from their questions that the commissioners were skeptical about the Azures' claims and those of the Assiniboine witnesses who provided testimony on their behalf. The commissioners poked holes in the testimonies, underscoring hazy genealogical claims and perceived inaccuracies in the Azures' personal narratives. Prophet, an Assiniboine man and Gabriel Azure's cousin who testified on Antoine Azure's behalf, faced the most direct questioning. If, as Prophet had testified, Antoine Azure claimed to speak fluent Assiniboine, the commissioners asked, why had Azure required the help of a Cree-speaking translator to help him with his application? One of the commissioners even alleged that the Azures had paid Prophet for his testimony and coached him on what to say.[37]

The commissioners focused in particular on the nature of the ties that linked the Azures to the Fort Belknap tribes and especially the claims of blood connections between them. Prophet, for example, faced close questioning on his knowledge of Antoine Azure's parents and grandparents. In response to a commissioner's question about the tribal affiliation of Hoop, Gabriel Azure's mother, Prophet indicated that she was Assiniboine. When asked whether she was "a full-blood," Prophet responded that she was. The commissioners were not satisfied.

> Q: Do you know what a person would have to be in order to be a full blood Assiniboine?
> A: Yes, their father and mother would have to be Assiniboines.
> Q: Then you say that Swift is a full-blood Assiniboine? How do you know that he was when you do not know his father?
> A: He is part Assiniboine.
> Q: And what is the other part?
> A: Half breed.
> Q: What do you mean by half breed?
> A: Mixed.

The commissioners returned to this point the following day, when they continued to question Prophet on the question of blood. This time, they turned to the tribal affiliation of Gabriel Azure's wife (and Antoine Azure's mother), Cecelia Laframboise.

> Q: Can you truthfully say to your knowledge, that Antoine Azure's mother was a full blood Assiniboine?
> A: Yes, she is an Assiniboine.
> Q: Was she a full blood?
> A: Yes, she is an Assiniboine.
> Q: Why did you say yesterday in your testimony that Swift was a full blood Assiniboine and today you say he is a half breed?
> A: I told you that he was an Assiniboine. I never said he was a half breed, I said he was an Assiniboine.[38]

Prophet's claims were simply baffling to anyone who believed that it was impossible to be "full-blood" Assiniboine if both parents were not themselves Assiniboine. More confusing still, his statements stood in sharp contrast with the Azure children's claims about their mother's ancestry. Admittedly, there was little agreement among them either. When asked, "What tribe did your mother belong to," Antoine Azure and his four children gave five different responses. According to them, Cecelia Laframboise was either "Half Chippewa and Half French," "Half Arrickaras and half French," "Half French and Half Cree," "Half Recree [Arickara] and Half Chippewa," or "Half Chippewa and mixed." Only Prophet claimed that Laframboise was Assiniboine.

Prophet's insistence on Laframboise's Assiniboine identity suggested that he relied on markers other than blood to determine identity and belonging on the Fort Belknap Reservation. In his testimony, he eschewed the term "full-blood," maintaining simply and repeatedly that Laframboise was Assiniboine. But the commissioners refused to let the matter drop. What was it, they asked, that made Prophet think that she was Assiniboine?

> A: The reason I claim that she is Assiniboine is because she was raised among them.
> Q: Did she talk Assiniboine?
> A: Yes.
> Q: Did you know her father and mother?
> A: No.
> Q: How can you say that she was an Assiniboine if you did not know her parents or did any one tell you that she was?
> A: No one told me for I know.

Q: How do you know that she was?

A: All that I know is that she was an Assiniboine when Swift married her.

Q: How can you truthfully say that she was an Assiniboine when you do not know her parents?

A: The reason that I did not know her parents is because they all died before I knew them.

Q: Did someone tell you that they were Assiniboine?

A: My father and the rest of the old people during my father's time and I understood that they were Assiniboines.

Q: How can you say that she or that they were Assiniboines when her own son states that she is part Cree and French?

A: They are descendants from the Assiniboine woman but on her father's side she might be a Cree. All I can say is she is mixed.

Q: What is the other part?

A: Assiniboine.

Q: You stated before that she was a full blood Assiniboine, what made you say that?

A: She is Assiniboine that is the reason I said that.

Q: Why do you say that she is Assiniboine when she is part Cree?

A: Her mother is an Assiniboine.

Q: How do you know that her mother is an Assiniboine?

A: I heard it through my grandmother, they told me that her mother was an Assiniboine.[39]

The exchanges between the commissioners and Prophet also suggested that the terms "full-blood" or "mixed-blood" held a different meaning for him than for the commissioners who cross-examined him. As Melissa Meyer suggests, such terms did not necessarily reflect *genetic* heritage, but were instead markers of *ethnic* differences among indigenous peoples. Their use demonstrated the common folk notion that blood transmitted human characteristics. They did not, however, necessarily match the presumed degree of "mixing" in an individual's make-up. Instead, "full-blood" and "mixed-blood" could serve as shorthand for the various ethnic markers or cultural attributes or affiliations that defined an individual's membership in a group. Thus, how someone dressed, what language he or she spoke, the person's lifestyle, and, perhaps most important, whom they married were key ways of determining ethnic differences.[40] Speak

Thunder, another Assiniboine witness who testified on Antoine Azure's behalf, pointed to such markers when he highlighted Gabriel Azure's participation in "a treaty at Fort Benton" and his help in the U.S. Army's 1877 campaign against the Nez Percés as evidence that he must be an Assiniboine.[41] Prophet's testimony made few direct references to such factors, but his repeated exchanges with the commissioners also suggested that there was no straightforward link between blood and belonging.

Prophet's insistence that the Azures were Assiniboine may also have reflected the importance that he placed on cultural and social practices and, specifically, the significance of being "raised among" Assiniboines as an important factor in determining belonging. Assiniboine society had long been structured around autonomous bands that, in turn, consisted of clusters of related families. The rules of kinship thus governed membership in these bands. According to Assiniboine custom, childrearing, insofar as it generally occurred within a matrilocal context, meant that a woman and her kin were initially responsible for the socialization of children. Among the Assiniboine, children often forged close bonds with their maternal grandparents, who typically helped raise children.[42] By Prophet's accounting, if Cecelia Laframboise was Assiniboine, then so too were her children.

But the Azures were unable to convince the enrollment commission of their rights. Despite the close questioning that Prophet endured on questions of blood and descent, what seems to have concerned the commissioners most was a more general lack of ties between the Azures and either the Assiniboines or Gros Ventres. Despite the fact that the Azures had lived on the reservation for at least thirty-two years, the commissioners wrote, "they have never affiliated with the Indians of this reservation, making their homes in the southeast corner of the reservation what is called the Bear Gulch country, taking no part in any of the affairs of the Indians and have never married into either of the tribes having rights on this reservation always marrying one of their own Cree blood."[43] In short, their physical marginalization at the reservation's edges and their apparent lack of marital or family ties to either the Assiniboines or Gros Ventres contributed to their separateness. The commission concluded that the Azures were "of no blood of either of the tribes of Indians living and entitled to allotments on this reservation" and thus had no rights to the reservation.

Determining Belonging

The commissioners' designation of these families as foreign, as lacking the necessary blood or kin ties to local tribes, and as otherwise unconnected to tribal affairs was part of an interrelated rationale for excluding them from tribal rolls. Their rationale was intimately bound up with broader contests on the reservation. After all, when community members agreed that an individual or family belonged, the commission added or maintained their names on the list. It was only in those instances where community members challenged someone's inclusion on the list that the enrollment commission began its investigations. Those challenges often pointed to deeper fissures and longstanding tensions that complicated the criteria for belonging.

For instance, by designating the Metis families as "half-breeds, half French Canadians and Cree," the commissioners invoked labels that marked the families as outsiders, by virtue of both their nationality and their tribal affiliation. In so doing, the commission gave renewed expression to longstanding Gros Ventre complaints about the growing presence of "Red River half-breeds," "Crees," and even "Canadian North Assiniboines" on the reservation. As early as the 1895 cession, for instance, Lame Bull and a group of "leading men of the Gros Ventres" asked for the removal of six hundred Assiniboines and "Red River Half-breeds" whom they claimed had no rights to the reservation. Agent Luke C. Hays dismissed the letter as "an old complaint" that re-emerged whenever "the relations between the tribes [became] strained."[44] And in subsequent years, Gros Ventre petitioners repeatedly lodged similar complaints with officials in Washington, D.C.[45]

The effectiveness of such complaints became clear when, in its final recommendations, the commissioners endorsed the view that the so-called Northern Assiniboines were interlopers who had come to the Milk River region "on hunting and raiding trips," but who always returned "to their northern country" where they received rations and cash payments from the Canadian government. They added that many had only arrived on the reservation as refugees from the 1885 Northwest Resistance. The commission recommended striking forty-four Northern Assiniboines from the rolls on the grounds that they were "Canadian Indians and of no blood of this tribe of Assiniboine Indians living and entitled to allotments on this reservation."[46]

The term "Northern Assiniboines" generally referred to those Assiniboine bands who occupied lands in present-day Saskatchewan, many of whom established treaty relations with the Canadian government in the 1870s. The Assiniboines' testimony in support of their applications, however, suggested a much longer, and more complicated, attachment to the Fort Belknap Reservation and its peoples than the name suggested. Those like Iron Horn, for example, recalled spending portions of their youth on both sides of the forty-ninth parallel. His family typically spent summers in or north of the Cypress Hills, and they usually wintered near the Little Rocky Mountains. Many had moved north to Canada after the buffalo disappeared, and they received treaty annuities on Canadian reserves; however, they then returned south to Fort Belknap after a period of years. Although their parents or grandparents typically represented different Assiniboine branches, all had some kin connections to the Fort Belknap Assiniboines, and all had spent some time in the vicinity of the reservation in their youth. Most had spent anywhere from thirty-two to fifty-six years on the reservation.[47] In their vigorous protests, Assiniboines also challenged their designation as newcomers, foreigners, and rebellion refugees and called for their reinstatement on the Fort Belknap rolls.[48]

Assiniboine protests eventually succeeded in convincing Indian commissioner Charles Burke to reverse course. Burke ordered Superintendent Marshall to re-investigate the claims of "northern Assiniboines" whose names were struck from the rolls. At a joint meeting of Assiniboines and Gros Ventres in August 1922, the former again used their numerical majority to reinstitute Assiniboines to the tribal rolls. Those assembled voted by a margin of 206 to 161 to restore the Assiniboines. According to Marshall, all the Assiniboines voted for enrollment, with all the Gros Ventres opposed.[49]

A mixture of policy and pragmatics was behind Commissioner Burke's decision to revisit the enrollment commission's decision to exclude virtually all the so-called northern Assiniboines. Whereas the commissioners had struck these individuals from the rolls on the basis that they had spent time in Canada or that they more properly belonged with Canadian bands of Assiniboines, Burke argued that different branches of the Assiniboines shared the same blood, and so long as there was evidence of longstanding affiliation with the Fort Belknap Indians (and no evidence of enrollment on other reservations or reserves in either Canada or the United States), they should be included on the tribal rolls. Behind his pronouncements was a set of legal and policy decisions that clarified, from the department's perspective, the rules of belonging on reservations. The decisions stemmed, as at Fort Belknap, from conflicts over enrollment. In the first, a U.S. Circuit Court decision about enrollment at Minnesota's White Earth Reservation stated that Indians, once recognized as members of a tribe, were entitled to those rights, even if they had not kept up tribal relations (although their children were not so entitled). The second arose from the enrollment at the Turtle Mountain Reservation. In that case, the assistant attorney general opined that nationality or participation in Canadian treaties or the like was not, by itself, sufficient grounds for exclusion from tribal rolls.[50]

The Bureau of Indian Affairs' reconsideration of Assiniboine exclusion also stemmed from recognition that the commission's recommendations would drive "old men and women" from their homes to an uncertain fate off the reservation. Officials acknowledged that the decision to strike so many people from the Fort Belknap tribal rolls seemingly contradicted Congress' earlier decision to establish Rocky Boy Reservation for landless Indians in 1919. The reservation had been created after years of lobbying by Chippewa chief Stone Child, Cree chief Little Bear, and their allies to have land set aside for a large population of so-called landless Indians (primarily Crees and Chippewas) in Montana. The enrollment commission's actions now threatened to undermine those earlier measures by creating a new population of landless Indians in Montana.[51]

The Gladues and Azures, by contrast, were unable to get the department to overturn the commission's decision on their applications. On the surface, their claims and those of the northern Assiniboines shared much in common. After all, most Montana Metis had been a part of the same borderland communities as Assiniboines. They had forged important ties with Assiniboine bands and even, in the case of the Azures and Gladues, had spent more time in the United States than some northern Assiniboines who had been reinstituted. Bound by denser webs of kinship and closer cultural ties, and more closely knitted into local communities, the links or associations between northern Assiniboines and Fort Belknap Indians, however, were more compelling than those that bound the Gladues and Azures to their neighbors.

Although the commissioners invoked blood as a marker of those ties, their rationale was only partly based on a concern about the degree of indigenous ancestry. After all, people of mixed ancestry had long been incorporated among the Fort Belknap Assiniboines and Gros Ventres. The leading Assiniboines, for instance, had secured the explicit inclusion of people of mixed ancestry as tribal members sharing in the proceeds of the 1895 cession. The final agreement even stated that "wherever the word Indian is used in this agreement it includes mixed bloods as well as full bloods."[52] Some of the most prominent Gros Ventre advocates for allotment, meanwhile, were of mixed ancestry, and they were enrolled in 1921 apparently without eliciting any comment from the commission.[53] The commission, however, did strike from the rolls various "half-blood Gros Ventres" who were living "as citizens." In these instances, however, it was a lack of tribal ties and their physical residence off the reservation, not the degree of blood, that appears to have been the overriding considerations. Moreover, the Bureau of Indian Affairs later reinstated many of these individuals.[54]

What mattered, apparently, was the perceived lack of "affiliation" or separateness. Although the commission cited the marriages between the Azures and Gladues and people "of their own Cree blood" as further evidence of their distinctiveness, it selectively overlooked those instances when members of these families did marry other members of the Fort Belknap tribes.[55] That these families lived at Bear Gulch, at the reservation's physical margins, seems only to have accentuated this perception. For the Azures and Gladues, this location put them close to the mills, mines, and residents of the mining towns like Zortman that provided markets for timber and other goods. Their involvement in timber cutting, however, was itself a recurrent source of complaint on the reservation. Although, as the agent maintained, they were entitled as members of the reservation to cut wood (so long as they secured the necessary permission and paid the required stumpage for wood sold off the reservation), others complained of a proliferation of outsiders who were crowding the reservation and stealing its timber.[56]

Indeed, the Bear Gulch settlement had a reputation as a gathering place for outsiders and became a source of complaints on the reservation. In the 1910s and 1920s, the rough mining communities that sprang up on the reservation's southern edges were also home to growing numbers of Metis people. The combined effects of drought and tough economic times after 1919 drove many Montanans from their farms. A number of the Judith Basin Metis families were among those who lost their lands during this time and migrated north to places like Zortman in search of work.[57] Members of Montana's so-called landless Indians, who were likewise in search of a place to settle, joined them there. The "half-breed Crees," whose presence the Fort Belknap Indians complained of, included a number of landless Chippewa–Cree who typically found employment on the Fort Belknap Reservation during the summers.[58] It is possible that others grouped the Azure and Gladue families, who were related to both the Judith Basin Metis and the members of the Turtle Mountain Chippewa, with this large population of non-status Indians and people of mixed ancestry in Montana. As Martha Foster notes, the label "Cree" in Montana encompassed various groups of landless or non-status people, especially those with some ties to Canada. As complaints from landowners, Indian agents, and even reservation Indians mounted about the presence of landless Indians in Montana's towns, cities, and reservations, the label "Cree" or "Cree half-breed" acquired a pejorative meaning.[59]

In this sense, the term "half-breed" was less a marker of descent than a social marker that distinguished Metis families from others on the reservation. That many on the reservation considered the Azures and Gladues families more "Cree" than Assiniboine spoke to the social distances that existed on the reservation. Antoine Azure gestured at this when he lamented that the question of enrollment had arisen after so many of the "old-timers" were dead. Their passing, he noted, "now makes it so hard to get proof as to my right here and my relationship among the Assiniboine Indians."[60] That events and details had receded into the recesses of memory perhaps spoke to the waning of these ties and their replacement by new relationships. Whereas Gabriel Azure and Cecelia Laframboise had forged or maintained the sorts of ties with local Assiniboine bands that had sustained their presence in the Milk River Valley in the 1860s and 1870s, their children and grandchildren were less successful in the reservation era.

When viewed through the lens of clear-cut racial or ethnic markers, those early borderland settlements were a confusing place. Mobility and intermixing between members of different tribes or branches of those tribes were defining features of life in the nineteenth-century borderlands. For government officials, this mobility and intermixing presented a recurring set of problems as they attempted to sort indigenous borderland peoples into discrete groupings of "Canadian" and "American" Indians, or into clear tribal groupings. The Fort Belknap Enrollment

Commission, for example, contrasted the relative ease with which it was able to generate the final roll of Gros Ventres with the difficulties that surrounded so many Assiniboine enrollments. "Unlike their neighbors the Assiniboines," the commissioners noted, "they stayed within the boundries of the old and present reservations."[61] When, in the 1870s, the Assiniboines petitioned the Canadian government for entry into the numbered treaties, or when individuals or groups of Assiniboines sought to join agencies in the 1870s and 1880s, officials discovered firsthand the difficulties of finalizing lists of "their Indians."[62] The resulting back and forth during the commission's hearings echoed these earlier attempts to situate Assiniboines on one side of the border or the other. It illustrated, moreover, just how difficult it was to disentangle the conditions and relationships that shaped or structured these communities.

The complex patterns of ethnic merger that had seen bands of Ojibwas, Assiniboines, Crees, and Metis fuse and mix with each other in the mid-nineteenth century were difficult to separate into their component parts and label as discrete ethnic groups. As a result, ethnographers looking backward at these communities, and even modern-day descendants of these groups, have had difficulty assigning or selecting a single ethnic marker.[63] From a policy perspective, this inability to select a single ethnicity created potential headaches, especially for bureaucrats charged with administering membership policies. Yet in instances such as the enrollment commission, these designations remained fluid or expansive enough to include others. What mattered was not an unambiguous racial or ethnic tie to a group, but a demonstrated and continued attachment to local communities. But, as the arrangements that sustained the borderlands communities of the nineteenth century faded, a more complicated dialogue about belonging emerged in its place.

In its place, colonial codes increasingly mediated decisions about belonging. These were not simple mandates that emanated from the Bureau of Indian Affairs. The specific decisions about enrollment and belonging— about who was Indian—rarely followed fixed criteria. They were instead rooted in the joint negotiations and dialogues in spaces such as enrollment commission hearings. They reflected the everyday understandings of exactly who belonged on the reservation and what it was that made someone Indian or Metis. As we have seen, such decisions embodied a multitude of factors, most of which had little to do with blood or race. Ironically, though, the final tribal roll became a critical marker of

Indian-ness in subsequent decades and the basis for its increasingly racialized definition in the twentieth century.[64]

Conclusion

The Tribal Enrollment Commission's deliberations offered a barometer of the changes that had occurred in borderland societies and the shifting basis for social relations within them. The enrollment requests by the Azure and Gladue families invoked the transnational and multiethnic nature of earlier borderland settlements. The descendants of Gabriel Azure and Cecelia Laframboise found, however, that without the kinds of interactions that had linked their parents and grandparents to their neighbors, their own claims to belonging had become more attenuated. The changed material and social circumstances of the twentieth-century borderlands no longer offered the same basis for the communities and relationships that had underpinned the Metis presence there through the nineteenth century.

Tribal enrollment councils sought to reassess and redefine relationships in these altered circumstances. The results were critical in fixing the twentieth-century legal and racial identities of their participants. Whether someone entered a treaty or became an enrolled member of a tribe had a lasting effect on his or her legal identity and that of any descendants. The designations an individual acquired papered over long and complicated histories of mixing and folded peoples with varied genealogies and histories into much simpler colonial categories. The goal behind the creation of such tribal rolls and band membership lists, as well as the delineation of sharper legal distinctions between Indians and Metis, was to create a "synoptic view" that collapsed the particularities of distant lands and peoples into simplified and standardized categories that state officials could document and replicate.[65] But the Fort Belknap Enrollment Commission's probes into family histories revealed the difficulties of untangling earlier borderland relationships and applying colonial taxonomies to their former residents. The changes in the enrollment commission's decisions, meanwhile, illustrated how tenuous those constructions remained. This tenuousness was attributable, in part, to the fact that the applicants who appeared before the commission and those who surrounded them were instrumental in shaping these discussions. The categories may have emanated from the state, but their application grew out of intensely local conversations that shaped their content and meaning.[66]

Ultimately, though, the law provided the markers of nationality or race with their power and durability. Their creation may have marked a gross oversimplification of the ties that had structured earlier relations, but they acquired a particular force over time as they became critical markers of belonging. The more rigid legal distinctions that separated U.S. and Canadian citizens and Indians and non-Indians on the twentieth-century plains suggest a human landscape marked as precisely as the forty-ninth parallel marked the territorial limits of Canada and the United States. The durability of such categories and markers stands as a testament to the success of nineteenth-century border-making projects.

Notes

An earlier version of this chapter appeared in Michel Hogue, "Between Race and Nation: The Plains Métis and the Canada-United States Border," Ph.D. diss., University of Wisconsin–Madison, 2009.

1. Affidavit of Antoine Gladue, 10 January 1922, file 4476-1921-053, pt. 1, box 7, Central Classified Files (CCF), Record Group (RG) 75, Bureau of Indian Affairs, National Archives and Records Administration (NARA). The Assiniboine refer to themselves as Nakota. Although the term "Assiniboine" is used increasingly to refer to bands who reside on the Canadian Prairies, I have retained its use as it is more commonly used among the Assiniboine who reside on Montana's Fort Peck and Fort Belknap Reservations. For consistency, I also retain the term "Gros Ventre." In addition, I have retained the original spelling used in direct quotes.

2. Antoine Azure to Commissioner of Indian Affairs, 16 November 1921, file 16996-1921-053, box 6, ibid.; and Affidavit of Antoine Azure, 20 December 1921, ibid.

3. [Fort Belknap Enrollment Commission] to Commissioner of Indian Affairs, file 54, box 16, Decimal Files, Records of the Fort Belknap Indian Agency, Bureau of Indian Affairs, Denver Federal Records Center (FRC), RG 75, NARA.

4. Harmon, *Indians in the Making*, 137–38.

5. Harmon, "Tribal Enrollment Councils."

6. Foster, *We Know Who We Are*, 61–62. The Chippewa are known variously as Plains Ojibwa, western Ojibwa, Bungi, Saulteaux, or Anishinaabeg. The term "Chippewa" is still commonly used in North Dakota and Montana, and I retain its use here.

7. U.S. Bureau of the Census, *1850 Minnesota Territorial Census*, 53; Morin, *Red River Settlement Censuses*, 6; and Morin, *Métis Families*, 1:65–66.

8. Foster, *We Know Who We Are*, 64, 69–72; and Ens, "Border, Buffalo, and Métis of Montana." Both Foster and Ens describe the conditions that brought growing numbers of Metis families to Montana in the 1860s and 1870s as well as the

effects of the buffalo's demise and the growing enforcement of the international boundary on Montana Metis communities.

9. The "Blackfeet" is the term given by nineteenth-century American observers to the three nations (the Pikuni/Piegan, Kainai/Blood, and the Siksika/Blackfoot) who are often collectively referred to as the "Blackfoot Confederacy," or the Niitsitapi. In Canadian documents, these people are known as the "Blackfoot."

10. Miller et al., *History of Assiniboine and Sioux*, 54–55. The tentative nature of this administrative presence was reflected in the many changes to Indian administration in north-central Montana. Five years after its opening, the Indian Bureau consolidated the Milk River agency with its neighbor, Fort Peck, and established a small subagency at Fort Belknap. Three years later, in 1876, the bureau closed Fort Belknap.

11. Father Van den Broeck, "Sketch of Ben Kline's Life," Ben Kline Reminiscence, Small Collection (SC) 942, Montana Historical Society (MHS). Beidler returned the following year and arrested Frank Ouellette, another Metis trader who had crossed the border from Canada hoping to trade for buffalo robes.

12. Hogue, "Between Race and Nation: Creation of a Métis Borderland."

13. Van den Broeck, "Sketch of Ben Kline's Life," SC 942, MHS; Ben Kline, "Reminiscence," SC 942, MHS; Samuel O'Connell, "Juneaux's Trading Post on Milk River, M.T." and "Reminiscence," both in Samuel O'Connell Papers, SC 597, MHS; and Foster, *We Know Who We Are*, 65–67.

14. Peers, *Ojibwa of Western Canada*, 112–14; and Albers, "Changing Patterns of Ethnicity," 99–102, 104–11.

15. Fowler, *Shared Symbols, Contested Meanings*, 49–50.

16. Capt. Constant Williams to A/Assistant Adjutant General, 27 February 1878, 2300 AGO 1878 (f/w 1056 AGO 1878), reel 394, microfilm (M) 666, RG 94, Records of the Office of the Adjutant General, NARA. Antoine Gladue's father, Modeste, had married Gabriel Azure's daughter, Melanie, and was also included on the list. Army campaigns to clear the reservation of "foreign" groups recurred throughout the early 1880s. See Hogue, "Disputing the Medicine Line."

17. Antoine Azure to Commissioner of Indian Affairs, 16 November 1921, file 16996-1921-053, box 6, CCF, RG 75, NARA; and "Testimony of Antoine Azure," 1921, file 100334-1921-053, pt. 1 (2 of 3), box 7, ibid.

18. Brown and Schenck, "Métis, Mestizo, and Mixed-Blood," 332.

19. Harmon, "Tribal Enrollment Councils," 176; and Meyer, "American Indian Blood Quantum Requirements," 231–33.

20. Meyer, *White Earth Tragedy*, 51–52; and Prucha, *Great Father*, 2:659–71.

21. Malone et al., *Montana: A History of Two Centuries*, 233–42.

22. Barry, *Fort Belknap Indian Reservation*, 167–68.

23. Kelley, "Report, Fort Belknap Agency, 18 August 1894," 181–82.

24. U.S. Congress, Senate, "Letter from Secretary of Interior, Transmitting an Agreement Made with Indians of Fort Belknap Reservation," 1–6.

25. "Proceedings of Councils of the Commissioners Appointed to Negotiate with the Fort Belknap Indians," in ibid., 7–11; and Fowler, *Shared Symbols, Contested*

Meanings, 71. Loretta Fowler also suggests that Assiniboine leaders may have been more eager to please government officials because one of their members had killed Indian agent Archer Simons just three years earlier. For a description of the grim socioeconomic situation on the reservation in the 1890s, see Foley, *Historical Analysis of Fort Belknap Indian Reservation*, 134–231.

26. Fowler, *Shared Symbols, Contested Meanings*, 70–72.

27. Ibid., 66–71.

28. "Proceedings of Councils," p. 21, in U.S. Congress, Senate, "Letter from Secretary of Interior"; and Fowler, *Shared Symbols, Contested Meanings*, 73, 90–91. A number of Gros Ventres families took advantage of the opportunity that existed under the 1895 agreement, which permitted individuals otherwise entitled to allotment to file claims to the amount of land allowed them under the act and establish themselves there.

29. [Fort Belknap Enrollment Commission] to Commissioner of Indian Affairs, 30 November 1921, file 54, box 16, Decimal Files, FRC, RG 75, NARA; and Chas H. Burke to John to Marshall et al., 24 May 1921, file 143, box 32, ibid.

30. [Fort Belknap Enrollment Commission] to Commissioner of Indian Affairs, 2 June 1921, File October 1920–December 1921, box 11, Letters Sent to Commissioner of Indian Affairs, FRC, RG 75, NARA.

31. *Rocky Mountain Husbandman*, 15 May 1879, quoted in research file "Judith Basin," box 1, Oscar O. Mueller Research Collection, Major Collection (MC) 93, MHS; and Foster, *We Know Who We Are*, 78–88.

32. LaPier, " 'Between Hay and Grass,' " 108–11; U.S. Department of Interior, Office of Federal Acknowledgment, *Proposed Finding, Little Shell Tribe*, 46–48. Some of the Azure children were enrolled in the mission school where Louis Riel taught in 1883 and 1884. See Riel, *Collected Writings of Louis Riel*, 378. Gabriel and Antoine Azure also gave Louis Riel power of attorney to attempt to secure scrip on their behalf when Riel traveled from Sun River to Manitoba in 1883 (Riel, *Collected Writings of Louis Riel*, 277–81).

33. Barry, *Fort Belknap Indian Reservation*, 58–60.

34. See, e.g., Indian Census Rolls, Fort Belknap, reels 126–27, Indian Census Rolls, 1885–1940, M595, RG 75, NARA; St. Paul's Mission, Montana, Reports on Indian School, 1890–1891, reel 13, Mission and Houses Collection, Jesuit Oregon Province Archives, Gonzaga University Archives; Quarterly School Reports, Fort Belknap Reservation, St. Paul's Mission School, Bureau Mission School Reports, reel 17, Bureau of Catholic Indian Missions, Marquette University Archives; and Fort Belknap Indians to Commissioner of Indian Affairs, ca. 7 March 1912, file "Lands, Allotment," box 12, Letters Received, FRC, RG 75, NARA.

35. Testimony of Antoine Azure, 1921, file 100334-1921-053, pt. 1 (2 of 3), box 7, CCF, RG 75, NARA.

36. See, e.g., testimonies of Joseph Azure, Julia Azure, Mellalia Gladeaux, and Cecelia Azure, ibid.

37. Testimony of Prophet, 1921, ibid.

38. Ibid.

39. Ibid.

40. Meyer, *White Earth Tragedy*, 118–22. Meyer notes that these meanings were not static but could evolve over time.

41. Testimony of Speak Thunder, 1921, file 100334-1921-053, pt. 1 (2 of 3), box 7, CCF, RG 75, NARA.

42. Rodnick, "Fort Belknap Assiniboine of Montana," 37–38.

43. "Summary of Findings by the Enrollment Commission," 30 November 1921, file 100334-1921-053, pt. 1 (2 of 3), box 7, CCF, RG 75, NARA.

44. Lame Bull et al. to William A. Jones, 25 July 1897, 31478-1897, Letters Received by the Office of Indian Affairs, LR 1881–1907, RG 75, NARA; and Luke C. Hayes to Commissioner of Indian Affairs, 21 August 1897, ibid.

45. John F. Healy to Commissioner of Indian Affairs, 9 October 1914, file 110428-1914-053, box 6, CCF, RG 75, NARA; Bobtail Bear et al., to A. B. Fall, Secretary of Interior, 9 December 1921, file 100334-1921-053, pt. 1 (1 of 3), ibid.; and Fowler, *Shared Symbols, Contested Meanings*, 201–206. Indeed, these complaints formed part of what Fowler terms a "here first" story. These accounts describe how each tribe came to settle on the Fort Belknap reservation and could be pressed into service to meet their varying political needs. In Gros Ventre accounts, they were native to the Upper Milk River valley area. Well-endowed with horses, food, and clothing, they had taken pity on a small group of Assiniboines and allowed them to share in their territory. They faulted Assiniboines for being ungrateful, disloyal guests who, by allowing greater and greater numbers of "Canadian" Assiniboines to join them on the reservation, undermined Gros Ventre primacy.

46. [Fort Belknap Enrollment Commission] to Commissioner of Indian Affairs, 2 June 1921, file October 1920–December 1921, box 11, Letters Sent to the Commissioner, FRC, RG 75, NARA; Chas. H. Burke to John T. Marshall, 21 June 1921, file 47096-1921-053, box 6, CCF, RG 75, NARA; and Summary and Findings, Enrollment Commission, 30 November 1921, file 100334-1921-053, pt. 1 (1 of 3), ibid. The commissioners had asked the Indian commissioner's advice about how to handle these applications. The commissioners stated that, although the Fort Belknap Assiniboines had allowed the Northern Assiniboines to remain, the tribe had not formally adopted these newcomers. Charles Burke said that, in the absence of such a formal adoption, they had no rights to the reservation.

47. See, e.g., testimonies of Iron Horn, Pity, and Strong Lodge Woman, file 100334-1921-053, pt. 1 (1 of 3), box 6, CCF, RG 75, NARA.

48. Assiniboine Indians of Fort Belknap to Commissioner of Indian Affairs, 18 July 1921, File 47096-1921-053, box 6, CCF, RG 75, NARA; Boy Chief et al. to Commissioner of Indian Affairs, 15 December 1921, file 100334-1921-053, pt. 1 (1 of 3), ibid.; August Moccasin to Secretary of the Interior, 27 March 1922, ibid.; and Fowler, *Shared Symbols, Contested Meanings*, 207, 212–15. Fowler notes how, in these accounts, the unwillingness of the Assiniboines to strike people from tribal rolls became evidence of their inclusiveness. According to one young woman, "We Assiniboines don't say things about breeds [métis]. Gros Ventres put others down—Assiniboines and breeds—we never did that" (p. 207).

49. August Moccasin to Secretary of the Interior, 16 September 1922, file 76486-1922-053, box 7, CCF, RG 75, NARA; and John T. Marshall to Commissioner of Indian Affairs, 29 September 1922, file 100334-1921-053, pt. 2, ibid.

50. Chas. Burke to John T. Marshall, 11 August 1922, file 100334-1921-053, pt. 2, box 7, CCF, RG 75, NARA.

51. John T. Marshall to Commissioner of Indian Affairs, 5 January 1922, file 100334-1921-053, pt. 1 (1 of 3), box 6, CCF, RG 75, NARA; [Mr. Shipe] to Unknown, 11 April 1922, ibid.; and Wessel, *History of Rocky Boy's Reservation*, pp. i–iv, 76–78.

52. "Proceedings of the Councils," pp. 16, 18–22, in U.S. Congress, Senate, "Letter from Secretary of Interior."

53. Barry, *Fort Belknap Indian Reservation*, 168.

54. [Fort Belknap Enrollment Commission] to Commissioner of Indian Affairs, 30 November 1921, file 54 "Census Matters," box 16, Decimal Files, FRC, RG 75, NARA; and J. T. Marshall to Commissioner of Indian Affairs, 29 September 1922, file 100334-1921-053, pt. 2, box 7, CCF, RG 75, NARA. The department overturned some of the enrollment commission's decisions regarding applicants who were of mixed Gros Ventre and white ancestry. Burke again pointed to the legal ruling in *Oakes et al. v. United States* to argue that those people who were born on the reservation and had been recognized as tribal members should continue to be enrolled. This policy meant reinstating a handful of individuals who had been left off the new lists. See Chas. H. Burke to Secretary of Interior, 26 March 1923, file 100334-1921-053, pt. 2, box 7, CCF, RG 75, NARA.

55. Antoine Gladue to Commissioner of Indian Affairs, 25 September 1922, file 16996-1921-053, box 6, CCF, RG 75, NARA.

56. See, e.g., S. K. Emerson to H. H. Miller, 9 September 1911, file Emerson, 1911, box 6, Letters Received, FRC, RG 75, NARA; H. H. Miller to S. K. Emerson, 12 September 1911, Letterbook 1911–12, Local Letters Sent, ibid.; and [Paul E.] Gradall to H. H. Miller, 24 March 1912, file Gradall, 1912, box 9, Letters Received, ibid.

57. Foster, *We Know Who We Are*, 199–200; and Verne Dusenberry, "Waiting for a Day that Never Comes," 134.

58. Peter Capture to Major Miller, 30 November 1913, file C, 1911–14, box 4, Letters Received, FRC, RG 75, NARA; [H. H. Miller] to W. D. Cochran, Letterbook 1914, box 2, Local Letters Sent, ibid.; and Wessel, *History of Rocky Boy's Reservation*, 53.

59. Foster, *We Know Who We Are*, 166.

60. Antoine Azure to Commissioner of Indian Affairs, 16 November 1921, file 16996-1921-053, box 6, CCF, RG 75, NARA.

61. [Fort Belknap Enrollment Commission] to Commissioner of Indian Affairs, 30 November 1921, file 54 "Census Matters," box 16, Decimal Files, FRC, RG 75, NARA.

62. For a discussion of North-West Mounted Police Colonel James Walsh's attempts to sort "British" Assiniboines from "American" Assiniboines in 1876–77 and determine who belonged on Canadian treaty pay lists, see Qu'Appelle

Agency, "Report Relative to Payment of Annuities," file 7088, vol. 3637, reel C-10112, RG 10, Library and Archives Canada (LAC); and Wood Mountain Agency, "Correspondence Regarding Payment of Annuities," file 8280, Volume 3649, reel C-10190, ibid.

63. Albers, "Changing Patterns of Ethnicity," 106–107.

64. Meyer, "American Indian Blood Quantum Requirements," 232–44. Cf. Valaskakis, *Indian Country*, 211–12, 223–25.

65. Scott, *Seeing Like a State*, 80–81.

66. Baud and Willem Van Schendel, "Toward a Comparative History of Borderlands," 217–19; and Harmon, *Indians in the Making*, 140–44. Cf. Schenck, "Border Identities," 241–46.

Works Cited

Archival Sources

Helena, MT
   Montana Historical Society (MHS).
      Kline, Ben. Reminiscence. Small Collection (SC) 942.
      O'Connell, Samuel. Papers, SC 597.
      Oscar O. Mueller Research Collection, Major Collection (MC) 93.
Milwaukee, WI
   Marquette University Archives.
      Bureau of Catholic Indian Missions. Bureau Mission School Reports, reel
         17. Quarterly School Reports, Fort Belknap Reservation, St. Paul's Mission School.
Ottawa, ON
   Library and Archives Canada (LAC).
      Qu'Appelle Agency. "Report Relative to the Payment of Annuities to the
         Indians of Treaty 4, submitted by J. M. Walsh." RG 10, reel C-10112, vol.
         3637, file 7088.
      Wood Mountain Agency. "Correspondence Regarding the Payment of
         Annuities to the Indians of Cypress Mountain." RG 10, reel C-10190, vol.
         3649, file 8280.
Spokane, WA
   Gonzaga University Archives.
      Jesuit Oregon Province Archives.
         Mission and Houses Collection, St. Paul's Mission, Montana.
         Reports on Indian School, 1890–1891, reel 13.
Denver, CO
   National Archives and Records Administration (NARA), Rocky Mountain
      Region (FRC).
      Bureau of Indian Affairs. Records of the Fort Belknap Indian Agency.
         Decimal Files. RG 75.

Letters Received. RG 75.
Letters Sent to the Commissioner. RG 75.
Local Letters Sent. RG 75.
Washington, DC
National Archives and Records Administration (NARA).
Bureau of Indian Affairs, Central Classified Files (CCF). RG 75.
Indian Census Rolls, 1885–1940. RG 75, M595.
Letters Received by the Office of Indian Affairs, LR 1881–1907. RG 75.
Records of the Office of the Adjutant General, microfilm (M) 666, reel 394, RG 94.

Published Sources

Albers, Patricia C. "Changing Patterns of Ethnicity in the Northeastern Plains." In *History, Power and Identity: Ethnogenesis in the Americas, 1492–1992*, edited by Jonathan D. Hill, 90–118. Iowa City: University of Iowa Press, 1996.

Barry, Edward E. *The Fort Belknap Indian Reservation: The First Hundred Years, 1855–1955.* Bozeman, MT: Big Sky Books, 1974.

Baud, Michiel, and Willem Van Schendel. "Toward a Comparative History of Borderlands." *Journal of World History* 8, no. 2 (1997): 211–42.

Brown, Jennifer S. H., and Theresa Schenck. "Métis, Mestizo, and Mixed Blood." In *A Companion to American Indian History*, edited by Philip Deloria and Neal Salisbury, 321–38. Malden, MA: Wiley-Blackwell, 2004.

Dusenberry, Verne. "Waiting for a Day That Never Comes: The Dispossessed Métis of Montana." In *New Peoples: Being and Becoming Métis in North America*, edited by Jacqueline Peterson and Jennifer S. H. Brown, 119–36. Winnipeg: University of Manitoba Press, 1985.

Ens, Gerhard J. "The Border, The Buffalo, and the Métis of Montana." In *The Borderlands of the American and Canadian Wests: Essays on the Regional History of the Forty-ninth Parallel*, edited by Sterling Evans, 139–54. Lincoln: University of Nebraska Press, 2006.

Foley, Michael F., comp. *An Historical Analysis of the Administration of the Fort Belknap Indian Reservation by the United States, 1855–1950s.* Report prepared for Indian Claims Commission, Docket Numbers 279-C and 250-A. 1975.

Foster, Martha Harroun. *We Know Who We Are: Métis Identity in a Montana Community.* Norman: University of Oklahoma Press, 2006.

Fowler, Loretta. *Shared Symbols, Contested Meanings: Gros Ventre Culture and History, 1778–1984.* Ithaca, NY: Cornell University Press, 1987.

Harmon, Alexandra. *Indians in the Making: Ethnic Relations and Indian Identities around Puget Sound.* Berkeley and Los Angeles: University of California Press, 1998.

———. "Tribal Enrollment Councils: Lessons on Law and Indian Identity." *Western Historical Quarterly* 32 (Summer 2001): 175–200.

Hogue, Michel. "Between Race and Nation: The Creation of a Métis Borderland on the Northern Plains." In *Bridging National Borders in North America: Transnational and Comparative Histories*, edited by Benjamin H. Johnson and Andrew R. Graybill, 59–87. Durham, NC: Duke University Press, 2010.

——. "Between Race and Nation: The Plains Métis and the Canada–United States Border." Ph.D. diss., University of Wisconsin–Madison, 2009.

——. "Disputing the Medicine Line: The Plains Crees and the Canadian–American Border, 1876–1885." *Montana the Magazine of Western History* 52, no. 4 (Winter 2002): 2–17.

Kelley, J. M. "Report, Fort Belknap Agency, 18 August 1894." In U.S. Office of Indian Affairs, *Report of the Commissioner of Indian Affairs to the Secretary of the Interior*. Washington, DC: Government Printing Office, 1907.

LaPier, Rosalyn R. " 'Between Hay and Grass': A Brief Examination of Two Métis Communities in Central Montana in the 1880s." In *Proceedings of the University of Great Falls International Conference on the Métis Peoples of Canada and the United States*, edited by William Furdell, 105–120. Great Falls, MT: University of Great Falls, 1997.

Malone, Michael P., Richard B. Roeder, and William L. Lang. *Montana: A History of Two Centuries*. Rev. ed. Seattle: University of Washington Press, 1991.

Meyer, Melissa L. "American Indian Blood Quantum Requirements: Blood Is Thicker Than Family." In *Over the Edge: Remapping the American West*, edited by Valerie J. Matsumoto and Blake Allmendinger, 231–52. Berkeley and Los Angeles: University of California Press, 1999.

——. *The White Earth Tragedy: Ethnicity and Dispossession at a Minnesota Anishinaabe Reservation, 1889–1920*. Lincoln: University of Nebraska Press, 1994.

Miller, David, Dennis J. Smith, Joseph R. McGeshick, James Shanley, and Caleb Shields. *The History of the Assiniboine and Sioux Tribes of the Fort Peck Indian Reservation, Montana, 1800–2000*. Poplar and Helena, MT: Fort Peck Tribal College and Montana Historical Society Press, 2008.

Morin, Gail, comp. *Métis Families: A Genealogical Compendium*. 5 vols. Pawtucket, RI: Quintin Publications, 2001.

——, comp. *Red River Settlement Censuses*. Pawtucket, RI: Quintin Publications, 1998.

Peers, Laura. *The Ojibwa of Western Canada, 1780–1870*. Winnipeg: University of Manitoba Press, 1994.

Prucha, Francis Paul. *The Great Father: The United States Government and the American Indians*. 2 vols. Lincoln: University of Nebraska Press, 1984.

Riel, Louis. *The Collected Writings of Louis Riel/Les Ecrits complets de Louis Riel*, edited by George F. G. Stanley. Vol. 2, *8 December/décembre 1875–4 June/juin 1884*, edited by Gilles Martel. Edmonton: University of Alberta Press, 1985.

Rodnick, David. "The Fort Belknap Assiniboine of Montana." Ph.D. diss., University of Pennsylvania, 1936.

Schenck, Theresa. "Border Identities: Métis, Halfbreed, and Mixed-Blood." In *Gathering Places: Aboriginal and Fur Trade Histories*, edited by Carolyn Po-druchny and Laura Peers, 233–48. Vancouver: University of British Columbia Press, 2010.

Scott, James C. *Seeing Like a State: How Certain Schemes to Improve the Human Con-dition Have Failed*. New Haven, CT: Yale University Press, 1998.

U.S. Bureau of the Census. *1850 Minnesota Territorial Census, Pembina District* (un-published manuscript census).

U.S. Congress. Senate. "Letter from the Secretary of the Interior, Transmitting an Agreement Made and Concluded October 9, 1895, with the Indians of the Fort Belknap Reservation." 54th Cong., 1st sess., 1896. S. Doc. 117, Serial 3350, 1–21.

U.S. Department of Interior, Office of Federal Acknowledgment. *Proposed Find-ing, Little Shell Tribe of Chippewa Indians of Montana*. Washington, DC, 2000.

Valaskakis, Gail Guthrie. *Indian Country: Essays on Contemporary Native Culture*. Waterloo, ON: Wilfrid Laurier University Press, 2005.

Wessel, Thomas R. *A History of Rocky Boy's Reservation*. 1973.

11

MÉTIS NETWORKS IN BRITISH COLUMBIA

Examples from the Central Interior

MIKE EVANS, JEAN BARMAN, *and* GABRIELLE
LEGAULT, *with* ERIN DOLMAGE *and* GEOFF APPLEBY

L ike much of Ontario, the areas of British Columbia west of the
Rockies sit on the fringes of the historic Métis Nation, and the nature of the connections between Métis families there and those of
the historic Métis Nation east of the mountains is not well understood.
In this chapter we examine the patterns of Métis[1] ethnogenesis in British
Columbia through two case studies from the central interior region—
specifically the network of families connected to Jean Baptiste Boucher,
a Métis who arrived in British Columbia from Rupert's Land as an employee in the fur economy at the beginning of the nineteenth century,
and a parallel network originating with Peter Skene Ogden, who came
as an officer a quarter of a century later. By tracing their descendents, we
show empirically the existence of an extensive network of linked families
with a geographical center west, not east, of the Rockies. We also explore
the character of the linkages between these British Columbian families
and the wider network of Métis in north-central North America. Finally, we reflect on the significance of these patterns—or, the authority
of the past—on the landscape of contemporary Métis politics and, more
particularly, on the inclusion of British Columbian Métis communities
within the scope of the historic Métis Nation.[2]

It's Complicated

The issues that swirl around the definition of contemporary Métis identity, be it a national identity or a personal one, are complex and difficult.[3] This difficulty is partly a reflection of the overlapping and often conflicting interests of the European and other indigenous communities with whom the Métis contend,[4] and partly a reflection of the subtle sociocultural differences between the historical trajectories of particular mixed-ancestry families and individuals.[5] As complicated as the terrain of Métis and colonial politics is today, it is matched by a history that is at least as difficult to describe. The conceptualization of Métis now, as in the past, requires sophisticated historiographical tools and equally subtle and sophisticated sociological and geographical ones.[6]

Arising at the intersections of indigenous and European contact, embedded as they were from their inception in intensely local and fundamentally global political economies, the Métis of north-central Canada manifest many elements and effects of globalization. Complex overlapping and sometimes multiple identities patterned and refracted economic and political processes, while the underlying course of life, love, and procreation formed a core of affinity and consanguinity that provided a bulwark for the expression of, first, family and, then, national interest. Events at Seven Oaks, the Red River, and Batoche made manifest the distinctive interests of the Métis and provided a history of great figures and cataclysmic events. This history, along with the enduring family ties and distinctive culture of the Métis, lies at the heart of the persistence of Métis communities in spite of attempts to render those communities invisible after the military defeats of 1885. But the marginalization of Métis after 1885 was not without effect; to a greater or lesser degree the networks of families and communities that have their national center in the heartlands of the historic Métis Nation were attenuated at the edges. They fragmented, to use Nicole St-Onge's term.[7] Today, as the Métis seek to reform and re-express a national presence, and to define a national homeland, the geographical and sociological margins of the Métis Nation homeland provide a basis for some sophisticated thinking about Métis nationhood and Métis identity.

Linkages between Families in British Columbia and the Wider Network of Métis in North-Central North America

At the outset let us be clear that we accept the position that being of mixed indigenous and European genetic heritage does not a Métis make.[8] A great many people who today identify as First Nations,[9] and many who identify and understand themselves to be unambiguously Euro-Canadians, have a complex ancestry arising from the interactions of indigenous and European peoples. Furthermore, we accept the notion that, like mixed-ancestry or interracial individuals, communities made up of linked interracial people and families may be aware of themselves as such and thus may comprise coherent interracial communities, though such communities may or may not be systematically related to the historic Métis Nation of the northern plains and parklands. The claim to nationhood made by Louis Riel and others in the 1800s, like the claim made by their descendants today,[10] turns on demonstrable sociological connection writ, literally, in political terms. Such claims neither negate nor exhaust the claims of other mixed-ancestry communities, but they are qualitatively different. The fundamental position of the Métis National Council, which is the principal national Canadian body representing and speaking for the historic Métis Nation, is that the Métis Nation is a distinct if geographically expansive entity consisting of related individuals and communities, and not simply interracial people related by virtue of a particular mixed genetic past. Thus, to define and describe Métis communities in British Columbia necessarily engages questions of who the members of the communities are and how those communities are related to others within the historic Métis Nation.[11] The answers to these questions speak directly, indeed tautologically, to the geography of the historic Métis Nation homeland.

Though identifying and defining Métis communities in British Columbia, especially communities located west of the Rockies, has its challenges, these challenges are not unique to British Columbia. Although one of the commonly accepted markers of Métis ethnogenesis is the development of endogamous marriage patterns,[12] even in the core areas of the Métis homeland marriages between Métis and non-Métis continued to take place, and marriages between Europeans and indigenous persons continued to give rise to interracial children. It is logical that processes of *métissage*, racial intermixing, unfolded in various locales more or less separate from the main network of families and communities that we now know as the historic Métis Nation, but these locales are not restricted to the geographical edges of the historic Métis Nation homeland. Indeed, even interracial/mixed-ancestry families in close proximity to the center of the historic Métis Nation homeland at the Red River in Manitoba might, in logical terms at least, be quite separate from the historic Métis Nation. Being of mixed ancestry is a necessary but not sufficient condition for being of the historic Métis Nation in any geographical location, including Manitoba. One might go so far as to argue that the dispersed and interspersed nature of the nodes and networks that make up the historic Métis Nation meant and means there are a great many sociological edges within the homeland itself.

The notion of networks and nodes also means that we can be systematic about how we describe the ways in which the geographical edges of the historic Métis Nation homeland are related. Rather than drawing (or, worse, assuming) boundaries, we can draw and trace connections between locales/communities/families at the edges—and in the core for that matter. This process is best exemplified rather than discussed in the abstract, in part because there is a dearth of language for describing a sociological and political entity such as the Métis Nation. Though at times and in places the Métis dominated particular regions, the areas in which they could claim exclusive control of territory in terms that would make sense to European nationalists are limited, for in many situations the Métis lived side by side with their indigenous cousins and with white trading partners and workmates. This historical circumstance does not negate the claims of Métis nationalists, but it does require clear thinking about the nature of Métis territoriality—and indeed territoriality of any nation, First Nations and the Canadian State included.

Two Case Studies from the Central Interior Region

Contemporary Métis identity is complex, and this complexity has historical roots. Again, the issue is most decidedly not whether people of mixed genetic heritage were present in any given area, though this is a precondition of the phenomenon that we seek to understand. For the purposes of this chapter, we focus on three basic elements of identity: (a) the degree to which sociological patterns of interaction present empirically and lead to the conclusion that a group of people share in a common identity,

(b) the degree to which people identify themselves and others as members of a group, and (c) the degree to which people outside the group identify and treat members of that group as a separate/distinct entity. These three elements reflect identity even as they inform and reinforce that identity; we are thus looking at both the results and sources of group formation.

For marginalized and mostly nonliterate communities like many of those of the historic Métis Nation, the forms of identity self-expression that are most likely to remain within the historical record are both limited and textured by the deposition process. We have accounts of momentous and fraught events, and we have the accounts of others that reflect with more or less accuracy the ways Métis thought of themselves.[13] This circumstance is not to suggest that the lives of British Columbia Métis and interracial persons were without drama or tension. Indeed, as we have argued elsewhere,[14] the Métis of British Columbia emerged as such in the context of systematic legal separation from their indigenous cousins and other forms of racism that are reflected in social, geographic, and occupational clustering.

We now turn to the nature of the Métis/interracial community at and around Fort St James and the broader area of the British Columbian central interior known historically as New Caledonia. Both the Hudson's Bay Company (HBC) and its principal competitor for control of the fur economy, the North West Company (NWC), crossed the Rockies in search of new sources of pelts at the beginning of the nineteenth century. They did so, and continued to trap and trade there, by employing a combination of men hired directly from Quebec, the Orkney Islands, and elsewhere alongside those already Métis by virtue of being the offspring of such born in the historic Métis Nation. Once men crossed the mountains, they mostly continued to be employed in New Caledonia or further south in the present-day states of Washington and Oregon, an area known historically as Oregon. Unlike the officers in charge, employees did not re-cross the mountains except on annual brigades or at the end of their employment. This policy was critical to the formation and persistence of intact families and communities.

The networks of Métis that developed in New Caledonia are evident in the surviving historical records. The quotidian of life, love, and procreation reflect overlapping networks of interrelated interracial families that stretch from the heartland of British Columbia, and also further south through Washington and Oregon, to the center of the historic Métis Nation.

Two such networks form the core of this chapter. Both originate in the fur economy but at opposite ends of the employment spectrum. The progenitor of the first network, Jean Baptiste Boucher, was an ordinary worker, whereas his counterpart, Peter Skene Ogden, was the man in charge.[15] The consequence is that, not unexpectedly, we know far less about the Bouchers through time than we do about the Ogdens.

The Bouchers

In 1805 Jean Baptiste Boucher, a young Métis born into the fur economy in Rupert's Land, journeyed over the Rockies with NWC partner Simon Fraser, whose mandate was to set up trading posts west of the mountains.[16] When Fraser returned east, Boucher stayed behind to work at the newly established post of Fort St James, located west of present-day Prince George. Upon the HBC taking charge from the NWC in 1821, Boucher continued in its employ to his death in 1849. Boucher was rooted in the area by occupation and by family, partnering with the daughter of an officer in the New Caledonia fur economy and of a local Carrier woman. Boucher's union with Nancy McDougall exemplifies the indigenization of the Métis in central British Columbia. Though one might argue that she was simply an interracial Carrier, her marriage to Boucher linked her, and her children, to the historic Métis Nation, while at the same time she linked Boucher and his children to a First Nation that was indigenous to British Columbia.

This dual linkage was realized again in the second generation of Bouchers, whose lives were characterized by residence west of the Rockies with recurring marital links to Métis east of the mountains, and by occupational clustering around the HBC (see table 11.1).[17] Two of the three eldest sons headed south to trading posts in Oregon, with James soon returning home. The two eldest daughters, Jane and Sophie, wed HBC men— one Métis, the other white—whose careers also took them to Oregon. Their younger sisters, Ellen, Elizabeth, and Amelia, also married HBC employees, two of them Métis, the third white but born at Red River. The returned eldest son James, along with his brothers Joseph, Jean Baptiste, Jean Marie, William, and Charles and their Métis brothers-in-law Charles Favel and Charles Desmarais, sustained the fur economy in central

TABLE 11.1. Known Children of Jean Baptiste Boucher and Nancy McDougall Reaching Adulthood

Name	Years	Location	Men's occupation	Marriage and no. of known children
James	1818–1910	Oregon	HBC	1 Rosalie Plouf (Oregon interracial)
		BC interior	HBC	2 Maria Tartinan (Carrier)–10
		BC interior	HBC	3 Nancy Ninza Murdoch (Carrier)
George	1819–	BC interior	Unknown	Cecile Aronhiowan (Iroquois/Nass)–4
Jane	1821–	Oregon	HBC	Wm McBean (Métis)–11
Sophie	1825–1915	Oregon	HBC	Edward Crete (White)–14
Jean Baptiste	1826–1852	Oregon	HBC	Isabelle Mainville (Oregon interracial)
Jean Marie	1830–	BC interior	HBC	1 Caroline Tatatz (Carrier)
		BC interior	HBC	2 Sophie Natai (Carrier)
		BC interior	HBC	3 Julie Hinnatchu (Carrier)
Ellen/Nellie	1831–1901+	BC interior	HBC	1 Charles Favel (Métis)–2
		Barkerville	Laborer	2 Ithiel/Edouard Nason (White)–5
Joseph	1833–1885	BC interior	HBC	Marguerite Joyal-Lapratte (BC interracial)–2
William	1833–1924	BC interior	HBC	Lizette Allard (BC interracial)–18
Elizabeth	1824–1874	BC	HBC	Peter Kirton (Red River White)–5
Charles	1845–1901+	BC interior	HBC	1 Agathe Unknown (Carrier)–2
		BC interior	HBC	2 Marguerite Touinatitnan (Carrier)–3
		BC interior	HBC	3 Unknown Carrier woman–1
Amelia	1850–	BC interior	HBC	Charles Desmarais (Métis)–9

Note: Information is drawn from surviving historical records, including vital statistics and the census. HBC = Hudson's Bay Company; BC = British Columbia.

337

British Columbia, or New Caledonia, through much of the nineteenth century.

Geographic and occupational networks facilitated marital choices. Second-generation Bouchers partnered with others of similar backgrounds and understandings where they were most likely to find social acceptance. Sons married a combination of indigenous or First Nations, Métis, and local interracial women; daughters primarily wed Métis men. These unions were reinforced by their being witnessed by relatives and others in the locality, many also Métis/interracial, with whom the Bouchers were linked by geography, occupation, or friendship (see table 11.4).

Linkages remained strong in the third generation (see tables 11.2 and 11.3). We have tracked the children of the three mainstays of the second generation—James, who had children with a Carrier woman; Ellen, who wed first a Red River Métis and then a white laborer born in Maine; and William, who married a British-Columbia-born interracial woman whose father had arrived in New Caledonia from Quebec in the employ of the HBC (table 11.1). They all made their lives in the New Caledonia homeland of their parents and grandparents, where most grandsons and grandsons-in-law worked in the fur economy either for the HBC or as trappers on their own.

Marital decisions of the third generation echoed those of parents and grandparents. The ten Boucher granddaughters we have tracked wed between them three and possibly four Red River Métis, five British-Columbia-born Métis (by virtue of having fathers connected to the historic Métis Nation), and five and possibly six white men (table 11.3). At this point in time, British Columbia still contained almost no Métis women among whom to find partners. The consequence was that the seven Boucher grandsons we have tracked opted between them for two local First Nations women, two British-Columbia-born Métis, one British-Columbia-born interracial woman, three white women, and two of unknown background. In other words, whereas Boucher daughters and granddaughters linked time and again with both the historic Métis Nation and British-Columbia-born Métis, their brothers were unable to do so to the same extent due to a lack of potential Métis partners (table 11.3). Their preferences were at the same time in good part similarly interracial.

What we see with the Boucher family is an ongoing process of ethnogenesis with strong local elements and significant white and First Nations involvement but located sociologically between the two and

TABLE 11.2. Known Children of Three of the Second-Generation Bouchers Reaching Adulthood

Name	Years	Location	Men's occupation	Marriage and no. of known children
James				
Maria	1849–	BC interior	HBC	James Bird (Métis)–11
Nancy	1850–			May have died young
Ellen	1852–	BC interior	HBC	Charles Ogden (BC Métis)–1
Sophie	1857–	BC interior	HBC	Pierre Roi (BC Métis)–8
Philomena	1858–	BC interior	HBC	1 Thomas Hamilton (White)
		BC interior	HBC	2 John Flett (Métis)
Jenny	1861–	BC interior	HBC	1 François Roi (BC Métis)
		BC interior	HBC	2 John MacDonald (White)
		BC interior	Blacksmith	3 Erich Wassener (White)
Margaret	1863–1966	BC interior	HBC	1 Antoine Flemmant (Métis)–8
		BC interior	Trapper	2 William Seymour (BC Métis)–6
James, Jr.	1865–	BC interior	Unknown	May have died young
Angela	1869–	BC interior	HBC	Samuel Sinclair (Métis?)
William	1871–1873	BC interior	HBC	Died young
Ellen				
Wm Favell	1853–1936	BC interior	Trapper	1 Marie Deschamps (BC interracial)–12
				2 Julia Roskoski (White)–1
				3 Julianne Perkowsni (White)
Duncan Favell	1856–	BC interior	Unknown	Milly (unknown)–2

339

TABLE 11.2. Known Children of Three of the Second-Generation Bouchers Reaching Adulthood (*continued*)

Name	Years	Location	Men's occupation	Marriage and no. of known children
Ithiel Nason	1864–	BC interior	Laborer	Amelia Boucher (BC Métis [cousin])
Frederick Nason	1867–	BC interior	Stage driver	Annie Willebrant (White)
Annie Nason	1870–	BC interior	Rancher	Thomas Mortimer (White)
Amelia Nason	1872–1922	BC interior	Unknown	Unknown–1
William				
Elizabeth	1866–	BC interior	Unknown	May have died young
Edward	1868–	BC interior	Laborer	Alice Moffitt (BC interracial)–4
Casimir	1869–	BC interior	Laborer	Agathe (Carrier)–2
William	1870–1914	BC interior	Laborer	Unknown
James	1872–ca. 1906	BC interior	Unknown	May have died young
Charles	1873–1918	BC interior	Laborer	1 Melany Pretty (unknown) 2 Theresa Ahool Hoola (Carrier)–2
Louisa	1878–1922	BC interior	Laborer	Adolphe Yargeau (White)–4
Amelia	1880–	BC interior	Laborer	Ithiel Nason (BC interracial [cousin])
Sophia	1883–	BC interior	Unknown	May have died young
Rosa	1885–	BC interior	Unknown	May have died young
Joseph	1888–1966	BC interior	Laborer	Unknown

Note: Information is drawn from surviving historical records, including vital statistics and the census. HBC = Hudson's Bay Company; BC = British Columbia.

TABLE 11.3. Known Partners of All Second- and Third-Generation Bouchers

Name	Spouse	Location	Men's occupation	Birthplace
Second-Generation Male Partners				
Wm McBean	Jane Boucher	Oregon	HBC	Red River (Métis)
Charles Favel	Ellen Boucher	BC interior	HBC	Red River (Métis)
Charles Desmarais	Amelia Boucher	BC interior	HBC	Red River (Métis)
Peter Kirton	Elizabeth Boucher	BC interior	HBC	Red River (White)
Ithiel Nason	Ellen Boucher	BC interior	HBC	Maine
Edward Crete	Sophie Boucher	BC interior	HBC	Quebec
Second-Generation Female Partners				
Maria Tartinan	James Boucher	BC interior	HBC	British Columbia (Carrier)
Nancy Ninza Murdoch	James Boucher	BC interior	HBC	British Columbia (Carrier)
Caroline Tatatz	Jean Marie Boucher	BC interior	HBC	British Columbia (Carrier)
Sophie Natai	Jean Marie Boucher	BC interior	HBC	British Columbia (Carrier)
Julia Hinnatchu	Jean Marie Boucher	BC interior	HBC	British Columbia (Carrier)
Agathe	Charles Boucher	BC interior	HBC	British Columbia (Carrier)
Marguerite Touinatitnan	Charles Boucher	BC interior	HBC	British Columbia (Carrier)
Cecile Aronhiowan	George Boucher	BC interior	Unknown	British Columbia (Iroquois/Nass)
Margeurite Joyal-Lapratte	Joseph Boucher	BC interior	HBC	British Columbia
Lizette Allard	William Boucher	BC interior	HBC	British Columbia (interracial)
Isabelle Mainville	Jean Baptiste Boucher	Oregon	HBC	Oregon (interracial)
Rosalie Plouffe	James Boucher	Oregon	HBC	Oregon (White)

(continued)

Name	Spouse	Location	Men's occupation	Birthplace
		Third-Generation Male Partners		
James Bird	Maria (via James)	BC interior	HBC	Red River (Métis)
John Flett	Philomena (via James)	BC interior	HBC	Red River (Métis)
Antoine Flemmant	Margaret (via James)	BC interior	HBC	Red River (Métis)
Samuel Sinclair	Angela (via James)	BC interior	HBC	Red River (Métis?)
Pierre Roi	Sophie (via James)	BC interior	HBC	British Columbia (Métis)
François Roi	Jenny (via James)	BC interior	HBC	British Columbia (Métis)
William Seymour	Margaret (via James)	BC interior	Trapper	British Columbia (Métis)
Charles Ogden	Ellen (via James)	BC interior	HBC	British Columbia (Métis)
Ithiel Nason (cousin)	Amelia (via William)	BC interior	Laborer	British Columbia (Métis)
John MacDonald	Jenny (via James)	BC interior	HBC officer	Scotland
Thomas Hamilton	Philomena (via James)	BC interior	HBC officer	Scotland
Erich Wassener	Jenny (via James)	BC interior	Blacksmith	Germany
Thomas Mortimer	Annie (via Ellen)	BC interior	Rancher	Ontario
Adolphe Yargeau	Louisa (via William)	BC interior	Laborer	Manitoba (White)
		Third-Generation Female Partners		
Agathe	Casimir (via William)	BC interior	Laborer	British Columbia (Carrier)
Theresa Ahool Hoole	Charles (via William)	BC interior	Laborer	British Columbia (Carrier)
Amelia Boucher (cousin)	Ithiel Nason (via Ellen)	BC interior	Laborer	British Columbia (Métis)
Marie Deschamps	William Favell (via Ellen)	BC interior	Trapper	British Columbia (Métis)
Alice Moffitt	Edward (via William)	BC interior	Laborer	British Columbia (interracial)
Julia Roskoski	William Favell (via Ellen)	Poland	Trapper	Poland
Juliana Perkowski	William Favel (via Ellen)	BC interior	Trapper	Poland?
Annie Willebrant	Frederick Nason (via Ellen)	BC interior	Stagedriver	White
Melany Pretty	Charles (via William)	BC interior	Laborer	Unknown
Milly (surname unknown)	Duncan Favell (via Ellen)	BC interior	Unknown	Unknown

Note: Information is drawn from surviving historical records, including vital statistics and the census. HBC = Hudson's Bay Company; BC = British

TABLE 11.4. Recorded Marriages among the Boucher Clan through the First World War, with Attention to Witnesses

Year	Generation	Male spouse	Female spouse	Witnesses
1844	2nd	William McBean	Jane Boucher	Forbes Barclay Esq. (HBC officer)
				Joseph Bourgeau (HBC)
1845	2nd	James Boucher	Rosalie Plouf	Fabien Malouin (his HBC friend)
				John Young (his friend)
				Angelique Dubois (her friend)
1855	2nd	George Boucher	Cecile Aronhiowan	Aime Leclaire (HBC)
				Ignace Aronhiowan (her father)
1864	2nd	William Boucher	Lizette Allard	Not given
1870	2nd	Jean Marie Boucher	Julie Hinnatchu	Not given
1872	2nd	Charles Boucher	Agathe	William Boucher (his brother)
				Lizette Boucher (his sister-in-law)
1874	2nd	Jean Marie Boucher	Sophie Ratai	Joseph Costely (unknown)
				Sophie Boucher (his niece)
1875	2nd	Thomas Hamilton	Philomena Boucher	Michel Deschamps (HBC White)
				William Favell (HBC Métis)
1875	2nd	Pierre Roy [Roi]	Sophie Boucher	Simon Rashiak (unknown)
				Angelique (her sister, Angela?)
1876	3rd	Antoine LaFrenier (La Flemmant)	Marguerite Boucher	Not given
1879	2nd	Joseph Boucher	Marguerite Joyal-Laptratte	Georges Joyal-Lapratte (her father)
				Pierre Sphiou (unknown)
1882	3rd	François Roi	Jenny Boucher	Pierre Roi (his father)

(continued)

TABLE 11.4. Recorded Marriages among the Boucher Clan through the First World War, with Attention to Witnesses (*continued*)

Year	Generation	Male spouse	Female spouse	Witnesses
1886	2nd	John William Flett	Philomena Boucher	J. M. S. Alexander (local HBC officer)
				A. C. Murray (local HBC officer)
1889	3rd	Edward Boucher	Alice Moffitt	Johnny Moffitt (her brother)
				Mary Moffitt (her sister)
1890	3rd	John MacDonald	Jane Boucher	Walter Traill (former HBC officer)
				Mary Murray (HBC officer's wife)
1890	3rd	Samuel Sinclair	Angela Boucher	Donald Todd (local HBC)
				McDonald (local HBC)
1894	3rd	Casimir Boucher	Agathe	J. Baptiste (unknown)
1896	3rd	Adolphe Yargeau	Louise Boucher	Mrs. A Kelly (local woman)
				Rev. A. G. Hutton (priest)
1899	3rd	Charles Boucher	Melany Pretty	Corinne Lebrun (HBC wife)
				Charley Lebrun (HBC Métis)
1900	3rd	Thomas Mortimer	Annie Nason	Ithiel Nason (her cousin-in-law)
				Amelia Nason (her cousin)
1904	3rd / 3rd	Ithiel Nason	Amelia Boucher (cousin)	Sophia Chapman (unknown)
				Joseph Boucher (her brother)
1911	4th	Robert Evans	Josephine Boucher	John MacDonell (local man)
				Joe Davies (local man)
1918	3rd	Erich Wassener	Jenny Boucher	Percy Pinker (unknown)
				W. Seymour (her brother-in-law)

Note: Information is drawn from surviving historical records, including vital statistics and the census. HBC = Hudson's Bay Company.

centered within an identifiably Métis and interracial context. Indeed, in the second and even more so the third generation, the Bouchers formed a node within the historic Métis Nation homeland by virtue of both their own connections and those forged with men from the historic Métis Nation. Seven or eight of the Boucher sons-in-laws and grandsons-in-law who we have tracked were Métis who had come west with the fur economy, and another five were the sons of such (table 11.3). None of the first-generation Métis appear to have had siblings or other relatives in British Columbia. Leaving home between their mid-teens and mid-twenties, they very likely cleaved to their in-laws more than they would have if at Red River or elsewhere and by doing so consolidated a little Métis homeland in the British Columbia central interior. As the nineteenth century drew to a close, and the effective European settlement of the interior progressed, the Bouchers and their networks were gradually marginalized occupationally, but nonetheless the imprint of a Métis community connected to both British Columbia First Nations and the historic Métis Nation remained.

The Ogdens

Whereas the Bouchers were in the mainstream of employees in the fur economy, the Ogdens were part of that small literate minority at its pinnacle, and for that reason we can observe the family much more closely over time.[18] Born into a leading anglophone Quebec City family in 1790, Peter Skene Ogden arrived in New Caledonia three decades after Jean Baptiste Boucher had established himself there. Entering the fur economy as a clerk in 1810 and rising in the ranks, Ogden was given charge of New Caledonia in 1835, by which time his eldest son Peter was already on the path that would see him occupy the same position a quarter of a century later.

Peter Skene Ogden had children by a Métis and two indigenous women. Peter was born in 1817 to an unnamed Cree woman when his father was at Île-à-la-Crosse in present-day Saskatchewan, followed by Cecelia to Marie Comptois (table 11.5). His second son, Charles, was born either to the same indigenous woman or to Julia Rivet, a high-status Flathead with whom Peter would have a second family.[19] Ogden lavished every care on his eldest son, sending him to Red River for his schooling. Young Peter, in turn, looked to his stepmother for the ideal qualities in a wife,

TABLE 11.5. Children of Peter Skene Ogden Reaching Adulthood

Name	Years	Location	Men's occupation	Marriage and no. of known children
By an unknown Cree woman				
Peter	1817–1870	BC interior	HBC officer	Phrisine Brabant (Fort Edmonton Métis)–11
By Marie Comptois (ca. 1795–1875)				
Cecelia	1882–1880?	Red River/Saskatchewan	HBC officer	Hugh Fraser (Scotland)–3
Unclear whether mother was the unknown Cree woman or Julia Rivet				
Charles	1819–1890	BC interior	HBC	Did not marry
By Julia Rivet (ca. 1794–1886)				
Michel	1824–	Oregon/Montana	HBC	1 Angelina (all or part indigenous) 2 Julia (unknown)–several
Sarah Julia	1826–1892	BC interior	HBC officer	Archibald McKinlay (Scotland)–6
Euretta Mary	1836–1861	Oregon	n/a	"Of weak mind and body"
Isaac	1839–1866	Oregon	HBC	Annie Manson (Oregon Interracial)–3

Note: Information is drawn from surviving historical records, including vital statistics and the census. HBC = Hudson's Bay Company; BC = British Columbia.

selecting Phrisine Brabant, born at Fort Edmonton of French Canadian and Snake descent. Married in 1844, they had at least ten children, who were by descent doubly Métis and for good measure spoke no English at home. The first two generations of Ogdens produced, as well as Peter, seven marriageable sons and eight marriageable daughters (tables 11.5 and 11.6).

A dearth of white women made the Ogden daughters extremely valuable to clerks and junior officers seeking advancement in the HBC fur economy (table 11.7). A consequence was large differences in age at marriage, not unlike those of some Boucher daughters and granddaughters, perhaps for the same reason. At age eighteen or nineteen, Peter Skene Ogden's eldest daughter Cecilia married a Scot two decades her senior who her father likely got to know when both were stationed at Île-à-la-Crosse. His other marriageable daughter, Sarah Julia, was only fourteen when in 1840 she wed a Scots Highlander fifteen years her senior, Archibald McKinlay, then a clerk in New Caledonia under her father.

Turning to the third generation, Peter Ogden acted similarly toward his daughters (table 11.6). A family story has him persuading recently arrived Orkney Islander Gavin Hamilton to serve under him in New Caledonia, eying him as much as a future son-in-law as a rising star in the fur economy, which he also was, being given charge of New Caledonia on Ogden's death in 1870. Peter Ogden's eldest daughter Margaret Julia was in her mid-teens when she wed Hamilton, at least a decade her senior. Peter Ogden's second daughter, Adelaide, was just fourteen when she married thirty-two-year-old clerk William Manson, a widower whose Scots father had succeeded her grandfather as head of Fort St James and whose mother was interracial. Sarah Julianna was seventeen when she wed James M. L. Alexander, a thirty-seven-year-old Scot then serving under her father at Fort St James. Rachel wed Robert Hall, an Englishman working for her brother-in-law Gavin Hamilton and perhaps selected by him for her on her father's death. In a pattern that would come to mark the Ogden clan, the two youngest daughters married within the family, Mary Elizabeth to her cousin Archibald McKinlay and Christine to her brother-in-law Gavin Hamilton's younger brother Thomas, a divorcé a decade her senior.

Indicative of the increasingly closed community that was the fur economy, Thomas Hamilton was one of several men in the Ogden clan who fraternized with Boucher women. He had been a clerk under his brother at Fort St James at the time of his marriage in 1875 to James Boucher's

TABLE 11.6. Known Children of Two of the Second-Generation Ogdens Reaching Adulthood

Name	Years	Location	Men's occupation	Marriage and no. of known children
Peter Ogden				
Peter Skene	1844–1870	BC interior	HBC officer	Died young
Charles Griffin	1844–1904	BC interior	HBC	Apparently did not marry Ellen Boucher (BC Métis)–1
Margaret Julia	1845–1918	BC interior	HBC officer	1 Gavin Hamilton (Scotland)–16 2 Ewan Duncan McKinlay (BC interracial [cousin])–0
Adelaide Victoria	1849–1879	BC interior	Farmer	William Manson (Oregon interracial)–6
Rachel Sarah	1852–	BC interior	HBC officer	Robert Hanley Hall (England)–2
Sarah Julianna	1854–1887	BC interior	HBC officer	James M. L. Alexander (Scotland)–10
Christine	1857–1945	BC interior	HBC officer	Thomas M. Hamilton (Scotland)–2
Mary Elizabeth	1858–1936	BC interior	Farmer	Archibald Isaac McKinlay (BC interracial [cousin])–0
Isaac	1861–1927	BC interior	Storekeeper	Rose Eagle (BC interracial)–3
Henry	1864–1948	BC interior	Farmer, hotelier	Apparently did not marry
Sarah Julia Ogden McKinlay				
James	1846–1889	BC interior	Farmer	Apparently did not marry
Sarah Ellen	1851–1898	BC interior	Hotelier	Adam Bell Ferguson (Ireland)–7
Ogden Allen	1852–1908	BC interior	Farmer	Apparently did not marry
Catherine Ann	1856–1894	BC interior	Farmer	Thomas McDougall (Ontario)–6
Archibald Isaac	1858–	BC interior	Farmer	Mary Elizabeth Ogden (BC Métis [cousin])–0
Ewan Duncan	1864–1939	BC interior	Farmer	Margaret Julia Ogden (BC Métis [cousin])–0

Note: Information is drawn from surviving historical records, including vital statistics and the census. HBC = Hudson's Bay Company; BC = British Columbia.

TABLE 11.7. Known Partners of Second- and Third-Generation Ogdens

Name	Spouse	Location	Men's occupation	Birthplace
Second-Generation Male Partners				
Hugh Fraser	Cecelia Ogden	Red River/Montana	HBC officer	Scotland
Archibald McKinlay	Sarah Julia Ogden	BC interior	HBC officer/trader	Scotland
Second-Generation Female Partners				
Phrisine Brabant	Peter Ogden, Jr.	BC interior	HBC officer	Fort Edmonton
Annie Manson	Isaac Ogden	Oregon	HBC	Oregon
Third-Generation Male Partners				
Gavin Hamilton	Margaret Julia Ogden	BC interior	HBC officer/farmer	Scotland
Ewan Duncan McKinlay (cousin)	Margaret Julia Ogden	BC interior	Farmer	British Columbia
William Manson	Adelaide Victoria Ogden	BC interior	HBC	Oregon
Robert Hanley Hall	Rachel Sarah Ogden	BC interior	HBC officer	England
James M. L. Alexander	Sarah Julianna Ogden	BC interior	HBC officer	Scotland
Thomas McCauley Hamilton	1 Philomena Boucher	BC interior	HBC officer	Scotland
	2 Christine Ogden	BC interior	Trader	Scotland
Archibald Isaac McKinlay (cousin)	Mary Elizabeth Ogden	BC interior	Farmer	British Columbia
Thomas McDougall	Catherine Ann McKinlay	BC interior	Laborer	Ontario
Adam Bell Ferguson	Sarah Ellen McKinlay	BC interior	Hotelier	Ireland
Third-Generation Female Partners				
Ellen Boucher	Charles Griffin Ogden	BC interior	HBC	British Columbia
Rose Eagle	Isaac Ogden	BC interior	HBC	British Columbia
Mary Elizabeth Ogden (cousin)	Archibald Isaac McKinlay	BC interior	Unknown	British Columbia
Margaret Julia Ogden (cousin)	Ewan Duncan McKinlay	BC interior	Unknown	British Columbia

Note: Information is drawn from surviving historical records, including vital statistics and the census. HBC = Hudson's Bay Company; BC = British Columbia.

daughter, sixteen-year-old Philomena (table 11.2). Divorcing her six years later on the grounds of adultery, he did so just two weeks before wedding Christine Ogden, whereas Philomena waited five years to marry a second time.

The Ogdens and Bouchers also brushed up against each other in other ways. Peter Skene Ogden and Jean Baptiste Boucher contributed equal amounts—£2 each—to a request for funds in 1841 to establish a Catholic mission in New Caledonia. Suggestive of the respect Ogden must have had for the Boucher patriarch, he referred to him in his journal by his full name and nickname as "J. Bte. Boucher ('Waccan')," whereas most other men merited only a single name or a nickname. Three decades later, in the mid-1870s, Peter Ogden's son-in-law Gavin Hamilton started a public school at Fort St James. All except three of the twenty-one pupils were Ogdens or Bouchers.

Ogden sons had fewer prospects than did their sisters. The HBC policy of limiting interracial sons to the local ranks of the fur economy was exceedingly difficult to disrupt. Although Peter Ogden secured a clerkship for his eldest son, Peter Skene (who died of illness soon thereafter), his brothers Charles, Michael, and Isaac and younger sons Charles, Isaac, and Henry followed modest paths similar to the Bouchers (tables 11.5 and 11.6). In a wife, the best that sons could hope for was a respectable interracial woman; thus, two sons, like their sisters, married within the family. A third initiated another pattern that would mark the Ogden clan in the next generations, which was to search out nearby interracial offspring of men attracted to British Columbia by the gold rush beginning in 1858. Others did not marry at all, although one had a child with James Boucher's daughter Ellen.

By this time the Ogden clan was transitioning from the node that was the New Caledonia fur economy to a successor node they created for themselves on the southern edge of New Caledonia around Lac la Hache, or 115 Mile, on the road to the Cariboo gold fields. The resulting cluster was a classic British Columbian mixture of *métissage*, or racial intermixing, and interraciality.

Peter Skene Ogden's death in 1854 and then those of his eldest son and grandson in 1870 might have fractured the Ogden family had it not been for their in-laws. Peter Skene Ogden's son-in-law Archibald McKinlay had, on retiring from the HBC in 1850, taken up land in Oregon. A decade later, just after the new British colony of British Columbia was created in response to the gold rush, his crops were flooded out. Recalling an area of British Columbia that, when stationed in New Caledonia from 1835 to 1841, reminded him of the Perthshire hills of his native Scotland, McKinlay headed off to find it, and in November 1862 he claimed 160 acres at 115 Mile. The next year his wife, Sarah, their five children, and Sarah's widowed mother, Julia Rivet—who would live with Archibald and Sarah until her death in 1886—followed him north.

The family's retreat from the now bustling American state of Oregon went beyond economics to the very core of Ogden self-worth. Their class status was their undoing. Peter Skene Ogden's estranged older brother, a leading government official on the Isle of Man, had on Peter's death in 1854 contested the will leaving his sizable estate to his children and to "the mother, commonly called Julia." Upset that Peter had never legally married Julia Rivet—supposedly because of a promise to his mother when young never to wed an indigenous woman—his brother sought to rectify what he considered to be a stain on the family honor. Informing HBC officials that under English common law "bastards" had no rights and the estate belonged to him and his siblings, he initiated a legal case in Oregon intended to humiliate the family by virtue of their being forced to testify.[20] It was on the dispute finally being resolved by compromise that the Ogdens turned inward on themselves on the southern edge of New Caledonia.

The Ogden clan consolidated itself around Lac la Hache extending between 100 Mile and 150 Mile (tables 11.7 and 11.8). Torn by the simultaneous deaths of their father and oldest brother in 1870, seven of Peter Ogden's nine living children moved there, along with his widow and two of his three living siblings. In 1868 former HBC employee William Manson, who a few years earlier had wed Peter's daughter Adelaide, took up 160 acres near 100 Mile. A decade later Gavin Hamilton, who married Adelaide's sister Margaret Julia, retired as chief factor at New Caledonia and, taking advantage of his HBC pension, acquired land at 150 Mile. His medical skills, ranging from remedies to bone setting, made him a particularly useful addition. Nearby lived Margaret Hamilton's younger sister Christine, who was married to Gavin Hamilton's brother Thomas. For a time, Thomas and Christine operated a stopping place at 100 Mile together with her younger brother Henry Ogden. Archibald Isaac McKinlay's brother-in-law Adam Bell Ferguson first ran a hotel at Clinton and then in 1883 moved his family south to Savona's Ferry. A McKinlay daughter who in 1882 married Ontarian Tom McDougall settled at 122 Mile. Gavin

TABLE 11.8. Members of the Ogden Clan Settling in the Lac la Hache (Mile 115) Area of British Columbia

Name	Years	Location	Men's occupation	Marriage
First Generation				
Julia Rivet	ca. 1794–1886	Lac la Hache	Widow	Peter Skene Ogden
Second Generation				
Sarah Julia Ogden and Archibald Mckinlay Family				
James	1846–1889	Lac la Hache	Farmer	Apparently did not marry
Sarah Ellen	1851–1898	Clinton/Savona	Hotelier	Adam Bell Ferguson (Ireland)
Ogden Allen	1852–1908	Lac la Hache	Farmer	Apparently did not marry
Catherine Ann	1856–1894	122 Mile	Farmer	Thomas McDougall (Ontario)
Archibald Isaac	1858–	Lac la Hache	Farmer	Mary Elizabeth Ogden (BC Métis [cousin])
Ewan Duncan	1864–1939	Lac la Hache	Farmer	Margaret Julia Hamilton (BC interracial [cousin])
Third Generation				
Adelaide Victoria Ogden and William Manson Family[a]				
Elizabeth	1863–1928	Lac la Hache	Farmer	John Rae Hamilton (BC interracial [cousin])
William "Billy"	1864–1921	Lillooet	Farmer	Alice Martley (BC White)
Margaret	1877–1964	Kamloops	Farmer	James Todd (BC interracial)
Margaret Julia Ogden and Gavin Hamilton Family				
Peter Ogden	1865–1933	Lac la Hache	Likely farmer	Apparently did not marry
John Rae	1866–1926	Lac la Hache	Farmer	Elisabeth Manson (BC interracial [cousin])

352

Colin Alexander	1868–	Lac la Hache	Unknown	Apparently did not marry Child with Clotilde Boitano (BC interracial)
Charles	1869–1954	150 Mile	Unknown	Apparently did not marry Child with Minnie Johnston (BC interracial)
Richard Rae	1870–1927	BC interior	Foreman	Apparently did not marry
Gavin Gaston	1872–1960	Lac la Hache	Farmer	Christine Eagle (BC interracial [cousin])
Hamilton Moffat	1873–1971	Lac la Hache	Farmer/trapper	Cecilia Boitano (BC interracial)
Margaret Helen	1874–1958	Unknown	Unknown	Apparently did not marry
William Rae	1875–1953	Lac la Hache	Laborer	Evelyne Lyne (BC interracial)
Isaac Ogden	1881–1963	BC interior	Cook	Apparently did not marry
Theodore Begue	1891–1967	BC interior	Rancher	Apparently did not marry

Christine Ogden and Thomas Macauley Hamilton Family

Mary Elizabeth	1883–1957	Lac la Hache	Farmer	Antonio Boitano (BC interracial)
William Charles	1888–	Lac la Hache	Farmer	Ellen McClughan (White)

Isaac Ogden and Rose Eagle Family

C. Peter	1892–	BC interior	Unknown	Unknown
Percy William	1894–1968	BC interior	Prospector	Elizabeth D. Nicholson (White)
John Moffat	1896–1942	BC interior	Farmer/logger	Wilhelmina Boitano (BC interracial)

Mary Elizabeth Ogden and Archibald Isaac Mckinlay (No children [cousins])

Henry Ogden (Unmarried)

Charles Griffin Ogden (Unmarried)

Note: Information is drawn from surviving historical records, including vital statistics and the census. BC = British Columbia.
^aThree others apparently died young.

Hamilton's oldest son Peter acquired 160 acres at 114 Mile, to which he moved his younger brothers and mother in 1891, so she could be closer to her younger brother Isaac Ogden, who ran a store there, and her younger sister Mary Elizabeth, who had married her cousin Archibald Isaac McKinlay. The only Peter Ogden sibling and children who did not settle around Lac la Hache were married to HBC officers Robert Hall, James M. L. Alexander, and Hugh Fraser, whose careers in the fur economy took them elsewhere.

Lac la Hache's remote location did not mean the Ogden clan forwent their achieved status. Sons were sent to private schools in the provincial capital and former HBC post of Victoria for a year or more to complete their education. Parents hoped they would, while there, connect with their friends from earlier days and perhaps thereby find spouses. This option did not work out, and the Ogden clan solved the marital situation by four principal means (tables 11.7 and 11.8). As had already begun to occur, they co-opted gold rush offspring, they intermarried, and they stayed single. Four of the Ogden clan turned to nearby successful rancher Augustine Boitano, arrived from Italy, and his Shuswap wife; a fifth wed an interracial woman whose paternal grandfather was American gold miner William Lyne and whose maternal grandfather was Joseph Dussault, a French Canadian fur economy employee. The fourth option was a husband or wife from away. Five daughters and three sons found such white partners, a Manson son by eloping and an Ogden son by marrying a war bride from Britain.

The Ogdens in their reformed British Columbian node engaged in a process not unlike ethnogenesis. They created for themselves a spatially contained collective identity that was in its essence neither white nor indigenous. That identity originated in pride of place in the fur economy and in their long-lived matriarch Julia Rivet, who despite her adopted surname never abandoned her identity as a "daughter of the Great Chief of the Flatheads." The attempt by Ogden's faraway brother to humiliate her and her children had the reverse effect of rallying them around her. According to Peter Skene Ogden's biographer, writing in the 1960s, her memory lived on in "simple things like putting pine cones in the embers of a winter fire to crack open and provide sweet seeds for the children; and little buckskin clothes, lovingly made, for dolls with painted faces."[21]

Scots, English, and Irish sons-in-law added a counterpoint to an Ogden collective identity at whose heart was a strong commitment to each

TABLE 11.9. Recorded Marriages among the Ogden Clan through the First World War, with Attention to Witnesses

Year	Generation	Male spouse	Female spouse	Witnesses
1878	3rd	Adam Bell Ferguson (Ireland)	Sarah Ellen McKinlay	Elizabeth Manson (her cousin's wife) James McKinlay (her brother)
1881	3rd	Thomas M Hamilton (Scotland)	Christine Ogden	Joseph Smith (not related) Mr. O Conner (not related)
1882	3rd / 3rd	Archibald I McKinlay	Mary Ogden (cousin)	William Abel (school teacher, settler) Emma Ogden (her aunt)
1882	3rd	Thomas McDougall (Ontario)	Catherine Ann McKinlay	William Abel (school teacher, settler) Emma Ogden (her aunt)
1887	4th	John Rae Hamilton	Elizabeth Manson (BC interracial [cousin])	Donald Manson (her half-brother) Margaret Hamilton (his sister)
1899	4th	Gavin Hamilton	Christine Eagle (BC interracial)	John Markley (unrelated) Margaret Hamilton (his sister)
1913	5th	Walter Farries (Ontario)	Rosie Hamilton	John Rae Hamilton (her uncle) Adelaide Hamilton (her cousin)
1913	4th	William Rae Hamilton	Evelyn Lyne (BC interracial)	Theodore Hamilton (his nephew) Addie Hamilton (his niece)
1915	4th	William Charles Hamilton	Ellen McClughan (BC White)	Two Oblate priests (unrelated)
1915	Likely 5th	Gustav Freeberg (Sweden)	Caroline Ogden	John Murphy (unrelated) Marguerite Murphy (unrelated)
1915	5th	John Wesley Moore	Sarah Hamilton (BC interracial)	Wilfred Hamilton (likely her cousin) Ella Boitano (her cousin by marriage)

(continued)

355

TABLE 11.9. Recorded Marriages among the Ogden Clan through the First World War, with Attention to Witnesses (*continued*)

Year	Generation	Male spouse	Female spouse	Witnesses
1915	5th	John Pigeon	Elizabeth Hamilton (BC interracial)	Alfred Hamilton (likely her cousin) Elizabeth Hamilton (her sister)
1915	5th	Raymond Wise (California)	Addie Hamilton	John Wesley Moore (her brother-in-law) Sarah Hamilton (her sister)
1917	3rd / 3rd	Ewan Duncan McKinlay	Margaret Ogden Hamilton	Rae Hamilton (his cousin/her son) Ike Hamilton (his cousin/her son)
1919	4th	John Moffatt Ogden	Wilhemina Boitano (BC interracial)	Percy William Ogden (his brother) Eliza Ogden (his cousin)

Note: Information is drawn from surviving historical records, including vital statistics and the census. BC = British Columbia.

other's economic and social well-being within a safe environment. Four out of every five marriages between 1878 and 1919 were witnessed by family members (table 11.8). A war bride arriving at Lac la Hache in 1919 as a fourth-generation wife found, she explained to Barman, "it was like a family down here—they had lots 1, 2, 3, and we had 4 . . . it was a Hudson's Bay settlement." This satisfactory state of affairs continued, she considered, until the 1920s, when the railway and sawmills began to bring in newcomers.

For virtually a century, the Ogdens masked the interracial identity that inwardly drove their lives.[22] Initially, progenitors' high status in the fur economy gave protection. With the progenitors' deaths, sons-in-law successfully negotiated a new node protecting the Ogdens into the fifth generation. Their veneer of respectability could not forever prevent family members from experiencing the consequences of mixed ancestry in a province that was becoming increasingly racist.[23]

Even earlier in time, Ogden descendants aligned with officers in the fur economy had to be circumspect on leaving New Caledonia. Peter Ogden's daughter Rachel (table 11.6) might have been the wife of the incoming head of the coastal trading post of Fort Simpson, but to the local Methodist missionary's wife who hailed from Ontario, she was "part Indian . . . speaks nothing but French," and "can neither read nor write."[24] A dozen years later, in 1890, Rachel's widowed brother-in-law arranged for his daughter Maggie to attend an elite girls' private school in Vancouver so as to mix "with educated and refined people." Earlier he had advanced his career by marrying post head Peter Ogden's daughter Sarah, and now he expended his resources to ensure his own daughters' future from his perspective, which included sending Maggie's two older sisters to England at an early age. Returning to Scotland for a visit two years later, he brought back as gifts a "small gun-metal pin on watches, all kinds of nice clothing and Scottish heather wool stockings." Maggie's marriage to a Vancouver accountant likely satisfied him, just as did those of most of her eight sisters.[25]

Two fifth-generation Ogdens born at the beginning of the twentieth century similarly lived outwardly as white but at the cost of submerging part of their identities. One described to Barman how when he suggested contacting her family, his mother cried and made him promise never to do so. As to the reason, they "were mixed up with Indians." The price of her marriage had been to cut off familial contact, which she gladly did in exchange for the "white gloved elegance" she maintained into her nineties. The second recalled his mother telling him of being taken as a child to visit an elderly aunt and, on passing an oil portrait of Peter Skene Ogden above the doorway, admonished by her mother, "don't look up, there's your grandfather," who in her view had led a deplorable personal life. He explained how "we would never admit we were darkies" because "the Indians were so far below us, so uncivilized." His family could not acknowledge "we had feathers too." The Ogdens had it all, except for one thing: they were not white. The respectability that whiteness gave they did not—could not—possess.

Bouchers and Ogdens

Most analysts have long since abandoned the notion that variation in the mix of occupation, language, and religion among Métis negates claims to sociological or political coherence. Nonetheless, a rough pattern of variations in occupational location, language, religion, ethnicity, and class has been noted elsewhere. Carol M. Judd traced the occupational marginalization of indigenous workers in the fur economy generally after 1821.[26] St-Onge and Gerhard J. Ens observed that class differences and cultural ones are likewise correlated (and perhaps causal) in the ethnic variations of the Red River in the nineteenth century, and St-Onge noted that the self-identification of Métis as such is directly linked to class in early twentieth-century Manitoba.[27]

As exemplified by the Ogdens and the Bouchers, mixed ancestry originating in the fur economy had different faces. For most, it followed the pattern of the Bouchers; for the handful of officers like the Ogdens, it had a more establishment character. Compared with the Bouchers, the Ogdens were much more deliberate in their identity formation. Growing out of their status or class position in the fur economy, the Ogdens had more means at their disposal, and they used them. Initially, both families formed nodes centered in the New Caledonia fur economy that had characteristics of ethnogenesis. Boucher descendants continued to make their lives there, but, on the death of the first three generations of Ogden oldest sons, sons-in-law took the lead in a process akin to re-ethnogenesis. They redefined the Ogdens as a new, post-fur-economy node that, between the last of the second into the fifth generations, enabled the clan to maintain their identity as a de facto Métis/interracial node well into the twentieth century.

It was when Ogden descendants by choice or circumstance disengaged from this second node sited at the southern edge of New Caledonia that their interracial identity had to be renegotiated, in some cases by submerging it from view, in others by taking pride in the past. The continuing tension between the two directions is captured by a sixth-generation Ogden who recollected to us in 2009 how her mother and grandmother "passed as white," even as her uncle nourished her pride in "a fiery and brave Flathead Princess" from whom she descended.

On one level, descendants in the second and subsequent generations of Ogdens and Bouchers behaved similarly in their patterns of work, residences, and personal lives. Sons continued in occupations made familiar by the fur economy, and they clustered together; sons and daughters followed different marital routes. Both families engaged in a process of ethnogenesis, but whereas the Bouchers did so in a pattern familiar from the Métis National homeland, the Ogdens were more ambiguous in their behavior.

Both the Bouchers and the Ogdens had to accommodate their interracial identities. At first view the Bouchers had fewer cultural and material resources with which to maneuver through time as an extended family of mixed descent in a province that was becoming increasingly fractured by race marked out by skin color and physical appearance. Paradoxically, the high fur-economy status that distinguished the Ogdens in their own eyes, and in the eyes of others, made it more difficult over time for some descendants to manage their mixed descent. As time passed and British Columbians lost touch with the province's earlier fur economy, their claim to a high standing lost its power.[28] The Ogdens had protected themselves by clustering and then reclustering together in a process akin to re-ethnogenesis, but then, as descendants sought other ways of life elsewhere, some of them were forced to respond by deliberately obscuring their inheritance.

In such circumstances the Bouchers had options denied to the Ogdens. In the second and third generations, Boucher daughters wed Métis from the prairies (table 11.3) and the Ogden daughters married white officers in the fur economy (table 11.7). The Bouchers continued to wed Métis, thereby consolidating links with the Métis National homeland, whereas the Ogdens sought out respectable interracial gold rush offspring. The Bouchers also had another option denied the Ogdens in that many of them felt comfortable with indigenous partners and, over time, felt comfortable defining themselves as indigenous if they chose to or circumstances prompted them to. For the Ogdens, such an option was unthinkable. It may have been for this reason the Ogdens clung together so tightly, witnessing each other's marriages in far higher proportions than did the Bouchers (tables 11.4 and 11.9). The Bouchers were more comfortable in their identities and did not need such external confirmation. The Ogdens walked a much finer line than did the Bouchers.

The histories of the Ogdens and Bouchers reflect, refract, and inform how Métis, interracial communities, and *métissage* are informed today. Both families were Métis in whole or part by the Métis Nation homeland definition, even though the category did not historically have that meaning in British Columbia. It was the Bouchers' and Ogdens' Métis/interracial inheritance, as the terms are used today, that defined their life courses, just as it was their indigenous descent based in physical differences that marked attitudes toward them in the dominant society. The two processes acted in ways very similar to their counterparts east of the Rockies. The two families' trajectories alert us that the concept of Métis is a construct that should inform a much broader interracial phenomenon in Canadian history. It is extremely important for us to acknowledge this broader phenomenon, for by doing so we come to realize the multiple and diverse ways in which *métissage*/interraciality has operated across Canada.[29] Because of, in part, a paucity of historical sources, there is no evidence that the category of Métis mattered for either family historically, though it is clear that a sociology rooted in *métissage*/interraciality mattered a great deal. Descendants were marked in ways very similar to their counterparts on the prairies.

Historical Patterns and Contemporary Métis Politics

In the last part of this chapter, we speculate on the significance of these historical patterns—or, the authority of the past—on the landscape of contemporary Métis politics. There is a great deal of contention about the geographical and sociological boundaries of the historic Métis Nation today. In our view, not only is the historic Métis Nation best conceptualized as a network, it is probably best conceptualized as a network of nested networks, that is, a nation of families and communities connected to each other, with each one nested and in turn connected to particular locales, including other indigenous peoples in those locales.[30]

The development of historiographical tools that are up to the challenge of describing the complexities of the Métis Nation is an ongoing project; it is also one that requires a sophisticated sociology, history, and geography. Family histories and the history of family networks are obvious candidates for inclusion within the canon of methodologies pertinent to the Métis—here then with the Bouchers and the Ogdens are two examples of how and why this is so. These families have deep roots in British Columbia, even though significant elements of the networks originate in Europe, Rupert's Land, or Red River.

One of the key problems with examining family histories is that as the generations lengthen, the empirical complexity compounds. We can use, and have used, census categories to describe the density of Métis in British Columbia,[31] but to do so we must assume that the categories used in the census overlap with the actual sociological networks we seek to comprehend. This assumption is problematic with any ethnicity and is particularly fraught for a category with boundaries as contested in the past and now as the Métis. Family histories are difficult to aggregate, but aggregate we must in order to move from "family" to "community" to "ethnicity" to "nation."

Given that we cannot assume the wider community is homogenous, when we move from "family" to "community" we must seek to understand whether or not a Métis community exists both within and amongst others in the same geographical space. To return to the Boucher and Ogden examples, it is revealing that when we "map" the social, occupational, and co-residential patterns of these family clusters across time, we do indeed see a particular intensity.

One attempt to do so has been undertaken as part of a larger research agenda. The British Columbia member organization of the Métis National Council,[32] Métis Nation British Columbia, has been collaborating with scholars at the University of British Columbia, Okanagan, under Evans to develop a "historical document database" pertaining to Métis in British Columbia. The intention of this database is to collect, digitize, and index any and all documents pertinent to Métis in the province. This database now contains over 16,000 documents (see www.bcmetis.ca). When a document is incorporated into the database, it is cataloged by document type, authorship, provenance, and similar metadata and then is indexed according to three criteria:

1) The subject areas to which the document pertains,
2) The patronymics of the actors to which the documents pertain,
3) The geo-locations to which the document pertains.

These elements are linked, so that each indexed entry arising from a document includes the three criterions. As a result, the index is relational and describes documents and parts of documents so that one may determine the relative weight (i.e., count) of references/documents within the database. A flexible mapping tool is attached to the database, but the indexing system is particularly helpful in mapping Métis communities by the density of the documents pertaining to that community on the landscape. When we geo-located the documentary references to the Boucher and Ogden family networks through the historical document database using the mapping tool, we could clearly distinguish nodes in a network of relationships centered in the interior of British Columbia and extending into the central plains and northern parklands.[33]

Although this representation of these families on the British Columbian landscape is not without some methodological caveats, the geographic image that maps to the narratives above is highly suggestive. These two networks of families are a demonstrable part of the historic Métis landscape of British Columbia. To push this point one step further, we might suggest—contrary to what might be assumed given the recent British Columbia Supreme Court decision overturning a related legal case, *R v Willison*[34]—that there is indeed a coherent historic Métis presence in the central interior of British Columbia and very likely elsewhere as well.

What is more, this presence was, in ethnogenic terms, an active one. We have a process of ethnogenesis that is consistent with the notion of the historic Métis Nation as a distinct entity, albeit a both geographically and sociologically complex one. Given that movement rendered coherent by familial ties is a core element in the development of Métis distinctiveness, we need not be surprised that this is so. We need to be cognizant that the Métis truly were, and indeed are, a dispersed people, and we need to craft a historiographical approach consistent with that reality.

One key tension in the contemporary debate over how Métis communities are to be defined is the identification of difference between the historic Métis Nation and other smaller, more localized communities of mixed ancestry or interracial people. The examples offered here suggest that, in the context of the central interior of British Columbia at least, this difference is easily overcome. As the cluster of Métis/interracial people living, working, and reproducing themselves in New Caledonia demonstrates, communities can be both locally rooted *and* nodes in the historic Métis Nation, with the same people acting as the glue for both local and wider ties. Though this might appear to be a phenomenon most evident at the geographical edges of the historic Métis Nation, another possibility exists. Given the presence of other racially diverse communities throughout the territories that Métis occupied, it is likely that these sorts of complex overlapping relationships are the norm within the historic Métis Nation, and not the exceptions.

Notes

1. This chapter uses its own terminology. We use the term "Métis" to refer to the group of sociologically connected families and communities of persons of mixed indigenous and European genetic heritage of north central North America—i.e., what is known as the historic Métis Nation. We use the term "interracial" to indicate a person is of genetically mixed indigenous and European descent, and in the tables we use "BC interracial" if the person's indigenous descent is derived from a First Nation, or indigenous people, in what is now British Columbia. These usages are heuristic. We are cognizant the term "interracial" is likely to attract the ire of some readers, and we use it advisedly to signal that the people to whom we apply the term likely felt the consequences of fitting in and between categories then premised on the use of "races" to distinguish between groups of persons so divided on the basis of physical features. Racial categories are cultural categories, not natural ones; nonetheless—and this is the point—once naturalized, such categories have tremendous sociological and actual force. We are aware we are substituting these terms for the common distinction between "Métis" and "metis," and we are aware that we are using the terms "mixed ancestry" and "interracial" interchangeably.

2. Our use of the phrase "historic Métis Nation" is derived from, and in dialogue with, the Métis National Council national definition of Métis (see http://www.metisnation.ca/who/definition.html). The contemporary political dialogues around these issues are treated in some detail in Barman and Evans, "Reflections on Being."

3. Saul, *Fair Country.*

4. Andersen, "From Nation to Population"; Lawrence, "Gender, Race, and Regulation"; and Sawchuk, "Métis, Non-Status Indians" and "Historic Interchangeability of Status."

5. Boisvert and Trimble, "Who Are the Métis?"

6. It is not, we think, coincidence that significant ground-breaking historiographic work (e.g., the gender-inflected re-analyses of fur trade life from Sylvia Van Kirk and Jennifer S. H. Brown) has come from this field (Van Kirk, *Many Tender Ties*; and Brown, *Strangers in the Blood*).

7. St-Onge, *Saint-Laurent, Manitoba*.

8. See especially Andersen, "From Nation to Population" and "Residual Tensions of Empire."

9. Here we follow the contemporary Canadian practice of identifying the original indigenous peoples of North America as "First Nations," replacing the earlier term "Indian." Note, however, the term "Indian" found in Section 35 of the Canadian Constitution, which identifies Indian, Métis, and Inuit as the aboriginal peoples of Canada. Like the term "Aboriginal" in the Canadian Constitution, in Canada the term "indigenous" includes all three of these communities but carries the extra meaning of a people autochthonous to a place. The intermarriage of Métis and others with local indigenous communities is thus potentially part of an indigenization (or, perhaps better, "autochthonization") process.

10. Weinstein, *Quiet Revolution West*.

11. Here we state rather than defend our understanding of these issues, which is the subject of extensive discussion in an earlier article (Barman and Evans, "Reflections on Being").

12. Peterson, "Many Roads to the Red River."

13. Among welcome exceptions are Heather Devine's methodical tracking of the mixed-descent Desjarlais family across the North American landscape and Brenda Macdougall's close interrogation of the northern Saskatchewan Métis community of Île-à-la-Crosse (Devine, *People Who Own Themselves*; and Macdougall, "Wahkootowin" and *One of the Family*).

14. Barman and Evans, "Reflections on Being."

15. For sourced biographies of Jean Baptiste Boucher and Peter Skene Ogden that include links to biographies of family members, see Watson, *Lives Lived*, 1:216–17 and 2:733–34.

16. Local Oblate priest and historian Adrien Morice (see Morice, *History of the Northern Interior*), who arrived in New Caledonia in 1880, described Boucher as a "French Cree half-breed"; earlier priests described both Boucher and his wife as "métis" as used in French to indicate mixed race at their children's baptisms and marriages, with her maternal heritage being given as Carrier. See Barman and Evans, "Reflections on Being," 61.

17. Our understanding of the Boucher family is based on historical records in the public domain—including archival and published materials, vital statistics, and the census. We are aware we may have misunderstood or misinterpreted some elements, and we apologize to descendants and others when we do so in the text or tables.

18. Our understanding of the Ogden family is based on historical records in the public domain—including archival and published materials, newspaper

articles, vital statistics, the census, and recorded interviews held in the British Columbia Archives—and on personal conversations with descendants. We are especially grateful to Ogden descendant Diane Dickert for her encouragement, support, and close reading of the text. We are aware we may have misunderstood or misinterpreted some elements, and we apologize to descendants and others when we do so in the text or tables.

19. Julia Rivet is described by Jennifer S. H. Brown as "the Nez Perce stepdaughter of an Old Canadian Voyageur" (Brown, *Strangers in the Blood*, 143). Rivet met Peter Skene Ogden at Spokane House, following his crossing of the Rocky Mountains in 1818. Although perhaps not interracial in genetic heritage, Julia was clearly raised in the intercultural space of the fur trade. Binns, *Peter Skene Ogden*; and Gloria Griffen Cline, *Peter Skene Ogden*.

20. Binns, *Peter Skene Ogden*, 356.

21. Ibid., 99.

22. Van Kirk, "Tracking the Fortunes," makes a similar point in respect to officer families living in the British Columbian capital city of Victoria.

23. Barman and Evans, "Reflections on Being."

24. Hare and Barman, *Good Intentions Gone Awry*, 135.

25. Barman, *Constance Lindsay Skinner*, 30–32.

26. Judd, "Native Labour and Social Stratification."

27. St-Onge, "Variations in Red River" and *Saint-Laurent, Manitoba*; and Ens, *Homeland to Hinterland*.

28. Somewhat poignantly, there is an excellent parallel of this process at Red River. Sylvia Van Kirk's portrayal of the tensions facing the Alexander Ross family there has striking similarities to the experience the Ogden family described here, albeit more dramatic (Van Kirk, " 'What if Mama is an Indian?' ").

29. This observation is as trite as it is true, and it extends to the other racial and ethnic categories of the day. It does not mean, however, that the historical and sociological linkages claimed by contemporary Métis are somehow "invented"; indeed, we have demonstrated exactly such ties here. The recontextualization of Métis and interracial identities today are part of ongoing sociological, political, and deeply historical processes.

30. Barman and Evans, "Reflections on Being."

31. Ibid.

32. The Métis National Council is made up of five governing members, one each from the five provinces from Ontario west.

33. For more information on the database and mapping tools described here, see Evans and Corbett, "New Media, Participatory Methodologies."

34. Ibid.

Works Cited

Andersen, Chris. "From Nation to Population: The Racialization of 'Métis' in the Canadian Census." *Nations and Nationalism* 14, no. 2 (2008): 347–68.

———. "Residual Tensions of Empire: Contemporary Métis Communities and the Canadian Judicial Imagination." In *Reconfiguring Aboriginal–State Relations. Canada, The State of the Federation, 2003*, edited by M. Murphy, 295–325. Montreal, QC, and Kingston, ON: McGill-Queen's University Press, 2005.

Barman, Jean. *Constance Lindsay Skinner: Writing on the Frontier*. Toronto, ON: University of Toronto Press, 2002.

Barman, Jean, and Mike Evans. "Reflections on Being, and Becoming, Métis in British Columbia." *BC Studies* 161 (Spring 2009): 59–91.

Binns, Archie. *Peter Skene Ogden: Fur Trader*. Portland, OR: Binfords & Mort, 1967.

Boisvert, David, and Keith Turnbull. "Who Are the Métis?" In *Readings in Aboriginal Studies*. Vol. 2, *Identities and State Structures*, edited by Joe Sawchuk, 108–41. Brandon, MB: Bearpaw Publishing, 1992.

Brown, Jennifer S. H. *Strangers in Blood: Fur Trade Company Families in Indian Company*. Vancouver: University of British Columbia Press, 1980.

Cline, Gloria Griffen. *Peter Skene Ogden and the Hudson's Bay Company*. Norman: University of Oklahoma Press, 1974.

Devine, Heather. *The People Who Own Themselves: Aboriginal Ethnogenesis in a Canadian Family, 1660–1900*. Calgary, AB: University of Calgary Press, 2004.

Ens, Gerhard J. *Homeland to Hinterland: The Changing Worlds of the Red River Metis in the Nineteenth Century*. Toronto, ON: University of Toronto Press, 1996.

Evans, Mike, and Jon Corbett. "New Media, Participatory Methodologies, and the Popularization of Métis History." In *Popularizing Research: Engaging New Genres, Media, and Audiences*, edited by Phillip Vannini. New York, NY: Peter Lang, 2012.

Hare, Jan, and Jean Barman. *Good Intentions Gone Awry: Emma Crosby and the Methodist Mission on the Northwest Coast*. Vancouver: University of British Columbia Press, 2006.

Judd, Carol M. "Native Labour and Social Stratification in the Hudson's Bay Company's Northern Department, 1770–1870." *Canadian Review of Sociology and Anthropology* 17, no. 4 (1980): 305–14.

Lawrence, Bonita. "Gender, Race, and the Regulation of Native Identity in Canada and the United States: An Overview." *Hypatia* 18, no. 2 (2003): 3–31.

Macdougall, Brenda. *One of the Family: Metis Culture in Nineteenth-Century Northwestern Saskatchewan*. Vancouver: University of British Columbia Press, 2010.

———. "Wahkootowin: Family and Cultural Identity in Northwestern Saskatchewan Metis Communities." *Canadian Historical Review* 87, no. 1 (2006): 431–62.

Morice, A. G. *The History of the Northern Interior of British Columbia*. London, UK: John Lane, 1906.

Peterson, Jacqueline. "Many Roads to Red River: Métis Genesis in the Great Lakes Region, 1680–1815." In *The New Peoples: Being and Becoming Métis in*

North America, edited by Jacqueline Peterson and Jennifer S. H. Brown, 37–71. Winnipeg: University of Manitoba Press, 1985.

Saul, John Ralston. *A Fair Country: Telling Truths about Canada*. Toronto, ON: Viking, 2008.

Sawchuk, Patricia K. "The Historic Interchangeability of Status of Métis and Indians: An Alberta Example." In *The Recognition of Aboriginal Rights*, edited by Samuel W. Corrigan and Joe Sawchuk, 57–70. Brandon, MB: Bearpaw Publishing, 1996.

———. "The Métis, Non-Status Indians and the New Aboriginality: Government Influence on Native Political Alliances and Identity." In *Readings in Aboriginal Studies*, vol. 2, edited by Joe Sawchuk, 70–86. Brandon, MB: Bearpaw Publishing, 1992.

St-Onge, Nicole. *Saint-Laurent, Manitoba: Evolving Métis Identities 1850–1914*. Regina, SK: Canadian Plains Research Center, University of Regina, 2004.

———. "Variations in Red River: The Traders and Freemen Métis of Saint-Laurent, Manitoba." *Canadian Ethnic Studies* 24, no. 2 (1992): 1–21.

Van Kirk, Sylvia. *Many Tender Ties: Women in Fur-Trade Society*. Winnipeg, MB: Watson and Dwyer; Norman: University of Oklahoma Press, 1980.

———. "Tracking the Fortunes of Five Founding Families of Victoria." *BC Studies* 115/16 (1997/98): 149–80.

———. " 'What if Mama is an Indian?': The Cultural Ambivalence of the Alexander Ross Family." In *The New Peoples: Being and Becoming Métis in North America*, edited by Jacqueline Peterson and Jennifer S. H. Brown, 207–217. Winnipeg: University of Manitoba Press, 1985.

Watson, Bruce McIntyre. *Lives Lived West of the Divide: A Biographical Dictionary of Fur Traders Working West of the Rockies, 1793–1858*. 3 vols. Kelowna: Centre for Social, Spatial, and Economic Justice, University of British Columbia, Kelowna, 2010.

Weinstein, John. *Quiet Revolution West: The Rebirth of Métis Nationalism*. Calgary, AB: Fifth House Publishers, 2007.

12

THE CREOLES OF RUSSIAN AMERICA

Laborers in the Borderlands

DANIEL J. BLUMLO

In 1799, Tsar Paul of Russia granted the Russian American Company (RAC) a monopoly for hunting, trading, and establishing settlements in present-day Alaska. Although the imperial charter broadly defined the reach of the RAC monopoly as "the American mainland to the northeast" of Russia, plus the Aleutian and Kuril Islands in the North Pacific, RAC merchants also established trading posts in northern California and the Hawaiian Islands.[1] From its creation, this government-backed enterprise faced severe labor shortages due to depopulation of conquered Native Americans and problems recruiting employees within Russia. These labor shortages limited the company's ability to extract fur and other resources from Alaska, and so the RAC decided to employ the colony's Creole population. In this chapter, I explore the forced employment of Creoles—the children of Russian fathers and Aleut, Alutiiq, and Tlingit women—during the nineteenth century. Once the RAC decided to use Creoles to fill its labor needs, especially for skilled workers, every aspect of the Creoles' lives became a political and public matter subject to Russian domination and influence. Because the RAC needed a secure and consistent work force, the company strove to control the Creoles and integrate them into the Russian Empire by altering their social status, marriages, and upbringing.

The Fur Trade

By the mid-eighteenth century, the lucrative Siberian fur trade attracted independent *promyshlenniki*, or fur trappers, to the Aleutian Islands. As in Siberia, overhunting forced adventurous trappers to expand their areas of operation in order to seek better profits. In the North Pacific, the promyshlenniki initially focused their attention on the seas off the western Aleutians, where they hunted fur seals, sea lions, and sea otters. The decimation of these fur-bearing animals, however, led the trappers to move their operations farther and farther east, to the eastern Aleutians, Kodiak Island, the Alaskan mainland, and the Alaskan panhandle.

From 1743 to 1867, Russian fur trappers, missionaries, and administrators encountered a number of indigenous peoples in Alaska. Although the Russians interacted with mainland tribes, like the Dena'ina and the Chugach, they had the greatest amount of contact with groups who lived on coastal islands near major offshore hunting spots. During their rule, the RAC categorized these tribes based on their degree of subjugation.[2] The Russians classified the Aleuts of the Aleutian Islands and the Alutiiq people of Kodiak Island and the Alaskan peninsula as "dependents." Early promyshlenniki first visited these islands in the 1740s, and by the time of the RAC's formation, Russians had already established several trading posts on the Aleutians and Kodiak. Fur-trapping entrepreneur Grigorii Shelikhov, for example, began the first permanent Russian settlement on Kodiak Island in 1784.[3] By the nineteenth century, the Aleuts and the Alutiiq had been completely conquered and forcibly enlisted into fur-hunting operations. By contrast, the RAC categorized the Tlingits who lived on the islands of the Alaskan panhandle as "independents." Though the RAC located their capital, Novo-Arkhangel'sk, in this area, the Russians never completely controlled or conquered the Tlingit. Of the numerous Tlingit clans, the RAC had a direct relationship, through warfare or trade, with only the Sitka Tlingit, who lived outside the Russian settlement.[4] To the Russian government, dependent people were the tsar's subjects, whereas independent people were not.

Throughout most of their rule over Alaska, including the early years of the RAC, the Russians treated the indigenous people of the Aleutian Islands and Kodiak in an excessively brutal manner. In order to amass as many pelts as possible, fur trappers impressed Aleut and Alutiiq men into employment through military coercion. This practice resulted in

FIGURE 12.1.   Sitka (formerly Novo-Arkhangel'sk) from the water, with
St. Michael's Cathedral on the right, late nineteenth century. Photo courtesy of
Alaska State Library, Michael Z. Vinokouroff Photograph Collection, P243-2-106.

constant exploitation and unofficial enslavement of these dependent
tribes.[5] The promyshlenniki, who were not familiar with hunting sea
mammals, or sailing in general, forced the Aleuts and Alutiiq to bring
furs to their outposts through a quota system, or *iasak*. In most cases—
probably because of distance—the Russians collected these only once
every few years.[6] As entrepreneurs could not launch an expedition into
the North Pacific without government authorization, Russian fur trappers had to promise to claim new lands for the crown and incorporate
local populations into the empire. The promyshlenniki then collected the
iasak from these "new citizens," which from the point of view of the state
signified their acceptance of Russian sovereignty.[7] To facilitate the payment of this tax, fur trappers often kidnapped relatives of Aleut and
Alutiiq clan leaders, forcing their relatives to pay the iasak in order to
obtain their release. The RAC and its predecessors also relocated entire
populations, sending young men to various hunting grounds and women
to company settlements. Because Aleut men had traditionally done the
hunting that provided their communities with enough food for the winter, their removal ensured that many Aleut families starved.[8] As a government inspector documented in 1789, "Leaving Unalaska for Alaska,
[Russian fur trappers] carried with them over a hundred Aleut men and
women; from those who were left on the islands they took all *baidarkas*
[kayaks], arrows, parkas, and foodstuffs. Only a few of the hundred

remained alive after four years' privation of food and clothing."[9] When the Aleuts in their communities scattered across the archipelago, or the Alutiiq on Kodiak resisted, the Russians responded with their gunpowder weapons and destroyed the indigenous villages.[10] The use of force enabled the Russians to stay in their fortified trading posts and aboard their ships as the indigenous population of the Aleutians and Kodiak set out on the Bering Sea and the North Pacific to hunt.

Although greed was perhaps the prevailing motivation for Russian brutality, first-hand witnesses observed that most early fur trappers were criminals who chose service in Alaska over jail time in Siberia. Pavel Golovin, a naval captain who visited Alaska in the 1860s, recalled that

> the first promyshlenniks [sic] mistreated the Aleuts, and even during the first period of the Company's existence the condition of the Aleuts improved very little. Even if Baranov [the first RAC manager] had wanted to protect them from oppression, he could hardly have done so, because he had to entrust the administration of the islands, offices, and stores to persons under his command, and with few exceptions, these persons were far from moral. In the first stages they sent whatever persons they could to the colony, without exception, because they had no choice.[11]

Georg Heinrich von Langsdorff, a physician who resided in Russian America from 1803 to 1807, witnessed similar behavior. He recorded that the promyshlenniki and their RAC overseers were generally dishonest and unprincipled, "the scum of Siberian criminals."[12] Von Langsdorff asserted that the main reason for the depopulation of the Aleuts was their complete dependency on the company for even basic needs. He wrote, "At present the Aleuts are so enslaved to the Company that they get *baidarkas*, the bones for their arrows, and indeed, even their clothing from the Company. The entire take of a hunt has to be turned over to the Company. The overseers and agents requisition as many persons of both sexes are necessary to go hunting or to carry out other work, to prepare skins, to sew clothing, to build *baidarkas*, to catch and dry fish, etc."[13] Russian fur companies' use of criminals helps explain atrocities committed against Native Americans, but it is not the only excuse.

In portions of the New World—namely Spanish colonies in the Caribbean and in Central and South America—European brutality and foreign diseases caused a continual depopulation of Native Americans. This situation also applied to the Russian occupation of Alaska. The size of the Aleut and Alutiiq population at the time of the Russian arrival is somewhat difficult to determine. Early accounts by Russian fur trappers are extremely dubious as they often exaggerated population numbers in order to entice the government into providing financial support for their expeditions.[14] Such was the case with Grigorii Shelikhov, who in the 1780s claimed that Kodiak had a population of 50,000.[15] Shelikhov, who had already consolidated several Alaskan enterprises under his ownership, no doubt misrepresented his figures in order to obtain a much coveted government monopoly over all hunting enterprises in Alaska. Based on the estimates of other early visitors and the number of Alutiiq settlements, the population of Kodiak in 1784 was more likely between 6,500 and 10,000.[16] Even when Russian violence subsided, Kodiak's population continued to decline. Decades later, following a smallpox epidemic in 1837–38, the Alutiiq population of Kodiak fell to under 2,000.[17] The population of the Aleutians, meanwhile, decreased from approximately 10,000 at the end of the eighteenth century to about 4,000 by 1840.[18] The same smallpox epidemic also hit the Tlingit of the Alaskan panhandle, a group who had suffered relatively less from Russian subjugation. The disease reduced their numbers from approximately 10,000 in 1835 to about 6,000 five years later.[19] Brutal treatment at the hands of fur traders and the introduction of diseases like smallpox caused a marked decline in the population of several Native American groups during the eighteenth and nineteenth centuries. This predicament caused labor shortages for the RAC.

Generally, the RAC and its predecessors in the fur-trading business did not employ large numbers of Russian laborers in Alaska. In 1839, the total number of Russian subjects (which included the Finnish and Baltic German colonial leadership) in Alaska peaked at 823 individuals.[20] Initially, the presence of the indigenous population and their virtual enslavement under tsarist rule made a large Russian presence unnecessary. However, other reasons account for the low number of Russian employees as well. Given the prevailing system of agricultural production in Russia at this time, large numbers of Russian serfs lacked freedom of movement.[21] Moreover, Alaska's distance from major population centers and the difficulty and expense of the voyage made it a hard sell for would-be Russian employees. Among those who did choose to go, the turnover rate was high. For most of Russian rule, the promyshlenniki had to leave the colonies once their seven-year passport expired, provided that they were not in debt. Although Russians had no legal right to reside in Alaska, it was more common to find indebted Russians who wanted desperately to go home versus those who wanted to stay.[22] Only in 1835, after several requests from the RAC, did an imperial decree allow permanent residence in Alaska to those few Russians who preferred to stay.

Most Russians who worked in Alaska were unskilled laborers. As the RAC began to increase its operations in Alaska, its leaders desperately needed, above all, a steady supply of skilled mid-level managers to sail company vessels and manage outposts. When the first naval officers to enter RAC service, Lieutenants Davydov and Khvostov, departed the port of Okhotsk for Kodiak aboard the RAC's *Elizaveta* in August 1802, the lack of competent sailors and sturdy ships shocked them. Davydov later wrote, "I honestly could not imagine that with the art of navigation at the stage of development it is at present, such bad ships as those in Okhotsk could exist."[23] The poor quality of the RAC sailors can be traced at least in part to the circumstances of their hiring. The company recruited heavily from the uneducated peasants and burghers around its regional office in Irkutsk. Because of their place of birth, such individuals had no experience in shipbuilding or sailing. As Davydov described, "Many of them had never seen the sea before," and one of the navigators "had hardly any idea what a compass was" and "had never seen maps."[24] A few days later he said, "The remoteness makes it difficult to attract people skilled in the art of navigation. . . . The work on our ship had been carried out extremely badly and, indeed, we could not have expected anything else, when not one of the hunters or sailors knew what he was about."[25] Not long after their voyage, the *Elizaveta* sank after it ran aground on a rock near Kodiak.[26]

Creoles as Laborers

Facing a steadily decreasing Aleutian population and insurmountable obstacles in bringing competent Russians to Alaska to work, the company decided to turn to Russian Creoles living in North America. The product of rape, prostitution, common-law unions, and official marriages, members of this marginalized group did not attract much attention from company officials until the early 1800s. The 1799 RAC charter did not mention them, nor had the RAC counted, categorized, or even given them a consistent label. During the first two decades of the nineteenth century, Europeans called the children of Russian and Native American unions everything from "Aleuts" to "children born to Russian promyshlen-nye" and "half-breeds."[27]

The origin of the Russian use of the term "Creole" is unclear. Alutiiq historian Sonja Luehrmann hypothesized that the mixed-race children of Russian America first received the term Creole in 1805 from the tsar's emissary to the colony, Chamberlain Nikolai Rezanov. Rezanov, who circumnavigated the world aboard the *Nadezhda*, adopted the term from Spain's Latin American colonies.[28] Lydia Black, however, traced the word's use only as far back as 1816, where it appears in Russian church records.[29] Regardless of origins, the RAC used the term Creole to categorize the children of Russians and Native Americans.

The RAC saw Creoles as a solution to their labor needs. Rezanov wrote that "the true strength of these regions lies in increasing the number of settlements and the population. The first objective of each administration should be to increase the population."[30] By this language, the Russian official meant that the company should increase the number of Creoles. As children of intermarriage, many were already under some degree of Russian and RAC influence. The RAC believed that the Creoles would eventually predominate over the Native Aleuts, "if not entirely replace them."[31] As the RAC historian Petr Tikhmenev wrote in the 1860s, "With the Aleuts fast diminishing in number, creoles will have to replace them in all their occupations."[32]

RAC policies regarding mixed-race children echoed those of earlier colonial societies elsewhere in North America. During the seventeenth century, French settlements along the St. Lawrence River Valley and in Acadia also depended heavily on the fur trade. New France, like Russian America, saw small numbers of predominantly male European immigrants—approximately 1,000—during company rule.[33] Although this number increased after the royal government implemented direct rule in 1663, the French had wanted to limit immigration to North America because of a mercantilist view that the strength of their kingdom depended on a large population.[34] In order to produce a larger colonial work force, New France trade officials sought to produce French nationals in North America through intermarriage with Native Americans.[35]

As the founder of New France, Samuel de Champlain reportedly said, "Our young men will marry your daughters, and we shall be one people."[36] Russian and French fur trading companies in the New World both sought to rely on American-born children of European descent in order to help their operations.

Once the RAC decided to use Creoles as a work force, it needed to find ways to control them. Through the 1810s, however, their legal status remained unclear. Consequently, the Russian government decided to reinforce company dominance over Creoles by placing them into a Russian social estate, or *soslovie*. This classification was a political act, for all Russian subjects, whether nobility, clergy, or peasants, belonged to and owed obligations to their soslovie. In 1818, RAC governor general Hagemeister suggested, "Children born here in America, it seems, ought to be equal to children of Russians born abroad."[37] The main office and the government heeded his advice, and the new 1821 RAC charter placed all Creoles into a Russian social estate. This decree stated that Creoles henceforth were subjects of Russia and "have the right everywhere to the legal protection of the government, just as all other subjects do who belong to the category of *meshchanstvo*."[38] The Creoles, in other words, gained the same rights as free townspeople, or petty burghers, in Russia.

The assignment to a Russian soslovie did not only apply to those Creoles who lived with their fathers or in Russian settlements. As RAC employee Kirill T. Khlebnikov added, "Creoles who do not belong to their fathers' families, that is, those whose birth has not been legitimized and who are not registered anywhere in the latest census, are citizens of the colonies, that is they are Russian subjects. They have all the rights of subjects and legal protection, and are at the same time obliged to obey the laws, and are accountable under them."[39] Thus all Creoles, even those who lived in their mothers' communities and considered themselves Aleut, Alutiiq, or Tlingit, were potential employees.

In addition to assigning Creoles to a social estate, the 1821 charter instructed the RAC to take accurate censuses for Russian America. The company not only had to keep track of marriages between Russian men and Native women, but it also had to "notify appropriate authorities of the number of births of these women."[40] The following year, the board of directors in St. Petersburg instructed the chief manager of Russian America to "prepare an accurate list of creoles, both male and female indicating age and present status, and . . . append a recommendation as to where each should be assigned. The Office Administrator shall attest to their capabilities and conduct, and sign this statement." [41] Whereas the government wanted an accurate census of the Russian American population, the RAC wanted to track their potential labor pool.

As these records indicate, the Creole population grew steadily throughout the nineteenth century. By the end of Russian rule, Captain Golovin assessed the total colonial population at 10,144 persons. Out of this total, there were 1,896 Creoles compared with just 595 Russians. [42] Golovin predicted that "in a few decades the creole population will become dominant in the colonies and completely replace the Aleuts, whose number is gradually diminishing." [43]

Historian Roxanne Easley concluded that because of differing racial views, nineteenth-century British and Russian fur companies had fundamental differences over how they incorporated mixed-heritage people into their social structures. In general, Easley contended that the Russian government had a direct role in RAC activities, whereas the British government preferred an indirect strategy for the Hudson's Bay Company (HBC). [44] Russian nationalism did not develop until the late nineteenth century, and so the RAC was more inclusive with Creoles than the HBC was with "countryborn." [45] Both the tsarist government and the RAC sought to assimilate mixed-heritage people into the empire through the Russian language, social estates, and Orthodox Christianity. [46] The Creoles only had to be Russian culturally in order to provide the RAC with a reliable and loyal work force in Alaska. [47] Furthermore, because the RAC had difficulties in employing Russians, Creoles could rise to leadership positions within the company. Although there was no fixed rule, according to Easley, the HBC did not try to impose their culture on the countryborn because they saw being of mixed race as a negative. This prejudice was especially true following the 1821 HBC merger with their Canadian rival, the North West Company. A temporary excess of employees led HBC officials to restrict the countryborn to positions as laborers. Because of British attitudes about race and the HBC's ability to hire more people of European descent, mixed-bloods had few opportunities for advancement. [48] In the nineteenth century, if countryborn children entered British society, gained an education, and advanced within the HBC, it was due to their father's social status and his active efforts to offset the perceived limitations of their mixed heritage. [49]

Marriages

Although many of the first Creoles born in Russian America came into existence after their mothers had been raped by promyshlenniki, it was inevitable that there would also be consensual relationships between Russian men and Native American women. Unconcerned with local practices, most Russian and European men in Alaska brought their brides to live with them in the company settlements and trading posts instead of moving to their wives' villages. When the RAC began to use Creoles as a labor source, the private relationships between Russian men and Native American women became a public matter. Prior to this decision, the RAC and its predecessors had encouraged concubines and common-law marriages instead of church marriages.[50] The leader of the first Orthodox mission to Alaska, Arkhimandrite Ioasaf, unsuccessfully tried to correct this behavior. In a 1795 letter to the entrepreneur Grigorii Shelikhov, the monk complained about the depravity of the Russian promyshlenniki. He wrote, "Only with great difficulty did I persuade a few Russian hunters to get married. The rest of them do not even want to listen to me. Everyone openly keeps one girl or several."[51] He continued by noting that future RAC manager Aleksandr Baranov and his staff blatantly disregarded church regulations and openly challenged his authority. Baranov allegedly told the monk, "We are not such hypocrites that we do not see that these regulations are made for fools."[52] Baranov apparently even encouraged and pressured company employees to keep mistresses. Ioasaf believed that he could have persuaded some of the Russian men to get married had it not been for Baranov, who even went so far as to say that "a married man is a poor hunter."[53] Early Orthodox missionaries found deeply entrenched resistance to legal marriages among Russian fur trappers.

As the RAC decided to enlist the Creoles into their ranks, the Orthodox Church and the company began to work together and gradually changed marriage practices for Russians in Alaska. In 1807, Father Gideon, a visiting clergyman who represented the tsar, gave instructions that employees who wished to get married needed to obtain permission from company management.[54] To some extent, the RAC must have followed this procedure because Chief Manager Baranov received numerous marriage petitions from 1809 to 1818. These requests were usually brief and included information such as the groom's name, status in the RAC, home province, and class. Information about the bride only included her first name, and perhaps some detail about her father and her race.[55] Once a couple petitioned for marriage, the RAC issued a certificate of permission, and a priest performed the marriage. A revived missionary effort in the 1820s helped the Russian government enforce legal church marriages. As more Orthodox Christian clergymen entered the colony, they established churches, won converts, and performed marriages. Although the effort was never completely successful, the Orthodox Church tried to eliminate what they considered to be immoral indigenous sexual practices, such as substitute wives, polygamy, and prostitution.[56]

Russian legal marriages were an effort to place Creole children under Russian dominance. Orthodoxy, along with autocracy and nationality, were the tenants of Tsar Nicholas I's doctrine of official nationality.[57] By expanding Orthodox Christianity and encouraging the production of children born in church-sanctioned marriages, the Russians sought to create a loyal population that identified with the tsar and empire. Ideally, parents would then raise these children within the church, give them Russian names, and raise them as Russians.

Concerning marriage, the fur trading communities of New France and British Canada held numerous similarities with Russian America. In New France, many unions between French Canadian trappers and Native American women took place *à la façon du pays*, or according to the custom of the country. Although the HBC initially forbade their European employees from having sexual relationships with Native American women, London-based policy was not able to alter reality at the forts along Hudson and James Bays.[58] Native Americans in Canada and Alaska viewed marriage as, among other things, an economic alliance that drew Europeans into indigenous trade in exchange for access to European goods.[59] As in Alaska, in New France these unions upset Christian missionaries. But it was not because they were between Europeans and Native Americans but, rather, because these unions took place outside of the church.[60] Lobbying by Jesuit missionaries won out, and in the 1660s the French began to enforce Christian marriages.[61] Furthermore, after a 1735 edict French trappers had to get permission from the governor or commanding officials to marry Native American women.[62] Although French and British toleration of intermarriage declined throughout the eighteenth and nineteenth centuries as European women began arriving in Canada in larger numbers, intermarriage and unions à la façon du pays continued west of the major cities.[63] In a similar manner, many Russian promyshlenniki stationed in *odinochkas*, or one-man posts, far removed from the settlements on Kodiak and at Novo-Arkhangel'sk, continued to have common-law wives and children outside of Christian wedlock.

In societies that practiced matrilocal residence patterns, like the Aleut, Alutiiq, and Tlingit, the husband joined the wife's family after the wedding ceremony. Furthermore, any children born to a couple often belonged to their mother's family, not their father's.[64] Maternal relatives also had the responsibility for raising children. The Russians, however, undermined local residential habits by bringing their wives to live with them in Russian settlements. Through the promotion of Orthodox marriages, the Russians sought to remove the mother's dominance in raising children. Russian fathers took control of their children's upbringing and often ceded it to RAC officials. By weakening matrilineal tendencies among indigenous people in this way, the Russians established a form of culture-based dominance.

Education

The raising and training of Creole children for service in the RAC was crucially important to the company. In order to address their labor shortage—particularly the lack of skilled seamen, navigators, clerks, shipbuilders, and doctors—the RAC needed to find ways to educate the Creoles and induce them to work for the company. Nikolai Rezanov, acting on behalf of the tsar, began this process. In 1805, the company began to educate the colony's children at RAC schools on Kodiak and in Novo-Arkhangel'sk. At the insistence of Rezanov, Russians, Creoles, and some Native Americans sent their children to these schools.[65] The same year, with five boys leaving aboard the *Neva*, Rezanov also started the tradition of sending Creole children to St. Petersburg for an education. Ideally, the RAC wanted to provide the Alaskan Creole youth with a vocational education locally and then take more promising students to Russia for advanced training.[66]

Most of the young men sent by the RAC to St. Petersburg went to the Kronstadt Pilot School. There, the Russian Navy successfully trained several young Creoles in navigation and ship building. Early successes encouraged the RAC to send more promising Creole children to the Russian capital. Several Russian-trained Creole navigators participated in the exploration of Alaska and the Arctic and went on to command company vessels and trading posts. One individual sent to St. Petersburg by Rezanov in 1805 was Andrei Klimovskiy. On his return to Russian America, Klimovskiy took part in an 1818 expedition that began to open up the Alaskan mainland to company control. A decade later, he commanded the company schooner *Aktsiya*.[67] Other Creole graduates of Kronstadt's navigation school were Petr Malakhov and Aleksandr Kashevarov, who learned arithmetic and geometry, how to calculate latitude and longitude, and how to use a compass, keep journals, and copy maps.[68] In the 1820s, the RAC's main office returned them to Alaska, as "such people are highly needed in the colonies."[69] In 1838, Kashevarov and Malakhov both took part in an expedition that explored the Bering Sea and the Arctic coast of Alaska. Kashevarov later commanded the port of Aian (in Russia) and eventually became a major general, whereas Malakhov helped establish a trading post at Nulato in the Alaskan interior.[70] Another talented young Creole, Kondratii Burtsev, learned ship building and worked at Kronstadt's naval dockyards during the 1810s.[71] By February 1817, the RAC decided to put Burtsev's training to use in the colonial capital Novo-Arkhangel'sk. The main office wanted to use Burtsev and his wife to encourage other Creoles to come to Russia and study, which would make them "more useful to the company."[72] The RAC found Burtsev extremely valuable, for he had learned how to draw nautical maps as well as repair and construct shallow-drought ships. Thus, as Rezanov had hoped, distinguished pupils found employment as ship builders and pilots, navigators, and commanders of company vessels.[73]

Despite some early success stories, by the late 1820s the RAC decided to stop educating Creoles in Russia. Expense was the overriding factor in this decision, but it came about in different ways. For instance, some Creoles learned skills in the classroom but were unable to apply those skills to practical situations. RAC employee Kirill Klebnikhov wrote that "there have been cases of some who studied shipbuilding and returned quite unfamiliar with both theory and practice and as a result were no use here."[74] In the official account of his circumnavigation of the world, Captain Litke echoed this sentiment. He wrote, "At various times, some of these [Creole] men were sent to Russia for instruction in navigation or the arts, but few of them were successful. Some did not take advantage at all of the instruction given them."[75] Thus, it was too expensive to educate Creoles in Russia, especially if many did not fulfill RAC expectations.

Some company officials opposed sending Creoles to Russia for their education because they often became susceptible to vice while living in St. Petersburg. Litke feared that some Creole pupils in Russia "lost the habit of their former, original way of life and picked up other ways of living which, on return, rendered them incapable of being usefully employed."[76] Khlebnikov agreed that vice corrupted many students: "Some of the pupils . . . acquired a taste for luxuries and learned bad habits."[77] In one case, the Russians employed Alaskan-born Andrei Larionov as a *prikashchik*, or supercargo, at Kronstadt. Accused of stealing and selling two ropes, as well as taking 200 rubles out of his till, Larionov confessed, but the main office suspected that he had stolen even more.[78] Thus, Khlebnikov argued that future Creole employees be educated in Alaska, because "in a small group dominated by one individual, who, with a paternal attitude supervises the conduct of each and every one, there cannot be so many open vices and evil tendencies as might occur in a large city."[79] After all, as some RAC officials pointed out, "such sins as thievery and deceit cannot be hidden, and the guilty person is found out right away."[80]

Creoles found more obstacles in Russia than unsavory habits. They also fell victim to European diseases from which their North American nativity offered them no immunity.[81] Many Creoles did not survive in Russia, which meant that the company was unable to recoup the loss of money spent on their travel to and training in Russia. In an 1817 letter to RAC manager Aleksandr Baranov, the main office informed him that Matrena Kuznetsova "came here with the other creoles you sent, but she is the only one still alive."[82] Khlebnikov recommended that the company prohibit Russians from taking their Creole or Aleut brides back to Russia, "where they experience the change of climate and do not live long."[83]

In 1805, under Rezanov's supervision, the RAC opened schools on Kodiak and in Novo-Arkhangel'sk for both sexes. The curriculum of these schools mirrored that of Russian primary schools, which since the reign of Peter the Great provided pupils with a utilitarian education. Members of the Orthodox mission and naval officers made up the teaching staff. Authorities divided the boys' schools into two classes, which taught reading, writing, and catechism during the first year and Russian grammar, arithmetic, geography, church history, and French during the second year.[84] After this stage in the students' training, the RAC sent some of them to Russia to pursue further studies, whereas others became

FIGURE 12.2.   Group portrait of Russian Orthodox Church clergy with Creole students in Sitka (formerly Novo-Arkhangel'sk). Bishop Vladimir Sokolovskii (*center, wearing black hat*), between 1888–1891. Photo courtesy of Alaska State Library, Michael Z. Vinokouroff Photograph Collection, P243-1-005.

apprentices and entered the company work force in Russian America. In the girls' schools, the RAC prepared female students for gender-specific tasks, emphasizing good morals, etiquette, and domestic skills.[85] The RAC used this education to turn Creole girls into potential wives for company employees. In an effort to cultivate close ties between Creoles and their Russian "benefactors," these schools not only educated young children, but also fed, clothed, and housed many of them.[86] Although company schools functioned, to some extent, as secular institutions designed to provide the RAC with skilled workers, they also existed to make loyal, Russian-speaking, Orthodox subjects.

Although the number of colonial schools increased and the quality of instruction improved over time, education within Alaska experienced its ups and downs. Captain Golovin wrote that until 1820 the school in Novo-Arkhangel'sk was in "deplorable condition."[87] In March 1827, when the main office decided to stop dispatching children to Russia, they instructed the governor general to improve the quality of the colonial schools and increase the number of teachers there. They proposed that the schools use naval officers and navigators operating in Russian America to teach science and navigation.[88] In 1860, under government decree, the RAC reorganized its schools in Alaska, but Russian rule there came to an end in 1867 before the changes could have an appreciable effect.

By the late eighteenth century, HBC employees in Rupert's Land also raised their mixed-heritage children within company trading posts and forts. A few HBC officials, like their contemporaries in the RAC, sent their children, predominantly sons, to England for an education.[89] Although education efforts were inconsistent, it was more likely for the children of HBC employees to receive some degree of schooling at the company's forts, especially during the winter months.[90] The London Committee of the HBC sent textbooks to Canada and sought to teach company offspring reading, writing, arithmetic, and basic principles of Christianity.[91] To some degree, the HBC wanted to educate their male children in order to train lower-ranking officials and supply the company with semi-skilled, locally born employees.[92] Company officials groomed their mixed-race daughters, meanwhile, to be the wives of incoming junior officers.[93]

Once Creoles received an education, the RAC still had to ensure that they remained in Alaska to work for the company. Company charters imposed by the Russian government assisted this effort. The 1821 RAC charter stated that children who received an education at the company's expense "must agree to serve in the colonies for at least ten years. They are to receive appropriate wages and maintenance expenses from the Company. When the set period has expired they may leave the colonies if they desire and be employed elsewhere, depending on their occupations."[94] The 1844 charter increased the Creoles' term of service to fifteen years.[95] The RAC focused their efforts on keeping Creoles active in the work force for as long as possible during their most productive years. This was often a life sentence, because diseases like tuberculosis, smallpox, and influenza claimed most Creoles by their mid-thirties.[96] Once their terms of service ended, surviving Creoles could do as they wished, so long as they were not in debt to the RAC.[97]

The RAC initially found it much easier to acquire those Creole youths who were raised by their fathers in Russian settlements. An 1822 board of directors decree, however, applied company education and service requirements to all Creoles. It directed that "Creoles born of legal marriages who are left without a father, as well as those born of a non-legalized union, are without exception to be educated at the Company's expense,

wherever and however possible."[98] The government later included this
provision in the 1844 company charter.[99] In their search for laborers, the
RAC sought to train and employ all Creoles, even those who resided
within their mother's communities. This policy was yet another way in
which the RAC broke down the traditional family structure of indigenous Alaskans. As a result, many Creoles never learned key elements of
their native relatives' culture, information that would have been immensely helpful once Russian rule came to an end.

Conclusion

The Creoles of Russian America were similar to the people of mixed European and American ancestry born during the early years of New France
and those born to HBC employees in the eighteenth and nineteenth centuries. French trappers gave their mixed-race children French names, and
by the 1660s governing officials considered them to be French, so long as
they were baptized.[100] These children then came to view themselves as
French or Indian, and depending on which parent had the dominant role
in raising them, identified with one parent's identity or the other.[101] A century later, a similar trend occurred when HBC employees sought to raise
their children as British subjects within the confines of company trading
posts. Thus, these Scottish and English fathers also played a large role in
determining their children's identities.[102]

This paternal involvement was also the case in the larger Russian
settlements, such as Novo-Arkhangel'sk, where Creoles saw themselves
as Russians because of their religion, education, names, language, and
social class. Meanwhile, those Creoles who lived in trading posts with a
more limited Russian presence had an easier time in remaining members
of their mother's communities. Perhaps if the Russians had stayed in
Alaska for a longer period of time, and had not sold the colony to the
United States in 1867, the Creoles might have developed their own identity. The United States, however, did not recognize mixed-race groups
and considered the Creoles as either whites or Indians.[103]

When the RAC decided to use the Creoles as a labor force, every aspect
of their lives became subject to company control. This politicization took
place because the Russians wanted to ensure that the Creole population
continued to both grow and loyally serve the RAC. The Russians, who before the early 1800s had not paid much attention to the Creoles, took

control of their marriages, living patterns, and upbringing. By exercising this control, they implanted Russian names, language, laws, and Orthodox Christianity on their new subjects. Attempts at integrating the Creoles into the Russian Empire influenced their identity and heightened their status as go-betweens. As mixed-race children in North America, some Creoles acted as culture brokers and operated in both Russian and Aleut/Alutiiq/ Tlingit worlds, whereas others identified with one group over the other.

Notes

I would like to thank the Woodrow Wilson International Center for Scholars, which granted me a residential fellowship that enabled me to conduct research at the Library of Congress during September and October 2008.

1. "The Charter of the Russian American Company, Granted by Imperial Decree of Emperor Paul I [8 July 1799]," in *Russian American Colonies, 1798–1867*, 12.

2. Golovin, *End of Russian America*, 13, 31.

3. In 1791, after an earthquake destroyed much of the original settlement, Aleksandr Baranov moved the Kodiak settlement to Pavlovskaia Gavan' (Paul's Harbor).

4. For recent works on Russian–Tlingit relations, see Kan, *Memory Eternal*; and Grinev, *Tlingit Indians in Russian America*.

5. Black, *Atka*, 81; Gibson, *Imperial Russia in Frontier America*, 9; and Forsyth, *History of the Peoples of Siberia*, 151–53.

6. Black, *Atka*, 78.

7. Ibid., 77.

8. Black, *Russians in Alaska*, 127.

9. Shelikhov, *Voyage to America*, 128.

10. Veniaminov, *Notes on the Islands of the Unalashka District*, 250–57; Black, *Atka*, 85–87; and Forsyth, *History of the Peoples of Siberia*, 151–53.

11. Golovin, *End of Russian America*, 22.

12. Von Langsdorff, *Voyage Around the World*, 35.

13. Ibid., 37.

14. Black, *Atka*, 78.

15. Von Langsdorff, *Voyage Around the World*, 29.

16. Crowell et al., *Looking Both Ways*, 32, 89.

17. Ibid., 60.

18. Sarafian, "Russian-American Company," 199–203.

19. Kan, *Memory Eternal*, 95–96.

20. Federova, *Russian Population in Alaska and California*, 155.

21. Okun, *Russian-American Company*, 162.

22. Sarafian, "Russian-American Company," 47.

23. Davydov, *Two Voyages to Russian America*, 82.

24. Ibid., 82, 86.

25. Ibid., 87, 88.

26. The *Elizaveta* sank on 19 December 1805. Many other Russian vessels suffered the same fate. See Gideon, *Round the World Voyage*, 95.

27. Von Langsdorff, *Voyage around the World*, 136; Gideon, *Round the World Voyage*, 132; and Khlebnikov, *Khlebnikov Archive*, 161.

28. Luehrmann, *Alutiiq Villages under Russian and U.S. Rule*, 117.

29. Black, *Russians in Alaska*, 215.

30. Nikolai Rezanov, quoted in Khlebnikov, *Colonial Russian America*, 48.

31. Federova, *Russian Population in Alaska and California*, 165.

32. Tikhmenev, *History of the Russian-America Company*, 446.

33. Harris, *Reluctant Land*, 52.

34. Dickason, "From 'One Nation,'" 21.

35. Ibid., 22–23; and Brown, *Strangers in Blood*, 4.

36. Dickason, "From 'One Nation,'" 21.

37. Governor-General Hagemeister to Russian American Company Main Office, 7 March 1818, in *Russian-American Company: Correspondence of Governors*, 44.

38. "A Personal Imperial Ukaz from Alexander I to the Senate Renewing Privileges of the Russian American Company and Approving Regulations for its Activities [13 September 1821]," in *Russian American Colonies, 1798–1867*, 360.

39. Khlebnikov, *Colonial Russian America*, 45.

40. "A Personal Imperial Ukaz from Alexander I . . . ," in *Russian American Colonies, 1798–1867*, 360.

41. Khlebnikov, *Colonial Russian America*, 46.

42. Golovin, *End of Russian America*, 141.

43. Ibid., 17.

44. Easley, "Demographic Borderlands," 73.

45. Easley used this term to refer to people of mixed English and Native American ancestry.

46. Ibid., 87.

47. Ibid., 86.

48. Ibid., 77, 88.

49. Ibid., 87.

50. As the Russian Orthodox Church was a branch of government, all legal marriages took place within the church.

51. Arkhimandrite Ioasaf to Shelikhov, 18 May 1795, in Pierce and Donnelly, *History of the Russian American Company*, 2:77.

52. Ibid., 2:81.

53. Ibid.

54. Gideon, *Round the World Voyage*, 117.

55. Sitka Matrimony, D398, reel 256, and Atka Matrimony, D39, reel 256, both in Russian Orthodox Church in Alaska, Library of Congress.

56. See Russian Orthodox Church in Alaska, Library of Congress, under headings "Matrimony Regulations" (D92 and D404) and "Cases" (D49, D248, and D327).

57. Lincoln, *Nicholas I*, 239. Nicholas I ruled 1825–1855.

58. Easley, "Demographic Borderlands," 74.

59. Van Kirk, *"Many Tender Ties,"* 28–29; de Laguna, *Under Mount Saint Elias*, 490; and Veniaminov, *Notes on the Islands of the Unalashka District*, 194.

60. Dickason, "From 'One Nation,'" 23.

61. Brown, *Strangers in Blood*, 4.

62. Dickason, "From 'One Nation,'" 28.

63. Van Kirk, *"Many Tender Ties,"* 4, 34–35.

64. Kamenskii, *Tlingit Indians of Alaska*, 33; and Dauenhauer and Dauenhauer, *Haa Kusteeyi*, 5–6.

65. Von Langsdorff, *Voyage Around the World*, 42.

66. Hans, *Russian Tradition in Education*, 8; and Edwards, "Count Joseph Marie de Maistre," 55.

67. Van Stone, *Russian Exploration in Southwest Alaska*, 8; and Michael, *Lieutenant Zagoskin's Travels in Russian America*, 9.

68. Main Office to Governor General Muraviev, 16 August 1820, Correspondence of the Governors General . . . , Russian American Company Documents, vol. 2, National Archives, Washington, DC.

69. Ibid.

70. Michael, *Lieutenant Zagoskin's Travels in Russian America*, 8–10.

71. Main Office to Governor General Baranov, 4 February 1817, Correspondence of the Governors General . . . , Russian American Company Documents, vol. 1, National Archives, Washington, DC.

72. "Instructions from the Main Administration of the Russian American Company to Aleksandr A. Baranov Concerning Education for Creoles [22 March 1817]," in *Russian American Colonies, 1798–1867*, 244.

73. Von Langsdorff, *Voyage around the World*, 42.

74. Khlebnikov, *Colonial Russian America*, 49.

75. Litke, *Voyage around the World 1826–1829*, 74.

76. Ibid.

77. Khlebnikov, *Colonial Russian America*, 49.

78. Main Office to Governor General Muraviev, 25 August 1820, Correspondence of the Governors General . . . , Russian American Company Documents, vol. 2, National Archives, Washington, DC.

79. Khlebnikov, *Colonial Russian America*, 49.

80. Ibid.

81. Ibid., 50.

82. "Instructions from the Main Administration of the Russian American Company . . . ," in *Russian American Colonies, 1798–1867*, 244.

83. Khlebnikov, *Colonial Russian America*, 50.

84. Gideon, *Round the World Voyage*, 74.

85. De Madariaga, "Foundation of Russian Educational System, 379.

86. Von Langsdorff, *Voyage Around the World*, 42.

87. Golovin, *End of Russian America*, 57.

88. Main Office to Governor General Chistiakov, 31 March 1827, Correspondence of the Governors General . . . , Russian American Company Documents, vol. 5, National Archives, Washington, DC.

89. Brown, *Strangers in Blood*, 156; and Van Kirk, "*Many Tender Ties*," 96.

90. Brown, *Strangers in Blood*, 163.

91. Van Kirk, "*Many Tender Ties*," 103.

92. Brown, *Strangers in Blood*, 79, 164.

93. Van Kirk, "*Many Tender Ties*," 108.

94. "A Personal Imperial Ukaz from Alexander I . . . ," in *Russian American Colonies, 1798–1867*, 360.

95. "From the Renewal of the Charter of the Russian American Company: The Russian Orthodox Church and to the Russian and Non Russian Inhabitants of the Russian American Colonies [11 October 1844]," in *Russian American Colonies, 1798–1867*, 469.

96. Golovin, *End of Russian America*, 17.

97. Most RAC employees, whether Russian, Creole, or Aleut, were heavily in debt. To cover their cost of living, employees received company credit to cover the purchase of clothing, footwear, and foodstuffs. This debt was then deducted from their low annual wages. In 1833 the RAC cancelled all Creoles' debt and after that would not give them credit (Sarafian, "Russian-American Company," 47, 138).

98. Khlebnikov, *Colonial Russian America*, 45.

99. "A Personal Imperial Ukaz from Alexander I . . . ," in *Russian American Colonies, 1798–1867*, 361.

100. Dickason, "From 'One Nation,'" 26.

101. Ibid., 29, 31.

102. Brown, *Strangers in Blood*, 79, 158.

103. Peterson and Brown, "Introduction," in Peterson and Brown, *New Peoples*, 5.

Works Cited

Archival Sources

Washington, DC
    Library of Congress. Manuscript Division.
        Russian Orthodox Church in Alaska.
            Atka Matrimony, reel 256. D39.
            "Cases." D49, D248, and D327.
            "Matrimony Regulations." D92 and D404.
            Sitka Matrimony, reel 256. D398.

National Archives.
Correspondence of the Governors General, Communications Received and Communications Sent. Vols. 1, 2, and 5. Russian American Company Documents, 1802–1867.

Published Sources

Black, Lydia T. *Atka: An Ethnohistory of the Western Aleutians*. Edited by Richard A. Pierce. Kingston, ON: Limestone Press, 1984.

―――. *Russians in Alaska, 1732–1867*. Fairbanks: University of Alaska Press, 2004.

Brown, Jennifer S. H. *Strangers in Blood: Fur Trade Company Families in Indian Country*. Vancouver: University of British Columbia Press, 1980.

Crowell, Aron L., Amy F. Steffian, and Gordon L. Pullar, eds. *Looking Both Ways: Heritage and Identity of the Alutiiq People*. Fairbanks: University of Alaska Press, 2001.

Dauenhauer, Nora Marks, and Richard Dauenhauer, eds. *Haa Kusteeyí, Our Culture: Tlingit Life Stories*. Seattle: University of Washington Press, 1994.

Davydov, G. I. *Two Voyages to Russian America, 1802–1807*. Translated by Colin Bearne. Edited by Richard A. Pierce. Kingston, ON: The Limestone Press, 1977.

De Laguna, Frederica. *Under Mount Saint Elias: The History and Culture of the Yakutat Tlingit*. Vol. 7, part 1, *Smithsonian Contribution to Anthropology*. Washington, DC: Smithsonian Institution Press, 1972.

De Madariaga, Isabel. "The Foundation of the Russian Educational System by Catherine II." *The Slavonic and East European Review* 57, no. 3 (July 1979): 369–95.

Dickason, Olive Patricia. "From 'One Nation' in the Northeast to 'New Nation' in the Northwest: A Look at the Emergence of the Métis." In Peterson and Brown, *New Peoples*, 19–36.

Easley, Roxanne. "Demographic Borderlands: People of Mixed Heritage in the Russian American Company and the Hudson's Bay Company, 1670–1870." *Pacific Northwest Quarterly* 99, no. 2 (Spring 2008): 73–91.

Edwards, David W. "Count Joseph Marie de Maistre and Russian Educational Policy, 1803–1828." *Slavic Review* 36, no. 1 (March 1977): 54–75.

Fedorova, Svetlana G. *The Russian Population in Alaska and California, Late 18th Century–1867*. Translated and edited by Richard A. Pierce and Alton S. Donnelly. Kingston, ON: Limestone Press, 1973.

Forsyth, James. *A History of the Peoples of Siberia: Russia's North Asian Colony, 1581–1990*. New York, NY: Cambridge University Press, 1992.

Gibson, James R. *Imperial Russia in Frontier America: The Changing Geography of Supply of Russian America, 1784–1867*. New York, NY: Oxford University Press, 1976.

Gideon, Hieromonk. *The Round the World Voyage of Hieromonk Gideon 1803–1809*. Translated by Lydia T. Black. Kingston, ON: The Limestone Press, 1989.

Golovin, Captain P. N. *The End of Russian America: Captain P. N. Golovin's Last Report 1862*. Translated by Basil Dmytryshyn and E. A. P. Crownhart-Vaughan. Portland: Oregon Historical Society Press, 1979.

Grinev, Andrei Val'terovich. *The Tlingit Indians in Russian America, 1741–1867*. Translated by Richard L. Bland and Katerina G. Solovjova. Lincoln: University of Nebraska Press, 2005.

Hans, Nicholas. *The Russian Tradition in Education*. London, UK: Routledge and Kegan Paul, 1963.

Harris, Cole. *The Reluctant Land: Society, Space, and Environment in Canada before Confederation*. Vancouver: University of British Columbia Press, 2008.

Kamenskii, Archimandrite Anatolii. *Tlingit Indians of Alaska*. Translated by Sergei Kan. Fairbanks: University of Alaska Press, 1985.

Kan, Sergei. *Memory Eternal: Tlingit Culture and Russian Orthodox Christianity through Two Centuries*. Seattle: University of Washington Press, 1999.

Khlebnikov, Kyrill T. *Colonial Russian America: Kyrill T. Khlebnikov's Reports, 1817–1832*. Translated by Basil Dmytryshyn and E.A.P. Crownhart-Vaughan. Portland: Oregon Historical Society Press, 1976.

———. *The Khlebnikov Archive: Unpublished Journal (1800–1837) and Travel Notes (1820, 1822, and 1824)*. Edited by Leonid Shur. Translated by John Bisk. Fairbanks: University of Alaska Press, 1990.

Lincoln, W. Bruce. *Nicholas I: Emperor and Autocrat of All the Russias*. Bloomington: Indiana University Press, 1978.

Litke, Frederic. *A Voyage around the World 1826–1829*. Edited by Richard A. Pierce. Kingston, ON: Limestone Press, 1987.

Luehrmann, Sonja. *Alutiiq Villages under Russian and U.S. Rule*. Fairbanks: University of Alaska Press, 2008.

Michael, Henry N., ed. *Lieutenant Zagoskin's Travels in Russian America, 1842–1844: The First Ethnographic and Geographic Investigations in the Yukon and Kuskokwim Valleys of Alaska*. Toronto, ON: University of Toronto Press, 1967.

Okun, S. B. *The Russian-American Company*. New York, NY: Octagon Books, 1979.

Peterson, Jacqueline, and Jennifer S. H. Brown, eds. *The New Peoples: Being and Becoming Métis in North America*. Winnipeg: University of Manitoba Press; Lincoln: University of Nebraska Press, 1985.

Pierce, Richard A., and Alton S. Donnelly, eds. *A History of the Russian American Company*, vol. 2. Translated by Dmitri Krenov. Kingston, ON: The Limestone Press, 1979.

The Russian American Colonies, 1798–1867: A Documentary Record (Volume Three to Siberia and Russian America, Three Centuries of Russian Eastward Expansion). Edited and translated by Basil Dmytryshyn, E.A.P. Crownhart-Vaughan, and Thomas Vaughan. Portland: Oregon Historical Press, 1989.

The Russian-American Company: Correspondence of the Governors Communication Sent: 1818. Translated by Richard A. Pierce. Kingston, ON: Limestone Press, 1984.

Sarafian, Winston Lee. "Russian-American Company Employees Policies and Practices, 1799–1867." PhD diss., University of California, Los Angeles, 1971.

Shelikhov, Grigorii I. *A Voyage to America, 1783–1786*. Translated by Marina Ramsay. Edited by Richard A. Pierce. Kingston, ON: The Limestone Press, 1981.

Tikhmenev, Petr Aleksandrovich. *A History of the Russian-American Company*. Vol. 1. Translated and edited by Richard A. Pierce and Alton S. Donnelly. Seattle: University of Washington Press, 1978.

Van Kirk, Sylvia. *"Many Tender Ties": Women in Fur-Trade Society, 1670–1870*. Norman: University of Oklahoma Press, 1983.

Van Stone, James, ed. *Russian Exploration in Southwest Alaska: The Travel Journals of Peter Korsakovskiy (1818) and Ivan Ya. Vasilev (1829)*. Translated by David H. Kraus. Fairbanks: University of Alaska Press, 1988.

Veniaminov, Ivan. *Notes on the Islands of the Unalaska District*. Translated by Lydia T. Black and R. H. Geoghegan. Edited by Richard A. Pierce. Kingston, ON: Limestone Press, 1984.

Von Langsdorff, Georg Heinrich. *Remarks and Observations on a Voyage around the World from 1803–1807*. Translated by Victoria Joan Moessner. Edited by Richard A. Pierce. Fairbanks, AK: Limestone Press, 1993.

13

Settling for Community?

Juridical Visions of Historical Metis Collectivity in and after *R. v. Powley*

CHRIS ANDERSEN

In *R. v. Powley* (2003), the Supreme Court of Canada (SCC) modified the test for section 35 aboriginal rights,[1] as set out in the 1996 *Van der Peet* decision,[2] to account for the Métis' supposedly unique "post-contact" origins. The *Powley* decision[3] recognized rights for the claimants in upper Great Lakes Métis communities (an important distinction from the "people" recognized in section 35 of the Constitution Act, 1982). In the decision, in fact, the court differentiated between at least three legal entities: the individual(s) who claimed the right; the site-specific communities within whom those rights are held under section 35 case law; and the peoples detailed in section 35 with whom those communities are presumably vested (though the *Powley* court stated that it "would not presume to enumerate"[4]). Like most decisions on aboriginal rights, the Supreme Court of Canada's final decision was not the result of mere contemplation or the dry attachment of facts to principles. Instead, it delved into the complex histories of the nineteenth-century upper Great Lakes society and bore legal witness to the demise of its fur trade communities. Like most Supreme Court of Canada decisions, however, its effects rippled far beyond the waters of the upper Great Lakes.

The *Powley* decision was, like all aboriginal rights cases that come before the Canadian courts, fundamentally enmeshed in complex webs of meaning, power, and, perhaps most relevantly to our present discussion, history. Legal scholarship advises us, however, that law is not necessarily a constructive forum for understanding historical nuance or complexity.[5] At one level, the central role of law in Canada's colonialism enormously complicates the recognition of indigenous historical accounts that clash with accepted legal orthodoxy. More technically, legal advocates tend to emphasize narrative elements favorable to their arguments while marginalizing or disregarding others that are not: this allows little purchase for shading or fine distinction. Likewise, a juridical desire for neat, ordered classifications attached to rules for how to distinguish those classifications leaves little ability for the law to handle contextual specificity or even the incompleteness of existing historical records. Law, in Canadian Supreme Court Justice Ian Binnie's words, "sees a finality of interpretation of historical events where finality, according to the professional historian, is not possible."[6]

However, courts do not simply require finality where none exists for the professional historian; rather, they manufacture one finality at the expense of others. Thus, if this were simply a matter of acknowledging that historians produce narratives and interpretation according to one set of disciplinary conventions and prescriptions and legal actors according to another, we might settle the matter by simply agreeing to disagree. However, the meanings and power of legal edicts and findings are never exhausted by their localized juridical application, nor can their broader legitimacy and impact be explained by the mere weight of their logic. Courts operate as a powerful field of knowledge production[7] that, given their tremendous symbolic power in Canadian society, accords them a broader cultural power (though, of course, not a monopoly) outside the juridical field to shape our understandings about who we are and how we relate to others. It does so in ways that are not readily recognizable as juridical yet, nonetheless, order the world according to norms and discourses produced in juridical arenas.[8]

Part of courts' broader legitimacy and distinctiveness as sites of knowledge production stems from their relative autonomy from society and other public sites of knowledge production and from their ability to surreptitiously draw on non-legal concepts and categories while naturalizing them juridically as their own (and vice versa). Courts operate as mediums of social and political struggle between legal actors who, invested with specific technical competencies, struggle according to distinctive and highly specialized methods to determine the very "stuff" of law.[9] These technical competencies and their associated labor require and produce a powerful forum through which the vagaries and various irrelevancies of social events are translated into legally relevant accounts.[10] Indeed, juridical translation of social events or concepts and their subsequent naturalization as universal or acontextual constitutes one of law's most powerful tools for playing its (often central) part in ordering social reality. One element of Métis collectivity lost in translation to section 35 court cases is an understanding of the *political* character of our historical social relations. Another is law's power to emphasize these historical realities as templates for *contemporary* use and occupancy modalities.

The conceptual thrust of this chapter lies in its discussion of the juridical translation of historical "aboriginal" communities into the seemingly familiar (yet nonetheless limiting) notions of juridical community. This discussion is animated by a single question: how do we make sense of *community* in ways that capture the distinctive features of historical Métis communities, particularly in relation to their mobility, while demonstrating the problems of attempting to reduce contemporary Métis polities to these historical modalities? Although community can mean many things, its typical juridical definition under section 35 shears it of much of its complexity. In this chapter, I explore this translative tension in four parts. Part one briefly explains the positioning and usage of the courts in terms of their *translative* power. This concept is particularly important for understanding how legal actors (particularly judges) manage the flow of information and expertise into—and out of—the juridical forum. Part two explores the meanings of community produced in *Powley* by paying particular attention to its conceptual differentiation from other, equally plausible forms of collectivity. Part three denaturalizes these juridically produced meanings to demonstrate their fundamental anchorage in western notions of agrarian land use and site-specificity. It details both the philosophical and juridical history of section 35 positioning in this context, and it offers a concept of community that is linked instead to webs of attachment (with both kinship and economic bases), the circulation of collective symbols and meanings, and the importance of social capital. Part four explores the meanings of community in the section 35 Métis harvesting cases produced in *Powley*'s wake. Although these decisions appear increasingly sensitive to the specificity of Métis historical land use and occupancy, they nonetheless remain wedded to settlement-based notions of community. The chapter concludes by exploring the ways in which use and occupancy modalities of thought emaciate more politically oriented understandings of territory.

Courts as Translators

In her classic contribution to the field of legal feminism, Carol Smart tells us that law's power lies not merely in its material effects (i.e., in its judgments), but additionally in its ability to produce its own legally relevant descriptions about non-legal social accounts in ways that "prune" and, in doing so, simplify the numerous elements deemed important to those originally involved in them.[11] Along these same lines, Robert Van Krieken suggests that law's power stems from its ability to either discount alternative conceptions of reality or reframe them, in juridical terms, without acknowledging the contextual specificity of such non-legal accounts in place prior to their conversion.[12] Furthermore, William Felstiner, Richard Abel, and Austin Sarat emphasize the importance of lawyers as gatekeepers in determining the suitability of transforming certain social events into juridically relevant grievances for which causes can be ascertained and remedies sought (and, likewise, determining which are best left outside the field).[13] In his work, Pierre Bourdieu points out the power of professional, specialized legal actors "to manipulate legal aspirations—to create them in certain cases, to amplify them or discourage them in others."[14]

Their disparate empirical subject matter notwithstanding, Smart, Van Krieken, Felstiner et al., and Bourdieu are each speaking to a crucial element of law's power in contemporary societies: its ability to *translate* social accounts into legal ones. The coupling of their translative power with their broader legitimacy affords Canadian courts not only an opportunity to package their knowledge for consumption as "truth" by non-legal actors, but also discretion as to what this truth will consist of. In an aboriginal rights context, these truths are bound up in complex ways with national narratives of the past and with memory more generally. Nancy Wood speaks of law as a privileged "site of memory," and Luke McNamara argues that juridical decisions amount to an endorsement of one collective understanding of memory over another.[15] In either case, historical discourses produced in juridical forums often radiate out to other arenas of social and political struggle, such as those of census takers, policymakers, educators, and popular discussion, to name but a few.

Juridical outcomes are the result of internal struggles between competing legal actors for the right to determine law's substance in any given
instance.[16] Bourdieu argues that the juridical field[17] is a site of ordered
competition between hierarchically organized legal actors who believe
deeply in the validity and effectiveness of law and who compete by using
the technical competencies "attached" to their (dis)positions. In this understanding of the courts, we may see how—despite the legitimacy that academic experts bring from their own disciplines (e.g., history, anthropology,
geography)—their arguments, positions, or logics are not easily, straight-
forwardly, or necessarily converted into juridically relevant accounts.
Indeed, Carole Smith argues that although the use of non-legal experts is
a growing reality of modern courts, legal actors (especially judges) "keep
them firmly in their place by negotiating and controlling the importation
of expert knowledge in particular cases."[18] In a similar manner, Van
Krieken suggests that, at least in the Australian courts, academic history
is often relegated to background knowledge from which justices may pick
and choose at their leisure.

Expert witnesses involved in Aboriginal rights litigation in Canada
have noted with some acerbity how the complexity of Aboriginal history is
simplified and distorted in its often rough journey into juridical discourse.
Arthur J. Ray argues, for example, that although the ostensible role of the
expert witness is to "provide the court . . . with knowledge that lies beyond
the realm of ordinary judgment and experience,"[19] in practice, opposing
legal actors use their own expert witnesses to challenge (as required) the
lines of evidence presented by opposing expert reporting and testimony.
Frank Tough argues that in this way court cases bring to light sharply contrasting understandings of the past: "The viability of contrasting historical
interpretations is put to a real test by the adversarial system."[20] Because
academic scholars hold different—often conflicting—historical accounts,
this disparity is often brought starkly to light in the adversarial system of
the Canadian courts, wherein judges, not non-legal experts, decide on the
relevancy of historical evidence to the legal issues before the court and,
thus, consecrate one understanding of the past at the expense of others.

Although such relegation or downgrading of academic knowledge
may constitute conscious attempts on the part of court justices to "keep
experts in their place," they are equally likely to be the simple result
of how law is structured; that is, academic accounts of history are often
secondary to precedent, a primary element of common law. Indeed,

Tough argues that non-legal evidence or expert opinion rarely figures conspicuously in the final decision. Justices may pick and choose from the reports and testimony as they please (and as it "feels" correct according to their professional habitus)—a power that holds important consequences for how the notion of "community," as enunciated in expert reports or testimony, is (or is not) eventually translated and woven into juridical decisions.

Rights-Bearing "Community" in *R. v. Powley*

R. v. Powley (2003) constituted the first section 35 Aboriginal-rights case pertaining to Métis to come before the SCC. Of the numerous elements that comprised the *Powley* court's definition of community, three are of particular relevance to the discussion here: distinctiveness, continuity and stability, and geographical proximity. Examining them last to first, *Powley's* vision of relevant geographical boundaries of a contemporary "rights-bearing" community defined it variously in the context of the municipality of Sault Ste. Marie;[21] "in the Sault Ste. Marie area";[22] "in and around Sault Ste. Marie";[23] and "in the environs of Sault Ste. Marie."[24] As I show below, such characterizations of a rights-bearing community are standard manifestations of "use and occupancy"-based notions of aboriginal rights-bearing communities. Although such use-and-occupancy notions appear natural or normal, they are in fact rooted in European-based notions of appropriate (and thus legally relevant) usage.

Although the *Powley* court also noted the emergence of "a distinctive Métis community . . . in the Upper Great Lakes region in the mid-17th century . . . [that] peaked around 1850,"[25] it avoided any possible implications of the geographically broader underpinnings of such a vision of community. Instead, it argued that "It is not necessary for us to decide, and we did not receive submissions on, whether this community is also a Métis 'people,' or whether it forms part of a larger Métis people that extends over a wider area such as the Upper Great Lakes"—though as I demonstrate in the conclusion, this is not entirely correct.[26] Nonetheless, Sault Ste. Marie was itself positioned as "one of the oldest and most important [Métis settlements] in the upper lakes area."[27] Geographical delimitation (i.e., settlement) was, for the *Powley* court, a major differentiating element between a "community" and a "people" and one that, though largely beyond the scope of this chapter, holds important consequences for how we position the relationship between Great Lakes communities and those of Red River.[28]

The court also commented on how rights-bearing communities might be differentiated from others, namely, by their continuity and stability. The SCC argued that these elements clustered around a number of important factors: "customs, way of life, and recognizable group identity";[29] "a new culture and a distinctive group identity";[30] "a distinctive collective identity, living together in the same geographic area and sharing a common way of life";[31] and "demographic evidence, proof of shared customs, traditions, and a collective identity."[32] As I explain further in the conceptual discussion around the notion of community, the *Powley* court's "stable community" is a conventional repetition of dated academic literature that emphasizes a narrowly conceived collective identity, distinctive culture/traditions, specific customs, and a recognized way of life, all of which are linked to *geographical proximity*. *Powley*'s emphasis on these characteristics is important not only because it distorts the actual character of many historical Métis communities,[33] but also because it limits the visions of community under which Métis claimants can seek section 35 legal redress today.

So, to sum up thus far: the *Powley* court fashioned a definition of community as conceptually interesting for what it excluded as legally relevant as for what it included. A rights-bearing Métis community under section 35 of the 1982 Constitution Act was thus: cultural rather than political (i.e., it had nothing to do with a collective ability or concern with governing territories, nor even for how settlement-based communities might be understood on a larger, interconnected scale); settlement-oriented rather than territory-oriented (i.e., legally relevant land use was conceived in the context of situated land use, presumably an agrarian context simply transferred to hunting use and occupancy); and contemporarily self-identifying as Métis, but not historically so (the case had no interest in cracking open the "Indian" and "Canadian" categories between which "Métis" communities were supposed to fit).

Although the *Powley* decision is widely viewed as a significant victory for Métis everywhere, and as representing a sea change in the ways that Métis are recognized officially in Canadian society, it nonetheless set into motion visions of Métis community that offer us only a partial glimpse of the circulation of bodies, goods, and meanings that comprised historical communities not only in nineteenth-century upper Great Lakes, but in

the sub-arctic fur trade more generally. In addition, it unnecessarily cal-
cified the kinds of collectivity through which Métis can seek constitutional protection today.

Community-As-Settlement Versus
Community-As-Attachment

Although the *Powley* case demonstrates a conventional juridical emphasis on the relationship between community and geographical proximity
(in the form of settlement), community can reasonably be positioned outside this proximity in the context of webs of attachment through shared
cultural meanings. In this section, I trace the conceptual and philosophical
underpinnings of juridical uses of community in section 35 to the contex-
tually specific instances of British land use. I then offer alternatives to this
construction that better capture historical Métis use and occupancy.

The SCC's logic in the *Powley* case is strongly indebted to the idea
that communities and settlements are largely synonymous—that is, that
communities begin with settlements and radiate outward (lessening
in attachment to the "core" community the farther away they move from
the settlement).[34] In his discussion of regionally based archaeology, John
Carman argues that the term "settlement" is often placed, in juxtaposition
to wilderness and landscape, as "a distinct location, a particular place,
and quite firmly bounded."[35] This notion is not necessarily surprising, he
argues, as many academic disciplines have entangled the idea of settlement "with concepts of domestication, civilization, the taming of the wild,
and the planting of new people in an empty and unused space. In short . . .
it is a very colonialist discourse that the concept of the 'settlement site'
invites us . . . to join."[36] Carman's argument helps us think about how
"settlement" is positioned as a bulwark against the unpredictability and
danger of "wilderness" or nature. This concept is particularly relevant in
the case of so-called New World sites, such as those in indigenous territories now claimed by Canada, and it has manifested itself in historical and
contemporary contexts for rendering harvesting rights claims.

Carman explains, however, that "off-site" archaeology positions settlements more complexly, as specific nodes of density for distinctive and
more geographically disparate patterns of human use and occupancy.
The logical consequence of this model is that "region" (or landscape),
rather than "settlement," may often represent a more appropriate scale

for understanding the specific "activity areas" represented by settlements. People and lives thus existed within a different and broader scope of use and, in some cases (though not necessarily and not always), sustained occupancy. He likewise suggests that an additional consequence of off-site investigation is that "instead of seeing a static concentration of people in the past, what is envisaged is people who are perhaps doing more things at one particular place than another, and spending more time at one place than another, but who are nevertheless generally understood to be constantly on the move."[37] Carman's model requires a replacement of "site" with "place," defined not in terms of fixed space or precise boundaries, but in the meanings accorded to those movements by those making them. This dynamic and deeply interrelational model holds important consequences for how we understand community in its relation to settlement and for how we might see them as related but not necessarily intersecting concepts. Carman concludes by stating that off-site archaeology "frees us from a static vision of people in fixed locations and puts them on the move through time and space."[38]

Though "putting people on the move through time and space" possesses the virtue of fidelity to historical and geographical context, it nonetheless lacks currency in western jurisprudential conceptions of use and occupancy. Various scholars have noted the extent to which the underpinnings of western philosophical thought from the sixteenth century onward denied the legal validity of modes of ownership and occupation favored by indigenous collectivities that did not presuppose or require geographical stillness.[39] Patrick Macklem argues, for example, that theories of property that emphasize the mixing of tracts of land with labor (what he calls "labor theories of property") or "providing sufficient notice" (presumably to others who might wish to invest in the same property), whether through agriculture or the building of settlements (what he calls "notice theories of property"), sit at the heart of the western European notions of legally relevant land use.[40] In turn, these came to dominate international legal norms for binding decisions about the legal availability of land.

In such an idiom, the property claims of highly mobile or seasonal collectivities that failed to follow these tenets tended to remain legally unrecognized by imperial powers. Because such ownership and occupation were understood to be of little legal consequence, associated territories were positioned as *terra nullius* (empty land). Paul Chartrand explains that such philosophical orientations are rooted in figurations of what he terms the "farmyard man" or "peasant standard" of use and occupancy, rooted in the specific context of historical Britain's population density and intensive competition over land. He argues that under such implicit orientations, aboriginal law or custom (and, thus, use and occupancy) is only "recognized and respected when it mirrors the laws or customs of the Crown's non-Aboriginal subjects."[41]

These theories continue to echo in contemporary Canadian Aboriginal site-specific rights law wedded to agrarian-based norms of collectivity, which, though overwhelmingly characteristic of European occupancy from the seventeenth century onward, might have appeared strange to indigenous collectivities living in territories now referred to as North America. Macklem captures this legal incommensurability nicely: "Defining occupancy by European standards of civilization and notice excludes from the outset legal consideration of the fact that many Aboriginal people related and continue to relate to land in ways that defy traditional European understandings of productive use and notice."[42] These orientations and philosophical commitments (whether recognized or not) are alive and well in Canadian court decisions about appropriate and constitutionally protectable indigenous land use.

However, the notion of site-specificity has a surprisingly short jurisprudential pedigree.[43] The justices in *Delgamuukw v. the Queen* (1997) distinguished between the use of land in title and non-title cases, arguing that even in cases where an aboriginal group could not make an argument for title, they might, nonetheless, prove a site-specific right to engage in particular activities. *R. v. Adams* (1996) and *R. v. Coté* (1996), both SCC cases preceding *Delgamuukw*, radically changed the jurisprudential landscape by turning Aboriginal title and rights on their head. Whereas Aboriginal rights were previously understood to stand under title, *Adams* and *Coté* flipped the relationship by arguing that title merely (though importantly) constituted a specific *kind* of right. In this same discussion, they defined for the first time the idea of a "site-specific" right to land use as follows: "An aboriginal practice, custom or tradition entitled to protection as an aboriginal right will frequently be limited to a specific territory or location, *depending on the actual pattern of exercise of such an activity* prior to contact. As such, an aboriginal right will often be defined in site-specific terms, with the result that it can only be exercised upon a specific tract of land."[44] Perhaps equally important, the court argued in *R. v. Adams* (a sister case) that although an aboriginal right might be exercised on a specific tract of land, it cannot be any land, but instead must be on the land in question.[45] In a sense, such thinking cuts to the bone of a section 35 "rights-bearing" community; its endogamous definition and boundaries (whether political or cultural) are of limited legal relevance because it is the community members' actual land-based activities that are legally significant, not the larger political context within which they occur.

Of course, this begs of the question of how we arrived at community as the appropriate lens through which to enforce and "give meat to the bones" of section 35. *R. v Van der Peet* (1996), notorious for its temporal infantilization of aboriginal rights, positioned site-specificity as an integral component of proving that right. However, with due respect to the Supreme Court in *Van der peet*, the decision's logic vacillated between a usage of community, nation, society, and culture as though they represented interchangeable terms for the same underlying concept.[46] Thus, in *Van der Peet* the court laid out a ten-part test to determine claimant eligibility for protection under section 35. The justices argued that "the existence of an aboriginal right will depend entirely on the practices, customs and traditions *of the particular aboriginal community claiming the right*."[47] Likewise, *Van der Peet* suggests that adjudication of rights must take place on a fact-by-fact, case-by-case basis, for "[t]he existence of the right will be specific to each aboriginal community."[48] Fact-by-fact, case-by-case logics make it difficult to sustain broader, regionally based conversations.[49]

Interestingly, because the court failed to explicitly define community, it equally failed to explain what separated it from other forms of collectivity, like society. As we will see, such important distinctions are apparently smoothed over in juridically commonsensical notions of community rooted to localized, site-specific activities. The failure to draw such analytical distinctions, however, becomes more problematic when we move away from settlement-based emphases focused narrowly on certain kinds of use and occupancy, toward a focus on the actual circulation of common meanings and symbols—that is, when we begin to examine community as a form of attachment.

Whereas mid-twentieth-century scholarship on community tended to understand it in terms of fixed locality, locality of social system, and shared sense of identity,[50] more recent scholarship has treated the latter two elements "like a set of points joined by lines, the lines indicating which individuals, groups or institutions interact with one another. *It is a matter for investigation whether or not this network is confined to a particular locality or not.*"[51] In a similar manner, Anthony Cohen (whose *The Symbolic Construction of Community* remains a powerful orienting grammar for such symbolic, meaning-centered and interactive discussions of community) argues that communities exist as such to the extent to which community members feel they hold things in common with other members that differentiate them from outsiders.[52] One concept that is used to make sense of these sinews and allows for conceptual movement beyond geographically constricted models of community is that of social capital.

David Studdert argues that social capital "encompasses norms, relationships, expectations that bind people together within all forms of community and as such, it is predominantly concerned with what creates stable communities and enhances their co-operative capacity."[53] Social capital is crucial for understanding how people understand the intensity of their attachments to others, attachments that are fundamentally linked to the creation of trust, the enforcement of group norms, and the basis of reciprocity central to community.[54] Such high levels of social capital, in the words of Robert Putman, "foster sturdy norms of generalized reciprocity and encourage the emergence of social trust. Such networks facilitate coordination and communication, amplify reputations, and thus allow dilemmas of collective action to be resolved."[55] Putman, in fact, differentiates between bonding social capital (linked to locality) and bridging social capital, meant to encapsulate more socially or geographically far-flung relationships.[56] And, although trust and obligation are important for face-to-face interactions, they are arguably even more important in establishing and maintaining relationships over distances.

European notions of community (or use, or occupancy) were not natural but, rather, were specific to the economic and social relations of seventeenth- and eighteenth-century European village economies.[57] Of course, indigenous ontologies of collectivity simply operated according to different criteria, and their relationship to land reflected this difference. The Royal Commission on Aboriginal Peoples noted the migratory way of life that characterized many aboriginal collectivities, even those who seasonally used and occupied territories in ways that might incidentally have met the approval of European philosophers and laws. East and West Coast societies were ordered in this sense. However, other nations, such as those on the Great Plains, lived distinctively migratory (as opposed to

nomadic) ways of life, even well after the initial arrival of European traders and, later, colonists.[58]

If we understand communities as hinging on the forms of social capital that garner resources, produce trust, establish reciprocity, and rely
on relatively common perceptions of symbols for establishing meaning,
what major sources characterize these social relations? Surely one of the
most powerful forms of internal identification and attachment in communities is the complex forms of kinship/trade relationships that marked
the nineteenth-century fur trade. Like the notion of community more
generally, kinship is part and parcel of the local social systems alluded to
by most community studies scholars, tacitly or not, in their understanding of community boundaries. Rules of kinship are of obvious importance in close-knit communities because they explain the biological relationships between its members, produce prohibitions (or ordinations)
about who can marry whom, set rules for the intergenerational transfer
of property, and, perhaps most important, distinguish us from them and
thus friend from foe.[59] Kinship constituted such a powerful element of
many aboriginal societies that it became inextricably linked to trade;
stable relationships of trust and obligation were produced primarily by
expanding kinship/trading networks. These networks allowed them to
avoid having to trade with strangers.[60] Heather Devine argues, in fact,
that, historically speaking, aboriginal "kin obligations generally superseded other commitments, resulting in social, economic, and political
behaviours that, to the modern observer, may seem at times to be unfair,
counter-productive, and even illogical."[61]

Rogers Brubaker and Frederick Cooper suggest that extended kinship
and trading systems required indigenous communities to operate rela-
tionally.[62] Such systems construed "the social world in terms of degree
and quality of connection among people rather than in terms of categories, groups, or boundaries. Social location is defined in the first instance
in terms of lineages, consisting of the descendents of one ancestor reck-
oned through a socially conventional line."[63] They note that building extensive kinship links demonstrates the "sliding scale" through which
mutual relations of different intensities (and for different purposes)
existed. And although certain "groups" are more closely affiliated than
others (who are similarly affiliated), the very social relations that distinguished them also demonstrated their attachment. Brubaker and Cooper
explain that attempts to mobilize a closely affiliated group against

another could always be upset by countermoves that demonstrated deeper or older genealogical connections: "This practice—and the ever-present possibility of construing relatedness on different levels—fosters relational rather than categorical understandings of social relations."[64]

These societies are "segmented": "Strangers—encountered via trade, migration, or other forms of movement—could be incorporated as fictive kin [i.e., godparents] or more loosely linked to a patrilineage via blood brotherhood."[65] Brubaker and Cooper suggest that migratory societies moved endlessly (though not randomly), and, as such, "traders stretched their kinship relations over space, formed a variety of relationships at the interfaces with agricultural communities, and sometimes developed a linga franca to foster communication across extended networks."[66] Brian Slattery has used the similar term "nested" to help make sense of the ways in which societies like the African Nuer (but also many North American aboriginal collectivities) incorporated strangers into their networks.[67] The point is that the scale of community in these kinds of situations is not usefully explicated in discussions of settlement-based idioms.

Among the most familiar notions of community that extend beyond settlement, fur trade literature has focused on the growth of a fur trade society (both in the Great Lakes and elsewhere), which, following in the footsteps of the early French fur-trading regime, produced distinctive markers distinguishing it from tribal and Euro-Canadian communities. Such factors as intermarriage between French fur traders and indigenous women (and the accompanying set of marriage patterns), visually distinct trading towns that began to dot the lake shores and rivers of the Great Lakes, distinctive occupational cultures attached to those towns and to the region more generally, a mixed-blood population exploding in size between the late seventeenth and early nineteenth centuries, and the changing gender roles of indigenous women all mark the contours of this new communality.[68]

Jacqueline Peterson tells us, however, that the Great Lakes fur trade—and with it its forms of communality—had largely collapsed prior to the mid-nineteenth-century era of Great Lakes treaty-making.[69] This was not the case, however, in the regions west of the Great Lakes on the broad, southern plains of what is now called Manitoba. Thus, the Great Lakes fur trade collapse did not change the fact that fur trading remained a staple feature of life in the territories of (now) western Canada. Historical geographer Frank Tough explains that the regionality of this system was the result of practical attempts to come to grips with the problem of how to transport furs and fur trade goods over a vast network of settlements and waterways. In such a system, he argues, settlements merely signposted the larger transport systems that circulated (mainly Métis) employees and freemen along fur trade corridors.[70]

These settlements were thus both fur trade communities *and* part of a larger fur trade community, either at Hudson's Bay Company (HBC) forts or in freeman settlements. Tough reconstructs, in painstaking detail, the regional flow of labor and commodities in the northern Manitoba fur trade region, for example, from camp to outpost to post to district headquarters.[71] This transportation system connected Red River to subarctic fur districts, and its commodities were transported mainly by Native labor. Likewise, so-called homeguard Indians often resided in communities around the forts, foraging to reduce food costs.[72] Teillet argues that "it is no coincidence that the major Métis settlements were all located at strategic points along these routes and in the wintering sites"[73] and explains further that the largest pockets of contemporary Métis community are situated on these historically strategic locations.

In addition, the plains of western Canada were marked by a growing exploitation of buffalo resources to provide fuel to send employees into regions with little carrying capacity (forcing them to ship their own provisions in the form of pemmican, which contained a large component of buffalo protein). By the middle of the nineteenth century, Red River Métis had exploited this economic niche by leading biannual buffalo hunts.[74] The cessation of the HBC trading monopoly in 1849 also provided a lively cross-border buffalo trade between Red River and St. Paul, Minnesota, and the extensive kinship networks had an economic reach far beyond the confines of Red River.[75]

Teillet nicely captures the centrality of this mobility in an account taken from a Métis memoir of a slice of mid-nineteenth-century Métis life:

We usually left [Red River] for the prairie early in spring, as soon as the grass was long enough for grazing—nippable, as we used to say. We would come back around the month of July, stay at the house one, two or three weeks and leave again, not to return this time until late in autumn. Sometimes we even spent the winter on the prairies. That's what we used to call wintering-over, in a tent, a cabin or a makeshift house on the plain. Normally we went to Wood Mountain, but when the buffalo drew back into the area of Cypress Hills, we followed them. Finally, later on when they took refuge in the rough country of Montana, Wyoming, Nebraska and Colorado, it was along the Missouri River we went to find the few remaining herds. Now that was a great life! *Cré mardi gras!*[76]

Étienne Rivard suggests a gap between how nineteenth-century mapmakers attempted to cartographically "settle" Métis in specific locations and the itinerant practicalities of their lived experiences: official "maps were at odds with the spatial reality of many Red River Métis. Not only was their life on the prairie not yet extinct by the 1870s but, with the bison progressively withdrawing further West, buffalo hunters and traders were left with even less time to farm their lots in Riviére Rouge."[77] We will see the ways in which such complex histories and regional scaling is translated (with uneven effects) in Métis harvesting rights cases.

In the next section, I touch on several notions of community, especially those that cast it in terms of geographical proximity (and its conceptual power in juridically produced understandings of community), but also in terms of the importance of attachments across time and space, through kinship and trade. Although these various constructions of community add valuable conceptual tools to our toolbox for thinking about how historical aboriginal communities made sense of their collective selves and ordered their social worlds, not all are equally valued in juridical discourse.

Juridical Visions of Historical Metis Collectivity after *Powley*

The practical effect of the *Powley* decision has been to let loose a deluge of Métis rights cases in nearly all provincial judicial systems. Court cases in British Columbia, Alberta, Saskatchewan, Manitoba, and Ontario provide a broad base for a discussion about how community has been taken up juridically since *Powley*. For example, although the three cases in British Columbia courts failed to find either a historical or contemporary Métis community, strands of their logic, undisturbed on appeal, appear to have moved the courts' logic toward a more regional and less settlement-based concept of community (in *R. v Willison*). In the 2002 *R. v Howse* case, the courts dismissed the idea that the claimants could claim "all of BC" as their territory by virtue of the nomadic nature of Métis. In *R. v Nunn*, the expert witnesses argued that the Métis had a strong historical presence in the region as "work horses" of the fur trade. As the trade expanded into interior British Columbia, the Métis came with it.[78] The judge ruled that "[t]he evidence of Mr. Nunn and the witnesses he called simply does not support the conclusion that there is a contemporary Métis community in the Okanagan Valley. There may be Métis families residing in the area, but there is no evidence to suggest that any significant number of them actively pursue the Métis way of life, in fact, the evidence is to the contrary."[79]

The most recent case, R. v Willison, originally found evidence of a historical and contemporary Métis community "in the environs of Falkland, BC."[80] With respect to a historical community, the judge found that Métis were an integral component of the brigade system that formed the fur trade in the area, with many fur trade employees marrying local First Nations women. Defining community for the purposes of the case, he stated that although we might look for evidence in a "cluster of dwellings" (i.e., a settlement), we also need to account for the mobility of the Métis.[81] Thus, his definition of the site specific to the facts of the case included the following:

> [T]he "environs of Falkland" for the purposes of understanding Métis life in British Columbia prior to control, but specifically in reference to Falkland, B.C., and specifically having regard to the "focus" of Dr. Angel's evidence, should be understood to include the environs of the Brigade Trail commencing in Fort Kamloops, moving south through the Falkland area itself and then the Okanagan Valley, and continuing south to what is today the US border en route to Fort Okanagan.[82]

The original judge's findings were overturned on appeal. The crown argued in the appeal that no site-specific community existed and that any Métis in the area were there incidental to their involvement in the fur trade. As such, they were "transients" rather than members of a site-specific community.[83] Willison's counsel argued sharply in reply that mobility was a distinctive characteristic of the Métis, and, as such, a purposive interpretation[84] of a rights-bearing community required sensitivity to this fact.[85] Although the appeal court overturned the trial judge, her discussion of community was instructive: "I am persuaded, as submitted by Mr. Willison, that the finding of a Métis community does not require evidence of a 'settlement' in the given area. However, there must be evidence of a community 'on the land.' "[86] Despite this finding, however, the court distinguished it from *Powley* by noting that while Métis were mobile, they maintained connections with, and returned periodically to, the settlement of Sault Ste. Marie: "There was found to be an established community on the site and in the environs of that settlement."[87] Equally important, this passage makes clear the fact that justices are translating non-legal expert evidence into the fabric of their juridical narrative and consistently tying settlements to larger regionality (i.e., that regions must contain settlements), rather than maintaining a fidelity to the expert narratives themselves.

If the courts in British Columbia and New Brunswick failed to find a historical or Métis community, the same cannot be said for Alberta, Saskatchewan, Manitoba, Ontario, or (possibly) Newfoundland and Labrador. In Alberta, the leading case is *R. v Kelley*. From a community standpoint, the trial judge originally found that the defendant had failed to demonstrate the existence of a Métis community in the Hinton area. *Van der Peet* and *Powley*, he suggested, demonstrated that rights were fact-driven and site-specific, and Kelley simply failed to adduce evidence that demonstrated historical settlement. The decision was overturned on appeal, where the appeal court justice decided that although the case was not, strictly speaking, about section 35 rights (because the issues related to an Interim Métis Harvesting Agreement signed with the province of Alberta the year before), he suggested that one could not place "an arbitrary limit on the geographical area which may be encompassed by a harvesting right. Site-specificity is an entirely fact driven determination, which in my view relates to historical antecedents rather than to the identification of a limited locality."[88]

In Saskatchewan, the leading case post-*Powley* is *R. v Laviolette* (2005), in which the court found the existence of a larger regional community in the area where the defendant was charged and, as such, argued that it could not be limited to specific settlements. Instead, these settlements needed to be understood in the context of a larger circulation of goods and kin as part of the historical fur trade. The court concluded that

the evidence led at this trial contains sufficient demographic information, proof of shared customs, traditions and collective identity to support the existence of a regional historic rights-bearing Metis community, which regional community is generally defined as the triangle of the fixed communities of Green Lake, Ile a la Crosse and Lac la Biche and includes all of the settlements within and around the triangle including Meadow Lake.[89]

In Manitoba, the leading case is *R. v Goodon* (2008). Goodon was charged while hunting ducks in southern Manitoba using a harvester's card issued by the Manitoba Métis Federation. Accepting his identification as Métis, the court argued that "[t]he issue in dispute is how the site or area where the right is claimed should be defined."[90] Although Goodon's legal team attempted to characterize the site as the entire (historical) Northwest, the court rejected the reasoning for two reasons. First, it argued that the presented evidence was tied to the region where the hunt took place (i.e., Turtle Mountain in southern Manitoba), and, second, that Turtle Mountain was being positioned as a specific geographical area.[91]

It is interesting that in explaining the existence of a separate historical community (as per *Powley*), the court noted approvingly one of the defendant's expert witnesses who argued that, by the beginning of the nineteenth century, those external to the community began to view them as separate from European and other aboriginal communities. Thus, externally imposed perceptions appear to have played a role in judicial consideration of their historical distinctiveness.[92] The court noted, as well, the extensive evidence of use and occupancy in the region in the larger context of the fur trade. The court clearly envisioned Métis in this case as a mobile, "transient" people, such that settlement-based notions of Métis community made little sense and would have made little sense to their ways of life. The court thus found that:

> The Metis community of Western Canada has its own distinctive identity. As the Metis of this region were a creature of the fur trade and as they were compelled to be mobile in order to maintain their collective livelihood, the Metis "community" was more extensive than, for instance, the Metis community described at Sault Ste Marie in *Powley*. The Metis created a large inter-related community that included numerous settlements located in present-day southwestern Manitoba, into Saskatchewan and including the northern Midwest United States.[93]

And furthermore:

> [w]ithin the Province of Manitoba this historic rights-bearing commu-
> nity includes all of the area within the present boundaries of southern
> Manitoba from the present day City of Winnipeg and extending south
> to the United States and northwest to the Province of Saskatchewan
> including the area of present day Russell, Manitoba. This community
> also includes the Turtle Mountain area of southwestern Manitoba even
> though there is no evidence of permanent settlement prior to 1880. I
> conclude that Turtle Mountain was, throughout much of the nineteenth
> century, an important part of the large Metis regional community.[94]

In Ontario, the *Powley* case is obviously the leading jurisprudence,
although subsequent cases have dealt with the issue of the Interim
Harvesting Agreement negotiated between the Métis Nation of Ontario
(MNO) and the Ontario Ministry of Natural Resources (MNR). In *R. v
Laurin et al.*, the court found that although the MNR disagreed with the
geographical boundaries of the MNO's harvesting areas designated
under the interim agreement, it (the MNR) had tacitly agreed to abide by
MNO boundaries when it signed the agreement (albeit with a two-year
limitation). The court thus stayed the charges against the defendants. The
court was quick to note, however, that it was not tacitly making a finding
that these harvesting areas were the territories of section 35 rights-bearing
Métis communities, only that the Interim Metis Harvesting Agreement
required good faith on the part of the provincial government of Ontario.
We see in this case that the parameters of a rights-bearing community are
no longer up for debate (or, at least, were not under the agreement).

Taken in total, these cases demonstrate that although the material
impact of *Powley* has been uneven, its conceptual impact has been almost entirely uniform. This unevenness is not necessarily unexpected,
given that part of the role of the appeal court is to iron out wrinkles of
logic contained in the lower courts. Yet, remnants of *Powley*'s community-
as-settlement logic—itself the legacy of a much older philosophical
orientation—nonetheless remain invested in these subsequent court
cases. Even in situations where the courts are willing to acknowledge
more regionally based logics, these logics remained pinned to settlements
as bases of that larger regionalism. Which is to say, settlements become a
primary indicator of bounding regionality.

The juridical unwillingness to untie settlement-based understandings of community, even in instances where larger regional depictions are allowed, is based in the more fundamental binaries pointed to by John Carman in the discussion of "civilization" versus "wilderness": one must occupy land in order to use it relevantly.[95] Arthur Ray similarly argues that legal analysis of historical land use and occupancy remains deeply embedded in a so-called nuclear theory, pioneered in U.S. land claim research. Nuclear theory is based, Ray explains, on the assumption that "Indian groups effectively used and occupied only a small portion of their tribal territories. A key related idea was that the boundaries of Indian territories were ill-defined because land-use intensity decreased from the core occupation area to the periphery."[96] He argues that this logic has manifested itself in Canadian court cases through similar assumptions that aboriginal people used only specific sites, regardless of the enormous amount of territory they traveled through to reach those sites or the situational-specific activities that accompany such travels. Hence, even in ostensible victories like *Powley*, use and occupancy are not equally valued concepts—that is, occupancy (rather than mere use) stands as the *real* juridical test of community.

Conclusion

In this chapter I have explored how juridical conceptions of community remain fundamentally tethered to settlement-based understandings reminiscent of historical British use and occupancy. Beginning with an explication of *Powley*'s construction of community as site-specific and its attendant disavowal of regional notions, I anchored this logic in older philosophical understandings of "civilized" land use and occupancy, then tied it into the surprisingly short pedigree of site-specific Canadian juridical understandings of community. From there, several alternatives to settlement-based understandings were explored—specifically, terms of the kinship and trade attachments through which indigenous community might be conceived. Then, a historical/empirical context was provided to give Métis context to these alternatives. Finally, the chapter explored how the case law following *Powley* remains rooted in a hierarchy that privileges occupancy over use, in which community is conflated with settlement.

The summary that ended the previous section emphasized the deeply rooted commitment of existing case law to both agrarian understandings of community and the implicit hierarchy of occupancy over use that grounds them. Although not surprising, such an envisioning of history is disheartening for the extent to which it attempts to fit the square peg of juridical logic into the round hole of historical Métis communality. Indeed, occupancy is used as a convenient substitution for discussions about ownership (a concept that need not require occupancy). These concepts were, as Arthur Ray showed, used to counter politically based accounts by expert witnesses for Indian tribes[97] based on the view that ecological, rather than political, models of use and occupancy were most relevant to tribal claims because " 'primitive' people . . . had not developed notions of territorial (land) ownership."[98]

Although Ray's discussion is clearly describing a vastly different context from the one of interest here, the use-and-occupancy logic that grounds contemporary Canadian juridical conversations about community bears a similarity to the logic discussed half a century earlier. The *Powley* court eschewed any politically rooted arguments about a Métis people that required them to step outside of the plodding, fact-by-fact, case-by-case use and occupancy logic handed down in *Van der Peet*. And although the *Powley* court suggested a lack of "submissions on . . . whether this community is also a Métis 'people,' or whether it forms part of a larger Métis people that extends over a wider area such as the Upper Great Lakes,"[99] it did receive an intervener factum, written for the Congress of Aboriginal Peoples by noted legal scholar Joseph Magnet, which spoke directly to the political context of the *Powley* case with respect to "peoplehood."[100]

In his factum, Magnet made the point, well entrenched in international law, that protecting individual harvesting rights must also be accompanied by larger protections accorded to the community within which that right is vested. And not just any community: "Only communities of sufficient critical mass, communities having the size and characteristics of nationhood, can self govern and determine culture. Local municipal communities are not capable."[101] Magnet argued forcefully that this realization, commonplace in other contexts, should animate the *Powley* court's juridical construction of community.[102] Needless to say, such thinking was not apparent in the final decision. Moreover, his oral argument to this effect was met with surprised chuckling from the Supreme Court justices, one of whom pointed out that even the Powleys' own lawyers did not pursue such an extreme strategy.[103]

In the end, perhaps the important point to take away from this chapter is that although courts operate as privileged sites of translation, their translations are neither neutral nor confined to the factual contexts of the cases themselves. Instead, they assume a broader legitimacy as their logics are reproduced in policy fields, media forums, and, more commonly, layperson palaver. These successive, extra-juridical translations strip them of much of their juridically contextual specificity while concomitantly fixing a broader legitimacy. Thus, a legally translated concept that began in response to a specific fact situation is, through its multiple interpretations by legal and non-legal actors alike, shorn of its partiality and contextuality and imbued with a legitimacy that, with a few notorious exceptions, largely insulates it from broader critique.

Like all forms of social power, however, legal relations do not mirror social realities but, rather, make them up (or at least, refract them in powerful ways that imbue them with the tremendous legitimacy of "truths" constructed in the juridical arena).[104] Moreover, they do so by muscling out (lately, with overwhelming success) competing accounts of social reality, like the mobility-based forms of attachment that characterized historical aboriginal collectivities, or the more politically rooted modalities that presuppose no necessary use and occupancy (e.g., the fact that no one lives on or uses the bottom of "Canada's" lakes or the top of its mountains does not prevent Canada from claiming ownership over them). And although acknowledging and legitimating the dispersed and mobile nature of historical Métis communality is an important middle step for avoiding the tyranny of settlement-based notions of community, it does not go far enough for helping us think about the contemporary or future collectivity of Métis society.

Notes

1. Section 35 of the Constitution Act, 1982, constitutes a dominant lens through which Aboriginal rights jurisprudence is carried out in Canada. Its relevant parts read as follows: "(1) The existing aboriginal and treaty rights of the aboriginal peoples of Canada are hereby recognized and affirmed. (2) In this Act, 'aboriginal peoples of Canada' includes the Indian, Inuit, and Metis peoples of Canada." We will see below that although the Constitution Act explicitly refers to Indian,

Inuit, and Métis peoples, and thus would appear to hold an explicitly political emphasis, much of this has been shorn away by a Supreme Court of Canada conflation of "community" with "settlement."

2. The *Van der Peet* decision (1996) is notorious for its relegation of legally relevant factors of Aboriginality to the pre-contact era, such that all contemporary Aboriginal rights seeking protection under section 35 must be rooted in that era. See Borrows, *Recovering Canada*; and Barsh and Henderson, "Supreme Court's *Van der Peet* Trilogy."

3. The facts of the *Powley* case are fairly straightforward. Steve and his son Roddy Powley shot a moose in the fall of 1993. Returning to their home in Sault Ste. Marie, Ontario, they were visited by game and fish officers who had received an anonymous phone tip that the Powleys had been poaching. A week later they were charged under Ontario's Game and Fish Act with hunting without a valid license and possession of illegally hunted wildlife.

4. *R. v. Powley*, 2003, para. 12.

5. See McNamara, "History, Memory and Judgment"; Ray, "Constructing and Reconstructing Native History"; Tough, "Prof v. Prof"; and Wicken, *Mi'kmaq Treaties on Trial*.

6. Binnie, *R. v. Marshall* 1999: 456 (para. 37); and *R. v. Marshall*, [1999] 3 S.C.R. 456.

7. See Van Krieken, "Law's Autonomy in Action"; and Valverde, *Law's Dream of a Common Knowledge*.

8. See Bourdieu, "Force of Law"; and Smart, *Feminism and the Power of Law*.

9. Bourdieu, "Force of Law."

10. Ibid.; Smart, *Feminism and the Power of Law*; and Van Krieken, "Law's Autonomy in Action."

11. Smart, *Feminism and the Power of Law*, 11.

12. Van Krieken, "Law's Autonomy in Action."

13. Felstiner et al., "Emergence and Transformation of Disputes."

14. Bourdieu, "Force of Law," 833–34.

15. Wood, "Memory on Trial."

16. See Bourdieu, "Force of Law."

17. This notion accords with our understanding of courts but might also, in another analytical context, be conceived of more broadly as including the entire assemblage of legal actors that produce all manner of juridical rulings, including, but in Canada not limited to, the courts, the parliament/legislature, and the executive arenas of social power.

18. Smith, "Sovereign State v. Foucault," 285.

19. Ray, "Native History on Trial," 254.

20. Tough, "Prof v. Prof," 55.

21. *R. v. Powley*, S.C.C. 43 (SCC) (2003), para. 23.

22. Ibid., paras. 6, 39.

23. Ibid., paras. 7, 12, 35.

24. Ibid., para. 19.

25. Ibid., para. 21.

26. Ibid., para. 12.

27. Ibid., para. 21.

28. See Andersen, *"Moya 'Tipimsook."*

29. *R. v. Powley,* para. 8.

30. Ibid., para. 11.

31. Ibid., para. 12.

32. Ibid., para. 23.

33. For example, various authors have noted kinship links between settlements that vastly complicate the Powley court's contemplation of settlement-based notions of community—this is explained in further detail, below.

34. See Ray, "Constructing and Reconstructing Native History."

35. Carman, "Settling on Sites," 21.

36. Ibid., 25.

37. Ibid., 26.

38. Ibid., 29.

39. See Chartrand, *"R. v. Marshall"*; Macklem, *Indigenous Difference and the Constitution*; and Tully, *Discourse on Property.*

40. Macklem, *Indigenous Difference and the Constitution,* 77–81.

41. Chartrand, *"R. v. Marshall,"* 140.

42. Macklem, *Indigenous Difference and the Constitution,* 81.

43. See Burke, "Left Out in the Cold." Jean Teillet notes, for example, that the SCC decision widely viewed as ushering in modern Aboriginal rights litigation, the *Calder* (1973) decision, makes "no requirement for fixed settlements or the use of 'community.'" See Teillet, "Métis of the Northwest," 79; and *Calder v. British Columbia (Attorney General)* S.C.R. 313 (1973).

44. *R. v. Coté,* 3 S.C.R. 139 (1996), para. 39 (emphasis added).

45. *R. v. Adams,* 3 S.C.R. 101 (1996), para. 30.

46. See Andersen, "Residual Tensions of Empire."

47. *R. v. Van der Peet,* 4 C.N.L.R. 177 (1996), para. 69 (emphasis in original).

48. Ibid., para. 69.

49. See Teillet, "Métis of the Northwest."

50. Lee and Newby, *Problem of Sociology,* 57–58.

51. Ibid., 63 (emphasis added).

52. Cohen, *Symbolic Construction of Community,* 12.

53. Studdert, *Conceptualizing Community,* 34.

54. Ibid., 35–36.

55. Putnam, "Bowling Alone," 67.

56. See Putnam, *Bowling Alone.*

57. Lee and Newby, *Problem of Sociology.*

58. See Royal Commission on Aboriginal Peoples (RCAP), *Looking Forward, Looking Back.*

59. See Bocock, "Cultural Formations of Modern Society," 155.

60. See Devine, *People Who Own Themselves*; and Sleeper-Smith, *Indian Women and French Men.*

61. Devine, *People Who Own Themselves*, 16–17.

62. Brubaker and Cooper, "Beyond Identity," 49–51.

63. Ibid., 49.

64. Ibid., 50.

65. Ibid.

66. Ibid., 51.

67. Slattery, "Our Mongrel Selves."

68. See Brown, *Strangers in Blood*; Peterson, "Many Roads to Red River," "Ethnogenesis," and "Prelude to Red River"; Sleeper-Smith, *Indian Women and French Men*; and Van Kirk, *"Many Tender Ties."*

69. Peterson, "Many Roads to Red River."

70. Tough, *"As Their Natural Resources Fail."*

71. Ibid., 45.

72. Ibid., 49–51.

73. Teillet, "Métis of the Northwest," 50.

74. See Gerhard J. Ens, *From Homeland to Hinterland*.

75. See Devine, *People Who Own Themselves*; Foster, *We Know Who We Are*; and Macdougall, *"Wahkootowin."*

76. Charette, *Vanishing Spaces*, 15 (as found in Teillet, "Métis of the Northwest," 45).

77. Rivard, "Colonial Cartography of Canadian Margins," 62.

78. *R. v. Nunn*, unreported, *Provincial Court of British Columbia*, Court File No. 30689H (Penticton) (2003), paras. 15–17.

79. Ibid., para. 32.

80. *R. v. Willison*, B.C.J. No. 924 (BCSC) (2005), para. 44.

81. Ibid., para. 76.

82. Ibid., para. 65.

83. *R. v. Willison*, B.C.J. No. 1505 (2006), para. 22.

84. Purposive reasoning, a rhetorical device constructed in *R. v. Sparrow*, 3 C.N.L.R. 160 (1990), is rooted in the idea that justices must seek to find the underlying purpose of a right.

85. *R. v. Willison* (2006), para. 23.

86. Ibid., para. 24.

87. Ibid., para. 34.

88. *R. v. Kelley*, No. 67 (ABQB) (2007), para. 15. However, see the most recent Alberta-based Métis rights case, *R. v. Hirsekorn* (2010), in which the judge argued that although a Métis community existed in central and northern Alberta, the same could not be said for southern Alberta because, prior to 1874 (the agreed upon date for "effective sovereignty"), the Métis had failed to establish a *settlement* and (thus) demonstrate consistent use and occupancy.

89. *R. v. Laviolette*, SK.P.C. 70 (2005), para. 30.

90. *R. v. Goodon*, MBPC 59 (CanLII) (2008), para. 15.

91. Ibid., paras. 20 and 21, respectively.

92. Ibid., para. 25.

93. Ibid., para. 46.

94. Ibid., para. 48.

95. See Carman, "Settling on Sites."

96. Ray, "Constructing and Reconstructing Native History," 20.

97. Ibid., 21.

98. Ibid., 22.

99. *R. v. Powley*, para. 12.

100. See Congress of Aboriginal Peoples, *Factum of the Intervener.*

101. Ibid., para. 20.

102. Ibid., para. 21.

103. See Supreme Court of Canada, *Oral Arguments in R. v. Powley* (2003), p. 103.

104. See Andersen *"Moya 'Tipimsook."*

Works Cited

Published Sources

Andersen, Chris. *"Moya 'Tipimsook* ('The People Who Aren't Their Own Bosses'): Racialization and the Misrecognition of Métis in Upper Great Lakes Ethnohistory." *Ethnohistory* 58, no. 1 (2011): 37–63.

———. "Residual Tensions of Empire: Contemporary Métis Communities and the Canadian Judicial Imagination." In *Reconfiguring Aboriginal–State Relations. Canada. The State of the Federation, 2003*, edited by M. Murphy, 295–325. Montreal, QC, and Kingston, ON: McGill-Queen's University Press, 2005.

Barsh, Russel, and James Youngblood Henderson. "The Supreme Court's *Van der Peet* Trilogy: Naïve Imperialism and Twisting Ropes of Sand." *McGill Law Journal* 42 (1997): 993–1009.

Bocock, John. "The Cultural Formations of Modern Society." In *Modernity: An Introduction to Modern Societies*, edited by Stuart Hall, David Held, Don Hubert, and Kenneth Thompson, 149–83. Cambridge, UK: Polity Press, 1995.

Borrows, John. *Recovering Canada: The Resurgence of Indigenous Law.* Toronto, ON: University of Toronto Press, 2002.

Bourdieu, Pierre. "The Force of Law: Towards a Sociology of the Juridical Field." *Hastings Law Journal* 38, no. 5 (1987): 814–53.

Brown, Jennifer S. H. "People of Myth, People of History: A Look at Recent Writings on the Métis." *Acadiensis* 17 (Autumn 1987): 150–63.

———. *Strangers in Blood: Fur Trade Company Families in Indian Country.* Vancouver: University of British Columbia Press, 1980.

Brubaker, Rogers, and Frederick Cooper. "Beyond Identity." In *Ethnicity Without Groups*. Cambridge, MA: Harvard University Press, 2004.

Burke, Brian. "Left Out in the Cold: The Problem with Aboriginal Title under Section 35(1) of the *Constitution Act, 1982* for Historically Nomadic Peoples." *Osgoode Hall Law Journal* 38, no. 1 (2000): 1–43.

Carman, John. "Settling on Sites: Constraining Concepts." In *Making Places in the Prehistoric World: Themes in Settlement Archaeology*, edited by J. Bruck & Melissa Goodman, 20–29. London, UK: UCL Press, 1999.

Charette, Guillaume. *Vanishing Spaces: Memoirs of Louis Goulet*. Translated by Ray Ellenwood. Winnipeg, MB: Editions Bois-Brûlés, 1976.

Chartrand, Paul. "*R. v. Marshall; R. v. Bernard:* The Return of the Native." *University of New Brunswick Law Journal* 55 (2006): 135–45.

Cohen, Anthony. *The Symbolic Construction of Community*. London, UK: Tavistock, 1985.

Congress of Aboriginal Peoples. *Factum of the Intervener—Congress of Aboriginal Peoples*. Court File No. C28533, 2001.

Devine, Heather. *The People Who Own Themselves: Aboriginal Ethnogenesis in a Canadian Family, 1660–1900*. Calgary, AB: University of Calgary Press, 2004.

Ens, Gerhard J. *From Homeland to Hinterland: The Changing Worlds of the Red River Metis in the Nineteenth-Century*. Toronto, ON: University of Toronto Press, 1996.

Felstiner, William, Richard Abel, and Austin Sarat. "The Emergence and Transformation of Disputes: Naming, Blaming, Claiming . . ." *Law & Society Review* 15, nos. 3–4 (1980–81): 631–54.

Foster, Martha. *We Know Who We Are: Métis Identity in a Montana Community*. Norman: University of Oklahoma Press, 2006.

Gorham, Harriet. "Families of Mixed Descent in the Western Great Lakes Region." In *Native People, Native Lands: Canadian Indians, Inuit and Métis*, edited by Bruce Cox, 37–55. Carleton Library Series 142. Ottawa, ON: Carleton University Press, 1987.

Lee, David, and Howard Newby. *The Problem of Sociology*. Victoria, Australia: Hutchinson & Co., 1983.

Macdougall, Brenda. "*Wahkootowin:* Family and Cultural Identity in Northwestern Saskatchewan Métis Communities." *Canadian Historical Review* 87, no. 3 (2006): 431–62.

Macklem, Patrick. *Indigenous Difference and the Constitution*. Toronto, ON: University of Toronto Press, 2001.

McNamara, Luke. "History, Memory and Judgment: Holocaust Denial, The History Wars and Law's Problems with the Past." *Sydney Law Review* 26 (2004): 353–94.

McNeil, Kent. *Common Law Aboriginal Title*. Oxford, UK: Clarendon Press; New York, NY: Oxford University Press, 1989.

Peterson, Jacqueline. "Ethnogenesis: The Settlement and Growth of a "New People" in the Great Lakes Region." *American Indian Culture and Research Journal* 6, no. 2 (1982): 23–64.

———. "Many Roads to Red River: Métis Genesis in the Great Lakes Region, 1680–1815." *The New People: Being and Becoming Métis in North America*, edited by Jacqueline Peterson and Jennifer S. H. Brown, 37–71. Winnipeg: University of Manitoba Press, 1985.

———. "Prelude to Red River: A Social Portrait of the Great Lakes Métis." *Ethno-history* 25, no. 1 (1978): 41–67.

Putnam, Robert. "Bowling Alone: America's Declining Social Capital." *Journal of Democracy* 6, no. 1 (1995): 65–78.

———. *Bowling Alone: The Collapse and Revival of the American Community*. New York, NY: Simon & Schuster, 2000.

Ray, Arthur J. "Constructing and Reconstructing Native History: A Comparative Look at the Impact of Aboriginal and Treaty Rights Claims in North America and Australia." *Native Studies Review* 16, no. 1 (2005): 15–39.

———. "Native History on Trial: Confessions of an Expert Witness." *Canadian Historical Review* 84, no. 2 (2003): 253–73.

Rivard, Étienne. "Colonial Cartography of Canadian Margins: Cultural Encounters and the Idea of Métissage." *Cartographica* 43, no. 1 (2008): 45–66.

Royal Commission on Aboriginal Peoples (RCAP). *Looking Forward, Looking Back*. Vol. 1. Canada: Ministry of Supply and Services, 1996.

———. *Restructuring the Relationship*. Vol. 2. Canada: Ministry of Supply and Services, 1996.

Slattery, Brian. "Our Mongrel Selves: Pluralism, Identity and the Nation." In *Community of Right/Rights of the Community*, edited by Ysolde Gendreau, 3–41. Montreal, QC: Éditions Themis, 2003.

Sleeper-Smith, Susan. *Indian Women and French Men: Rethinking Cultural Encounter in the Western Great Lakes*. Amherst: University of Massachusetts Press, 2001.

Smart, Carol. *Feminism and the Power of Law*. New York, NY and London, UK: Routledge, 1989.

———. "The Sovereign State v. Foucault: Law and Disciplinary Power." *The Sociological Review* 48, no. 2 (2000): 283–306.

Studdert, David. *Conceptualizing Community: Beyond the State and Individual*. Hampshire, UK: Palgrave Macmillan, 2005.

Supreme Court of Canada (SCC). *Oral Arguments in R. v. Powley*. Transcription of cassettes, Monday, March 17, 2003. No. 28533.

Teillet, Jean. "The Métis of the Northwest: Toward a Definition of a Rights-Bearing Community for a Mobile People." LLM thesis, University of Toronto, 2008.

Tough, Frank. *'As Their Natural Resources Fail': Native Peoples and the Economic History of Northern Manitoba, 1870–1930*. Vancouver: University of British Columbia Press, 1996.

———. "Prof v. Prof in the Trial of the Benoit Treaty Eight Tax Case: Some Thoughts on Academics as Expert Witnesses." *Native Studies Review* 15, no. 1 (2004): 53–72.

Tully, James. *A Discourse on Property: John Locke and his Adversaries*. Cambridge and New York, NY: Cambridge University Press, 1980.

Valverde, Mariana. *Law's Dream of a Common Knowledge*. Princeton, NJ: Princeton University Press, 2003.

———. "Social Facticity and the Law: A Social Expert's Eyewitness Account of Law." *Social & Legal Studies* 5, no. 2 (1996): 201–17.

Van Kirk, Sylvia. *"Many Tender Ties": Women in Fur Trade Society, 1670–1870.* Winnipeg, MB: Watson and Dwyer, 1980.

Van Krieken, Robert. "Law's Autonomy in Action: Anthropology and History in Court." *Social & Legal Studies* 15, no. 4 (2006): 574–90.

Wicken, William. *Mi'kmaq Treaties on Trial: History, Land, and Donald Marshall Junior.* Toronto, ON: University of Toronto Press, 2002.

Wood, Nancy. "Memory on Trial in Contemporary France: *The Case of Maurice Papon." History and Memory* 11, no. 1 (1999): 41–76.

Court Cases

Calder v. British Columbia (Attorney General). 1973. S.C.R. 313 (BCSC).

Delgamuukw v. the Queen. 1997. 1 C.N.L.R. 14 (SCC).

R. v. Adams. 1996. 3 S.C.R. 101 (SCC).

R. v. Coté. 1996. 3 S.C.R. 139.

R. v. Goodon. 2008. MBPC 59 (CanLII).

R. v. Hirsekorn. 2010. ABPC 385.

R. v. Howse. 2002. B.C.J. No. 379 (B.C.S.C.).

———. 2000. B.C.J. No. 905 (B.C. Prov Ct.).

R. v. Kelley. 2007. No. 67 (ABQB).

———. 2006. No. 353 (APC).

R. v. Laviolette. 2005 SK.P.C. 70.

R. v. Laurin et al. 2007. O.J. No. 2344 (OCJ).

R. v. Marshall. [1999] 3 S.C.R.

R. v. Nunn. 2003. Unreported, *Provincial Court of British Columbia,* Court File No. 30689H (Penticton).

R. v. Powley. 2003. S.C.C. 43 (SCC).

R. v. Sparrow. 1990. 3 C.N.L.R. 160 (SCC).

R. v. Van der Peet. 1996. 4 C.N.L.R. 177 (SCC).

R. v. Willison. 2006. B.C.J. No. 1505 (BCSC).

———. 2005. B.C.J. No. 924 (BC Prov Ct.).

14

THE MYTH OF METIS CULTURAL AMBIVALENCE

BRENDA MACDOUGALL

Ⅰn *A Fair Country*, John Ralston Saul boldly proclaimed, "We are a métis nation."[1] While some Metis may be seduced by this statement—
superficially, at least, it appears to be a positive affirmation of our
identity and history—Saul's declaration really has little to do with us.
Saul was not concerned with Metis history, culture, or nationalism but
instead used the term to advance the argument that politically Canada is
a hybrid of western European and First Nations philosophical traditions.
Although he made reference to seminal figures and events in Metis
history—Metis leaders Louis Riel and Gabriel Dumont as well as the
1885 Resistance when the Metis went to war against Canada—to ground
his notion of Metis-ness in a Canadian-specific historical narrative, he
also asserted that "anyone whose family arrived before the 1760s is probably part Aboriginal."[2] The implication of course is that mixed blood,
mixed ancestry, or just an Indian great-great-great-grandmother is all
that is required to be Metis. We often hear the phrase, "You don't look
like one," or have someone say, "I'm Metis too. My great-great-great-
grandmother was part Indian." Both these types of statements instantly
negate the stories of our families, the histories of our communities, and
the authenticity of our aboriginality, reducing us to an in-between, in-
complete, "not-quite-people" who are stuck somewhere on the outside of

the discourse. However unintended, declaring Canada to be a "Métis nation" perpetuates the fallacy that the Metis do not hold a distinct place in North American history as a new nation or culture, but instead are simply a by-product of the interactions between First Nations women and French or British men. Saul's statement only diminishes what it is to be Metis because it reduces a people's identity to the act of miscegenation and obscures the historical processes that gave rise to their cultural, political, and economic traditions. It is the sharing of these types of historical processes as a community of people that defines the Metis, not the degree of Indian blood in their veins or number of Indians in the family tree.

Before proceeding, a note on spelling is necessary. By now, readers should have noticed that my spelling of Metis does not conform to the usual French spelling, as adhered to by Saul. Instead, my use of Metis without an accent is meant to be inclusive of cultural backgrounds and experiences that are nonetheless grounded within a shared historical context and community experience. There is a great deal of debate about the terminology (as this chapter seeks to explore), but "Métis" is typically applied in historical contexts to those people with French Canadian paternity and who had a sense of political nationalism, whereas the term "Half-breed" (or the less commonly used "country-born") has been applied to the Scottish English-speaking communities who may have shared the Metis sense of nationalism but were less populous and more likely to be connected to the Hudson's Bay Company (HBC) hierarchy. Throughout the nineteenth century, the term Half-breed was commonly used and applied across Canada to a variety of populations and communities, as the English language dominated historical, political, and legal discourses. By the 1960s and 70s, national and provincial political organizations began to use Métis, in form and spelling, as the preferred term. These organizations initially represented mixed-ancestry peoples—Métis, Half-breed, and non-status Indian populations—in a broad, pan-aboriginal context.[3] In the early 1980s, the Métis National Council (MNC) and its provincial counterparts adopted Métis as the appropriate term and spelling for their constituents—Métis and Half-breeds exclusively—whom they defined as those descended from peoples of historic Métis ancestry and residing within the historic Métis Nation homeland.[4]

In line with the MNC, scholars made a distinction between groups of Metis but settled the issue based on spelling. The edited collection titled *The New Peoples* used Métis or métis, noting that the uppercase *M* was

reserved for those people who were a part of the New Nation born at Red
River in the first half of the 1800s, whereas the lowercase *m* was used for
those who were mixed racially and culturally, but who had no political
sense of distinctiveness. The authors in that collection borrowed this sty-
listic usage from the MNC, which, at the time, determined that there was
a significant difference between its constituency—whom they defined as
a distinct indigenous people who had evolved during a certain historical
period in a certain region of Canada—and others of a similar background but dissimilar sociopolitical historical experience.[5] The issue of
uppercase and lowercase *m*'s has remained with us ever since and influenced subsequent historiographical trends. This attempt to establish a
definition inclusive of both Métis and Half-breeds, however, emphasizes
a French paternal ancestry that obscures the Scottish and English paternal origins as well as the maternal indigenous ancestries—Cree, Anishinaabe, Sioux, Dene—of this New Nation. Part of the problem is that the
term Métis tends to be used uncritically and ahistorically in all of these
contexts, which has diminished the historical contexts and experiences
of Metis in North America and the nature of their collective identity. Our
collectively clumsy use of terms and conflation of historical experiences
with contemporary political aspirations has led to a fixation on how to
best define a people whose very existence defies traditional ontological
systems.[6]

So-called mixed-race people in North America have proven to be a
challenge to intellectual thought since the eighteenth and nineteenth
centuries, and contemporary scholarship on Metis history continues to
struggle with how to describe this new people. What has developed is
a scholarly tradition concerned with one question: which way did the
Metis tilt—were they more Indian or European?[7] As a result, the prevailing articulation of Metis-ness is that the people are necessarily and fatally culturally ambivalent because they do not fit understood categories
of authenticity. One of the stronger articulations of this notion of cultural
ambivalence is found in Sylvia Van Kirk's assessment of the life and career of "Anglophone mixed-blood" James Ross. In her 1985 article, " 'What
if Mama is an Indian?': The Cultural Ambivalence of the Alexander Ross
Family," Van Kirk explicated the lives of the children born to Scottish-
born trader and historian Alexander Ross and Sally, an Okanogan woman.
Van Kirk primarily focused on their son James Ross, concluding that his
cultural ambivalence caused a personal identity crisis "so profound that it

destroyed him."[8] Furthermore, she concluded, "the tragedy of his life is suggestive for the fate of anglophone mixed-bloods as a whole. Unlike the métis, this group was not permitted to build a cultural identity based on the recognition of their dual racial heritage."[9] Van Kirk concluded that James Ross was excluded from a Métis experience because he was anglophone, because there was racist bigotry in Red River directed toward the Ross children, and because of his father's strong desire for his children to assimilate into his British, Protestant social world—all of which negatively impacted James Ross's ability to be a healthy and productive adult.[10]

In order to establish the veracity of the cultural ambiguity thesis, Van Kirk made several speculative assessments about the physical and social well-being of the Ross family. Noting that only one Ross child lived past age thirty (the rest possibly succumbing to inherited health ailments), Van Kirk mused, "One wonders to what extent psychological stress contributed to their poor health. The degree of psychological dislocation which they suffered appears to have been proportional to the degree to which they attempted to assimilate, accompanied as this was by the hazards of personal ambivalence and the threat of rejection."[11] In addition, Van Kirk noted that four of the six Ross daughters married white men, leading her to conclude that "marriage would be the key to their continued assimilation," and that "these marriages to white men not only underscore the Ross family's desire to be viewed as 'British,' but also symbolize the way in which the family identified with the forces of 'progress' in Red River."[12]

The final manifestation of the Ross children's trauma and crises of identity is summed up by Van Kirk's appraisal of a single letter written by James Ross to his brothers and sisters following the death of their father. Ross asked the question that now frames the historical interpretation of him, his family, and the entirety of the so-called anglophone mixed-bloods: "What if Mama is an Indian?" According to Van Kirk, this simple sentence is definitive proof that the Rosses specifically, and anglophone mixed-bloods more generally, shared an "ambivalence toward their native mothers, which was in essence an ambivalence toward their own Indian blood and heritage, [a trait] not uncommon among British-Indian children."[13] Van Kirk treated Ross's statement as a negative assessment of his mother's aboriginality. Van Kirk claimed that "it is hard to interpret this statement as a positive defense of his Mother's Indian-ness," because, according to her, what Ross meant was that *"even* if their mother was an Indian, she was a most exemplary mother and for that reason was entitled to the love and respect of her children."[14] There are alternate interpretations of this evidence that will be explored shortly. For now, however, it seems that Van Kirk was ensnared in a paradoxical argument. Because of a rigid classification structure based on racial authenticity (in this case, white or Indian) there was, as a result, no room for anglophone mixed-bloods—Half-breeds—to exist independently of their parental legacies, as a separate and definable category, as Metis people. Instead, because they were "mixed," they had to choose one category or another. Yet any attempt to meet the criteria of being one or the other denies the authenticity of a singular Metis identity. Instead, by virtue of their inauthenticity, the existence of the Metis raises the specter of an internalized cultural ambivalence. And, indeed, scholarship has continued to emphasize the differences between, say, French Métis and Scottish Half-breeds to the exclusion of exploring the indigenous origins of this new people.[15] Because of this fixation on French and British ancestry, two nations known for their historical animosity toward one another, Metis scholarship has described their mixed-blood offspring as "a people in between," "caught between two worlds," or, more generally, as the physical manifestation of a "middle ground" between Indians and Europeans.[16] Consequently, Metis history has become rife with descriptions of the Metis being either/or—either European or Indian, either French or British, either Christian or followers of indigenous religious and spiritual practices.[17] At the same time, however, the Metis do not actually fit these categories. Their very existence abrogates the relevancy of the classification structure. Collectively, the Metis are denied entrance into those categories that would provide them with the authenticity of an Indian or white identity. And so we are all caught within a paradox, one that Van Kirk did not create but that she, like many others, could see no way out of. And so she expressed her own ambivalence about how to best assess the circumstances surrounding the Rosses and others like them when they did not fit the only accepted categories of racial authenticity. To better understand Van Kirk's ambivalence, it is useful to first deconstruct the manner in which she interpreted the Ross family and, in particular, Alexander Ross's goals and ambitions for himself and his children.

Apart from James, Alexander Ross is the central character in Van Kirk's analysis. More than any other person, she concludes, Alexander was the architect of his children's cultural ambivalence. Before becoming a writer, Alexander Ross was a fur trader employed by the Pacific Fur, North West, and Hudson's Bay Companies. While posted at Fort Okanagan in 1813, Ross met and married Sally according to the custom of the country, a marriage renewed according to Christian rite in 1828. Ross and his family moved to Red River in 1825, where he served as sheriff of Assiniboia and then as a member of the Council of Assiniboia. In spite of his choice of wife (a woman whom he married twice and never abandoned, unlike others of his stature) and, therefore, the heritage of his children, Ross felt that Metis were inferior, and he often asserted that they needed to work harder than others to overcome their disadvantages in life.

In his 1855 publication, *The Fur Hunters of the Far West*, Ross wrote a particularly harsh critique of Metis, or rather those people he called the Half-breeds or *brules*. Ross observed:

Half-breeds, or as they are more generally styled, brules, from the peculiar colour of their skin, being of a swarthy hue, as if sunburnt, as they grow up resemble, almost in every respect, the pure Indian. With this difference that they are more designing, more daring, and more dissolute. They are indolent, thoughtless, and improvident. Licentious in their habits, unbounded in their desires, sullen in their disposition. Proud, restless, and clannish, fond of flattery. They alternately associated with the whites and the Indians, and thus became fatally enlightened. They form a composition of all the bad qualities of both.[18]

One could rebuke Ross for such comments, as Van Kirk did, for his insensitivity toward his own children. However, although his comments were, at best, ethnocentric, there is no indication that they were directed at his progeny or reflected any personal assessment of their character. By the very title of his book, it is clear that Ross was referring to a very specific group who lived as hunters, an occupation and lifestyle that the Ross children did not, and would never, share. It seems reasonable to assume that Ross, a man who worked and lived in the economic zone of the fur trade and amongst indigenous people, recognized differences based on occupation, class, lifestyle, and religion—historical categories or distinctions that we, far removed from Ross's socioeconomic and temporal context, often gloss over. As a member of the Council of Assiniboia, Ross held a position of authority and privilege. Sally Ross, furthermore, was the daughter of an Okanagan chief and would have had a sense of her own class and position within a society where everyone may have worked within the same economy but not existed within the same class. The Ross children were raised, no doubt, to understand their status within this socio-cultural context intrinsic to fur trade society. Surely, given this context, Alexander Ross was not equating his children with the fur hunters. Even by Van Kirk's assessment, Ross ensured that his children had the opportunities befitting a man of his stature—his sons were well-educated and daughters well-married—and so the family's position in Red River society, a community of Metis people, was secured.[19]

What Van Kirk regarded as an assimilationist agenda of a father erasing the stigma of his children's Indian-ness can instead be viewed as the efforts of a politically well-connected, well-educated, socially prominent man to ensure that his children had the best opportunities in life. Furthermore, providing one's children with the best opportunities possible should not be equated with manipulating them to ensure their assimilation into the dominant society. Yet this is the manner in which the Ross family history is characterized. Van Kirk's treatment of the Rosses permitted no positive or hopeful interpretation of their identity but instead fixated on the idea that their in-betweenness—really, their biraciality—fostered a psychologically damaging cultural ambivalence. According to Van Kirk, the Rosses epitomized what must have been true for other anglophone mixed-bloods. This group, she concluded, never developed a distinct sense of self or cultural identity like their "French métis" counterparts, a group with whom they shared a "bond of kinship."[20] Van Kirk made no explanation for why the "French métis" did not develop the same crippling cultural ambivalence, nor did she make clear the difference between culture, class, or race within Red River or fur trade society. Furthermore, the lack of critical engagement with how the "French métis" may have been different from other Metis makes it difficult to know how Van Kirk understood them. They were presumably more "Indian" because of their style of life and economic engagement as hunters, as well as being politically and socially removed from the day-to-day machinations of Red River society. What Van Kirk clearly articulates, however, was that the Rosses and others like them who were anglophone and Protestant aspired to whiteness and rejected their Indian-ness because their European ancestry meant access to privilege, power, and psychological well-being. When denied claims of white authenticity and relegated to the status of "just another Indian," however, they did not become more

Indian like the métis, but rather became alienated from both themselves and others like them. There was no opportunity for the Rosses to be Metis and, therefore, no possibility for them to be anything except white, in Van Kirk's analysis, because of the desires of Alexander Ross. In her assessment, Alexander Ross, ashamed of his children's Indian-ness, had an overwhelming desire to have them assimilate and become white. Perhaps what should be explored is the cultural ambivalence of scholars who, when faced with people who defy accepted racial (or even cultural) categorization, find fault with those populations instead of the ontological ordering that denies their existence.

Van Kirk's conclusion that James Ross (and others like him) was culturally ambivalent is an idea pervasive in Metis scholarship. Scholars of Canadian Metis history have been inordinately preoccupied with how to classify the Metis—were they more white or more Indian, more French or more British? Even Louis Riel, the archetype of nineteenth-century Metis political leadership, has had the authenticity of his Metis identity questioned. Some have reflected that Riel is best characterized as French Canadian because he had only one Dene grandparent and three French Canadian grandparents, which would make him only one-eighth Indian.[21] In this rendering, Riel's life course and his personal and political decisions are all meaningless. Instead, his identity is evaluated at the moment of conception rather than within his own historical cultural context.

American scholars, on the other hand, have been more concerned with figuring out why there are no Metis in the United States today.[22] In these instances, the root of discourse is on race and, more importantly, how so-called mixed-race people can fit into a world designed around categories that appear even more inflexible today than they were two centuries ago. By not confronting this paradigm, academic scholarship has fixated on the idea that the Metis were destined to face personal identity crises because they were neither Indian nor white. In this rendering of history, Metis were not a people in their own right because their basic origins and experiences denied that possibility. As such, there is no way to describe them except in terms of being caught in the middle, between the expectations and aspirations of their paternal or maternal antecedents. Van Kirk's article on the Ross family is part of a long scholarly tradition that has been most comfortable addressing Metis identity within the framework of racial and cultural ambivalence.

Since the onset of the colonial era, lay people and scholars alike have found it problematic to reconcile the Metis with existing social, cultural, economic, or political reference points because of their implicit and explicit defiance of those basic systematic categories that define our understanding of the world.[23] At various points in their history, collectivities of people begin to regard themselves as "real" because of their shared religious beliefs and cultural worldviews. Christians thought that they were more real than Jews, Muslims thought that they were more real than Christians, and all thought that they were more real than pagans. Even the first indigenous peoples of North America established for themselves identities that marked them as real people based on their socioreligious concepts. For instance, Inuit translates as "the people"; Dene is most often translated as "the people," but another translation is "the people who flowed from our female (earth)" (*De* or *deh* means flow or river, and *ne* means "our female"); Anishinaabe, usually translated as "first, original, or good people" is more precisely "the people from nothing"; and Nehiyaw (Cree) means "people of the four worlds."[24] Recognizing that the standard definitions of these terms all relate to the idea of "the people," traditional philosophical teachings further unpack the terms according to the etymology of the language as well as religious knowledge of whom the people were in the place where they existed. For indigenous peoples in North America, as it is with all people, the act of naming yourself shapes an ontological system of categorization—as you define yourself, you also define others.

Although we mostly rely on European languages to establish the appropriate terminology for the Metis, there were indigenous words applied to these populations that reveal an alternate ontological system of categories. The Cree had several names for the Metis that reveal a great deal about how they understood communities of Metis in different eras and locations. *Otipimsuak*—which translates in a number of ways, including "the free people," "people who own (or command) themselves," or "their own bosses"—is a term that has gained currency in contemporary scholarship and has been applied to the community at Batoche, northwestern Saskatchewan and, more generally, western Canadian communities.[25] Cree speakers, however, might argue that the term has been misapplied to those communities and that it refers only to the buffalo hunters of the Great Plains who operated independently of any specific company. Otipimsuak, in this context, is similar to the concept of *les gens libre,* the free traders, or the freemen, as they have been described in a variety of scholarly works.[26] The more common Cree and Anishinaabe terms for Metis were *âpihtawkosisan,* from *âpihtaw* "half" and *kosis* "son"; or *aay-aabtawzid* or *aya:pittawisit,* "one who is half."[27] Ontologically, "half son" references a familial relationship between the Cree and the Metis, whereas "one who is half" establishes a connection between Anishinaabe and Metis that is personal—the Metis are "half" of the Anishinaabe.

These Cree and Anishinaabe terms are little different from either "Métis" or "half-breed," yet they implicitly echo a familial relationship between the old and the new peoples that is missing from the French and English terminology. Perhaps it is this lack of relationship that makes explaining the Metis in French or English so difficult. "Half-breed" is most definitely a racial and biological term that references the offspring of distinct races, whereas métis simply means mixed, and although it has no inherently racial connotation, it is accepted to mean a person of mixed European and Indian blood. However, by the mid-nineteenth century, racial categories were conceptualized as discrete, neatly bounded, genetically determined means to group or classify humans: Caucasoid (white), Negroid (brown), Mongoloid (yellow), and Australoid (black).[28] Within each of these racial categories, individuals were identifiable by physical, inheritable characteristics, such as color, height and stature, cranial shape, facial features, and hair texture. Still, nuance was accepted and subcategories recognized. For instance, not all Caucasoids looked alike—there were differences between Nordic and Slavic peoples, for example, but they were all regarded as a part of a single racial category.

There were no nuances, however, that recognized the movement of people across or between categories. Over time, the idea that race not only existed but was meaningful came to be regarded as natural and immutable in western European thought. Within such a system of classification, there was little room for those who did not easily fit. When these discrete categories mixed—when miscegenation occurred between races rather than between subcategories of the same race—these systems became problematic. Those who had invested themselves in the creation and maintenance of those strict borders of identity (those who belonged to discrete, bounded, racial categories) had to find a way to reinforce these categories or else lose the very thing that made them real.[29] But these racial categories proved inadequate for peoples who, by virtue of their birth, defied such simplistic binaries. Instead of recasting the categories to fit

emerging contexts on the colonial frontier, it became commonplace to
find fault with those who defied categorization.

Nineteenth-century newcomers and visitors to western Canada, like
Alexander Ross, wrote descriptions of Metis people that reflected the racial ambiguity with which these new people were regarded, thus revealing their personal ambivalence. While traveling through the Northwest
Territories in the 1890s, Edgerton Ryerson Young expressed a hope that
the racial mixing of people of Red River would prove a strength rather
than an insurmountable character flaw. He noted, "The intermixture
of races, however, is there, and doubtless in sufficient amount to aid in
the development of characteristics which, it is to be hoped, will not be
defects, but blessings, in the coming generations."[30] Young's interactions
with the people of the Northwest Territories led him to conclude that the
Metis were clearly in a position to embrace civilization, but he also felt
that the Scottish Metis were more advanced than their French brethren.
According to Young, "The French half-breeds have retained in their looks
and also in their habits much more of the peculiar characteristics of their
Indian ancestry than the Scotch half-breeds," but they were also "physically superior to their Indian and French ancestors." He continued, "With
such antecedents it is no wonder that these half-breeds were ever vastly
superior to the Indian tribes around them, with whom they had become
so allied by marriage. The word 'Métis' is the one used by themselves to
designate the children of these peculiar marriages."[31]

On his tour of Rupert's Land between 1859 and 1860, the Earl of Southesk wrote of the difference between the French and Scottish Metis at
Lower Fort Garry in Red River. Southesk was, at the time, reflecting on
the difficulty of finding laborers to support the settlement's agricultural activities and other needs. It was within this context that Southesk
remarked,

Moreover, there is reason to doubt if much aptitude for labour belongs
to the constitution of the native-born inhabitants, especially those of
French origin. As a rule the French half-breed is said to dislike continuous work. No man will labour more cheerfully and gallantly in the
severe toils of the voyageurs calling, but these efforts are of short duration, and when they are ended his chief desire is to do nothing but eat,
drink, smoke, and be merry,—all of them acts in which he greatly
excels.

Though there is much general resemblance, the English or rather Scottish, half-breeds differ considerably from those of French origin both in looks and character; the former often possessing the fair hair and other physical characteristics of a northern race, while in disposition they are more industrious and more actuated by a sense of duty,— for though the word "devoir" is frequently on the lips of the semi-French man, the principle of "devoir" is not so strong in their hearts as the impulses of passion or caprice.[32]

Southesk proceeded to state that he "cannot think so ill of the half-breed population as most writers appear to do," and he went on to describe their general physical appearance as being superior to their paternal and maternal ancestors.[33] Commenting on Metis appearance, Southesk observed,

In countenance the half-breed is swarthy, with dark hair and eyes; his features are often good and aquiline in character, but sometimes they are coarse,—though invariably well proportioned, and utterly removed from the baboon jaw and flat nose of the Old World savage. With some cleverness and cheerfulness, their faces generally betray a certain moodiness of temper; neither the frank self-reliant generosity of the English countenance, nor the sagacious honest respectability of the Scottish, are commonly stamped on the aspect of these men, at once more meditative and more impulsive.[34]

So, while feeling that these Half-breeds were generally attractive, he nevertheless found them to be wanting in other capacities. And, of course, Alexander Ross contributed to this debate in his publications, although his presentation of the Metis was much less admiring than Southesk's, and he was much more pointed than Young in his assessment of their social behavior, capabilities, and intellect. Ross, by far the most critical, found few redemptive qualities in this nineteenth-century people, but perhaps he only said bluntly what others expressed in softer prose. These nineteenth-century descriptions, no matter how often they are cited for their ethnocentric and bigoted assessments, have had an indelible influence on the manner in which the Metis are portrayed in twentieth-century academic scholarship.

We can certainly trace the roots of this paradigm to pioneering scholars Marcel Giraud and George Stanley, both of whom evaluated Metis history as an epic battle between civilization and savagery.[35] In the 1936 preface to his work, Stanley wrote, "Both the Manitoba insurrection and the Saskatchewan Rebellion were the manifestation in Western Canada of the problem of the frontier, namely the clash between primitive and civilized peoples."[36] Stanley further argued that the problem was that the "half-breed," like Indians, were not only unfit to compete with whites or even share with them the duties or responsibilities of citizenship, but they did not want to be civilized.[37] Giraud, meanwhile, quite specifically argued that individual and collective deficiencies amongst the Metis were the results of miscegenation and that the culture itself was horribly socially underdeveloped.[38]

Changing the focus, but not challenging notions surrounding race, Frits Pannekoek concentrated on religious differences in nineteenth-century Red River as the source of conflict. Relying on records from the local Protestant clergy to evaluate the mood and situation in the community on the eve of the 1869–70 Resistance, Pannekoek concluded that religious differences between English-speaking Protestant country-born and French-speaking Catholic Métis were significant. These differences in the population, according to Pannekoek, were so great that Red River was unable to unite in common self-interest against the Canadian state in 1869–70.[39] Pannekoek's emphasis was on religion, but his descriptions of the English-speaking and French-speaking peoples align with older notions of race as articulated by nineteenth-century writers as well as Stanley and Giraud. What seems more pertinent, however, is the recasting of the terms of reference. Within the historiography of Red River, scholars have regularly racially subdivided the Metis population according to nineteenth-century ideas, even though this system is both imprecise and inappropriate in this particular context. We now have a myriad of categorical options from which to choose: French-speaking, English-speaking, anglophone mixed-bloods, francophone métis, half-breed, mixed-bloods, Métis, country-born, Catholic Métis, or Protestant half-breeds—all terms found in the records as created and maintained by newcomers and representing a variety of economic, political, and religious interests. But the continued reliance on these classificatory terms fosters a notion that pulled the Metis community apart more than bound it together.

There is an alternative interpretive approach to the story of Metis cultural ambivalence predicated on a fixation on race and difference. Historian Irene Spry refuted the existence of racial and/or cultural divisions along French and British lines amongst the Red River Metis population and sought to explore whether these categories were meaningful to the people themselves by surveying non-clerical sources. Her research showed that the community was linked by "ties of blood and long association on the hunt and trip."[40] Intermarriage between Metis families at Red River was, according to Spry, fairly widespread, and so the emphasis on division was less useful in assessing the community's social make-up. What Spry highlighted was that Red River was a place where race was less important than family, which is the organizing principle of aboriginal societies. Spry offered a methodological and theoretical possibility that warrants greater attention and asks only that we refocus our gaze. Spry looked to what communities of Metis had in common, rather than continuing to reinforce a dichotomous argument that centered Metis authenticity on French-speaking, Catholic, buffalo-hunting, resistance fighters of Red River, thus ensuring that all mixed-blood communities were measured against this group. What invariably happens is that those who are deficient in these qualities are judged inauthentic, non-Metis. Spry suggested that the whole paradigm of French-speaking Métis/English-speaking Half-breeds limited the discourse because the wrong questions were being asked.

Despite Spry's insight, we continue to fixate on race—really, the purity of race—which has led to scholarship that argues that mixed-ancestry individuals have chosen either "European-ness" or "Indian-ness," rather than a third, far more compelling option—the choice to be Metis.[41] This third option is clearly an intellectually complex problem that forces us to confront how a people are created, emerge, or develop. The Metis are often used within hybridity and postcolonial discourse as the epitome of a bicultural middle ground.[42] But this still maintains the fallacy that accepts the authenticity of white and Indian societies but denies the legitimacy of the third. This discourse is further unsatisfactory because these theories promote notions that ambivalence rests with the hybrids, not the parental societies' interpretations.

American scholars have recently begun to explore "Metis" or hybridized communities in the United States, particularly along the Great Lakes and northern Plains borderlands. Studies by Martha Harroun Foster, Susan Sleeper-Smith, Tanis C. Thorne, and Lucy Eldersveld Murphy have explored the interrelationship between family and community as both a personal and social construction amongst Metis in the United States.[43] Methodologically, each of these scholars has combined ethnographic and genealogical practice to explore the existence of a people whose multiethnic and multiracial sociocultural complexion often defied categorization. However, they also have sought to explain why American Metis, unlike in Canada, no longer exist as a separate, recognized aboriginal people with an enduring cultural legacy. The focus has almost inevitably focused attention on racism, government policies, and nomenclature that reproduced illusions of purity amongst the races rather than how the people conceived of themselves collectively.

The question, then, is why do we still rely on racial classification when discussing the Metis? Natural scientists would argue that definitions of race, including its corresponding subcategories that further divide people, are imprecise and laden with exceptions. Yet race in social scientific and humanist scholarship continues to dominate our ideas of human categorization, infiltrating our thinking when it comes to categorizing and identifying such dynamic historical populations like the Metis. Perhaps, as Nancy Shoemaker has suggested, it is because, regardless of what we nominally believe to be true about race, it is clear that nineteenth-century people ascribed to this type of thinking.[44] Perhaps it is because our language is ill-suited to fully articulate what it means to not fit the categories. Or maybe it is that race, although scientifically unremarkable, is connected to social categories that have important cognitive meanings for us and are necessary for establishing a well-ordered world. However, it is the very nature of this cognitive ordering that has led Metis academics like sociologist Chris Andersen to argue that we constitute the Metis as a "(part of) a race," rather than attempt to understand them according to an indigenous national construct.[45] I would take that one step further still and argue that in the field of Metis Studies, Canadian scholars, like their American colleagues, have been overly and unproductively preoccupied with race at the expense of culture and the categories within each cultural ontology that establishes who and how people are real.

As a means of exploring some different questions that we should be asking, I want to present a number of experiences of family and geography that are expressions of Metis-ness yet do not fit this dichotomous model. The first requirement, however, is to recast the categories by which to evaluate the Metis. In an article entitled "Categories," Nancy Shoemaker suggested that part of the categorization problem is rooted in a scholarly tradition that dictates that historical human behavior must be evaluated in terms of race, class, and gender. She argued that these categories are inappropriate within the context of Indian communities—and, I would add, Metis communities—on the colonial frontier because they were irrelevant to their sociocultural context. As an alternative, Shoemaker suggested that we should pursue categories more historically relevant to Indian communities, such as gender, kinship, and age.[46] In the case of defining the Metis experience, kinship is probably the most appropriate starting point for understanding their identity formation; in addition, homeland, geographic associations, and involvement in the fur trade writ large may be more relevant categories than age or race.[47] Gender remains a useful category because the Metis defined their relationship to each other, their homeland, and the economy based on their paternal and maternal ancestry. Listening to (or seeking out) the clues to how Metis people understood themselves in relation to others (as Spry did) will expand the frameworks of analyses in numerous geographies and across different eras. The relationship between people, place, and economy was significant to how Metis peoples came to define themselves as a community with collective or corporate interests. This shared historical context reveals who the Metis were more so than the terms used to describe them.

This connection between a sense of self, family, and homeland was articulated in the late nineteenth century in northwestern Saskatchewan. Addressing the question of the Halfbreed Claims Commission for the Treaty 6 adhesion, fifty-seven-year-old Raphaël Morin had occasion to express who he was in relation to his mother and father and, in turn, to express a concept of homeland and identity not often so well articulated in Metis historiography. Morin explained that in his youth he had lived at both Athabasca and Île à la Crosse, where his father had been employed in the service of HBC, before coming to reside at Devil's Lake, near the Shell River (located just south of Green Lake, Saskatchewan).[48] Morin further stated that he had taken his family to Devils Lake "to live in the land of my mother who was originally from the lands of [her] parents [because] we most of the time were in the said lands of her relatives as we had no interest in the lands . . . where my father and myself" were born and raised.[49] In this statement, Raphaël Morin was clear that his identity was encompassed in his maternal connection to home, land, and family. His sister, Marie Morin, echoed his words in her own scrip application taken two years later. According to her declaration, after her husband's death in 1880, Marie, the widow of HBC servant Peter Lin-klater, took her three youngest children to the Shell River area to live in the "country of her mother."[50]

There are several converging issues in the Morin family's scrip applications that bear further scrutiny. Some would argue that simply by applying for scrip, the Morins were asserting themselves to be Metis. More relevantly, though, they were asserting themselves to have particular rights that flowed from their maternal ancestry to land. In their scrip applications, Raphaël and Marie Morin clearly articulated their relationship to a homeland that was geographically broad and covered a significant range of northwestern Saskatchewan. Notably, Raphaël denied any connection or claim to his father's homeland in eastern Canada. Homeland in their world encompassed a sizable region where people worked, traveled, and socialized with one another. For this nineteenth-century Metis people, family and homeland were inextricably interconnected, and sense of self was defined in relation to these two elements.

The history of the Morin family in northwestern Saskatchewan dates to the early 1800s, when the family matriarch, Pélagie Boucher, the mother of Raphaël and Marie, was born. In a scrip application filed at Green Lake in 1887, the then-eighty-four-year-old Pélagie Boucher Morin was recorded by the commissioners as being known "by the HalfBreeds and Indians generally as a halfbreed, the child of a French Canadian and an Indian [Montagnais] woman."[51] It is very likely that Pélagie's father was Louis Boucher of Berthierville, Quebec, and her mother was Marie-Joseph LeBlanc, a Dene woman from the region. Louis Boucher had worked for the North West Company at Île à la Crosse in the late eighteenth century, but by 1811, he and some of the family apparently returned to Quebec.[52] However, at least two women carrying the Boucher surname remained in northwestern Saskatchewan well after Louis's retirement. Born around 1803 at Portage La Loche, Pélagie Boucher married Antoine Morin, a Quebec-born French Canadian servant of the HBC, at Île à la Crosse when she was fifteen years of age. Several years later, by 1817, a Marguerite Boucher, likely Pélagie's sister, married Jean Baptiste Riel at Île à la Crosse. Marguerite Boucher and Jean Baptiste Riel were the parents of Jean Louis Riel, father to Metis political leader Louis Riel. However, Marguerite's life at Île à la Crosse ended early. By 1821, she was dead and her husband and young son had relocated to Quebec.[53] Meanwhile, Pélagie remained in the subarctic, married, and had fifteen children, seven of whom were born at Athabasca or Portage La Loche, and the remainder at Île à la Crosse. Ten of the Morin children are known to have married and lived throughout the subarctic region, from Portage La Loche in the north to Devils Lake in the south and as far west as Meadow Lake. After her husband's death at Île à la Crosse in 1873, Pélagie lived with several of her children and grandchildren in the Green Lake region until her own death in 1907 at 104 years of age.[54]

Genealogical analysis of the Metis communities in northwestern Saskatchewan reveals that, beginning in the eighteenth century and continuing throughout the nineteenth-century fur trade, the Morins belonged to a society defined by a regional matrilocal family organization. That is, indigenous women (Indian and Metis) were the stabilizing force who remained in the region, whereas men, typically trade employees, were more migratory inside and outside of the region because of employment demands. In the Morin family, matriarch Pélagie Boucher—the daughter of a French Canadian trader and Dene mother—remained in the region of her birth and eventually married a French Canadian trader, Antoine Morin. In this area, and in many others, women became the centripetal force that pulled the community together and shaped it as outsider males entered the region and integrated themselves into the prevailing society.

Although she was not as specific in articulating her sense of belonging to the lands of her mother, Sophie Morin, Raphaël's and Marie's sister, provided some hint by her actions. Sophie left her homeland for a period of time (unusual for a woman from this region and during this time period) with her husband, William Linklater. According to her scrip application, Sophie and William lived at Île à la Crosse until 1868, when they moved to Lake Manitoba, William's home territory. A year later, according to Sophie, "they" moved to Waterhen River, Northwest Territories, where they lived until 1874, when she and her husband moved to Shell River near Devil's Lake.[55] Sophie gave no further information about what prompted the first move to Lake Manitoba or the return to the Saskatchewan region. However, an 1874 letter written by Father Alexander Taché of Red River provided further elaboration on Sophie's marital life. In the letter, Taché described Sophie as being brought to Red River by her first husband, William Linklater, who then "gave her" to Paul Delaronde, Sr., who was, at the time, the husband of Marguerite Sinclair. Paul and Sophie left Red River for the "prairies or somewhere north," while William went to

Duck Bay to find himself another wife.[56] The "they" in Sophie's scrip application was a reference to her and Paul Delaronde, not her and Linklater.[57] In Taché's account, Sophie was little more than an object brought to Red River and then given away by her husband to another man. At this stage in the story, it would be tempting to condemn William Linklater for "giving" his wife to Paul Delaronde (as in Taché's interpretation). However, if we alter the categories of analysis to look at kinship, gender, and homeland, different conclusions can be reached. Sophie Morin, far from her mother's country, her relations, and her homeland, found a means of returning home when her first husband William decided to remain in Manitoba (presumably to be nearer to his own family).[58] By marrying Paul Delaronde, Sr., Sophie was able to return to the country of her mother. Like other men before him, Paul Delaronde, Sr., was then integrated into the community through his marriage to Sophie. In the Northwest, as in other regions, it was indigenous women who carried the history of the land and identity of the people, which they then shared with their families. An individual's connection to a place was made through family, but those connections were derived from their maternal ancestry.

In a similar manner, in the eighteenth-century American South during the deerskin trade, there emerged a community of Metis people whose sense of self was shaped by maternal connections to land. These Metis developed as a distinct and identifiable community with shared corporate interests, born of relations between Scottish and English traders in the deerskin trade and local Cherokee, Creek, and Yamasee women. This population was described by outsiders as Half-breeds and clearly constituted a separate community of people from Indian and colonial societies. Religious scholar Joel W. Martin suggested that although the southeastern children of the deerskin trade and plantation economies were labeled Half-breeds by Anglo-Americans, these people should be considered a "nascent southeastern 'métis' people" because "by birth, vocation, and lifestyle" they "embodied the cutting edge of the great material, social, and political transformation reshaping Muskogee."[59] Martin further noted that their distinctiveness was that they lived differently from their Muskogee relatives by focusing on farming and trading rather than hunting and also by assuming greater control of trade by the 1750s.[60] The story of these people, however, is likewise situated in the contested space between those who define others' identities and those being defined.

In the southern deerskin trade, as in the Canadian fur trade, children belonged to their mother's country and so inherited a maternally derived social structure born of that landscape. As eighteenth-century adventurer John Lawson lamented, "But one great Misfortune which oftentimes attends those that converse with these Savage Women, is, that they get Children by them, which are seldom educated any otherwise than in the State of Infidelity; for it is a certain Rule and Custom, amongst all the savages of America . . . to let the Children always fall to the Woman's Lot."[61] Children of Indian–white marriages were accepted into Indian society according to the cultural expectations of their mother's people, but the idea that there was a Metis social organization built on the foundation of matriarchal and matrilineal relationships, as well as that of the economy of trade in this region, has been ignored. Instead, the focus has been on how acculturated they were to their father's society. Historian Claudio Saunt's research into the life and times of Alexander McGillivray, a man of Scottish–Creek lineage, continues to frame a narrative of cultural ambivalence. Born in Creek country in 1750, McGillivray spent the first six years of his life among his mother's people and then moved to Augusta to live on the plantation of his father, Lachlan McGillivray. Educated in Charleston between the ages of thirteen and nineteen, Alexander apprenticed in two trading companies. After the American Revolution, Lachlan retired to Scotland and Alexander returned to his mother's country, where he ran a trade operation, served in a number of militaries, and owned a plantation with slaves.[62] Saunt emphasized the ambivalence of Alexander's identity, arguing that although his maternal line gave him membership in the Wind Clan and he attained the rank of a "most beloved man," he was "deeply alienated from most Creek traditions and from the vast majority of the Creek people."[63] This contradiction placed McGillivray at the "center of a growing fissure" between colonial and Indian society.[64] Furthermore, Saunt cited as evidence of his ambivalence Alexander's lack of warrior tattoos common among Creek men and his decision to leave his possessions at the time of his death to his son rather than his daughters, contrary to Creek customary law.[65] However, it could be argued that McGillivray's behavior was not ambivalent but rather consistent with his identity as a Metis man. Like the Morins, he ascribed to an identity that combined paternal and maternal heritages within a complex socioeconomic and political milieu.

As with the Morins, a similar story of land, family, and identity was played out a century earlier in the American South, when another woman asserted her ancestral claim to the lands of her maternal relatives. In the 1750s, Mary Musgrove Mathews Bosomworth, or Coosaponakeesa, a woman of Creek and English ancestry, asserted proprietary rights to the islands of Ossabow, Sapelo, and St. Catherines, lands also claimed by co-lonial Georgia. Mary was born in the early eighteenth century to an un-named Creek woman and an English trader. Her maternal uncle, Brims, and her brother, Malatchi, were Creek *micos* (headmen). The environ-ment that fostered relationships such as that of Mary's parents was the lucrative and important deerskin trade that was central to the early colo-nial economy. As with other children born to these types of economic alliances, whether in the American South or northern Canada, Mary re-ceived a formal education and was eventually baptized a Christian. All these familial circumstances ensured Mary's prominent status within a society that characterized the social and cultural milieu of the southern deerskin trade. She married three times between 1717 and 1743, always to men whose positions in both the Creek and English colonial worlds further enhanced her own personal status, as well as that of her family's economic, social, and political network.[66]

By the time of her final marriage to Reverend Thomas Bosomworth, an English adventurer and agent for Indian Affairs in Georgia, Mary was in her own right a prosperous businesswoman, a diplomat who negoti-ated trade and land agreements between the Creek and colonial English, and a land owner, largely because she "could speak both English and Creek languages [and] had great influence among Indians."[67] On a mis-sion into Creek territory in July 1752, Thomas Bosomworth traveled with Mary and met with Chiggilli, the new mico of the Creek town Cowetus and one of Mary's relatives.[68] Culturally framing the visit with public declarations that reinforced familial connections, Chiggilli welcomed Thomas, stating that, because his "Relation," Mary, accompanied her husband, the visit must be important, and that the Creek would listen at-tentively. Mary's work as a diplomat for the Creek nation and colonial government of Georgia, where she acted as an interpreter and facilitated treaty negotiations because of her personal relationship with several prominent Creek micos and colonial officials, shaped her reputation as a powerful woman and eventually brought her into conflict with Georgia.

Mary's family connections and place in the territory were characteristics valued by Georgia until she asserted an identity contrary to the colony's interests.[69] It was, however, Mary's familial connections that influenced the developing relationship between the town of Cowetus and colonial governments. In time, Mary eventually sought public acknowledgement of her role in bringing these communities together. In a formal letter to the governor, Thomas explained "that [Mary] has always used the Utmost of her Authority, Influence, and private Fortune (to the utter Ruin of herself and Family) to continue those Nations of Indians steady and steadfast in their Friendship and Alliance to the English."[70] If she were not paid for her services, Bosomworth argued, Mary would be disgraced and cease to be of any help to the English because to maintain standing with her community and family she had to demonstrate generosity by giving "a few Presents to bestow amongst her Relations."[71]

Mary, using her husband as her public representative with Georgia officials, further asserted a right to the three islands off the coast, which, she asserted, were granted to her in 1747 by Malatchi, the Creek mico.[72] The officials in Georgia adamantly refused to recognize her ownership of the islands. Mary asserted an identity that was based on aboriginal notions about how land and people were connected. She was reared in a society that gave equal consideration to women, and so her assertion of land rights was not unusual. Furthermore, colonial society had given Mary great latitude as a woman of influence amongst the Creek. So, even within an English colonial framework, her claim to the islands should not have appeared inappropriate. Mary understood her position and asserted both her maternally derived land rights and her paternal connections to colonial Georgia to amass wealth and prestige within an English colonial setting as a Metis woman.

Denying her claim, colonial administrators attempted to ascribe to Mary an identity that suited their own notions of authenticity. First, they demanded to know why Mary did not consider herself to be an English woman, noting that her father was English, and that she had been baptized a Christian. Because she had been baptized, these officials concluded that Mary, as a Christian, was not "Indian," which proved that she held no rights based on her Creek maternity. Worse, these same officials claimed that Mary had insulted them with her claim to the islands. She pretended to be descended in a maternal line from an Indian king, who held from nature the territories of the Creeks, and [Thomas] Bosomworth now persuaded her to assert her right to them, as superior not only to that of the Trustees, but also to that of the King. Accordingly Mary immediately assuced the title of an independent empress, disavowing all subjection or allegiance to the King of Great Britain, otherwise thus by way of treaty and alliance, such as one independent sovereign might make with another.[73]

Georgia's response to Mary's assertion of a distinct cultural identity highlighted the debate over the right of Metis people to assert their aboriginality. The ambivalence expressed by colonial officials when faced with having to acknowledge those rights was manifested in their attempts to construct arguments to deny Mary's identity as a Metis woman able to capitalize on both her lineages as it suited her for the benefit of her family.

Mary vehemently disagreed with what was said about her, declaring that there was nothing contradictory in her behavior or about her identity. In response, colonial officials altered their approach. They argued that English laws regarding inheritance and ownership rights based on gender superseded traditional Creek laws favoring maternity. Ignoring Mary's personal influence and abilities, and implying that her prestige and position in colonial society was a result of her three husbands' successful enterprises rather than her own efforts or her maternal connections, colonial officials claimed that Mary, as a woman, had no right to claim the islands because her brother, Mico Malatchi, had a more legitimate claim as a male (despite sharing the same ancestry as his sister). Before she could prove herself in English courts, Mary went bankrupt. She eventually gave up her claim to the islands and died on St. Catherines in 1767. Georgian officials, as well as subsequent biographers, determined that her lack of racial authenticity contributed to her inability to articulate a clear sense of identity. However, Mary tried many times to articulate to others who she was, how she understood her place on the land, and her rights as a woman in her society. The ambivalence of colonial officials in Georgia and later scholars has prevented Mary's own voice from being heard.

It should be noted that the term Metis was never used in the context of the American southeast, but certainly Half-breeds was well used and understood to apply to a specific group of people much as it was in Canada. It could, of course, be argued that the term Metis should not be used here because it was not used in Mary's lifetime to refer to her. But the term "Half-breed" definitely was, and regular reference to groups or communities of Half-breeds belies the notion that they were not considered a separate or distinct society. The term Half-breed or Metis, like the term "Indian," should perhaps be interpreted more broadly to apply to different groups or tribes of people who lived in different regions and have separate experiences but nonetheless share something in common as expressed through categories of gender, family, geography, and economy. The Creek perhaps saw Mary as a Creek woman. Certainly her relatives claimed her, and it was a matriarchal society where the father's bloodline was less significant in their understanding of who she was. However, when her mother died, Mary "was brought Down by her Father from the Indian Nation to Pomponne in South Carolina where she was educated, baptized, and raised."[74] Arguably, Mary, although a descendant of an important Creek family, was not fully regarded as Creek, but rather as a Half-breed or Metis, otherwise she would have been raised by a maternal uncle and not her biological father. As the Creek and English established their relationship politically and economically, they did indeed treat the children of their alliances differently than they did non-Half-breed children. It seems fairly certain that such children were still regarded as relatives, albeit with a different status than other relatives.

Likewise, the sense of relatedness between Indians and Half-breeds was evident in the Canadian treaty process as federal treaty negotiators were faced with requests from Indian chiefs that the claims and rights of their Half-breed relatives be recognized as well. Alexander Morris, treaty negotiator for Treaties 3 through 6, and responsible for renegotiating Treaties 1 and 2, reflected on these requests in his published account of the negotiations process.[75] Although not present at the Robinson Huron and Superior treaty negotiations twenty years earlier, Morris reprinted the commissioner's report and noted that, "The relations of the Indians and half-breeds, have long been cordial; and in the negotiations as to these initial treaties, as in the subsequent ones, the claims of the half-breeds, to recognition, was urged by the Indians."[76] At Fort Francis, during the negotiation of Treaty 3, otherwise called the North West Angle Treaty, in 1873, Chief Ma-We-Do-Pe-Nais commented, "some of my children that are around me—those children that we call the Half-breed—those that have been born of our women of Indian blood. We wish that they should be counted with us, and have their share of what you have promised."[77] Again in 1874 during the negotiations for Treaty 4, Morris noted that "the Chiefs then agreed to accept the terms offered and to sign the treaty, having first asked that the Half-breeds should be allowed to hunt, and having been assured that the population in the North-West would be treated fairly and justly, the treaty was signed."[78] One could argue that these Half-breeds were really Indians with mixed-blood, but each of these chiefs was quite precise in identifying them as both relatives and a separate people. As relatives, the Half-breeds shared certain indigenous rights and were, therefore, to be included in treaties, but they were not being included as members of the bands negotiating the treaties.

What Mary shared in common with the people during treaty negotiations, the Morins, and (as we shall see) others was an assertion of her rights to a physical landscape as defined and supported by her connection to her maternal relatives. In short, her rights flowed from her membership in the family and, through that membership, a claim to being part of the land itself. She used her position and status as an indigenous woman to facilitate a relationship between colonial and Creek governments while also carving out a space for herself as a Half-breed woman. Mary Bosomworth's role as a woman with strong family connections and sense of self in a specific landscape was a particular role played by other women who created and nurtured for their families their space within their homelands.

To bring a bit of clarity to this issue, consider those Metis whose lifestyle ensured that their communities moved freely across the forty-ninth parallel in pursuit of economic opportunities. This was the case for the Round Prairie (Prairie du Ronde) community of the Great Plains.[79] In the early nineteenth century, waves of Metis from the Red River region ventured westward as free traders in pursuit of buffalo. Dating to the late 1830s, Round Prairie, south of modern-day Saskatoon, Saskatchewan, was one of the oldest wintering sites. Within twenty years, however, Round Prairie had become the home territory of a group of approximately thirty Metis families led by patriarch and chief Charles Trottier but grounded in their homeland by their relationship to the Laframboise women.[80] Because of his role as a captain of a brigade, a position of importance and prestige within buffalo-hunting culture, Trottier was the leader of this community and widely discussed by many scholars and contemporaries.[81]

However, close inspection of genealogical connections between the brigade's men revealed that this community had, at its foundational core, three Laframboise sisters and, therefore, a broad connection to the Laframboise family. Sisters Ursule, Philomène, and Angélique Laframboise—daughters of Jean Baptiste Laframboise and Susanne Beaudry—were married to Charles Trottier, Moise Landry, and Antoine Trottier, respectively. Another leading man in the community, Isadore Dumont, Sr., was likewise married into the Laframboise family via his wife Louise Laframboise, the sister of Jean Baptiste and therefore the aunt of Ursule, Philomène, and Angélique. Also at Round Prairie were two sons of Jean Baptiste Laframboise and Suzanne Beaudry. Jean Baptiste was married to Elise Roussain dite Thomas, and François was married to Marie Trottier, sister of Charles, Antoine, and Andre.[82] The Laframboise family, one of the oldest Metis families in North America, was spread throughout the borderland regions in the southern Great Lakes and west to the Maple Creek, Cypress Hills, and Badlands regions.[83] By the mid-nineteenth century, this family was located as far north as Round Prairie and as far south as Lewistown in the Montana territories.

As plains hunters, the Round Prairie community as a whole moved on a seasonal route between Round Prairie on the South Saskatchewan River (about twenty miles south of Saskatoon) to Havre and Lewistown, Montana, from 1850 until after 1885. Many of the Round Prairie children were born on the plains because of the nature of their parents' work and lifestyle. Round Prairie soon became the community's home space, where they lived in seasonal permanence and from where they operated their hunting brigades. In 1885, Charles and the other men of the community went to fight alongside their relatives from Batoche, Fish Creek, and Petite Ville against the Canadian state. Although there is little evidence to suggest that the women of Round Prairie were directly involved in the 1885 Resistance, the role of the Round Prairie men in the fighting was attributable to the strong female kinship ties between these two communities. Isadore Dumont, Sr., Charles Trottier's uncle, lived in the Batoche/St. Laurent region but by 1885 was at Round Prairie, likely because of his wife, Louise Laframboise, and her relationship to the many other Laframboise women living there. Two of Isadore's and Louise's sons—Isadore, Jr., and Gabriel—were central to political and military events at Batoche and St. Laurent throughout the 1870s and 1880s. Indeed, the family connections between these two communities were quite complex. Louise Laframboise, sister to Jean Baptiste Laframboise, Sr., had both a brother and a sister who married into the South Branch communities, and two sons actively engaged in political organizing during the 1880s.[84]

After the Metis defeat at Batoche, the Round Prairie families (along with others from Batoche, St. Laurent, and other communities and Cree and Saulteaux relatives from across the Great Plains) retreated into Montana as refugees, a region well known to them because of their economic pursuits. The Round Prairie families lived in the Havre and Lewistown regions until 1903, when they began returning to Round Prairie to take up homesteads in their old community. After almost twenty years absent from Round Prairie, one must ask why they returned. By examining the affidavits in the homestead files, we can begin locating answers for this decision to return home. Upon their arrival, the Metis heads of household applied for homesteads on their traditional lands. In his petition for a homestead, for instance, Charles Trottier claimed that he had "taken up this land as far back as in the year 1855, when I was with my parents hunting the buffaloes in the plains," and "that [he] wintered there every year since up to 1885."[85] Charles went on to explain,

> In 1884 before survey I broke there at least fifteen acres of land with the intention of sowing it in the next year and that I had their a dwelling house of 18 × 20 feet and a stable. That in 1885, on account of the rebellion, I had to go to the United States, and that I lived in said States up to July 1903, when I came back to my old house.[86]

In this 1903 declaration, Charles explained his historic ties to Round Prairie by referencing his family and the community's economy. In a similar manner, Charles Trottier's nephew, Norbert, declared his right to the Round Prairie land based on prior occupation and as one of the "oldest settler" in the area.[87] In a letter to the Department of the Interior, dated 1907, Norbert stated that in 1880 he had been "squatting" at Round Prairie prior to the land being surveyed in 1884. Norbert claimed that he had already made the necessary improvements, including building a house and two stables. He further stated that he had cleared and fenced eighty acres of this land.[88] Norbert said that he had resided at Round Prairie for six years until his buildings were burned and eight of his horses killed by the Canadian army during the Resistance. Following the Resistance,

Norbert fled to Montana with the rest of his family, remaining there until the early 1900s.[89]

Like his uncle, Norbert Trottier obtained title to land at Round Prairie in 1908 through the homesteading process.[90] What is significant is that both Trottiers claimed the lands as "original" occupiers/users, indicating that they understood their proprietary rights as indigenous peoples of Round Prairie. It seems fairly certain that this was a part of an ongoing connection to a home that shaped their sense of self. Although there was a clear determination to remain on this land—their homeland—this determination should also be regarded as a subtle assertion of their sense of collectivity. The homestead process privileged a single individual's right to own a specific quarter-section of land. However, these people took out applications within the same area in order to reclaim Round Prairie because it connected them as a people. Round Prairie was not just subsumed in a foreign land, however, because it was more than a place that people simply passed through while on the hunt. The connection these people had to Round Prairie was important to their identity because it honored the relationships of the community's founding sisters. As such, these two men asserted their indigenous claims to these lands based on an understanding of their place in a landscape created by their relationship to the Laframboise women. Although these men did not specifically cite the Laframboise women in their declarations, it seems fairly certain that Round Prairie was formed via this core group of women who drew the buffalo hunters together into a community of shared familial interests, while the buffalo hunt underpinned their corporate identity.

In the context of the fur trade, buffalo-hunt economy, or deerskin trade, the emergence of Metis cultural identities was a factor of social, political, and economic competition between Indians and Europeans. But this is not the be-all story to the Metis experience—it is only the starting point. The Metis formed complex systems of relationships amongst each other based on family ties and shared homeland while also establishing themselves as indispensable to a variety of geopolitical relationships. Across the North American continent, Metis forged amongst themselves communities defined by their maternal ancestors and then continued to redefine themselves via ongoing female familial connections to land. Metis identity, therefore, is based on the historical interconnections to land and women.

Despite being separated by a century and 2,500 miles, the Morin siblings, Mary Bosomworth, and the Trottiers shared in common maternal connections to land, something that was constant for similar indigenous communities across North America. It would be easy to separate the stories into simple narratives that distinguish Canadian from American history, Metis from Half-breed, and declare that they bear no relation to each other. And, indeed, there are certainly clear distinctions in these histories. The history of Canada's Metis, for example, has been marked by overt expressions of collective political and social independence. Furthermore, because of these overt expressions of nationalism through free-trading efforts in the 1840s and 1850s, and the political independence movements in 1869–70 and 1885, the Canadian state was forced to acknowledge their existence and, via the scrip process, recognize their rights to land, albeit defining those rights narrowly. The opportunity to take scrip set Metis people apart from their Indian relatives and established a legal difference between Metis and Indian aboriginality. This opportunity, however, was not available to Metis in all parts of Canada; thus, lack of participation should not be criteria for denying contemporary communities their historical Metis-ness. Nevertheless, this legal distinction has since become a part of Canada's discourse about race and authenticity. The United States, conversely, has not had this same historical acknowledgement, and although Metis people have clearly existed and asserted their rights in that country, there has been no recognition for them as a people under American law. Despite these differences, what is telling in each case is how the people defined and categorized themselves as having rights to the lands of their mothers and rooted in the economic pursuits of their father's society. The role of family and inherent relationships of kith and kin connected groups to one another and brought cohesion to their societies across time and space. The reaction to these assertions, furthermore, reveals that the root of cultural ambivalence rests with non-Metis people, not with the Metis themselves.

The colonial era's ambivalence about people who did not fit fixed racial categories was recreated within the academic arena, where scholars ascribed meanings to events and categorized Metis people as either more Indian or more white, which is to say more authentically or inauthentically aboriginal. This conceptualization of self through the acknowledgment of ancestors and living relatives is not unique to any particular aboriginal group. It was, and is, how North America's Aboriginal people—Indian, Metis, and Inuit—laid the foundations for their individual and collective identity, one culturally distinct from Europeans. The notion of identity formation as grounded in family structures, sense of place, and economic pursuits is often overlooked by scholars analyzing the historical manifestation of Metis communities and their reckoning of identity. The issue for Metis people is twofold: their identity is rooted in a familial experience where responsibility and obligation to relatives supersedes all else, but because of the duality of their parentage their identities often shift to fit those two sets of familial expectations. Furthermore, and perhaps more importantly, scholars who deal with questions of historical identity construction do not typically address the ramifications that rigid categorization systems have on those who did the categorizing. Those who do not face issues of shifting cultural realities may feel insecure when something that they assume to be coherent and fixed is displaced by people who refuse simple categorization. The issue of shifting identities is not a problem necessarily experienced by Metis communities but is instead experienced by the parent cultures and communities that use their own social, cultural, political, and legal institutions to create systems of categories that reflect their conceptions of reality. Identities, however, are not rigid or singularly created but, rather, are constructed through multiple processes that are simultaneously intersecting, antagonistic, and complementary.[91] Clearly, there is a problem. How can a group of people that is inherently biracial and bicultural by virtue of their mixed Indian and white ancestries establish a new and singular culture and society founded on what appears to be a duality? Are we wrestling with the limitations of language—do we lack the frames of reference within the English and French languages to clearly articulate how duality can be singularly identified and authenticated within a people's shared experience? Are we limited by an ideology that links race and culture as so ingrained we cannot escape from it? If the answer to these questions is yes, then the roots of cultural ambivalence must rest with others, not with Metis who have, throughout the historical record, attempted to express who they were to those who asked—only to be ignored or redefined in ways compatible with someone else's ontological system.

The expression of Metis-ness as a separate space culturally and socially in Canada and the United States is more than an in-between space. People chose to identify themselves in ways that underscored their own notions of self. It has been argued that we do not know how the Metis understood themselves because they did not leave us clearly articulated statements in the available records. We do not have many moments when individuals stood up and declared their Metis-ness definitively. But perhaps it is just that we have not understood the clues to their identity and sense of self that were left behind. The Morins, Trottiers, Rosses, and Mary Bosomworth all articulated who they were. It is the scholars who have failed to listen to them, who have instead reinforced a restrictive paradigm about race. We need to be less concerned with race and focus on the other meaningful characteristics—family, connections to specific locations in the midst of a life of mobility, the role of women in coalescing communities, and the economy in which they operated—if we are to unpack what it means to be Metis historically. Louis Riel articulated what we have long found so perplexing when he wrote, "It is true that our Native roots are humble, but it is right for us to honour our mothers as well as our fathers. Why should we concern ourselves with the extent of our European blood or our Indian blood? If we have any sense of appreciation or filial devotion to our parents, are we not obliged to say, 'We are Métis'?"[92] Years later, Metis historians D. Bruce Sealy and Antoine S. Lussier succinctly summed up the assertion of a new identity by Canadian Metis:

> The dominant question was how cultures and environment could be modified and this fundamental question was personified in the Metis. To observers at that time it seemed the choices were clear cut. The mixed bloods could become nomads of the woods and the plains or they could become as Europeans and be governed by the pen and the plough. The Metis chose neither one, they pulled both ways incessantly and sought a compromise between European and Indian ways; between hunting and agriculture.[93]

The question is not whether there was ambivalence but, rather, where the ambivalence rests—with the Metis or with outsiders who fail to understand how a people can assert an identity that is not dual but is instead rooted in their biculturality? Perhaps contemporary scholars have inadequately accounted for the behavior of the Metis because it is difficult to categorize them within the simplistic binaries of white and Indian, Native and newcomer, colonized and colonizer. Historically, miscegenation was met with a fear born of uncertainty as to what Metis meant to people with "pure" bloodlines. The reaction of so-called pure races to the Metis is where the seeds of ambivalent discourse lie. Both have sought mixed-ancestry people's knowledge, connections, and experiences when it benefited their agendas but have equally feared their potential to assert separate rights and values and cultural independence from their parental groups. These expressions of self should not be mistaken for contradictory behavior, confusion, ambivalence, or, worse, crass opportunism. Rather, Metis people and communities established for themselves a niche that they used to capitalize on their opportunities within colonial societies, which, over time, increasingly attempted to constrain them within rigid categories of either Indian or white. Only when Metis people, individually or collectively, asserted an alternative set of values was their ability to self-identify as a distinct people challenged.

Notes

1. Saul, *Fair Country*, 106.

2. Ibid., 8.

3. In Canada, the Indian Act is the legislation that defines who is legally an Indian. Those who are legally Indians are registered as such and are therefore conferred the "status" of Indian. Non-status Indians are those people who are culturally, but not legally, Indians. Until about 1985, Metis and non-status Indians were often politically united as they attempted to have the Canadian government recognize and acknowledge their rights as Aboriginal people.

4. See the Métis Nation website (http://www.metisnation.ca/who/index.html) for the complete definition of that organization's citizenry. Since the 1980s, this political body has restricted its membership in such a way as to exclude non-status populations and other mixed-ancestry populations, such as those found in Labrador who refer to themselves as the Labrador Métis Nation. To date, there is no national definition of the Metis in Canada that is legislated by either federal or provincial governments, unlike "Indian" and "Inuit," which are defined in federal statutes.

5. See Peterson and Brown, "Introduction," 6.

6. St-Onge, "Uncertain Margins."

7. See Devine, *People Who Own Themselves*. Devine's work on the Desjarlais family in North America emphasized the French Canadian paternal origins of this family and determined that those who were French-speaking and Catholic were Métis, whereas those who lived a more "Indian" lifestyle in the subarctic never managed to establish this new identity. Similarly, Brown's *Strangers in Blood* emphasized that assimilation of the country-born into the British Protestant worlds of their fathers occurred because of the active and pervasive paternal influence evident in these British–Indian families. See *Strangers in Blood*, 20–26.

8. Van Kirk, "'What if Mama is an Indian?,'" 208.

9. Ibid., 207–17.

10. Ibid., 208.

11. Ibid., 214.

12. Ibid., 209–10.

13. Ibid., 211.

14. Ibid (emphasis in original).

15. See Ens, *Homeland to Hinterland*; Pannekoek, *Snug Little Flock*; Stanley, *Birth of Western Canada*; Giraud, *Les Métis Canadien*; and John Foster, "Wintering, the Outsider Adult Male."

16. See Nicks, "Mary Anne's Dilemma," and Harrison, *Métis*, for two works on material culture that speak to the ambivalence of cultural heritage institutions as they attempt to catalogue artifacts from Metis people. Nicks and Harrison, however, do not characterize their work as ambivalent, but instead emphasize the cultural confusion of the people who created the artifacts. Scholars of Metis history have recently picked up on Richard White's theory of the middle ground, an explanation for cultural, economic, and political accommodation in the Great Lakes pays d'en haut (high country) during the seventeenth century and applied it to the Metis as a manifestation of a physical middle ground. It is important to note that White was discussing a hybridized landscape as existing between European and Algonquian people, and he did not apply his theory to the Metis themselves. See White, *Middle Ground*.

17. Devine noted two Desjarlais brothers who lived very different lives, with one being more "Indian" because he followed traditional Indian religious conventions, whereas the Metis in the family were Catholic. See Devine, *People Who Own Themselves*, 90–91. Kenneth S. Coates and William R. Morrison argued that the Yukon developed as a bi-cultural society—Indian and white—and that mixed-bloods, with the exception of a few prominent fur trade families, were forced to choose between those two races. See Coates and Morrison, "'More Than a Matter of Blood,'" 269.

18. Ross, *Fur Hunters of the Far West*, 196.

19. For instance, James was sent to the University of Toronto after going to the Red River Academy; William attended the Red River Academy; and Sandy (Alexander) was educated by Presbyterian minister John Black, who also tutored sisters Henrietta and Jemima. James served on the Council of Assiniboia and became the political spokesman for the anglophone mixed-bloods in 1869–70. William was appointed assistant sheriff and governor of the jail and was a member of the Council of Assiniboia. He also held the offices of petty judge, auditor of public accounts, and postmaster. Ross and Sally's children also found good marriage partners befitting their stature as the children of Alexander Ross. Henrietta eventually married Rev. John Black, and Mary married the Presbyterian minister George Flett. Jemima Ross married William Coldwell, who, along with his wife's brother James and another partner, founded the first newspaper in the settlement, the *Nor'Wester*. Margaret married Hugh Matheson, a Scottish settler

in Kildonan, Manitoba, and Isabella's second husband was James Stewart Green, an American free trader. See Van Kirk, " 'What if Mama is an Indian?,' " 209–210, 215; and *Dictionary of Canadian Biography*, s.v. "Alexander Ross."

20. Van Kirk, " 'What if Mama is an Indian?,' " 208.

21. Lussier, "Metis."

22. For examples of the American scholarship, please see Martha Haroun Foster, *We Know Who We Are*; Sleeper-Smith, *Indian Women and French Men*; Thorne, *Many Hands of My Relations*; and Murphy, *Gathering of Rivers.*

23. Shoemaker, "Categories," 51. Although I recognize that Shoemaker is not making specific reference to the Metis, her work is useful for understanding how people create categories to manage complexity.

24. For alternative translations of the term Dene, see the Canadian Broadcasting Corporation's piece "Dene Oppose Nunavut Boundaries," in which the broadcaster explores the etymology of Dene as a means to explain who they are to Canadians. For alternative translations of Anishinaabe, see Rheault, *Anishinaabe Mino-Bimaadiziwin*. For Nehiyaw, please see Lee, "Traditional Teaching," who further notes that the Cree are named for the four parts of human beings: emotional, mental, spiritual, and physical.

25. Payment, *Free People*; Devine, *People Who Own Themselves*; and Tough and McGregor, " 'Rights to the Land May be Transferred.' "

26. John Foster, "Wintering, the Outsider Adult Male"; Podruchny, *Making the Voyageur World*; and Macdougall, *One of the Family*.

27. Bakker, *Language of Our Own*, 65.

28. Indians are a subcategory within the Mongoloid race. These four categories have been contested and not always been agreed upon by scientists, and the evolution of these ideas cannot be unpacked here. The point is merely that humankind has a history of establishing difference as a means of making categorical sense of the world in which we live. See Huxley, "On the Geographical Distribution."

29. Paige Raibmon's history of labor and culture amongst First Nations in British Columbia during the nineteenth century explores the ideology of authenticity. More specifically, Raibmon explains how nineteenth-century settler society created a paradigm of oppositional authenticities between whites and Indians. In short, Indians represented everything that whites were not, and, from the perspective of the colonizer, Indians could not contest or step away from the category that defined them. See Raibmon, *Authentic Indians*.

30. Young, *Stories from Indian Wigwams*, 59–60.

31. Ibid., 60–61. Young's use of the term "half-breed" indicates, perhaps, that he saw no linguistic distinction between it and Métis.

32. Southesk, *Saskatchewan and the Rocky Mountains*, 359.

33. Ibid.

34. Ibid., 360.

35. Stanley, *Birth of Western Canada*; and Giraud, *Les Métis Canadien*.

36. Stanley, *Birth of Western Canada*, p. xxv.

37. Ibid., p. xxv.

38. Giraud, *Les Métis Canadien*, 329.

39. Pannekoek, *Snug Little Flock*.

40. Spry, "Métis and Mixed-Bloods," 97.

41. We especially see this in American scholarship on mixed-ancestry people. See Saunt, *New Order of Things*; and Perdue, *Mixed Blood Indians*.

42. Hybridity theory is most clearly articulated within literary criticism, with its emphasis on concepts grounded in postmodern and postcolonial scholarship. Even if the original authors themselves did not regard Metis and/or "half-breeds" as the physical representation of hybridity, their writing is assessed by literary critics as discursive strategies to create and maintain in-betweenness. See Andrews, "Irony, Métis Style."

43. Martha Haroun Foster, *We Know Who We Are*; Sleeper-Smith, *Indian Women and French Men*; Thorne, *Many Hands of My Relations*; and Murphy, *Gathering of Rivers*.

44. Because it is such a dominant ideology, Shoemaker suggests that scholars should not be too quick to dismiss notions of race. The people whom we study had much different perceptions and conceptions, and we need, therefore, to take those ideas seriously. Shoemaker, "How Indians Got to Be Red," 644.

45. Andersen, however, argued that what has occurred as a result is that any-one of mixed racial ancestry has been included in the definition of Metis because of a fixation on the "mixed" part of race, instead of concepts grounded in indig-enous notions of nationalism. Indeed, Andersen concluded, "mixed ancestry," rather than cultural distinctiveness, came to be naturalized as a legitimate signi-fier for Métis, an ordering reflected in subsequent census classifications. Ander-sen, "From Nation to Population," 347–48.

46. Shoemaker, "Categories," 55–56.

47. This notion is not new. In the mid-twentieth century, Sioux scholar Ella Deloria published the first-ever account of Sioux family and social life—the *tiyospaye*—from a cultural insider's perspective, bringing forth an awareness of the intricate web of Sioux social obligations and responsibilities. Deloria, *Speaking of Indians*.

48. Raphaël Morin, 1 March 1887/17 October 1887, file 167727, vol. 557, RG 15, Library and Archives Canada (hereafter cited as LAC); Canadian Census Re-turns for 1881 and 1891, Green Lake, both in LAC. It is unclear whether "Atha-basca" refers to a location within the Athabasca District or to living at or near Lake Athabasca.

49. Raphaël Morin, 1 March 1887/17 October 1887, file 167727, vol. 557, RG 15, LAC. Raphaël's father, Antoine Morin, was French Canadian, and so the family had no association with the land of their father's birth.

50. Marie Morin, 8 March 1889, file 320835, vol. 682, RG 15, LAC.

51. Pilagie Morin, 22 October 1887, file 167786, vol. 558, RG 15, LAC. Montagnais was a term used by French speakers to indicate the Dene people, also known as Chipewyan.

52. Duckworth, *English River Book*; and Morice, *Dictionnaire Historique Des Canadiens*.

53. After Jean Louis's birth at Île à la Crosse in 1817, the family lived in English River for another five years and then left for Quebec after the merger of the companies. Jean Louis married Julie Lagimodiere in 1844 at Red River, and their son Louis was born that same year. The couple's next child to live past infancy was Sara Riel, who became a Grey Nun and served at the mission at Île à la Crosse from 1872 until her death in 1883.

54. In 1881, according to census records, Pélagie was living with her grandson, Pierre Marie. By 1887, according to her scrip application, she was living with her son, Louis Morin, on the east side of Green Lake. Louis, like his sisters, was born in Île à la Crosse, but by 1870 he was living and working for the HBC at Green Lake. By the time of the 1901 Canadian census, Pélagie was living at Green Lake with her daughter Sophie and Sophie's custom-of-the-country husband, Paul Delaronde, Sr. Overall, the Morin family of the English River District, all of whom were descended from Antoine Morin and Pélagie Boucher, lived in most of the communities throughout northwestern Saskatchewan and married extensively into both Metis and Indian (Cree and Dene) families across the territory. Pilagie Morin, 22 October 1887, file 167786, vol. 558, RG 15, LAC; Canadian Census Returns for 1881 and 1901, Green Lake, both in LAC.

55. Sophie Morin Linklater, 8 March 1899, vol. 1360, RG 15, LAC.

56. St-Onge, *Saint-Laurent, Manitoba*, 38, 66. Paul Delaronde's first wife, according to St-Onge's research, was listed in the 1891 census at St.-Laurent as the forty-eight-year-old widow of Paul Delaronde and headed a household that included her son William, who was then working as a salaried farm hand.

57. Registres paroissiaux, 1867–1912, Eglise catholique, Mission de Saint-Jean-Baptiste, Ile à la Crosse, Saskatchewan, Church of Jesus Christ of Latter Day Saints Family History Search Center; and William De Laronde, 11 July 1900, vol. 1343, RG 15, LAC.

58. According to the 1881 census for the region, Paul, Sr., Sophie Morin Linklater, and their daughter Marie were living in the household of Jean Baptiste Aubichon, Sr., at Green Lake. By the 1891 census, Marie and her husband Adolphus Primo, age twenty-three, were living in the household of Paul Delaronde, Sr., although they were listed as "domestic[s]" rather than dependents. Canadian Census Returns, 1891, Green Lake, LAC.

59. Martin, *Sacred Revolt*, 79–81.

60. Ibid.

61. Lawson, *New Voyage to Carolina*, 192.

62. Saunt, *New Order of Things*, 67–89.

63. Ibid., 69, 75, and 83.

64. Ibid., 69.

65. Ibid., 75 and 89.

66. For complete biographies of Mary Musgrove Mathews Bosomworth, see Green, "Mary Musgrove"; Fisher, "Mary Musgrove"; Todd, *Mary Musgrove*;

Gillespie, "Sexual Politics of Race and Gender"; Corkran, *Creek Frontier, 1540–1783,* 31, 63, 115; McDowell, *Documents Relating to Indian Affairs,* 396; and Braund, *Deerskins and Duffels,* 35, 41.

67. Hewatt, *Historical Account,* 2:20–21.

68. Mary's Uncle Brims, the Cowetus mico, had died in 1733 and was succeeded by his clan relatives Chigilli and Malatchi.

69. Braund, *Deerskins and Duffels,* 41; and Corkran, *Creek Frontier,* 91–110.

70. McDowell, *Documents Relating to Indian Affairs,* 270–76, 349, 495.

71. Ibid., 495. Ritualized reciprocity through "gifting" is a fairly common trait across North American aboriginal nations. The best-known example is the West Coast Potlaches, which have been heavily commented on by European and Canadian spectators because of their lavishness. However, gift giving received historians' attention because of the ritual's importance as part of a trading ceremony that took place before the commencement of individual exchanges at posts and treaty-signing ceremonies.

72. By the late 1740s, Mary's holdings included the original Musgrove depot at Yamacraw Bluffs; 500 acres in Georgia; Yamacraw lands granted to her by the Yamacraw mico, Tomachichi; Creek lands given her by her relatives and Creek micos Chigilli and Malatchi; and the Creek islands (Corkran, *Creek Frontier,* 99; and Green, "Mary Musgrove," 33).

73. Hewatt, *Historical Account,* 2:153. Original spelling has been retained in direct quotes.

74. Gillespie, "Sexual Politics of Race and Gender," 190.

75. Morris, *Treaties with Indians of Manitoba.*

76. Ibid., 7.

77. Ibid., 44.

78. Ibid., 54.

79. One of my former graduate students, Cheryl Troupe, wrote her thesis on the history of the Round Prairie Metis families, focusing on the role of women as community organizers, both traditionally and as they moved into the city of Saskatoon in the mid-twentieth century. From Troupe's excellent research, I have been able to draw on a great deal of material that she located on the Trottiers. Troupe, "Métis Women."

80. Norbert Welsh, Trottier's peer and brother-in-law, recounted that in the 1850s and 1860s he belonged to the Round Prairie buffalo hunting brigade, adding that Trottier's community was made up of families that included Charles's brothers, Antoine and Andre Trottier, Moise and Louis Landry, and Isadore Dumont, Sr. (Weekes, *Last Buffalo Hunter,* 37, 45–72).

81. The life and times of Charles Trottier has been recounted in several publications, including Schilling, *Gabriel's Children;* Stonechild and Waiser, *Loyal Till Death;* and Weekes, *Last Buffalo Hunter.*

82. After Marie's death in 1867, Francois remarried Louise Chaboyer, with whom he had one son, Joseph, born at Round Prairie in 1869.

83. A number of scholars have explored the lives and experiences of several generations and branches of the Laframboise family. See Martha Haroun Foster, *We Know Who We Are*; and Sleeper-Smith, *Indian Women and French Men*.

84. Stonechild and Waiser, *Loyal Till Death*, 151.

85. Charles Trottier, Duck Lake, North West Territories, to Department of the Interior, 17 December 1903, Saskatchewan Archives Board (SAB).

86. Ibid.

87. Norbert Trottier, Swift Current, North West Territories, to Department of the Interior, 24 October 1906, SAB.

88. The land was not surveyed until 1884, and as a result he could not file a homestead application until afterward. Presumably, he did not get a chance to do so because of the Resistance (Norbert Trottier, Swift Current, North West Territories, to Department of the Interior, 8 June 1907, SAB).

89. Ibid.

90. Charles Trottier, homestead application, 16 December 1908, SE16, S3, T32, R6, W3, Department of the Interior, SAB; and Norbert Trottier, homestead application, 11 September 1908, NW20, Q20, T32, R5, W3, Department of the Interior, SAB.

91. Over the past decade, there have been a number of studies that have dealt with identity-construction theories and identity politics that are particularly useful for understanding Metis peoples historically. See, e.g., Clifford, *Predicament of Culture*; Hal B. Levine, *Constructing Collective Identity*; Lawrence W. Levine, *Unpredictable Past*; Woods, *Marginality and Identity*; and Dominquez, *White by Definition*. In addition, although he does not deal specifically with Metis people, Cohen in *Self Consciousness* argues that we need to recognize that social groups are collections of complex selves, and because all individuals are multidimensional we must acknowledge people as deeply complicated. Therefore, we require more subtle and sensitive descriptions of identities.

92. Stanley, *Collected Writings of Louis Riel*, 3:278–79.

93. Sealy and Lussier, *Metis*, 13.

Works Cited

Archival Sources

Ottawa, ON
  Library and Archives of Canada (LAC).
    Canadian Census Returns, 1881, 1891, and 1901, Green Lake.
    De Laronde, William. 11 July 1900, vol. 1343, RG 15.
    Linklater, Sophie Morin. 8 March 1899, vol. 1360, RG 15.
    Morin, Marie. 8 March 1889, file 320835, vol. 682, RG 15.
    Morin, Pilagie. 22 October 1887, file 167786, vol. 558, RG 15.
    Morin, Raphaël. 1 March 1887/17 October 1887, file 167727, vol. 557, RG 15.

Salt Lake City, UT
    Church of Jesus Christ of Latter Day Saints Family History Search Center.
        Registres paroissiaux, 1867–1912. Eglise catholique, Mission de Saint-Jean-
        Baptiste, Ile à la Crosse, Saskatchewan.
Saskatoon, SK
    Saskatchewan Archives Board (SAB), Homestead Records.
    Trottier, Charles. Homestead Application, 16 December 1908. Department of
        the Interior. SE16, S3, T32, R6, W3.
    ———. Letter sent from Duck Lake, North West Territories, to the Depart-
        ment of the Interior, 17 December 1903.
    Trottier, Norbert. Homestead Application, 11 September 1908. Department of
        the Interior. NW20, Q20, T32, R5, W3.
    ———. Letters sent from Swift Current, North West Territories, to the Depart-
        ment of the Interior, 24 October 1906 and 8 June 1907.

Published Sources

Andersen, Chris. "From Nation to Population: The Racialisation of Métis in the
    Canadian Census." *Nations and Nationalism* 14, no. 2 (2008): 347–68.
Andrews, Jennifer. "Irony, Métis Style: Reading the Poetry of Marilyn Dumont
    and Gregory Scofield." *Canadian Poetry Studies/Documents/Reviews* 50 (Spring/
    Summer, 2002). http://www.uwo.ca/english/canadianpoetry/cpjrn/vol50
    /andrews.htm.
Bakker, Peter. *A Language of Our Own: The Genesis of Michif, the Mixed Cree–French
    Language of the Canadian Métis.* New York, NY: Oxford University Press, 1997.
Braund, Kathryn E. Holland. *Deerskins and Duffels: The Creek Trade with Anglo-
    America, 1685–1815.* Lincoln: University of Nebraska Press, 1993.
Brown, Jennifer S. H. *Strangers in Blood: Fur Trade Company Families in Indian Coun-
    try.* Vancouver: University of British Columbia Press, 1980.
Canadian Broadcasting Corporation (CBC). "Dene Oppose Nunavut Boundar-
    ies," 5 May 1992. http://archives.cbc.ca/politics/provincial_territorial_politics
    /clips/660.
Clifford, James. *The Predicament of Culture: Twentieth-Century Ethnology, Literature
    and Art.* Cambridge, MA: Harvard University Press, 1988.
Coates, Kenneth S., and William R. Morrison. "'More Than a Matter of Blood': The
    Federal Government, the Churches and the Mixed Blood Populations of the
    Yukon and Mackenzie River Valley, 1890–1950." In *1885 and After: Native Soci-
    ety in Transition*, edited by F. Laurie Barron and James B. Waldram, 253–77.
    Regina, SK: Canadian Plains Research Centre, University of Regina, 1986.
Cohen, Anthony P. *Self Consciousness: An Alternative Anthropology of Identity.* New
    York: Routledge, 1994.
Corkran, David H. *The Creek Frontier, 1540–1783.* Norman: University of Oklahoma
    Press, 1967.

Deloria, Ella. *Speaking of Indians.* Lincoln: University of Nebraska Press, 1998. First published in 1948.

Devine, Heather. *The People Who Own Themselves: Aboriginal Ethnogenesis in a Canadian Family, 1600–1900.* Calgary, AB: University of Calgary Press, 2004.

Dictionary of Canadian Biography Online, s.v. "Alexander Ross" (by Frits Pannekoek), http://www.biographi.ca.

Dominquez, Virginia R. *White by Definition: Social Classification in Creole Louisiana.* New Brunswick, NJ: Rutgers University Press, 1986.

Duckworth, Harry W., ed. *The English River Book: A North West Company Journal & Account Book, 1796.* Montreal, QC, and Kingston, ON: McGill-Queen's University Press, Rupert's Land Record Society Series, 1990.

Ens, Gerhard J. *Homeland to Hinterland: The Changing Worlds of the Red River Metis in the Nineteenth Century.* Toronto, ON: University of Toronto Press, 1996.

Fisher, Doris. "Mary Musgrove: Creek Englishwoman." Ph.D. diss., Emory University, 1990.

Foster, John. "Wintering, the Outsider Adult Male and the Ethnogenesis of the Western Plains Metis." *Prairie Forum* 19, no. 1 (1994), 1–14.

Foster, Martha Haroun. *We Know Who We Are: Métis Identity in a Montana Community.* Norman: University of Oklahoma Press, 2006.

Gillespie, Michele. "The Sexual Politics of Race and Gender: Mary Musgrove and the Georgia Trustees." In *The Devil's Lane: Sex and Race in the Early South,* edited by Catherine Clinton and Michele Gillespie, 187–201. New York, NY: Oxford University Press, 1997.

Giraud, Marcel. *Les Métis Canadien: son rôle dans l'histoire des provinces de l'Ouest.* Paris, France: Institut d'ethnologie, 1945.

Green, Michael D. "Mary Musgrove: Creating a New World." In *Sifters: Native American Women's Lives,* edited by Theda Perdue, 29–47. London, UK: Oxford University Press, 2001.

Harrison, Julia. *Métis: A People between Two Worlds.* Calgary, AB: Glenbow-Alberta Institute, 1985.

Hewatt, Alexander. *An Historical Account of the Rise and Progress of the Colonies of South Carolina and Georgia, 1779.* 2 vols. London, UK: Printed for Alexander Donaldson, 1779.

Huxley, Thomas Henry. "On the Geographical Distribution of the Chief Modifications of Mankind." *Journal of the Ethnological Society of London* 2 (1870). http://alepho.clarku.edu/huxley/SM3/GeoDis.html.

Lawson, John. *A New Voyage to Carolina.* Edited by Hugh T. Lefler. Chapel Hill: University of North Carolina Press, 1967.

Lee, Mary. "Traditional Teaching." http://www.fourdirectionsteachings.com/transcripts/cree.html.

Levine, Hal B. *Constructing Collective Identity: A Comparative Analysis of New Zealand Jews, Maori and Urban Papua New Guineans.* Frankfurt am Main, Germany: Peter Lang, 1997.

Levine, Lawrence W. *The Unpredictable Past: Explorations in American Cultural History*. Oxford, UK: Oxford University Press, 1993.

Lussier, Antoine S. "The Metis: Contemporary Problem of Identity." *Manitoba Pageant* 23, no. 3 (1978). http://www.mhs.mb.ca/docs/pageant/23/metisidentity.shtml.

Macdougall, Brenda. *One of the Family: Metis Culture in Nineteenth Century Northwestern Saskatchewan*. Vancouver, BC: University of British Columbia Press, 2010.

Martin, J. W. *Sacred Revolt: The Muskogees' Struggle for a New World*. Boston, MA: Beacon Press, 1991.

McDowell, William L., ed. *Documents Relating to Indian Affairs, May 21, 1750–August 7, 1754*. Columbia: University of South Carolina Press, 1958.

Morice, A. G., OMI. *Dictionnaire historique des Canadiens et des Métis français de L'Ouest*. Montreal, QC: Chez Granger Freres, 1908.

Morris, Alexander. *The Treaties with the Indians of Manitoba, the North-West Territories, Including the Negotiations on Which They Were Based, and Other Information Relating Thereto*. Toronto, ON, 1880. http://www.gutenberg.org/catalog/world/readfile?fk_files=1465851 (accessed 24 April 2011).

Murphy, Lucy Eldersveld. *A Gathering of Rivers: Indians, Métis, and Mining in the Western Great Lakes, 1737–1832*. Lincoln: University of Nebraska Press, 2000.

Nicks, Trudy. "Mary Anne's Dilemma: The Ethnohistory of an Ambivalent Identity." *Canadian Ethnic Studies* 17, no. 2 (1985), 103–114.

Pannekoek, Frits. *A Snug Little Flock: The Social Origins of the Riel Resistance, 1869–1870*. Winnipeg, MB: Watson and Dwyer, 1991.

Payment, Diane. *"The Free People—Otipemisiwak": Batoche, Saskatchewan, 1870–1930*. Ottawa, ON: Canadian Parks Service, 1990.

Perdue, Theda. *Mixed Blood Indians: Racial Construction in the Early South*. Athens: University of Georgia Press, 2003.

Peterson, Jacqueline, and Jennifer S. H. Brown. "Introduction." In Peterson and Brown, *New Peoples*, 3–16.

———, eds. *The New Peoples: Being and Becoming Métis in North America*. Winnipeg: University of Manitoba Press, 1985.

Podruchny, Carolyn. *Making the Voyageur World: Travelers and Traders in the North American Fur Trade*. Toronto, ON: University of Toronto Press, 2006.

Raibmon, Paige. *Authentic Indians: Episodes of Encounter from the Late-Nineteenth-Century Northwest Coast*. Durham, NC: Duke University Press, 2005.

Rheault, D'Arcy. *Anishinaabe Mino-Bimaadiziwin: The Way of a Good Life*. Peterborough, ON: Debwewin Press, 1999. http://eaglefeather.org/series/Native%20American%20series/anishinaabe%20Tradition%20D'Arcy%20Rheault.pdf.

Ross, Alexander. *The Fur Hunters of the Far West*. 1855. Reprint edited by Kenneth A. Spaulding. Norman: University of Oklahoma Press, 2001.

Saul, John Ralston. *A Fair Country: Telling Truths about Canada*. Toronto, ON: Viking Canada, 2008.

Saunt, Claudio. *A New Order of Things: Property, Power, and the Transformation of the Creek Indians, 1733–1816.* Cambridge, UK: Cambridge University Press, 1999.

Schilling, Rita. *Gabriel's Children.* Saskatoon, SK: Saskatoon Métis Local 11, 1983.

Sealy, D. Bruce, and Antoine S. Lussier. *The Metis: Canada's Forgotten People.* Winnipeg, MB: Pemmican Publications, 1975.

Shoemaker, Nancy. "Categories." In *Clearing a Path: Theorizing the Past in Native American Studies,* edited by Nancy Shoemaker, 51–74. New York, NY: Routledge, 2002.

———. "How Indians Got to Be Red." *American Historical Review* 102, no. 3 (1997): 625–44.

Sleeper-Smith, Susan. *Indian Women and French Men: Rethinking Cultural Encounter in the Western Great Lakes.* Amherst: University of Massachusetts Press, 2001.

Southesk, Earl of. *Saskatchewan and the Rocky Mountains: A Diary and Narrative of Travel, Sport, and Adventure, During a Journey Through the Hudson's Bay Company's Territories, in 1859 and 1860.* Edmonton, AB: M.G. Hurtig, 1969.

Spry, Irene M. "The Métis and Mixed-Bloods of Rupert's Land before 1870." In Peterson and Brown, *New Peoples,* 95–118.

Stanley, George F. G. *The Birth of Western Canada: A History of the Riel Rebellions.* 5 vols. London, UK: Longmans, Green, and Co., 1936.

———, ed. *The Collected Writings of Louis Riel/Les écrits complets de Louis Riel.* Edmonton: University of Alberta Press, 1985.

Stonechild, Blair, and Bill Waiser. *Loyal Till Death: Indians and the North-West Rebellion.* Calgary, AB: Fifth House, 1997.

St-Onge, Nicole. *Saint-Laurent, Manitoba: Evolving Métis Identities, 1850–1914.* Winnipeg: University of Manitoba Press, 2004.

———. "Uncertain Margins: Métis and Saulteaux Identities in St-Paul des Saulteaux, Red River, 1821–1870." *Manitoba History* 53 (October 2006): 1–8.

Thorne, Tanis C. *The Many Hands of My Relations: French and Indians on the Lower Missouri.* Columbia: University of Missouri Press, 1996.

Todd, Helen. *Mary Musgrove: Georgia Indian Princess* Chicago, IL: Adams Press, 1981.

Tough, Frank, and Erin McGregor, " 'The Rights to the Land May Be Transferred': Archival Records as Colonial Text—A Narrative of Métis Scrip." In *Natives & Settlers, Now & Then: Historical Issues and Current Perspectives on Treaties and Land Claims in Canada,* edited by Paul DePasquale, 33–64. Edmonton: University of Alberta Press, 2007.

Troupe, Cheryl. "Métis Women: Social Structure, Urbanization and Political Activism, 1850–1980." Master's thesis, University of Saskatchewan, 2009.

Van Kirk, Sylvia. " 'What if Mama is an Indian?': The Cultural Ambivalence of the Alexander Ross Family." In Peterson and Brown, *New Peoples,* 207–217.

Weekes, Mary, as told to her by Norbert Welsh. *The Last Buffalo Hunter.* New York, NY: T. Nelson, 1939.

White, Richard. *The Middle Ground: Indians, Empires, and Republics in the Great Lakes Region, 1650–1815*. Cambridge, UK: Cambridge University Press, 1991.

Woods, F. J. *Marginality and Identity: A Colored Creole Family through Ten Generations*. Baton Rouge: Louisiana State University Press, 1972.

Young, Egerton Ryerson. *Stories from Indian Wigwams and Northern Campfires*. London, UK: Charles H. Kelly, 1893.

CONTRIBUTORS

CHRIS ANDERSEN is Michif (Métis), from Saskatchewan, and is an associate professor in the Faculty of Native Studies at the University of Alberta. His research focuses on the (il)logics of Canadian state classifications of the Aboriginal category "Métis." Currently, he has completed the first draft of a book-length manuscript entitled " 'Metis': Canada's Misrecognition of an Indigenous People."

PETER BAKKER is a linguist and associate professor at the University of Aarhus, Denmark. His research interests include languages created by twins, Romani, Basque–American Indian contacts, the genesis of the Michif language, mixed languages, the typology of creole languages and the first African Americans in the New World, and deep connections between the Salish and Algonquian language families.

JEAN BARMAN has published extensively on the history of British Columbia and of indigenous peoples. She is professor emeritus at the University of British Columbia and a fellow of the Royal Society of Canada. She was recently awarded the Canadian Historical Association's Clio Prize for Service to British Columbia History.

DANIEL J. BLUMLO received his PhD in Russian history from Florida State University in August 2010. His dissertation, "The Creoles of Russian America," addressed the identity of people of mixed Russian and Native American ancestry in nineteenth-century Alaska. He currently teaches world and Middle Eastern history at Rock Valley College in Rockford, Illinois.

ERIN DOLMAGE completed her MA at the University of British Columbia, Okanagan, in indigenous studies and is working on her PhD in Canadian Aboriginal history at York University. Her interests focus on Metis biography, genealogy, and the construction of family history.

GERHARD J. ENS is a professor of history at the University of Alberta in Edmonton. He has spent his professional career researching and writing about the fur trade, the Metis, and First Nations communities in Canada. He has also worked as a consultant and testified as an expert witness in various court cases concerning Metis and First Nations land claims and treaty rights.

MIKE EVANS is professor and head of the School of Arts and Social Sciences at Southern Cross University in Australia. Previously he taught at the University of Northern British Columbia, the University of Alberta, and Okanagan University College, which was later renamed the University of British Columbia, Okanagan. Dr. Evans has a long-term relationship with the Prince George Métis Elders Society and has worked extensively with colleagues at the Métis Nation of British Columbia on historic and contemporary Métis communities in British Columbia, some of which are discussed in this volume.

MICHEL HOGUE is assistant professor of history at Carleton University in Ottawa, Ontario. His published work has appeared in several anthologies on the history of the Canadian West and the American West. He received his PhD in 2009 from the University of Wisconsin, Madison, and his doctoral dissertation is entitled "Between Race and Nation: The Plains Métis and the Canada–United States Border."

GABRIELLE LEGAULT is Métis from southwest Saskatchewan and has a background in historical archaeology and indigenous studies. Her master's research examined the indigenous identities of the Okanagan's historic McDougall family. She is a board member of the Métis

Community Services Society of BC and has been working collaboratively with Métis Nation British Columbia (MNBC) since 2008. Her current PhD research at the University of British Columbia–Okanagan explores the cultural ecology of Métis traditional land use activities in British Columbia.

VICTOR P. LYTWYN is an independent consultant from Orangeville, Ontario. His work involves historical and geographical research relating to Aboriginal issues in Canada. He has worked with many First Nations and Aboriginal organizations as well as the federal and provincial governments and private companies. Dr. Lytwyn has written two books and many articles on Aboriginal and fur trade history.

BRENDA MACDOUGALL is the current chair of Métis studies at the University of Ottawa. She has worked extensively with Metis communities in Saskatchewan documenting their history. Her first book, *One of the Family: Metis Culture in Nineteenth-Century Northwestern Saskatchewan*, published by the University of British Columbia, received the Clio Prize for best book in prairie history in 2011.

LUCY ELDERSVELD Murphy is an associate professor of history at Ohio State University, Newark. She is the author of *A Gathering of Rivers: Indians, Métis, and Mining in the Western Great Lakes, 1737–1832* (2000). She coedited *Native Women's History in Eastern North American before 1900: A Guide to Research and Writing* (2007) with Rebecca Kugel, and with Wendy Hamand Venet she coedited *Midwestern Women: Work, Community, and Leadership at the Crossroads* (1997). Currently, she is working on a history of Prairie du Chien's Creole families in the mid-nineteenth century.

DIANE P. PAYMENT is author of *The Free People—Li Gens Libres: A History of the Métis Community of Batoche, Saskatchewan* (2009) and numerous publications relating to the Métis and francophone communities of western and northern Canada. She was a historian at Parks Canada in Winnipeg, Manitoba, for thirty years and is now an independent scholar. Past president of La Société historique de Saint-Boniface, she is an active member of the Union Nationale Métisse Saint-Joseph du Manitoba (the oldest Métis association in Canada, which was founded by Louis Riel in 1884). She received an award from the Canadian Historical Association for her work on Batoche and was the recipient of the Canada 125th anniversary commemorative medal for her contribution to Métis history.

JACQUELINE PETERSON is professor emerita from Washington State University. She has published widely on Indian and European relations in western North America, including *Sacred Encounters: Father De Smet and the Indians of the Rocky Mountain West* (1993) and *The New Peoples: Being and Becoming Metis in North America* (edited with Jennifer S. H. Brown). She is currently writing a book on Metis ethnogenesis in the Great Plains.

CAROLYN PODRUCHNY is associate professor of history and past director of the Graduate Program in History at York University. She has published widely on fur trade, Aboriginal, and French colonial history. She is currently exploring the mingling of oral traditions and material cultures in the context of the fur trade, and she is also working on language materials compiled by Roman Catholic missionaries on the prairies in the nineteenth century.

ÉTIENNE RIVARD received his PhD in geography from the University of British Columbia and is a historical and cultural geographer. His main fields of research are on Métis territoriality and its cartographic expression and on the idea of métissage. He also works on North American francophone geographies and on the place of Aboriginal peoples in planning and territorial development in Canada.

NICOLE ST-ONGE, professor of history at the University of Ottawa, has long been a specialist in Metis history. Her prize-winning book, *Saint-Laurent, Evolving Metis Identities, 1850–1914* (2004), was one of the first to weave Metis oral histories with documentary sources. She has developed extensive databases of voyageurs and Metis peoples to produce macrohistories to contrast with her earlier case studies. Her recent work on Metis histories and their voyageur paternal ancestors has concentrated on the moment of genesis from a river world community to a Metis homeland and the variations of this process.

PHILIP D. WOLFART works in identity formation and the history of cartography, drawing on archival sources for regions as far apart as Rupert's Land and the northern rim of the Alps. Educated at St. John's

Ravenscourt School in Winnipeg and at Moûtiers-en-Tarentaise (Savoie), he holds a BA (Oxford) in geography; for his MA and PhD (Queen's, Kingston) he concentrated on historical geography. He has taught at Queen's and the University of Toronto and has experience (with an MLIS from the University of Western Ontario) as a law librarian and at the University of Manitoba's Dafoe Library.

INDEX

Page numbers in italic type refer to illustrations.

471

CPSIA information can be obtained
at www.ICGtesting.com
Printed in the USA
LVHW090105200421
684916LV00007B/384

9 780806 144870